Strategies for Managing Behavior Problems in the Classroom

SECOND EDITION

Mary Margaret Kerr
UNIVERSITY OF PITTSBURGH

C. Michael Nelson
UNIVERSITY OF KENTUCKY

MERRILL PUBLISHING COMPANY
A BELL & HOWELL INFORMATION COMPANY
COLUMBUS TORONTO LONDON MELBOURNE

Cover Photo: Larry Hamill

Published by Merrill Publishing Company
A Bell & Howell Information Company
Columbus, Ohio 43216

This book was set in Souvenir.

Administrative Editor: Vicki Knight
Production Coordinator: Sharon Rudd
Art Coordinator: Lorraine Woost
Cover Designer: Brian Deep
Photo Editor: Gail L. Meese

Photo Credits: Jean Greenwald/Merrill Publishing,
p. 2; Harvey Phillips, pp. 32, 172; Lloyd Lemmer-
man/Merrill Publishing, p. 64; Mary Hagler/Merrill
Publishing, pp. 102, 134; Gail Meese/Merrill Publishing, pp. 212, 311, 356; Bruce Johnson/Merrill
Publishing, pp. 247, 274, 395; Marie Hanak, p. 79;
Marianne Bookmyer, pp. 179, 188.

Library of Congress Catalog Card Number:
  88-63286
International Standard Book Number:
  0-675-21033-X
Printed in the United States of America
1 2 3 4 5 6 7 8 9—92 91 90 89

. . . when we met, the pace of life altered at once; all its atoms were recombined, and we lived in another, lighter time-medium . . .
—Nabokov, 1968

For Bruce, who has magically altered my life with his love.

M.M.K.

To Cheryll, who has changed and enriched me.

C.M.N.

Preface

The field of behavioral disorders has undergone dramatic changes since 1983 when the first edition of this book appeared. We are gratified to have so many new strategies to offer you, our readers. To reflect the recent developments in the field, we have revised our textbook to include

- updated material on definition, identification, and assessments
- a new section on systematic school-wide screening procedures
- a new chapter on social skills and school survival skills
- expanded guidelines for analyzing data
- a new section on prereferral interventions
- updated material on enhancement and reductive techniques
- expanded guidelines for selecting interventions
- a new chapter on maintenance and generalization strategies
- current research on intervention strategies
- a new chapter format: objectives, discussion questions, and references at the end of each chapter.

We are indebted to colleagues and students who studied the first edition and suggested many of these changes.

Also in keeping with your feedback, we have maintained several features of the original text:

1. *Empirical validation.* For each problem behavior, we present methods that have been validated empirically and replicated across numerous settings. We wanted to ensure that these methods will be successful in the varied settings and conditions in which you might work.
2. *In-depth descriptions.* We give you enough information to use the procedures. No additional reading is required.
3. *Coverage of methods for severe behavior disorders.* Because schools now accommodate severely handicapped students, educators must learn how to handle more extreme behavior disorders. We cover the management of such severe behavior problems as self-injury, self-stimulation, extreme social withdrawal, and serious aggression.
4. *Inclusion of adolescent problems.* We offer tactics for preschool through secondary school students.
5. *Topics for support personnel outside the classroom.* In many cases, someone who is not a teacher must manage problem behaviors at home or in the community. To ease this process, we include a unique chapter describing strategies for working outside of the classroom.
6. *Case Studies.* We illustrate problem behaviors and their interventions in case studies conducted by professionals in public schools and clinical residential treatment centers.

7. *Emphasis on social behaviors.* We highlight social rather than academic problems because the former are not as well handled in teacher training texts.

8. *Recognition of other professionals.* For many specific and complex problems, such as depression or phobias, the educator may need to refer the child to a mental health professional. We describe the teacher's role as collaborator with these professionals and agencies and give some basic guidelines on how to make referral decisions.

To give you a logical plan for working with problem children and adolescents, we've organized the book in the same way you would address a behavior problem: identifying and assessing the problem, planning and monitoring objectives, designating strategies for treating behavior patterns, instituting behavior change across time and setting, and supporting changes outside the classroom. You will find case studies that demonstrate how a program is developed and organized and how it is actually put into practice.

Additionally, we have emphasized collecting and using data to make good program decisions. We explain and illustrate (with many tables, figures, and charts) a number of strategies for assessing student behavior and for monitoring student performance. Each problem behavior chapter features a decision-making chart. It should help you assess the usefulness of an intervention by comparing the characteristics of the pupil and the setting with the resources required for its use.

We invite your personal response to our book so that we may improve it in future editions. If you have any comments or case studies you would like us to consider, we would be delighted to examine them.

M.M.K.
C.M.N.

Acknowledgments

Many persons have contributed to the development of this text. Although we cannot name all of those whose ideas, suggestions, and criticisms are reflected in these pages, we hope that our friends and colleagues will recognize their influences on this volume.

However, we do wish to acknowledge specific persons who devoted much of their time and energy to the production of this work. These include our colleagues at the University of Pittsburgh:

Kelly Bassler, for her assistance with references and permissions

Jamey Covaleski, for turning our rough drafts into "readable" form

Lynne Cummings, for sharing her expertise on social skills instruction

Jeanne Kostishack, for advice on early drafts of the manuscript

Deborah Lange Lambert, for producing the glossary and index

Robert W. Staub, for his suggestions for strategies chapters

Merope Versi, for designing the strategy selection charts

We also thank our co-workers at the University of Kentucky:

Colleen Ryall, for her insightful reviews and comments on chapter manuscripts

Steve Eversole, for his careful editing of manuscripts

Marcia Bowling, for her willing and skillful preparation of manuscripts, despite many other demands on her time

David Gast and Mark Wolery, for sharing their work and expertise with us

We also wish to thank Elizabeth U. Ragland, George Peabody College for Teachers of Vanderbilt University, for helpful comments on stereotypic behaviors. Robert B. Rutherford, Jr., Arizona State University, reviewed the entire manuscript and offered helpful comments. George Sugai, University of Washington, provided comprehensive reviews of each phase of the project and made invaluable contributions to this edition. Frank H. Wood, University of Minnesota, offered many good suggestions from a teacher training perspective as he reviewed the text.

Finally, our special thanks go to Vicki Knight, our editor, who has once again guided us through the writing process.

Contents

Chapter 9.   Stereotypic Behaviors   274

Chapter 10.   Deficits in Social Skills   311

Strategies and Considerations

Part One

Identifying and Serving Students with Behavioral Problems

Chapter 1

OUTLINE

Behavior Disorders or Problem Behaviors?
Identifying Behaviorally Disordered Pupils
The Continuum of Behavioral Problems and Educational Services

OBJECTIVES

After completing this chapter, the reader should be able to:

- Indicate what a defintion of behavioral disorders should accomplish and indicate some weaknesses of current definitions.
- Compare traditional procedures for identifying behaviorally disordered students with more recent approaches.
- Discuss prereferral intervention strategies and the role of teacher assistance teams.
- Describe the process of determining pupil eligibility for special education services, including the assessment data that should be collected and the decisions that should be made.
- Describe the continuum of educational services available for students with behavior problems and indicate where special education becomes involved.
- Give a rationale for systematic screening, identification, and prereferral intervention services as part of comprehensive educational programming for students who exhibit problem behaviors.

Aggressive, disruptive, noncompliant, socially inadequate, stereotypic, or withdrawn behaviors constitute a difficult set of problems for educators. Among the many questions raised in reference to pupils exhibiting these behaviors are the following:

- Should they be considered handicapped and served by special education, or should they remain in regular programs and be treated as disciplinary problems?
- To be served by special education, must these pupils display significant deficits in academic performance in addition to their behavior problems?

- Can the needs of identified behaviorally disordered students be addressed in mainstream educational settings, or do they require services in self-contained special classes or in even more restrictive settings?
- Are there two groups of students: those who are emotionally disturbed and those who are behaviorally disordered? If so, do they have different educational needs? Is the former group "mentally ill" and the latter group socially maladjusted or simply "naughty"?
- Regardless of their educational placements, what approaches to managing these pupils' behavior problems are most effective? What

skills and resources are needed to accomplish desired behavior changes?

The Education of the Handicapped Act of 1975 (PL 94-142) represented a major accomplishment in terms of guaranteeing appropriate educational experiences for handicapped children and youth. However, pupils handicapped by their behavior problems have not benefited greatly from this legislation; compared with a very conservative prevalence estimate of 2 percent of the school-age population, less than 1 percent are receiving special education across the nation (Braaten, Kauffman, Braaten, Polsgrove, & Nelson, 1988). This means that three-quarters of a million behaviorally handicapped pupils are not receiving appropriate special education services (Apter, 1982). Moreover, there is little evidence that schools are effectively dealing with the behavior problems of students who are not identified as handicapped.

The Education of the Handicapped amendments of 1986 (PL 99-457) substantially expand the scope of PL 94-142. Its provisions include increased funding incentives for states that provide services to preschool handicapped children (ages three to five), greater emphasis on programs for improving the transition of handicapped students to adult life and services, and a call for early intervention services to handicapped infants and toddlers (birth to age two) and their families. The effects of this legislation on children and youth with behavioral disorders remain to be seen, but it is reasonable to expect that although more children with severe behavioral disorders (e.g., **autism**) may be identified, little or no increase in overall services to the total population of students who are handicapped by their behavior will result.

In this text, we attempt to present methods for successfully remediating the behavior problems of students across the range of educational labels and settings. The strategies presented have been carefully researched and proven effective with student populations ranging from the severely and profoundly developmentally disabled to the nonhandicapped, from preschool children to adults. Further, they have been applied by educators in a variety of professional roles (regular and special classroom teachers, consultants, psychologists, guidance counselors, and administrators) as well as by parents. This is not to suggest that the effective management of behavior problems is easy, nor that it can be done by untrained persons without supervision. On the contrary, it involves a complex technology and careful decision making.

The systematic analysis of behavior and setting variables and making appropriate decisions based on these factors are essential to effective management of problem behaviors. These assessments and decisions concern student behavior and environmental characteristics that affect their behavior. Chapter 1 describes assessment procedures used to identify and classify those students whose behavior interferes with their educational progress, as well as the early intervention strategies designed to avoid the necessity of special education classification. Chapter 2 deals with assessment for the purpose of intervention planning. The focus of Chapter 3 is assessment for the purposes of monitoring and facilitating student progress, and that of Chapter 4 is assessment for evaluating and adjusting interventions. The selection of interventions, which is part of the assessment/decision-making process, is also described in Chapter 4. Chapter 5 presents considerations and strategies for effective classroom behavior management. In the present chapter, we take up the broad question of which students should be considered handicapped by their behavior for educational purposes. We also present an overview of special education for behaviorally disordered students —specifically, who these pupils are, how they are identified, and the services available to them in school programs.

Behavior Disorders or Problem Behaviors?

Howell and Morehead (1987) point out that assessment procedures may be grouped into two categories of educational decisions: classification, which involves deciding how students should be grouped, where they should be placed, or whether they are eligible for special services; and treatment, which includes decisions about what to teach and how to teach. The focus of this chapter is classification decisions — specifically, determining whether students with problem behaviors should be classified as handicapped and placed in special education or not classified and retained in the regular education program. Assessment for the purpose of deciding what to teach and how to teach (i.e., what behaviors to target for intervention, determining whether interventions are effective, and matching interventions to student and setting characteristics) is discussed in Chapters 2 through 4.

An initial decision that you have already made, or are contemplating, is whether to work with children or youth who exhibit problem behaviors. As you know, such pupils may carry a variety of labels from "emotionally disturbed" or "behaviorally disordered" to "autistic" or "psychotic"; from "juvenile delinquent" or "socially maladjusted" to "discipline problem". These students may display behavior characteristic of their labels to a greater extent than "normal" children — or they may not. Often, these labels are given as a matter of administrative convenience to facilitate removal and placement of a student in a particular classroom or program.

All teachers, whether in special or regular education, must deal with problem behavior. Pupils labeled "emotionally disturbed" are no more homogeneous than children labeled any other way. Furthermore, labeling a student

"learning disabled," "mentally retarded," or even "gifted" provides no guarantee that behavior problems may be ruled out. Our focus, therefore, is on techniques for dealing with problem behaviors, rather than on dealing with students labeled "behaviorally disordered" or "emotionally disturbed." We feel that such a focus will better serve your pupils' interests and will make you a better practitioner.

We also believe it will lessen your anxiety to think of working with specific behavior problems rather than of dealing with a group of pupils described as emotionally disturbed. If you realize that such children may be more like so-called normal students than they are different and that their labels may reflect the system's intolerance for their deviation more than their alleged psychopathology, you will be a better advocate for maintaining them in, or returning them to, less restrictive environments.

Nevertheless, Public Law 94-142 requires that pupils who are provided with special education services because of their behavior deviations be defined and labeled in order for the programs serving them to receive state and federal funds. This law defines students labeled as **seriously emotionally disturbed** (SED)[1] as those who exhibit one or more of the following characteristics over a long period of time and to a marked degree, which adversely affects educational performance:

---

[1] Use of the term *seriously emotionally disturbed* has been contested by many professionals and the Council for Children with Behavioral Disorders (Huntze, 1985). The term *behavioral disorders* is preferred by CCBD on the grounds that it is more useful for educational purposes, less stigmatizing, and more representative of the population of students who are handicapped by their behavior. State departments of education may adopt their own labels for this population. The labels used include behaviorally handicapped, behaviorally impaired, emotionally disturbed, and emotionally handicapped, as well as behaviorally disordered and seriously emotionally disturbed. All such labels should be considered synonymous. In this text, we prefer to use the term behavioral disorders.

1. An inability to learn, which cannot be explained by intellectual, sensory, or health factors
2. An inability to build or maintain satisfactory interpersonal relationships with peers and teachers
3. Inappropriate types of behavior or feelings under normal circumstances
4. A general pervasive mood of unhappiness or of depression
5. A tendency to develop physical symptoms or fears associated with personal or school problems

The term includes children who are schizophrenic or autistic.[2] The term does not include children who are **socially maladjusted,** unless it is determined that they are seriously emotionally disturbed (Department of Health, Education, and Welfare, August 23, 1977, p. 42478).

This definition has been widely criticized by authorities in the field of behavioral disorders (e.g., Bower, 1982; Gresham, 1985; Kauffman, 1987) as vague, contradictory, confusing, arbitrary, and impractical. For example, what constitutes a "long period of time," "to a marked degree," or "adversely affects educational performance"? Or, for that matter, what is meant by "inability" and "pervasive"? The exclusion of the so-called socially maladjusted has been attacked by professionals as arbitrary and meaningless, and the inclusion of children who are schizophrenic or autistic is seen as redundant with the five characteristics (Kauffman, 1987). The basic weakness of the definition is that it fails to provide a rational or objective basis for discriminating between the behaviorally disordered and the nonhandicapped.

The **Council for Children with Behavioral Disorders** (CCBD), the major professional organization for special educators serv-

ing behaviorally disordered students, issued a position paper criticizing the federal definition and current identification practices (CCBD, 1987). This paper also points out that the federal Education of the Handicapped Act permits states to adopt their own definitions of this population, as long as state definitions identify an equivalent group of pupils. However, so much variety exists among states in terms of definition and identification procedures that whether students are identified as behaviorally disordered for special education services is, to some extent, contingent on which state they reside in (CCBD, 1987). The CCBD recommended that the federal definition be revised and that the arbitrary exclusion of the socially maladjusted be removed.

The test of any definition of behavioral disorders is whether it is useful in discriminating between those pupils who need special education services and those who do not. In other words, a definition should assist in identification. Gerry (1984) states that three criteria must be met in order for a student to qualify for special education as behaviorally disordered: (1) The disorder must constitute a condition (i.e., a relatively persistent pattern of behavior, as opposed to a transient or situational problem), (2) the condition must have an adverse effect on the student's educational performance or progress, such that (3) special education and related services are required. Nevertheless, simply meeting these criteria will not eliminate the subjectivity of a definition. Gresham (1985) indicates that a useful definition should (1) specify the excesses, deficits, or situational inappropriateness of behavior in operational terms, (2) specify the objective features of behavior and its dimensions (e.g., frequency, duration, intensity), (3) specify the behavioral system or systems through which the excesses and deficits are expressed (e.g., cognitive-verbal, overt-motoric, or physiological-emotional), (4) demonstrate the occurrence of the behavior across situations and over time, (5) establish that multiple methods of assessment agree upon the occurrence of the behav-

---

[2] The National Society for Autistic Citizens successfully lobbied to have autism moved from the category of "seriously emotionally disturbed" to "other health impaired," primarily because of the stigma attached to the former label.

ior, and (6) establish that the behavior continues at an unacceptable level subsequent to school-based intervention. Similar criteria have been incorporated into some state definitions and identification procedures, for example, in Oregon (Waksman & Jones, 1985).

For the purposes of this text, the issue is not whether a pupil should be identified as behaviorally disordered (BD) and served through special education. Rather, the issue is whether an intervention strategy needs to be designed. Unfortunately, in many cases, students who are not identified and labeled behaviorally disordered receive no services, or inadequate services, because schools tend to lack effective strategies for helping nonhandicapped pupils who exhibit behavior problems. The effectiveness of such traditional disciplinary practices as corporal punishment, suspension, and expulsion has not been proven for the majority of students with which they are used. Therefore, the dilemma is whether to identify and label the student as behaviorally disordered, which has potentially negative social and educational consequences (i.e., stigmatization, separation from behaviorally normal peers and from the regular academic program), or not to identify and label in the hope that the student's problem behaviors can be remediated by using resources available in the regular education program. Procedures for identifying and serving behavior problem students within the regular education program have been improved through systematic screening and **prereferral intervention** services. These procedures are discussed in the following section.

Identifying Behaviorally Disordered Pupils

Identification procedures may be described in three stages: (1) *Screening* to determine who may be behaviorally disordered, (2) *assess-*

ment to determine who actually is behaviorally disordered for educational purposes, and (3) *certification* of the assessment decision by a team of individuals who also determine the nature and extent of the services to be provided. These stages constitute assessment for making classification decisions (i.e., for determining whether students are eligible for special education). Whereas systematic school-wide **screening** procedures are applied to detect other handicapping conditions (e.g., hearing, vision, postural defects, learning disabilities, mental retardation), screening for behavioral disorders typically amounts to a referral from the regular classroom teacher. And once referred, teacher-nominated students are very likely to be certified as behaviorally disordered, especially if they exhibit externalizing (acting-out) behavior patterns. On the other hand, students manifesting internalizing (withdrawn, depressed) behavior patterns tend not to be referred and therefore not identified because they are less bothersome to classroom teachers (Walker & Fabre, 1987). Assessment data typically include an individualized intelligence scale, norm-referenced achievement tests, standardized behavior rating scales, direct observations, and a test of perceptual-motor skills. Less frequently, personality or projective tests are administered, although the poor reliability and validity of the latter render them suspect for diagnosing behavioral disorders (Waksman & Jones, 1985). In any case, as Walker and Fabre (1987) observe, research suggests that the behavioral characteristics and performance deficits of referred and nonreferred pupils are quite similar, and the assessment data typically collected have little impact on certification decisions.

Recent improvements in screening and identification procedures have made this process more objective and systematic. For example, the state of Iowa has adopted a comprehensive assessment model for students exhibiting behavior problems (Wood, Smith, & Grimes, 1985). Other states are also developing systematic procedures for the screening of, the identification of, and the provision of services to such pupils. Figure 1-1 presents a checklist contained in a technical assistance paper developed by Waksman and Jones (1985) to facilitate the identification of and the provision of services to seriously emotionally disturbed students in Oregon. This checklist provides operational guidelines for applying Oregon' definition (which closely resembles the definition used in the federal law) to determine whether a student should be considered SED for special education purposes. The items pertaining to the pupil's behavior document that the problems are severe (i.e., occur to a "marked degree"). A "long period of time" is defined as eight months (note the exception in the case of behavior that is dangerous), and "adverse effects on educational performance" are documented *either* through academic performance markedly below capacity *or* through deficiencies in social skills or social competence. Finally, note the requirement that attempts to solve the problem through consultative intervention in the regular program must be documented. Wood et al. (1985) and CCBD (1987) also recommend using multiple sources of data for identification and documenting efforts to modify the student's behavior in regular education settings. The CCBD, Iowa, and Oregon all urge that multidisciplinary teams be used to make special education eligibility decisions.

Although such procedures make the identification of behaviorally disordered students more objective and accountable, they do not remove the bias that exists when identification is based on teacher referral. As Gerber and Semmel (1984) observe, referral-driven identification procedures place the regular classroom teacher in the role of a "gatekeeper," who determines which students will be considered for special education services. We have already noted that the referral process is biased toward externalizing behavior problems, whereas students with internalizing behavior patterns are underreferred. Also, some pupils are referred because their teachers are simply less tolerant of disruptive behavior.

STANDARDIZED SCREENING AND IDENTIFICATION

Walker, Severson, and Haring (1986) developed a school-wide standardized screening and identification procedure that reduces this bias by using a series of progressively more precise and expensive assessments or gates. At the first gate, classroom teachers systematically evaluate all pupils in their classes in terms of whether they are at risk for either internalizing or externalizing behavioral disorders. This brief procedure results in a rank-ordered list of up to ten students in each group. The second gate involves teachers rating the three highest ranked students in each group on two short scales. Those pupils whose ratings exceed local norms are advanced to the third gate, which consists of two sets of observations by a trained observer in a classroom and in an unstructured play situation. These data are compared to age- and sex-appropriate norms. In the second and most expensive part of the third gate, a range of standardized tests and diagnostic procedures relevant to a certification decision may be administered.

The advantages of this procedure include the systematic and routine screening of all students to determine their potential need for special education services, the equal consideration given to withdrawn (internalizing) pupils, and the use of standardized and locally normed procedures. Furthermore, this procedure provides several points at which prereferral intervention strategies may be applied. Prereferral interventions consist of systematic modifications in the student's regular education program, including altering the instructional setting, academic curriculum, or behavior management system. These changes are planned and supervised by regular education personnel, and the data collected regarding their effects may comprise one of the criteria for de-

Figure 1-1. Suggested SED Evaluation Checklist

	YES	NO

1. At least two of the following five apply.
    a. The student is rated at or above the ninety-eighth percentile on two different acceptable problem rating scales (or similarly named subscales by *two* or more current teachers.
    b. The student is rated at or above the ninety-eighth percentile on two different acceptable problem-behavior rating scales (or similarly named subscales) by his or her current teacher and by at least one previous year's teacher.
    c. The student is rated at or above the ninety-eighth percentile on two different acceptable problem-behavior rating scales (or similarly named subscales) by one or more parents or guardians.
    d. The student is currently displaying behavior that is endangering his or her life or seriously endangering the safety of others.
    e. The student's observable school or classroom problem behavior is documented to be more severe than approximately 98 percent of his or her peers.
 	
All of these apply:
 	
2. Behavior management consultation has been provided to the classroom teacher(s) over a period of at least four weeks by a behavioral specialist, and documentation indicates that specifically prescribed and consistently employed classroom management interventions have not reduced the inappropriate behavior within acceptable limits suggested by these eligibility criteria.
3. The problem behaviors have been exhibited for over six months. This may be waived if the child is endangering his or her life or seriously endangering the safety of others.
    Waived: ____ Yes ____ No
4. No recent acute stressor or isolated traumatic event in the child's environment (e.g., divorce or death in the family, loss of property) can adequately explain the problem behavior.
5. No medical problem or health impairment can adequately explain the problem behavior pattern.
6. An inappropriate educational program cannot adequately explain the problem behavior pattern.
7. Culturally different norms or expectations cannot adequately explain the problem behavior pattern.
8. The child is either
    a. performing markedly below his or her academic potential on acceptable academic tests or school report cards (____ Yes ____ No), or
    b. severely deficient in social skills or social competence (____ Yes ____ No).
9. Direct observation by a school psychologist or behavior specialist has documented that either
    a. the student is displaying problem behaviors at a high frequency (____ Yes ____ No), or
    b. the student is displaying low-frequency behaviors that grossly deviate from acceptable social norms (____ Yes ____ No).		

Source: Waksman, S. and Jones, V. (1985, August). A suggested procedure for the identification and provision of services to seriously emotionally disturbed students. *Technical assistance papers: A series on PL 94-142 and related Oregon laws.* Portland, OR: Department of Education.

termining the student's eligibility for special education (Gresham, 1985).

PREREFERRAL INTERVENTION STRATEGIES

Interventions at this level should consist of program modifications that are straightforward and relatively easy to implement by the regular classroom teacher. Interventions that are too complex or time-consuming will not be properly applied by busy teachers responsible for twenty-five to thirty other pupils. However, some of the most effective interventions are also the most straightforward. Clearly explaining expectations, modifying instructions, providing peer assistance, changing seating arrangements, removing obstacles to desired behavior, having students monitor their behavior, and providing feedback or praise for desired performances are strategies familiar to most regular educators. Figure 1-2 is a form used to document prereferral intervention strategies and their effects. It indicates a substantial range of available regular classroom interventions, which may be used singly or in combination.

The difference between an informal tactic and a prereferral intervention strategy is that the latter should be applied and evaluated systematically. To ensure this, it is desirable to create building-based **teacher assistance teams** as a resource for teachers experiencing difficulty with specific pupils (Chalfant, Pysh, & Moultrie, 1979; McGlothlin, 1981). Teacher assistance teams are typically composed of regular education teachers, support staff (e.g., school counselor, psychologist), and a special educator. The core team of three to five members is available to all school staff in order to provide immediate crisis intervention, short-term consultation, continuous support, information, resources, or training (Stokes, 1982). For example, if a student is screened as being at risk for a behavioral disorder, or if a teacher (or parent) expresses a concern, the team may respond by assisting the teacher in assessing

the problem and implementing a systematic program modification. The team may act in a consultative capacity until the problem is solved or until it is determined that more intensive action is needed (e.g., referral for special education evaluation). Figure 1-3 is a form included in a document compiled by the National Association of School Psychologists (1986) to help schools develop teacher assistance team models. This form is used to request team assistance with a problem student. Note that information is requested concerning specification of the problem and the teacher's prior efforts to solve it. The lower half of the form is used by the team in designing and evaluating systematic interventions.

There are no hard-and-fast rules concerning the duration of prereferral interventions, but twenty to forty school days (i.e., one to two months) should constitute an adequate period for determining whether the problem can be managed without more formal procedures. To avoid the tendency to turn such problems over to special services personnel, it is important that both ownership of the problem and of intervention plans be vested in the regular education program. Therefore, we recommend that teacher assistance teams be composed of staff identified with the regular education program. Specialized staff (e.g., special education teachers, school psychologists) may serve as ancillary team members on specific cases. Schools should seek in-service staff training before adopting a consultative prereferral intervention model.

Prereferral interventions are important for two reasons: first, they emphasize that attempts should be made to solve students' behavior problems using resources available in the regular education program before special education referrals are considered; and second, their results provide assessment information useful to those making decisions about pupils' eligibility for services and for determining the services that are needed. School-wide screening and prereferral intervention procedures, if systematically applied and evaluated, will make the determination of who is and is not behaviorally disordered more objective and accountable, and they will make available services to students who have behavior problems, not just those who are classified as behaviorally disordered. For more information about prereferral interventions and teacher assistance teams, consult Chalfant et al. (1979), McGlothlin (1981), and Stokes (1982).

ASSESSMENT FOR IDENTIFICATION

This stage initiates formal consideration of the student's eligibility for special education services. The question of whether a student is educationally handicapped is a serious matter. Therefore, PL 94-142 requires that the student's parents be notified of the school's intent to assess, and it requires that they give their approval. These **due process** safeguards protect students' and parents' rights.

As we mentioned previously, traditional assessment for identifying behavioral disorders consists of administering a battery of psychoeducational instruments, including an individual intelligence scale, norm- and criterion-referenced measures of achievement, instruments that assess perceptual-motor skills, and less frequently, measures of personality characteristics. Data from these instruments may be supplemented with teacher or parent interviews, direct observation of the pupil, and anecdotal information from school records. Most of the responsibility for this stage of the classification process falls on school psychologists. However, as Gresham (1985) observes, school psychologists are more comfortable and competent in assessing mental retardation and learning disabilities than in assessing behavioral disorders.

Mental Health Assessment

Many school districts do not have staff psychologists to perform assessments for the purpose of classifying pupils. These districts must rely on other agencies or professionals (e.g., men-

tal health clinics, psychologists or psychiatrists in private practice) to conduct these evaluations. The assessment model used by mental health professionals is considerably different from models that are useful for educational purposes. One of the chief differences is that the mental health assessment model is based on the identification of emotional or cognitive pathology that is presumed to underlie the student's behavior problems. Until recently, this **medical model** dominated other approaches to the assessment of behavioral disorders. It is still widely used by mental health practitioners and by school districts in some states.

The classification decisions resulting from mental health assessment often result in diagnostic labels that come from the Diagnostic and Statistical Manual, third edition (DSM-III) published by the American Psychiatric Association (1980). The DSM-III classifies psychological disorders along five axes or dimensions. Axis I consists of the major pattern of symptoms, or **clinical syndrome**, that the student exhibits. Axis II describes personality disorders; Axis III addresses physical disorders or conditions; Axis IV describes psychosocial factors that are imposing stress on the individual; and Axis V involves consideration of the pupil's level of adaptive functioning over the past year. A diagnosis may or may not be made on every axis, depending on the student and how much information the evaluator has about the case. Axis I diagnoses are always made, however. The Axis I diagnostic categories for behavior disorders of children and adolescents are grouped into five broad classes, as follows (American Psychiatric Association, 1980, pp. 35-36):

I. Intellectual
   Mental Retardation
II. Behavioral (overt)
   Attention Deficit Disorder
   Conduct Disorder
III. Emotional
   Anxiety Disorders of Childhood or
   Adolescence

Figure 1-2. Alternative Regular Classroom Interventions

Please check the various educational strategies that have been employed in attempts to enable the student to overcome the suspected problem(s) in the regular classroom and WRITE in the space provided the student's performance after the application of the strategies.

INSTRUCTIONAL MODIFICATION

1. Provided structured routine. _____
2. Provided a place with limited visual and auditory distraction. _____
3. Changed seat if auditory or visual problems were suspected. _____
4. Gave abbreviated assignments. _____
5. Provided clear, concise directions (verbally or orally). _____

6. Matched assignments with ability; taught at instructional level, not frustration level. _____
_____

ACADEMIC STRATEGIES

7. What learning aids have you used (e.g., language master, games, stencils)? _____
   Describe their effect on the student. _____

8. What modalities were used in the approach to reading and math (e.g. visual, auditory, tactile, kinesthetic)? _____
   Describe their effect on the student. _____
_____

RESPONSIVITY TO LEARNING

9. Describe the student's attitude toward learning (e.g., gives up easily, perseveres, etc.). _____
10. Describe the parent's participation in this student's educational process (e.g., degrees of interest, time spent with child, standard of excellence). _____

11. How does the student view his or her ability to be successful in accomplishing school work (academic and non-academic)? _____

BEHAVIOR MANAGEMENT STRATEGIES

12. Ignored inappropriate behavior. _____
13. Reinforced appropriate behavior. _____
14. Increased positive statements. _____
15. Gave extra privileges and responsibilities as a reward for completed assignments. _____

16. Utilized time out area. _____
17. Eliminated privilege. _____
18. Used modeling. _____
19. Established specific goals for student—one at a time. _____
20. Charted good behavior. _____
21. Provided student with chart of progress. _____
22. Set up contracts with consistent follow through. _____
23. Provided successful experiences. _____
24. Held parent conferences for home reinforcement. _____

CLASSROOM INTERACTION

Describe your interaction with this student. _____
_____

Describe this student's interaction with you. _____
_____

Describe this student's interaction with his peers. _____
Describe his or her peers' interaction with him or her. _____
Describe his or her interactions with other staff members in the building (e.g., lunch aides, custodians, music teacher, etc.) _____
_____

Source: Adapted from National Association of School Psychologists. (1986) *Intervention assistance teams: A model for building level instructional problem solving.* Washington, D.C.: Author.

Figure 1-3. Request for Assistance Form

Date _____

Student's Name _____ Grade Level _____ D.O. B. _____

Class/Cluster/Subject _____ Teacher _____ Bldg. _____

I. Describe the problem in specific terms: _____

_____

_____

The following checklists may also be of assistance:

1. ____ Disruptive
2. ____ Poor attendance
3. ____ Off task
4. ____ Disorganized
5. ____ Doesn't complete assignments
6. ____ Poor attitude

7. ____ Distractible
8. ____ Slow rate of work
9. ____ Cannot follow oral directions
10. ____ Cannot follow written directions
11. ____ Poor retention

12. ____ Poor study habits
13. ____ Lacks initiative
14. ____ Lack of participation
15. ____ Hyperactive
16. ____ Inconsistent
17. ____ Poor peer relationship
18. ____ Works below grade level

II. What modifications or adjustments have you made to remediate the problem? _____

_____

What instructional material changes have you made? _____

_____

Have you involved the parents? ____ Yes ____ No

Have you reviewed the student's cumulative record folder? ____ Yes ____ No

FOR CONFERENCE USE ONLY

III. Date of Planning Conference: _____ Observer: _____

Recommended strategies and changes: _____

_____

Implementation Period: _____ Review Conference Date: _____

Plan approved by: _____

_____ _____ _____
Observer Teacher Principal

_____ _____
Other Other

IV. Measurable or Observable Changes during the Implementation Period.

_____

_____

Modification has provided satisfactory progress: _____

Multifactored evaluation will be requested: _____

(Use other side if additional space is needed in any area.)

Source: National Association of School Psychologists. (1986). *Intervention assistance teams: A model for building level instructional problem solving.* Washington, D.C.: Author.

Other Disorders of Infancy, Childhood
or Adolescence
IV. Physical
Eating Disorders
Stereotyped Movement Disorders
Other Disorders with Physical
Manifestations
V. Developmental
Pervasive Developmental Disorders
Specific Developmental Disorders

More specific diagnoses are made within these categories and subcategories for individual cases. For example, *conduct disorder, undersocialized, aggressive,* is a diagnosis made on the basis of a set of symptoms:

1. A repetitive and persistent pattern of aggressive conduct . . . manifested by either of the following (American Psychiatric Association, 1980, pp. 47–48):
   (a) physical violence against persons or property
   (b) thefts outside the home involving confrontation with the victim
2. Failure to establish a normal degree of affection, empathy, or bond with others, as evidenced by no more than one of the following indications of social attachment:
   (a) has one or more peer-group friendships that have lasted over six months
   (b) extends himself or herself for others even when no immediate advantage is likely
   (c) apparently feels guilt or remorse when such a reaction is appropriate
   (d) avoids blaming or informing on companions
   (e) shares concern for the welfare of friends or companions
3. Duration of pattern of aggressive conduct of at least six months
4. If eighteen or older, does not meet the criteria for Antisocial Personality Disorder

As the preceding example suggests, the DSM-III approach to assessment is descriptive in that the diagnosis is based on a pattern, or

syndrome, of behavior. It is also clinical because portions of the diagnosis are based upon judgments and inferences made from the presenting symptoms (e.g., "failure to establish a normal degree of affection, empathy, or bond with others"). It is pointed out in DSM-III that the categories are not mutually exclusive, that youths often have problems not subsumed within the categories, and that many behavior problems do not warrant diagnostic classification. To these cautions we must reiterate our previous observation that students who have other handicaps may also exhibit behavioral disorders. Moreover, traditional diagnostic procedures usually occur in the clinician's office where the verbal reports of the client and others (e.g., parents) must be used instead of direct behavioral observation. This affects the reliability of the diagnosis (i.e., two clinicians may not arrive at the same diagnostic label because they each receive a different report or interpret the same information differently). In some cases the diagnosis is applied to internal processes or **constructs** (theoretical constructions of traits or attributes, e.g., overanxious disorder). The validity of these constructs (i.e., the extent to which the construct really exists) may also be questionable.

The limitations of the DSM-III diagnostic and classification system have been widely discussed (see Rizzo & Zabel, 1988). Perhaps the major weakness stems from its reliance on a disease analogy, that is, on the assumption that psychological disorders are analogous to disease processes that exist within the individual. The addition of Axis IV (psychosocial stressors) classification notwithstanding, DSM-III diagnoses tend to attribute the causes of behavior disorders to conditions within the individual. This is in contrast to the preferred practice of viewing disordered behavior as the outcome of interactions between characteristics of the individual and the environmental settings in which behavior occurs (Rizzo & Zabel, 1988).

Traditional mental health assessment begins with a referral that includes a statement of the presenting problems or the reason for referral.

And as we suggested earlier, the reason for referring a student has been shown to bias the outcome of assessment. In one study, for example, pupils referred for behavior problems were more often labeled emotionally disturbed than pupils who were referred for academic difficulties (Ysseldyke & Algozzine, 1982). The study was based on a computer simulation, but we feel the same bias operates in the real world as well. Therefore, there is a better than average possibility that a student who is referred for mental health assessment will be given a label. Ysseldyke and Algozzine (1982) suggest that when referring a student for assessment, the first steps should be (1) to clarify the nature of the referral problem, and (2) to articulate the decision that must be made (e.g., should the student be enrolled in a special class for behaviorally disordered children?). Such clarification reduces the likelihood that the diagnostician will miss the real problem or that inappropriate assessment procedures will be used when the decision is made.

The next step is to conduct the assessment. The procedure followed depends on the discipline of the evaluator (psychiatrist, psychologist, social worker), the evaluator's skills, and the diagnostic tools available. Many diagnosticians conduct structured or unstructured interviews with the student, the student's parents, or others (e.g., classroom teachers). In some cases, standardized assessment procedures or instruments may also be used. These may include individually administered intelligence tests, personality tests, tests of interest or preference, rating scales, or self-concept inventories. Table 1-1 lists a number of such tests that may be used with your students. It is important to recognize that many of the instruments, especially those using **projective techniques** (those in which the client "projects" his personality through responses to ambiguous stimuli, such as ink blots or pictures) offer poor reliability and validity, as well as inadequate norms (Salvia & Ysseldyke, 1985). The inadequacy and educational irrelevance of personality tests, as well as the threat of legal sanction

arising from decisions based on their results, has led to increasing reliance on more objective procedures (Salvia & Ysseldyke, 1985).

Nevertheless, clinical assessment procedures that result in a diagnostic mental health label are still employed with children and youth. And despite its weaknesses (tests that are often static, subjective, narrow in scope, and inferential), a good diagnostic evaluation can be helpful, especially if the outcomes include multidisciplinary planning and follow-up activities. We have chosen to organize this text in terms of educationally relevant behavioral categories rather than the DSM-III categories; therefore, you may need to ignore psychiatric labels or translate them into more useful terms. The label "emotionally disturbed" or "behaviorally disordered" is sufficient to qualify pupils for special education, and once more, we stress that it is not necessary to label students in order to work with them.

School-Based Assessment

A more functional process for determining whether students should be classified as behaviorally disordered consists of building upon the information gathered from systematic screening and prereferral intervention procedures through comprehensive assessments directed by school personnel. This process begins with a referral for formal evaluation and involves the compilation of information from attempts to manage the problem at the prereferral level, as well as systematic assessments by school staff and other professionals. This process is summarized in Figure 1-4. The *compilation of prereferral screening and intervention data* may include such documentation as is included in Oregon's evaluation checklist (Figure 1-1). This documentation should demonstrate that: (1) problem behaviors are perceived as extreme by more than one observer across more than one setting; (2) prereferral interventions have been attempted and have failed; (3) the problem has existed over a reasonably long period of time (except in the case of behavior

Table 1-1. Commonly Used Measures of Personality, Interests, and Traits

General Personality and Emotional Development

Bender Visual Motor Gestalt Test (Bender, 1938)

Blacky Pictures (Blum, 1967)

California Psychological Inventory (Gough, 1969)

California Test of Personality (Thorpe, Clark, & Tiegs, 1953)

Children's Apperception Test (Bellak & Bellak, 1965)

Draw-a-Person (Urban, 1963)

Early School Personality Questionnaire (Coan & Cattell, 1970)

Edwards Personal Preference Schedule (Edwards, 1959)

Edwards Personality Inventory (Edwards, 1966)

Eysenck Personality Inventory (Eysenck & Eysenck, 1969)

Family Relations Test (Bene & Anthony, 1957)

Holtzman Ink Blot Technique (Holtzman, 1966)

House-Tree-Person (Buck & Jolles, 1966)

Human Figures Drawing Test (Koppitz, 1968)

Jr.-Sr. High School Personality Questionnaire (Cattell, Coan, & Belloff, 1969)

Minnesota Multiphasic Personality Inventory (Hathaway & McKinley, 1967)

Rorschach Ink Blot Technique (Rorschach, 1966)

School Apperception Method (Solomon & Starr, 1968)

Sixteen Personality Factor Questionnaire (Cattell, Eber, & Tatsuoka, 1970)

Thematic Apperception Test (Murray, 1943)

Interests or Preferences

Kuder Personal Preference Record (Kuder, 1954)

School Interest Inventory (Cottle, 1966)

School Motivation Analysis Test (Sweney, Cattell, Krug, 1970)

Personality or Behavior Traits

Burks Behavior Rating Scale (Burks, 1969)

Devereux Adolescent Behavior Rating Scale (Spivack, Spotts, & Haimes, 1967)

Devereux Child Behavior Rating Scale (Spivack & Spotts, 1966)

Devereux Elementary School Behavior Rating Scale (Spivack & Swift, 1967)

Revised Problem Behavior Checklist (Quay & Peterson, 1983)

Pupil Behavior Inventory (Vinter, Sarri, Vorwaller, & Schafer, 1966)

Walker Problem Behavior Identification Checklist (Walker, 1970, Revised, 1983)

Self-Concept

Piers-Harris Children's Self-Concept Scale (Piers & Harris, 1969)

Tennessee Self-Concept Inventory (Fitts, 1965)

Source: Salvia, John, and Ysseldyke, James E. "Commonly Used Measures of Personality, Interests, and Traits," *Assessment in Special and Remedial Education,* Fourth Edition. Copyright © 1988 by Houghton Mifflin Company. Adapted with permission.

Figure 1-4. Pupil Identification Assessment Process

I. Compilation of Screening and Prereferral Data
Documentation that student's problem behaviors occur more frequently or more intensely than nonreferred peers, that such behaviors have occurred for a long period of time, and that they have not been solved through systematic management in the regular education setting

Acceptable procedures:
- Standardized behavior ratings completed by two or more teachers, or by teachers and parents
- Direct observation data (including data on nondeviant peer)
- Evidence that problems have occurred for a prolonged period
- Evidence that problems are not due to temporary stress or to curriculum or cultural factors
- Evidence that interventions in regular program have been systematically implemented and have not been effective
- Verification by school personnel that behavior is dangerous to student or to others

II. Intellectual Assessment
Documentation that behavior is not due to impaired cognitive functioning, or if cognitive deficits are present, that appropriate programming has not solved behavior problems

Acceptable procedures:
- Acceptable individual measure of intelligence or aptitude, administered by qualified examiner

III. Academic Assessment
Documentation that academic performance or progress has not been satisfactory for a period of time

Acceptable procedures:
- Individually administered norm-referenced measures of academic achievement
- Group administered achievement tests *and* written analysis of classroom products and documentation of classroom academic progress
- Curriculum-based or criterion-referenced assessments documenting progress across curriculum
- Direct observation of academic time on task
- Samples of classroom work across time and tasks

IV. Social Competence Assessment
Documentation that student is deficient in social skills or that social status is seriously affected

Acceptable procedures:
- Administration of approved standardized social skills inventories or checklists
- Administration of adaptive behavior scales
- Administration of sociometric scales or procedures
- Direct observation in unstructured social setting (include peer comparison data)

V. Social, Developmental, and School History
Documentation that problem is not due to any previously undiscovered factors or cultural differences

Acceptable procedures:
- Interviews with parents or guardians, referring teacher, other teachers, student
- Review of student's cumulative school records

VI. Medical Evaluation
Documentation that problem is not due to health factors

Acceptable procedures:
- Medical screening by physician, school nurse, or physician's assistant
- Comprehensive medical evaluation if student fails to pass screening

that poses a hazard to life or safety); (4) the problem cannot be explained by such factors as temporary stress, medical problems, inappropriate educational programming, or cultural differences; (5) the pupil is deficient in academic performance or social skills; and (6) the problem behaviors occur at a high rate or are markedly deviant from acceptable norms.

Intelligence tests have very limited utility for assessing behavior problems. However, an *intellectual assessment* can document that the problem is not due to cognitive impairment. (If the student is mentally handicapped, it should be documented that specific programming related to this handicap has not solved the student's behavior problems.) It is important to realize that students may be mentally retarded *and* have behavior problems or disorders. Therefore, schools should be able to bring the needed services to the pupil in his current school placement, rather than moving the student to another program, unless it is decided that the latter is more appropriate. Changes in school placement require invoking due process, as well as reassessment and decision making by the committee established to supervise the pupil's educational program, and thus cannot be made quickly or easily. Taking services to the student is more expedient and less disruptive, and so it is the preferred strategy.

The *academic assessment* may be accomplished through a variety of procedures, including individually administered norm-referenced achievement tests, curriculum-based assessments, analysis of classroom work samples and data regarding academic progress, and direct observation of time on task. Several sources of academic data should be provided in order to rule out the possibility that conclusions are based on inadequate samples of student performance.

Academic assessment is important for two reasons. First, in most states, a diagnosis of behaviorally disordered (seriously emotionally disturbed) can be made only if educational performance is adversely affected. Second, behavior problems and academic difficulties are often functionally related. Students who are frustrated by academic tasks and expectations that are beyond their current skill levels may act out or withdraw to avoid such tasks or to express their feelings. Conversely, problem behaviors may interfere with academic learning because they are incompatible with academic performance or because they result in disciplinary actions that cause pupils to be removed from the instructional setting.

The *social competence assessment* is likely to reveal social skills deficits in students considered for classification as behaviorally disordered because failure to establish satisfactory

social relationships is a defining characteristic. Therefore, it is important that skills related to social interactions with peers and adults be assessed. Recall that in some states (e.g., Oregon), social skill deficits carry as much weight as academic deficiencies when identifying pupils as behaviorally disordered. **Social competence** is a general domain referring to summative evaluative judgments regarding the adequacy of a student's performance on social tasks by an informed social agent (Walker & McConnell, 1988). Gresham and Reschly (1987) indicate that social competence is composed of two subdomains: adaptive behavior and specific social skills. Measures of adaptive behavior typically assess general independent functioning, which includes physical development, self-direction, personal responsibility, economic or vocational skills, and functional academic skills (Walker & McConnell, 1988). The American Association of Mental Deficiency (AAMD) Adaptive Behavior Scale, School Edition (Lambert, Windmiller, Tharinger, & Cole, 1981) or the Vineland Adaptive Behavior Scale (Scarrow, Balla, & Cicchatti, 1985) are appropriate measures of social competence. The format of these scales consists of ratings that are completed through interviews with persons familiar with the pupil's functioning or development in relevant settings. **Social skills** are the specific strategies one uses to respond to social living tasks (Walker & McConnell, 1988). Several social skills assessment instruments have recently been developed, among them the Social Behavior Assessment (Stephens, 1979), the Teacher Ratings of Social Skills (Clark, Gresham, & Elliott, 1985), the Social Skills Rating Scales (Gresham & Elliott, 1986), and the Walker-McConnell Scale of Social Competence and School Adjustment: A Social Skills Rating Scale for Teachers (Walker & McConnell, 1988). As the names of these instruments suggest, they consist of rating scale items that are completed by persons who are familiar with the student's functioning.[3] Alternate procedures for assessing social competence include sociometrics and direct observations of the pupil's behavior in unstructured social situations.

The direct observation of social behavior is an important assessment tool for pupils being considered for special education services. It provides an opportunity to analyze the student's behavior in the immediate social context, enabling the assessor to identify excess and deficit problem behaviors, adaptive behavior patterns, as well as the antecedents and consequences of specific behaviors. Potential biases associated with personal judgment are reduced when using direct observation procedures. Behavioral observation strategies are described in Chapter 2.

Additional data may be collected about social, developmental, and school history through interviews with the student's caretakers, the referring teacher, other teachers, and the student. A thorough search of the pupil's cumulative school records should be conducted to assess such variables as attendance, health history, discipline reports, and previous screenings or referrals for special education evaluation. Concurrently, a *medical evaluation* should be performed to rule out possible health factors. Students who do not pass this screening should be referred for a comprehensive medical examination.

It is also important to assess the extent to which *cultural differences* may contribute to behavior problems in school. Although membership in a racially or ethnically different cultural group should not be used to overlook a student's maladaptive behavior, school personnel must be sensitive to the effects of cultural attitudes and of customs on behavior. Culturally different students may exhibit patterns of language and social behavior that conflict with the normative standards and expectations of the school. Moreover, pupils' awareness of their deviation from school norms regarding dress, extracurricular activities, and financial status may cause them to withdraw from or rebel against persons exemplifying these norms. The expectations and reactions of other pupils and school staff may also be affected by cultural stereotypes, which can intensify difficulties involving cultural issues. Therefore, in assessing culturally different students, evaluators should attempt to determine the function that "deviant" behaviors may serve for the student (e.g., "playing the dozens", avoiding direct eye contact) with reference to his cultural group before concluding that such behavior patterns are maladaptive. When culturally appropriate behaviors conflict with staff or peer expectations, assessors should be open to the conclusions that the expectations are in error and that intervention should address these in addition to (or instead of) the student's behavior.

Cultural differences should be considered during prereferral screening and during identification too, of course. In fact, sensitivity to cultural factors underlying presumed behavior problems may be even more important at this level, as culturally related behavior patterns and stereotypes may trigger a sequence of events that lead to certification and labeling of pupils as handicapped. Algozzine, Christenson, and Ysseldyke (1982) demonstrated that initiation of special education referrals is likely to result in special education certification. They surveyed a national sample of state directors of special education and found that 92 percent of students referred for psychoeducational evaluation were actually tested, and 73 percent of those evaluated were declared eligible for special education.

Thus, an adequate assessment of students referred for possible classification as behaviorally disordered is comprehensive and complex. However, the seriousness of the decision being considered justifies this detailed evaluation pro-

---

[3] Standardized instruments and informal procedures for assessing student behavior and social status are described in Chapter 2.

cess. Also, this process is multidisciplinary. No one professional is qualified to perform all of these assessments. It is appropriate and desirable to involve professionals in other roles within the school, as well as professionals outside the schools, in the assessment process. However, it is important that a staff member or a team of staff from the pupil's school be responsible for compiling and analyzing the assessment data then presenting it to the persons who will make the classification (certification) decision.

CERTIFICATION

The decision to classify a pupil as behaviorally disordered is too important to be made on the basis of limited information or by persons not familiar with all facets of the student's personality and environment. Thus, PL 94-142 requires that eligibility decisions be made by a team of persons, which must include the parents or guardians (if they are not available, a **parent surrogate** may be appointed), the referring teacher, a school administrator, the special education teacher, and a person able to interpret the results of the diagnostic procedures. Other individuals should be included as necessary. This team is usually labeled the child study team or the special education **admission and release committee** (ARC). The ARC's responsibilities are to determine whether the assessment information supports the need for special education certification, to make decisions regarding the most appropriate educational program and placement, and to evaluate the student's progress and the effectiveness of the educational services provided.

The validity of the classification decisions made by ARCs has been questioned, however. Potter, Ysseldyke, and Regan (1983) gave a large group of school professionals assessment information on a hypothetical student that reflected performance in the average range for the student's age and grade placement. They indicated that the student had been referred for

special education and asked the professionals whether they believed the pupil was eligible for special education. Fifty-one percent of these professionals declared the student eligible for special education services. This study verifies that assessment data are often not used in making certification decisions (Walker & Fabre, 1987). The procedures we described in the previous sections should help to remedy this problem; however, decisions involving the judgments of persons are inescapably subjective. Careful analysis and review are therefore important.

The decision to certify a student as behaviorally disordered actually consists of a set of decisions. If the ARC decides that the pupil is eligible for services, it must decide what services are needed and in what settings they should be provided. In the past, these decisions were guided by the limited range of services available in schools. Often, the only alternatives were special academic instruction or behavior management in a self-contained special classroom or resource room. The availability of an increased range of special education and support services reduces the ARC's dependency on placing students in restrictive educational settings in order to provide them with needed services. Thus, the ARC may determine that a pupil needs systematic behavior management, highly structured academic instruction, and social-skills training. However, because the school offers consulting teacher services and has adopted a social skills teaching curriculum, these services can be provided without requiring a change in the student's current educational placement. Even in schools where a wide range of services is not available, decisions regarding what services pupils need should precede and be separate from decisions about where students will access these services (i.e., where they will be placed).

Finally, we advocate that when students are certified as eligible for special education, criteria for their **decertification** be set. This means that the ARC should specify the goals and objectives for the pupil's special education program (which is required by law) and also indicate that when these are met, the student should be declared no longer handicapped and returned to regular education. (The decision to retain the pupil in special education should be justified through a comprehensive reevaluation and should be made by the student's ARC.) This strategy would reduce the tendency to leave pupils in special education for the rest of their school careers.

Figure 1-5 summarizes the eligibility decision-making process, from screening through decertifying and returning pupils to the regular program. For a complete, step-by-step guide to the assessment of behavioral disorders, see the Iowa Assessment Model (Wood et al., 1985).

The Continuum of Behavioral Problems and Educational Services

The range of problem behaviors encountered in schools can be described in many ways. For practical reasons, this range is generally matched to a continuum of special education interventions: the more severe the problem behavior, the more restrictive the special education program (the further removed from the educational mainstream). In the past, special education interventions have been "place-oriented" (Reynolds & Birch, 1977) — that is,

Figure 1-5. Eligibility Decisions

Question	*Action*
I. Screening	
A. Is student "at risk"?	A. Administer screening procedure, activate teacher assistance team
B. Can student be helped through regular program?	B. Modify or adapt regular program
II. Identification	
A. Has student benefited from adaptations made in regular program?	A. Evaluate effects of regular education interventions
B. Is additional support or service needed?	B. Implement consultative intervention
C. Should student be identified as behaviorally disordered?	C. Conduct assessment; hold staffing
III. Certification	
A. Should student be referred for BD services?	A. Conduct ARC meeting
B. What services are needed?	B. Develop individualized education plan (IEP)
C. Where should services be provided?	C. Identify least restrictive settings for pupil
D. What expectations must the pupil meet to return to the regular classroom?	D. Specify criteria for decertification
IV. Program Evaluation	
A. Is the program working?	A. Implement formative and summative evaluation procedures
V. Decertification	
A. Is special education no longer needed?	A. Evaluate progress against exit criteria, conduct exit ARC

confined to special places such as self-contained classrooms or resource rooms. This orientation has created an expectation that pupils who are referred for special education will be removed from the regular program and treated in some "special" place with a "special" set of methods. Nowhere is this expectation more prevalent than in the area of behavioral disorders. Students who are unruly, aggressive, disrespectful, threatening, or just "weird" are aversive to regular classroom teachers; teachers find themselves unable to manage such students effectively. For years, special education has served these students in segregated programs, thereby reinforcing the expectation that behavior problem pupils cannot be taught in the mainstream, and that regular educators are not responsible for their management.

It is unfortunate that this refer-and-remove pattern also reinforces the assumption that the referred pupil always owns the problem. Seldom is it acknowledged that the source of the behavioral disorder may be inappropriate expectations, curriculum, or teaching methods. Thus, the referring teacher emerges from this process without a problem, and with a reinforced attitude that the problem was the student's fault. The referred child, on the other hand, comes out of this process stigmatized by a label and transferred to a "special" environment to be "treated" and, perhaps, never returned to the educational mainstream.

Fortunately, the emphasis on place-oriented services is giving way to a philosophy of providing a continuum of services that are brought to the pupils and their teachers. For example, Oregon's suggested continuum of behavior management services is presented in Figure 1-6. Note that the first three steps in this continuum involve procedures and resources provided in the regular classroom. A change in educational placement (from regular to special) is not considered until step 4.

We stress repeatedly throughout this text that problem behaviors occur without regard

for a student's educational placement or labels. Thus, pupils who have been labeled and placed in programs for other categories of handicapping conditions are as likely to require intervention services as students in regular programs or in programs for the behaviorally disordered. Regular and special education administrators should view behavior problems as indications of a need for services rather than as a need for change in a student's educational placement. The latter requires considerably more elaborate and time-consuming activities, which are likely to disrupt the student's program, and there is no guarantee that the new placement will benefit the pupil any more than the old.

Figure 1-7 describes the continuum of services to students who have been certified as behaviorally disordered. In contrast to Figure 1-6, this continuum gives more emphasis to placement. Levels I and II include identified behaviorally disordered pupils who are mainstreamed into regular classes without consultative assistance to the regular classroom teacher (Level I) or with consultative assistance (Level II). Subsequent levels indicate more restrictive placements, including placement outside the public school setting.

When special education placement is deemed necessary, a decision must be made as to which level in the continuum is least restrictive for the student. **Least restrictive placement** is not synonymous with the regular classroom. The educational environment that imposes the fewest obstacles to the pupil's optimal social and academic functioning depends on that student's individual needs. We believe this decision cannot be made without a comprehensive and thorough assessment of the pupil and his or her total environment.

If the pupil is causing a management problem in one setting, a consultation with the teacher regarding effective management strategies may be all that is needed (i.e., Level II services). Should the pupil's behavior problems occur across more settings (e.g., all

Figure 1-6. Continuum of Services for Managing Student Behavior

Step	Responsibility	Procedure	Resources
#1	Classroom teacher	Regular classroom placement	The teacher utilizes instructional and classroom management methods that include posted classroom rules and consequences for behavior.
#2	Classroom teacher and school staff	Regular classroom placement and referral to school resources	This involves advice and support from colleagues, involvement of the school support staff, or student referral to a systematic school discipline system.
#3	Classroom teacher, school staff, and district staff	Regular classroom placement and request for district resources	The district provides consultation resources such as a special education school psychologist, or behavior specialist.
#4	Classroom teacher, school staff, and district staff	Request for special education evaluation and eligibility decision. Placement in a special building, program, or regular classroom.	The multidisciplinary team determines eligibility, the IEP team determines the placement and programming, and the special education staff provides and coordinates services.
#5	School staff, special education, district staff, and community resources	Placement within district resources and referral to community resources	District and community resources.

Source: Waksman, S., and Jones, V. (1985, August). A suggested procedure for the identification and provision of services to seriously emotionally disturbed students. *Technical assistance papers: A series on PL 94-142 and related Oregon laws.* Portland, OR: Department of Education.

classes, on the playground, in the lunchroom, on the bus), or if the pupil exhibits academic difficulties needing special remedial methods, a more restrictive placement might be considered, such as a resource room or self-contained special class (i.e., Level III or IV). In our view, severe and widespread behavior problems or serious communication difficulties should be present before placement in more restrictive settings (i.e., Levels V, VI, and VII) is considered.

Placements that eliminate students' opportunity for contact with the normal environment should be avoided if possible. The only advantage afforded students in these placements is more intensive programming by a qualified team. For example, segregated day schools may offer psychologists, social workers, and other mental health professionals to assist in designing a consistent and therapeutic program. Some pupils need this degree of structure and support. Still others require a twenty-

Figure 1-7. Continuum of Services for Behaviorally Disordered Children and Youth

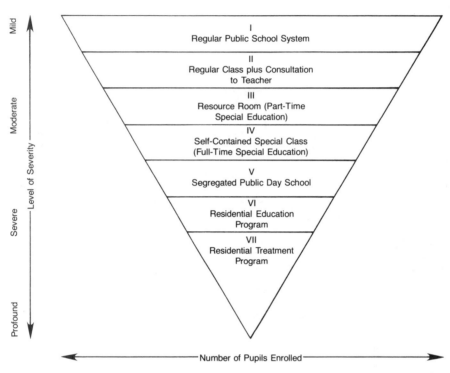

four hour structured program such as that in a residential school. The last level, a residential treatment program, is available for children and youth who require a psychiatrically oriented treatment program, which may include medical treatment and intensive psychotherapy.

Figure 1-7 suggests that more students, with less severe behavior problems, will be found at the upper levels of the continuum. This observation holds for students who have *not* been certified as behaviorally disordered; however, as Walker and Fabre (1987) indicate, three-fourths of all certified behaviorally disordered pupils are currently served in self-contained (Level IV) or more restrictive settings. Furthermore, approximately 41 percent of all students receiving homebound instruction are behaviorally disordered (Walker & Fabre, 1987). In contrast, 68 percent of the overall handicapped population are receiving most of

their education in regular classes (U.S. Department of Education, 1985). Thus, it appears that, in general, schools are reluctant to identify students as behaviorally disordered, and if they do, they prefer to remove them as far as possible from the mainstream. The assumption that certified behaviorally disordered pupils are placed in more restrictive settings because their behavior problems are more severe is intriguing, but is essentially untestable because judgments of the severity of behavior problems are subjective. Even with standardized rating scales and direct observation, behavioral disorders cannot be quantified along a continuum, as is the case with IQ and achievement test scores.

Again, the least restrictive placement depends on the individual student, and we urge that special education be conceptualized as a continuum of services first, with consideration given to more restrictive educational placements after interventions have been tried and proven unsuccessful in less restrictive settings. We also recommend that the behavioral requirements of educational settings be assessed and that those competencies be targeted for instruction in more restrictive placements so that the curriculum is functional in terms of promoting student progress to less restrictive educational settings. Procedures for assessing the behavioral expectations of less restrictive environments have been developed (see Walker & Rankin, 1983) and are described in Chapter 12.

As a professional working with problem behavior, you may function anywhere within this continuum, from a consultant to regular classroom teachers to a teacher in a residential psychiatric hospital. The methods presented in this book can be applied effectively in all of these settings, and they have been. Although the focus of our discussion is the classroom, the techniques and procedures described may be used elsewhere — in the lunchroom, library, gym, playground, home, and neighborhood. Often, you will find that you must generalize your classroom procedures to these settings because it is here that youths with behavior problems experience their greatest difficulty. Then too, unless you want to be the exclusive caregiver of six to ten students for the entire school day, you must teach others to implement your management procedures. Not only do your pupils need to learn to cope with the larger environment but also the environment (other school staff, parents, other children) must learn how to cope with them.

Finally, to change problem behavior—to teach pupils and their caregivers to use new and better skills in their total environment—you must systematically prepare these skills to be generalized and maintained in other settings (Rutherford & Nelson, 1988). What good have you accomplished when you have taught a student to accept your correction of his or her behavior or not to steal in your classroom, if the student blows up when corrected in algebra class or steals money from a purse at home?

Working with behaviorally disordered pupils requires that you spend a good deal of time outside your classroom, and later, we will offer techniques and suggestions for working effectively in other settings.

The concepts and strategies presented in this chapter are not currently in widespread use in many school programs. In addition, their implementation may depend on school policies developed by boards of education and administrators. Therefore, you may feel powerless to use these models in your role. Nevertheless, we have presented these concepts and strategies because, far from being futuristic ideals, they are part of a currently developing technology for serving pupils who have behavior problems. In the following chapters you will learn some of this technology, as well as guidelines for judging when and where to apply it. We hope that skills you acquire will help you function more effectively in your professional role and advocate for more effective services for students whose behavior reduces their chances of succeeding in the educational system.

Summary

The assessment of students exhibiting behavior problems is a complex and technical process that leads to decisions about student classification and intervention procedures. This chapter has focused on assessment for the purposes of identifying and classifying pupils as behaviorally disordered for special education services. Unfortunately, the identification of students as behaviorally disordered has typically been influenced by numerous subjective and political factors, resulting in this population being among the most underserved of all groups of handicapped pupils. Even more unfortunately, students who fail to meet definitional criteria for special education have historically been inadequately served by the regular education system. These problems are currently being addressed through the development of systematic screening and identification procedures, prereferral interventions, and the use of systematic assessment data to match pupil needs with a continuum of educational services.

Discussion Questions

1. Why is the identification of students who are handicapped by their behavior more difficult than that of other handicapped populations? How does this affect prevalence estimates?
2. How does assessment for classification purposes differ from assessment for treatment planning? What instruments and procedures would you include in an "ideal" classification system?
3. Would you advocate the identification and certification of students as behaviorally disordered in order to provide them with educational services, or would you favor serving them through systematic interventions in regular programs? Support your position.
4. Increasingly, children and youth with behavioral disorders are being served in residential treatment programs outside of local school districts. Discuss this trend in terms of its effects on students' likelihood of successful reintegration into the educational mainstream.

References

Algozzine, B., Christenson, S., & Ysseldyke, J. (1982). Probabilities associated with the referral to placement process. *Teacher Education and Special Education, 5,* 19-23.

American Psychiatric Association, Committee on Nomenclature and Statistics. (1980). *Diagnostic and statistical manual to mental disorders* (3rd ed.). Washington, DC: Author.

Apter, S. J. (1982). *Troubled children: Troubled systems.* New York: Pergamon.

Bellak, L., & Bellak, S. (1965). *Children's Apperception Test.* Cleveland: Modern Curriculum Press.

Bender, L. (1938). *A visual motor gestalt test and its clinical use* (Research Monograph No. 3). New York: American Orthopsychiatric Association.

Bene, E., & Anthony, J. (1957). *Family Relations Test: An objective technique for exploring emotional attitudes in children.* Windsor, England: NFER-Nelson Publishing Company.

Blum, B. (1967). *Blacky Pictures: A technique for the exploration of personality dynamics.* Santa Barbara: Psychodynamic Instruments.

Bower, E. M. (1982). Defining emotional disturbance: Public policy and research. *Psychology in the Schools, 19,* 55-60.

Braaten, S., Kauffman, J. M., Braaten, B., Polsgrove, L., & Nelson, C. M. (1988). The regular education initiative: Patent medicine for behavioral disorders? *Exceptional Children, 55,* 21-27.

Buck, J., & Jolles, I. (1966). *House-Tree-Person.* Los Angeles: Western Psychological Services.

Burks, H. (1969). *Burks Behavior Rating Scales.* Los Angeles: Western Psychological Services.

Cattell, R. B., Coan, R., & Belloff, H. (1969). *Jr.-Sr. High School Personality Questionnaire.* Indianapolis: Bobbs-Merrill.

Cattell, R. B., Eber, H., & Tatsuoka, M. (1970). *Sixteen Personality Factor Questionnaire.* Champaign, IL: Institute for Personality and Ability Testing.

Chalfant, J. C., Pysh, M., & Moultrie, R. (1979). Teacher assistance teams: A model for within-building problem solving. *Learning Disabilities Quarterly, 2,* 85-96.

Clark, L., Gresham, F. M., & Elliott, S. N. (1985). Development and validation of a social skills measure: the TROSS-C. *Journal of Psychoeducational Assessment, 4,* 347-356.

Coan, R., & Cattell, R. B. (1970). *Early School Personality Questionnaire.* Champaign, IL: Institute for Personality and Ability Testing.

Cottle, W. (1966). *School Interest Inventory.*

Chicago: The Riverside Publishing Company.

Council for Children with Behavioral Disorders (1987). Position paper on definition and identification of students with behavioral disorders. *Behavioral Disorders, 13,* 9-19.

Department of Health, Education, and Welfare, Office of Education, (1977, Tuesday, 23 August). Education of handicapped children: Implementation of Part B of the Education of the Handicapped Act. *Federal Register, 42,* 163.

Edwards, A. (1966). *Edwards Personality Inventory.* Chicago: Science Research Associates.

Edwards, A. (1959). *Edwards Personal Preference Schedule.* Cleveland: The Psychological Corporation.

Eysenck, H., & Eysenck, S. (1969). *Eysenck Personality Inventory.* San Diego: Educational and Industrial Testing Service.

Fitts, W. (1965). *Tennessee Self Concept Inventory.* Nashville: Counselor Recordings and Tests.

Gerry, M. (1984). Expert witness deposition from *Lavon v. Turlington.* Class action lawsuit settled in State of Florida.

Gerber, M., & Semmel, M. (1984). Teacher as imperfect test: Reconceptualizing the referral process. *Educational Psychologist, 19,* 137-148.

Gough, H. (1969). *California Psychological Inventory.* Palo Alto: Consulting Psychologists Press.

Gresham, F. M. (1985). Behavior disorders assessment: Conceptual, definitional, and practical considerations. *School Psychology Review, 14,* 495-509.

Gresham, F. M., & Elliott, S. N. (1986). *Social Skills Rating Scales.* Circle Pines, MN: American Guidance Service.

Gresham, F. M., & Reschly, D. (1987). Issues in the conceptualization, classification, and assessment of social skills in the mildly handicapped. In T. Kratochwill (Ed.), *Advances in school psychology,* Vol. 6, (pp. 203-264). Hillsdale, NJ: Lawrence Erlbaum.

Hathaway, S., & McKinley, J. (1967). *Minnesota Multiphasic Personality Inventory.* Cleveland: The Psychological Corporation.

Holtzman, W. (1966). *Holtzman Ink Blot Technique.* San Antonio, TX: The Psychological Corporation.

Howell, K. W., & Morehead, M. K. (1987). *Curriculum-based evaluation for special and remedial education.* Columbus, OH: Merrill.

Huntze, S. (1985). A position paper of the Council for Children with Behavioral Disorders. *Behavorial Disorders, 10,* 167-174.

Kauffman, J. M. (1987). Forward: Social policy issues in special education and related services for emotionally disturbed children and youth. In N. Haring (Ed.), *Measuring and managing behavior disorders* (pp. x-xx). Seattle: University of Washington Press.

Koppitz, E. M. (1968). *Human Figures Drawing Test.* New York: Grune & Stratton.

Kuder, R. (1954). *Kuder Personal Preference Record.* Chicago: Science Research Associates.

Lambert, N., Windmiller, M., Tharinger, D., & Cole, L. (1981). *AAMD Adaptive Behavior Scale (school edition).* Monterey, CA: Publishers Test Service.

McGlothlin, J. E. (1981). The school consultation committee: An approach to implementing a teacher consultation model. *Behavioral Disorders, 6,* 101-107.

Murray, H. (1943). *Thematic Apperception Test.* Cambridge, MA: Harvard University Press.

National Association of School Psychologists. (1986). *Intervention assistance teams: A model for building level instructional problem solving.* Washington, DC: Author.

Piers, E., & Harris, D. (1969). *The Piers-Harris Children's Self-Concept Scale.* Nashville: Counselor Recordings and Tests.

Potter, M. L., Ysseldyke, J. E., & Regan, R. R. (1983). Eligibility and classification decisions in educational settings: Issuing "passports" in a state of confusion. *Contemporary Educational Psychology, 8,* 146-157.

Quay, H., & Peterson, D. (1983). *Revised Problem Behavior Checklist*. Coral Gables, FL: University of Miami.

Reynolds, M. C., & Birch, J. W. (1977). *Teaching exceptional children in all America's schools*. Reston, VA: Council for Exceptional Children.

Rizzo, J. V., & Zabel, R. H. (1988). *Educating children and adolescents with behavioral disorders: An integrative approach*. Boston: Allyn & Bacon.

Rorschach, H. (1966). *Rorschach Ink Blot Technique*. New York: Grune and Stratton.

Rutherford, R. B., Jr., & Nelson, C. M. (1988). Generalization and maintenance of treatment effects. In J. C. Witt, E. N. Elliott, & F. M. Gresham (Eds.), *Handbook of behavior therapy in education* (pp. 227–324). New York: Plenum.

Salvia, J., & Ysseldyke, J. E. (1985). *Assessment in special and remedial education* (4th ed.). Boston: Houghton Mifflin, p. 300.

Solomon, I., & Starr, B. (1968). *School Apperception Method*. New York: Springer.

Sparrow, S. S., Balla, D. A., & Cicchetti, D. V. (1985). *Vineland Adaptive Behavior Scales*. Circle Pines, MN: American Guidance Service.

Spivack, G., & Spotts, J. (1966). *Devereux Child Behavior Rating Scale*. Devon, PA: The Devereux Foundation Press.

Spivack, G., Spotts, J., & Haimes, P. (1967). *Devereux Adolescent Behavior Rating Scale*. Devon, PA: The Devereux Foundation Press.

Spivack, G., & Swift, U. (1967). *Devereux Elementary School Behavior Rating Scale*. Devon, PA: The Devereux Foundation Press.

Stephens, T. M. (1979). *Social behavior assessment*. Columbus, OH: Cedars Press.

Stokes, S. (Ed.). (1982). *School-based staff support teams: A blueprint for action*. Reston, VA: ERIC Clearinghouse on Handicapped and Gifted Children.

Sweney, A., Cattell, R. B., & Krug, S. (1970). *School Motivation Analysis Test*. Champaign, IL: Institute for Personality and Ability Testing.

Thorpe, L., Clark, W., & Tiegs, E. (1953). *California Test of Personality*. Monterey, CA: CTB/McGraw-Hill.

Urban, W. (1963). *Draw-A-Person*. Los Angeles: Western Psychological Services.

U. S. Department of Education (1985). *Seventh annual report to Congress on the implementation of the Education of the Handicapped Act*. Washington, DC: U.S. Department of Education, Office of Special Education and Rehabilitative Services.

Vinter, R., Sarri, R., Vorwaller, D., & Schafer, E. (1966). *Pupil Behavior Inventory*. Ann Arbor: Campus Publishers.

Waksman, S., & Jones, V. (1985, August). A suggested procedure for the identification of and provision of services to seriously emotionally disturbed students. *Technical assistance papers: A series on PL 94-142 and related Oregon laws*. Portland: Oregon Department of Education.

Walker, H. (1983). *Walker Problem Behavior Identification Checklist*. (Revised). Los Angeles: Western Psychological Services.

Walker, H. M., & Fabre, T. R. (1987). Assessment of behavior disorders in the school setting: Issues, problems and strategies revisited. In N. Haring (Ed.), *Measuring and managing behavior disorders* (pp. 198-243). Seattle: University of Washington Press.

Walker, H. M., & McConnell, S. R. (1988). *The Walker-McConnell Scale of Social Competence and School Adjustment: A Social Skills Rating Scale for Teachers*. Austin, TX: PRO-ED Publishing Co.

Walker, H. M., & Rankin, R. (1983). Assessing the behavioral expectations and demands of less restrictive settings. *School Psychology Digest, 12*, 274-284.

Walker, H. M., Severson, H., & Haring, N.

(1986). *Standardized screening and identification of behavior disordered pupils in the elementary age range: Rationale, procedures and guidelines.* Eugene: University of Oregon.

Wood, F. H., Smith, C. R., & Grimes, J. (Eds.). (1985). *The Iowa assessment model in behavioral disorders: A training manual.* Des Moines, IA: Department of Public Instruction.

Ysseldyke, J. E., & Algozzine, B. (1982). *Critical issues in special and remedial education.* Boston: Houghton Mifflin.

Assessment for Intervention Planning

Chapter 2

OUTLINE

The Assessment Process
A Model for the Assessment of Social Behavior
Intervention Objectives and Task Analysis
Case Study

OBJECTIVES

After completing this chapter, the reader should be able to

- Describe the purposes and outcomes of the behavioral-ecological assessment process.
- Indicate the difficulties of evaluating discrepancies between social behaviors and standards, and describe some procedures for assessing these discrepancies.
- Describe assessment decisions based on the model presented in Figure 2-1 given information about target behaviors.
- Explain how the following influence the selection of social behavior targets: the communicative function, the fair pair rule, the criterion of ultimate functioning, and the criterion of functioning in the next environment.
- Write terminal intervention objectives and analyze these objectives by breaking them down into three to five task steps, given descriptions of target behaviors.

In Chapter 1 we described two sets of assessment decisions: those regarding students' educational classification and placement, and those involving their educational treatment, which include what to teach and how to teach (Howell & Morehead, 1987). This chapter concerns assessment for the purpose of planning educational interventions directed at pupils' social behaviors (i.e., what to teach). At this point we assume that placement decisions have been made and that you are concerned with assessments for the purpose of identifying and evaluating behaviors for intervention. In other words, the assessment decisions we are concerned with here are those you make as an intervention agent, whether you are a classroom teacher, a school counselor or psychologist, or some other support person in the school setting. We begin by describing the process of behavioral-ecological assessment (Polsgrove, 1987) then present a systematic model for assessing social behavior that leads to intervention planning decisions. This model encompasses a range of instruments and procedures, including norm- and criterion-referenced assessment scales, direct observation procedures, interviews, and sociometric techniques for selecting and analyzing targeted social behaviors. We conclude with a discussion of the outcomes of treatment planning assessment;

namely, intervention goals and objectives, as well as how to task-analyze terminal objectives for intervention. The case study at the end of the chapter illustrates a portion of an IEP concerning social behaviors. Chapters 3 and 4 extend the assessment process, including monitoring students' progress through intervention programs, evaluating the program, and making data-based decisions, and selecting intervention strategies.

Although we describe assessment in terms of two distinct sets of decisions—those involving educational classification and those concerned with intervention—we are not suggesting that these processes are separate or unrelated. On the contrary, they are closely linked. For example, in conducting systematic school-wide screening procedures, prereferral interventions planned by teacher assistance teams or school-based specialists may be attempted. The results of these interventions constitute another set of assessment data that include the pupil's response to the intervention, the characteristics of the intervention strategy (how complex, how intensive), and the resources needed to deliver a successful intervention (if it was, in fact, successful). These data may be used by appropriate school personnel (e.g., teacher assistance teams, assessment or behavioral specialists) to make subsequent decisions, such as whether to continue a prereferral intervention, adjust it, replace it with a more intensive strategy, or refer the student for formal special education evaluation. Assessments for classification and for treatment planning also involve many of the same instruments and procedures, such as rating scales, checklists, and behavioral observations. Thus, we view the assessment process as a continuum of procedures and decisions, each assessment providing information to help make subsequent decisions and each decision influencing the interventions that follow. Assessment may begin at a general level with a question: Which students are at risk for behavioral disorders? But assessment becomes much more specific when the question is asked: What intervention will

maintain the student in a regular education program?

Intervention planning also requires data from various levels of assessment in order to tailor interventions to the characteristics of the students to which they are to be applied, the persons applying them, and the settings in which they are used. The purposes of these assessments are (1) to verify that a problem exists and that it warrants intervention; (2) to analyze the problem in terms of what behaviors are occurring, where they occur, and which characteristics compose the environmental settings (which persons, expectations, degrees of structure, etc.); and (3) to develop hypotheses about the factors that may cause or contribute to the problem, as well as about the potential intervention strategies that address the relevant characteristics.

The Assessment Process

Behavioral-ecological assessment is the evaluation of observable student behaviors across the range of environmental settings in which they occur. As we indicated in the previous chapter, traditional mental health assessment focuses on internal processes that are assumed to underlie overt behavior patterns. In contrast, behavioral assessment focuses upon the objective analysis of the overt behavior itself, which minimizes inferences about underlying conditions. This leads to differences in the types of procedures and instruments used for measurement; that is, tests that measure personality constructs, attitudes, and feelings are not typically used in behavioral assessment. Because behaviors occur in a variety of settings (e.g., home, school, community), and because the behaviors that occur in one setting may not happen in others, it is important to assess student behaviors across various settings. A single **ecological setting** is actually comprised of many subsettings. For example, the school set-

Table 2-1. Guidelines for Ecological Assessment

Information to be Obtained	Potential Sources of Information
1. What are the pupil's major environmental settings and reference groups?	1. Pupil, parents, other teachers, peers.
2. Who are the significant persons in these settings?	2. Pupil, parents, other teachers, peers, direct observation
3. What behaviors occur in these settings? (List both desired and undesired behaviors.)	3. Parents, other teachers, peers, direct observation.
4. (For settings in which problem behavior occurs): Who sees the behavior as a problem?	4. Significant others in the setting.
5. What behaviors are expected in the setting?	5. Significant others in the setting.
6. How does the pupil's behavior differ from these expectations?	6. Significant others in the setting.
7. How *should* the pupil behave?	7. Significant others in the setting.

ting consists of classrooms, offices, a lunchroom, a gymnasium, hallways, a bus waiting area, a playground, and so forth. Even students placed in self-contained classrooms function in many settings, each of which differs in terms of other persons, behavioral expectations, degree of structure, and the interactions likely to occur. The concept of behavioral-ecological assessment emphasizes the need to conduct behavioral assessments in the ecological settings relevant to planning and implementing effective interventions. Polsgrove (1987) articulated the goals of behavioral-ecological assessment as (1) identifying specific interpersonal and environmental variables within each setting that influence behavior, (2) analyzing the behavioral expectations of various settings, and (3) comparing expectations and the pupil's behavior across settings. These analyses provide a comprehensive picture of the student's behavior in a range of places and among a variety of persons. They also reveal differences in expectations, structure, and social interaction patterns that characterize these settings. Table 2-1 presents guidelines for assessing behavior across the settings in which the student functions. The procedures used to obtain assessment data include checklists, rating scales, sociometric devices, direct observations, and interviews.

Thus, behavioral-ecological assessment procedures address the range of behaviors and settings that characterize each student's total environment. Such broad assessments are particularly useful in identifying potential target behaviors, where they occur, the environmental factors that influence their occurrence, and the general types of intervention required to achieve a successful outcome. Within and across these ecological settings, increasingly specific and precise assessments are conducted to identify, analyze, and monitor the behaviors targeted for intervention. The decisions made by an intervention agent guide this process as the agent evaluates the student's behavior relative to the characteristics of the ecological settings in which the student functions. A decision model for assessing specific social behaviors is described in the following section.

A Model for the Assessment of Social Behavior

Assessment of behavior problems is essentially a process of collecting information and making decisions based on this information. The decision-making process that guides intervention planning is described in Figure 2-1. This process includes the assessment procedures and instruments useful in collecting the data for making initial intervention decisions and is described in the following sections.

DOES A PROBLEM EXIST?

Your initial assessment task is to evaluate pupils' social behaviors across the settings in which they are expected to perform. Data from behavioral-ecological assessment procedures will suggest which student behaviors are problems in which settings relative to the expectations for social behavior in these different settings. As Howell and Morehead (1987) point out, a problem exists if there is a discrepancy between student behavior and a standard. Determination that a discrepancy exists between pupil behavior and the standard involves a judgment. In other words, someone must decide that there is a discrepancy and that it is serious enough to justify proceeding further. In the case of academic behaviors, making judgments about discrepancies between standards and behaviors is relatively straightforward and objective (e.g., the student is performing four grade levels below expectations in language arts). But standards for social behavior are based on the expectations of other persons, and such expectations are both personal and subjective. For example, Mrs. Smith believes that pupils should not talk to each other while working; therefore she expects students to speak only when called upon. But Ms. Pearson believes that pupils should talk to each other while working; therefore she expects some level of noise in her classroom.

In the case of a serious social behavior problem (e.g., aggression, stereotypic behavior), discrepancies between standards and behavior are more obvious. Students who are severely handicapped and display "psychotic" behaviors clearly depart from expectations for "normal" behavior. However, judgments about the seriousness of less extreme behavior problems

are more difficult due to the absence of instruments and procedures for accurately measuring behavioral standards and student performance relative to these standards. Fortunately, the assessment technology needed to accomplish such measurement is being developed. Procedures that may be used for this purpose are described below.

Methods of Assessment

Evaluation to determine whether a problem exists corresponds to screening. Therefore, the procedures used should be relatively brief and efficient so that persons in each relevant setting will be inclined to cooperate. Alternately, screening assessments may be conducted by persons who are familiar with the student's performance across most or all of the relevant settings. The school-wide screening procedures discussed in Chapter 1 serve the purpose of establishing whether a problem exists, but these are not widely used. The traditional method of screening students for behavioral problems is through teacher referral. You will recall that referral-driven identification procedures are unreliable and biased against students who are socially withdrawn. The more systematic and reliable procedures for identifying behaviorally disordered students described in Chapter 1 may also be used to determine the existence of a significant discrepancy between behavior and expectations, irrespective of whether the student is being considered for special education. The methods we describe here include rating scales, teacher rankings, self-report measures, and sociometric procedures. In addition, we describe procedures designed to measure teacher expectations and pupil social skills. Screening for intervention planning addresses the following questions: Is intervention required? If so, in which settings should they be applied? The assessment procedures used to answer these questions are likely to involve more time and more sophisticated procedures across more ecological settings than those re-

Figure 2-1. Assessment Model

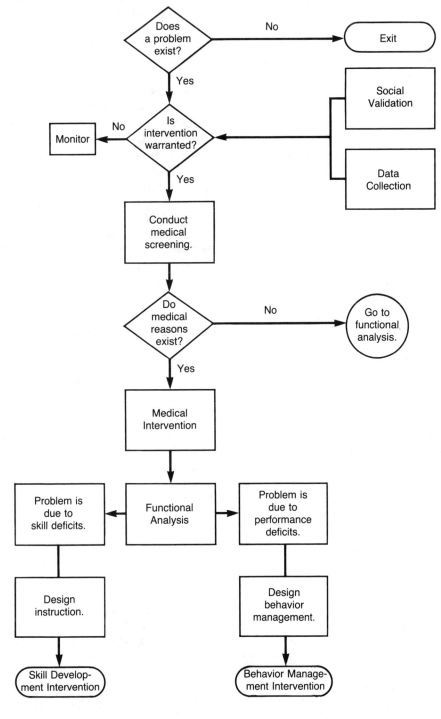

quired by general screening to identify pupils at risk. However, this level of screening focuses on a limited number of students, and the importance of the decisions to be made justifies the greater expenditure of time and resources needed for these assessments.

A *rating scale* generally uses information supplied by a significant other (e.g., teacher, parent, sibling, or peer) to produce a picture of a target child's behavior. The rater is given a set of items and asked to evaluate these items with respect to a particular student. Sometimes, you as a teacher, may be asked to rate how often a student engages in a particular behavior (never, rarely, occasionally, often, very frequently). If you are asked to complete a rating scale as part of a formal screening program, be sure that you have had enough experience with the child to provide valid responses. Re-

member, screening is not a fine-tuned stage in the assessment process.

Behavior rating scales may be *standardized*, meaning that tests were administered to a number of persons and, on the basis of their responses, norms and criteria for discriminating between groups were established (e.g., a conduct problem/not a conduct problem). Some of the better-known standardized rating scales include the Revised Behavior Problem Checklist (Quay & Peterson, 1983), the Walker Problem Behavior Identification Checklist (WPBIC) (Walker, 1983), and the Behavior Rating Profile (Brown & Hammill, 1983). Others are listed in Table 1-1. Figure 2-2 shows illustrative items from WPBIC. Rating scales may also be informal and nonstandardized, such as the instrument shown in Figure 2-3. The format shown here has the advantage of rating a

Figure 2-2. Sample Items from the *Walker Problem Behavior Identification Checklist* (1983)

		Scale			
	1	2	3	4	5
20. Has nervous tics: muscle-twitching, eye-blinking, nail-biting, hand-writing.					3
21. Habitually rejects the school experience through actions or comments.	1				
22. Has enuresis (wets bed).					1
23. Utters nonsense syllables and/or babbles to himself.				4	
24. Continually seeks attention.			1		
25. Comments that nobody likes him.				2	
26. Repeats one ideal, thought, or activity over and over.				4	
27. Has temper tantrums.	2				
28. Refers to himself as dumb, stupid, or incapable.				3	
29. Does not engage in group activities.		2.			
30. When teased or irritated by other children, takes out his frustration(s) on another inappropriate person or thing.	2				

Directions: The rater identifies those statements that describe the student and circles the number in the column corresponding to these statements. The circled values in each column are then added to yield a score for each of the 5 scales. The scales are: Acting Out (column 1), Withdrawal (column 2), Distractibility (column 3), Disturbed Peer Relations (column 4), and Immaturity (column 5).

Source: Walker, H. M. (1983) *Walker Problem Behavior Identification Checklist.* Los Angeles: Western Psychological Services. Copyright © 1970, 1976, 1983 by Western Psychological Services. Reprinted by permission of the publisher, Western Psychological Services, 12031 Wilshire Boulevard, Los Angeles, CA 90025, U.S.A.

Figure 2-3. Teaching Rating Form

Students	Child has close friends	Child is frequently chosen by classmates to play on a team, study together, etc.	Child spends most of recess time playing with others	Child volunteers for classroom "jobs."	Child answers appropriately when the teacher asks questions of the group	Child follows most teacher instructions independently or with minimal assistance	Child brings materials and ideas to school for inclusion or class discussions and projects	Child initiates conversations with the teacher	Child completes most assignments within allotted time	Child's academic performance is about right or better than expected for his grade level	Child regularly follows classroom rules of conduct	Child checks over most work papers before submitting them	Child's statements about school are usually positive	Child attends school regularly	Child has no known major health problems
1.															
2.															
3.															
4.															
5.															
6.															
7.															
8.															
9.															
10.															
11.															
12.															

Teacher: _____

Grade: _____

Interviewer: _____

Date: _____

School: _____

Time: _____

group of students on the same sheet, thereby permitting comparisons. Rating scales may contain items that assess undesired or maladaptive behaviors, desired or adaptive behaviors, or both. Many rating scales are commercially available, and we suggest that you study their items, reliability, validity, norms, and recommended uses in order to identify those that are likely to be most appropriate and useful for your purposes (see McMahon, 1984).

A discrepancy between student social behavior and standards or expectations for behavior is the basis for determining that a problem exists. However, these expectations are likely to vary among ecological settings and among the persons in these settings who evaluate student behavior. To make the assessment of **teacher expectations** less subjective, Walker and Rankin (1980) developed a standardized rating scale format, the SBS Inventory of Teacher Social Behavior Standards and Expectations. It asks teachers to rate the importance of adaptive behaviors (e.g., child takes turns, uses free time appropriately) and their own tolerance for maladaptive pupil behaviors (e.g., child whines, has tantrums, uses obscene language) in terms of how these affect their willingness to work with the students in their classrooms. This instrument is also a component of the Assessment for Integration into Mainstream Settings system (AIMS) (Walker, 1986), which is a procedure used to identify the minimal skill requirements of mainstream settings, to prepare the student to meet these requirements, and to assess the pupil's adjustment following mainstream placement. The other instruments in the AIMS system include (1) the SBS Correlates Checklist, which asks teachers to check behaviors that would cause them to oppose placement or for which they would require technical assistance in order to accept the placement; (2) a criterion-referenced rating scale to assess the pupil's behavioral status on the SBS items that the teacher has indicated as important classroom skills or that the teacher rates as unacceptable behaviors; and (3) two interval observational coding

systems for observing the target student's behavior in academic and free-play situations. Sample items from the AIMS system are presented in Figure 2-4. We describe the AIMS system in greater detail in Chapter 12.

Teacher rankings on the basis of social criteria (e.g., frequency of peer verbal interactions) have been shown to be a reliable and valid method of identifying pupils who are not socially responsive (Walker, Severson, & Haring, 1986). Figure 2-5 illustrates one such ranking procedure. The teacher initially ranks all students in the class then divides them into two groups according to the behavior pattern being considered (e.g., most and least talkative) and finally ranks all pupils according to the criterion (Hops & Greenwood, 1981). The systematic school-wide screening procedure (Walker et al., 1986) described in Chapter 1 includes this ranking procedure. Teacher rankings offer the advantages of being quick and establishing the relative standing of pupils in the group with respect to the criterion on which they are ranked.

Another format for problem identification screening is a **self-report.** As the name implies, this type of instrument requires that the students describe their own behavior in response to a number of questions or statements. For young students or nonreaders, the questions may be read orally with subsequent directions for students to color in a response area, to circle a happy or sad face, or to sort pictures into groups (Finch & Rogers, 1984). Self-report instruments have been designed to assess a variety of general (e.g., Locus of Control) and specific (e.g., anger, depression) constructs. Self-reports provide useful information, but they should be supplemented with data from other sources, such as behavioral ratings and observations (Finch & Rogers, 1984).

Although **sociometric procedures** may not be considered traditional screening devices, they can nevertheless play an important role in identifying students at risk for social behavior problems (Hops & Lewin, 1984). Sociometric measures have been shown to be valuable pre-

Figure 2-4. Sample Items and Rating Formats from the SBS Inventory and Correlates Checklist

SBS Inventory			
Section I	Critical	Desirable	Unimportant
____ Child responds to requests and directions promptly.	( )	( )	( )
____ Child completes tasks within prescribed time limits.	( )	( )	( )
Section II	Unacceptable	Tolerated	Acceptable
____ Child disturbs or disrupts the activities of others.	( )	( )	( )
____ Child is physically aggressive with others, e.g., hits, bites, chokes, holds.	( )	( )	( )

Section III *

In the line space to the left of the Section I (critical) items, indicate whether:
(a) You would insist that the child have mastered the skill or competency *prior* to entry into your class, or
(b) Following entry, you would accept responsibility for developing the skill/competency, but you would expect technical assistance in the process of doing so, or
(c) Following entry, you would accept responsibility for developing the skill/competency and would not require technical assistance.

Similarly, for Section II (unacceptable) items, indicate whether:
(a) The child must be within normal limits on the social behavior in question *prior* to entry into your class, or
(b) Following entry, you will take responsibility for moving the child to within normal limits on the social behavior but only with technical assistance provided, or
(c) Following entry, you will take responsibility for moving the child to within normal limits on the social behavior and would not require technical assistance.

* Please indicate your answer by placing an a, b, or c in the space to the left of the item.

SBS Correlates Checklist	
Child has severely dysfluent speech and/or impaired language.	____
Child is eneuretic, e.g., has inadequate bladder control.	____
Child requires specialized and/or adapted instructional materials to progress academically.	____

Source: Walker, H. M. (1986). The AIMS (*Assessment for Integration into Mainstream Settings*) assessment system: Rationale, instruments, procedures, and outcomes. *Journal of Clinical Child Psychology, 15* (1), 55-63.

Figure 2-5.   Student Ranking Form

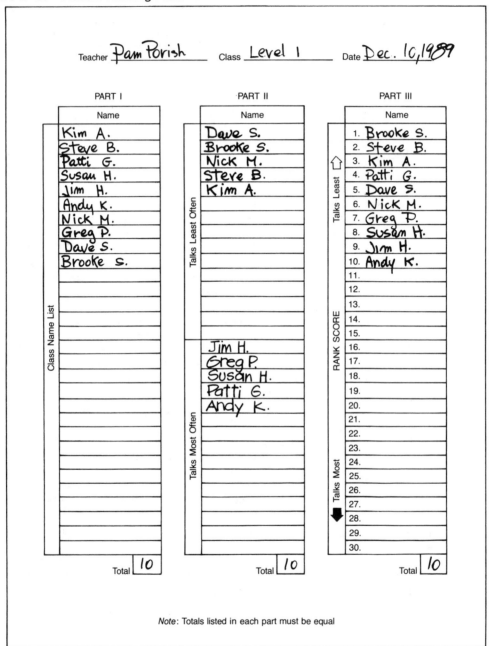

Source: H. Hops & C. R. Greenwood, Social skills deficits. In E. J. Mash and L. G. Terdal (Eds.), *Behavioral assessment of childhood disorders.* New York: Guilford Press, 1981, p. 359.

dictors of later social behavior problems such as dropping out of school (Ullmann, 1952) and delinquency (Roff, Sells, & Golden, 1972). Before using a sociometric procedure in your classroom, check with your supervisor to determine what, if any, parental permissions are required in order for students to participate in this assessment procedure. In general, a sociometric procedure requires that students describe one another according to a predesignated set of criteria. For example, students might be asked to name their best friend or to list classmates they do not like. In this type of peer nomination, the student is making an acceptance or rejection choice about a selected number of peers. Because peer acceptance and rejection appear to be independent dimensions, both positive (e.g., "Who would you *most* like to go with to a movie?") and negative (e.g., "Who would you *least* like to go with to a movie?") choices should be obtained (Hops & Lewin, 1984). Asking students to make negative nominations raises ethical questions that should be weighed before using this procedure.

Another drawback of peer nomination sociometric procedures is that students who are socially isolated may never be nominated at all. A sociometric procedure that does not have these limitations is the peer-rating method. In using this procedure, a student is asked to rate each of his classroom peers according to a scale. For example, a young child might be asked to circle a number from one to five to indicate how much he likes a particular peer. Faces depicting expressions ranging from frowns to smiles might accompany the number to make the directions clearer. Each child in the classroom thus earns a score, the average of his ratings from his peers. Another procedure for young children is to show each child a picture of peers and ask the child to rate that peer (Bower & Lambert, 1961).

For screening purposes, sociometric techniques are limited by their relatively high cost in teacher time, especially for younger pupils.

Also, elementary schools are adopting more flexible scheduling, which means that pupils move from class to class more often. This makes it difficult to establish a stable reference group (e.g., a homeroom) for nominations or ratings.

Instruments that measure student's social skills are relatively new additions to behavioral-ecological assessment technology. The Social Behavior Assessment (SBA) (Stephens, 1981) is a teacher rating scale of 136 social skills that are grouped into four behavioral domains (environmental behaviors, interpersonal behaviors, self-related behaviors, and task-related behaviors). The Social Skills Rating Scales (SSRS) (Gresham & Elliott, 1986) consist of three rating scales: one for parents to complete, one for teachers, and one self-report format for the pupil. The SSRS include a version for elementary-age pupils and one for junior and senior high school students. Unlike the SBA, it is standardized on a national sample. The Walker-McConnell Scale of Social Competence and School Adjustment (Walker & McConnell, 1988) consists of 43 positively worded items describing social skills. Three subscales were identified through factor analysis. Subscale I, Teacher Preferred Social Behavior, includes sixteen items measuring peer-related social behaviors that are highly valued by teachers (e.g., shows sympathy for others, controls temper). Subscale II, Peer Preferred Social Behavior, consists of seventeen items that assess peer-related social behaviors that are valued by the peer group (e.g., makes friends easily with other children, plays games and activities at recess skillfully). The ten items in Subscale III, School Adjustment Behavior, measure adaptive social-behavioral competencies that are highly valued by teachers in classroom settings (e.g., displays independent study skills, listens carefully to teacher directions and instructions for assignments.)

In addition to these methods, *direct observation* and *interviewing* may be used to establish that a problem exists. However, because they are more specific and may require more time to administer, we have elected to describe these procedures in the section dealing with the analysis of problem behaviors. Remember that it is important to assess student behavior across several settings and to obtain data from multiple sources in order to get a valid and comprehensive picture of pupils' behavioral assets and liabilities.

Pinpointing Target Behaviors

In completing the assessment steps previously described, you will have determined the student's eligibility for special education services (if this is an issue), identified his problem behavior areas, identified his behavioral strengths, and determined the settings in which desired and undesired behaviors occur. Now you are ready to select and define the student behaviors you consider for intervention. **Pinpointing** refers to the specification of behaviors to be modified or taught. Behavior pinpoints may include behaviors to be decreased (refusal to complete assignments, tantrums, self-injurious behavior) or behaviors to be increased (completion of assignments, making appropriate requests of peers, keeping hands to self). Both classes of pinpoints are referred to as **target behaviors** if they are observable, measurable, and definable so that two persons can agree on their occurrence or nonoccurrence. A criterion can then be set for a desired level of performance. We wish to emphasize the importance of pinpointing target behaviors to be increased, rather than those to be decreased, whenever possible. The tendency to identify behaviors to be decreased leads to an emphasis on aversive consequences that create an unpleasant atmosphere for both students and teachers. Greater emphasis on teaching appropriate and useful social skills should be the aim of intervention strategies. A positive focus is also much more palatable to parents and other professionals, and it is a good model for other educators.

Moreover, excessive reliance on aversive control has influenced several professional organizations (e.g., The Association for the Severely Handicapped, The Association for Retarded Citizens) to establish policies severely limiting the use of punishment procedures. If your objective is to reduce undesired target behaviors, we recommend that you follow the **fair pair rule** (White & Haring, 1980); that is, simultaneously identify a desired social behavior to replace the behavior to be reduced (e.g., target an increase in appropriate social initiations to peers in addition to targeting a reduction in verbal or physical aggression).

It is also important to pinpoint behaviors to be increased that are adaptive, that are desirable, and that contribute to the development of social competence (McConnell, 1987). Unfortunately, research indicates that the behaviors educators target for intervention tend to lack social relevance. Black (1985; cited in Gresham & Reschly, 1988) had teachers rate pupil behaviors as to importance. The ten highest rated behaviors corresponded to what Hersh and Walker (1983) describe as the *model behavioral profile:* compliance with teacher expectations and acceptable academic performance. Although such targets appear desirable, it is necessary to ask whether compliance and academic achievement are the only critical target behaviors for a given pupil and whether changes in these behaviors are important to students, their caregivers, and significant others. These questions have been a major concern of educators working with more severely handicapped students. Brown, Nietupski, and Hamre-Nietupski (1976) developed an approach to curriculum design based on the **criterion of ultimate functioning,** which refers to the functional skills needed by adults to participate freely in community environments (e.g., interviewing for a job). Although this criterion may seem to lack relevance for younger pupils or for those who do not exhibit severe developmental disabilities, you may find it useful to think in terms of the **criterion of**

functioning in the next environment (Vincent et al., 1980) when pinpointing behaviors to increase. This means identifying the skill requirements and expectations of less restrictive environments (e.g., a regular classroom, playground, school club) and teaching these in order to increase pupils' chances of successful participation. For example, a student may need to learn how to participate in class discussions.

We have already indicated that behavioral pinpoints should be observable, measurable, definable so that persons can agree regarding their occurrence, and they should include a criterion for desired performance. These characteristics describe an **operational definition** of target behaviors. Sometimes you will be working from the verbal descriptions of behavior provided by others or from statements contained in behavior checklists. Also, you will be writing behavioral objectives from definitions of behaviors. For these reasons, it is important that your definitions be observable and precise. Table 2-2 provides examples of target behavior definitions derived from general statements. Study these operational definitions and prac-

tice writing some of your own in order to gain fluency in this skill.

IS INTERVENTION WARRANTED?

The procedures we have just described will provide a wealth of information about pupil behaviors and setting characteristics that are useful in documenting that a problem exists. However, keep in mind that in most schools, awareness of student behavior problems reaches assessors and supervisors much more informally; through a conversation in the teachers' lounge or through a referral by a classroom teacher. Also, if you are the teacher of the student in question, simply recognizing that the pupil's behavior is a concern constitutes problem identification. No matter how the problem is brought to the attention of the person or persons responsible for making decisions about interventions, the next step is to anlayze the behavior and the settings in which the student functions in order to decide whether intervention is warranted. For example, one teacher may regard students who are noisy and boisterous, or who violate her standards for order and routine, as

Table 2-2. Examples of Target Behavior Definitions

General Statement	Target Behavior
1. Kim does not comply with teacher requests.	1. When asked to do something by the teacher, Kim will respond appropriately within ten seconds without being asked again.
2. Andy is hyperactive.	2. Andy will remain at his desk, keeping desk legs on the floor, for twenty consecutive minutes.
3. Fred cannot ride the school bus appropriately.	3. Fred will get on the bus without pushing, hitting, or shoving; walk to his assigned seat; remain there without disturbing others throughout the ride; and exit from the bus without pushing, hitting, or shoving.
4. Betsy is aggressive.	4. Betsy will play with other children during recess without hitting, kicking, pushing, or calling them names during the entire period.
5. Billy is withdrawn.	5. Billy will initiate at least two peer interactions during any given fifteen-minute recess period.

serious problems who require intervention, but the behavior of the same students is seen as "normal" by other staff members in other settings. We are not suggesting that students who act out in only one classroom should not be considered candidates for intervention; we mean only that persons' standards and tolerance for pupil behavior are subjective and vary from setting to setting or from one occasion to another. Also, because students with behavioral problems seldom display only one undesired behavior and seldom lack only one appropriate social skill, it is necessary to decide which behaviors to act upon first. As Figure 2-1 indicates, social validation and direct observation procedures will help you evaluate the discrepancy between pupil behavior and standards. With this information, you can determine whether intervention is justified and which behaviors should receive priority for intervention.

Social Validation of Problem Behaviors

Social validation (Wolf, 1978) is a strategy for evaluating whether significant persons agree that a problem is serious enough to require intervention.[1] Several procedures can be used to validate the existence and severity of a behavior problem. The most obvious is simply to ask other persons who have daily contact with the student (e.g., parents, teachers, peers) whether the identified target behaviors are serious problems. If systematic screening procedures such as those just described have been used, the data from various sources and instruments can be compared in order to see whether the same problems occur in multiple settings and in the presence of several persons. This is not a complex process, but it provides

---

[1] Social validation also encompasses the acceptability of intervention procedures and goals to professionals and caregivers, as well as their satisfaction with the results of interventions (Wolf, 1978). The latter two facets of social validation are discussed in Chapters 4 and 5.

some assurance that a student is not singled out for intervention because one person has unreasonable standards for behavior.

Collection of Observational Data in Natural Settings

Another procedure for assessing the severity of problem behavior is to observe the student in those settings in which the target behavior occurs. Direct observation formats include a functional analysis (see pages 000–000), event recording, and interval recording procedures that measure single or multiple behaviors of one or more pupils (see Chapter 3). Direct observation data will tell you little about the need for intervention, however, unless the target behavior is dangerous or intolerable if it occurs at any level, or unless you have some indication of what level of the behavior the setting will tolerate. For example, even a single instance of physical aggression during a classroom work period is likely to be intolerable, but what about off-task, out-of-seat, or noncompliant behavior? Almost all students display some levels of undesired social behaviors, as well as some deficits in appropriate social skills. Pupils who are identified as behaviorally disordered are usually distinguished from those who are not by excesses or deficits in the frequency or rate at which they exhibit such behaviors rather than by differences in the kinds of behaviors they exhibit. It is possible that the teacher simply notices the designated student's disruptive behavior more than he notices the same behavior in others. One way to assess the discrepancy between the target student's behavior and the standard for that behavior in the classroom is to simultaneously observe the target pupil and a peer who the teacher designates as nondeviant for the target behavior (Walker & Fabre, 1987). Comparing the frequencies of the two students will help you assess the relative severity of the target behavior. Figure 2-6 displays a sheet of interval data collected on a target student and a selected peer. Note that on some behaviors the target student was much like his behaviorally acceptable peer.

Ranking Target Behaviors

If students were in only one setting for the entire school day or presented only one behavior to be changed, setting priorities for intervention would be easy. However, behaviorally disordered pupils, whether they are identified as handicapped or not, usually exhibit several or many problem behaviors in a variety of settings. Not every problem can be addressed simultaneously. Therefore, the persons responsible for the student's education and welfare must agree upon a set of priorities for changes in the student's behavior. In school settings, a forum for this decision-making activity is provided in the evaluation and the individual education program conferences (i.e., ad-

Figure 2-6. Target Student and Peer Comparison Observational Data

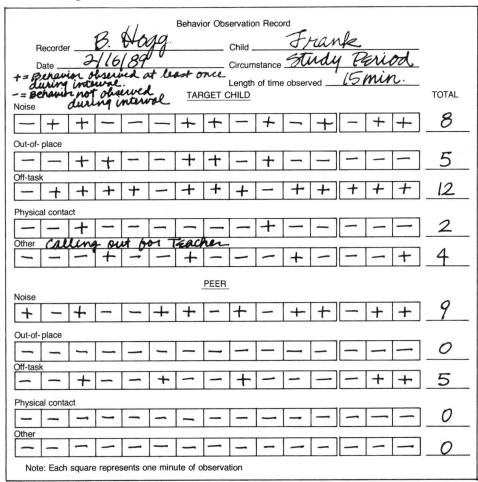

Source: S. Deno & P. Mirkin. *Data-based program modification.* Reston, Va.: Council for Exceptional Children, 1978.

mission and release committees) required by PL 94-142. In other treatment agencies (e.g., residential treatment programs) habilitation planning conferences or case conferences are held for the same purpose. It may be difficult to achieve group consensus regarding which of the student's behaviors should be addressed first. Behaviors that are intervention priorities can be identified by asking such questions as the following (Wolery, Bailey, & Sugai, 1988):

1. Does the behavior cause injury to the student or others?
2. Does the behavior interfere with the student's or other pupils' learning?
3. Does the behavior present a safety risk to the student or to others?
4. Is the behavior age-appropriate or likely to be transient?
5. Does the behavior occur at frequencies similar to that of peers' behavior?
6. Is the behavior due to skill deficits in other areas?
7. Does the behavior cause others to avoid interacting with the student?

Other high priority target behaviors include self-help skills (e.g., dressing, feeding, toileting, identifying environmental dangers), behaviors that restrict access to less restrictive environments (e.g., aggression, noncompliance, defiance), and "survival" skills or information (e.g., following directions, staying on task, bringing required materials to class).

One way to achieve consensus on which targeted social behaviors should have priority for intervention is to ask persons who have frequent contact with the student to develop a rank-ordered list of these behaviors. The average of their rankings provides a basis for deciding which behaviors should receive top priority. Figure 2-7 shows a form used to list and rank target behaviors of a student whose teacher has requested consultation services. Each person who works with this pupil may be asked to rank the target behaviors, and the average of their rankings may be used to determine the priority of each target.

ARE THERE MEDICAL REASONS FOR THE PROBLEM BEHAVIOR?

A student who lacks functional communicative skills may be unable to tell you that he is striking his head because he has an earache. Or a non-handicapped pupil whose listlessness, lethargy, and inattention to tasks interfere with her educational performance may be unaware that she has diabetes. Mild or potentially serious medical problems may underlie student behavior problems, and educators should not assume that managing the environment is the only effective way to control behavior. Particularly if an undesired behavior pattern has a sudden onset, and if behavioral-ecological screening procedures reveal no apparent environmental factors that affect its occurrence, you should ask the parents if they have observed any recent changes in their child's behavior, and whether the child has had a recent physical examination. In any case, it may be wise to ask the school nurse or health practitioner to conduct a brief medical screening (with parental permission). If the screening reveals any indicators of potential health problems, ask the parents to obtain a *medical examination* and indicate specifically the suspected medical cause of the problem. If the parents approve, you may contact the examining physician to explain the behavioral manifestations of concern.

If an underlying health problem is revealed, the next step is appropriate *medical intervention*. While the pupil is receiving treatment, continue to observe the behaviors of concern and note any changes. You should be aware that in cases where medical problems have been long-standing, successful medical treatment may not solve the problem immediately. For example, if the student has missed out on instruction in important skills, or if the undesired behavior originally caused by her health problem has been reinforced (e.g., she has been able to avoid tasks), solving her physical problem may not alleviate the corresponding behavior pattern. Thus, whether or not medical explanations have been ruled out, you

Figure 2-7. Priority-Ranking Form

Directions: Ask each person concerned with student to complete a form. Items may be listed by the consultant or each person may generate his/her own list.

Referee: _Ricky_   Age/Grade: _9/Gr. 3_   Date: _9/12/89_

Name of person completing this form: _Ms. B./Classroom Teacher_

Specify those goal (terminal) behaviors which you would most like to see attained through program modification.

Academic   Acceptable Level of Performance
Rank

_1_	_Reading_	_1 yr. below grade level_
_3_	_Spelling_	_75% correct_
_4_	_Math_	_75% correct_
_5_	_Handwriting_	_faster and legible_

Social

| _2_ | _Noise_ | _none_ |
| _2_ | _Fights_ | _none._ |

After you complete your list, rank order the list in terms of those most requiring immediate attention.

Source: S. Deno & P. Mirkin. *Data-based program modification.* Reston, Va.: Council for Exceptional Children, 1978, p. 71.

may need to proceed to a functional analysis of behavior.

PERFORMING A FUNCTIONAL ANALYSIS

A **functional analysis** of behavior involves assessing student behavior in the context of environmental variables that occur before, during, and after the target behavior itself. This entails careful observation in the immediate environment in which the behavior occurs. The skill requirements and behavioral tolerances of other current or potential environments in which the pupil might function should also be considered. The procedures that may be used include direct observation, interviews, assessments of current and potential future environmental expectations and skill demands.

Direct Observation

Human behavior occurs in environmental contexts that contain a variety of stimuli. Some of these stimuli influence behavior directly or indirectly. It is helpful to know precisely which stimuli affect behavior and which do not. Environmental variables should be analyzed systematically to sort out those that potentially influence what the student does. Direct observation may enable you to identify variables that affect what the student does. An antecedent-behavior-consequence (A-B-C) analysis is a direct observation format that accomplishes this by organizing events into those that are present or that take place immediately before a behavioral event and those that occur immediately afterward. Some of the antecedent stimuli that may affect pupil behavior include environmental obstacles that prevent the student from performing as desired (e.g., he may be in a location where you cannot see him when he needs to ask for your assistance). Or certain **setting events,** such as time of day or transition periods, may set the occasion for some behaviors. Other antecedent events such as the task the student is expected to perform, the other

persons present, or the instructions provided to the student may be important. On the other hand, stimuli that occur subsequent to the pupil's behavior may prove to be conseqences that influence that behavior. For example, does the student receive social attention, praise, or criticism following specific behaviors? Does her behavior result in avoiding or escaping task demands? Does her behavior enable her to obtain things she otherwise does not get?

An A-B-C analysis involves carefully observing and recording events that occur immediately before the target pupil's behavior, the behavior itself, and the events that take place immediately afterward. Figure 2-8 illustrates an A-B-C analysis. Note that the observer logs the time and narratively describes the immediate antecedents, the student's response, and the consequences in the sequence in which they occur. An analysis of recurring antecedent and consequent events provides some clues as to which of these stimuli potentially influence behavior. Can you identify some of these events in the example? An A-B-C analysis is only useful for observing students individually; it would become too unwieldly if it were attempted with several pupils at the same time. Also, it is not something you can do while you are involved in direct instruction. However, you can organize the informal observations you make about specific incidents into an A-B-C format at a later time.

Touchette, MacDonald, and Langer (1985) devised a format that enables observers to monitor targeted behaviors across extended periods of time. This procedure, called a **scatter plot,** is a system for rating behavior in time intervals. This format is presented in Figure 2-9. Each day is represented by a vertical column divided into thirty-minute blocks of time. During each interval, the observer indicates whether the behavior occurred by filling in the cell representing the day and time. If desired, symbols may be used to indicate whether the behavior occurred at a high rate (e.g., a completely filled cell) or at a low rate (e.g., a slash). A blank grid indicates that the behavior

Figure 2-8. Sample A-B-C Record

STUDENT _Raymond_   DATE _Oct. 29, 1989_

OBSERVER _Dianne McInerney_   TIME _2:15_ to _2:25_

BEHAVIOR _Talking out during class discussion; off task._   ACTIVITY _Social Studies_

ANTECEDENT	BEHAVIOR	CONSEQUENCE
Teacher says, "Everyone please get out your Social Studies notebook and pencil."	Raymond asks student next to him, "What did she say?"	Teacher says, "No talking."
Teacher asks Tommy to name the capital of Alabama.	Raymond shouts out, "Montgomery".	Tommy yells, "Shut up, Raymond!"
Teacher says. "Please, Raymond, sit quietly until it is your turn."	Raymond yells, "What did I do?"	Teacher says, "Raymond, be quiet!"
Teacher asks, "Which state has the largest population? Raymond, can you answer?"	Raymond says, "Uh? I didn't do anything!"	Class laughs.
Teacher asks, "Alice, which state is nicknamed the Keystone State?"	Raymond calls out, "I know. It's Pennsylvania."	Teacher says, "Raymond, I've had enough. . Put your head down on your desk."

Source: Dianne McInerney, Personal Communication, 1986.

did not occur. Although a scatter plot does not indicate the actual frequency with which a target behavior occurs, it does reveal patterns of responding over time. Therefore, this procedure is useful for doing functional analyses; that is, it may be used to identify relationships between problem behaviors and time of day, the presence or absence of certain persons, a physical or social setting, a particular activity, and so forth. (Touchette et al., 1985).

Analysis of direct observation data also may reveal that some undesired student behaviors

Figure 2-9. Scatter plot grid with a key at the top to indicate response frequencies corresponding to filled, slashed, and open boxes. Each location on the grid identifies a unique time interval on a given day.

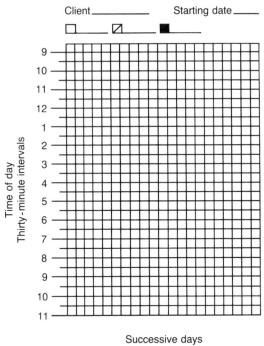

Source: Touchette, P.E., MacDonald, R. F., & Langer, S.N. (1985). A scatter plot for identifying stimulus control of problem behavior. *Journal of Applied Behavior Analysis 18,* 343-351.

serve a **communicative function.** Some maladaptive behaviors may occur because the student lacks more effective means of communicating her needs or of obtaining reinforcement. Donnellan, Mirenda, Mesaros, and Fassbender (1984) suggested that maladaptive behaviors of severely handicapped persons may occur because they serve such communicative functions as (1) requesting attention, interactions, or items; (2) expressing protests, refusals, or desire to terminate an event; or (3) making declarations or comments; or because they are noninteractive functions that have personal meaning. Carr and Durand (1985) demonstrated that developmentally disabled children who received functional communication training reduced their rates of maladaptive behavior that had previously been their means

of sending messages. Assessment of the communicative functions of undesired behavior is not just useful with persons who are severely handicapped. For example, the student who displays disruptive behavior during certain classroom activities that result in his being removed from the classroom may be indicating that the work is too difficult. In this case, providing remedial instruction or adjusting the level of task difficulty is a more appropriate response than punishing the student's undesired behavior. Thus, knowledge about recurring antecedent-response-consequence relationships is important for intervention planning.

Interviews

Not all stimuli that influence student behavior occur immediately before or after a behavior.

Moreover, other important information, such as the skills pupils need to gain access to less restrictive environments or the events taking place at home that affect pupils' school behaviors, cannot be obtained through an A-B-C analysis. Behavioral interviews are a useful assessment tool for obtaining assessment data from both children and adults. For example, an interview may be used (1) to gather information about concerns and goals, (2) to identify factors that maintain or occasion problem behaviors, (3) to obtain historical information, and (4) to identify reinforcers (Gross, 1984). Information from two or more sources can be compared to evaluate the reliability of informants or to obtain individual perceptions of behaviors and environmental events across ecological settings. Figure 2-10 is an interview format for identifying and analyzing target behaviors. Note that the questions are open-

Figure 2-10. Anecdotal Interview Recording Form

Teacher: _____

Consultant: _____

Date: _____

Student(s): _____

1. Can you describe for me in your own words what the problem behavior seems to be?

2. Could you be a little more specific? For example, when you say that the student disrupts the class, what exactly does he do?

3. Now I'm getting the picture. Tell me, does this behavior take place every day (period)?

4. (If no) Would you say it happens every week? Every other week?

5. Let's try to figure out what the student gains from this behavior. Can you recall what happens to the student (that is, what do you do) after this behavior occurs?

6. Have you been able to notice what other students in the room do when this behavior takes place?

7. Is there anything else you can tell me about this behavior or this student?

ended (they do not limit answers by requiring only one-word responses or by asking the respondent to hypothesize as to why the pupil's behavior occurs) and include probes for following up on previous answers. Consult Gross (1984) or Polsgrove (1987) for more information on conducting behavioral interviews.

Assessing the Skill Requirements of Current and Future Environments

We previously indicated that the skills needed to succeed in current and future school settings are important assessment data. This is also true of other environments in which students currently, or will be expected to, function (e.g., community and work settings). Behavioral interviews, direct observation, and the AIMS system are three methods that can be used to obtain these data. Information regarding these skill requiremments is important for two reasons. First, the absence of these skills may prevent pupils' access to these settings. For instance, if a student lacks the skills needed to buy a theater ticket, she may be prevented from attending a movie. An adolescent who cannot initiate a telephone conversation is restricted from an important source of social learning and reinforcement. Second, desired social skills may serve as targeted **replacement behaviors** to be strengthened as undesired maladaptive behaviors are reduced (Gast & Wolery, 1986).

Evans and Meyer (1985) suggest a five-step process for assessing discrepancies between environmental expectations and student behavior. In step 1, the teacher lists some least restrictive settings in which the pupil presently can function (e.g., home room, regular physical education class). Next, some future least restrictive environments in which the student could function (e.g., school cafeteria, school bus, playground, regular classrooms) are listed. In step 3, the teacher lists those skills the student currently has that allow her to participate in current settings (e.g., follows teachers' direc-

tions, participates in games and sports). Skills that the pupil does not currently have but that would allow her to participate in future least restrictive settings (e.g., appropriate table manners, conversational skills, appropriate verbal responses to peer initiations, controlling temper) are lised in step 4. Step 5 involves a discrepancy analysis. The skills that nonhandicapped students will perform in those settings listed as future least restrictive are entered first (e.g., share toys, take turns, use appropriate table manners, initiate and respond to peers). If the target student can perform the skill, a plus is entered beside that skill. A minus is recorded if she cannot perform the skill. For those skills the student cannot perform, the teacher lists the behaviors that she exhibits instead of the needed skill (e.g., cries, has tantrums, eats with fingers). Thus, Evans and Meyer's (1985) procedure not only provides information about the skillls that are needed in current and future enviroments, but it also evaluates the pupil's status with regard to these skills, as well as any undesired behaviors that should be reduced to increase her chances of succeeding in these settings.

IS THE BEHAVIOR PROBLEM THE RESULT OF SKILL OR PERFORMANCE DEFICITS?

In order to design an appropriate intervention, it is critical to know whether targeted undesired behaviors are due to the lack of appropriate skills or due to the absence of motivation to perform as desired (Howell & Morehead, 1987). If the desired behavior is one the pupil cannot do (i.e., it is *never* performed because the student lacks the necessary information or component skills), the appropriate intervention is instruction in these skill areas. Attempting to change the student's motivation to perform the skill through arranging positive or aversive consequences will be ineffective, unless also accompanied by relevant skill instruction. On the other hand, if the skill is something the student can perform (i.e., he has done it before or does it in other settings) the problem is due to a performance deficit. A performance deficit may be caused by a lack of motivation or of opportunity to perform as desired. In this case, the appropriate intervention consists of providing opportunities for the student to perform and reinforcing the desired behavior when it occurs, at the same time removing reinforcement or applying consequences in order to reduce undesired behaviors. Thus, knowing whether targeted behavioral excesses and deficits are the result of skill or performance deficits is an important factor in selecting alternate intervention procedures. Intervention decisions regarding strategies for responding to undesired behavior when it occurs are discussed in Chapter 4.

It is important that educators who assess student social behavior be sensitive to the possibility that pupils may be deficient in social skills. Often, teachers assume that undesired student behavior reflects the pupil's decision to misbehave. However, the student who lacks appropriate social behavior does not really have a choice (i.e., alternative social behaviors are missing from his repertoire). As Howell and Morehead (1987) emphasize, students should be taught the social skills they lack, rather than just receiving behavior management interventions to control their maladaptive behavior when it occurs. When targeting undesired social behaviors for intervention, remember to consider whether the behavior serves a communicative function. If it does, or if the pupil lacks alternate adaptive social behaviors, identify and teach a desired replacement behavior that (1) serves the desired communicative function, or (2) is a skill the student will find useful in a current or future ecological setting.

Kaplan, McCollum-Gahley, and Howell (1988) argue that **criterion-based assessment** (CBA) procedures represent the best practice for both academic and social skills, and involves assessing pupils' status with regard to specific curriculum content and objectives. However, the absence of a widely accepted and carefully sequenced social skills curriculum limits the use of CBA with social skills instruction. This results in a tendency to confuse classroom control problems with social skills deficits. That is, teachers wait for a pupil to misbehave then respond with a behavior management (i.e., control intervention), when in fact, the student's behavior is a direct outcome of her lack of particular social skills (e.g., she responds to being teased with physical aggression). Several excellent social skills curriculum packages have been developed (see Chapter 10), and some (e.g., the ACCEPTS Program, Walker et al., 1983) include CBA scales. We recommend that you examine several social skills curricula and ask your school district to purchase one or more of them for your program. If you do not have access to these curricula, Kaplan, et. al. (1988) suggest a task analytic approach to social skills assessment, which involves evaluating the pupil with respect to prerequisite and specific subskills of appropriate social behaviors (see the next section and Chapter 10).

Intervention Objectives and Task Analysis

The beginning point of intervention, whether it consists of skill instruction or behavior management, is to write **behavioral objectives** that describe the behavior to be achieved following intervention. A well-written behavioral objective specifies in observable and measurable terms the **terminal behavior** the student is to demonstrate, the **conditions** under which the behavior should occur, and the **criteria** for acceptable performance (Mager, 1962). Figure 2-11 contains examples of acceptable and unacceptable terminal instructional objectives. It has been our experience that many objectives for social behaviors are inappropriate not be-

Figure 2-11. Acceptable and Unacceptable Instructional Objectives

Instructional Objectives	Acceptable?	Reason (If Unacceptable)
1. Arnold will behave in gym class.	No	Behavior and criteria not specified
2. Given a forty-five minute study hall, Sally will remain on-task 90 percent of the time.	No	On-task behavior not specified; impossible to assess "90 percent of the time"
3. Yen-Su will interact with her peers with no hitting, kicking, biting, pushing, or verbal taunting for thirty-minute lunch periods for five consecutive days.	Yes	
4. Washington will be punctual in arriving at school for fifteen consecutive days.	No	"Punctual" not defined
5. When given a task request, Tanya will begin the task within ten seconds without saying "I can't."	Yes	
6. Karen will refrain from biting or scratching herself for any given one-hour period.	No	Conditions not specified (i.e., instructions, prompts, or supervision to be provided during the hour)
7. Yolonda will not take any drugs during school for twenty consecutive days.	No	Impossible to monitor drug intake accurately
8. When approached by a peer, Philip will emit an appropriate greeting response (make eye contact, extend his right hand, smile, shake hands, and say "hello") on ten out of ten trials.	Yes	

cause the teacher could not specify the behavior in observable and measurable terms, but because the conditions or criteria for the objective are meaningless ("90 percent of the time"); are not matched to the skill ("Tony will demonstrate that he understands the classroom rules by coming to class on time"); or are not matched to the instructional strategy used ("Given immediate positive consequences for completing her math assignments, Renee will remain on-task for 80 percent of five consecutive math periods"). With practice and feedback, you will become proficient at writing good instructional objectives for social skills. As Mager (1962) noted, if your objectives are writ-

ten precisely, there may be little more you need to do, other than provide appropriate materials or learning trials.

Terminal behavioral objectives indicate relatively long-range desired outcomes of intervention strategies. The student may have none or some of the skills he needs to perform the desired behavior. It is important to know whether he can perform all necessary components of the terminal behavior, once you have written the objective, because this information will affect the strategies you will use to get him there. The best way to assess the skills pupils need in order to perform a particular task (or to engage in a desired social behavior) is to perform a

task analysis. Essentially, task analysis is a fine-grained assessment of a task; that is, the task is broken down into sequential component steps. The number of components depends on the complexity of the task and the entry skills of the pupil (the skills the pupil brings to the task).

Analyzing academic or motor tasks is relatively simple. Most teachers are familiar with the component steps involved in solving two-place addition problems with carrying, for example. Social skills are more difficult to analyze by task, however. One reason is that many social behaviors are performed without obvious, discrete steps. Another reason is that most persons are not accustomed to analyzing social skills systematically. We suggest that you organize task steps according to one, or a combination, of the following:

1. A change in response criterion (e.g., a systematic increase in percentage of time on-task across days or trials)
2. A progression through a sequence of discrete skills (e.g. learning social greeting responses)
3. A change in response topography (e.g., controlling one's temper by substituting verbal for physical reactions, such as counting to ten silently)

Once you have constructed a task sequence, you should assess the pupil wth respect to the component steps. The evaluation will help you determine where to begin instruction and how to revise your sequence if needed. The steps included in your program can be written as instructional objectives and matched to teaching methods and materials. This, then, constitutes your intervention plan for a target behavior. It should be described in general terms on the student's IEP, and developed more specifically in your weekly and daily lesson plans. Your plan is not inflexible; it should be adjusted and revised as indicted by your continued assessment of the student's progress. This phase of assessment is described in the following chapter.

Summary

Assessment for intervention planning is a decision-making process involving multiple sources of information and assessment strategies. To guide this process, we have presented a model that uses behavioral assessment procedures across and within the ecological settings in which the student functions. It is important to assess both pupil and setting variables. The outcomes of behavioral-ecological assessments include information about the following (Polsgrove, 1987):

1. The variety and severity of the student's problem behaviors across various settings
2. The significant persons in these settings who object to the pupil's behavior and why they object to it
3. The discrepancies between the student's behavior and the expectations that significant others have for behavior
4. The differences among the behavioral expectations of persons in various settings
5. Persons who are more or less effective in managing the pupil's behavior
6. The cultural norms in these settings and the differences among settings in terms of norms and values
7. The specific antecedents and consequences associated with problem behavior in each setting in which it occurs
8. The sources of support for problem behavior in each setting
9. The specific antecedents and consequences associated with desired behavior in each setting
10. The sources of support for appropriate behavior in each setting

If student behavior problems are few, relatively mild, or confined to one or two settings, the assessments needed to generate such information are not too involved. However, if the converse is true, the assessment burden is proportionately greater. This is one reason multidisciplinary assessment involving several professionals is recommended for students who may be handicapped by their behavior.

Assessment information is used to identify both adaptive and maladaptive target behaviors, to decide which behaviors to address first, and to decide whether the intervention should be instructional or motivational. The step-proceeding intervention consists of writing terminal behavioral objectives and breaking these down according to a task analysis that is based on the characteristics of the behavior and the changes that are accomplishable and desired.

CASE STUDY

An IEP for Improving Social Interactions

Susan was identified in the first grade as an isolate child. The teacher first noticed that Susan was different from the other students when she failed to interact with anyone during recess times. Attempts on the teacher's part to introduce Susan to the other children and to have her participate in classroom games were unsuccessful. During a parent-teacher conference, the teacher shared this problem with the parents who stated that Susan had only one playmate with whom she would play in the afternoons. During academic activities, Susan worked hard and almost always finished her assignments. Still, she did not speak up during classroom discussions or volunteer for special jobs in the classroom. She seemed especially fond of the gerbils, however, and was occasionally noticed playing with them. When a child approached Susan to play, Susan would leave immediately.

In the second grade, the problem continued, so Susan's teacher tried a peer-mediated procedure. Because the teacher had never observed Susan playing with classroom toys, she did not know whether Susan actually possessed play skills. Because Susan typically played alone, her parents could not confirm that she possessed the skills to play cooperatively with toys such as telephones or blocks. She preferred to do puzzles or to color by herself, at home as well as at school. Therefore, the teacher selected a short-term peer imitation program to assist Susan in learning basic play skills. The Individual Education Plan shown in Figures 2-12 and 2-13 was written by Susan's teacher and a consultant.

Susan's teacher chose a friendly female classmate to assist in the peer imitation training. The teacher then selected three of the most popular toys in the classroom and asked the peer trainer to demonstrate for Susan how to use the toys. She conducted the peer imitation training sessions, assisting Susan in participating with the other child, for one week. Then the teacher determined that Susan had the skills to use these toys but had simply been reluctant to play with them. At this point she decided to use the peer-mediated social initiation procedure with Susan, and asked the same child to serve as the peer trainer. Using the same three toys, the peer trainer made initiations toward Susan in a quiet area of the classroom each day for fifteen minutes. This intervention session lasted for three weeks, and the teacher maintained simple records of Susan's progress during these sessions. By observing the students playing together twice a week, the teacher could record the number of times Susan responded to her peer trainer's initiation to play. She also recorded which toys Susan enjoyed.

After three weeks of this intervention, Susan's teacher decided to introduce three new toys to Susan. The peer trainer used the new

Figure 2-12. Individual Education Program: Total Service Plan

Child's Name Susan Thurman

School Rosebank Elementary School

Date of Program Entry 9/7/89

Prioritized Long-Term Goals:

1. Susan will participate successfully in group goal setting and feedback activities.
2. Susan will play with friends.
3. Susan will socially interact with friends in a nonplaying context.

Summary of Present Levels of Performance: Susan was identified as an isolate child, never interacting during recess times. Susan completed assignments, but never played with others afterwards.

Short-Term Objectives	Specific Educational and Support Services	Person(s) Responsible	Percentage of Opportunities	Beginning and Ending Date	Review Date
1. Susan will imitate Alicia.	Teacher will reinforce Susan for playing with peers.	Teacher and the student Alicia	90% (during recess)	9/15/89-11/5/89	6/10/90
2. Susan will play blocks with Alicia during recess.	Teacher will prompt and reinforce Alicia and classmate for interacting with Susan.		90% (of offers)	9/15/89-11/5/89	
3. Susan will use the free play area and play 10 minutes with a classmate.	Cooperative toys will be available for recess and free play.	Classroom peers and teacher	100% (ten consecutive minutes)	9/15/89-11/5/89	

Percent of Time in Regular Classroom

100%

Placement Recommendation

Committee Members Present

Anne Thompson—Principal

Melissa Rutter—School Consultant

Bonnie Edwards—Teacher

Mark & Jamie Thurman—Parents

Dates of Meeting 11/2/89; 12/5/89

Figure 2-13. Individual Education Program: Individual Intervention Plan

Child's Name ___Susan Thurman___

School ___Rosebank Elementary School___

Date of Program Entry ___9/7/89___

Goal Statement ___To increase social skills.___

Short-Term Objective ___When told to play building blocks or to share blocks with Alicia, Susan will comply for 10 minutes during free play.___

Task Analysis/ Instructional Sequence	Criteria for Mastery	Strategies and/or Techniques	Materials and/or Resources	Start Date	End Date	Comments
1. Teacher will talk to Alicia saying, "Try your best to get Susan to play blocks with you."	Spend 10-20 min./day until Alicia can initiate 80%. 1 wk/peer imitation training.	Prompting & reinforcement by teacher & Alicia. Susan will be positively praised for playing & will be hugged by teacher & rewarded. Recording of toys Susan enjoyed.	Cooperative play toys: building blocks, dolls & ball.	9/15	10/5	If program is successful with building blocks, Susan will be introduced to other toys and other peers besides Alicia. Eventually a group goal setting and feedback will be used for Susan and entire class.
2. Role play activity with Alicia. Train Alicia to initiate, verbally and gesturally, towards Susan.	Use different toys 80% for 2 consecutive days.					
3. Carry out role play with building blocks, then dolls, then a ball.	80% daily.					
4. Have Alicia initiate towards Susan with building blocks.						
5. When told to play, Susan should share blocks during recess with Alicia.	10 minutes of playing together.					
6. Susan will repeat sequence, this time with dolls (new toys will be introduced once a week for two weeks).	2 weeks, 10 minutes a day with Alicia or another peer.	Teacher prompting & reinforcement.	Dolls	11/8	12/8	If the program is successful, Susan's parents and neighborhood friends will be involved. Other toys will continue to be introduced.
7. Susan will repeat sequence with ball. (Susan can return to play with blocks.) During this period she will at least be introduced to new toys.		Peer prompting & social reinforcement	Ball	1/5	13/5	
8. Teacher will involve other classmates. Children will take turns using same procedure described on IEP.				10/15	6/10	

toys for an additional week. At this point, the teacher decided to bring in two new playmates who would take turns carrying out the peer initiation procedures. This particular intervention lasted for two weeks, after which the teacher made a decision to involve Susan with the classroom group since she now had three playmates with whom she played comfortably for fifteen minutes each day.

To involve the entire classroom group, the teacher set up a group goal-setting and feedback procedure. Susan's goal was simple: to play with one of her friends during recess. In maintaining this simple goal, the teacher was ensuring that Susan could participate successfully in the group goal-setting and feedback while playing with the same friends with whom she had established some rapport. Other mem-

bers of the classroom group had goals either related to academic or social skills. The group goal-setting and feedback procedure was maintained for the rest of the school year. The only modifications in Susan's goal were to expand the number of friends with whom she played and to introduce some nonplay social interactions.

To maintain the effects of the peer-mediated procedure outside of school, Susan's teacher met with Susan's parents and explained the procedure very simply. She suggested they attempt the same procedure with Susan's friend in the neighborhood. Susan's teacher hoped Susan would be introduced to various new toys and to other children in her neighborhood in the same sequence that new activities and friends had been introduced to her at school.

Discussion Questions

1. A student has been referred to you because his behavior is a concern to school staff. How would you design a strategy to assess both the pupil's behavior and the expectations of the settings in which he functions?
2. For the situation described in Question 1, indicate several alternate instruments and procedures you could use to assess the pupil's behavior and setting expectations. What would you use as a criterion for deciding whether intervention is needed? Where should it be applied?
3. What procedures are used in performing a functional analysis? How does a functional analysis affect intervention decisions?
4. If you were asked to assist a teacher in designing an intervention to reduce a student's physical aggression, what questions would you ask in order to identify target behaviors? What procedures would you use to identify behaviors with which to replace the pupil's aggression?
5. Write a behavioral objective for reducing physical aggression and analyze it into three to five sequential tasks.

References

Black, F. (1985). *Social skills assessment for mainstreamed handicapped students: The discriminative efficiency of the Teacher Ratings of Social Skills.* Unpublished doctoral dissertation, Louisana State University.

Bower, E. M., & Lambert, N. M. (1961). *In-school screening of children with emotional handicaps.* Sacramento: California State Department of Education.

Brown, L. L. & Hammill, D. D. (1983). *The Behavior Rating Profile—teacher rating scale.* Austin, TX: Pro-Ed.

Brown, L., Nietupski, J., & Hamre-Nietupski, S. (1976). The criterion of ultimate functioning and public school services for severely handicapped students. In A. Thomas (Ed.), *Hey, don't forget about me: Education's investment in the severely, profoundly, and multiply handicapped* (pp. 2-15). Reston, VA: Council for Exceptional Children.

Carr, E. G., & Durand, M. (1985). Reducing behavior problems through functional communication training. *Journal of Applied Behavior Analysis, 18,* 111-126.

Deno, S. L., & Mirkin, P. K. (1978). *Data-*

based program modification: A manual. Reston, VA: Council for Exceptional Children.

Donnellan, A. M., Mirenda, P. L., Mesaros, R. A., & Fassbender, L. L. (1984). Analyzing the communicative functions of aberrant behavior. *Journal of the Association of the Severely Handicapped, 9,* 201-212.

Evans, I. M., & Meyer, L. H. (1985). *An educative approach to behavior problems: A practical decision model for intervention with severely handicapped learners.* Baltimore: Paul H. Brookes.

Finch, A. J., Jr., & Rodgers, T. R. (1984). Self-report instruments. In T. H. Ollendick & M. Hersen (Eds.), *Child behavior assessment: Principles and procedures* (pp. 106-123). New York: Pergamon Press.

Gast, D. L., & Wolery, M. (1986). Severe maladaptive behaviors. In M. E. Snell (Ed.), *Systematic instruction of the moderately and severely handicapped* (3rd ed.) (pp. 300-322). Columbus, OH: Merrill.

Gresham, F. M., & Elliott, S. N. (1986). *Social Skills Rating Scales.* Circle Pines, MN: American Guidance Service.

Gresham, F. M., & Reschly, D. J. (1988). Issues in the conceptualization, classification, and assessment of social skills in the mildly handicapped. In T. R. Kratochwill (Ed.), *Advances in school psychology,* Vol. 6, (pp. 203-247). Hillsdale, NJ: Lawrence Erlbaum.

Gross, A. M. (1984). Behavioral interviewing. In T. H. Ollendick & M. Hersen (Eds.), *Child behavioral assessment: Principles and procedures* (pp. 61-79). New York: Pergamon Press.

Hersh, R. H., & Walker, H. M. (1983). Great expectations: Making schools effective for all students. *Policy Studies Review, 2,* 147-188.

Hops, H., & Greenwood, C. R. (1981). Social skills deficits. In E. J. Mash & L. G. Terdal (Eds.), *Behavioral assessment of childhood disorders* (pp. 347-396). New York: Guilford Press.

Hops, H., & Lewin, L. (1984). Peer sociometric forms. In T. H. Ollendick & M. Hersen (Eds.), *Child behavioral assessment: Principles and procedures* (pp. 124-147). New York: Pergamon Press.

Howell, K. W., & Morehead, M. K. (1987). *Curriculum-based evaluation for special and remedial education.* Columbus, OH: Merrill.

Kaplan, J. S., McCollum-Gahley, J. M., & Howell, K. W. (1988). Direct assessment of social skills. In R. B. Rutherford Jr., C. M. Nelson, & S. R. Forness (Eds.), *Bases of severe behavioral disorders in children and youth* (pp. 143-162). San Diego: College-Hill Press.

Mager, R. F. (1962). *Preparing instructional objectives.* Palo Alto, CA: Fearon Press.

McConnell, S. R. (1987). Entrapment effects and the generalization and maintenance of social skills training for elementary school students with behavioral disorders. *Behavioral Disorders, 12,* 252-263.

McMahon, R. J. (1984). Behavioral checklists and rating scales. In T. H. Ollendick & M. Hersen (Eds.), *Child behavioral assessment: Principles and procedures* (pp. 80-105). New York: Pergamon Press.

Polsgrove, L. (1987). Assessment of children's social and behavioral problems. In W. H. Berdine & S. A. Meyer (Eds.), *Assessment in special education* (pp. 141-180). Boston: Little, Brown.

Quay, H. C., & Peterson, D. R. (1983). *Interim manual for the revised Behavior Problem Checklist.* Coral Gables, FL: University of Miami.

Roff, J. E., Sells, S. B., & Golden, M. M. (1972). *Social adjustment and personality development in children.* Minneapolis: The University of Minnesota.

Stephens, T. M. (1981). *Technical information: Social Behavior Assessment.* Columbus, OH: Cedars Press.

Touchette, P. E., MacDonald, R. F., & Langer, S. N. (1985). A scatter plot for identifying stimulus control of problem behavior. *Journal of Applied Behavior Analysis, 18,*

343-351.

Ullman, C. A. (1952). Identification of maladjusted school children. *Public Health Monograph No. 7.* Washington, DC: Federal Security Agency.

Vincent, L. J., Salisbury, C., Walter, G., Brown, P., Gruenewald, L. J., & Powers, M. (1980). Program evaluation and curriculum development in early childhood/special education: Criterion of the next environment. In W. Sailor, B. Wilcox, & L. Brown (Eds.), *Methods of instruction for severely handicapped students* (pp. 303-328). Baltimore: Paul H. Brookes.

Walker, H. M. (1983). *Walker Problem Behavior Identification Checklist.* Los Angeles: Western Psychological Services.

Walker, H. M. (1986). The AIMS (Assessments for Intregration into Mainstream Settings) assessment system: Rationale, instruments, procedures, and outcomes. *Journal of Clinical Child Psychology, 15* (1), 55-63.

Walker, H. M., & Fabre, T. R. (1987). Assessment of behavior disorders in the school setting: Issues, problems and strategies revisited. In N. G. Haring (Ed.), *Assessing and managing behavior disabilities* (pp. 198-243). Seattle: University of Washington Press.

Walker, H. M., & McConnell, S. R. (1988). *The Walker-McConnell Scale of Social Competence and School Adjustment: A social skills rating scale for teachers.* Austin, TX: PRO-ED Publishing Co.

Walker, H., McConnell, S., Holmes, D., Todis, B., Walker, J., & Golden, N. (1983). *The Walker social skills curriculum: The ACCEPTS program.* Austin, TX: PRO-ED Publishing Co.

Walker, H. M., & Rankin, R. (1980). *The SBS inventory of teacher social behavior standards and expectations.* Eugene, OR: SBS Project, University of Oregon.

Walker, H. M., Severson, H., & Haring, N. (1986). *Standardized screening and identification of behavior disordered pupils in the elementary age range: Rationale, procedures and guidelines.* Eugene, OR: University of Oregon.

White, O. R., & Haring, N. G. (1980). *Exceptional teaching* (2nd. ed.). Columbus, OH: Merrill.

Wolery, M., Bailey, D., & Sugai, G. (1988). *Effective teaching: Principles and procedures of applied behavior analysis with exceptional children.* Boston: Allyn & Bacon.

Wolf, M. M. (1978). Social validity: The case for subjective measurement or how applied behavior analysis is finding its heart. *Journal of Applied Behavior Analysis, 11,* 203-214.

Classroom Measurement
of Student Progress

Chapter 3

OUTLINE

Overview of Classroom Measurement

Monitoring Student Progress

OBJECTIVES

After completing this chapter, the reader should be able to

- Select alternate measurement strategies that take into consideration the characteristics of the behavior, the setting, constraints on data collection, and the person collecting the data, given descriptions of target behaviors.

- Explain and illustrate the following measurement strategies so that a parent or paraprofessional could use them: permanent product recording, event recording, trials to criterion recording, duration and response latency recording, interval recording, and time sampling.

- Design an appropriate recording strategy, given two or more target behaviors, or given more than one student exhibiting targeted behaviors.

- Select the appropriate reliability formula and calculate interobserver agreement correctly, given event or interval data collected simultaneously by two observers.

- Summarize and graph or chart data using techniques appropriate for the data.

In the previous chapters, we discuss assessment strategies and procedures that guide screening, identification, and assessment planning. If you follow the assessment sequence that we have been describing, you should be able to determine who will be the targets of social behavior interventions and what behaviors you are going to target for intervention (i.e., what to teach). This chapter presents strategies and techniques for measuring and summarizing student progress. It serves as an important bridge to Chapter 4, in which we present strategies for evaluating and adjusting interventions on the basis of your measures of student performance, as well as guidelines for selecting the most appropriate intervention procedures. Thus, the precise and systematic monitoring of student progress provides data upon which to base decisions about how to teach.

Evaluating intervention programs involves many complex decisions: Should you continue with an intervention, discard it, or modify it? Is the pupil ready to move on to more complex skills or to less restrictive settings, or does she need more training at her current skill level and in the present setting? To make good decisions, you must have useful data. In behavior change programs using powerful methods that can be misapplied, student progress cannot be evaluated subjectively or casually. As White (1986, p. 522) explains, "to be responsive to the pupil's needs the teacher must be a student of the pupil's behavior, carefully analyzing how that behavior changes from day to day and adjusting the instructional plan as necessary to facilitate continued learning." Careful monitoring is a critical element of your role as an intervention agent.

To be an effective teacher—that is to ensure that your students are progressing as rapidly as their capacities and present educational technology allow—you need a system for monitoring their progress on a frequent and regular basis. Because you must act upon the information you obtain from such monitoring, you are, in effect, conducting on-going assessments of your students throughout the school year. The data you obtain serve as a basis for evaluating pupil growth, for locating flaws or deficiencies in your instructional or management programs, and for evaluating the effects of program modifications. Another factor that will improve your use of pupil data is data decision rules, which are rules that suggest how to respond to patterns in student performance. **Data decision rules** are developed by the teacher to facilitate the efficient and effective evaluation of instructional and behavior management programs. You will find guidelines for developing data decision rules in Chapter 4.

Many special educators are able to function adequately without using systematic procedures such as those described in this text. Continuous data collection for the purpose of monitoring and evaluating student progress is one of the most time-consuming and burdensome of these procedures. Because most public school and educational agencies do not require teachers to continuously collect data, it is the first set of skills lost from a beginning teacher's repertoire. Nevertheless, *good* teachers constantly monitor, evaluate, and revise their instructional and behavior management programs. They are consequently more sensitive to the instructional needs of their pupils, and they are accountable to students, supervisors, and parents for the methods they use. If

you want to be a good teacher, you must expect to spend somewhat more time collecting student performance data and planning and implementing systematic interventions. The result will be greater pride in your own skill as a teacher, the recognition of fellow professionals, and more rapid progress by your students. Fuchs and Fuchs (1986) found that students whose programs are systematically monitored and adjusted through ongoing data-based evaluation procedures make greater gains than students whose programs are not monitored systematically or formatively evaluated.

We begin this chapter with an overview of measurement procedures, including common objections to data collection, frequent pitfalls of monitoring student performance, and the use of measurement in IEPs. Next, we present measurement considerations, followed by step-by-step procedures for data collection, for reliability assessment, and for summarizing and visually displaying data. A number of alternate strategies are described and illustrated.

Overview of Classroom Measurement

TEACHER OBJECTIONS TO SYSTEMATIC DATA COLLECTION

Unfortunately, it is common for educators and supervisors to lament the tendency of classroom teachers to avoid data collection, despite the emphasis placed on this function in preservice training. The most common objections are presented below, and alternative remedial strategies are mentioned. These strategies are described in greater detail later in this chapter.

"I don't have enough time to collect data—I have to teach." This objection suggests a basic misunderstanding of the role of data collection. Frequently, it is seen as impractical or as a useless activity required by an administrator or

bureaucrat. We understand why many teachers hold this attitude. School districts and state and federal agencies require teachers to gather and report such data as daily attendance, which students will be eating the school's hot lunch, who will be taking the early (or late) bus home, and so on, in addition to periodic surveys, questionnaires and lists. Because these data have little application to what the teacher does, it is no wonder that practitioners develop a repugnance for data collection in general.

Still, teachers are notorious data collectors. Their gradebooks are full of checkmarks showing assignments turned in, scores on daily or weekly tests, counts of disciplinary actions, and so forth. Unfortunately, these data are used infrequently as a basis for evaluating the pupils or their programs. One solution to the problem of not enough time, then, is to make sure the data you keep are data you can, and will, use. This does *not* include IQ scores, test profiles, who owes you milk money, and the like. It *does* include daily reading or math performance rates, spelling test scores, rates of targeted social behaviors, number of time-outs (or other disciplinary actions), and student progress toward individual behavioral objectives. As a rule of thumb, you should carefully decide what to measure then measure it as precisely as you can.

Another solution is to simplify your data collection chores. Later we describe several alternate strategies. These include using data probes or time samples instead of continuous measurement, and auto-graphing. You may also train someone else to observe and record data, such as an aide, a fellow teacher or other staff person, another pupil, or the student whose behavior is being measured. (See page 74 for guidelines to use in training observers.)

"Collecting data doesn't help me teach." This objection also suggests that the teacher is not gathering useful data—that is, data that can be used to make educational decisions and upon which to base program adjustments. In

response to this objection, we offer this guideline: If you do not use the data frequently, do not collect it. (Note: This guideline does not apply to data you are required to collect by your agency.) On the other hand, failure to gather data you *should* use is inexcusable. If your data are not useful to you, perhaps you need to select measures that are more sensitive to what you are trying to accomplish. A common mistake is to measure the results of behavior instead of the behavior itself. For example, if you are trying to increase a pupil's use of specific social skills, do not record the number of points he earns for appropriate social behaviors each day. Instead, directly record the frequency with which these skills are exhibited.

Scott and Goetz (1980) indicate that data collection can facilitate understanding of pupil strengths and weaknesses, basic observation skills, awareness of student behaviors that recur or are just beginning to occur, effectiveness in interacting with other school personnel (school psychologists, social workers, or speech therapists) by providing more accurate information, and monitoring of program effectiveness precisely enough to make program adjustments without wasting instructional time. We hope you will reconsider the value of data collection by the time you complete this text.

"I don't get any support or reinforcement for data collection." Obviously, if you do not gather data, you cannot expect to be reinforced for doing so. However, many teachers enter their profession with an earnest desire to use systematic teaching and measurement procedures, and a year later, their teaching is guided by guesses and hunches. Frankly, there *are* no explicit reinforcement contingencies for data-based instruction in most schools. Neither your salary nor your effectiveness, as measured by most parents or administrators, depends on the objective documentation of student progress. Therefore, to maintain such a complex and sometimes difficult task, you will need to "recruit" reinforcement (Stokes and Baer, 1977). One way is to share your data

with those to whom you report student progress. Parents should be more receptive to graphs or charts detailing their child's progress in, for example, learning a functional speaking vocabulary than they would be to a letter grade in Language Arts. Administrators too can learn to view your performance in the school by progress made toward individual student objectives. (We feel this perception would be an immense help to public education in general.) So, share your student data with everyone with whom you communicate. Show them what you are trying to do and how you are trying to measure and evaluate progress. Solicit their assistance in solving your measurement problems. In addition to getting valuable feedback and support, you are more likely to gain their cooperation with data collection activities such as beginning to record student performances in their own classrooms.

COMMON PITFALLS OF DATA COLLECTION

In addition to recruiting reinforcement for data-based instruction from others, you must also minimize the response cost to yourself, if you are to keep it up. Here we will list a few teacher behaviors that tend to make data collection *less* relevant and more aversive.

1. *Trying to collect data about everything.* As Scott and Goetz (1980) point out, some teachers collect data seemingly for its own sake. Gast and Gast (1981) suggest that the question "To what practical end can the data be used?" be employed as a guideline for describing how much data are needed and how often it should be collected. And, as we said earlier, there is little purpose in gathering data to which you do not respond. So, if you intend to do something about a behavior, even if your intention is only to monitor it, record it. If you have no such design, ignore it. Some behaviors will have to be ignored simply because they are not a top priority for immediate intervention. For example, if the student's IEP committee has ranked her physical aggression and name-

calling as priority targets, and her occasional out-of-seat behavior as a much lower priority, you will probably want to devote more effort to monitoring the first two behaviors and let the third go until later. Or you may wish to conduct periodic measurement probes (see p. 76) of lower priority targets in order to verify that abrupt changes in their rates are not occurring.

If you follow the rule of collecting only those data you can use in decision-making, you also may find that you can consolidate some data. For example, if you are concerned with general classroom disruptions and have no desire to respond differently to specific behaviors in this category, such as out-of-seat or talking out, count the number of disruptions rather than the number of out-of-seat and the number of talk-outs.

2. *Collecting data on nonessential behaviors.* The points we mentioned above obviously apply here also. If you rank objectives and target behaviors, if you consolidate measures of behaviors, if you gather only those data to which you will respond, you should be able to cut down on this problem significantly. It does not hurt to ask the question, "Do I need this?" every time you review data sheets and displays. Our emphasis on using data to make frequent program adjustments applies to your data collection procedures as well. Remember, your recording strategy is also part of your program.

3. *Recording the results of behavior.* Whereas academic performances result in a permanent product that is a reasonably sensitive measure of the behaviors that produced it, social behaviors leave no such record. Behavioral indexes such as teacher ratings or point earnings are affected by variables other than the pupil's behavior (e.g., the teacher's mood) and therefore are less sensitive as measures of actual behavior. These data are convenient, and they perhaps provide a rough estimate of student progress, but they are not sufficient for making specific educational decisions. Further, the time and effort used in obtaining and summarizing these data can be spent more produc-

tively in more precise recording. For example, some teachers monitor classroom behavior by charting daily token earnings. Token earnings may be affected by factors other than the behaviors the teacher wishes to measure (e.g., the teacher may award more tokens to a pupil during the process of shaping a complex new behavior). Indirect measures such as these are not as sensitive to changes in the behaviors of interest as are more direct approaches. Therefore, instead of counting the number of tokens earned, count the behaviors that earn tokens (completing assignments, following directions). Finally, if your students are interested in such information as their daily point earnings, teach *them* to record and chart these data.

Teachers are not always present to observe and record student behavior when it occurs. Further, some behaviors (e.g., stealing, verbal threats) are almost never emitted when an authority figure is around. However, sometimes these behaviors do have effects on the environment that can be measured. For example, the number of items stolen, papers torn, marks made on furniture, or objects damaged represent **permanent products** that can be accurately counted. Unlike recording points earned or lost, these results of behavior are not based on teachers' subjective evaluations of pupils' responses, and so they are more reliable indicators of the behaviors that produced them.

4. *Not responding to the data collected.* If you follow our suggestions thus far, you should have little difficulty avoiding this pitfall. Still, it is wise to review periodically all student programs with your supervisor or colleagues to ensure that you are gathering important data, that your data collection procedures are appropriate, and that you are making the best use of these data. We have found a number of teachers who are interested in biweekly informal meetings to talk about programs and review data.

A major reason teachers fail to use the data they collect is that the data are not summarized graphically. This process takes time and is frequently put off until it is too dated to be useful (Fabry & Cone, 1980). Teachers' gradebooks or planbooks are often full of data regarding academic performances and social behaviors. However, these data are not arranged so as to show change over time. Graphing or charting serves to organize these data to show such changes and is critical to the effective use of data for making program adjustments based on student performance (Fabry & Cone, 1980). More efficient techniques have been devised, some of which combine the functions of data recording and graphing or charting (e.g., Fabry & Cone, 1980; Nelson, Gast, & Trout, 1979). We illustrate these procedures later in the chapter.

Finally, because measures of pinpointed social behaviors occur repeatedly over time and cover a relatively narrow range of behaviors, you should select your monitoring points carefully. Just as a physician knows where to find a pulse that tells important things about a patient, so too should you measure a few behaviors that describe the student adequately and that are sensitive to the changes you are attempting to achieve. You should neither measure too much nor too little, nor should you monitor behaviors that are not directly related to the changes you want to occur. That's like searching for a pulse in the wrong place — the data will tell you nothing.

THE ROLE OF PROGRAM MONITORING AND EVALUATION IN IEPS

PL 94-142 mandates that the total service plan for a pupil's education be reviewed annually, at least. However, as White and Haring (1980) point out, an annual review of goals and objectives is far too infrequent for any child, especially one who has a great deal of catching up to do. Annual, semiannual, or quarterly reassessments relative to the goals and objectives stated in a pupil's IEP are **static measures**; that is, they provide a report of progress at a single point in time. In addition to the potential inaccuracy or unreliability of static measures, they are not made often enough to allow the teacher to make timely program decisions or precise program adjustments.

That educational decisions (e.g., to change a pupil's grade placement) are frequently made on the basis of such static measures is no excuse for perpetuating these practices in your classroom. As Gast & Gast (1981) state:

> To go beyond perfunctory "paper compliance" with the static assessment of a child's progress annually, it is necessary to evaluate and measure the efficacy of a child's program on a frequent and regular basis. The pretest/posttest methods of determining pupil performance are only the peripheral ends of a continuum of evaluating and monitoring individual education plans. Systematic procedures that result in formative data, from which decisions of program maintenance and modification can be made, are imperative if the IEP is to be a truly functional tool for assuring appropriate education for exceptional children. (p. 3)

The following sections present a number of measurement principles and techniques. Very likely, as you read, you will find yourself thinking, "I can't do all this!" If so, you are quite right. The measurement principles and strategies presented here describe an ideal situation, one that can be achieved only when sufficient resources are available. Our goal is for you to understand these principles and procedures well enough to make intelligent compromises about fitting these methods to your teaching situation. For example, if you are a beginning teacher, we suggest that you attempt *some* systematic data collection (e.g., on your top-ranked instructional or management targets). As you gain skill and confidence, you can increase the amount and sophistication of your data collection. Furthermore, it is not necessary to do everything we suggest in order to be a good teacher. Experienced educators develop their own decision-making strategies. You will notice that the chapter case studies do not follow all of our guidelines regarding data collec-

tion. As you gain more experience, you will develop your own strategies, many of them perhaps less formal than those we describe. Nevertheless, we hope you will strive for the principles presented here, and will find the measurement strategies useful in your attempt to become a systematic and effective teacher.

Monitoring Student Progress

Progress monitoring involves four basic steps, several of which we have already highlighted: selecting a measurement strategy and procedures; recording data; assessing reliability; and summarizing the data for analysis. In this section, we describe and illustrate procedures for accomplishing each of these steps.

SELECTING A MEASUREMENT STRATEGY

This step includes several components: determining what aspects of student behavior to measure, selecting an appropriate recording procedure, and deciding what data to collect. We mention these separately, but in practice, you will probably evaluate these components simultaneously.

Deciding what to measure requires that you must first have some knowledge of what properties of behavior can be measured. Obviously, human behavior does not have the dimensions of a physical object; therefore, it cannot be measured in terms of height, weight, volume, or mass. However, behavior does have properties that can be observed and reliably measured. The first of these is *frequency* or rate, which refers to how often a behavior occurs in a period of time. For example, the number of times a child hits, self-stimulates, or is out of his seat in an hour may be measured. Second, behavior may be described or measured in terms of its *duration:* the length of time out of seat, the duration of temper tantrums, and so forth. Third, the *latency,* or time between the presentation of a prompt, or verbal instruction, and the initiation of a response, may be observed. Behavior also may be measured in terms of *intensity,* which includes its frequency and its duration: for example, recording the number and the length of a pupil's temper tantrums. Finally, behavior is sometimes measured in terms of its *magnitude,* or force, although this is difficult to do objectively without laboratory apparatus. The decision of which of these properties to measure depends upon which is best suited to the pupil, the situation, and the changes you want to occur. For instance, if your target is a student's temper tantrums, you may consider whether tantrums are best characterized in terms of their frequency or their duration, and then, whether your goal is to lessen the number of tantrums, or their length of occurrence, or both (i.e., intensity).

The selection of a measurement strategy therefore is partly based on the characteristics of the behavior being emitted and how you want it to change. If you want to increase fluency, measure rate. If you want to reduce time, measure duration. However, another important consideration is convenience. Although you may want to reduce the duration of out-of-seat behavior, for instance, keeping track of it with a stopwatch is highly inconvenient, unless you have nothing else to do. We suggest alternative strategies for such problems later.

Thus, you have several decisions to make regarding the choice of the behaviors you will measure and attempt to change. The range of these **dependent measures** is described in Table 3-1. Study it carefully to determine which option best suits your purposes and situation.

If you are not accustomed to observing behavior systematically, it is easy to make mistakes that adversely affect the data you collect. Because unreliable data increase the probability

of bad decisions, it is imperative that your procedures be as sensitive and precise as possible. To help you accomplish this goal, we offer the following guidelines.

1. Select a direct and sensitive measurement strategy. Consider several factors before deciding upon a measurement strategy: What constraints does the observation setting place on measurement and recording? What is it about the behavior observed that you want to change? How do you want the behavior to change? As we have stressed, you should measure behavior *directly* (i.e., measure the behavior itself, not the results of the behavior). For example, many persons monitor their eating by measuring their weight. They are dismayed if decreases in eating are not accompanied by immediate reductions in their weight. This may occur because weight also is affected by other factors, such as fluid retention. (See our previous discussion of indirect measures.)

Direct measures of behavior are more sensitive to the effects of your instructional and management programs. Therefore, the data are more useful to you in analyzing and "fine-tuning" your program. The more experience you acquire with observation and recording techniques, the easier it will become to tailor measurement strategies to the behaviors you want to monitor. The major exception to measuring behavior directly is in the case of permanent products. Written responses on worksheets, number of objects stolen, and so forth, are indirect measures of the behaviors contributing to responses, but they are also more convenient, and unless it is possible for students to cheat on every written assignment, or items reported as stolen were simply misplaced, there is generally only one way to produce the outcome that is measured.

2. Observe and record daily for as long as possible. A busy teacher decided to monitor a pupil's fighting during the first thirty minutes of school. She was disappointed that her baseline data showed zero fights, even though the stu-

Table 3-1. Summary of Dependent Measures

Dependent Measure	Definition	Considerations
1. Number	Simple count of the number of times a behavior or event occurs	1.1 Requires constant time across observational periods when response opportunities are not controlled 1.2 Requires constant number of trials across sessions/days with teacher-paced instruction
2. Percent	Number of occurrences divided by the total number of opportunities for the behavior to occur multiplied by 100	2.1 Equalizes unequal number of opportunities to respond across sessions/days 2.2 Easily understood 2.3 Frequently used measure for accuracy 2.4 Efficient means for summarizing large numbers of responses 2.5 No reference to the time over which behavior was observed 2.6 Generally, should be used only when there are 20 or more opportunities to respond
3. Rate	Number of occurrences divided by the number of time units (minutes or hours)	3.1 Converts behavior counts to a constant scale when opportunities to respond or observation time varies across sessions/days 3.2 Reveals response proficiency as well as accuracy 3.3 Reported as responses per minute or responses per hour 3.4 Appropriate for behaviors measured under conditions in which opportunities to respond are not controlled

dent had been in several battles that week. The problem was that fighting occurred rather infrequently, and her observation sample was too brief to capture it. Therefore, the behavior "escaped." Unless the behaviors you want to monitor occur fairly often across all settings and times, you should plan to observe, or have others record the events, long enough to obtain an adequate sample. This is particularly important with regard to social behaviors that are not limited to certain settings or antecedent stimuli. Usually, by the time you decide a behavior warrants measurement, you will have a fairly good idea of when and where it occurs, and

can design your measurement strategy accordingly.

Longer observation and recording periods yield more accurate samples of behavior, and provide a better check of your intervention program. In addition, you will be able to check for generalization of behavior changes across settings or time. If the behavior is discrete, not constant, and apparent when it occurs (e.g., tantrums and physical aggression), you should be able to observe and record several times during the day. On the other hand, if it is more subtle or continuous (e.g., stereotypic behavior, off-task), you may be able to use one of the

Table 3-1. *continued*

Dependent Measure	Definition	Considerations
		3.5 Cumbersome to use with behaviors measured under teacher-paced conditions
4. Duration (total)	Amount of time behavior occurs during an observation period	4.1 Expressed as the percentage of time engaged in behavior
		4.2 Does not yield information about frequency or mean duration per occurrence
5. Duration per occurrence	Amount of time engaged in each episode of the behavior	5.1 Yields behavior frequency: mean duration per occurrence and total duration information
6. Latency	Elapsed time from the presentation of the discriminative stimulus (S^D) and the initiation of the behavior	6.1 Appropriate measure with compliance problem behaviors (long response latency)
		6.2 May yield information regarding high error rate when there is a short response latency
7. Magnitude	Response strength or force	7.1 Direct measure requires automated-quantitative instrumentation
		7.2 Indirect measure of magnitude possible by measuring effect response has on environment
8. Trials to criterion	Number of trials counted to reach criterion for each behavior	8.1 Yields information on concept formation (learning-to-learn phenomenon)
		8.2 Post hoc summary measure

Source: Tawney, J. W., and Gast, D. L. (1984) *Single subject research in special education.* Columbus, OH: Merrill.

momentary time sampling techniques described below that permit you to sample behaviors across the day.

Determining the optimal length for observation periods is a decision for which no hard and fast guidelines exist. Generally, you should adjust the interval to the "typical" rate at which the behavior occurs; that is, you should get a representative sample. If the target behavior is infrequent, longer observation periods will be required. If it occurs frequently, on the other hand, briefer time samples are possible, provided they represent the rate of occurrence accurately. Ask yourself, "Do these data reflect the behavior as I evaluate it?" If the answer is "No," adjust your recording period (or reevaluate your subjective assessment of the behavior).

Although daily measurement provides the best data base for making intervention decisions, research supports the conclusion that twice weekly monitoring of student academic performance is as adequate as daily monitoring in terms of promoting academic achievement (Fuchs, 1986). However, priority social behaviors should be monitored daily during the initial phases of intervention (i.e., when programs are being tested and revised). Less frequent measurement probes may be taken when students have advanced to maintenance or generalization phases.

3. Observe and record behavior where it occurs. The teacher we mentioned in connection with the second point also violated this guideline. Obviously, your measures of behavior are not going to be valid if your observation periods do not coincide with the times or activities during which the behavior occurs. Thus, if fighting occurs only during lunch or recess, observe in the lunchroom or playground instead of the study hall. And, as we stated earlier, if the behavior does not occur in your presence, train someone to monitor it who is present when it happens. Given proper training and supervision, peers are reliable observers of behavior (Fowler, 1986). Also, do not overlook other school staff who may *not* be discriminative stimuli for good behavior: the janitor, cafeteria workers, aides, and so forth. The following guidelines are suggested for training others to observe behavior systematically and reliably. It is very important that you train observers well, if you are going to base decisions on the data they collect.

A. Develop a specific, observable definition of the behavior(s) to be observed. Include all instances (what is counted as an occurrence) and noninstances (what is not counted as an occurrence). Review this with the observer.

B. Explain recording sheets and apparatus to the observer. Teach the observer to use the recording equipment (e.g., wrist counter, stopwatch) as well as the recording procedures (response codes, interval data sheets, etc.). Go over these procedures several times.

C. Ask the observer to practice data collection. At first, you may label the behavior and have the observer record it according to your procedure. Later, you may role-play the behavior while the observer records, or use a video tape to simulate an actual situation. Be sure to stop immediately to answer questions or correct mistakes.

D. Ask the observer to collect data in the actual situation with you (or another qualified observer) present to provide assistance.

E. Ask the observer to collect data while a more experienced observer simultaneously observes and records. Assess the reliability of the novice's data, answer questions, correct errors, and so forth. Continue reliability checks until interobserver agreement is 80 to 90 percent. Do not use any of the data until this has been achieved!

F. The observer is now ready to begin formal data collection. Continue frequent reliability checks (e.g., once a week, depending on the frequency of data collection). If reliability falls below 80 percent, stop formal data collection and retrain this observer.

Unless there are no reliabile differences in the level of the behavior across settings or activities, you should observe and record in the same setting, activity, or time period each day. Not only will this result in more comparable data, it also will be easier for you to remember to monitor specific performances.

4. Keep observation time relatively constant. If you are maintaining a numerical count of behavior, your data will be affected by the length of time you observe. For instance, there is twice as much opportunity to commit physical aggression in sixty minutes as in thirty minutes. If your observation period is not controlled, your data may reflect variations in the opportunity to respond rather than in the response itself. If you are unable to observe for the same amount of time each session or day, use a rate, or percent of time, recording procedure (discussed later) to control for these variations. Rate data are particularly useful because they permit comparison of measures taken across different settings or for varying lengths of time.

5. Once a behavior is defined, observe and record only responses meeting that definition. One of us supervised a teacher who was working on a preschool child's self-injurious behavior. The teacher was counting the number of times the child slapped herself in the head or bit her fingers. The teacher reported that intervention was successful, and our observations in the classroom confirmed this. However, when the data was turned in, we could see very little change! Our questioning revealed that the teacher's definition of self-injurious behavior gradually had shifted from slaps and bites to touches and mouthings.

This change in response definition is called **observer drift** (Gelfand & Hartmann, 1984), and there are two solutions to it. The first is to decide on what constitutes the behavior. Thus, self-injurious behavior could be defined as slaps to the face or head, bites to the fingers or hands that result in an audible sound and, perhaps, reddening of the skin. Noninstances would include covering face with hands, twisting hair with fingers, and so forth. The latter would not be counted as instances of self-injurious behavior. The best way to discriminate instances from noninstances when developing behavioral definitions is to observe the child continuously for a period of time, writing down every response made, as well as their antecedents and consequences. This initial A-B-C analysis will not only help you establish all the forms of the behavior you will be observing, it will also help identify environmental variables associated with it (see Chapter 2).

Sometimes, as in the case of self-injurious behavior, behavior definitions encompass several different but related responses. These are called **response classes,** of which there are two types. A **functional response class** consists of behaviors that have the same effect on the environment. Self-injurious behavior belongs in this category, because although there are many forms of self-injurious behavior (striking, biting, scratching, or pinching oneself), they all have the same result — pain or injury. Disruptive behaviors (see Chapter 6) also constitute a functional response class, as does attention-seeking and door-slamming. On the other hand, behaviors belonging to a **topographic response class** are related in terms of their form, or the movements comprising the

response (Gelfand & Hartmann, 1984). For example, hand-raising, out-of-seat, and head-weaving may be described in terms of a set of physical movements, all of which may not be emitted in any given instance. Some response classes may involve both functional and topographic descriptions (e.g., bullying). Knowing how to group behaviors into response classes is useful if you want to consolidate data on behaviors for which you are not going to develop individual programs, as, for example, when a student exhibits a variety of disruptive classroom behaviors.

The second solution to the problem of observer drift is to conduct periodic reliability checks. These are especially helpful if, after each reliability session, the observers discuss their agreements and disagreements. It is still possible that **consensual observer drift** (Gelfand & Hartmann, 1984) will occur. This amounts to both observers gradually changing their response definitions as they become accustomed to the behavior, and is more likely to occur if some element of subjectivity is involved in scoring response instances or noninstances. The best way to avoid consensual observer drift is to avoid using subjective response criteria and to retrain observers frequently (Gelfand & Hartmann, 1984).

6. Monitor only as many behaviors in as many settings as you can manage. There is little purpose in observing and recording so many behaviors that you have no time left for instruction or you confuse yourself and your students. Likewise, the purpose of data collection is lost if you have more data than you can act upon. Cooper (1981) suggested that the more severe the pupil's educational problem, the more behaviors should be monitored. Teachers of mildly handicapped students should monitor all responses to direct (planned academic) instruction, whereas teachers of the severely and profoundly handicapped should monitor all student responses to planned academic instruction and those during social activities.

Cooper also provided several practical suggestions for initiating data-based instruction:

A. Begin observing one or two behaviors of one student. Gradually expand observations of the same behavior in another student, a third, and so on. Experiment with different measurement strategies (duration, time sample, interval) to find those that are most useful, sensitive, and direct for a particular setting.

B. Measure behavior for the shortest time possible to get an adequate sample (i.e., without occurrences of behavior "escaping" measurement).

C. Use other persons, especially students, to observe, to record, and to collect observer agreement information.

D. Ask persons who are skilled in recording and graphing behavior to help you analyze your measurement strategies.

You will find it possible to monitor a larger number of behaviors if you adjust your data collection procedures to the behavior you are recording. All behavior does not *need* to be monitored constantly. For example, if you are evaluating the maintenance or generalization of a previously taught skill, daily measurement is not required. In such cases, you might employ periodic (weekly or biweekly) **measurement probes.** For example, you may observe a student once a week to see whether that student continues to play appropriately with others during recess. Data probes also are useful for

general monitoring (e.g., spot-checking pupils' on-task behavior) and for monitoring programs in which student progress is slow. Table 3-2 summarizes guidelines for adjusting the frequency of measurement to student and program characteristics.

7. *If you are not observing in your own classroom or school building, follow established procedures.* Each institution, residential facility, or school district has its own policies regarding visitors. Although we cannot prepare you for every situation, we have summarized general guidelines. Experience has taught us that these procedures are important, if you are to obtain accurate data without offending anyone.

Do obtain permission to observe the student. Consult the building or program administrator and the teacher. Some agencies require parental consent also. Check with the teacher or supervisor to find out whether this is the case.

Do sign in and out when entering and leaving the building.

Do talk with the teacher beforehand about the purpose of your observations, what to tell the class about your visits, and the extent of your participating with the class.

Do enter and leave the classroom unobtrusively, ideally, during a normal break in the routine.

Table 3-2. Guidelines for Adjusting Frequency of Monitoring

Student or Program Characteristics	Monitoring Strategy
Rapid student progress or progress through small-step sequence	Session-by-session recording (one or more per day)
Daily progress or fluctuation in student behavior, daily program adjustments	Daily recording
Slow rate of student progress	Data probes (biweekly, weekly)
General monitoring of behavior, less frequent program adjustments	Data probes (biweekly, weekly)
Evaluating maintenance or generalizing previously mastered programs or steps	Data probes (biweekly, weekly, monthly)

Do avoid being conspicuous. Sit where you can see the pupil and monitor the behavior you want to observe, but in general, sit out of the student's direct line of vision.

Don't interact or make eye contact with any of the students or the teacher during your observations.

Don't participate in classroom activities.

Don't begin systematic observations until the pupils have become accustomed to your presence.

Do thank the teacher for allowing you to observe and share your data with the teacher if you can do so without disrupting the classroom.

RECORDING PROCEDURES

Advances in the technology of behavior measurement have resulted in a variety of alternatives for recording. The alternatives you select depend on a number of factors, some of which are presented in Table 3-3. Your answers to the questions posed in this table will help determine which recording procedure you should use. For example, if observations must be done while you are involved in direct instruction involving pupils other than, or in addition to, the target student, you would likely choose a sampling technique or train someone other than yourself to observe and record. The following discussion and examples illustrate alternative approaches you may use to record behavior.

Permanent Products

If your measurement strategy is based on permanent products, your choices of recording techniques are fairly straightforward. You may obtain numerical counts, rate or percent, or trials to criterion. The decision among these will be based upon some of the considerations listed in Table 3-3. For example, does the student not attempt work, or is the work inaccurate? Will you be recording student responses in a one-to-one instructional situation, in which you are presenting discrete learning trials? Do

Table 3-3. Considerations in Selecting a Measurement Strategy

1. Definition of the behavior target	Movement/function/both?
2. Characteristics of target behavior	Frequency/duration/latency/intensity? Individual/group? High rate/low rate?
3. Goal of intervention	Change rate/duration/latency/intensity?
4. Observation situation	Your class/another class? Group/one-to-one? Teacher giving lesson/individual seatwork/recess or free time/lunch/other?
5. Person doing observation	Trained observer/untrained observer? Adult/child?
6. Time available for observation	All day/one period/portion of several periods/portion of one period?
7. Equipment available for measurement	Automatic recorder/cumulative recorder/multiple event recorder/wrist counter/timing device/pad and pencil?
8. Accuracy	High/medium/low? Interobserver agreement critical/not critical? Reliability observers trained/untrained?
9. Audience for whom data are intended	Professionals/parents/students?

you want to increase the pupil's speed of responding, accuracy, or both? Will you be giving daily or weekly probes over the objective you are attempting to reach? Will the student monitor and record the target behavior himself? Will you use a peer observer? Permanent product recording is useful primarily for monitoring academic behaviors that result in written student responses, although, as we suggested earlier, some social behaviors may have results that can be measured as permanent products. Also, you can use audio or video recordings as permanent products of social behaviors (Tawney & Gast, 1984). Consult Cooper (1981), Deno and Mirkin (1978), or White and Haring (1980) for information about permanent product recording strategies.

To measure behaviors that do not result in a permanent product (e.g., most human social behavior), you must rely upon observational recording techniques. A variety of these are available, or you may adapt or design a recording procedure suited to your own situation. We briefly describe and illustrate several approaches. Other examples may be found in Chapters 6 through 11.

Event Recording

If you have defined target behaviors specifically and objectively, recording their frequency of occurrence is relatively easy. Event recording is the method of choice for most behaviors that are brief and discrete (i.e., have a definite beginning and end, and are best characterized in terms of their frequency rather than their duration). In some cases, a simple numerical count will be sufficient (e.g., keeping track of the number of times a pupil is tardy), but it is generally better to record the time period in which the behavior occurred or keep observation time constant to permit comparison across observation sessions. If recording sessions vary in length, you may convert event data to rate by dividing the numerical count by the time

observed (e.g., Kathy was out of her seat seven times in thirty minutes. Rate = 7/30 or .23 times per minute). This will permit comparison of your data across unequal observation periods.

Event recording may be accomplished with a paper and pencil, or you may use one of several devices (see Figure 3-1). Although sophisticated recording instruments are available, a variety of inexpensive devices are equally useful for recording event data. For example, a piece of masking tape can be attached to a clipboard, watchband, or pencil, and marked on whenever a target behavior occurs. Or coins or paper clips can be transferred from one pocket to another or to a container whenever a target behavior occurs. Golf counters, knitting counters, button counters, and even digital stop watches or wrist watches can be purchased at department stores for under ten dollars.

Trials to Criterion Recording

When you are providing skill instruction through **discrete learning trials** (i.e., presenting a fixed number of trials that consist of a specific instruction or model, the pupil's response, and a subsequent teacher response), or when you are otherwise controlling the student's opportunities to respond (e.g., through teacher-paced instructions), it is useful to record data concerning each trial. Figure 3-2 shows a discrete trial-recording format for teaching a pupil to take time-outs in the classroom. Note that the teacher has set ten trials per training session and that the criterion for moving to the next level of response duration is specified on the recording sheet. Trials to criterion data sheets may be attached to a separate clipboard for each student. Trials to criterion is an appropriate measurement strategy for monitoring progress through a task analysis sequence (as in Figure 3-2), or for measuring skill generalization (Tawney & Gast, 1984).

Figure 3-1. Manual Recording Devices

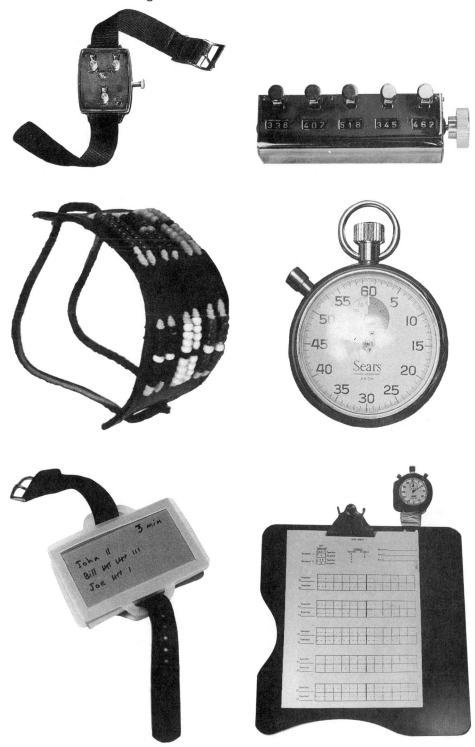

Figure 3-2. Trials to Criterion Data Sheet

Objective: When instructed to "show me the time-out position," Robert will demonstrate the correct time-out position (sitting or standing) for thirty seconds. *Criterion*: eight out of ten consecutive correct trials for two consecutive sessions.

Duration	Session	Trials									
		1	2	3	4	5	6	7	8	9	10
5 seconds	1	O	XP	XP	O	XP	XP	X	X	X	X
	2	XP	O	XP	XP	X	X	X	X	X	X
	3	XP	XP	X	X	X	X	X	X	X	X
	4	X	X	X	X	X	X	X	X	X	X
15 seconds	1	O	O	OP	OP	XP	XP	OP	OP	XP	XP
	2	XP	XP	OP	OP	X	X	O	O	XP	XP
	3	X	X	X	O	XP	XP	X	X	X	X
	4	O	XP	X	X	X	X	X	X	X	X
	5	X	X	X	X	X	X	X	X	X	X
30 seconds	1	XP	XP	O	XP	X	X	X	X	X	X
	2	O	O	XP	X	X	X	X	X	X	X
	3	X	X	X	X	X	X	X	X	X	X
	4	X	X	X	X	X	X	X	X	X	X

Scoring Key: X = correct
O = incorrect
XP = correct prompted (verbal)
OP = incorrect prompted (verbal)

Duration Recording

If the length or the latency of a response is its major characteristic or the one you most want to change, duration recording may be the best method. For example, a student may have a low frequency of out-of-seat behavior, but each episode lasts several minutes. Or, a student may be extremely slow in following directions or in joining group activities.

Response duration or latency may be monitored by any watch or clock with a second hand or second counter, but a stopwatch is best for precise measurement. By starting and stopping a stopwatch without resetting it, you may record cumulative time out-of-seat or off-task across several instances. Although a *total duration* recording procedure such as this is more convenient, it is less descriptive than *duration per occurrence* because the latter keeps track of each event and its duration. Both of these procedures are easier to use if the observer is not occupied in direct instruction or management.

Response latency is measured by starting the timer when a cue (verbal instruction, visual signal, etc.) is presented and by stopping the time when the pupil complies with the request (e.g., "Take your seat"). Although teachers generally want to decrease latency, as when a student is exhibiting noncompliance with teacher requests or instructions, sometimes it is desirable to increase latencies, as when students respond impulsively and thereby increase their errors (Tawney & Gast, 1984).

Interval Recording

Even with a stopwatch, duration recording tends to be unreliable and awkward. Interval recording is a versatile technique for recording both discrete and continuous responses. It does require that you devote your full attention to observing and recording, but you can observe several behaviors or pupils simultaneously. Interval recording also may be the most practical strategy if a response occurs too frequently for each instance to be counted (e.g., hand flapping or other stereotypic behaviors). When using this technique, break the observation period down into small intervals of equal length (ten, fifteen, or thirty seconds) and observe whether the behavior occurs or does not occur in any given interval. Gelfand and Hartmann (1984) recommend that the size of the interval be at least as long as the average duration of a single response, but small enough so that two complete responses cannot occur in the same interval. You may count a behavior as occurring according to a proportion of the interval during which it took place (e.g., 50 percent or more of the interval) or if the behavior occurred at all during the interval (Gelfand & Hartmann, 1984). The latter procedure is easier and more

reliable. If you are observing several behaviors simultaneously, it may be easier to observe for one interval and use the next to record your observations (ten seconds to observe, ten seconds to record, and so forth). It also is possible to arrange your recording sheet to allow more time for observing than for recording (fifteen seconds to observe, followed by five seconds to record, or three observation and recording intervals per minute). Figure 3-3 shows interval data collected in fifteen-second blocks. Another option for coding more than one behavior is to preprint recording sheets with the behavior codes written in each interval, as in Figure 3-4. The observer indicates the occurrence of a coded behavior by drawing a slash through the appropriate code. Other examples of interval recording are found in subsequent chapters.

In addition to being versatile, interval recording does not require sophisticated equipment. A clipboard and a stopwatch or watch with a sweep second hand are all you need.[1] Because interval recording does not provide a measure of absolute frequency, it is not appropriate to report the total number of target behaviors occurring in a given observation period. Instead, you should report the percent of the intervals in which the behavior was observed to occur. This is calculated by the formula:

$$\frac{\text{Number of intervals in which behavior occurred}}{\text{Total number of intervals}} \times 100 = \begin{array}{l}\text{percent of}\\\text{occurrence}\end{array}$$

---

[1] However, to increase the reliability of interval recording, it is advisable to use a device to signal the beginning and end of an observation interval. For example, beeps or verbal signals ("fifty seconds . . . one minute . . . ten seconds") may be recorded on an audiotape and replayed via an earphone for the observer to use while recording. Calculators that signal time intervals, such as the Casio ST-24 and PW-80 models, may also be used for this purpose. The audible signal they produce may distract students, however, and therefore, we recommend that these devices be used when the observer is separated from the group (e.g., in an observation room).

Figure 3-3. Sample Interval Recording Form

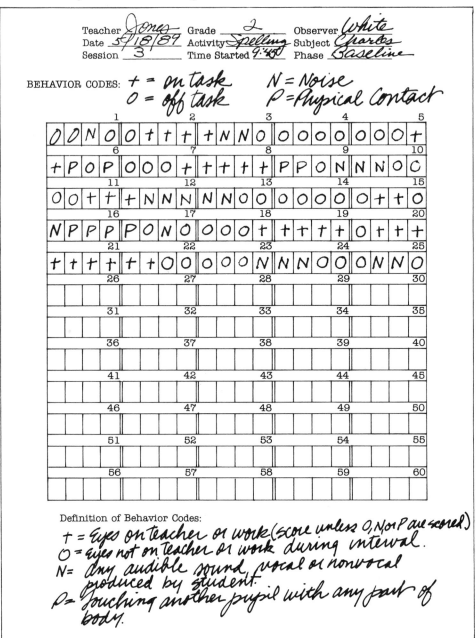

Figure 3-4. Interval Recording Form

OBSERVER *Dianne McInerney*   STUDENT(S) *John*

DATE *Oct. 29, 1989*   ACTIVITY *Science*

T=talking out, N=not attending,

BEHAVIOR CODE(S) *O=out of seat*   TIME *10:45* to *10:60*

	10 secs.		20 secs.		30 secs.		40 secs.		50 secs.		60 secs.	
1	T	N	T	N	T	~~N~~	T	~~N~~	T	~~N~~	T	~~N~~
	O		O		O		O		O		O	
2	T	N	T	N	~~T~~	N	T	~~N~~	T	~~N~~	T	N
	~~O~~		~~O~~		O		O		O		O	
3	~~T~~	N	T	N	T	N	T	N	T	~~N~~	T	~~N~~
	~~O~~		O		O		O		O		O	
4	T	N	T	N	T	N	T	N	T	N	~~T~~	N
	O		O		O		O		O		O	
5	T	N	~~T~~	N	T	N	~~T~~	N	T	N	T	N
	O		O		O		~~O~~		O		O	

DEFINITION OF BEHAVIOR CODES:

T = *talking, whispering, or making vocalizations without permission*

N = *looking out the window, around the room, out into the hall, or sitting with eyes closed*

O = *leaving seat or seated position during lesson*

TOTAL % OF INTERVALS

T = *16.6%*

N = *26.6%*

O = *13.3%*

With a little practice, you will become proficient in collecting interval data.

Time Sampling

If you do not have a block of time to devote to observing and recording, if you want to sample behaviors across an extended time period or across settings, or if you are monitoring a number of pupils or behaviors, a time sampling technique may suit your needs. **Time sampling** is similar to interval recording, but the intervals are much longer (one to twenty minutes), are less frequent, and may be variable. There are many variations to this approach. For example, you may take a five-minute sample out of every hour, or take one momentary sample every five minutes, or sample behavior on a variable interval schedule. If you employ a **momentary time**

sampling procedure, you should rate the occurrence or nonoccurrence of the target behavior immediately following a specified interval of time (Cooper, 1981). In this case, it is advisable to use a kitchen or wrist watch timer to signal when to observe. Set the timer for the desired interval (e.g., five minutes), and when it rings, record whether the behavior is occurring (remember to reset the timer after recording). Kubany and Slogett (1973) developed a recording form to use in conjunction with a timer set for variable schedules averaging four,

eight, or sixteen minutes (see Figure 3-5). The advantage of a variable observation schedule is the unpredictability of each interval. Students may be aware of the behavior being observed, but cannot predict each interval and change their behavior when the timer is due to ring. This strategy is particularly useful for measuring the behavior of a group of pupils relative to classroom rules, for example. When the timer rings, you can check which pupils are on task, in-seat, and so forth. A smiliar procedure is PLACHECK (Hall, 1973), which involves re-

Figure 3-5. Variable Interval Recording Form

Target Behavior __On task (V)__   Date __5/18/89__
Schedule __VI 4 min.__   Student __Rob__
    Teacher __Jones__
    Starting time __8:40__
    Activity __Language arts__

VI Schedule (in minutes)

Comments		Four		Eight		Sixteen
	2	V	12		12	
	5	—	2		8	
	7	V	10		28	
	1	V	4		2	
	3	V	6		24	
	6	—	14		6	
	4	V	8		24	
	6	—	2		6	
	4	—	10		30	
	1	V	14		12	
	2	V	8		16	
	5	V	10		4	
Came in from fire drill	3	—	6		8	
	7	—	4		30	
	2	—	12		28	
	1	V	4		6	
	7	—	12		24	
	3	V	14		16	
	4	—	2		12	
	5	V	6		2	

Scoring Key: V = on-task
        — = off-task

Source: E. S. Kubany & B. B. Slogett. Coding procedure for teachers. *Journal of Applied Behavior Analysis*, 1973. *6*, 330-344.

cording which students are engaged in a particular activity at the end of specified intervals. Pupils may be trained to take momentary time sample data also.

Observing and Recording Multiple Behaviors or Students

As some of the examples we have presented indicate, event, interval, and time sampling formats can be adapted to monitor several behaviors simultaneously. Sometimes researchers measure quite a number of behaviors at the same time, but we do not recommend that you attempt such complex recording systems without appropriate training. Teachers can usually observe and record up to four behaviors accurately by using appropriately constructed interval recording formats. There are occasions when you may want to monitor two students who are exhibiting the same behaviors or when you may want to collect simultaneous data on the target pupil's behavior and that of selected peers, either as a basis for comparison with the target pupil or for setting a criterion level (see Chapter 2). One way to accomplish this using an interval format is to observe and record one student's behavior for ten seconds then observe and record the second pupil's, and so on, until you have sampled the behavior of all the pupils you wish to observe. You should observe pupils in the same sequence (Jim, then Ted, then Carol, then Alice, etc.) during any single observation session, but vary the sequence from session to session to avoid unintentional bias. Kubany and Sloggett's (1973) variable interval procedure or Hall's (1973) PLACHECK strategy may be used if you are observing the same behavior for each student. Figure 3-6 shows an interval recording form developed for this purpose. When recording more than one behavior or the behavior of more than one student, you should be careful not to make your data collection task too great. The advantages of having more data may be erased by the problem of low reliability. When attempting new or complex recording procedures, you

should practice collecting data with a reliable observer until you reach 80 to 90 percent agreement. Remember also to recheck your reliability frequently.

Using Computers to Observe and Record Behaviors

The computer revolution has affected nearly every aspect of education, and data collection technology is no exception. A variety of computer software and hardware is available for observing behavior and for recording and plotting data from direct observations. Portable laptop computers are capable of recording and storing data on a number of coded behaviors. Or the data can be simultaneously fed into a monitor that displays a graphic record of the data as they are recorded. For example, the UPWARD system developed by Reith, Haus, and Bahr (in press) consists of eleven categories that include ninety-seven specific teacher, student, and class behaviors. The observer codes data on a Zenith A-181 lap-top computer. The system automatically formats and stores the data for direct use with most statistical analysis programs. Sophisticated computer technology is not out of the reach of classroom observers. Many schools now have microcomputers in some or all classrooms. Programs are available that will turn a classroom computer into a data collection and plotting instrument (e.g., Zuckerman, 1987). You should investigate these labor-saving data collection and analysis systems with your school's technology specialist.

ASSESSING RELIABILITY

If all human behavior could be observed and recorded automatically by machines (as the disk pecks or lever presses of laboratory animals are recorded), reliability of measurement would be a minor concern. However, we must rely upon our own powers of observation to measure the majority of human performances. This raises the question of the accuracy of the

Figure 3-6. Interval Recording Form for Monitoring Four Students

+ = On-task
√ = Off-task
O = Out-of-seat
V = Talking-out

Date __5/18/89__
Activity __Reading__
Starting time __10:15__

Students

	Alice (15 secs.)	Jimmy (15 secs.)	Owen (15 secs.)	Fred (15 secs.)
1	+-	OV	V	√
2	+	O	√	+
3	+	V	+	+
4	√	V	+	+
5	O	V	V	+
6	+	+	+	+
7	+	V	+	+
8	+	V	V	V
9	+	+	+-	+
10	V	OV	V	√

Minutes

Comments: _Reprimanded class at minutes 6 and 9_

observer's estimates. In the classroom, if the target behaviors result in a permanent product (math worksheet, spelling test, carburetor assembled), reliability of measurement is relatively certain. But most social behaviors are ephemeral: they leave no trace. Unless you are able to obtain an audio or video recording of the students' performance, your accuracy in observing and recording behavioral occurrences is a major concern. One reason to be concerned about reliability is that human observers are biased rather easily, and their measures may be influenced by many subjective factors. Another reason is that changes in observed behaviors may be due to our errors of measurement rather than to actual changes in behavior caused by intervention procedures.

For observational measures to be reliable, the behaviors to be observed must be specifically and objectively defined (Cooper, 1981). By specific, we mean observations must be confined to what the student actually does rather than reflecting a generalization or impression. Consider the difficulty you might have in measuring hostile remarks or pesky noises, for example. Human behaviors are objectively defined if two or more persons agree on whether they occurred. It is unlikely that high interobserver agreement could be obtained for either of the behaviors we just mentioned. What is "hostile" or "pesky" to one person may not be to another. To make these behavioral definitions specific and objective, we would have to ask: What does the pupil *do* that makes us interpret her remarks as hostile or her noises as pesky? To answer this question we might prepare a list of specific behaviors, the occurrence or nonoccurrence of which two independent persons could agree upon. She says to others, "Go to hell," "I don't like you," "Your momma," and so forth; she taps her pencil against her desk; she squeaks her chair; she belches, and so on.

It is not sufficient to develop definitions of target behavior about which two observers *could* agree, however. The primary criterion for evaluating the adequacy of a behavioral definition is the extent to which independent observers *do* agree that they have observed the same levels of behavior during the same observational period (Hall, 1973). Only then can we feel relatively confident that the data reflect what the pupil is actually doing and not measurement error. Several methods are used to assess the agreement between observers. The simplest is **total reliability** (Kelly, 1977), determined by dividing the smaller obtained frequency by the larger and multiplying by 100. This method is appropriate for comparing total numerical counts of behaviors or products (Koorland & Westling, 1981). For example, if two observers counted seven and eight episodes of self-stimulation in a thirty-minute period, their reliability would be $7/8 \times 100 = 88$ percent. **Point-by-point reliability** is used when discrete units of observation, such as time intervals or trials, are being compared (Koorland & Westling, 1981). For each time interval or opportunity to observe the behavior, two observers may agree or disagree as to its occurrence (i.e., they both may "see" the behavior as defined, or they both may not see it, or one may see it although the other does not). Thus reliability is calculated by:

$$\frac{\text{Number of Agreements}}{\text{Agreements} + \text{Disagreements}} \times 100 = \frac{\text{percent of}}{\text{agreement}}$$

If, for instance, off-task behavior is being observed in ten-second blocks for thirty minutes,

there would be six observations per minute, or 180 observations for the thirty-minute period. If two observers agreed (that off-task behavior occurred or *did not* occur) on 150 of these observations, their reliability would be

$$\frac{150}{150 + 30} \times 100 = 83 \text{ percent}$$

The point-by-point method may also be used to assess the reliability of occurrences and nonoccurrences separately by using the number of intervals in which one or both observers scored an occurrence (or nonoccurrence) as the denominator (e.g., agreements and disagreements regarding occurrences).

Tawney and Gast (1984) recommend that interobserver agreement regarding occurrences be computed when the target behavior is reported to have occurred in less than 75 percent of the intervals observed. Only the intervals in which at least one observer recorded an occurrence are compared. On the other hand, agreement regarding nonoccurrences should be computed when the target behavior is observed in more than 75 percent of the intervals. This comparison involves only those intervals in which at least one observer recorded a nonoccurrence. Computing occurrence and nonoccurrence reliabilities separately provides a more rigorous and conservative estimate of interobserver agreement.

Reliability is actually a statistical concept. The above formulas yield **percent of interobserver agreement** rather than true reliability. Statistical reliability of observational measures is typically computed by using Pearson's r or a comparable procedure. It is used when comparing data obtained from numerous recordings of behavior (Koorland & Westling, 1981). You are not likely to encounter occasions when it is important to determine statistical reliability; therefore, we recommend that you use one of the percent agreement methods instead.

There are no hard and fast rules for determining how much agreement is enough. If low levels of behavior are observed, a single disagreement may make a difference of several percentage points when the total reliability method is used. Generally, 80 percent agreement is considered satisfactory, but 90 percent or better is preferred (Gast & Gast, 1981; Koorland & Westling 1981). To rule out gradual changes in the observers' interpretation regarding the occurrence or nonoccurrence of a behavior, periodic reliability checks are recommended. We feel you should conduct reliability checks at least once during each program phase, and otherwise once a week, unless you are measuring permanent products. If interobserver agreement is below 80 percent, you should check with your reliability observer regarding scorable instances and noninstances of the behaviors observed before resuming formal data collection. If agreement is below 90 percent, the same procedure should be followed but without interrupting formal data collection. However, in both cases you should conduct additional reliability checks to ensure that disagreements have been resolved.

The procedure you select to assess reliability will depend upon the measurement strategy you use. Total reliability is better suited to event, frequency, or rate data, or for determining scoring agreement on permanent products. The point-by-point approach is more useful when several behaviors are being observed and recorded simultaneously, when interval data are recorded, or when pupil responses to discrete learning trials are being measured. It is best to consult someone more experienced in behavioral measurement if you are unsure of which approach to use.

SUMMARIZING DATA

Obviously, if your observations are recorded with a wrist counter, on scraps of paper, or on an interval data sheet, you will want to transfer the data to a central form, both for convenience and safekeeping. Such forms need not be elaborate, but they should contain all relevant information: dates, sessions, observation time, data taken, and program phase. Figure

3–7 is a data summary sheet for rate data, measured in terms of responses (movements) per minute. Such forms centralize your data for easy reference, and for transfer to a chart or graph.

Data summaries can also be organized to eliminate the necessity of graphing or charting. For example, Nelson, Gast, and Trout (1979) developed an IEP performance chart to monitor progress on task steps or short-term objectives. Figure 3–8 shows how the system can be used to summarize performance regarding several targeted social behaviors. In this figure, an X indicates that criterion was met for a particular behavior, a / (slash) indicates that criterion was not met, and the daily total indicates whether the short-term objective was met for that day.

Another procedure was developed by Fabry and Cone (1980) for trial-by-trial recording (for recording student responses to individual prompts given by the teacher over a set of discrete trials). In this procedure, an X indicates a correct response and an O designates an error response. Three uses of this procedure are illustrated in Figure 3–9. The left-hand portion displays a summary of pupil responses to each trial across sessions. The middle portion shows these same data, but the recording procedure was changed so that correct responses are charted cumulatively from the bottom of the chart, whereas errors are entered from the top down. This variation allows the teacher to plot correct responses for each session cumulatively. A graph of these data may be produced by connecting the Xs representing the cumulative total of correct responses for each session. The right-hand portion summarizes the same students' performance, but the teacher also entered the number of each trial according to whether the response was correct or incorrect. Thus, trials 3, 4, 6, and 9 in session 1 were correct. These data have also been transformed into a graph by connecting the cells representing the last correct trial per session. The advantage of this procedure is that the teacher can collect, summarize, and graph student perfor-

Figure 3-7. Rate Data Summary Sheet

Advisor Magee   Jerry
        (last)   (first)

Manager Swenson   Margaret
        (last)   (first)

Protege Issacs   Jean
        (last)   (first)

Target **Offers to share with peers**

Phase	Session	Number of responses	Time (minutes)	Rate (number of responses per minute)	Consequence
baseline	1.	0	30	0	
	2.	0	30	0	
	3.	10	30	.33	
	4.	0	20	0	
	5.	0	30	0	
Intervention 1	6.	9	30	.30	1 min free
	7.	11	30	.35	time .33
	8.	5	30	.18	per min.
		9	30	.30	
	10.	13	30	.42	
	11.	8	30	.27	
	12.	5	30	.18	
Intervention 2	13.	16	30	.52	Loss of
	14.	13	30	.42	morning re-
	15.	18	30	.58	cess if .42
	16.	11	30	.35	per min.
	17.	16	30	.52	
	18.	20	30	.62	
	19.	17	30	.55	
	20.	20	30	.64	Loss of re-
	21.	17	30	.55	cess if less
	22.	20	30	.64	than .52 per
	23.	20	30	.64	min.
	24.	18	30	.58	
	25.	20	30	.64	
	26.	20	30	.64	
	27.	20	30	.64	
	28.				
	29.				
	30.				

mance while administering the instructional trials.

A final variation of Fabry and Cone's (1980) system is to substitute time intervals for trials. Interval lengths are set according to a predetermined variable interval schedule (see the left side of Figure 3-9). The teacher sets a timer for the designated interval lengths, and when it rings, enters the appropriate symbol for the pupil's response, as in Kubany and Slogett's (1973) procedure. These data may be arranged to create a graph, just as when trial-by-trial data are recorded.

GRAPHING AND CHARTING

In this section, we describe and illustrate methods of creating a visual display of your data. If you employ either of the charting sys-

Figure 3-8. IEP Performance Chart

Area:	Math	Reading		Social Skills			Teacher: _Ron Williams_ Student: _Charlotte Jenks_

Dates: _March 2_ _March 19_

10.

9.

8. baseline   intervention

7. / / | X / X | / X X | X X X | X X X

6. *Daily Total*

5. *Arguing with teacher* X / | / / | X X X | X X / | X X X

4. *Doing name-calling* / | X X X | X X X | / X X | X X X

3. *Failing to work independently* / | X X | / / | X X | X X X

2. *Whining and/or crying* X / | X X | X X / | X X X | X X X

1. *Not yelling, hitting* / / | / X | X X X | X X X | X X /

Date: 3/2 3/3 3/4 3/5 3/6 3/9 3/10 3/11 3/12 3/13 3/15 3/16 3/17 3/18 3/19

Objective: _Charlotte will exhibit no more than one of her target behaviors per day for 10 consecutive days._

Legend:

☒ = Criterion met

◫ = Criterion not met

Program Phases

1. Baseline
2. Response cost: minus 10 points per behavior
3.
4.

90

Figure 3-9. Auto-Graphing Data Forms

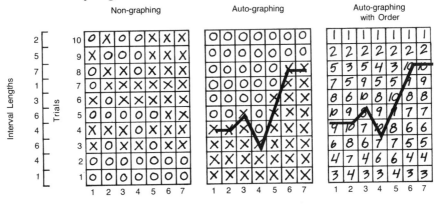

Source: B. D. Fabry & J. D. Cone. Auto-graphing: A one-step approach to collecting and graphing data. *Education and Treatment of Children*, 1980, 3: 361-368.

tems just presented, you may already have a useful visual display.

To reiterate our previous observation, most teachers can get many kinds of data pertaining to student performance. Much of it is work samples, weekly test scores, or results of standardized achievement tests. Such data are used infrequently for program decision making because these samples are not organized to be useful for this purpose: they do not show trends in student performance or compare performance to predetermined criteria. Non-graphic data summary forms, such as that depicted in Figure 3-7 do organize the data, but they fail to display trends or communicate clearly to anyone who is not intimately familiar with the program or student they represent. Graphs and charts, on the other hand, meet these goals. Graphs and charts are distinguished by the type of data they display. A **graph** typically uses only one or two symbols to represent data (e.g., a dot or a triangle). A **chart,** however, displays from several to many symbols to represent the data. All types of graphs and charts serve three important purposes: they summarize data in a manner convenient for precise, daily decision making; they communicate program effects; and they provide reinforcement and feedback to those persons involved with the program.

Potentially, there are as many types of charts and graphs as there are behaviors to monitor. However, these can be grouped into a few categories. The selection of any particular type depends on the considerations listed in Table 3-3, as well as on the type of data to be presented. A **bar graph** may be used to show progress toward a specific goal or objective. For example, Figure 3-10 shows a student's progress toward earning a class party through appropriate classroom behavior. This type of graph is useful for presenting data to be used by students because it is easily interpreted and may be reinforcing. Pupils may also be reinforced by filling in the graph each day. Another type of bar graph is shown in Figure 3-11. This graph provides a better display of daily fluctuations in student performance. Bar graphs may be used to plot any kind of data you wish, and they are easily understood by pupils, parents, and other lay persons. An even simpler presentation is a star chart, shown in Figure 3-12. Charts such as these can be sent home to parents as daily or weekly reports. Charts that report the results of behavior (points earned, stars) instead of the behavior itself are reinforcing and do communicate readily, but they do not provide the kind of data useful to teachers for decision-making purposes.

Figure 3-10.   Susan's Progress Toward a Class Party

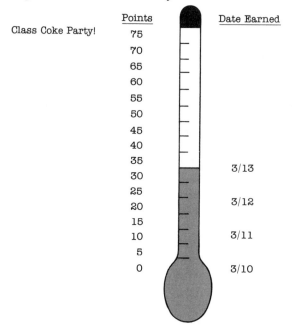

Figure 3-11.   Arnold's Percent of Assignments Completed

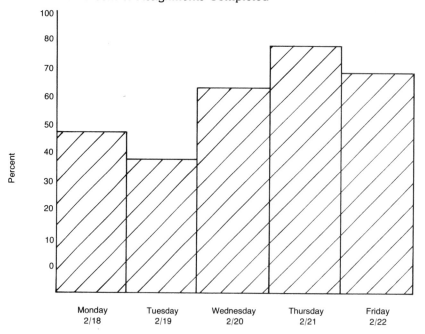

Figure 3-12. Mary's Good Behavior Chart

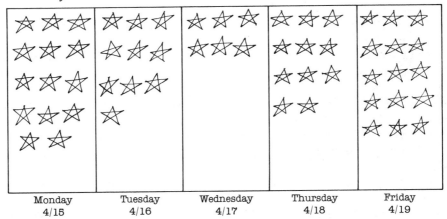

| Monday 4/15 | Tuesday 4/16 | Wednesday 4/17 | Thursday 4/18 | Friday 4/19 |

15 stars = a perfect day
10 stars = good
5 stars = unsatisfactory

Figure 3-13. David: Math Facts Learned

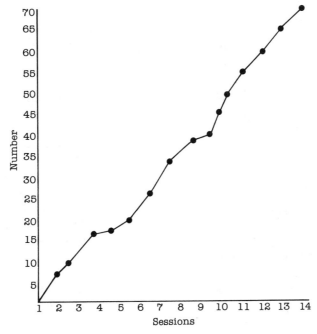

The graph pictured in Figure 3-10 is **cumulative;** each day's total is added to the previous day's earnings. Line graphs may also be cumulative, as shown in Figure 3-13. Although you may plot cumulative time, percentages, frequencies, or rates of either appropriate or inappropriate behavior, we recommend that you plot appropriate behavior (e.g., time in-seat instead of time out-of-seat) if the graph is to be used by the student so that increases in level will be associated with gains, not losses.

A noncumulative frequency graph, or **frequency polygon,** is the most common type used in behavioral research, and is the type most useful in data-based decision making. It may be used to report frequency, rate, or percent data. Frequency polygons are illustrated in Figures 3-14 and 3-15. Numerical frequency is plotted in Figure 3-14 and rate movements per minute is graphed in Figure 3-15.

Figure 3-14 illustrates plotting on **equal interval** graph paper (i.e., the difference between a frequency of 15 and 16 is equal to the difference between 19 and 20). Figure 3-15 shows data plotted on **equal ratio** or semilogarithmic graph paper, on which equal changes in rate show up as identical changes in the slope of the data path regardless of their absolute rate (e.g., a change in rate from .1 to .2 movements per minute or from 5 to 10 movements per minute, or an acceleration in rate of times 2, show up as identical slopes on the graph). Although equal ratio graph paper may be confusing to those who are not accustomed to it, the rules for plotting data are learned quickly. Also, this standard semilogarithmic charting paper offers several advantages: (a) it saves time in drawing and scaling graphs; (b) it allows behaviors occurring anywhere between 1 time in 24 hours and 1,000 times per minute to be plotted on the same graph; (c) it permits comparison across different times and activities when the amount of time or number of opportunities to respond varies; and (d) once persons

become familiar with the ratio scale, time is saved in reading and interpreting the plotted data (White, 1986). The major disadvantage of equal ratio graphing is that it is cumbersome to collect data on students' responses per minute when each response is controlled by the teacher's instruction (e.g., "Do this" . . . "Now do this" . . .) because, in order to measure only the pupil's rate of response, the teacher would have to subtract the time required to give each instruction from the time period in which response rate was measured (Tawney & Gast, 1984). Standard semilogarithmic graph paper, called the Standard 'Celeration Chart, may be purchased from Behavior Research Company, Box 2251, Kansas City, KS 66103.

Graphs and charts may be designed to display either student progress or performance. A **progress graph** or **chart** shows the time it takes a student to master a set of objectives (Deno & Mirkin, 1978). For example, Figure 3-16 is a chart of a student's progress toward mastery of 110 words in the Dolch list. A **performance chart** or **graph,** on the other hand, reports a change on a single task or behavior (Deno & Mirkin, 1978). The same type of data may be charted either way. For example, Figure 3-17 shows student daily performance on the same set of Dolch words. Whether you select progress or performance graphs depends on the kind of data you will be using to make decisions: daily performance or sequential progress (Deno & Mirkin, 1978). Your choice will also be influenced by your instructional strategy. If you have task-analyzed your terminal objective, for instance, progress charting will be more suitable. Performance graphs or charts are better suited for monitoring most social behaviors, unless you are using direct teaching procedures to shape a particular skill or behavior.

The communication function of charts and graphs is not fulfilled if they are cluttered, if they are inconsistent, or if the reader cannot follow what is being reported. Tawney and Gast (1984) indicate that graphic presentations

Figure 3-14. Kay: Talk-Outs

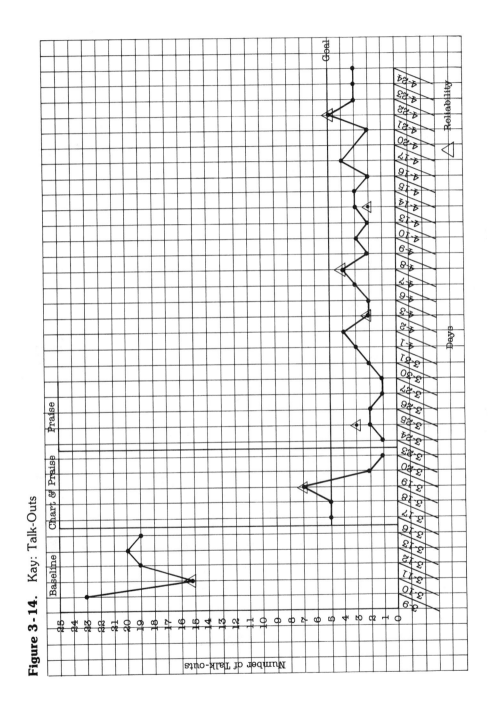

Figure 3-15. Doug: Rate of Assignment Completion

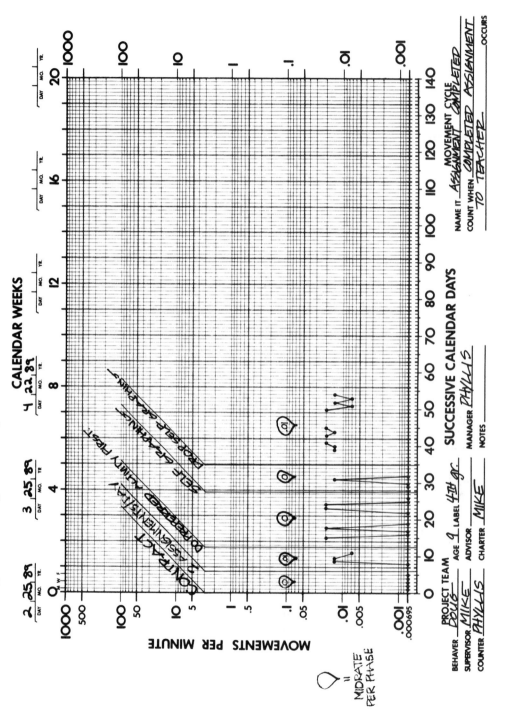

Figure 3-16. Progress Chart: Dolch Words

IEP Performance Chart

Teacher __Williams__   Student __Ronnie__

Dates: __Oct. 1__ to __Oct. 26__

Area:	Math	Reading (circle one)	Social Skills

	10/1	2	3	4	5	10/8	9	10	11	12	10/15	16	17	18	19	10/22	23	24	25	26
10																				
9																				
8																				
7																				
6 — 6th 10 words									T/7	T/6	T/8	T/X	T/X	T/X	T/X	T/X	X			
5 — 5th 10 words										T/X	T/X	T/X	T/X	T/X	-/8					
4 — 4th 10 words										T/X	T/X	T/X	T/9	T/X						
3 — 3rd 10 words							T/9	T/X	T/X	T/X	T/X	T/X	-/8	T/X	X					
2 — 2nd 10 words						T/7	T/9	T/X	T/X	T/X	-/9	T/X	X	X	X					
1 — 1st 10 words	10/6	T/7	T/9	T/X	T/X	19/8					X				X					X
Date:	10/1	2	3	4	5	19/8	9	10	11	12	19/15	16	17	18	19	19/22	23	24	25	26

* Objective: __Given 110 Dolch sight words presented on flash cards, Ronnie will call each word correctly the first time for 5 consecutive sessions.__

* T/# = Training/number correct   X = Assessment, criterion met

T/X = Training/criterion met (10/10 words)   -/# = Assessment, criterion not met/# correct

Legend

T/# = Training/number correct

T/X = Training/criterion met (10/10 words)

Comments:

Figure 3-17. Performance Graph: Dolch Words

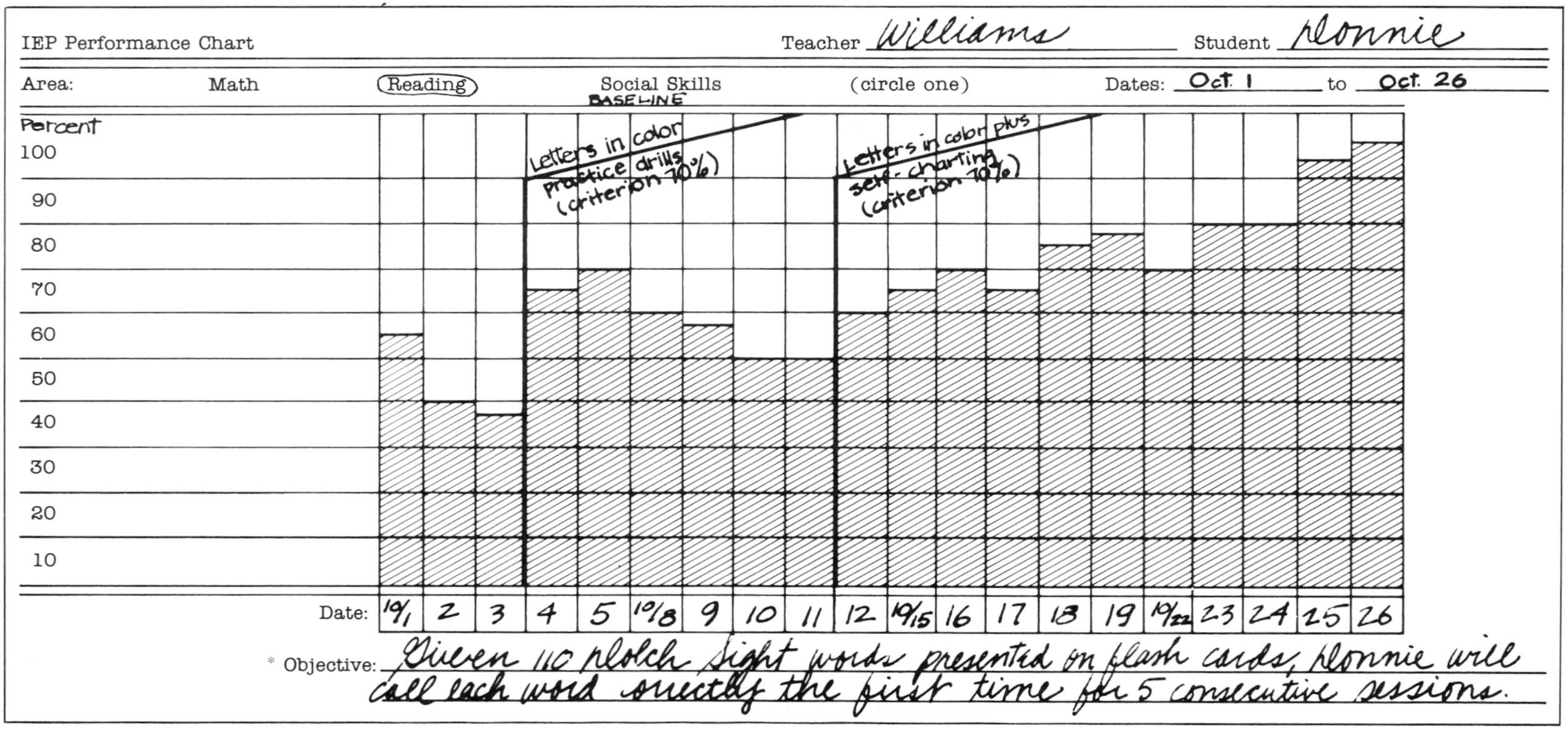

IEP Performance Chart

| Area: | Math | (Reading) | Social Skills | (circle one) | Teacher _Williams_ | Student _Ronnie_ |
| | | | | | Dates: _Oct. 1_ to _Oct. 26_ | |

Percent
100
90
80
70
60
50
40
30
20
10

Letters in color
Practice drills
(criterion 70%)

BASELINE

Letters in color plus
self charting
(criterion 70%)

Date: 19₁ 2 3 4 5 10₈ 9 10 11 12 19₁₅16 17 18 19 19₂₂23 24 25 26

* Objective: _Given 110 Dolch sight words presented on flash cards, Ronnie will call each word quickly the first time for 5 consecutive sessions._

Figure 3-18. Basic Components of a Simple Line Graph

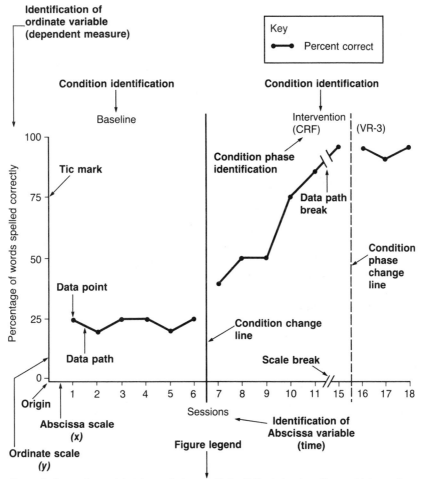

Figure 5. Percentage of words spelled correctly by K.G. during baseline and intervention
(CRF and VR-3) conditions.

Source: Tawney, J. W., & Gast, D. L. (1984) *Single subject research in special education.*
Columbus, OH: Merrill.

of data should communicate to the reader: (1) the sequence of baseline and intervention conditions, (2) the time spent in each condition, (3) the independent and dependent variables, (4) the experimental design used, and (5) the relationship among variables. Figure 3-18 identifies the major components of a frequency polygon or simple line graph. Because charts use a variety of symbols to represent the data, they require more elaborate legends, but the basic parts are the same. Phase lines are used

to designate where changes in conditions are made. Generally, behavior graphs begin with a baseline phase, followed by intervention conditions that may include phase changes (adjustments in the intervention; e.g., a change in the schedule of reinforcement). Intervention conditions and phases should be labeled descriptively, but briefly, so the reader knows basically what conditions are in effect at any given time. The examples we have provided in this chapter illustrate the range of options possible without grossly violating these guidelines. With practice, you will be able to construct useful graphs quickly and efficiently. Your pupils can learn to construct graphs and plot data too (self-graphing may be a reinforcer for students interested in their own progress). Readers interested in a more in-depth discussion of graph construction should consult Tawney and Gast (1984).

Summary

This chapter has addressed the important area of monitoring student performance. The range of procedures for measuring human behavior is expanding rapidly. We have attempted to present important considerations concerning the collection and use of behavioral data in educational settings, and to provide sample strategies from which you may draw or which you may use to design your own procedures for monitoring students' educational progress. Although there are no tangible incentives to encourage data-based instruction or intervention, research indicates that pupils whose teachers monitor their performance make greater progress than those who do not (Fuchs, 1986). Practice in data collection and graphing will increase your fluency and confidence.

Discussion Questions

1. What are some of the factors that contribute to teachers' unwillingness to collect behavioral data? Suggest strategies for overcoming these resistances.
2. Suggest alternate recording strategies for the following behaviors and situations: a low-rate behavior that occurs on the playground; a high-rate behavior that occurs across a number of settings; a behavior that is characterized by its duration; a behavior that is continuous; several behaviors exhibited by more than one pupil.
3. Why is interobserver agreement an important consideration in measuring social behavior? How can it be influenced by such factors as low or high rates of targeted behaviors?
4. Describe the features of well-constructed graphs and charts, and how these contribute to clear communication.
5. Differentiate between equal interval and equal ratio graphs, and between performance or progress charts. What circumstances influence decisions about which to use?

References

Cooper, J. O. (1981). *Measuring behavior* (2nd ed.). Columbus, OH: Merrill.

Deno, S. L., & Mirkin, P. K. (1978). *Data-based program modification: A manual.* Reston, VA: Council for Exceptional Children.

Fabry, B. D., & Cone, J. D. (1980). Autographing: A one-step approach to collecting and graphing data. *Education and Treatment of Children 3*, 361–368.

Fowler, S. A. (1986). Peer-monitoring and self-monitoring: Alternatives to traditional teacher management. *Exceptional Children, 52*, 573–581.

Fuchs, L. S. (1986). Monitoring progress among mildly handicapped pupils: Review of current practice and research. *Remedial and Special Education, 7* (5), 5–12.

Fuchs, L. S., & Fuchs, D. (1986). Effects of systematic formative evaluation: A meta-analysis. *Exceptional Children, 53*, 199–208.

Gast, D. L., & Gast, K. B. (1981). Educational program evaluation: An overview of data-based instruction for classroom teachers. In *Toward a research base for the least restrictive environment: A collection of papers* (pp. 1–30). Lexington, KY: College of Education Dean's Grant Project.

Gelfand, D. M., & Hartmann, D. P. (1984). *Child behavior analysis and therapy* (2nd ed.). New York: Pergamon Press.

Hall, R. V. (1973). *Managing behavior — behavior modification: The measurement of behavior* (Part 1). Lawrence, KS: H & H Enterprises.

Kelly, M. B. (1977). A review of the observational data-collection and reliability procedures reported in the Journal of Applied Behavior Analysis. *Journal of Applied Behavior Analysis, 10,* 97–101.

Koorland, M. A., & Westling, D. L. (1981). An applied behavior analysis research primer for behavioral change personnel. *Behavioral Disorders, 6,* 164–174.

Kubany, E. S., & Slogett, B. B. (1973). Coding procedure for teachers. *Journal of Applied Behavior Analysis, 6,* 339–344.

Nelson, C. M., Gast, D. L., & Trout, D. D. (1979). A charting system for monitoring student progress in instructional programs. *Journal of Special Education Technology, 3,* 43–49.

Reith, H., Haus, G. J., & Bahr, C. M. (in press). The use of portable microcomputers to collect student and teacher behavior data. *Journal of Special Education Technology.*

Scott, L. C., & Goetz, E. M. (1980). Issues in the collection of in-class data by teachers. *Education and Treatment of Children, 3,* 65–71.

Stokes, T. F., & Baer, D. M. (1977). An implicit technology of generalization. *Journal of Applied Behavior Analysis, 10,* 349–367.

Tawney, J. W., & Gast, D. L. (1984). *Single subject research in special education.* Columbus, OH: Merrill.

White, O. R. (1986). Precision teaching—precision learning. *Exceptional Children, 52,* 522–534.

White, O. R., & Haring, N. G. (1980). *Exceptional teaching* (2nd ed.). Columbus, OH: Merrill.

Zuckerman, R. A. (1987). *Data* [Computer program]. Kent, OH: Department of Special Education, Kent State University.

Selecting and Evaluating Interventions

Chapter 4

OUTLINE

Principles of Applied Behavior Analysis

Systematic Procedures to Influence Behavior

Guidelines for Selecting Interventions

Evaluating Behavioral Interventions

OBJECTIVES

After completing this chapter, the reader should be able to

- Describe six principles of applied behavior analysis and give examples from school situations.
- Describe professional, legal, and ethical guidelines affecting the use of behavioral interventions.
- Identify appropriate and inappropriate intervention alternatives for given behaviors and circumstances, and provide a rationale for each decision.
- Visually analyze graphed data and write data decision rules.
- Identify the major types of single-subject research designs and give the uses and limitations of each.

In the preceding chapters, we describe procedures for screening and identifying students who require intervention for their behavior problems, for assessing these students for the purpose of intervention planning, and for monitoring students' progress during intervention. In following these procedures, you should have decided with which students you will intervene and what behaviors will be the focus of your interventions. Further, you should have assessed these behaviors and formed some tentative hypotheses regarding why they are occurring. Finally, you should have designed strategies to monitor behaviors in the settings in which they occur or where they are expected to occur. This chapter describes strategies for selecting and evaluating interventions based upon your assessments.

Behavioral interventions are derived from a set of principles that explain the relationship of human behavior to immediate environmental variables that exert powerful influences over it. We begin with a brief explanation of these principles, followed by a description of systematic procedures used by behavior analysts to influence behavior. Next, we present guidelines that affect the choices made among these procedures, followed by a discussion of intervention planning. We conclude the chapter with a description of specific procedures for evaluating interventions formatively, that is, for the purposes of determining their effectiveness and making adjustments to intervention strategies based on these evaluations.

Principles of Applied Behavior Analysis

Applied behavior analysis implies that the practitioner is interested in more than the simple management of behavior. It implies an interest in understanding behavior and its functional relationship to environmental events (Baer, Wolf, & Risley, 1968). The behavior analyst therefore studies behavior in the context of the immediate situation. Specifically, stimuli that precede and follow the behavior are examined. Diagrammatically, the model may be represented as A→B→C; A stands for antecedent stimuli, which precede behavior (B), and C designates those stimuli that occur predictably as consequences of the behavior (Worell & Nelson, 1974; see also Chapter 2). The following principles describe how this model operates.

However, a word of caution before proceeding: Under no circumstances should specific behavior analysis techniques be used by teachers who do not thoroughly understand the principles upon which they are based. These techniques are a powerful set of tools, but they are easily misapplied. Therefore, you should master them through reviewing such basic texts as Alberto and Troutman (1986), Cooper, Heron, and Howard (1987), Ferster and Culbertson (1982), or Wolery, Bailey, and Sugai (1988), as well as through competent supervised practice in the implementation and evaluation of behavior management procedures.

PRINCIPLE I

Behavior is controlled by its **consequences.** This principle is the heart of behavior analysis, yet it is also the one that is least understood. Most persons assume that behavior is controlled by preceding, or antecedent, stimuli.

Consider the teacher who wants a pupil to sit down. She might say, "Sit down." This clearly is an antecedent (A) to the student sitting (B). If the child sits, it is obvious that the antecedent controlled his behavior. But what if the pupil *does not* sit down after receiving the instruction? The normal tendency is to repeat the command until it is followed, varying voice intensity and adding gestures or threats. Antecedent stimuli effectively control behavior when they enable the behaver to discriminate that certain consequent stimuli will follow certain behavior. Thus, the pupil is more likely to sit if he knows there is a predictable relationship between sitting (or remaining standing) and consequent events. Antecedent stimuli facilitate such discriminations through repeated association with consequences. The student who has learned that sitting upon command will likely be followed with positive consequences, or that remaining standing is likely to result in aversive consequences, has acquired a discrimination. If he consistently sits upon request, this behavior is under antecedent **stimulus control.** Unfortunately, many teachers fail to provide predictable consequences for students who fail to follow their instructions, with the result that pupils learn to rely on other discriminative stimuli: how often the command has been repeated, how loudly, or how red the teacher's face is.

There are three possible ways in which consequences can affect behavior. Some consequences *strengthen* or *increase* the frequency of the behavior they follow; others *weaken* or *decrease* behavior; whereas other consequences *maintain* preceding behavior at a pre-established level. *Neutral* consequences have no effect on the behavior they follow. Only consequences that strengthen, weaken, or maintain behavior have a functional relationship to that behavior. Moreover, consequences are always defined by their effects: strengthening consequences increase behavior, weakening consequences decrease it, and maintaining consequences keep behavior at the current level.

PRINCIPLE II

Behavior is strengthened or maintained by reinforcement. **Reinforcement** functions in two ways. **Positive reinforcement** occurs when the presentation of a consequence maintains or strengthens behavior over time. It is important to remember that procedures, as well as consequences, are defined by their effects. For example, Madsen, Becker, Thomas, Koser, and Plager (1968) found that when first grade teachers told their pupils to sit down, higher rates of out-of-seat behavior occurred. Thus, the command to sit down, given when students were out-of-seat, actually served as positive reinforcement for out-of-seat.

Behavior also may be strengthened or maintained if it avoids or terminates an aversive stimulus. This is called **negative reinforcement.** Examples of behaviors controlled by negative reinforcement include slowing down upon seeing a radar trap, closing the window to stop a draft, adjusting the water temperature before stepping into the shower, or sitting upon command to avoid a reprimand from the teacher. Negative reinforcement, because it emphasizes aversive stimuli, promotes escape and avoidance behaviors other than those the teacher intends to be strengthened. For instance, a child may learn to avoid reprimands by not coming to school. Therefore, the major emphasis in behavior management is on positive reinforcement.

PRINCIPLE III

Behavior is weakened by removing the consequences that have been maintaining it. This process is called **extinction.** For example, if your attention has consistently followed a pupil's out-of-seat behavior, and you withhold attention each time the student is out-of-seat, such behavior will be weakened over time. However, for extinction to work, you must know *which* consequences have been supporting the behavior, and these consequences must

be under your control. Out-of-seat behavior, for instance, may be maintained by reinforcement from the student's peer group instead of (or in addition to) teacher attention. If so, ignoring out-of-seat behavior will have little effect. Such examples emphasize the *analysis* component of behavior analysis, for only through careful study of antecedents, behaviors, and consequences can you understand their interrelationships and apply appropriate procedures.

Attempting to weaken behavior through extinction takes time. At first, you will likely see an immediate, but temporary, *increase* in the undesired behavior. Hold your ground when this occurs and give the procedure time to work. If you do not achieve the desired effect after a fair trial (depending on the student's past history of reinforcement for the behavior), attempt another procedure.

PRINCIPLE IV

Behavior is also weakened by **punishment.** As in the case of reinforcement, there are two classes of punishment. The first involves presenting an aversive consequence immediately after a response has occurred (a verbal reprimand for being out-of-seat). The second involves removing a positive consequence following a response (taking away a minute of recess time or a token for being out-of-seat). This type differs from extinction because the consequence being removed is arbitrarily chosen rather than the consequence that maintains the undesired behavior. Also, something actually is taken away, rather than being withheld. Just as with reinforcement or extinction, punishment is defined by its effects (i.e., the behavior must decrease in frequency when the aversive consequence is applied). Therefore, you must analyze the procedure over a period of time. For example, if your verbal reprimands result in increased out-of-seat behavior, punishment has not been implemented.

PRINCIPLE V

Consequences must consistently and immediately follow the behaviors they are meant to control. A planned, systematic relationship between a behavior and a consequence is referred to as a **contingency.** Although some contingencies in the environment are naturally systematic and predictable (failing to adjust cold water to warm before stepping into the shower results in goose pimples), many are not. A teacher may sometimes allow pupils to leave their seats without permission and at other times reprimand them. To the extent that such practices diminish the predictability of a contingency, so too is the teacher's control over behavior weakened. Consistency is one of the most taxing requirements of effective behavior management, but in the long run, effort expended here will save you a great deal of frustration and suffering.

PRINCIPLE VI

Behavior also is strengthened, weakened, or maintained by **modeling** (Bandura, 1969). Modeling involves the alteration of one's behavior through imitating a model. Models may be live or imagined, adults or children, and the behavior imitated may be appropriate or inappropriate. Children more readily imitate the behavior of models who are similar to them in some way, who have high status, and who have been reinforced. If a model's behavior is punished, the same behavior is more likely to be suppressed by the imitator (Bandura, 1969). It is important to apply planned consequences consistently to all students who serve as models for others.

Although these principles have been described separately, they seldom operate in isolation. For example, teachers often apply positive reinforcement to desired behavior (e.g., in-seat) and extinction to incompatible undesired behavior (e.g., out-of-seat). In this and the following chapters, we will present a number of strategies based on these principles or combinations of principles. First, however, remember that the complexity of behavior analysis and of behavior management interventions requires that practitioners be well versed in the foregoing principles, as well as in data collection and evaluation procedures. An alternative is to have access to a consultant with demonstrated competence in the principles and techniques of behavior analysis.

Systematic Procedures to Influence Behavior

The principles we just described explain the effects of environmental events on behavior, and how these effects may be enhanced or weakened. Using their knowledge of these principles, behavior analysts have designed procedures to strengthen or weaken behavior. These are summarized in Table 4–1. Note that we have arranged them in two groups, according to their influence on behavior: those that maintain or increase behavior (enhancement procedures) and those that decrease behavior (reductive procedures). You also may have heard these sets of procedures referred to as those that *accelerate* or *decelerate* behavior. Within each category, we have listed procedures from those that are least intrusive or restrictive to those that are most intrusive or restrictive. **Intrusiveness** refers to the extent to which interventions impinge or encroach on students' bodies or personal rights (Wolery et al., 1988) as well as the degree to which they interrupt regular educational activities. Thus, more intrusive interventions potentially involve the risk of interferring with students' rights (e.g., to freedom of movement, bodily integrity), of exposing them to physical risks (e.g., through restraint or aversive stimuli), or of interrupting their normal educational programs.

Table 4-1. Enhancement and Reductive Procedures

Enhancement Procedures	Reductive Procedures
Self-regulation	Differential reinforcement
Social reinforcement	Extinction
Modeling	Verbal aversives
Contracting	Response cost
Activity reinforcement	Time-out
Token reinforcement	Overcorrection
Tangible reinforcement	Physical aversives
Edible reinforcement	
Tactile and sensory reinforcement	

(We also consider those interventions that pull the teacher away from normal instructional routines intrusive because such an interruption affects the educational program for other students as well). **Restrictiveness** involves the extent to which an intervention inhibits students' freedom to be treated like all other pupils (Barton, Brulle, & Repp, 1983). We describe each of the major enhancement and reductive procedures briefly here. More detailed descriptions appear in Chapters 6 through 10, along with examples of how these are applied singly and in combination with other methods. In reviewing these, it is important to keep in mind that this hierarchy is based on our own beliefs regarding which interventions are more or less intrusive or restrictive. Other authorities may place the same interventions in a different hierarchy, although there is growing consensus about the relative intrusiveness/restrictiveness of alternate reductive procedures in particular (e.g., see Nelson & Rutherford, 1988; Wolery et. al., 1988). You should also be aware that whereas we describe these procedures separately, in practice they are usually combined as intervention packages that are applied together to increase their effects on behavior.

BEHAVIORAL ENHANCEMENT PROCEDURES

Self-Regulation

Self-regulation actually includes three procedures: **self-monitoring, self-evaluation,** and **self-reinforcement.** We consider these the least intrusive and least restrictive of the enhancement procedures because, after students have been trained in self-regulation, they may apply these procedures across a wide range of situations without interrupting ongoing activities. Most students learn to monitor their own performance ("Am I doing this right?"), evaluate it ("Yes, that's right"), and administer reinforcement or corrective feedback ("I'm doing a good job so far") without systematic training. However, pupils exhibiting behavioral disorders often appear deficient in these skills (Polsgrove, 1979). Although self-regulation procedures have shown much promise in terms of changing behavior (Nelson & Polsgrove, 1984), because they are usually private events, it is difficult to objectively establish the degree to which students use them. Changes in overt behaviors that result from self-regulation procedures (e.g., self-recording, verbal reports, target behaviors) may be monitored to evaluate the extent to which these strategies are used, however. Training in self-regulation prior to allowing students to control reinforcing events (i.e., to decide when they have earned reinforcement) appears to be a factor in its success (Polsgrove, 1979). A number of self-regulation strategies are described in the self-mediated interventions sections of Chapters 6 through 10.

Social Reinforcement

Like self-regulation, **social reinforcement** consists of several operations: feedback, attention, and approval. However, social consequences are mediated by another person. Social reinforcement may be delivered easily and nonintrusively. Used by itself, contingent social feedback has been shown to have only weak effects, but attention and approval have been found to be powerful reinforcers for both handicapped and nonhandicapped students, particularly those who are developmentally younger (Nelson, 1981). Teacher attention, even when paired with frowns, warnings, and reprimands, may be a potent reinforcer, especially with students who tend to be ignored except when they misbehave (Walker, 1979). Furthermore, it has been shown that such students receive proportionately more teacher attention than nondeviant pupils (Walker, Hops, & Fiegenbaum, 1976), which may strengthen their undesired behaviors. Nevertheless, teacher attention and approval (e.g., praise), when contingent upon desired student behavior, are very effective in strengthening or maintaining these behaviors. Naturally, for attention and praise to control student behavior successfully, they must have been established as **conditioned reinforcers** through repeated pairings with previously established reinforcers. Their effectiveness also depends upon whether strong competing reinforcers exist for undesired behavior, and whether the teacher uses them contingently and delivers them immediately following desired behavior (Nelson,

1981). Praise is more effective when it is genuine, describes the desired behavior exhibited, and is applied consistently. However, it should not disrupt the behavior being emitted and should not involve the same phrase (e.g., "Good") time after time (Wolery et al., 1988). With older or more severely disordered pupils, social consequences tend to work better in combination with other behavior enhancement procedures.

Modeling

Having another person demonstrate desired behavior has been used successfully to accelerate these behaviors in students of all ages and levels of disability (Stainback, Stainback, & Dedrick, 1979). Also, vicarious modeling through films or printed materials has been effective with students who do not have severe cognitive impairments. Modeling is especially useful for teaching complex behaviors such as social skills (Gelfand & Hartmann, 1984). Modeling is most effective if (1) the model is highly regarded by the student (e.g., a school athlete), (2) the model is like the student in some way (e.g., age or sex), (3) the student observes the model receive reinforcement for the desired behavior, (4) the modeled behavior is in the target student's repertoire, and (5) the target student is reinforced on other occasions when he displays the desired behavior (Bandura, 1969). Undesired behaviors may also be reduced if students observe a model who receives aversive consequences as a result of the target behavior. As with social reinforcement, modeling is likely to be used in conjunction with other procedures and is a component of behavioral rehearsal and role-playing, both of which are used in several social skills training packages.

Contracting

A behavioral **contract** is a formal, written agreement negotiated between the student and other persons. A contract usually specifies the behavior(s) to be increased (or decreased), the consequences to be delivered contingent upon satisfaction of the contract's terms, and the criterion for determining whether the terms of the contract have been fulfilled (Rutherford & Polsgrove, 1981). Although contracts are relatively more intrusive in terms of the time required to negotiate, write, monitor, and fulfill them, they do not restrict the student's freedom to participate in normal educational activities.

Activity Reinforcement

Providing opportunity to engage in preferred or **high-probability behaviors** contingent upon completion of less preferred or **low-probability behaviors** (Premack, 1959) is an effective reinforcement procedure with both handicapped and nonhandicapped students. It is a relatively intrusive procedure because the reinforcing activity must be identified and access to it made contingent upon the occurrence of desired target behaviors. However, high probability behaviors do not necessarily have to be such major events as a class party or an extra recess; the opportunity to engage in a preferred academic task (e.g., reading, tutoring a peer) can be used as a reinforcer for a less desired academic activity (e.g., working on a composition). Activity reinforcers are often used as **back-up reinforcers** in token systems or behavioral contracts.

Token Reinforcement

A **token economy** is a behavior management system involving nonsocial conditioned reinforcers (e.g., points, chips, paper clips, etc.) that are earned for exhibiting desired academic or social behaviors and that may be exchanged for back-up reinforcers of predetermined token value. Although tokens may be delivered quickly and easily, the time required to develop a token system makes this a more intrusive intervention. Token economies may be used with students individually, but they are more often applied with groups (see Chapters 5 and

6). They have been used with an extraordinarily wide range of populations and age groups and in numerous educational and treatment settings (Kazdin, 1983). A major problem with token systems is teachers' failure to fade out tokens in preparation for moving pupils to less restrictive environments.

Tangible Reinforcement

Tangible reinforcers are nonedible items that are reinforcing for particular students. Often they are used as back-up reinforcers in token economies, but they may also be delivered immediately contingent upon desired student behavior. Many types of tangible reinforcers are inexpensive (e.g., stickers), but because the same item may not be reinforcing to every student, delivering the correct reinforcer to each student immediately contingent upon desired behavior makes this an intrusive procedure.

Edible Reinforcement

Edible reinforcers suffer the same drawbacks as tangibles, but also involve several other disadvantages. First, the student must be in a state of relative deprivation for the edible item. Thus, pretzels, popcorn, or even M & Ms may be ineffective immediately after breakfast or lunch. Second, students may have varying food preferences, which again makes delivering the right reinforcer to every student immediately contingent upon desired behavior rather difficult. Third, because these are consumable items, health factors (e.g., food allergies) and parental preferences must be taken into account. Finally, many public schools have policies restricting the use of edible items in classrooms (Stainback et al., 1979). Edibles have been widely effective, especially with developmentally younger pupils. Fortunately, behavior analysis technology has advanced to the point where teachers seldom must rely exclusively on edible reinforcement.

Tactile and Sensory Reinforcement

The application of tactile or sensory consequences that are reinforcing has been used almost exclusively with severely and profoundly handicapped students, especially in attempts to control self-stimulatory behaviors (SSB) (Stainback et al., 1979). The teacher must first identify sensory consequences that appear to be reinforcing (e.g., vibration, movement, touch) and then arrange for these consequences to follow desired behavior. For example, if the student self-stimulates by rubbing her palm, the teacher can rub the pupil's palm immediately contingent upon a desired behavior. Alternately, the teacher can allow the student to rub her own palm when the desired behavior occurs. Among the risks of such a procedure is that of strengthening SSB even further. Before considering **tactile or sensory reinforcement,** you should evaluate such possibilities as well as consider parental wishes and whether the SSB interferes with the acquisition of more adaptive behaviors. Another way of programming tactile or sensory reinforcement is to select toys or other devices for the student to use that provide sensory stimulation or feedback like that he receives through his SSB.

BEHAVIORAL REDUCTION PROCEDURES

Procedures for reducing undesired student behavior have received an enormous amount of attention from professionals who deal with children and adults exhibiting behavioral disorders. Consequently, the professional literature on the topic of reductive strategies and techniques is extensive. It is matched by the tradition in our schools of attempting to control unwanted pupil behavior through the administration of aversive consequences. Fortunately, the preoccupation with aversive management techniques is giving way to a recognition of the influence of a sound and relevant curriculum, interesting instructional activities, appropriate stimulus control, and positive classroom structure on increasing desired student behaviors.

These antecedent events are clearly prerequisite to the effective management of maladaptive behavior and are discussed at greater length in Chapter 5. In addition, more attention is being given to analyzing the communicative function of aberrant behavior (e.g., Carr & Durand, 1985) as well as to identifying and strengthening desired replacement behaviors through differential reinforcement (LaVigna & Donnellan, 1986). However, we agree with others (e.g., Axelrod, 1987; Gast & Wolery, 1987; Walker, 1979) that behavioral enhancement procedures alone are not sufficient to decelerate undesired behavior in pupils with moderate to severe behavioral disorders. The following continuum of reductive procedures is arranged from least to most intrusive and restrictive. It also is likely that the more intrusive and restrictive procedures we describe will be experienced as aversive by both students and teachers.

Differential Reinforcement

Differential reinforcement actually consists of four strategies. **Differential reinforcement of low rates of behavior** (DRL) is applied by providing reinforcement when the targeted behavior occurs no more than a specified amount in a given period of time (e.g., if fewer than three talk-outs are observed in a one-hour period, the student earns five bonus points). **Differential reinforcement of other behaviors** (DRO, which Dietz and Repp, 1983, renamed differential reinforcement of the *omission of behavior*) requires that the target behavior be suppressed either for an entire interval (whole interval DRO), or only at the end of an interval (momentary DRO). **Differential reinforcement of incompatible behaviors** (DRI) and **differential reinforcement of alternate behaviors** (DRA) involve reinforcing behaviors that are functionally incompatible with (i.e., cannot occur at the same time) or that are simply alternatives to the target behavior (Dietz & Repp, 1983). DRL is appropriate for relatively minor behavior problems that can be tolerated at low rates, whereas DRO, DRI, and DRA may be used with severe behavioral disorders. However, because direct consequences (i.e., loss of reinforcement) are not provided for target behaviors under DRI and DRA, they may take longer to work than DRL or DRO, and they may be ineffective if the target behavior has a long history of reinforcement or has been maintained by other sources of reinforcement (Polsgrove & Reith, 1983).

Extinction

Withholding reinforcers (e.g., attention) will reduce undesired behavior if the reinforcer being withheld is the one that maintained the target behavior and is consistently and contingently withheld. However, it is a relatively weak procedure for controlling severe maladaptive behavior (Stainback et al., 1979) and is inappropriate for behaviors reinforced by consequences that are not controlled by the teacher (e.g., talking out, aggression, SSB) or that cannot be tolerated during the time required for extinction to work, such as self-injurious behavior (SIB). Nevertheless, many pupil behaviors are maintained because they result in peer or teacher attention, and therefore extinction can be effective, particularly when combined with reinforcement procedures (differential reinforcement). **Sensory extinction** (Rincover, 1981) is an intrusive procedure in which the sensory consequences of SSB or SIB are masked so that reinforcement is effectively withheld (e.g., covering a table top with felt to eliminate the auditory feedback produced by spinning objects). The need to monitor student behavior carefully and to use special equipment limit the usefulness of sensory extinction beyond very specific circumstances (see Chapter 9).

Verbal Aversives

Verbal reprimands have been used effectively with many mild and moderate behavior problems (Rutherford, 1983), but by themselves, they are less successful with severe behavior disorders. Van Houten, Nau, MacKenzie-Keating, Sameoto, and Colavecchia (1982) demonstrated that reprimands are more effective when accompanied by eye contact and when delivered in close proximity to the target pupil, and they demonstrated that reprimanding one student for behavior also exhibited by another student reduced both students' behavior. When reprimands are associated with other aversive back-up consequences (e.g., response cost, time-out), they acquire conditioned aversive properties and are subsequently more effective when used alone (Gelfand & Hartmann, 1984).

Response Cost

The removal of reinforcers contingent upon the occurrence of undesired target behaviors, or **response cost,** differs from extinction in that the reinforcer is taken away, rather than simply withheld, and is not the reinforcer that has maintained the target behavior. This procedure is most often used in token systems, in which tokens may be lost for displaying undesired behaviors. Variables that influence the success of response cost include the type of behavior on which it is used, the ratio of fines to reinforcers, and the amount of cost imposed (Polsgrove & Reith, 1983).

Time-Out

Like differential reinforcement, **time-out** from positive reinforcement involves several possible strategies, ranging from planned ignoring to putting the student in a secluded place for a period of time (Nelson & Rutherford, 1983). Its effectiveness varies with the level of time-out used, with its duration, with whether a warning signal precedes placement in time-out, with how it is applied, with the schedule under which it is administered, and with procedures for removing pupils from time-out (Gast & Nelson, 1977; Polsgrove & Reith, 1983; Rutherford & Nelson, 1982). Perhaps the most important variable affecting the success of time-out is whether the time-in setting is more reinforcing. When students may escape or avoid unpleasant demands or persons, or when they may engage in more reinforcing behavior (e.g., SSB) while in time-out, this clearly is not a good intervention to choose. It is also an inappropriate option when the student is likely to harm himself while in time-out. Time-out has been effective in reducing severe maladaptive behaviors when combined with procedures to enhance desired behavior (Nelson & Rutherford, 1988).

Overcorrection

Two types of **overcorrection** procedures may be used. **Positive practice overcorrection** involves having the student repeat an arbitrarily selected behavior (e.g., arm movements) contingent upon the occurrence of an undesired target behavior (e.g., stereotypic hand wringing). **Restitutional overcorrection** requires the student to overcorrect the effects of her behavior on the environment (e.g., returning stolen items and giving one of her possessions to the victim). In general, both types of overcorrection have been effective, but the procedures are time-consuming and often aversive to both students and staff.

Physical Aversives

Substances having aversive tastes and odors, electric shock, slaps, pinches, and spankings illustrate the range of physically aversive stimuli that have been used. Such procedures have been shown to be an efficient and effective means of reducing severe maladaptive behaviors (Rutherford, 1983; Stainback et. al., 1979). However, the frequency with which such aversives are abused; the occurrence of undesired side effects; and the objections by parents, educators, and community groups have limited the application of these most intrusive and restrictive procedures. Even less de-

fensibly, many school districts sanction the use of corporal punishment with students in spite of the absence of empirical studies demonstrating its effectiveness (Rose, 1983). The general trend has been away from using aversives and toward greater use of procedures to decrease undesired behaviors by increasing functional and desired replacement behaviors through behavior enhancement strategies.

Other Procedures

Other reductive procedures, such as in-school suspension and temporary exclusion from school, also are available. These procedures are quite disruptive to student's educational programs, and their use with certified handicapped pupils is carefully regulated (Warboys, 1987). The development of an expanded range of reductive procedures has fortunately opened up numerous options to educators concerned with reducing maladaptive student behaviors. However, the increase of intervention alternatives has placed greater demands on practitioners to make appropriate choices from among these options. Behavior analysts have made this decision-making process easier by developing guidelines and decision models. We present these considerations in the next section.

Guidelines for Selecting Interventions

With the exception of changing antecedent conditions and using differential reinforcement or extinction, the procedures used to reduce undesired behaviors involve the application of aversive consequences. (Based upon observations of its side effects, extinction is also perceived as an aversive event by students.) Verbal reprimands, response cost, time-out, overcorrection, and any physical aversive are all considered punishment procedures if they result in the deceleration of behaviors upon which they are contingent. As Nelson and Rutherford (1988, p. 143) observe, "the excessive and inappropriate use of aversive procedures constitutes one of the more sensitive areas of special education practice." Concerns regarding the potential and real abuse of aversives have led some professional organizations (e.g., the Association for Retarded Citizens, The Association for the Severely Handicapped) to adopt policies severely limiting the use of reductive procedures that involve aversive stimuli. For example, the Association for Retarded Citizens' resolution "calls for a halt to those aversive practices that (1) deprive food, (2) inflict pain, and (3) use chemical restraint in lieu of programming . . ." (*The Association for the Severely Handicapped Newsletter,* 1986). The Association for the Severely Handicapped (1981) resolution

> supports a cessation of the use of any treatment option which exhibits some or all of the following characteristics: (1) obvious signs of physical pain experienced by the individual; (2) potential or actual physical side effects, including tissue damage, physical illness, severe stress, and/or death, that would properly require the involvement of medical personnel; (3) de-humanization of the individual experiencing a severe handicap because the procedures are normally unacceptable for persons who are not handicapped in community environments; (4) extreme ambivalence and discomfort by family, staff, and/or caregivers regarding the necessity of such extreme strategies or their own involvement in such intervention; and (5) obvious repulsion and/or stress felt by peers who are not handicapped and by (community) members who cannot reconcile extreme procedures with acceptable standard practice . . .

Other professional groups (e.g., the Council for Children with Behavioral Disorders) are preparing position statements addressing the use of punishment procedures. In addition, the Council for Exceptional Children, the National Education Association, and the National Association of School Psychologists have adopted positions against the use of corporal punishment with all students.

LEGAL AND ETHICAL GUIDELINES

The position statements quoted above were adopted for the purpose of guiding professional practice. However, they clearly do not prohibit all use of aversive procedures, nor are practitioners, especially those not belonging to the respective professional organizations, legally bound to follow these policies. Educators are legally required to follow local school district policies regulating the use of aversives, but many districts do not have such policies. In the absence of local regulations, your best source of guidance is case law. Barton et al. (1983) reviewed judicial rulings concerning the use of aversive techniques and found that except for *Morales v. Turman* (1973), which allowed slaps in extreme circumstances, all decisions have expressly forbidden corporal punishment with handicapped persons. In *Wyatt v. Stickney* 1972) the use of electric shock was upheld under carefully defined conditions. Physical restraint and seclusionary time-out also must be used under supervised conditions and only when the failure of less restrictive techniques has been documented. To our knowledge, other aversive procedures have not been litigated.

The absence of legal precedent for many reductive procedures and the observation that corporal punishment is used in many schools despite rulings against it may cause you to wonder whether to be concerned with these issues. The precaution offered by Barton et al. (1983, p. 5) should clear up this ambiguity: "Any person who provides aversive behavioral therapies for handicapped persons without knowledge of the current legislative and litigative mandates governing such provision and concern for the rights of the individual invites both professional and personal disaster." In fact, the United States Supreme Court has ruled that if punishment is found to be excessive, the teacher or school officials who are responsible may be held liable for damages to the student (Singer & Irvin, 1987). Thus, you may avoid using punishment procedures altogether or use them carefully and with proper attention to student and parental rights (Wood & Braaten, 1983). Again, we believe that reductive procedures are necessary with highly disruptive and aggressive pupils, but we agree with Wood and Braaten that they should be used in combination with procedures for teaching desired replacement behaviors. We further agree that corporal punishment "has no place in special education programs" (Wood & Braaten, 1983, p. 71).

The possibility of legal sanctions is a compelling reason for school districts to adopt policies regulating the use of reductive procedures. Singer and Irvin (1987) suggest that students' and teachers' rights concerning intrusive or restrictive procedures should be safeguarded through establishing school district procedures that include the following:

1. Obtaining informed consent, which includes a detailed description of the problem behavior, previously attempted interventions, proposed intervention risks and expected outcomes, data collection procedures, and alternative interventions; and a statement of consent from the parents, which includes the right to withdraw consent at any time
2. Review by a school district human rights committee (Such review procedures are not found in most school districts, but they should be developed.)
3. Due process procedures to regulate school district actions when intrusive behavior management techniques are used (Again, few school districts have developed such procedures. However, "formal IEP processes must be used if disciplinary methods

of any kind are a regular part of a handicapped child's educational program" [p. 50]. Intrusive interventions require a level of review beyond regular IEP procedures [e.g., human rights committee review].)
4. Use of the **least restrictive alternative,** which refers to interventions that restrict a student's freedom no more than is necessary to achieve the desired goals (Budd & Baer, 1976) (Restrictive interventions must be aimed at educational objectives and those proposing an intervention must prove that less intrusive methods are not the best approach and that the proposed intervention is the least restrictive alternative.)

Wood and Braaten (1983) suggest that school district policies regarding the use of punishment procedures include (1) definitions and descriptions of procedures that are permitted and those that are not allowed; (2) references to relevant laws, regulations, court decisions, and professional standards; and (3) procedural guidelines that contain the following elements:

a. Information concerning the use and abuse of punishment procedures
b. Staff training requirements for the proper use of approved procedures
c. Approved punishment procedures
d. Procedures for maintaining records of the use of punishment procedures
e. Complaint and appeal procedures
f. Punishment issues and cautions
g. Procedures for periodic review of procedures used with individual students

Resources that can be used in drafting such policies include guidelines in the professional literature for specific interventions such as differential reinforcement (Deitz & Repp, 1983), response cost (Walker, 1983), time-out (Gast & Nelson, 1977; Nelson & Rutherford, 1983) and for aversive procedures in general (Polsgrove & Reith, 1983; Wood & Braaten, 1983). Some professional and parental organizations, such as the Association for Retarded Citizens, have adopted guidelines for behavioral interventions (Sajwaj, 1977), and others (e.g., CCBD) are developing these.

This discussion has considered the impact on and acceptability by persons directly affected by behavioral interventions (i.e., students and parents). The IEP committee format provides a means of *socially validating* the goals, the appropriateness, and the acceptability of intervention procedures, that is, the extent to which caregivers and significant others agree with the objectives and methods of intervention programs (Wolf, 1978). In planning interventions for nonhandicapped students, care should be taken to assure that intervention objectives and procedures are seen as appropriate and necessary by those persons who are involved and concerned with pupils' well-being and educational progress. School policies regulating the use of behavior reduction procedures should therefore apply to all students, not just to handicapped students.

The acceptability of interventions by practitioners is also a relevant issue, especially because some procedures will be recommended to regular educators working with handicapped pupils in mainstream settings. Research on this issue has revealed that, in general, more restrictive interventions (e.g., time-out and psychoactive medications) are viewed as less acceptable than such interventions as positive reinforcement of desired behavior, although more restrictive procedures are seen as more acceptable with students exhibiting highly deviant behavior (Kazdin, 1981; Witt, Elliott, & Martens, 1984). Student and teacher ethnicity have also been suggested as factors affecting treatment acceptability (Pearson & Argulewicz, 1987). Witt and Martens (1983) recommend that professionals ask five questions regarding the acceptability of an intervention before implementing it: (1) Is it suitable for mainstream classrooms? (2) Does it present unnecessary risks to pupils? (3) Does it require too much teacher time? (4) Does it have negative side ef-

fects on other pupils? (5) Does the teacher have the skill to implement it?

CONSIDERATIONS IN SELECTING REDUCTIVE PROCEDURES

Legal and ethical factors, as well as school district policies, place limits on what reductive procedures can be used with pupils. However, these do not provide specific guidelines concerning which procedures represent the appropriate alternative for specific problem behaviors. Although decisions regarding these choices should be made by students' IEP committees, it is important that this group have guidance from persons who are technically knowledgeable about intervention procedures and their effects, side effects, advantages, and drawbacks. Furthermore, committees should feel comfortable that the recommendation to intervene with a reductive procedure occurs in the context of an educational environment that is positive, structured, and productive. Since we are assuming that you will be the professional with the technical expertise to make intervention recommendations, in this section we provide you with guidelines from the professional literature.

Braaten (1987) suggests three principles that govern the appropriate use of reductive procedures: (1) The priority given the target behavior justifies the level of intervention; (2) interventions based on positive reinforcement of incompatible or alternative behaviors have been demonstrated to be ineffective; and (3) less restrictive or intrusive procedures are attempted first. We elaborate on each of these principles in the following discussion.

Priority of Target Behavior

In Chapter 2, we introduced the *fair pair rule* (White & Haring, 1980), which applies to the identification of desired replacement behaviors for each undesired behavior targeted. Further, we indicated that desired replacement behaviors could be selected by assessing the skills pupils need in their current or potential future environments. But what criteria should be used in deciding which of the student's undesired behaviors to target first? Braaten (1987) suggests a hierarchy of such behaviors. *Low priority* target behaviors are those that are annoying but not harmful to others (e.g., teasing, off-task). *Mild priority* targets include behaviors that frequently interfere with the achievement of classroom or individual student goals (e.g., defiance, pushing, minor property damage). *Moderate priority* targets are behaviors that repeatedly or significantly interfere with goal achievement or with other class members (e.g. fighting, avoiding school, abuse of staff). Behaviors that are *high priority* targets involve persistent, generalized alienation or agitation that is excessively disruptive to self and others (e.g., physical assault, stereotypic behaviors, total noncompliance). Finally, *urgent priority* targets involve extreme risk and require expert intervention (e.g., behaviors that are life-threatening or that risk serious injury to self or others). By reviewing the student's problem behaviors with regard to this hierarchy, you can determine which behaviors may be ignored or monitored to ensure that they are not increasing to obtrusive levels, and target these for intervention after higher priority undesired behaviors have been reduced.

Demonstrated Ineffectiveness of Enhancement Interventions

We hope that you have seen ample need to attempt interventions that strengthen desired behaviors before considering reductive procedures. By differentially reinforcing behaviors that are incompatible with or alternative to undesired targets, you may be able to avoid using punishment procedures entirely. In targeting replacement behaviors, remember also to consider the possible *communicative function* of the pupil's maladaptive behavior (Carr & Durand, 1985). If you can identify a replacement behavior that serves the same communi-

cative function *and* that you can systematically reinforce, the chances are doubly good that you will not have to use aversive consequences to reduce the undesired target behavior. However, for strategies based on enhancement procedures to be most effective, remember our caution that you should identify reinforcers for both desired and undesired behaviors and be able to control the pupil's sources of positive reinforcement. Furthermore, in demonstrating that reinforcing interventions are ineffective, we assume that you have systematically implemented the intervention, have collected data on its effects over an adequate period of time, and have evaluated its effects on the target behavior with respect to level, trend, and stability (see pp. 119 for guidelines on data-based evaluation of interventions).

Use of Less Restrictive or Intrusive Procedures

This principle suggests that, once the decision to use reductive procedures has been made, you should consider those that intrude the least upon the student's body, rights, or curriculum. A wide range of alternatives that address both the antecedents to and consequences of the undesired target behavior may be considered. Wolery et al. (1988) describe four categories of setting events that may influence behavior. The *instructional dimensions of the environment* include the types of materials, activities, and instruction that are provided, as well as the sequence of activities. For example, if the target behavior occurs mainly when certain activities are scheduled, perhaps these activities are too difficult or are boring to the student. The *physical dimensions of the environment* that may influence behavior include lighting, noise, heat, the physical arrangement of the environment, and the time of day. Variables related to the *social dimensions of the environment* include the number of other students, the number of adults, the behavior of others toward the student, and the pupil's physical proximity to others. Finally, *changes in the environment* that potentially affect student behavior include changes in schedule, physical arrangement of the setting, and changes in the home environment. By being a careful student of the pupil's behavior and staying informed of changes in his other ecological settings, you should be able to identify antecedent conditions or variables that affect him. If a functional relationship between the target behavior and any of these variables is discovered, interventions that address these factors should be attempted before reductive consequences are considered.

If you cannot identify a relationship between antecedent variables and undesired behavior, and if you have tried nonpunishment reductive procedures (i.e., differential reinforcement, extinction) and found them ineffective, you are now faced with choices from among the punishment options listed in Table 4-1. Two principles will help you select from among these options. The principle of the **least intrusive alternative** (Gast & Wolery, 1987) indicates that the simplest effective intervention should be chosen when data are available regarding the general effectiveness of a given procedure. This principle implies that intervention agents must keep up with current research literature on behavioral interventions, which is reported in a variety of professional journals. We encourage you to subscribe to some of these journals independently or through your professional organization (e.g., CCBD), and to allow some time each week for professional reading.

Although behavioral interventions have been proven effective across numerous settings, intervention agents, and target individuals, because outcomes vary with the unique characteristics of persons and settings, effectiveness is always relative. Thus, the question of what works must address with whom and under what circumstances (Nelson, 1987). Another principle, the criterion of the **least dangerous assumption,** is useful when conclusive data are not available regarding the effectiveness of a particular intervention and the circumstances surrounding it. As stated by Donnellan (1984, p. 142), "in the absence of conclusive data, educational decisions should be based on assumptions that, if incorrect, will have the least dangerous effect on the student." For example, an intervention package involving DRI and response cost could be assumed to have less dangerous effects than one that includes overcorrection.

Although the focus of this discussion has been on reductive procedures, you should be aware that strategies based on positive reinforcement can also be misapplied and abused (P. S. Strain, personal communication, April 1986). For example, inappropriate contingencies of reinforcement may directly support undesired behavior, as when teachers attend to maladaptive student performances while ignoring adaptive behavior when it occurs. One reason that interventions involving aversive procedures are evaluated more critically is that their misuse usually involves greater risks to the student (although we can think of several exceptions, e.g., the teacher who attends to SIB).

DECISION MODELS FOR REDUCING UNDESIRED BEHAVIORS

The guidelines and considerations we have described provide a basis for making tentative decisions about intervention alternatives. However, a more detailed analysis is necessary to match precisely the intervention strategy to the characteristics of the pupil, the setting, and the target behavior. Several decision models have been devised for this purpose (e.g., Evans & Meyer, 1985; Gaylord-Ross, 1980; Wolery et al., 1988). The common elements of these models are the formation of hypotheses regarding why problem behavior is occurring and systematic assessment of these hypotheses through manipulation of potential maintaining variables. For example, the model developed by Gaylord-Ross (1980) includes reinforcement, ecology, curriculum, and punishment components. In terms of reinforcement, if it is hypothesized that the student's behavior is maintained by positive reinforcement and that the teacher controls the reinforcer, extinction would be a viable intervention. On the other hand, if the behavior is maintained by negative reinforcement (e.g., the student escapes or avoids tasks or settings by engaging in the target behavior), the task itself can be modified to make it less aversive, or the opportunity to escape can be removed by putting the student through the task. Or if the behavior occurs due to an insufficient amount of positive reinforcement, increasing the density of reinforcement through differential reinforcement might be the best choice.

Interventions based on ecological hypotheses stress determining whether problem behaviors occur because of crowding, the lack of engaging objects, or the presence of environmental pollutants (heat, noise, light). Changes in these variables constitute the appropriate intervention in such cases. (However, remember the observation of Wolery et al., 1988 that more remote events occurring in other settings, such as the home, may need to be considered.) Hypotheses based on curriculum variables derive from the observation that problem behaviors vary according to particular tasks. Interventions addressing this component involve making appropriate adjustments in the curriculum (e.g., modifying overly difficult tasks, changing nonpreferred tasks).

Punishment is the last component in the Gaylord-Ross (1980) model, which indicates that the other hypotheses should be entertained first. Only when reinforcement, ecological, or curricular variables affecting the student's problem behavior cannot be identified should punishment be considered. We cannot overemphasize the importance of trying to "read" the pupil's behavior correctly; interventions chosen without regard for maintaining variables may be doomed to failure. For example, if a student's disruptive behavior is

maintained by escape from undesired tasks, time-out would be ineffective in reducing this problem. The systematic, continuous assessment of pinpointed target behaviors in the settings in which they occur is crucial to identifying their relationships to variables that may influence them, to selecting appropriate intervention strategies, and to evaluating and adjusting these interventions.

DEVELOPING AN INTERVENTION PLAN

IEPs for pupils certified as behaviorally disordered should contain objectives and strategies for targeted social behaviors. (We are often surprised to read IEPs for such pupils that contain no plans for intervening with their social behavior problems.) However, these strategies lack the specificity needed to guide intervention efforts on a day-to-day basis, Moreover, students who are not certified as handicapped will not have IEPs. Wolery et al. (1988) indicate that a specific intervention plan should be developed for each social behavior that is targeted for reduction. The components of an intervention plan include: a *behavioral objective, what* will be done, *who* will do it, *how* it will be done, *when* it will be done, *when* it will be reviewed, *who* will review it, and *what* will happen if the plan is ineffective or if undesired side effects occur. Given the many legal, ethical, and practical considerations that must be taken into account in using reductive procedures, Wolery et al. (1988) recommend that such plans are best worked out by a team. Initial intervention plans can be developed by IEP committees, but for daily decision making and for those students who do not have IEPs, planning teams should include persons who are readily available to review data, discuss problems, and make decisions about plan revisions as required. Data-based evaluation strategies are valuable tools for intervention teams. These are discussed in the following section.

Evaluating Behavioral Interventions

Powerful intervention strategies, especially if they are restrictive or intrusive, require precise and sensitive evaluation procedures to ensure that students do not spend unnecessary amounts of time in ineffective programs. Good evaluation procedures also protect those who carry out interventions, in that they provide feedback that may be used to adjust or change procedures that are inappropriate, incorrectly applied, or simply do not work as planned. Unlike assessment, which yields information regarding the current status of a student, evaluation involves assessing the impact of a program on a pupil's current status. Evaluation may be **summative,** occurring after teaching and learning have taken place, or **formative,** which means it occurs as skills are being formed (Howell, Kaplan, & O'Connell, 1979). Traditionally, most educational programs are evaluated summatively (e.g., once or twice a year), when it is too late to make any program changes based on the data obtained. Formative evaluation, however, is an integral part of the teaching process.

There are two sets of behavioral procedures that are used in conducting formative evaluations of student programs. The first, **data-based decision making,** involves comparing student performance or progress to a desired level and making adjustments based on this comparison (Deno & Mirkin, 1978). The second procedure is to apply a **single-subject research design** to identify and isolate specific variables that have a direct cause-effect relationship to target behavior. We discuss these procedures separately, although both have much in common and may be used simultaneously.

DATA-BASED DECISION MAKING

Although we have stressed the importance of making team decisions about which interventions to use with specific target behaviors, especially if aversive procedures are involved, the professional who is directly responsible for managing the target student in settings where targeted behaviors occur must be able to evaluate interventions continuously and make or recommend adjustments in intervention procedures on the basis of these evaluations. Data-based decision making is a technology designed to assist practitioners in conducting ongoing formative evaluations of student performance as part of the teaching process. It uses data that are collected systematically to measure targeted academic and social behaviors.

One of the first skills required for data-based decision making is determining what the data you have collected are telling you. In other words, you must know how to analyze data. There are two approaches to behavioral data analysis: statistical and visual. The debate between proponents of both approaches has been long-standing and lively. We side with those advocating the visual method, who maintain that visual analysis is more conservative (Parsonson & Baer, 1978). In addition, visual inspection is more practical and realistic for busy practitioners.

Formative evaluation, then, is based upon ongoing data collection. These data are used to decide when to change an instructional or behavior management program as well as which components of a student's program to alter, remove, or replace. Obviously, this task cannot be accomplished without data that are sensitive to variations in students' daily performances and that are reliable measures of those performances. If your data are sensitive and reliable, you can make good program evaluation decisions from **visual analysis.**

Formative evaluation based on visual data analysis (data-based decision making) is a search for **functional relationships.** Specifically, this means looking for environmental variables that affect the level of the target behavior being measured. This is accomplished by systematically manipulating certain independent variables (curriculum, reinforcement, instructions, etc.) one at a time while keeping other variables constant, insofar as possible.

Before implementing an academic or social intervention, you should assess the student's current performance. Instead of a static pretest approach, which may not represent the pupil's typical performance, you should measure target behavior across several sessions or days. Your intervention data can then be compared to this preintervention or **baseline** data to determine whether your program is effective. Thus, the purpose of collecting baseline data is to determine current levels and trends in behavior, as well as to see whether any environmental variables present during the baseline period are affecting it.

There are no hard and fast rules for determining the length of a baseline condition. Length depends on the level of the behavior, its variability, and whether it shows a **trend** in the direction of the criterion level, as well as such factors as the effects of the target student's behavior on others, the amount of time left in the school term, and so forth (Gelfand & Hartmann, 1984). If baseline data are highly variable or show a trend in the direction of the desired criterion level, you should consider extending this phase of the program while looking for sources of variation or factors contributing to trends. A minimum of three baseline data points are generally recommended for academic target behaviors (e.g., White & Haring, 1980), although White (1971) demonstrated that a minimum of seven data points are needed to project a reliable performance trend. We recommend that you collect five to seven baseline data points on social behavior targets, unless circumstances prohibit it.

Baseline data provide a relative standard against which subsequent program changes may be evaluated, so it is essential to analyze these data as carefully as those gathered during intervention conditions. The visual display of data via graphs and charts provides a convenient summary of data across various baseline and intervention conditions. Within these conditions, the data may be characterized in terms of level, trend, and stability. Straightforward and useful procedures for analyzing data with respect to these characteristics on simple line graphs have been developed.

Analyzing Level

Level refers to the magnitude of the data in terms of the scale value on the ordinate, or Y-axis, of the graph. Tawney and Gast (1984) describe two characteristics of level that are important in data analysis. Within a given condition, level may be analyzed with regard to stability and change. *Level stability* refers to the variability of the data points around their median. (The median is determined by finding the middle data point on the ordinate. To do this, simply count up from the abcissa, or X-axis, until you reach the middle data point; for example, if there are seven data points in the condition, the median is the fourth data point — there are three data points above and three below it. If there are an even number of data points in a condition, the median will fall halfway between two data points.) Data that vary no more than 15 percent from the median value would be considered stable. Level stability reflects the degree to which behavior is affected by planned or unplanned variables. For example, unstable data following the introduction of an intervention suggest that the other variables may be influencing the behavior as much as the intervention procedures (Tawney & Gast, 1984).

Level change refers to the amount of relative change in the data within or between conditions. To compute level change within a condition, find the ordinate values of the first and last data points in the condition, subtract the smallest from the largest, and note whether the change is occurring in a therapeutic (improving) or contratherapeutic (decaying) direction, based on the intervention objective. Knowledge of the amount of level change within a condition is useful for deciding whether it is appropriate to change conditions. For example, if a level change is occurring in a therapeutic direction during baseline conditions, it may be unnecessary to begin an intervention. *Level change between adjacent conditions* (e.g., baseline and intervention) is computed by identifying the ordinate values of the last data point of the first condition and the value of the first data point of the second condition, subtracting the smaller from the larger, and noting whether the change is in an improving or decaying direction. The amount of level change between baseline and intervention conditions is an indication of the immediate impact of the intervention on the target behavior (Tawney & Gast, 1984).

Another important characteristic to consider when evaluating changes in data between conditions is the amount of *overlapping data points*. This is calculated by noting the proportion of data points in adjacent conditions that fall within the same range. For example, if more than 50 percent of the data points during an intervention condition fall within the range of baseline data points, it may be concluded that the intervention has only weak effects (Parsonson & Baer, 1978). (However, the trend of the intervention data must also be considered; see the following sections.)

Analyzing Data Trends

Data paths seldom follow straight lines, nor do they increase or decrease in even increments. This can make it difficult to make reliable judgments about whether rates of behavior are accelerating, decelerating, or remaining relatively stable. A relatively simple way to analyze data trends is to draw **trend lines** (also called lines of progress) that depict the general path of the

data within a condition. This can be done by the *freehand method*, which involves drawing a line of "best fit" that bisects the data points (Parsonson & Baer, 1978). This method takes very little time, but the trend lines produced are likely to be inaccurate (Tawney & Gast, 1984). A more reliable procedure is the *split-middle method* (White & Haring, 1980), which is explained in Figure 4-1. This method may be used to analyze trends in data plotted either on equal interval or semilogarythmic graph paper, and with a little practice, you can do it quickly.

Data trends often reveal important and useful information. For example, an increasing (accelerating) trend indicates that the target behavior is probably being reinforced. A level trend suggests that reinforcement is also occurring but that it is serving to maintain the behavior at its current rate. A decreasing (decelerating) trend indicates that extinction or punishment contingencies are in effect. Such trends may show that contingencies unknown to or unplanned by intervention agents are operating. If a baseline trend is in the direction of your intervention criterion, for example, and you were to implement an intervention, it would be difficult to attribute a continued change in a therapeutic direction (were this to occur) to the intervention, because the behavior was changing anyway. On the other hand, if the baseline trend is stable or in a direction opposite to the intervention criterion, you could justifiably hypothesize that therapeutic changes following the initiation of an intervention condition were the result of your procedure.

Analyzing Data Stability

The stability of data is the variability of individual data points around the trend line. Gable, Hendrickson, Evans, and Evans (1988) suggest drawing a **window of variance** around the trend line to indicate the amount of desired stability around the trend. This is done by drawing parallel dotted lines representing a 15

Figure 4-1. Line of Progress

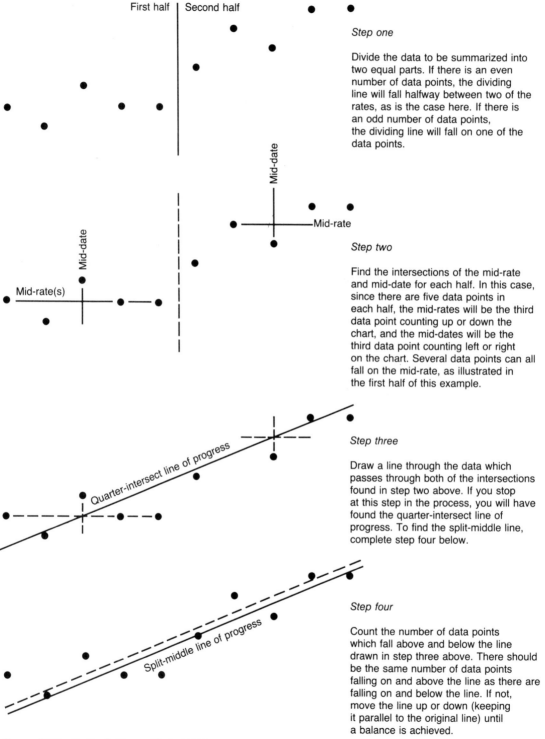

First half | Second half

Step one

Divide the data to be summarized into two equal parts. If there is an even number of data points, the dividing line will fall halfway between two of the rates, as is the case here. If there is an odd number of data points, the dividing line will fall on one of the data points.

Mid-date

Mid-rate

Step two

Find the intersections of the mid-rate and mid-date for each half. In this case, since there are five data points in each half, the mid-rates will be the third data point counting up or down the chart, and the mid-dates will be the third data point counting left or right on the chart. Several data points can all fall on the mid-rate, as illustrated in the first half of this example.

Mid-date

Mid-rate(s)

Quarter-intersect line of progress

Step three

Draw a line through the data which passes through both of the intersections found in step two above. If you stop at this step in the process, you will have found the quarter-intersect line of progress. To find the split-middle line, complete step four below.

Split-middle line of progress

Step four

Count the number of data points which fall above and below the line drawn in step three above. There should be the same number of data points falling on and above the line as there are falling on and below the line. If not, move the line up or down (keeping it parallel to the original line) until a balance is achieved.

Source: White, O. R., & Haring, N. G. (1980). *Exceptional teaching* (2nd ed.). Columbus, OH: Merrill.

percent range above and below the trend line. (This range can be computed by determining the medians for both halves of the data within a condition and calculating values within 15 percent of these, but it is simpler to estimate this variance visually.) Howell and Morehead (1987) recommend that the window of variance should encompass at least 80 percent of the data points. Any extreme variation or sudden change in your data that is not associated with a planned condition indicates that something unanticipated is affecting the target behavior, and you should attempt to find out what it is through conducting further functional analyses. This information may help you to adjust the intervention or to control extraneous variables affecting the student's performance.

Determining data trends during intervention may also help you assess functional relationships and troubleshoot your program. Parson-son and Baer (1978) provided several guidelines. For example, stable intervention data following a variable baseline indicates that recurring baseline variables are perhaps the treatment variables (e.g., differential teacher attention that was not controlled systematically during baseline). Weak program effects are suggested by variable intervention data, or by considerable overlap between data points in baseline and intervention phases. This problem is less critical if the overlap diminishes later during the intervention phase. A delayed therapeutic trend in the intervention data (i.e., no positive change followed by a change in the desired direction) may indicate the presence of training steps that are redundant or a waste of time. Figure 4-2 presents stylized graphs illustrating several intervention trends, and their interpretation. As you become more proficient in analyzing data visually, you also will be able

Figure 4-2. Interpretation of Data Trends

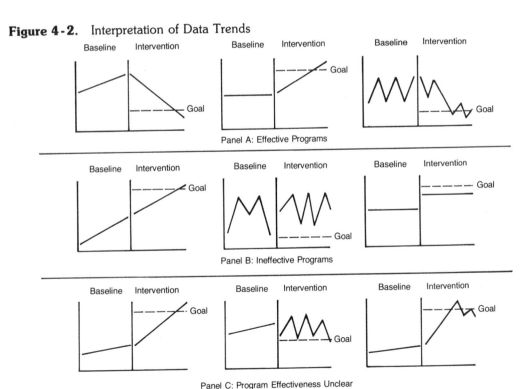

Panel A: Effective Programs

Panel B: Ineffective Programs

Panel C: Program Effectiveness Unclear

to interpret trends more accurately. Interested readers are referred to Parsonson and Baer (1978) for a complete discussion of graphic data presentation and analysis.

Data trend analysis tells you whether a program is working and can prompt you to remove or revise an intervention, but waiting for a trend to emerge may take too long. Practitioners who must make day-to-day program decisions need rules to expedite their decision making. Fortunately, empirical data decision rules have been developed for academic targets (Deno & Mirkin, 1978; White & Haring, 1980). To implement these rules, follow these steps:

1. Determine desired terminal goals. These may be established arbitrarily, by the curriculum, by assessing peers, from data obtained from previous programs with the student or from normative data on the target behavior, if available.
2. Set a date when you want to meet this goal. Also plot this on the graph.
3. Obtain and plot baseline assessment data for three days (or sessions), if more than one instructional session takes place each day.
4. Draw a **line of desired progress** from the last day of baseline to the goal level and date.
5. Change the program if the student's progress fails to meet or exceed the line of desired progress for three consecutive days or sessions (White & Haring, 1980).

Figure 4–3 illustrates a data decision graph for an academic target.

Data decision rules for social behaviors are not as clear-cut, because student performance, rather than sequential progress, is generally measured. Therefore, it is more difficult to establish a line of desired progress. You may, however, set your goal in terms of a daily level of performance, and base your decisions on the following steps:

1. Set and graph terminal goal level and date, just as for academic targets.

2. Obtain five to seven days (or sessions) of baseline data (more if the data are extremely variable or a therapeutic trend is apparent).
3. Write a data decision rule for the program (e.g., change program if performance is below criterion in a particular phase for three consecutive sessions or days).
4. Collect intervention data and adjust the program according to your rule.

These steps should be regarded as guidelines rather than rules; they are intended to be applied flexibly. Different behaviors and circumstances will require different data decision guidelines. Figure 4–4 shows data regarding a social behavior change program employing these data decision guidelines.

When setting criterion levels for targeted social behaviors, a good concept to keep in mind is that of an **ecological ceiling** (Howell & Morehead, 1987). This means simply to acknowledge that it is unrealistic (and unfair) to expect target behaviors to increase or decrease to rates above or below those of peers in the same settings. Thus, a zero rate of talk-outs is an unreasonable goal if the usual rate of peer talk-outs is five per hour. By assessing peers who are exhibiting acceptable rates of the target behavior, you can establish what are reasonable criterion levels (see Chapter 2). Lines of desired progress or performance should terminate at the appropriate ecological ceiling rather than at an arbitrarily chosen rate.

SINGLE-SUBJECT RESEARCH DESIGNS

By using data decision rules and by learning to visually analyze data, you should become skilled at systematically evaluating interventions and making appropriate decisions. However, although data-based decision-making procedures are extremely useful in determining whether an intervention is working, they cannot prove that the intervention is responsible for changes in target behaviors. Other uncon-

Figure 4-3. Data Decision Graph: Academic Program

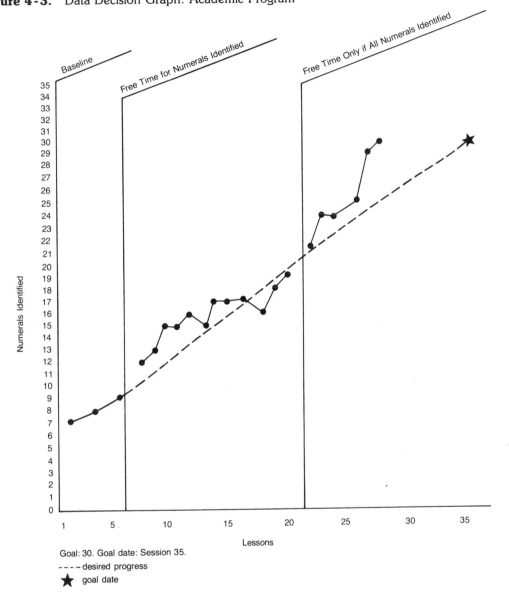

Goal: 30. Goal date: Session 35.

- - - - desired progress

★ goal date

trolled factors may influence the behavior simultaneously with the intervention, and these offer **competing explanations** for observed changes (e.g., something else in the setting was altered, the student became more mature, gained insight, etc.). Single-subject research designs control for the effects of such extrane-

ous variables through systematic manipulation of intervention variables over time while the target behavior continues to be monitored.

At this point, many teachers say they do not *care* whether these variables are uncontrolled, as long as something works to change behavior. The problem with this attitude is that it may

Figure 4-4.   Data Decision Graph: Social Behavior Program

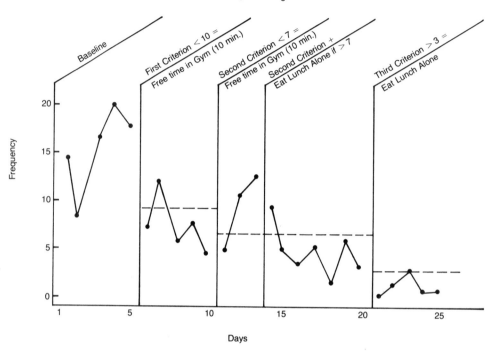

Billy: Swearing

Data decision rule: Change program if criterion isn't met any two consecutive days.

lead to using nonfunctional procedures or complex interventions that place extensive demands on the teacher. For instance, a teacher designed a good behavior game (see Chapter 5) to control a group's disruptive behavior. The game involved points, back-up consequences, and much of the teacher's time. It was, however, very effective and the teacher used the game with subsequent groups for several years. Unfortunately, the effects weren't always as dramatic as the first time. Had the teacher been able to determine which components of the game were responsible for its effectiveness, the interventions could have been adjusted to the demands of each new situation. Further, some components could have been dropped, thereby simplifying the procedure and reducing the response cost to the teacher. The point is, use the simplest procedures that are also effec-

tive. If praise is an effective reinforcer, why develop an elaborate token economy?

Single-subject research designs are not only useful in controlling for the effects of unsystematic variables and for isolating the essential components of intervention "packages," but understanding them will help you interpret studies reported in the research literature. (Published research is a source of many good ideas on instructional procedures and interventions.) We hope you will enhance your professional growth by reading journals and perhaps subscribing to one or more. The reference lists at the end of each chapter give you an idea of the journals reporting research in areas of interest or concern to you.

Now, we briefly describe three single-subject research designs: reversal designs, multiple baseline designs, and changing criterion designs. For more comprehensive explanations, you may wish to consult a single-subject design book (e.g., Tawney & Gast, 1984). The information we presented in our discussion of data-based decision making regarding the length of baseline phases and the determination of stability or trends in data through visual analysis applies here as well. You may even apply data-decision rules within phases of a single-subject design.

Withdrawal and Reversal Designs, also referred to as A-B-A-B designs, involve collecting preintervention data (A), followed by an intervention condition (B), a withdrawal or reversal of intervention procedures (A), and finally reinstatement of the intervention (B). If the target behavior, continuously measured during all conditions, changes in accordance with the condition in effect, it may be concluded that the intervention is effective. Although A-B-A-B designs are commonly referred to as **reversal designs,** Tawney and Gast (1984) indicate that a "true" reversal design involves a reversal of intervention contingencies in which the intervention is withdrawn from one behavior (e.g.,

in-seat) and simultaneously applied to an incompatible behavior (e.g., out-of-seat). The purpose of this manipulation is to demonstrate that the intervention procedure (e.g., teacher attention delivered contingent on the target behavior) has a functional relationship to the behaviors with which it is applied. Reversal designs are uncommon in the applied research literature because of the understandable reluctance of researchers and practitioners to directly reinforce undesired behavior once it has been reduced. **Withdrawal designs,** on the other hand, involve simply removing the intervention during the second A condition. In other words, baseline conditions are reinstated. Figure 4–5 shows a withdrawal design used to evaluate the effects of time-out contingent on a student's temper tantrums. It may be concluded that time-out was effective in this case, because the pupil's rate of crying decreased when the intervention was applied. (The second replication of baseline and intervention conditions establishes time-out as the critical variable. Without this replication we could not be sure that time-out was responsible for

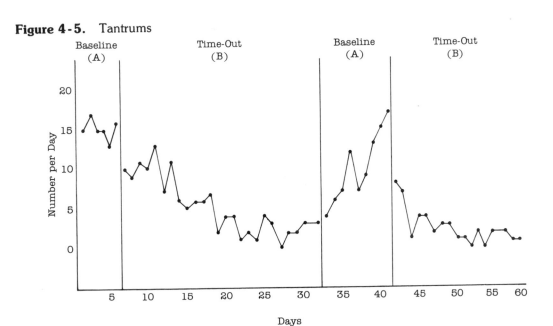

Figure 4-5. Tantrums

Figure 4-6. Percent of Verbal Responses per Opportunity

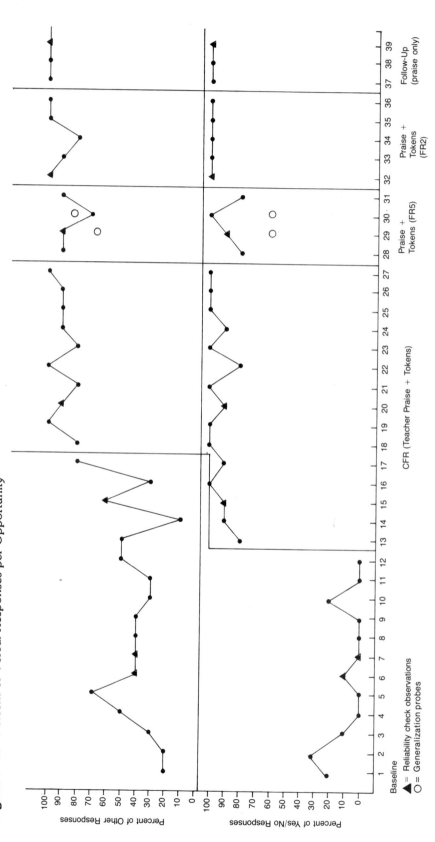

changes in the target behavior, because other uncontrolled events may have been introduced at the same time as the time-out contingency.) Changes in levels and trends of the target behavior in accordance with repeated introduction and withdrawal of the intervention demonstrates that manipulation of the time-out contingency controlled the student's tantrums, regardless of any uncontrolled events that may have taken place.

Multiple baseline designs provide a means of evaluating an intervention without a return to baseline conditions. The effectiveness of a program is demonstrated by applying it sequentially across different students, across different behaviors in the same student, or across different conditions or settings with the same student and behavior. If the measured behaviors change in the desired direction only when the intervention is applied, it may be concluded that the intervention is effective. Figure 4-6 illustrates a multiple baseline design across behaviors. The teacher's goal was to increase the pupil's oral responses to questions. Baseline data were collected on two classes of oral responses: simple yes-no answers, and more elaborate verbal responses. Next, intervention was applied to yes-no responses only, while baseline data were collected on other verbal responses. After a stable trend in the former was apparent, intervention was applied to other verbal responses. The conclusion that the teacher's procedures were responsible for the changes in the pupil's oral responses is allowed because neither class of verbal behavior changed until the intervention was applied. The same sequence is followed in the other types of multiple baseline designs; that is, baseline data are collected across multiple students or settings, then the intervention is staggered across students or settings.

Multiple baseline designs are applicable to a variety of situations. However, they require two or more replications (two or more students, settings, or behaviors), prolonged baselines, and target behaviors that can be sepa-

Figure 4-7. Chris: Time Spent in Classroom

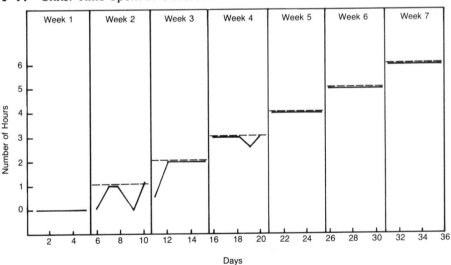

_ _ _ _ _ Criterion Level

Source: J. Worell & C. M. Nelson. Managing instructional problems: A case study workbook. New York: McGraw-Hill, 1974, p. 216.

rately altered without changing the rate of the behavior still in baseline (Tawney & Gast, 1984).

A variation on the multiple baseline is the **multiple probe design.** It differs from the former in that data probes, rather than continuous data, are recorded for the settings, behaviors, or students to which the intervention has not yet been applied. This variation is particularly useful if you are unable to monitor all target behaviors each day (Tawney & Gast, 1984).

The **changing criterion design** (Hartmann & Hall, 1976) is actually a variation on the multiple baseline design, but it may be used with only one student, one behavior, or in only one setting. Following the baseline phase, an intervention program is applied through a series of increments in criterion levels. If the rate of the target behavior changes as the criterion is altered, it may be concluded that the intervention was responsible (Hartmann & Hall, 1976). For example, Figure 4–7 shows a changing criterion design used to evaluate a program to increase a child's time in his classroom. Each week, the criterion was increased in terms of time in the classroom. Chris' performance also increased in response to these criterion changes. This design is especially appropriate for evaluating programs in which a stepwise progression is desired (Tawney & Gast, 1984).

Summary

Designing intervention strategies from among the variety of behavior change procedures currently available involves complex decisions that are best made by a team of professionals and advocates for the students affected. Professional guidelines and school district or agency policies should be considered in making such decisions, but ultimately, it is the responsibility of primary behavior change agents to make informed choices (based on their knowledge of the current research literature, of ethical and legal constraints, and of the characteristics of the student and the settings in which interventions are to be applied) from among the range of available behavior enhancement and reductive procedures. Frequently these procedures must be combined or used in novel ways to fit the circumstances in which they are to be used. Formative evaluation procedures based on continuous and precise measurement of target behaviors are therefore needed for studying and for adjusting interventions. Formative evaluation reduces the chances that students will be subjected to ineffective or unnecessarily aversive procedures. These skills are the basic tools of applied behavior analysis practitioners.

Discussion Questions

1. Give an example showing how each of the following principles affects behavior in classroom situations: positive reinforcement, negative reinforcement, extinction, punishment, modeling.

2. Why is the concept of a contingency important in determining how effectively behavioral change procedures work? Give examples of both planned and unplanned contingencies.

3. What procedures and policies should be addressed in developing guidelines for behavioral interventions in schools? Develop a model set of guidelines.

4. A student engages in disruptive behavior almost every day in math class. This results in his being placed in time-out for the remainder of the math class. Comment on the effectiveness and appropriateness of this intervention.

5. Describe alternate intervention strategies for reducing the disruptive behavior of the student described in question 4.

6. How do data levels, trends, and stability affect decisions about changing intervention conditions?

7. What is a functional relationship? How is a functional relationship demonstrated be-

tween an intervention and a target behavior?

8. For what behaviors and circumstances are the following designs appropriate: withdrawal, reversal, multiple baseline, multiple probe, changing criterion?

References

The Association for the Severely Handicapped Newsletter. (1986, February). Volume 12, No. 2.

The Association for the Severely Handicapped. (1981, October). *Resolution on Intrusiveness Interventions.*

Alberto, P. A., & Troutman, A. C. (1986). *Applied behavior analysis for teachers* (2nd ed.). Columbus, OH: Merrill.

Axelrod, S. (1987). Doing it without arrows: A review of Lavigna and Donnellan's *Alternatives to punishment: Solving behavior problems with non-aversive strategies. The Behavior Analyst, 10,* 243–251.

Baer, D. M., Wolf, M. M., & Risley, T. R. (1968). Some current dimensions of applied behavior analysis. *Journal of Applied Behavior Analysis, 1,* 91–97.

Bandura, A. (1969). *Principles of behavior modification.* New York: Holt, Rinehart, & Winston.

Barton, L. E., Brulle, A. R., & Repp, A. C. (1983). Aversive techniques and the doctrine of least restrictive alternative. *Exceptional Education Quarterly, 3,* 1–8.

Braaten, S. (1987, November). *Use of punishment with exceptional children: A dilemma for educators.* Paper presented at the 11th annual Conference on Severe Behavior Disorders of Children and Youth, Tempe, AZ.

Budd, K. S., & Baer, D. M. (1976). Behavior modification and the law: Implications of recent judicial decisions. *Journal of Psychiatry and the Law, 4,* 171–244.

Carr, E. G., & Durand, V. M. (1985). Reducing behavior problems through functional communication training. *Journal of Applied Behavior Analysis, 18,* 111–126.

Cooper, J. O., Heron, T.E., & Heward, W. L. (1987). *Applied behavior analysis.* Columbus, OH: Merrill.

Deno, S. L., & Mirkin, P. K. (1978). *Data-based program modification: A manual.* Reston, VA: Council for Exceptional Children.

Dietz, D. E., & Repp, A. C. (1983). Reducing behavior through reinforcement. *Exceptional Education Quarterly, 3,* 34–46.

Donnellan, A. M. (1984). The criterion of the least dangerous assumption. *Behavioral Disorders, 9,* 141–150.

Evans, I. M., & Meyer, L. H. (1985). *An educative approach to behavior problems: A practical decision model for interventions with severely handicapped learners.* Baltimore: Paul Brookes.

Ferster, C. B., & Culbertson, S. (1982). *Behavior principles* (3rd ed.). Englewood Cliffs, NJ: Prentice-Hall.

Gable, R. A., Hendrickson, J. M., Evans, S. S., & Evans, W. H. (1988). Data decisions for instructing behaviorally disordered students. In R. B. Rutherford, Jr., C. M. Nelson, & S. R. Forness (Eds.). *Bases of severe behavior disorders in children and youth* (pp. 75–89). San Diego, CA: College-Hill Press.

Gast, D. L., & Nelson, C. M. (1977). Legal and ethical considerations for the use of timeout in special education settings. *Journal of Special Education, 11,* 457–467.

Gast, D. M., & Wolery, M. (1987). Severe maladaptive behaviors. In M. E. Snell (Ed.). *Systematic instruction of the moderately and severely handicapped* (3rd ed., pp. 300–322). Columbus, OH: Merrill.

Gaylord-Ross, R. (1980). A decision model for the treatment of aberrant behavior in applied settings. In W. Sailor, B. Wilcox, & L. Brown (Eds.). *Methods of instruction for severely handicapped students* (pp. 135–158). Baltimore: Paul Brookes.

Gelfand, D. M., & Hartmann, D. P. (1984).

Child behavior analysis and therapy (2nd ed.). New York: Pergamon.

Hartmann, D. P., & Hall, R. V. (1976). The changing criterion design. *Journal of Applied Behavior Analysis, 9,* 527-532.

Howell, K. W., Kaplan, J. S., & O'Connell, C. Y. (1979). *Evaluating exceptional children: A task analysis approach.* Columbus, OH: Merrill.

Howell, K. W., & Morehead, M. K. (1987). *Curriculum-based evaluation in special and remedial education.* Columbus, OH: Merrill.

Kazdin, A. E. (1981). Acceptability of child treatment techniques: The influence of treatment efficacy and adverse side effects. *Behavior Therapy, 12,* 493-506.

Kazdin, A. E. (1983). Failure of persons to respond to the token economy. In E. B. Foa & P. M. G. Emmelkamp (Eds.). *Failures in behavior therapy* (pp. 335-354). New York: Wiley.

LaVigna, G. W., & Donnellan, A. M. (1986). *Alternatives to punishment: Solving behavior problems through non-aversive strategies.* New York: Irvington.

Madsen, C. H., Jr., Becker, W. C., Thomas, D. R., Koser, L., & Plager, E. (1968). An analysis of the reinforcing function of "sit down" commands. In R. K. Parker (Ed.). *Readings in educational psychology* (pp. 265-278). Boston: Allyn & Bacon.

Morales v. Turman, 364 F. Supp. 1078 (1973).

Nelson, C. M. (1981). Classroom management. In J. M. Kauffman & D. P. Hallahan (Eds.). *Handbook of special education* (pp. 663-687). Englewood Cliffs, NJ: Prentice-Hall.

Nelson, C. M. (1987). Behavioral interventions: What works and what doesn't. *The Pointer, 31*(3), 45-50.

Nelson, C. M., & Polsgrove, L. (1984). Behavior analysis in special education: White rabbit or white elephant? *Remedial and Special Education, 5,* 6-17.

Nelson, C. M., & Rutherford, R. B., Jr. (1983). Timeout revisited: Guidelines for its use in special education. *Exceptional Education Quarterly, 3,* 56-67.

Nelson, C. M., & Rutherford, R. B., Jr. (1988). Behavioral interventions with behaviorally disordered students. In M. C. Wang, M. C. Reynolds, & H. J. Walberg (Eds.). *The handbook of special education: Research and practice* (Vol. 2, pp. 125-153). Oxford, England: Pergamon.

Parsonson, B. S., & Baer, D. M. (1978). The analysis and presentation of graphic data. In T. R. Kratochwill (Ed.). *Single subject research: Strategies for evaluating change* (pp. 101-165). New York: Academic Press.

Pearson, C. A., & Argulewicz, E. N. (1987). Ethnicity as a factor in teachers' acceptance of classroom interventions. *Psychology in the Schools, 24,* 385-389.

Polsgrove, L. (1979). Self-control: Methods for child training. *Behavioral Disorders, 4,* 116-130.

Polsgrove, L., & Reith, H. J. (1983). Procedures for reducing children's inappropriate behavior in special education settings. *Exceptional Education Quarterly, 3,* 20-33.

Premack, D. (1959). Toward empirical behavior laws: I. Positive reinforcement. *Psychological Review, 66,* 219-233.

Rincover, A. (1981). *How to use sensory extinction: A non-aversive treatment for self-stimulation and other behavior problems.* Lawrence, KS: H & H Enterprises.

Rose, T. L. (1983). A survey of corporal punishment of mildly handicapped students. *Exceptional Education Quarterly, 3,* 9-19.

Rutherford, R. B., Jr. (1983). Theory and research on the use of aversive procedures in the education of moderately behaviorally disordered and emotionally disturbed children and youth. In F. H. Wood & K. C. Lakin (Eds.). *Punishment and aversive stimulation in special education* (pp. 41-64). Reston, VA: Council for Exceptional Children.

Rutherford, R. B., Jr., & Nelson, C. M. (1982). Analysis of the response-contingent timeout literature with behaviorally disordered students in classroom settings. In R. B. Rutherford, Jr., (Ed.). *Severe behavior disorders of children and youth* (Vol. 5, pp. 79-105). Reston, VA: Council for Children with Behavioral Disorders.

Rutherford, R. B., Jr., & Polsgrove, L. (1981). Behavioral contracting with behaviorally disordered and delinquent children and youth: An analysis of the clinical and experimental literature. In R. B. Rutherford, Jr., A. G. Prieto, & J. E. McGlothlin (Eds.). *Severe behavior disorders of children and youth* (Vol. 4, pp. 49-69). Reston, VA: Council for Children with Behavioral Disorders.

Sajwaj, T. (1977). Issues and implications of establishing guidelines for the use of behavioral techniques. *Journal of Applied Behavior Analysis, 10,* 531-540.

Singer, G. S., & Irvin, L. K. (1987). Human rights review of intrusive behavioral treatments for students with severe handicaps. *Exceptional Children, 54,* 46-52.

Stainback, W., Stainback, S., & Dedrick, C. (1979). Controlling severe maladaptive behaviors. *Behavioral Disorders, 4,* 99-115.

Tawney, J. W., & Gast, D. L. (1984). *Single subject research in special education.* Columbus, OH: Merrill.

Van Houten, R., Nau, P. A., MacKenzie-Keating, S. E., Sameoto, D., & Colavecchia, B. (1982). An analysis of some variables influencing the effectiveness of reprimands. *Journal of Applied Behavior Analysis, 15,* 65-83.

Walker, H. M. (1979). *The acting-out child: Coping with classroom disruption.* Boston: Allyn & Bacon.

Walker, H. M. (1983). Applications of response cost in school settings: Outcomes, issues, and recommendations. *Exceptional Education Quarterly, 3,* 47-55.

Walker, H. M., Hops, H., & Fiegenbaum, E. (1976). Deviant classroom behavior as a function of combinations of social and token and cost contingency. *Behavior Therapy, 7,* 76-88.

Warboys, L. M. (1987, November). *Special education and school discipline: Legal issues.* Paper presented at the 11th annual Conference on Severe Behavior Disorders of Children and Youth, Tempe, AZ.

White, O. R. (1971). A pragmatic approach to the description of progress in the single case. Unpublished doctoral dissertation, University of Oregon, Eugene.

White, O. R., & Haring, N. G. (1980). *Exceptional teaching* (2nd ed.). Columbus, OH: Merrill.

Witt, J. C., Elliott, S. N., & Martens, B. K. (1984). Acceptability of behavioral interventions used in classrooms: The influence of amount of teacher time, severity of behavior problem, and type of intervention. *Behavioral Disorders, 9,* 95-104.

Witt, W. C., & Martens, B. K. (1983). Assessing the acceptability of behavioral interventions used in classrooms. *Psychology in the Schools, 20,* 510-517.

Wolery, M., Bailey, D. B., & Sugai, G. M. (1988). *Effective teaching: Principles and procedures of applied behavior analysis with exceptional students.* Boston: Allyn & Bacon.

Wolf, M. M. (1978). Social validity: The case for subjective measurement or how applied behavior analysis is finding its heart. *Journal of Applied Behavior Analysis, 11,* 203-214.

Wood, F. H., & Braaten, S. (1983). Developing guidelines for the use of punishing interventions in the schools. *Exceptional Education Quarterly, 3,* 68-75.

Worell, J., & Nelson, C. M. (1974). *Managing instructional problems: A case study workbook.* New York: McGraw-Hill.

Wyatt v. Stickney, 344 F. Supp. 373 (1972).

Classroom Behavior Management

Chapter 5

OUTLINE

Goals of Behavior Management

Situations That Create Management Crises

Effective Classroom Behavior Management

Considerations for Severe Behavior Disorders

Case Study

OBJECTIVES

After completing this chapter, the reader should be able to

- Explain what is meant by "bringing a student's behavior under stimulus control" and give examples of behaviors and of the antecedent stimuli that control them.
- Describe how a cycle of pupil misbehavior and teachers' use of aversive behavior management practices may create a crisis situation.
- Indicate which aspects of classroom structure are likely to influence pupil behavior and how they may be altered to increase the probability of desired behavior.
- Describe the characteristic features of token systems and three types of group-oriented contingencies.
- Indicate how the characteristics of severely handicapped and adolescent students, as well as the settings in which they are educated, affect classroom behavior management.

Perhaps the most complex and demanding task of educators who work with students exhibiting serious problem behaviors is the day-to-day management of their behavior in the classroom. Pupils who are chronically disruptive, defiant, withdrawn, aggressive, or who engage in nonfunctional stereotypic behaviors and possess minimal social or functional communicative skills are often difficult to handle, even in one-to-one situations. The teacher who works with such pupils must be able to manage them in group settings, which means establishing a productive and orderly classroom environment in which to implement IEPs and in which to work on specific target behaviors. In other words, effective programming for individual students cannot occur if the classroom atmosphere is chaotic or is in a constant state of crisis. The purpose of this chapter is to help you develop the skills necessary to create productive learning environments.

Classroom behavior management, as discussed here, refers to the management of pupil behavior in group settings, which, in its broadest sense, is only part of classroom management. How you organize the curriculum, structure the daily schedule and physical environment, arrange and individualize instruction, evaluate students' learning, and communicate the outcomes of instruction to others are also important components. However, managing behavior is a necessary, if not sufficient, condition for accomplishing your major goal — facilitating pupils' learning. The teacher who cannot maintain behavior within reasonable limits, through positive management procedures, will face constant frustration and personal dissatisfaction, and is likely to find those same feelings expressed by students and their parents.

Therefore, this chapter focuses on management decisions and strategies aimed at the prevention of crisis situations (i.e., occasions in which one or more students exhibit behaviors that are dangerous or extremely disruptive and not under your stimulus control). We emphasize variables that have been shown to affect the classroom environment: teacher social attention and praise; establishing stimulus control over pupil behavior; the use of rules and consequences; applying interventions appropriately; and using group behavior management strategies. The objective of preventative classroom behavior management is to analyze and structure classroom social interactions in such a way that behaviors requiring crisis intervention are minimized. Management procedures and systems intended for specific behavior problems are emphasized in subsequent chapters. Our position is that many crisis situations can be prevented through careful assessment, effective educational programming, and appropriate group behavior management.

Our focus on acting-out (externalizing) behavior problems may appear to overlook behavioral deficits; that is, the absence of socially desirable behaviors. However, many students exhibiting behavioral excesses that create classroom management problems are also deficient in appropriate social behaviors. Classroom behavior management, aimed at preventing or reducing the occurrence of behaviors that interfere with productivity and learning, will be more effective if the curriculum simultaneously addresses pupils' social skill deficits. Students who consistently break rules of conduct, whose inappropriate behaviors repeatedly disrupt classroom order, or who fail to correct their undesired behavior when exposed to the teacher's available disciplinary measures should be assessed with respect to desired social and school survival skills, and their deficits in these areas should be remediated through appropriate curricular interventions (see Chapters 8 and 10).

This chapter begins with a discussion of the goals of classroom behavior management. Because students with behavior problems may react catastrophically to certain management practices, situations leading to behavioral crises are described next. We then discuss the kinds of assessment decisions teachers must make each day in order to stay tuned-in to students' behavior. This is followed by an overview of classroom behavior management interventions, including how to use them appropriately. Next, special considerations for working with severely handicapped pupils and with secondary age pupils are presented. Finally, procedures for evaluating management strategies are described.

Goals of Behavior Management

The primary goal of behavior management, especially for students exhibiting problem behavior, is to bring their behavior under **stimulus control.** This means that pupils should respond appropriately to antecedent stimuli (A) without always having to experience the consequences (C) of their behavior. For example, stimulus control over behavior has occurred when students respond to the request "Take out your science books" by getting out the appropriate text and not leaving their seats, shouting, or daydreaming. The teacher who has stimulus control over pupil behavior experiences a minimum of crisis situations, and both teacher and pupils work in an orderly and productive atmosphere.

The behavior of most children is at least partially under stimulus control by the time they begin public school. However, a significant number (both handicapped and "normal") do not respond appropriately to antecedent stimuli. Limited stimulus control over pupils' behavior greatly increases the probability of a crisis situation occurring. Therefore, your first management task is to prevent crises by bringing pupil behavior under the control of such antecedent stimuli as teacher directions and instructional materials. This is accomplished by systematically applying positive consequences to appropriate responses made in the presence of those stimuli. For instance, if you want pupils' desks to be the stimulus that controls in-seat behavior, you should apply positive consequences (attention, praise, tokens) for students who sit at their desks, and you should apply different consequences (ignoring, verbal reprimands, loss of tokens or privileges) for students who are not at their desks.

Developing stimulus control over the behavior of "problem" students requires many systematic applications of consequences. You must begin by reinforcing approximations to the desired behavior (e.g., praising a student for only a few seconds of in-seat behavior). Gradually, you can increase the requirement for reinforcement (e.g., praising only when the pupil has been in-seat for a minute or longer), until the desired goal has been reached (e.g., the student remains in-seat as long as the others). The process of reinforcing closer and closer approximations to desired behavior must

be carried out slowly and systematically, and the hierarchy of steps must be adjusted according to the behavior of individual students. This again emphasizes the importance of behavior *analysis* and underscores the need for a thorough understanding of behavior principles and their application.

The specific management goals expressed by teachers are likely to include increasing such desired student behaviors as attending to tasks, remaining in-seat, following teacher directions, using time productively, and giving correct academic responses (Gresham & Reschly, 1987). As we noted in Chapter 2, these behaviors correspond to a "model behavioral profile" (Hersh & Walker, 1983), but they have little to do with developing students' peer relationship skills (Gresham & Reschly, 1987). Teachers are also concerned about decelerating behaviors that are dangerous, disruptive, or incompatible with the completion of academic tasks. The majority of pupils likewise want to achieve these goals, and therefore, it is prudent to negotiate with students when setting expectations for classroom behavior. Your expectations are more likely to be accepted if you also consider the expectations of your students.

Situations That Create Management Crises

You may be tempted to blame behavior problems on underlying "pathology" supposedly inherent in students who have been given the label of behaviorally disordered or emotionally disturbed. We have not taken this position in this book. Pupils who have been reinforced for their tantrums, defying authority, aggressive acts against others, or being noncompliant *will* exhibit such behavior in situations when others will not, but the key to effective control of these behaviors lies in the teacher's ability to analyze and adjust variables in the immediate environment; specifically, antecedents and consequences.

These same variables also happen to be responsible for most crisis situations. This observation has been documented in a number of studies. For example, White (1975) and Thomas, Presland, Grant, and Glynn (1978) studied rates of teacher approval and disapproval, and found that most teachers gave disapprovals at higher rates than they gave approvals. Both sets of investigators suggested that teachers are more reinforced for using disapprovals (by negative reinforcement; disapprovals quickly, though temporarily, terminate undesired child behavior). Thomas et al. (1978) also conjectured that teachers feel that appropriate behavior deserves little recognition.

Walker and Buckley (1973) and Walker, Hops, and Fiegenbaum (1976) investigated the rates of teacher praise and disapproval toward behaviorally deviant and nondeviant children, and also studied the behaviors upon which these responses were contingent. They found that teachers interacted significantly more with deviant children, and that the majority of these interactions consisted of attending to inappropriate behavior. Walker (1979) observed that negative teacher attention to acting-out children increases inappropriate child behavior. Recall that Madsen, Becker, Thomas, Koser, and Plager (1968) also found that teacher attention to inappropriate behavior (out-of-seat) in behaviorally "normal" children increased the rate of this behavior. Thus, teacher attention to undesired behavior, *even though negative*, may function as positive reinforcement. This has been documented in studies by Buehler, Patterson, and Furniss (1966) and Solomon and Wahler (1973). Furthermore, both of these studies demonstrated that peer attention to inappropriate responses exerted more powerful control over child behavior than did the reactions of adults.

As Walker (1979) pointed out, the cumulative effect of disproportionate teacher attention

(in addition to peer support and attention) to acting-out children's misbehavior is to strengthen inappropriate behavior patterns. The unfortunate result of this combination of events is a classroom situation in which the teacher relies on progressively more aversive management practices (public scoldings, sending children to the principal's office, spankings, etc.). These measures may have temporary suppressive effects for some students, but they have no effect or a strengthening effect on undesired behaviors of other pupils, and these measures are not likely to succeed over time, particularly if the peer group reinforces deviant behavior. Moreover, continued use of aversive consequences that are ineffective in reducing undesired behavior may result in increased tolerance for such consequences (Azrin & Holz, 1966). The persistence of undesired behavior under such circumstances may encourage teachers to use aversive consequences in attempts to control the behavior. Patterns of unintentional teacher reinforcement of problem behaviors, resulting in increased rates of such behaviors, followed by increasingly more aversive teacher interventions to which pupils become adapted, lead to cycles characterized by high levels of student misbehavior and aversive teacher counter control.

A common side effect of aversive teacher control is power struggles between the teacher and some, or all, pupils. Like adults, children react negatively to aversive management. If they sense that the teacher is reacting from frustration or feels out of control of the situation, they may respond with even more intensive misbehavior. Thus, behavior management practices that are not carefully and thoughtfully chosen, that involve little or no pupil input, and that consist largely of reacting negatively to inappropriate student behavior are to be avoided.

In addition to excessive reliance on aversive control and inadvertently attending to maladaptive student behaviors, we have observed two related mistakes that are made even by experienced teachers of behaviorally disordered pupils. The first is to assume that students know what is expected of them. An indication that this problem is occurring is the absence of clear rules for classroom behavior. Either rules are not stated at all, or they are worded so generally as to invite multiple interpretations (e.g., "show respect for other persons," "use good manners"). Vague rules may be operationalized so that pupils understand them (e.g., showing respect means keep hands and feet to yourself, do not interrupt when others are talking, take turns, etc.), but often they are not. The second mistake is to punish students for their failure to exhibit a behavior that they do not know how to perform (e.g., following directions, remaining in-seat). This problem relates to the failure to correctly discriminate the difference between a skill deficit and a performance deficit, which was discussed in Chapter 2. We see it most often in response to students' noncompliance. Although noncompliance may reflect a pupil's decision not to follow a rule or direction, it may also indicate that the student does not know what behavior is expected, that there are obstacles to the student performing as desired, or that the student lacks the skills to exhibit the desired behavior. Therefore, be sure that your students can line up properly, can bring required materials to class, can take time-outs appropriately, or can tie their shoelaces before punishing their nonperformance. Also remember to attempt to correct the problem first through interventions based on positive reinforcement.

Another potential cause of crisis situations involves setting goals or selecting curricula that are inappropriate for particular students. Appropriate goals and curricula are those that are fair, functional, and meaningful to students. Undesired behavior may be one way (perhaps the only way) the student has of saying "This is too hard," "I don't like this," or "This is baby stuff." Inappropriate expectations or curricula generate frustration, dissatisfaction, and rebellion, thus setting the stage for behavior problems. If the teacher reacts punitively, a self-perpetuating cycle of crises may be initiated. By functionally analyzing problem behaviors in relationship to variables inherent in specific curricula and settings, you can identify potential causes and address these without resorting to procedures that involve aversive consequences. To the extent that your goals and curricula are fair and important to students, you can also prevent many problems from occurring in the first place.

To summarize, the following questions make up an informal checklist that you can use to assess the potential sources of problem behaviors:

Is what I am teaching useful or important to the students?

Do the pupils know what I expect them to do?

Are there any obstacles to the students performing as desired?

What are the consequences of desired performance?

What are the consequences of nonperformance?

When does the problem behavior occur?

What is different about the students who *are not* displaying the problem behavior?

How can I change my instruction to help the pupils develop the skill I am trying to teach?

Effective Classroom Behavior Management

We have indicated that the goals of classroom behavior management are to develop stimulus control over pupil behavior and to prevent crisis situations from occurring. These must be accomplished in group settings where the teacher is responsible for delivering instruction. Consequently, appropriate classroom management interventions are those that are less intrusive and restrictive; they may be accomplished without significant interruption of ongoing activities and without removing students or instructional staff from the teaching setting.

The least intrusive and most natural behavior management strategies are, of course, good teaching practices. The literature on effective teaching indicates that such teaching behaviors as using brisk instructional pacing, reviewing students' work frequently, giving systematic and constructive corrective feedback, minimizing pupil errors, providing guided practice, modeling new behaviors, providing transitions between lessons or concepts, and monitoring student performance are strongly related to pupil achievement and attitudes toward learning. These instructional behaviors are beyond the scope of this text but are clearly important elements of effective classroom management. Consult Bickel and Bickel (1986), Brophy and Good (1986), and Rosenshine and Stevens (1986) for reviews of the research on effective teaching. Because of their impact on students' classroom behaviors, you should also ensure that you are competent in these vital teaching skills.

The classroom behavior management procedures we consider here are designed to specifically influence the behaviors that teachers desire in their pupils: compliance with teacher requests and instructions, on-task behaviors, cooperative interactions with others, and low rates of noise and disruptions. Most practitioners have a logical preference for the least intrusive management strategies that produce these results. Although group behavior management systems require that you spend time outside the classroom to plan and arrange their implementation, we concur that the most appropriate group behavior management procedures are those that are more natural and easier to implement. For example, praise and attention are more natural and easier to administer than tokens, and tokens are easier to deliver than edible reinforcers. Similarly, extinction and response cost are less intrusive behavior reduc-

tion procedures than time-out or overcorrection. Each teacher must decide what range of interventions is best for her particular classroom. In practice, the procedures that you choose will be based on your own experience and feelings of competence with them. Effective classroom behavior managers use a range of enhancement and reductive interventions, and they develop the ability to "read" situations and behaviors on the spot and apply interventions appropriately and in a timely fashion. We encourage you to develop a level of proficiency with a range of interventions so that you too can use them effectively. A wide variety of management procedures are described in literature dealing with both handicapped and normal students. We present those found useful for organizing social interactions with your pupils and in preventing most extreme behavior problems from occurring—or if they do occur, for helping you decide what to do. Thus, we see a management system as a flexible, operating framework, not as a rigid, intolerant set of rules and consequences. As a matter of principle, we believe in using the system most natural (i.e., most like management practices used in regular classrooms) and easy to operate. Artificial systems must usually be diminished in order for pupil behavior to generalize to classroom environments in which naturalistic management practices prevail. In accordance with this principle, we present management procedures in an ascending order of complexity. In any management system, there are factors that influence the effectiveness of the procedures used. We will discuss these first.

FACTORS AFFECTING CLASSROOM MANAGEMENT

In addition to positive and aversive consequences, five environmental variables are known to affect behavior. These are the antecedent stimuli; the contingencies of reinforcement or punishment; the **contiguity,** or timing, of reinforcement or punishment; the schedule of reinforcement in effect; and the persons who control the available consequences. These are the variables you must consider, and can adjust, in developing or altering a management system. For example, what rules and instructions will you provide students? How will you relate specified desired and undesired behaviors to planned consequences? Can you deliver these consequences immediately following behavior so as to maximize their effectiveness? If not, what alternatives can you use? Which schedule of reinforcement is best under various circumstances? Do you control the consequences of pupil behavior? If not, who does, and how can you enlist the aid of these agents to help you establish desired behavior patterns? Thinking about how you will answer these questions before entering the classroom can avoid serious problems later. However, do not expect to prevent all problems at this stage, and do not walk into the classroom with a fully developed management system to impose on students. Each system must be individually tailored, and should be developed in cooperation with students, not imposed upon them. In the following discussion, we describe four basic approaches to group classroom management: structuring, informal or naturalistic techniques, token systems, and group-oriented contingencies.

STRUCTURING

As defined by Haring and Phillips (1962), *structuring* refers to clarifying the relationship between behavior and its consequences. For many children and youths exhibiting behavior disorders, this relationship has been anything but clear, either because of an absence of rules, inconsistent application of consequences for behavior, or ability to out-manipulate adults controlling these consequences. Such pupils enter special education programs with the expectation that their wishes will prevail or that the social world is a chaotic place where noth-

ing can be predicted. The structured approach developed by Haring and Phillips was designed to make these youngsters' environment more predictable, as well as to provide a basis for behavior change.

Our use of the term **structuring** differs somewhat from that of Haring and Phillips. For our purposes, *structuring* refers to a range of antecedent variables that the teacher may use to control pupil behavior: planning of physical space, daily schedule, rules, and stimulus change.

Physical Space

For a moment, imagine you have just walked into the room where you are going to spend the next nine months with six to fifteen students who have behavior problems. Perhaps the room is arranged as the previous teacher left it; or maybe you find yourself staring at nothing more than boxes and packing crates. Your first thought might be, "How can I arrange this to suit what I want to do here?" The answer to the first part of this question depends on how much thought you have given to the second part; that is, the arrangement of your classroom is determined by how you intend to use it.

With this in mind, we offer several considerations. They are intended to help you plan for the full use of your classroom, not restrict it. The first is *how many students* will you have in the room at one time? Twenty students impose more restriction on room use than ten. However, you can plan to use different areas for more than one activity; a science area can also be used for art, provided equipment can be stored and retrieved easily. A related concern is *how close together* should you place your pupils? The answer to this depends on both the behavior patterns of your students and the activities that will be going on. Extremely active or disruptive children should sit farther apart, and independent seatwork generally calls for less physical proximity than a group project.

Regarding activities, have you thought about what *kinds of activities* will be taking place in your classroom? You will want to provide for some physical activity, particularly if you have younger children with nowhere else to go for recess on inclement days, or if your curriculum includes activities requiring space for free movement. Ask yourself whether *two or more kinds of activities* will be going on simultaneously. One student listening to rock music as earned reinforcement can be disruptive if done in the middle of your civics group. In this situation it is wise to set up separate areas if space permits. If not, adjust your schedule so that quiet activities go on at one time and noisy or physical activities at another.

Consider also whether any students need to be *isolated,* and if so, whether only for certain activities or for most of the day. By "isolation" we mean physical (usually visual) separation from classmates, not time-out (although this too is a consideration in planning the physical layout of your classroom). **Study carrels** or **cubicles** are a popular method of isolating easily distracted pupils, but they are expensive when purchased commercially. Perhaps students in a workshop program can construct one or two for you. Or you can make one yourself out of an old refrigerator crate. If none of these options is possible, a desk in the corner gives at least some limiting spatial structure. Using a cubicle or separate desk space need not be punishing. If you explain it as a way to get work done on time, a student may appreciate the opportunity. When cubicles are called offices and students understand they are used to facilitate studying, competition frequently develops over access to them. One word of caution, however: Under no circumstances should a study carrel be used as a means of permanently separating a disruptive or slow student, or as a time-out area. All children deserve as much educational and personal assistance as you can provide. Using a cubicle and forgetting the student is there is hardly an acceptable strategy.

Finally, you should consider how *movement in the classroom* is to be regulated. When pupils need help, will they come to you or will you go to them? Will student movement be restricted ("Raise your hand to get permission") or free? Will you require them to line up before leaving the room or not? How will you regulate movement to and from learning centers or the free-time area? How will students be monitored in these areas? Regardless of whether you want an open, free classroom or a highly structured one, you will need to make decisions such as these and design your classroom accordingly. (See Figure 5-1.)

There are other factors to consider when planning your classroom. Those discussed here are only illustrative, not exhaustive. Much of what you do will be dictated by elements you will not discover until you see your room — amount of storage space, location of windows, lights, blackboards, sink, and counters, for example. We strongly recommend that you look at your potential classroom when you are interviewed for a job. Otherwise, you might end up in a storage closet.

Daily Schedule

This part of structure has to do with your *general daily routine* — how you order your classes and activities. A dependable classroom routine is good for both you and your pupils; pupils generally like the security of routine, and if you nearly suffer a breakdown trying to get through the algebra period, there is some comfort in knowing that in thirty minutes you can get to that biology project both you and the pupils like.

Fortunately, the job of setting up a daily schedule is often half done for you. Recesses, lunch, and planning periods are usually determined by school administrators, and like it or not, you will have to organize your day around these set activities. Such scheduled events can be used to good advantage, simply by applying

Figure 5-1. Floorplan of an Engineered Classroom

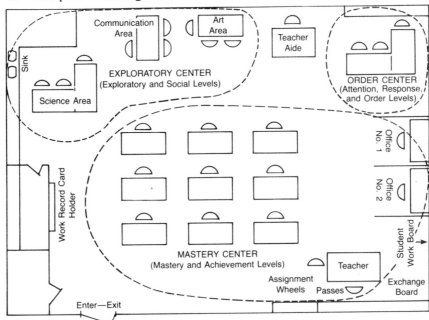

Source: F. M. Hewett. *The emotionally disturbed child in the classroom.* Boston: Allyn & Bacon, 1968, p. 243.

Grandma's Law:[1] "First eat your vegetables, then you may have your dessert" (Homme, 1970). Applying the law to a schedule means having handwriting just before recess and requiring it to be done before recess.

You might also consider Grandma's Law when trying to decide *what should come first* in the school day. We have found it useful to schedule the least enjoyable tasks first (math, reading, spelling, or whatever for a given student or class). Thus, you not only reward task completion with a higher probability behavior, you also get pupils over a big hurdle early in the day. On the other hand, Hewett (1968) suggested beginning with a warm-up activity, usually a simple direction-following task, to get the children settled and ready for work. Figure 5-2

shows a sample class schedule for primary-age children with behavioral and learning problems.

There are several other things you should consider when setting up a daily schedule. Earlier, we stated that a consistent routine was a worthwhile goal. Obviously, routine should be balanced by a *reasonable variety* of activity, lest school become boring or aversive. But variety does not mean keeping your pupils guessing what is going to happen from one day to the next. You can plan both variety and routine if you vary specific tasks frequently but depart from the routine schedule less often.

Another consideration is the *physical activity* of your pupils during the day. Young children especially need to have some times in the day set aside for physical games and activities. Even though you can work for long periods in one place, do not assume that nine-year-olds can do the same. Plan for some physical activ-

---

[1] Grandma's Law is actually a euphemism for the **Premack Principle** (Premack, 1959).

Figure 5-2. Daily Program for a Primary Self-Contained Classroom

Time	Task
	Task
8:50	Enter room, take seats, get ready to work
9:00	Math
9:45	Juice and cookie break
10:00	Social skills (group)
10:30	Recess
10:45	Reading, language arts (group)
11:30	Reading, language arts, other (individual)
12:00	Lunch
12:30	Recess
12:45	English, social studies, science (group)
1:30	Finish individual work (PE Tues/Thurs)
2:00	Music, library, or arts and crafts (outside room)
2:30	Finish group work
2:45	Listen to story
2:55	Clean up, ready for dismissal
3:00	Dismissal

ity every hour or so, even if it's only to stand and stretch or to get a drink of water.

Another feature of schedule planning is to make sure your *pupils understand the schedule.* Telling them is not enough. Take them through the schedule several times before assuming they know the routine. However, do not be afraid to change the schedule if it is not working satisfactorily. This is good advice for secondary school teachers also. Junior and senior high school schedules can be complicated, and pupils without the skills to get around properly may get into trouble in the building. Specific suggestions for schedules are explained in Chapter 8.

Rules

Rules are verbal statements regulating behavior. Not only do they tell pupils which behaviors will be tolerated and which will not, they also serve as cues to the teacher as to which behaviors should be followed with which consequences. Worell and Nelson (1974) provided some guidelines for establishing rules:

1. Select the *fewest possible number* of rules. Too many rules are difficult to remember, and are frequently so specific that pupils can easily find exceptions to them. For example, one teacher, who was concerned about fighting in the classroom, developed a long list of rules: "no hitting," "no shoving," "no biting," "no name-calling," and so forth. She later substituted just one rule, "remain in your seat unless you have the teacher's permission to be up," because in-seat behavior was incompatible with behaviors leading to and involved in fighting.

2. Use *different rules* for different situations. Obviously, rules for classroom activities should be different from playground, lunch line, or bus waiting area rules. Some pupils need to be taught that different situations call for different behavior. Clearly stated rules can help them make this discrimination.

3. Rules should be *stated behaviorally* and they should be *enforceable.* Thus, the rule "show respect toward others" invites differing interpretations of what constitutes re-

spect or disrespect and is not easily enforceable. The rule "no talking when my back is turned" is behaviorally stated, but obviously would be very difficult to enforce. Rules that are not enforceable invite tattling as well as testing, both of which can lead to disruptions.

4. Rules should also be *stated positively;* that is, they should describe appropriate and desired student behaviors rather than those that are to be avoided. This focuses attention on positive replacement behaviors rather than on inappropriate pupil activity. For example, the rule "Get the teacher's permission before speaking" is preferable to "No talking."

5. Rules should be *reasonable.* The most common response to an unreasonable rule is to challenge it, which may lead to a serious power struggle. Another option is to give up, rather than try to meet the expectation. Thus, the rule "all homework must be in before first period" is reasonable only if all students are capable of meeting it—that is, no one has a night job, and the homework is within all pupils' ability to complete. The best way to ensure that rules are reasonable is to develop them with students.

6. There must be *consistent consequences* for rule fulfillment or infraction. This does not mean the use of threats or lectures. Rule consequences should be posted with the rules themselves or taught until all pupils know them thoroughly. Posted rules and consequences, incidentally, are a tremendous help to substitute teachers or new classroom aides. It has been demonstrated that without consequences, rules have little effect on behavior (Madsen, Becker, & Thomas, 1968; O'Leary, Becker, Evans, & Sudargas, 1969; Walker, 1979). Therefore, consistent teacher follow-through is critical, including praise or points for following rules and systematic withdrawal of attention or other reinforcers (or presentation of aversive consequences) for their infraction. Bending the rules for specific pupils or

situations should be avoided, unless this has been planned with students in advance.

Stimulus Change

Stimulus change means altering the discriminative stimuli for a particular response. For example, students who talk excessively or fight may be separated. Stimulus change can produce changes in behavior, though the effects are usually temporary, unless accompanied by differential application of consequences (Nelson, 1981; Sulzer-Azaroff & Mayer, 1977). Transfer to a special class is a type of stimulus change, and Walker et al. (1976) observed a thirteen percent increase in appropriate behavior when acting-out children were placed in an experimental classroom. However, the effects of this stimulus change were confused by a number of accompanying alterations (e.g., a change in teacher, classroom expectations). By itself, this technique does not have the power to alter more disruptive behavior (Walker, 1979).

INFORMAL OR NATURALISTIC TECHNIQUES

Modeling

As a behavior management strategy, modeling has been infrequently studied. Broden, Bruce, Mitchell, Carter, and Hall (1970), and Strain, Shores, and Kerr (1976) observed positive behavior changes in some nontarget children when positive consequences were applied to target pupil's behavior. Kazdin (1973) suggested that reinforcement becomes a discriminative stimulus (a stimulus that indicates that responses made in its presence will be reinforced) for nonreinforced peers, because it signals the probability that similar behavior on their part will be reinforced. If students have a history of positive reinforcement for appropriate behavior, a statement such as "I like the way Tommy is waiting his turn" increases the probability that other pupils will imitate his behavior. However, to be effective with more disruptive children, modeling should be accompanied by the consistent application of consequences.

Teacher-Administered Social Reinforcement

As we indicated in Chapter 4, this category includes three kinds of teacher behavior: feedback, attention, and approval. *Feedback* typically occurs as a consequence of particular behaviors (finishing a task, breaking a rule). However, by itself, the effects of feedback are weak (Madsen, Becker, & Thomas, 1968; O'Leary et al., 1969). On the other hand, contingent teacher *attention* has been shown to influence behavior strongly, particularly with young children. Attention differs from approval, in that it need not involve any verbal behavior, nor is it necessarily positive.

Manipulating teacher attention involves applying differential reinforcement. When appropriate behavior occurs, the teacher attends, stands near, touches, looks at, or interacts with the student. Inappropriate behavior is placed on extinction by looking away, moving to another part of the room, or calling attention to another child. Providing differential attention has been successful in eliminating regressive crawling (Harris, Johnston, Kelly, & Wolf, 1964), aggression (Brown & Elliot, 1965), and in increasing following instructions (Schutte & Hopkins, 1970), and correct academic performance (Zimmerman & Zimmerman, 1962).

However, in order for teacher attention to function effectively, it must become a **conditioned reinforcer** (a consequence that has acquired reinforcing properties through association with previously established reinforcers). To establish attention as a conditioned reinforcer, it should be repeatedly paired with the presentation of a consequence that has already been demonstrated to be reinforcing, such as praise, points, or tangibles (e.g., food). The lat-

ter consequences are gradually and systematically faded until attention alone is demonstrated to exert the desired effect. This process may take time for many behaviorally disordered pupils. Other students may reveal an extensive repertoire of inappropriate attention-getting behaviors (e.g., raising a hand and saying, "Hey teacher!"; getting up to ask a question). Clearly stated rules governing how teacher attention may be solicited are helpful, but they serve little purpose if you even occasionally respond to the inappropriate activity. Managing such pupils requires a high degree of self-monitoring and self-control.

Teacher *approval* or praise involves the same contingencies as attention, and may be verbal or nonverbal. However, in using approval, the teacher usually specifies the desired behavior verbally, such as "I like the way you are working" or "You really did a good job on your algebra assignment." Nonverbal approval (smiles, pats on the back) may also be effective (Kazdin & Klock, 1973). The contingent use of approval is more critical than the amount of approval, *per se* (Becker, Thomas, & Carnine, 1971; Kazdin & Klock, 1973), but you should use contingent praise four times as often as verbal aversives.

A major problem with attention and approval is getting teachers to use the technique. Breyer and Allen (1975) were unsuccessful in their attempts to train a teacher with twenty-three years of teaching experience to praise appropriate behavior and ignore inappropriate behavior. However, they did persuade the teacher to implement a token system, which resulted in positive changes in rates of teacher approval and disapproval. Some teachers feel the number of available ways to praise student performance is limited. Table 5-1 illustrates that this is not the case. We hope you will make liberal use of these and other statements in your daily interactions with students.

Also remember that reductive procedures are more effective when they occur in a reinforcing social climate. Therefore, we urge you

Table 5-1. Sample Praise Statements

1. You're doing a good job!	42. You're doing beautifully.
2. You did a lot of work today!	43. You're really working hard
3. Now you've figured it out.	44. That's the way to do it!
4. That's RIGHT!!!	45. Keep on trying!
5. Now you've got the hang of it.	46. THAT'S it!
6. That's the way!	47. You've got it made.
7. You're really going to town!	48. You're very good at that.
8. You're doing fine!	49. You're learning fast.
9. Now you have it!	50. I'm very proud of you.
10. Nice going.	51. You certainly did well today.
11. That's great!	52. That's good.
12. You did it that time!	53. I'm happy to see you working like
13. GREAT!	that.
14. FANTASTIC!	54. I'm proud of the way you worked
15. TERRIFIC!	today.
16. Good for you!	55. That's the right way to do it.
17. GOOD WORK!	56. You're really learning a lot.
18. That's better.	57. That's better than ever.
19. EXCELLENT!	58. That's quite an improvement.
20. Good job, (name of student).	59. That kind of work makes me very
21. You outdid yourself today!	happy.
22. That's the best you've ever done.	60. Now you've figured it out.
23. Good going!	61. PERFECT!
24. Keep it up!	62. FINE!
25. That's really nice.	63. That's IT!
26. WOW!	64. You figured that out fast.
27. Keep up the good work.	65. You remembered!
28. Much better!	66. You're really improving.
29. Good for you!	67. I think you've got it now.
30. That's very much better.	68. Well look at you go!
31. Good thinking!	69. TREMENDOUS!
32. Exactly right!	70. OUTSTANDING!
33. SUPER!	71. Now that's what I call a fine job.
34. Nice going.	72. You did that very well.
35. You make it look easy.	73. That was first class work.
36. Way to go!	74. Right on!
37. Superb!	75. SENSATIONAL!
38. You're getting better every day.	76. That's the best ever.
39. WONDERFUL!	77. Good remembering!
40. I knew you could do it.	78. You haven't missed a thing.
41. Keep working on it, you're getting	79. You really make my job fun.
better.	80. You must have been practicing.

Source: Reprinted with permission from H. M. Walker, N. Golden, D. Holmes, J. Y. McConnell, G. Cohen, J. Anderson, A. Connery, and P. Gannon. *The SBS social skills curriculum: Teaching interactive competence and classroom survival skills to handicapped children.* Eugene, Ore.: University of Oregon, 1981.

administer positive reinforcers (e.g., attention, praise, points) four times more than you use reductive procedures. When students are used to receiving positive reinforcement and know which behaviors are likely to earn reductive consequences, your withholding reinforcement is more effective in controlling desired behavior, thereby reducing the probability that more intrusive and aversive procedures will be needed (Ferster & Culbertson, 1982).

Finally, you should be aware that verbal praise and approval may be ineffective if misapplied. As Brophy (1981, p. 15) has pointed out, much teacher praise "is not systematically contingent on desirable behavior, lacks specification of the behavioral elements to be reinforced, and/or lacks credibility." To be effective, praise should: (1) be genuine, warm, and spontaneous; (2) specifically describe the desirable student behavior; (3) be used with all pupils, even those with large repertoires of undesirable behaviors (i.e., find some behaviors to praise in every student each day); (4) avoid disrupting ongoing appropriate pupil behavior; and (5) be varied in delivery, and not overused so that it becomes meaningless (Wolery, Bailey, & Sugai, 1988).

RATIONALE FOR GROUP MANAGEMENT SYSTEMS

Whereas modeling and teacher reinforcement are more or less informal and naturalistic management techniques, token systems and group-planned contingencies are formal systems that require proportionately more strategic planning and effort during implementation. However, in programs for behaviorally disordered students (as well as those in a significant minority of regular classrooms) the number of pupils who require some type of behavior management is sufficient to require a group plan. Behavior analysis techniques could be applied on an individual basis, but this tactic would present several problems. First, it would be necessary to identify and deliver individual consequences to each pupil. Although tokens, for example, can be delivered easily to many students, and later exchanged for individual back-up reinforcers, delivering different consequences immediately contingent upon the behavior of individual pupils can be complicated and exhausting. (One reason the number of pupils in classes for students with severe behavior disorders is restricted by state laws is because so much individual programming of this sort is required.)

Delivering reinforcers immediately is virtually impossible unless a conditioned reinforcer can be established for all students. As we have seen, praise can become a conditioned reinforcer, but with many students this takes a great deal of time and is less likely to be effective than tangible consequences. Both points and praise statements should be used as conditioned reinforcers, with points offering the advantage of being concrete and additive; once a specified total is reached, the student may exchange points for back-up reinforcers.

Group management systems also are flexible: They may be applied to intact groups of students, to individuals within the group, or to any combination. Thus, two pupils may receive the same number of tokens for performing different tasks or for reaching different criterion levels. Within such a system, individualization is accomplished by adjusting reinforcement contingencies. The same conditioned reinforcer is given to all pupils, but for different behaviors or on different reinforcement schedules.

TOKEN SYSTEMS

The token economy is a widely used classroom management system. Token systems have been used in regular and special classrooms, with mildly to severely handicapped children, with preschoolers and adults, and with social and academic behaviors (Kazdin & Bootzin, 1972). They may also be adapted to fit any situation, or they may be combined with a variety of other management strategies (see Walker, 1979).

The essential ingredients of a token system include tokens, **back-up reinforcers** (tangible or activity) for which tokens may be exchanged, **contingencies** specifying the conditions under which tokens may be obtained or lost, as well as the exchange rate of tokens for back-up reinforcers.

A variety of back-up reinforcers is possible: classroom or school privileges, activities, trinkets, clothes, costume jewelry, toys, or even such large items as bicycles. Some community agencies (e.g., the chamber of commerce, Volunteers of America, church groups, labor unions) may be willing to conduct drives or donate items. Cast-off items from your basement or attic may prove valuable in a token system. Chapter 6 provides guidelines for selecting back-up reinforcers.

Because tokens are conditioned reinforcers, their value derives from association with previously established consequences. You may teach students to value tokens by pairing their presentation with an existing social or tangible reinforcer (e.g., see Hewett & Taylor, 1980) or by reinforcer sampling; that is, giving pupils a number of tokens and letting them purchase back-ups immediately (Ayllon & Azrin, 1968). Over a period of days, you can fade out the paired reinforcer or delay token exchange and make receipt of tokens contingent upon desired behaviors. As your system evolves, we recommend that you increase the length of intervals between token exchange. This teaches pupils to delay gratification and encourages saving for larger items, which, incidentally, are desirable behaviors in our economic system.

Token systems offer a number of advantages. Because each student can select from a variety of back-up reinforcers, pupil satiation and loss of reinforcer power are not likely problems. Also, tokens can be delivered more easily than individualized tangibles, and simply by announcing that a student has earned a token, you can develop your praise and approval as a conditioned reinforcer. If tokens are awarded contingent upon academic performance, in-compatible social behaviors are reduced in most cases (Ayllon & Roberts, 1974; Hundert & Bucher, 1976; Marholin & Steinman, 1977; Robinson, Newby, & Ganzell, 1981). Also, with such contingencies, little time is lost from teaching functions as a result of behavior management. The requirement that tokens be awarded often also forces the teacher to interact frequently with pupils. By using activities as backups, the cost of the system is minimal. Specific guidelines for setting up a classroom token system are presented in Chapter 6.

GROUP-ORIENTED CONTINGENCIES

Token systems are powerful behavior management systems, but they do not necessarily take into account the dynamics of children in group settings. Also, because reinforcement is based on individual performance, the teacher must deal with record-keeping logistics. Differences among individuals in amount of reinforcement may create jealousy, competition, and theft of tokens (Hayes, 1976).

On the other hand, contingencies related to group characteristics take advantage of social reinforcers controlled by the peer group and are adaptable to a variety of situations. **Group-oriented contingencies** also reduce the number of individual consequences the teacher must deliver, which saves time from behavior management duties.

The basic characteristic of group-oriented contingencies is group reinforcement. Whether the target is an individual student or the entire class, the group shares in the consequences of the target's behavior. In many cases, group-oriented contingencies are devised to deal with specific problem behaviors. Nevertheless, they can be used to establish appropriate behaviors and to prevent problems from occurring; hence, we have included these systems here. Litow and Pumroy (1975) described three categories of group-oriented contingencies: dependent, independent, and interdependent.

With **dependent group-oriented contingencies,** the performance of certain group members determines the consequences received by the entire group. For example, Carlson, Arnold, Becker, and Madsen (1968) eliminated a second-grader's tantrums when a class ice cream party was made contingent on the child going without a tantrum for two days. Coleman (1970) improved appropriate behaviors and decreased out-of-seat and talking-out in four elementary pupils in separate classrooms by awarding them candy to be shared with peers.

Dependent group-oriented contingencies are most effective when group members are less disruptive than the target child or children (Hayes, 1976). Therefore, these contingencies may not be suitable with groups of behaviorally disordered students whose behavior is not under appropriate stimulus control. If used, the teacher must be careful that peer influence does not become peer pressure (Hayes, 1976). This is not likely to occur if the contingency involves group reinforcement rather than cost, if the desired behavior is in the pupil's repertoire, and if the initial contingency is not set too high.

The identifying characteristic of **independent group-oriented contingencies** is that the same consequence (e.g., free time) is applied to individual group members (Litow & Pumroy, 1975).[2] One of the best-known variations of independent group-oriented contingencies is **contingency contracting** (Homme, 1970). In contracting, access to a high-probability behavior (one that has a high probability of occurrence) is made contingent upon a low-probability behavior. Contracts are individually negotiated, but access to high-

probability behaviors may be arranged on a group basis by setting aside a special area for such activities, called a reinforcing event (RE) area. Pupils also may select a variety of reinforcing events from an **RE menu** (Homme, 1970). Even undesired behavior may be used as a reinforcer for low-probability desired behavior (Homme, 1971). Contracting is low-cost and effective (Cantrell, Cantrell, Huddleston, & Woolridge, 1969; White-Blackburn, Semb, & Semb, 1977), but the process takes time. Suggestions for contracting with pupils and sample contingency contracts are shown in Chapter 6.

Contingent access to a common reinforcer by individual pupils is also a successful variation of independent group-oriented contingencies. Osborne (1969) made free time contingent upon the in-seat behavior of six preadolescent, hearing-impaired girls. Schulman, Bailey, and Huntsinger (1976) used masking tape to mark one-square-yard "territories" around fourth-graders' desks. Violation of classroom rules caused an immediate twenty-minute loss of territory. This contingency effectively controlled out-of-seat and inappropriate verbal behavior. Wolf, Hanley, King, Lachowicz, and Giles (1970) devised a timer game to control the out-of-seat behavior of sixteen students in an after-school remedial class. A kitchen timer was set for intervals varying around an average of twenty minutes. When the timer went off, all pupils in their seats earned tokens exchangeable for a variety of activities and tangibles. We have found the timer game useful not only for shaping pupil behavior, but also in training teachers to use tokens and praise. However, it is important to fade out the timer gradually, so that appropriate pupil behavior becomes the discriminative stimulus for reinforcement rather than the timer bell.

The occurrence of unfavorable peer pressure is less probable with independent group-oriented contingencies because each student earns consequences independent of the group. However, this procedure also fails to take advantage of the peer group's potent social rein-

---

[2] Token systems actually fall within this definition as well, in that the same consequence (tokens) is received by individual pupils and the amount of reinforcement is independent of what others earn. Token systems were treated separately mainly for convenience. However, independent group-oriented contingencies are more frequently directed at a common target behavior, whereas token systems may be used with individual target behaviors.

forcement and thus may have less impact on children who seek peer attention through deviant behavior. Speltz, Shimamura, and McReynolds (1982) found that dependent group-oriented contingencies were better than independent contingencies in producing higher rates of academic productivity and improved group interactions with most of the learning disabled children they studied.

In **interdependent group-oriented contingencies,** consequences are applied to the group, contingent upon each member reaching a specified level of performance (Litow & Pumroy, 1975). Such contingencies may be positive or negative. The "Good Behavior Game" (Barrish, Saunders, & Wolf, 1969) is an interdependent group-oriented contingency that is easy to operate. A class is divided into two or more teams, and each team accumulates marks, which are written on the blackboard indicating that a target behavior (desired or undesired, depending on the contingency) has occurred in the team. At the end of the day, the team with the most (fewest) marks gains a privilege. This game has been successful in reducing disruptive behavior (Barrish et al., 1969; Harris & Sherman, 1973; Medland & Stachnik, 1972), and to increase group on-task behavior (Darch & Thorpe, 1977).

Sulzbacher and Houser (1968) conducted a classic study involving interdependent group-oriented contingencies. Fourteen mildly handicapped, special class students displayed high rates of using the "naughty finger" (third finger, extended) or referring to it. It was arranged for students to receive a special ten-minute recess at the end of the day. Ten cards, each one corresponding to a minute of recess time, were mounted in the front of the room. If the teacher saw the naughty finger, or heard anyone refer to it, she turned over one card, indicating that a minute of recess had been lost. The contingency quickly reduced the target behaviors.

Switzer, Deal, and Bailey (1977) effectively reduced stealing in a second-grade class by using contingent recess time. Interdependent contingencies are particularly well suited to problems such as stealing because of the difficulty in identifying the guilty parties. However, you should carefully monitor peer interactions. Axelrod (1973), for example, found both group and individual contingencies equally effective in two special classes, but the interdependent group contingency resulted in more verbal threats.

With some special equipment and a little ingenuity, you can manage even difficult problems with interdependent contingencies. For instance, Schmidt and Ulrich (1969) used a decibel meter to monitor the noise level of a fourth-grade class. After determining the baseline level, a criterion of forty-two decibels was used as a basis for awarding additional gym and break time. If the noise level did not exceed forty-two decibels for ten consecutive minutes, a two-minute addition to gym or break time was awarded. Wilson and Hopkins (1973) linked a voice-operated relay to a decibel meter and a radio. Classroom noise above a set criterion level automatically turned off a radio that was tuned to a popular music station. This strategy was effective in reducing the noise level in four junior high school home economics classes.

Comparisons of the two show that group-oriented contingencies are at least as effective as individual contingencies, and are easier for teachers to manage (Axelrod, 1973; Darch & Thorpe, 1977; Drabman, Spitalnik, & Spitalnik, 1974; Kazdin & Geesey, 1977; Rosenbaum, O'Leary, & Jacob, 1975). The social status of some children may be improved by group-oriented contingencies, and cooperative peer interactions may be fostered (McCarty, Griffin, Apolloni, & Shores, 1977). However, pupils with high peer social status may become more disruptive under group contingencies, and one pupil may be reinforced at the cost of others (Hayes, 1976; O'Leary & Drabman, 1971). Individual child characteristics, peer interaction patterns, and situational influences should be considerd in setting up group contingencies (Hayes, 1976). A combination of contingencies may be more effective than group or individual contingencies alone (Hayes, 1976; O'Leary & Drabman, 1971).

USING REDUCTIVE PROCEDURES IN CLASSROOM BEHAVIOR MANAGEMENT

Although behavior enhancement procedures should dominate classroom management, many students are adept at manipulating situations so that their inappropriate behavior results in positive reinforcement. Also remember that teacher attention, even when accompanied by reprimands or other negative reactions, may be positively reinforcing to some pupils. Students who are constantly punished may develop a tolerance for aversive consequences, and the attention that accompanies their use may be a powerful reinforcer, especially if the pupils' appropriate behaviors are largely ignored. Used by itself, positive reinforcement of appropriate behavior is generally thought to be effective in maintaining low rates of undesired behavior of pupils with relatively mild behavior disorders, but even with these students, it should not be assumed that positive reinforcement alone will be effective. For example, Pfiffner and O'Leary (1987) found that increasing the density of positive reinforcement alone was ineffective in maintaining acceptable levels of the on-task behavior and the academic accuracy of first-through third-grade students with academic or behavioral problems, unless they had previously experienced negative consequences. Research with individuals exhibiting more severe behavior disorders consistently indicates that a combination of positive reinforcement and punishment procedures is superior to either reinforcement or punishment alone (see Axelrod, 1987). Walker (1979, p. 178) observed that "as a general rule, a combination of both positive reinforcement and mild punishment techniques will be required to effectively change the behavior of moderately to severely deviant/disruptive children."

Guidelines and policies regarding the use of aversive consequences are provided in Chap-

ter 4. In subsequent chapters, we present intervention procedures for dealing with inappropriate behavior and problem or crisis situations. Our purpose in discussing reductive procedures here is to help you establish a repertoire of interventions that can be applied to behavior *before it gets out of control.* For example, what should you do if a pupil breaks a rule, ignores a direct request, or persistently engages in off-task or disruptive behavior? Having command of a range of reductive interventions can help you move in and quickly resolve such problems before they become crisis situations.

As we indicated previously, the range of reductive procedures that can be used in classroom management is limited by the need for strategies that are less intrusive and restrictive. Nevertheless, there are several procedures that can be applied with minimal interruption of instructional interactions: extinction, verbal reprimands, response cost, and time-out. We suggest how each can be designed for maximum effectiveness, but keep in mind that we advocate the use of such techniques only in the context of systematic positive reinforcement of desired behaviors.

Extinction

You will recall from the previous chapter that extinction involves withholding reinforcement thought to be maintaining maladaptive behavior. Therefore, extinction is likely to be ineffective in reducing behaviors for which you cannot identify or control the reinforcer (e.g., social interactions between pupils, bullying, or SSB) or in reducing a behavior that has been maintained by intermittent positive reinforcement (Gelfand & Hartmann, 1984). It has been used with success in reducing mild behavior problems (e.g., disruptive classroom behavior, off-task, and tantrums) and, in combination with differential reinforcement of appropriate behavior, in reducing more serious problems such as aggression (Alberto & Troutman, 1986). If the target behavior has been maintained by your attention, and you initiate an extinction procedure, be prepared for a temporary increase in rate and intensity. Thus, the student who repeatedly calls out to get your attention may increase her calling out and perhaps add standing up, yelling, or coming to you for several days after you first apply extinction. Alberto and Troutman (1986) suggest some strategies to help you control your attention under such circumstances: become involved with another student, read or write something, recite something to yourself, carry a worry rock or beads, or leave the room (if possible). Again, if you cannot tolerate a temporary increase in the behavior, extinction is not a good choice. Alternatives should also be considered if you cannot control other sources of reinforcement (e.g., peer reactions) for the target behavior, if the target behavior is likely to be imitated by other pupils, if you are not able to withhold your attention consistently, or if alternative behaviors that can be reinforced have not been identified (Alberto & Troutman, 1986).

Verbal Reprimands

Of the range of verbal aversives used by adults to influence children's behavior (i.e., warnings, threats, sarcasm, ridicule, etc.) reprimands are the most effective and ethical. Other types are not usually consistently applied immediately following undesired behavior; they imply consequences that may not be carried out (e.g., "If you do that one more time, I'll kick you out of class for a week!"), or they involve evaluations that are personally demeaning to students (e.g., "You're the worst student I've ever had."). Reprimands provide immediate feedback to students that their behavior is inappropriate, and they serve as **discriminative stimuli** that punishment contingencies are in effect. Their effectiveness in controlling mild and moderate behavior problems has been amply demonstrated (Rutherford, 1983). However, they should be used with caution because to deliver a reprimand, one must also provide attention, which may be a potent reinforcer. Therefore, reprimands should be brief

and to the point (e.g., "No hitting") rather than accompanied by lectures or explanations. Obviously, the student should know in advance which behaviors are not allowed so that a reprimand is not an occasion for a discussion (e.g., the pupil says "What did I do?"). O'Leary, Kaufman, Kass, and Drabman (1970) found that soft, private reprimands were more effective than those given loudly and in public. When reprimanding, get close to the student, make eye contact, give the reprimand, and move on. If the student fails to correct his behavior, provide a more intrusive back-up consequence (e.g., response cost) instead of another reprimand or a threat. Note: you should never ask a pupil whether he "wants" to go to time-out, the principal's office, and so forth. Such verbalizations merely invite the student to call your bluff or to challenge your statement (e.g., "You can't make me!").

Response Cost

This punishment technique involves the loss of reinforcer, contingent upon an undesired behavior (Kazdin, 1972). The consequence lost may be an activity, such as a privilege or a portion of recess time, or a token (Rutherford, 1983). Response cost has been used successfully with various children in different settings without the undesirable side effects (escape, avoidance, aggression) sometimes observed with other forms of punishment (Kazdin, 1972). It is easily used in conjunction with a token system (Walker, 1979, 1983), and compares favorably with positive reinforcement in controlling behavior (Hundert, 1976; Iwata & Bailey, 1974). On the other hand, McLaughlin and Malaby (1972) found positive reinforcement to be more effective, presumably because the teacher had to attend to disruptive students when taking away points.

However, response cost contingencies can be arranged so as to limit this kind of attention. For example, the number of points or minutes of an activity that can be lost for given rule violations may be posted, and you simply may give the pupil a nonverbal signal (raising a finger, pointing) indicating what has been lost. Examples of cost penalties are given in the next chapter. It is important to maintain a balance between cost penalties and reinforcers earned, so that a pupil does not get "in the hole" with no chance of obtaining any positive reinforcers. Once all opportunity to earn reinforcers has been lost, you hold no contingencies over undesired behavior; that is, there's no reason for the student to behave appropriately. As with any aversive system, we strongly urge you to negotiate systematic response cost penalties with your pupils before they are used.

Time-out

Exclusionary levels of time-out (i.e., when the pupil is removed from the immediate instructional setting) are intrusive and restrictive. Therefore, they should only be used as back-up consequences when less intrusive interventions have not been effective. However, these forms of time-out (*exclusion* and *seclusion*) are only two of six time-out levels that have been used (Nelson & Rutherford, 1983; Rutherford & Nelson, 1982). Three levels of time-out may be used in the instructional setting. *Planned ignoring* involves the systematic withdrawal of social attention for the length of the time-out period. Like extinction, it will be effective if teacher attention during time-in is associated with positive reinforcement, and other sources of reinforcement can be controlled during time-out. *Reduction of response maintenance stimuli* is based upon systematically enriching the time-in setting through the addition of positive reinforcers for behaviors incompatible with or alternative to the undesired behavior (i.e., using differential reinforcement). When time-out is imposed, these reinforcers are withdrawn. For example, Foxx and Shapiro (1978) gave disruptive students a "time-out ribbon" to wear while they were exhibiting appropriate behavior. The ribbons were discriminative stimuli for staff to deliver high levels of reinforcement.

When a student misbehaved, his ribbon was removed and reinforcement was withheld for three minutes. Salend and Gordon (1987) used a group contingency time-out ribbon procedure to reduce inappropriate verbalizations in mildly handicapped students. **Contingent observation** requires the student to remain in a position to observe the group without participating or receiving reinforcement for a specified period. As we have emphasized before, time-out is not a good choice if time-in activities are not reinforcing to the student or if time-out provides her the opportunity to engage in behavior that is more reinforcing. Having the pupil take time-out without leaving the setting offers the advantage of being able to observe her behavior during the time-out condition. We do not recommend using another level of time-out (*time-out with restraint*) because of the possibility that physical contact may be highly reinforcing to the student. However, Rolider and Van Houten (1985) successfully applied a movement suppression time-out procedure, in which the pupil was positioned in a corner with his chin against the corner, hands behind his back, and both feet touching the wall for two to three minutes. You should plan in advance the levels of time-out and procedures to follow when using this intervention. Also, time-out periods should be brief (one to five minutes) and students should be taught how to take time-out appropriately before it is used.

No matter how mild, procedures that involve aversive stimuli should be used systematically in conjunction with positive reinforcement, and their effects should be carefully monitored. We advise you to master a hierarchy of such consequences and to plan specific techniques for each level in the hierarchy so you will have alternate intervention strategies for any given behavior or situation. Then, when you apply a selected consequence, use it at maximum intensity (e.g., a firm "No" instead of a plaintive "It hurts my feelings when you do that"). You may give students choices when applying consequences (e.g., "You may go back to work or you may take a time-out"). This indicates to pupils that they have control over the consequences they receive. If the student returns to work, give positive reinforcement (e.g., praise, a point). If undesired behavior persists, apply the stated consequence. Student decisions to take point or time-out penalties should be reinforced by praise and attention *after* the penalty has been paid (e.g., "I appreciate the way you took your time-out"). Note, however, that reinforcement for accepting consequences appropriately should not be equal to or greater than the reinforcement the student would receive for appropriate behavior in the first place. If pupils can obtain strong reinforcers by engaging in undesired behaviors then taking a mild penalty, they will learn to exhibit such behaviors to initiate the chain of events leading to reinforcement. More restrictive procedures (e.g., overcorrection, physical aversives, or suspension) should be reserved for situations in which it is documented that the above procedures have been ineffective, and they should involve careful attention to due process and to other procedural considerations discussed in Chapter 4.

Considerations for Severe Behavior Disorders

The classroom behaviors of severely handicapped[3] children and youths present some-

what different management problems than their less involved peers. Basically, their teachers can expect to see a more limited repertoire of behavior, including more limited social, academic, and self-help skills as well as more stereotypic behavior patterns that interfere with learning (Kauffman, 1985; Gast & Wolery, 1987; Spradlin & Spradlin, 1976). Here we identify some of these differences and the management procedures that have proven to be effective with this population.

Your selection of appropriate target behaviors for change and appropriate strategies for continuously measuring them are critical to your success in managing the behavior of severely handicapped pupils (Spradlin & Spradlin, 1976). Spradlin and Spradlin recommend concentrating on the following initial targets:

1. *Limiting behaviors.* This category includes behaviors that limit the student's access to public education programs. Often, these are the behaviors that cause management problems. To be a pupil in most public schools, the individual must be able to function in a group setting (i.e., for the most part, behavior must be under stimulus control by the teacher or by the setting). Many of the behaviors that limit pupils' access to public schools also interfere with learning: stereotypic behaviors (rocking, hand-flapping, finger plays, etc.); tantrums; seriously disruptive behaviors; and behaviors that are dangerous to the pupil or to others, such as headbanging, throwing objects, or aggression.

---

[3]Although *severe behavior disorders* are traditionally used to refer to individuals displaying autistic or psychotic behavior patterns, it has not been demonstrated that differentially labeling such pupils has any educational utility (Kauffman, 1985). The topography, or form, of the behaviors exhibited by children labeled autistic may vary from that of children labeled severely retarded, but these differences have not proven sufficiently reliable to warrant differential diagnosis. Furthermore, the function, or effect on the environment, of the various topographies of severely handicapped

behavior is the same: whether a child is self-abusive or has tantrums, the teacher should perform an A→B→C analysis and systematically apply appropriate consequences. Finally, the behavioral repertoires of severely handicapped children and the educational goals and intervention strategies developed for them as a group are similar. Therefore, in this text, we do not attempt to differentiate a set of methods unique to persons with severe behavior disorders from those used with the severely handicapped in general.

2. *Self-help skills.* These include toileting, dressing, feeding, and getting around in the environment. Deficits in these areas also impose practical limitations on the student's ability to function in a public school.
3. *Social skills.* To be successful in a group setting, pupils need to exhibit appropriate social interactions, to attend to teacher instructions and educational materials, to follow verbal instructions, and to have a repertoire of imitative behaviors.

These behaviors, then, comprise the initial teaching targets for severely handicapped persons. Classroom management of such individuals will be easier if you assess your pupils regarding these areas and design individualized education programs to fit the unique characteristics of each student.

Behaviors in these three categories follow the same principles as outlined at the beginning of Chapter 4, and they respond to systematic alteration of consequences. However, the learning needs and behavioral characteristics of these pupils are sufficiently different to require specialized procedures. The first of these is a greater emphasis on one-to-one instruction, which dictates a smaller pupil-teacher ratio. Generalized stimulus control is more difficult to establish, and therefore, the teacher and classroom aides must work more intensively with each child. Precise command of such techniques as differential reinforcement, stimulus fading, prompting, time delay and other procedures for developing appropriate stimulus control are invaluable skills (Gast & Wolery, 1987; Spradlin & Spradlin, 1976). These procedures are described in subsequent chapters.

Identifying effective reinforcers can also be more difficult with severely handicapped learners. Although most of these pupils respond to contingent social behavior (attention and praise), primary reinforcers (food, water) must be used in some cases. Public school policy often forbids the contingent feeding of meals (Spradlin & Spradlin, 1976). Teachers who

work with low-functioning, severely behaviorally disordered students must work with less potent reinforcers, attempt to alter school policies, or identify alternate consequences.

In using reinforcement with severely behaviorally disordered pupils, you should reinforce desired behavior immediately. This means you must have a reinforcer that you can deliver promptly in small units. Pieces of crackers, pretzels, potato chips, raisins, bites of cereal, or sips of milk are good alternatives to candy, cookies, and ice cream. By pairing these items with praise, the procedure can be developed into an effective conditioned reinforcer, even for low-functioning pupils. If a pupil's responsiveness to social praise and attention is not established after a fair trial, consider using such stimuli as lights, buzzers, or bells. These have been developed into conditioned reinforcers by some researchers.

It is also crucial to design an appropriate curriculum for each student. Individual programs must be broken down into small, sequential steps presented repeatedly and systematically until the pupil reaches a specified behavioral criterion.

If this gives you the impression that a major key to effective behavior management of severely handicapped persons is sound educational programming, you are exactly right. Actually, this is the essence of good behavior management with any group or population. If your curriculum is not based on functional skills that pupils need to learn in order to be more effective both in and out of school, education will not be reinforcing. We stress it here because we have seen too many programs for severely handicapped children in which the curriculum consisted largely of cutting and pasting, coloring and painting, playing with blocks or other toys, or making pot holders. Such activities take up time; if students find them more reinforcing than inappropriate behavior (which is often not the case), behavior problems are under control. However, no functional (useful and generalized) skills are developed.

Finally, as a teacher of severely handicapped students, you must consider how to control behaviors that interfere with learning. Some of these behaviors (e.g., self-stimulation through rocking, twirling objects, engaging in finger plays) are more reinforcing than the behaviors you want. Also, some pupils may have developed extensive repertoires of disruptive or dangerous behavior that, through intermittent reinforcement, have become highly resistant to extinction. Before you can teach more functional and appropriate skills, therefore, you must often employ procedures for reducing these behaviors. The contingent presentation of aversive consequences has demonstrated the best results, but punishment is also the most controversial approach, even for this population (Stainback, Stainback, & Dedrick, 1979).

Alternatives include extinction, overcorrection, response cost, and time-out. However, all of these techniques are difficult to implement if the pupil's behavior is not under stimulus control. Consequently, you must shape appropriate responses to these interventions through the procedures mentioned earlier: differential reinforcement, prompting and stimulus fading.

CONSIDERATIONS FOR SECONDARY SCHOOL STUDENTS

The difficulties in working with adolescents exhibiting behavior disorders are so imposing that until recently, few special programs existed. Even recently, school exclusion was not uncommon as an intervention with adolescents displaying behavior problems (Nelson, 1977). Programs for these youths, whether in regular classrooms or special alternative settings, must provide two essential ingredients: structure and consistency. These are not easy to accomplish in traditional secondary schools where students change classes and are managed by five or six separate teachers.

With behaviorally disordered adolescents, there is a greater probability of power struggles and defiance of authority figures. A structured curriculum, in which both teacher and pupils know the expectations, consequences, and routine, will be invaluable. Rules and consequences should be established well in advance of potential crisis situations and should be developed in conjunction with pupils. Another aspect of structuring is to have in mind a continuum of interventions for undesired behavior, such as described earlier. This permits you to match consequences more fairly to offenses, and it reduces the likelihood that a given intervention will lose its effectiveness through overuse. The same is true of reinforcers. Praise and attention should be delivered liberally, and a variety of reinforcers available in the classroom, the school, the home, and the community should be used. We also suggest that teacher verbalizations accompanying the use of aversive procedures be reduced and simplified. This technique will help avoid unproductive confrontations and arguments.

As with any population, it is extremely important to analyze continuously and to adjust the curriculum for adolescents. Both subject matter and learning activities must be relevant to pupils' immediate lives, otherwise they either will not attend classes or will engage in more reinforcing behaviors, which may be highly undesirable. Therefore, the curriculum must be individualized, and adjustments must be made in students' programs on the basis of continuous evaluation of their performances. Social skills and school survival skills that students will find useful in their current settings are important components of curricula for this age group (see Kerr, Nelson, & Lambert, 1987; also Chapters 8 and 10).

We strongly recommend that you encourage pupils to participate in all aspects of the curriculum. Specifically, they should be involved in selecting and ordering their own academic and social goals, in making decisions about the classroom structure, and in setting consequences and contingencies. Contingency contracting is a productive technique for involving adolescents in decisions about their educational programs (see Rutherford & Polsgrove, 1981). Bear in mind that pupil participation does not mean pupil control. Disordered adolescents are not likely to possess decision-making skills (Rutherford, 1975), yet they can be adept at manipulating social situations, especially if the teacher lacks confidence. The teacher remains the final authority, but as students develop greater competency in making decisions, their participation can be increased systematically. The ultimate goal of pupil participation in decision-making is self-regulation. Students must be taught to set goals for themselves, to monitor and evaluate their behavior accurately, and to self-administer reinforcement (Polsgrove, 1979).

Regarding the application of consequences with adolescents, several adaptations are useful. First, whenever possible, teachers should emphasize consequences that are the natural outcomes of behavior. For example, the natural consequence of stealing is arrest, not sympathetic counseling or exoneration. In school, the natural consequence of being tardy may be detention. Although it is difficult to identify many truly "natural" consequences to human social behaviors that can be applied systematically, even those that must be contrived can be presented as natural and consistent outcomes of behavior. Thus, if a rule is broken, the stated consequence is applied. This reduces the occurrence of power struggles, because pupils learn to see the teacher as someone who follows the rules and not as one who capriciously or maliciously applies punishment. Consistency in applying such consequences also teaches self-control; pupils learn to anticipate predictable consequences for behavior, and therefore can choose to engage in or suppress their behavior based on this knowledge.

Second, in designing behavior management systems, the teacher of adolescents must consider the reinforcers controlled by the peer group. Peer reinforcement can be much more powerful than adult reinforcement for almost any age group, but this is especially true for adolescents. The behavior reinforced by peers may be contrary to the goals of the program (see Buehler et al., 1966). Therefore, it is prudent to design systems that increase the probability that peer influence will be exerted in accordance with your objectives. Group-oriented contingencies are ideally suited for this purpose.

Third, we recommend the use of conditioned reinforcers that can be easily administered or withheld. Further, it should be possible to conduct transactions involving these reinforcers with a minimum of teacher verbalization. Many special education programs for adolescents use point systems. Points meet the requirements just mentioned and are especially useful when response cost contingencies are employed.

Fourth, back-up reinforcers for adolescents should be considered carefully. The range of activities and tangibles that serve as reinforcers for secondary-aged pupils is wide, and the same reinforcer is not likely to work with all students. The potent influence of peers can be harnessed by including peer interactions as back-up reinforcers. Also, because many adolescent reinforcers lie outside the school, it is wise to arrange contingencies in the home and local community. This involves enlisting the aid of parents, social agency personnel, employers, and girlfriends and boyfriends as agents of reinforcement. For example, MacDonald, Gallimore, and MacDonald (1970) trained volunteer mothers to serve as attendance counselors for adolescents. These counselors made "deals" with their clients and other persons who controlled client reinforcers. One such contingency required that a boy fulfill the terms of his contract before being allowed into a local pool hall. Another boy's girlfriend saw him only if he had met his contingency. Parents can control access to cars, peers, television, and special events such as concerts. By negotiating for such back-up reinforcers to be delivered or withheld at home, the teacher can increase effective control of behavior in school.

Finally, you should give thought to the selection and application of techniques for managing undesired behaviors. The physical size of adolescents renders some interventions impractical (e.g., physical punishment). Other techniques should be avoided because they increase the probability of further conflict (e.g., public reprimands). We suggest that you incorporate response cost contingencies into your group management system, as a first step intervention. Such contingencies help develop control over inappropriate pupil reactions when other aversives must be employed. For example, students will learn to take self-imposed time-outs if there are meaningful cost penalties for failure to do so and if points and social reinforcers are used to shape appropriate responses to time-out contingencies. However, response cost contingencies should be developed thoughtfully and evaluated continuously. Under some conditions, the removal of reinforcers has increased rates of undesired pupil behaviors (Santogrossi, O'Leary, Romanczyk, & Kaufman, 1973).

In every secondary program we have observed, the bottom line of the reductive continuum has been temporary exclusion from school. However, if the pupil for whom this intervention is considered has been certified as handicapped, legal restrictions on the use of both suspension and expulsion must be considered. The prevailing view of the courts is that a student cannot be expelled from school if the behavior occasioning such an intervention is related to his handicap (*Honig v. Doe*, 1988). Furthermore, in such cases the school has the burden of proving that the handicap and the behavior problem are not related. If the handicap and behavior are related, the school may take emergency measures, but courts disagree regarding what these measures are. The Office of Civil Rights has offered the opinion that suspensions totaling less than ten days of the school year are not in violation of a handicapped pupil's right to a free and appropriate education (Warboys, 1987). However, some

school districts interpret the Supreme Court's *Honig v. Doe* decision to mean ten-day suspensions for each incident. Any school district that finds it necessary to use more than one suspension should carefully examine its policy and instructional program. Suspension should never be substituted for adequate instructional programming and disciplinary measures that permit students to remain in school. If temporary suspension is contemplated, it must be negotiated with school officials and parents. Procedures for communicating with parents when this consequence is applied should be worked out. Ideally, parents should be instructed in how to manage their child during exclusion (what privileges should be withheld, what activities should be permitted, etc.), and home visits should be conducted to ensure that the procedures agreed upon are being implemented effectively. Homework should be assigned and enforced during the exclusion period. The period itself should be brief (one to three days), and alternative procedures should be developed for students who approach the ten-day limit. This intervention is specifically *not* recommended if a responsible adult will not be home to supervise the pupil, if the adult has no control over the student's behavior, or if that individual is unlikely to implement the strategy as designed. If school exclusion is contemplated as an intervention, school personnel should carefully evaluate the potential for competing reinforcers (e.g., access to drugs, peers, delinquent activities, avoidance of school demands) to strengthen patterns of behavior that result in school exclusion. Therefore, it is important that this intervention be closely monitored.

In-school suspension is a less restrictive alternative to sending students home, and it permits better supervision of pupils while they are in suspension. It is somewhat like a detention hall where students work and receive a minimum of privileges. Adequate space and personnel to manage the suspension room limit this intervention. It can also be completely ineffective if avoiding their scheduled classes is more reinforcing than participation, and supervisory staff may not be qualified to work with handicapped students. Therefore, the effects of in-school suspension should be monitored continuously for all students. For handicapped pupils, this restrictive intervention should be subjected to human rights review, it should be written into students' IEPs, and its effects should be carefully evaluated. If it can be argued that suspension has denied a pupil her civil rights, you may be subject to litigation. This is another reason for giving careful thought to using this intervention. In-school suspension is discussed in Chapter 6.

EVALUATING CLASSROOM MANAGEMENT PROGRAMS

The basic question teachers ask about a classroom management program is, "Has it been effective?" Generally, this refers to whether the teacher's goals have been met. Yet this is only one part of evaluation. Other important questions are: Did pupil behavior change as a result of the program, or because of uncontrolled variables? What components of the program were responsible for these changes? The answers to these questions require systematic data collection and experimental manipulation, which are imposing tasks for the classroom teacher. However, you should be sufficiently competent in using single-subject research designs to identify the mechanisms of your management system responsible for its success or for any problems. These designs are described in Chapter 4.

Published research on classroom management systems has yielded the following general results:

1. Total management packages appear more effective than separate components or combinations of components (Greenwood, Hops, Delquadri, & Guild, 1974; Herman & Tramontana, 1971; MacPherson, Candee, & Hohman, 1974; Walker, Hops, &

Fiegenbaum, 1976).
2. The most important component of management systems is the application of contingent extrinsic consequences (Ayllon, Garber, & Pisor, 1975; Becker, Madsen, Arnold, & Thomas, 1967; Hayes, 1976; Porterfield, Herbert-Jackson, & Risley, 1976).
3. Reinforcement and cost seem to work equally well (Hundert, 1976; Iwata & Bailey, 1974; Kazdin, 1972), although this may not be the case if teacher attention accompanies the removal of reinforcers (McLaughlin & Malaby, 1972).
4. Group-oriented contingencies seem as effective as individual contingencies and are more efficient to administer (Drabman et al., 1974; Kazdin & Geesey, 1977; Rosenbaum et al., 1975); however, negative peer interactions with group contingencies are possible (e.g., Axelrod, 1973).
5. The optimum management package, particularly for highly disruptive students, appears to be a combination of group and individual contingencies (O'Leary & Drabman, 1971; Polsgrove & Nelson, 1982; Walker, 1979).

Summary

Planning and operating a positive and productive classroom environment are important elements of success in teaching any group of students at any level. Without effective behavior management, teachers and pupils are both likely to be dissatisfied with the time they spend in school. This chapter has provided information about classroom management strategies that will help you establish stimulus control over student social behaviors in group settings. When the group norm is appropriate and desirable behavior, individual behavior problems are less likely to occur, and if they do, the teacher can manage them without having to worry simultaneously that other students are going to be out of control. The following points summarize the procedures we feel are critical to your success in managing classroom social behavior.

1. *Collect data on target behaviors.* This is the most critical feature of effective classroom management, but it is also the one most often left out. Without objective, reliable measures of the behaviors targeted for change, you will have no basis on which to judge the effectiveness of your management program or for determining program adjustments. Data collection should occur on a daily basis, and if you relate it to the academic program (such as when the system is based on academic performance rates or accuracy), this process need not be a significant additional burden. Remember too that students can be taught to monitor and record their own academic and social behavior.

2. *Set goals that are specific, clear, and fair.* The most effective classroom management goals are stated behaviorally and include clear criterion statements. This enables you, your pupils, and others to evaluate progress clearly. Your management goals should be based upon baseline data and communicated to everyone having an interest in the management program.

3. *Set contingencies that are clear and fair.* Contingencies are the "rules" of the system; they specify which consequences will follow which behaviors. The best contingencies are few in number, are positively stated, and are easily understood. The ideal contingency is one in which the response automatically produces the consequence, but in education, the natural consequences of behavior are often long-term and tend to be ineffective in the short run (e.g., failure to turn in assignments results in a failing semester grade). Therefore, devise contingencies that relate behavior to immediate consequences, even if these contingencies must be arbitrary and artificial.

4. *Negotiate the system with pupils.* If you open yourself to pupil input you are likely to find that your students also are distressed by a chaotic and confusing classroom environment or by being unable to meet teacher or parental expectations for academic performance. Students can participate in identifying target behaviors and setting goals for classroom management. In addition, they can help you operate the program: monitoring behavior, giving tokens, tutoring classmates, keeping records of points saved and spent, or operating a token store. If you develop a management system with students, it will be more to their liking than if you impose it on them.

5. *Make systematic program adjustments based upon observable change in target behaviors.* Conscientious data collection, if not accompanied by responding to the data with improvements and adjustments, is a pointless activity. Depending on the kind of data you collect and the trends and patterns you observe, you may find it necessary to add or delete components, revise them, or create program modifications for individual pupils.

6. *Base the selection and application of any management system on a careful study of each individual situation.* Classroom management programs are not fixed entities applied to all groups of children. Rather they are infinitely flexible and varied and may be designed to suit any set of circumstances. The variables you should take into account in setting up a program include the target behaviors, the sociometric status, age, and other characteristics of your group, the enthusiasm and effort you are willing to put into the program, your ability and willingness to adjust the program, and the long-range effects of the system on students and on you. This may seem like an overwhelming array of variables, but it is actually no more than you should consider when implementing any intervention, whether it be a new reading curriculum or a recess period.

CASE STUDY

Using the Timer Game to Reduce Disruptive Classroom Behavior

Karen Hensley

In my first year as a special education teacher, I was assigned to a primary level (ages six through eight) self-contained class for children with behavioral disorders. Not being trained in this area, I was pretty nervous and insecure from the beginning. The first few weeks of school reinforced my apprehension.

I had established a token system, using points for completing academic assignments and for following classroom rules. Points were exchanged each day for free time to engage in such quiet play activities as puzzles, games, assembling models, and coloring. However, the system didn't prevent off-task behavior and inappropriate social interactions, which frequently disrupted the classroom routine and atmosphere. My pupils (four boys and one girl) would attempt to gain attention or distract others through talking, namecalling, arguing, and occasional open warfare.

Strategy

I had enrolled in a graduate-level behavior management class during my first semester of teaching, so I elected to do my project on disruptive classroom behaviors. I realized that if the students followed my classroom rules requiring teacher permission to talk or to leave one's seat, disruptive behavior would occur less often. Therefore, I selected talking-out and out-of-seat as target behaviors. I also identified nonverbal noises as a target, because my students often used this tactic to distract other pupils or to get my attention. For recording purposes, I defined these as follows:

1. Talking out — pupil speaks or makes verbal noises without turning over his "Help" sign and waiting for teacher attention.
2. Out-of-seat — pupil's bottom is no longer touching the chair without teacher permission to be up.
3. Nonverbal noises — repeated kicking, tapping, or other motions that result in an audible sound that is noticeable to me.

Baseline data were collected on these behaviors for six days; I observed three ten-minute time samples each day, scattered across a one-hour-forty-minute independent work period. For recording purposes, I divided each ten-minute period into 40 fifteen-second intervals. If any of the target behaviors occurred in an interval, I entered a code in the box corresponding to that interval (T = talking-out, O = out-of-seat, N = noises). Only one symbol per behavior was entered in each interval, no matter how many times it occurred or how many students were doing it. Thus, I could measure these behaviors reliably while performing other teaching duties. I attached recording sheets to the clipboard I normally carry with me during independent work.

The intervention strategy consisted of a timer game. I set a kitchen timer for an average of ten minutes. When the timer rang, my aide or I gave all students who were showing appropriate behavior a point, along with verbal praise. At the end of the period, these points could be exchanged for a "special" free time, provided the student had earned eighty percent of the possible points. Students who failed to meet this criterion had to remain in their seats during free time.

During baseline, I observed that talking-out occurred more frequently than out-of-seat or nonverbal noises. Since it was also the problem of greatest concern to me, the timer game

Figure 5-3. Reduction of Disruptive Behavior

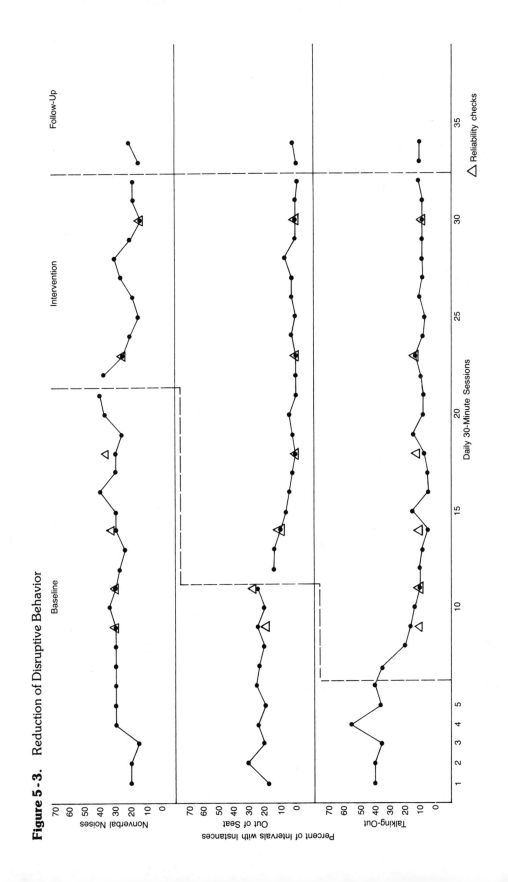

began with this behavior alone (a multiple base-line design was used in my study). After six days, out-of-seat behavior was added to the contingency and nonverbal noises were added on day twenty-two. Reliability observations were made by my aide at regular intervals. Our independent records showed that we were consistently in agreement (see Figure 5-3).

On day thirty-three, I began phasing out the timer. Gradually the interval between timer rings was lengthened from an average of ten minutes to an average of twenty minutes. I did this so that students' good behavior would become a discriminative stimulus for awarding points rather than the sound of the timer. Also, I conducted two follow-up checks, to assess generalization and maintenance. The first was conducted in the school library during independent work supervised by the librarian. The second was done during another period in my class.

Outcome

Figure 5-3 shows the percentages of disruptive behavior for all students. All three behaviors steadily decreased. This decrease was least dramatic for nonverbal noises, probably because these were most difficult to detect. By the end of my intervention, all three behaviors were occurring less than 10 percent of the work period. These changes were maintained during my follow-up observations.

At this writing, I am still fading out the timer game. Soon I will drop the timer altogether and just catch my pupils "being good" as a basis for awarding points. I also plan to drop the special free time. My original goal, which was to reduce the occurrence of these three behaviors to less than 20 percent has been met, and my classroom is a much quieter and more productive place in which to work.

Discussion Questions

1. When Ms. Pearson says to her students, "Please line up quietly to go to the lunch room," her first-grade pupils immediately line up in single file with no disruptive behavior. When Ms. Thomas issues the same request to her class, there is a great deal of running, shouting, and fighting among her first-grade students to be first in line. Explain the difference between the behavior of these two groups in terms of stimulus control and suggest how Ms. Pearson may have established stimulus control over her students' lining up behavior.
2. Ms. Thomas often uses a loud voice, threats, and spankings to attempt to control her class, but her pupils are among the most unruly in the building. Use your knowledge of behavior analysis to explain why this happened.
3. If you were to set up a resource room for elementary-age, behaviorally disordered pupils, how would you structure it? How would you structure a resource room differently for junior high school behaviorally disordered students?
4. Design group behavior management systems based on each of the following: dependent group-oriented contingency; independent group-oriented contingency; interdependent group-oriented contingency.
5. How would you plan a behavior management strategy for a school day for severely handicapped adolescents? How would your strategy differ for mildly handicapped adolescents?

References

Alberto, P. A., & Troutman, A. C. (1986). *Applied behavior analysis for teachers* (2nd ed.). Columbus, OH: Merrill.

Axelrod, S. (1973). Comparison of individual and group contingencies in two special classes. *Behavior Therapy, 4,* 83–90.

Axelrod, S. (1987). Doing it without arrows: A review of Lavigna and Donnellan's *Alternatives to punishment: Solving behavior problems with non-aversive strategies. The Behavior Analyst, 10,* 243-251.

Ayllon, T., & Azrin, N. H. (1968). *The token economy: A motivational system for therapy and rehabilitation.* New York: Appleton-Century-Crofts.

Ayllon, T., Garber, S., & Pisor, K. (1975). The elimination of discipline problems through a combined school-home motivational system. *Behavior Therapy, 6,* 616-626.

Ayllon, T., & Roberts, M. (1974). Eliminating discipline problems by strengthening academic performance. *Journal of Applied Behavior Analysis, 7,* 71-76.

Azrin, N. H., & Holz, W. C. (1966). Punishment. In W. K. Honig (Ed.), *Operant behavior: Areas of research and application* (pp. 380-447). New York: Appleton-Century-Crofts.

Barrish, H. H., Saunders, M., & Wolf, M. M. (1969). Good behavior game: Effects of individual contingencies for group consequences on disruptive behavior in a classroom. *Journal of Applied Behavior Analysis, 2,* 119-124.

Becker, W. C., Madsen, C. H., Arnold, C. R., & Thomas, B. A. (1967). The contingent use of teacher attention and praise in reducing classroom behavior problems. *Journal of Special Education, 1,* 287-307.

Becker, W. C., Thomas, D. R., & Carnine, D. (1971). Reducing behavior problems: An operant conditioning guide for teachers. In W. C. Becker (Ed.), *An empirical basis for change in education* (pp. 129-165). Chicago: Science Research Associates.

Bickel, W. E., & Bickel, D. D. (1986). Effective schools, classrooms, and instruction: Implications for special education. *Exceptional Children, 52,* 489-500.

Breyer, N. L., & Allen, G. J. (1975). Effects of implementing a token economy on teacher attending behavior. *Journal of Applied Behavior Analysis, 8,* 373-380.

Broden, M., Bruce, C., Mitchell, M. A., Carter, V., & Hall, R. V. (1970). Effects of teacher attention on attending behavior of two boys at adjacent desks. *Journal of Applied Behavior Analysis, 3,* 205-211.

Brophy, J. (1981). Teacher praise: A functional analysis. *Review of Educational Research, 51,* 5-32.

Brophy, J., & Good, T. L. (1986). Teacher behavior and student achievement. In M. C. Wittrock (Ed.), *Handbook of Research on Teaching* (3rd ed., pp. 328-375). New York: MacMillan.

Brown, P., & Elliott, R. (1965). Control of aggression in a nursery school class. *Journal of Experimental Child Psychology, 2,* 103-107.

Buehler, D., Jr., Patterson, G. R., & Furniss, J. M. (1966). The reinforcement of behavior in institutional settings. *Behavior Research and Therapy, 4,* 157-167.

Cantrell, R. P., Cantrell, M. L., Huddleston, C. M., & Woolridge, R. L. (1969). Contingency contracting with school problems. *Journal of Applied Behavior Analysis, 2,* 215-220.

Carlson, C. S., Arnold, R. R., Becker, W. C., & Madsen, C. H. (1968). The elimination of tantrum behavior of a child in an elementary classroom. *Behavior Research and Therapy, 6,* 117-119.

Coleman, R. (1970). A conditioning technique applicable to elementary school classrooms. *Journal of Applied Behavior Analysis, 3,* 293-297.

Darch, C. B., & Thorpe, H. W. (1977). The principal game: A group consequence procedure to increase classroom on-task behavior. *Psychology in the Schools, 14,* 341-347.

Drabman, R., Spitalnik, R., & Spitalnik, K. (1974). Sociometric and disruptive behavior as a function of four types of reinforcement programs. *Journal of Applied Behavior*

Analysis, 7, 93-101.

Ferster, C. B., & Culbertson, S. (1982). *Behavioral Principles* (3rd ed.). Englewood Cliffs, NJ: Prentice-Hall.

Foxx, R. M., & Shapiro, S. T. (1978). The timeout ribbon: A non-exclusionary timeout procedure. *Journal of Applied Behavior Analysis, 11,* 125-143.

Gast, D. M., & Wolery, M. (1987). Severe maladaptive behaviors. In M. E. Snell (Ed.), *Systematic instruction of the moderately and severely handicapped* (3rd ed., pp. 300-322). Columbus, OH: Merrill.

Gelfand, D. M., & Hartmann, D. P. (1984). *Child behavior analysis and therapy* (2nd ed.). New York: Plenum.

Greenwood, C. R., Hops, H., Delquadri, J., & Guild, J. (1974). Group contingencies for group consequences in classroom management: A further analysis. *Journal of Applied Behavior Analysis, 7,* 413-425.

Gresham, F. M., & Reschly, D. J. (1987). Issues in the conceptualization, classification, and assessment of social skills in the mildly handicapped. In T. R. Kratochwill (Ed.), *Advances in school psychology.* Hillsdale, NJ: Lawrence Erlbaum.

Haring, N. G., & Phillips, E. L. (1962). *Educating emotionally disturbed children.* New York: McGraw-Hill.

Harris, F. R., Johnston, M. K., Kelly, C. S., & Wolf, M. M. (1964). Effects of positive social reinforcement on regressed crawling of a nursery school child. *Journal of Educational Psychology, 55,* 35-41.

Harris, V. W., & Sherman, J. A. (1973). Use and analysis of the "good behavior game" to reduce disruptive classroom behavior. *Journal of Applied Behavior Analysis, 6,* 405-417.

Hayes, L. A. (1976). The use of group contingencies for behavioral control: A review. *Psychological Bulletin, 83,* 628-648.

Herman, S. H., & Tramontana, J. (1971). Instructions and group versus individual reinforcement in modifying disruptive group behavior. *Journal of Applied Behavior Analy-*

sis, 4, 113-119.

Hersh, R. H., & Walker, H. M. (1983). Great expectations: Making schools effective for all students. *Policy Studies Review, 2,* 147-188.

Hewett, F. M. (1968). *The emotionally disturbed child in the classroom.* Boston: Allyn & Bacon.

Hewett, F. M., & Taylor, F. D. (1980). *The emotionally disturbed child in the classroom: The orchestration of success* (2nd ed.). Boston: Allyn & Bacon.

Homme, L. E. (1970). *How to use contingency contracting in the classroom.* Champaign, IL: Research Press.

Homme, L. E. (1971). Human motivation and environment. In W. C. Becker (Ed.), *An empirical basis for change in education.* Chicago: Science Research Associates.

Honig v. Doe (1988). 108 S. ct. 592.

Hundert, J. (1976). The effectiveness of reinforcement, response cost, and mixed programs on classroom behaviors. *Journal of Applied Behavior Analysis, 9,* 197.

Hundert, J., & Bucher, B. (1976). Increasing appropriate classroom behavior and academic performance by reinforcing correct work alone. *Psychology in the Schools, 13,* 195-200.

Iwata, B. A., & Bailey, J. S. (1974). Reward versus cost token systems: An analysis of the effects on students and teacher. *Journal of Applied Behavior Analysis, 7,* 567-576.

Kauffman, J. M. (1985). *Children's behavior disorders* (3rd ed.). Columbus, OH: Merrill.

Kazdin, A. E. (1972). Response cost: The removal of conditioned reinforcers for therapeutic change. *Behavior Therapy, 3,* 533-546.

Kazdin, A. E. (1973). The effects of vicarious reinforcement on attentive behavior in the classroom. *Journal of Applied Behavior Analysis, 6,* 71-78.

Kazdin, A. E., & Bootzin, R. R. (1972). The token economy: An evaluative review. *Journal of Applied Behavior Analysis, 5,* 343-372.

Kazdin, A. E., & Geesey, S. (1977). Simultaneous-treatment design comparisons of the effects of earning reinforcers for one's peers versus for oneself. *Behavior Therapy, 8,* 682-693.

Kazdin, A. E., & Klock, J. (1973). The effects of nonverbal teacher approval on student attentive data. *Journal of Applied Behavior Analysis, 6,* 643-654.

Kerr, M. M., Nelson, C. M., & Lambert, D. L. (1987). *Helping adolescents with learning and behavior problems.* Columbus, OH: Merrill.

Litow, L, & Pumroy, D. K. (1975). A brief review of classroom group-oriented contingencies. *Journal of Applied Behavior Analysis, 8,* 341-347.

MacDonald, W. S., Gallimore, R., & MacDonald, G. (1970). Contingency counseling by school personnel: An economical model of intervention. *Journal of Applied Behavior Analysis, 3,* 175-182.

MacPherson, E. M., Candee, B. L., & Hohman, R. J. (1974). A comparison of three methods for eliminating disruptive lunchroom behavior. *Journal of Applied Behavior Analysis, 7,* 287-298.

Madsen, C. H., Jr., Becker, W. C., & Thomas, D. R. (1968). Rules, praise, and ignoring: Elements of elementary classroom control. *Journal of Applied Behavior Analysis, 1,* 139-150.

Madsen, C. H., Jr., Becker, W. C., Thomas, D. R., Koser, L., & Plager, E. (1968). An analysis of the reinforcing function of "sit down" commands. In K. R. Parker (Ed.), *Readings in educational psychology* (pp. 265-278). Boston: Allyn & Bacon.

Marholin, D., & Steinman, W. (1977). Stimulus control in the classroom as a function of the behavior reinforced. *Journal of Applied Behavior Analysis, 10,* 465-478.

McCarty, T., Griffin, S., Apolloni, T., & Shores, R. E. (1977). Increased peer-teaching with group-oriented contingencies for arithmetic performance in behavior-disordered adolescents. *Journal of Applied*

Behavior Analysis, 10, 313.

McLaughlin, T. F., & Malaby, J. (1972). Intrinsic reinforcers in a classroom token economy. *Journal of Applied Behavior Analysis, 5,* 263-270.

Medland, M. B., & Stachnik, T. J. (1972). Good behavior game: A replication and systematic analysis. *Journal of Applied Behavior Analysis, 5,* 45-51.

Nelson, C. M. (1977). Alternative education for the mildly and moderately handicapped. In R. D. Kneedler & S. G. Tarver (Eds.), *Changing perspectives in special education* (pp. 185-207). Columbus, OH: Merrill.

Nelson, C. M. (1981). Classroom management. In J. M. Kauffman & D. P. Hallahan (Eds.), *Handbook of special education* (pp. 663-687). Englewood Cliffs, NJ: Prentice-Hall.

Nelson, C. M., & Rutherford, R. B., Jr. (1983). Timeout revisited: Guidelines for its use in special education. *Exceptional Education Quarterly, 3,* 56-67.

O'Leary, K. D., Becker, W. C., Evans, M. B., & Sudargas, R. A. (1969). A token reinforcement program in a public school: A replication and systematic analysis. *Journal of Applied Behavior Analysis, 2,* 3-13.

O'Leary, K. D., & Drabman, R. (1971). Token reinforcement programs in the classroom. *Psychological Bulletin, 75,* 379-398.

O'Leary, K. D., Kaufman, K. F., Kass, R. E., & Drabman, R. S. (1970). The effects of loud and soft reprimands on the behavior of disruptive students. *Exceptional Children, 37,* 145-155.

Osborne, J. G. (1969). Free-time as a reinforcer in the management of classroom behavior. *Journal of Applied Behavior Analysis, 2,* 113-118.

Pfiffner, L. J., & O'Leary, K. D. (1987). The efficacy of all-positive management as a function of the prior use of negative consequences. *Journal of Applied Behavior Analysis, 20,* 265-271.

Polsgrove, L. (1979). Self-control: Methods for child training. *Behavioral Disorders, 4,*

116-130.

Polsgrove, L., & Nelson, C. M. (1982). Curriculum interventions according to the behavioral model. In R. L. McDowell, F. H. Wood, & G. Adamson (Eds.), *Teaching emotionally disturbed children* (pp. 169-205). Boston: Little, Brown.

Porterfield, J. K., Herbert-Jackson, E., & Risley, T. R. (1976). Contingent observation: An effective and acceptable procedure for reducing disruptive behavior of young children in a group setting. *Journal of Applied Behavior Analysis, 9,* 55-64.

Premack, D. (1959). Toward empirical behavior laws: I. Positive reinforcement. *Psychological Review, 66,* 219-233.

Robinson, P. W., Newby, T. J., & Ganzell, S. L. (1981). A token system for a class of underachieving hyperactive children. *Journal of Applied Behavior Analysis, 14,* 307-315.

Rolider, A., & Van Houten, R. (1985). Movement suppression time-out for undesirable behavior in psychotic and severely developmentally delayed children. *Journal of Applied Behavior Analysis, 18,* 275-288.

Rosenbaum, A., O'Leary, K. D., & Jacob, R. G. (1975). Behavioral intervention with hyperactive children: Group consequences as a supplement to individual contingencies. *Behavior Therapy, 6,* 315-323.

Rosenshine, B., & Stevens, R. (1986). Teaching functions. In M. C. Wittrock (Ed.), *Handbook of research on teaching* (3rd ed., pp. 376-431). New York: MacMillan.

Rutherford, R. B., Jr. (1975). Behavioral decision model for delinquent and predelinquent adolescents. *Adolescence, 11,* 97-106.

Rutherford, R. B., Jr. (1983). Theory and research on the use of aversive procedures in the education of moderately behaviorally disordered and emotionally disturbed children and youth. In F. H. Wood & K. C. Lakin (Eds.), *Punishment and aversive stimulation in special education* (pp. 41-64). Reston, VA: Council for Exceptional Children.

Rutherford, R. B., Jr., & Nelson, C. M. (1982). Analysis of the response-contingent timeout literature with behaviorally disordered students in classroom settings. In R. B. Rutherford, Jr. (Ed.), *Severe behavior disorders of children and youth* (Vol. 5, pp. 79-105). Reston, VA: Council for Children with Behavioral Disorders.

Rutherford, R. B., Jr., & Polsgrove, L. (1981). Behavioral contracting with behaviorally disordered and delinquent children and youth: An analysis of the clinical and experimental literature. In R. B. Rutherford, Jr., & A. G. Prieto (Eds.), *Severe behavior disorders of children and youth* (Vol. 4, pp. 49-69). Reston, VA: Council for Children with Behavioral Disorders.

Salend, S. J., & Gordon, B. D. (1987). A group-oriented timeout ribbon procedure. *Behavioral Disorders, 12,* 131-137.

Santogrossi, D. A., O'Leary, K. D., Romanczyk, R. G., & Kaufman, K. R. (1973). Self-evaluation by adolescents in a psychiatric hospital school token program. *Journal of Applied Behavior Analysis, 6,* 277-287.

Schmidt, G. W., & Ulrich, R. E. (1969). Effects of group contingent events on classroom noise. *Journal of Applied Behavior Analysis, 2,* 171-179.

Schulman, J. A., Bailey, K. G., & Huntsinger, G. M. (1976). Territory and classroom management: An exploratory case study. *Behavior Therapy, 7,* 240-246.

Schutte, R. C., & Hopkins, B. L. (1970). The effects of teacher attention on following instructions in a kindergarten class. *Journal of Applied Behavior Analysis, 3,* 117-122.

Soloman, R. W., & Wahler, R. G. (1973). Peer reinforcement control of classroom behavior. *Journal of Applied Behavior Analysis, 6,* 49-56.

Speltz, M. L., Shimamura, J. W., & McReynolds, W. T. (1982). Procedural variations in group contingencies: Effects on children's academic and social behaviors. *Journal of Applied Behavior Analysis, 15,* 533-544.

Spradlin, J., & Spradlin, R. (1976). Developing the necessary skills for entry into classroom teaching arrangements. In N. G. Haring & R. Schiefelbusch (Eds.), *Teaching special children* (pp. 232-267). New York: McGraw-Hill.

Stainback, W., Stainback, S., & Dedrick, C. (1979). Controlling severe maladaptive behaviors. *Behavioral Disorders, 4,* 99-115.

Strain, P. S., Shores, R. E., & Kerr, M. M. (1976). An experimental analysis of "spillover" effects on the social interaction of behaviorally handicapped preschool children. *Journal of Applied Behavior Analysis, 9,* 31-40.

Sulzbacher, S. I., & Houser, J. E. (1968). A tactic to eliminate disruptive behaviors in the classroom: Group contingent consequences. *American Journal of Mental Deficiency, 73,* 88-90.

Sulzer-Azaroff, B., & Mayer, G. R. (1977). *Applied behavior analysis procedures with children.* New York: Holt, Rinehart, & Winston.

Switzer, E. B., Deal, T. E., & Bailey, J. S. (1977). The reduction of stealing in second graders using a group contingency. *Journal of Applied Behavior Analysis, 10,* 267-272.

Thomas, J. D., Presland, I. E., Grant, M. D., & Glynn, T. L. (1978). Natural rates of teacher approval and disapproval in grade-7 classrooms. *Journal of Applied Behavior Analysis, 11,* 91-94.

Walker, H. M. (1979). *The acting-out child: Coping with classroom disruption.* Boston: Allyn & Bacon.

Walker, H. M. (1983). Applications of response cost in school settings: Outcomes, issues, and recommendations. *Exceptional Education Quarterly, 3,* 47-55.

Walker, H. M., & Buckley, N. K. (1973). Teacher attention to appropriate and inappropriate classroom behavior: An individual case study. *Focus on Exceptional Children, 5,* 5-11.

Walker, H. M., Golden, N., Holmes, D., McConnell, J. Y., Cohen, G., Anderson, J.,

Connery, A., & Gannon, P. (1981). *The SBS social skills curriculum: Teaching interactive competence and classroom survival skills to handicapped children.* Eugene, OR: University of Oregon.

Walker, H. M., Hops, H., & Fiegenbaum, E. (1976). Deviant classroom behavior as a function of combinations of social and token reinforcement and cost contingency. *Behavior Therapy, 7,* 76-88.

Warboys, L. M. (1987, November). *Special education and school discipline: Legal issues.* Paper presented at the 11th annual Conference on Severe Behavior Disorders of Children and Youth, Tempe, AZ.

White, M. A. (1975). Natural rates of teacher approval and disapproval in the classroom. *Journal of Applied Behavior Analysis, 8,* 367-372.

White-Blackburn, G., Semb, S., & Semb, G. (1977). The effects of a good-behavior contract on the classroom behaviors of sixth-grade students. *Journal of Applied Behavior Analysis, 10,* 312.

Wilson, C. W., & Hopkins, B. L. (1973). The effects of contingent music on the intensity of noise in junior high home economics classes. *Journal of Applied Behavior Analysis, 6,* 269-275.

Wolery, M., Bailey, D. B., Jr., & Sugai, G. M. (1988). *Effective teaching principles and procedures of applied behavior analysis with exceptional students.* Boston: Allyn & Bacon.

Wolf, M. M., Hanley, F. L., King, L. A., Lachowicz, J., & Giles, D. K. (1970). The timer game: A variable interval contingency for the management of out-of-seat behavior. *Exceptional Children, 37,* 113-117.

Worell, J., & Nelson, C. M. (1974). *Managing instructional problems: A case study workbook.* New York: McGraw-Hill.

Zimmerman, E. H., & Zimmerman, J. (1962). The alteration of behavior in a special classroom situation. *Journal of the Experimental Analysis of Behavior, 5,* 59-60.

Strategies for Specific Problem Behaviors

Part Two

Disruptive Behaviors

Chapter 6

OUTLINE

School-Wide Interventions

Environmentally Mediated Interventions

Teacher-Mediated Interventions

Peer-Mediated Interventions

Self-Mediated Interventions

Case Study

OBJECTIVES

After completing this chapter, the reader should be able to

- Explain the five types of behavior management interventions and give examples of each.
- List ten reinforcers appropriate for an elementary or secondary classroom.
- Design a token economy with levels.
- Select and implement a group contingency.
- Design and implement a self-monitoring procedure.
- Select the best intervention for a given disruptive behavior.

The focus of this chapter is on behaviors that serve to disrupt the ongoing learning process in a classroom. Behaviors that we refer to as *disruptive* are a serious problem for regular classroom and special education teachers. There is no single precise description of disruptive behavior because youngsters can misbehave in a variety of ways. Students can climb on furniture, grab other classmates' materials, make obscene noises or gestures, throw spitballs, verbally or physically defy the teacher, touch their classmates, or run through the hallways. We are concerned about these behaviors not only because they disrupt the ongoing educational activities of the classroom but because they demand a lot of teacher time and attention. The teacher's feelings of pressure and emotional tension that result from coping with disruptive behaviors may have a negative effect on classroom management practices. Yet teachers are expected to manage this problem effectively. To face this difficult challenge, we offer strategies and tactics for dealing with behaviorally disruptive students.

The Worell and Nelson (1974) guidelines cited in Chapter 5 help you decide whether to intervene to correct a problem behavior. These guidelines offer objective criteria to balance against your subjective feelings. Disruptive behaviors that "interfere with the freedom or personal comforts of another individual" (Worell & Nelson, 1974, p. 50) include crying, having temper tantrums, pushing, yelling, throwing objects, stealing, and talking out of turn.

Table 6-1. Sample Definitions of Disruptive Behaviors

1. *Talking Out* — The student speaks without permission or interrupts the teacher and another student who are talking to each other.
2. *Out-of-Chair* — Movement of the student from his chair when not permitted. Such movement may include leaving the chair to open the window, remove items or threaten to remove items from the teacher's or other students' desks, name-calling, and moving around the room.
3. *Modified Out-of-Chair* — Movement of the student from his chair with some part of the body still touching the chair (excluding sitting on feet).
4. *Noise* — The student creates any audible noise other than vocalization.
5. *Rocking* — The student lifts one or more of his chair legs from the floor while he is seated in his chair.
6. *Noncompliance* — Failure by the student to initiate the appropriate response as requested by the teacher.
7. *Other* — The student clearly violates school or classroom rules or engages in behavior which prevents him from engaging in learning tasks and which are not otherwise specifically defined. Such behavior must be determined by the rules in operation in students' classrooms. Examples of such behavior may include engaging singly in activities or tasks not approved by the teacher or related to the assigned academic tasks (i.e., combing hair, writing on desk, looking at or handling objects within the immediate area surrounding the student's desk or work area, not appropriate to the academic task at hand).

Source: The information in this table was reprinted with permission from Rhode, G., Morgan, D. P., & Young, K. R. (1983). Generalization and maintenance of treatment gains of behaviorally handicapped students from resource rooms to regular classrooms using self-evaluation procedures. *Journal of Applied Behavior Analysis, 16,* 171-188.

Table 6-1 illustrates disruptive behaviors. You might find these target behaviors helpful as you plan interventions, conduct direct observations, or write individualized education programs. Remember that the better your target behavior definition, the more reliable your observations will be. Team agreement on exactly what the problem behaviors are will also ease intervention planning.

Now that you have an idea of the kinds of behavioral problems this chapter addresses, let us turn to the intervention strategies available to you. We present five categories of interventions: **school-wide, environmentally mediated, teacher-mediated, peer-mediated,** and **self-mediated.** In each section we define the approach and provide multiple examples of strategies to use in your classroom or school.

School-Wide Interventions

Behavior management approaches taken by districts or by schools are the focus of this section. Most school districts have adopted some of the practices described here, including rules, detention, and in-school suspension.

RULES

Every school has a general discipline code. One of the ways to assist your school is to design effective **rules.** Recall the guidelines for establishing rules (Worell & Nelson, 1974) in Chapter 5. Rules should be communicated to parents, staff, and students. Too often discipline codes change without the input of those close to the problems. All communications should be written simply and clearly. (For a reference on analyzing readability levels, see Gilliland, 1974, pp. 100-101.)

DETENTION

Detention takes place either before or after school for a thirty- to ninety-minute period. At the beginning of the year, plan a school-wide or an individual detention program:

1. Determine students' transportation options. Contact parents to explain detention and to work out transportation.
2. Establish certain days and times for detentions. A limited number of "detention days" allows you to supervise the detention students without being distracted by other activities.
3. Choose assignments students will complete. Telling students to complete work they did not finish in class may not be feasible if it requires your help or special materials (e.g., film, lab equipment).

Once you have planned detention, consider the following implementation guidelines:

1. Assign detention through written forms that explain the rule violation and the date of the assigned detention. These detention slips should be convenient to use, even when a teacher stops a student in the hall between classes. That is, the slips should be small and handy for teachers who are in the halls. Because others will need notification, either carbon-set slips or slips with a perforated "receipt" work best. You can make one copy of the important information for communication with parents and one copy for school records.
2. Notify parents in writing before the detention is to be served. This allows parents to arrange for transportation. The parental detention notice should describe the rule violation and the date and time of the detention. Include the telephone number of a school staff person who can answer parental questions. Figure 6-1 shows a detention slip with these features. Notice the clarity of the detention slip; it is designed for students as well as for parents.

Figure 6-1. Detention Slip

Dear Parent/Guardian,
 Your child, _____ , broke a rule at school today. This is what s/he _____ did: _____

 The school has a rule that your child must now go to a detention. In other words, your child will have to come to school at 3:00 P.M. on ___*January 16*___ to do school assignments. Your child will be able to go home at 4:00 P.M. To get home from school, your child can take the school activities bus for $0.50. Or, you may make other travel plans for your child.

 Please know that detention is serious. If your child does not come on time, with schoolwork, to the detention period, then we will have to keep your child in the In-School Suspension Room for one school day. This means that your child will have no regular classes for one entire day.

 We have told your child about the detention. If you have any questions, you may call Dean Whittaker at 556–9087 between 9:00 A.M. and 3 P.M. tomorrow. If you do not call us, we will look for your child at the detention.

                                                                            Mrs. Marsh, Teacher

January 15

Source: Reprinted with permission from Kerr, M. M., Nelson, C. M., & Lambert, D. L. (1987). *Helping adolescents with learning and behavior problems.* Columbus, OH: Merrill.

3. Plan detention for a time when it will be enforceable. For example, an early morning detention may have to be rearranged for an afternoon time.

4. Have adequate work on hand for students. If students fail to bring their own work, then apply a consequence. For example, you might impose another detention. Do not excuse students from detention because they do not bring work—they will learn to beat the system.

5. Post and review firm rules for behavior during detention.

6. Establish rules for "excused" absences from detention. For example, require that parents contact you directly in the case of dental visits that conflict with the detention schedule.

7. Consider having a coordinator who is responsible for detention schedules and parental contacts; this may make the system more efficient. Perhaps a dean or a vice-principal can handle the parental phone calls, and a secretary can take care of scheduling detentions, in-school suspensions, and make-ups.

8. Reinforce colleagues who conduct the detention periods, whether the duty is assigned or voluntary. Managing a disgruntled group after school is no picnic.

9. Be sure that detention is assigned for less serious infractions and that in-school suspension is assigned for more serious ones.

10. You may wish to run your own detentions for infractions of classroom rules. In this case, "central detention" may be used exclusively for violations of school-wide rules, or it may also be used for violations of your classroom detentions.

11. As with all disciplinary programs, build into the detention system a regular review. Some discipline committees meet on a regularly scheduled basis for this purpose.

12. At the end of each month (at least), review the list of students assigned to detentions. See how many are repeat offenders. Con-

sider an alternative punishment for these students, or revamp detention. Students should hesitate before committing a rule violation that incurs detention. Remember that rules must be reasonable in the first place if the system is to work properly.

IN-SCHOOL SUSPENSION

In-school suspension (ISS) varies widely in its applications. The crucial elements include

A reinforcing setting from which the student is removed

A nonreinforcing environment to which the student is sent

Carefully articulated contingencies that govern the student's passage from one environment to the other.

The in-school suspension room serves as the nonreinforcing environment, so the regular (or special education) class should be the more reinforcing environment, and the rules governing ISS should outline how a student enters and exits from ISS. Specific guidelines for in-school suspension appear in Table 6-2.

Because in-school suspension is misused so often, we offer some troubleshooting ideas (Kerr et al., 1987):

- Do communicate the rules for ISS to *all* staff members, students, and parents.
- Do inform students' parents about each instance of ISS.
- Do select ISS teachers with care, ensuring that they possess good behavior management skills.
- Do not let ISS become just another study hall or tutorial program.
- Do not allow students to misbehave in ISS without firm, negative consequences.
- Do not allow teachers to overrun the ISS room with students who have engaged in only minor infractions.
- Do monitor referrals for ISS and give teachers feedback on their referrals.

Table 6-2. Guidelines for In-School Suspension

1. Be sure that the individual in charge of ISS can manage misbehavior. Preferably, teachers should be hand-picked for this assignment. If one individual is not in charge all day, then rotate teachers through the ISS duty, with perhaps a permanent paraprofessional on duty.

2. Do not allow students to enter ISS at any time except the beginning of the school day. Mid-day entries are disruptive and create additional problems (e.g., parents who are not notified in advance, failure to get enough appropriate assignments from regular teachers, etc.).

3. When students check into school on the day of their ISS, have them meet in a central location. In one successful program, students meet in the dean's office, where they receive a brief orientation to the ISS policies and a reminder of the infraction that earned them ISS. Students then go to ISS in a group, accompanied by the dean.

4. Have students' work already organized when they arrive to serve their ISS day. Do not allow students to circulate throughout the building collecting assignments — this may turn into a reinforcer!

5. When students go to the restroom, do not let them go in groups. One or two students per trip should be the rule.

6. ISS students probably should have lunch in the ISS room. The alternative, allowing them to eat with other students, may earn them vocal recognition from their peers and create cafeteria disruption.

7. Students who misbehave in ISS should be required to return for an additional day.

8. Time spent in ISS should be work time — no talking to one another or to the adults unless the talk relates to assignments. You may choose to set up carrels to facilitate this atmosphere.

9. At the end of the student's ISS time, an adult should review with the student alternatives to the behavior that warranted ISS placement. Somehow, the ISS teacher should communicate to the regular staff the student's compliance with the punishment.

Source: Reprinted with permission from Kerr, M. M., Nelson, C. M., & Lambert, D. L. (1987). *Helping adolescents with learning and behavior problems.* Columbus, OH: Merrill.

- Do check to see if ISS is reducing behavior problems. If not, review the guidelines and adjust the ISS program accordingly. Remember, a disciplinary consequence is not punishing, by definition, unless it reduces the behavior you designate!
- Do keep all staff informed on the ISS program and any revisions made in it.

Thus we conclude our discussion of school-wide strategies and turn to classroom-level strategies.

Environmentally Mediated Interventions

In an environmentally mediated strategy, some aspect of the environment is altered to prevent or to manage behavioral problems. Aspects of the environment that can be changed include rules, curricula, schedules, seating, and the overall physical plan of the classroom. Two important concepts may help you when considering environmental strategies. First, altering the environment is not itself a powerful intervention strategy. Second, all other strategies depend on a sound environment that discourages disruptive behavior and that supports the other, more powerful interventions. In other words, *environmental modifications may not be sufficient to change a target behavior, but they are necessary if other strategies are to be*

Figure 6-2. Physical Plan Checklist

Directions: Ask yourself these questions about your classroom's present physical plan (+ means *yes*, − means *no*, and question mark means that you need assistance on this item).

Doorway:
_____ Clearly marked so that visitors can find it.
_____ Has an envelope/pad/pencil for messages for others so that they will not have to interrupt class.
_____ Has plenty of room just inside for children to line up in without knocking things.

Walls:
_____ Displays are at children's eye level.
_____ Displays either offer entertainment _____, teach _____, or provide classroom information.
_____ Children's work, _____ art, is displayed.
_____ Blackboards are located within each child's visual range.
_____ Schedule for daily and nondaily activities is posted, _____ is written so that children can read it, _____ is written in no more than thirty-minute time blocks, _____ is current.
_____ Some walls are clean for visual "rest."
_____ Chipping paint and malfunctioning electrical outlets have been reported.

Furniture:
_____ Each child's desk is the correct size.
_____ Each child's desk is arranged so that the child can see and participate readily in seatwork activities, _____ teacher presentations, _____ and chalkboard lessons.
_____ Each child has own desk.
_____ Each child's desk is organized for ready access to materials and supplies.
_____ Desks are in their best arrangement for pupil activities. _____ You can move easily from one desk to another.
_____ There are other types of room furniture, carpets, and so forth so that children are not always seated at their desks.
_____ Children are seated with other children with whom they can work successfully.

Storage:
_____ Instructional materials are stored so that you can find anything within ten minutes.
_____ Materials are stored in a logical order and place.
_____ Student records are kept in a convenient, _____ orderly place.
_____ Storage areas are safe.

Other Concerns:

---

successful. Review the environmental modification suggestions for the grade level of concern to you before you attempt subsequent intervention activities. The first step in creating an environment that fosters appropriate rather than disruptive behaviors is to analyze the classroom setting. Disruptive behavior can result when students experience difficulties caused by the physical environment of a classroom or school. For instance, disruptive behavior may occur when too many students are crowded into a small area, as when students from an entire grade level are sent to a single classroom to view a film. A number of checklists and rating scales are available to help teachers arrange their teaching environments to facilitate classroom management and optimum learning situations. However, it is rare to find any checklist or rating scale that describes every environmental element of an "effective" classroom. We have observed extremely good classrooms that were located in former storage rooms, furnished with leftovers, or decorated with a coat of lime-green paint. Teachers create good learning environments through effective teaching. Nevertheless, it is helpful to have a physical environment suited to the needs of the students and their teacher. Figure 6-2 may assist you in analyzing the physical environment of your classroom, in determining whether environmental modifications may prevent or deter disruptive behavior, and by suggesting variables that should be considered in the general physical environment.

SUGGESTIONS FOR PRESCHOOL AND PRIMARY SCHOOL ENVIRONMENTS

Two simple modifications can help students stay in their assigned areas. The first strategy is to mark the floor around each child's desk with masking tape, thereby designating his "yard" or assigned area. Reinforce pupils for remaining in their yards, and do not reinforce students who are out of their yards. The second inter-

Figure 6-3. Signaling Device for a Child's Desk

vention is a signaling device (see Figure 6-3) that the student can use to indicate whether teacher assistance is needed. This procedure reduces the need for students to be out-of-seat to get teacher attention.

SUGGESTIONS FOR ELEMENTARY AND MIDDLE SCHOOL ENVIRONMENTS

One handy and proven environmental intervention is a **clock light,** described by Greenwood, Hops, Delquadri, and Walker (1977) as a wireless, remote-control clock used by the teacher to signal on-task and off-task behavior to students. A green light attached to the clock shows students that they are on-task; a red light reminds students that they are not attending to their work. During a lesson, teachers can operate the clock light from a remote-control switch at their desks. Immediate feedback to students is one of the featues of this successful intervention. By designating a length of time that students must be on-task (the clock measures the time cumulatively), teachers can assign reinforcing activities tied to the on-task contingency. An inexpensive design for assembling a clock light in your classroom is described in Adams (1984).

Many of the suggestions offered for young children are applicable to older students as well. Students in the older group, however, are more likely to travel from classroom to classroom and may therefore require assistance in transitions from one location to another. Hall passes are recommended for this age level and may be made of inexpensive materials. In addition, you may wish to mark the traffic pathways with colored tape or decorative footprints.

SUGGESTIONS FOR SECONDARY SCHOOL ENVIRONMENTS

Large-scale environmental changes are not practical at the secondary level. Instead, it is important to emphasize to students the specific behavioral requirements for each classroom. For example, students should have a clear notion of the criteria for arriving at class on time. Does a student need to be in a seat, in the classroom, or at the door when the bell rings? Areas of the school building that are off-limits to students should be clearly marked, and differential reinforcement should be applied to pupils who respect these limits.

Visibility of adults is important. A recent survey in urban middle schools (Kerr, 1986) indicated that disruptions in the hall were less common when deans and faculty members remained visible during the changing of classes. This all-out effort lets students know that staff members support each other in a consistent program of discipline.

SUGGESTIONS FOR SPECIAL EDUCATION ENVIRONMENTS

It is crucial that your special education environment prepare students for the regular education placements to which they will be main-

streamed. Be sure that you have ample spaces and opportunities for students to practice group participation skills that will help them succeed in the regular education setting. To the extent possible, model your classroom after the mainstream classrooms to which your students will be going.

The use of cubicles is a common practice in many special education settings. Like many aspects of environmental planning in the classroom, the effectiveness of cubicles has not been thoroughly examined. However, two research studies provide information on the effectiveness of this environmental manipulation. Shores and Haubrich (1969) found that attending behavior was increased by the use of cubicles but that children's performance on math and reading activities was not affected. In a follow-up study, these authors found that a reinforcement intervention was necessary to improve academic performance, despite improvements in attention obtained through the cubicles (Haubrich & Shores, 1976). We recommend that each classroom provide quiet spaces in which students may work individually. Cubicles may serve this function adequately, but they will not replace appropriate academic programming. It is not necessary for each student to have a cubicle. A few cubicles can be shared by all students. Overreliance on individual cubicles will defeat the purpose of teaching children to interact appropriately in a group.

Teacher-Mediated Interventions

The classroom teacher, through direct interaction with students, plays a primary role in modifying their behavior. This section centers on such interventions; however, be sure to consult the Strategy Selection Chart (Figure 6-14) at the end of this chapter to select the appropriate initial intervention before searching for one in this section.

PUBLIC POSTING

Public posting is a successful, yet relatively simple strategy that combines an environmental intervention with a teacher-directed approach. In public posting, students receive visual feedback about their performance (e.g., a poster telling them how well they have performed a given behavior). Two recent studies illustrate the versatility of this intervention. Both were conducted with secondary school students, but there is no reason why the public posting strategy would not be effective with younger students, as long as they understand the contents of the poster. Jones and Van Houten (1985) used public posting to change seventh graders' disruptive behavior (i.e., noises, pushing, teasing, "showing off," leaving seats) during science and English classes. Before trying the posting, the authors instituted pop quizzes to see whether these would remediate the misbehavior, but they were not entirely successful, so the authors turned to the public posting of each student's daily quiz score. The public posting resulted in decreased disruptive behaviors as well as in similar or improved quiz scores for the seventh graders. Here is a description of the poster that Jones and Van Houten used:

> Three 70 cm x 56 cm white bristol board sheets covered with clear plastic laminate were used as feedback posters. Each poster contained the names of the students in whose classroom it was used. In addition, the poster provided space to record five consecutive daily academic quiz scores, the highest daily quiz score and the highest weekly score by each student's name. Further, the daily scores, the highest daily score and the highest weekly score of the class as a whole were recorded on the poster. Red and black grease crayons were used to record the quantitative data noted above on each poster. Black ¾″ and 1″ lettering was used for all printed material on the chart. Letters were formed with the use of letter stencils and filled in with felt-tipped black markers. (p. 94)

In a second study of public posting, Staub (1987) sought to improve the rambunctious hall behavior of middle school students during change of classes. Large posters (see Figure 6-4) at each end of a very busy corridor gave students the following information: percent change in the daily occurrence of disruptive behavior (as compared with the day before), and the "best record to date" of decreasing disruptive behaviors. To enhance the public posting strategy, the Dean gave verbal feedback and praise matching the posters to each classroom during the first minute of classes.

This simple and inexpensive intervention proved successful in reducing the disruptive behaviors of the middle school students.

MONITORING TEACHER VERBAL BEHAVIOR

What you say or do not say may be your most powerful strategy for remedying disruptive

Figure 6-4. Public Posters to Reduce Hallway Disruptions

DISRUPTIVE HALLWAY BEHAVIOR WORSE THAN YESTERDAY BY
5%
BEST RECORD TO DATE
BETTER BY   15%

DISRUPTIVE HALLWAY BEHAVIOR BETTER THAN YESTERDAY BY
10%
BEST RECORD TO DATE
BETTER BY   15%

behavior. We all know teachers who are "naturals" at disciplining students. These individuals have distinctive speaking voices that command students' attention without screaming. You, too, can have an authoritative but courteous voice. First, ask a colleague to role-play some situations with you. Pretend that you are stopping a rambunctious student in the corridor. Ask your colleague to tell you honestly how you sound. Do you sound angry and out of control? Do you convey authority without losing your "cool"? Are you meek or apologetic? Now, practice again. This activity might seem silly at first, but it helps you become more aware of your verbal reactions, especially in stressful situations. Once you realize how you sound, concentrate on your facial expressions and ask a colleague for feedback on how you look.

Monitoring yourself is a great way to gain control of your verbal messages. Table 6-3 offers steps in monitoring verbalizations (e.g., praise, reprimands, nags, repeated requests).

Reprimands

Admonishing students who misbehave is a teaching tradition. Studies have shown that you can reprimand more effectively by

1. Making your reprimand privately, not pub-

Table 6-3. Guidelines for Modifying Teacher Verbalizations

1. Obtain at least fifty pennies or paperclips.
2. Place the pennies or paperclips in one pocket.
3. Each time you find yourself giving a designated verbal statement, move a penny or a paperclip to the other pocket.
4. At the end of the day, count the items in each pocket and record your score.
5. Tally the number of times you gave the designated verbal statement and record this on an individual chart. Try to improve your record the next day.

licly (O'Leary, Kaufman, Kass, & Drabman, 1970)
2. Giving the target student direct eye contact while you are scolding him (Van Houten, Nau, MacKenzie-Keating, Sameoto, & Colavecchia, 1982)
3. Standing near the student while you are talking to her (Van Houten et al., 1982).

We generally recommend that you find another way to handle misbehavior (e.g., a contingency arrangement that will not lead to a power struggle).

The Praise-and-Ignore Approach

Sometimes we ignore problem behaviors, only to be disappointed in the results. Our failure to control behavior may be due to a misunderstanding of the basic principles that underlie this intervention. Here are four guidelines for an effective praise-and-ignore approach:

1. Remember that ignoring will not work unless the reason for the student's behavior is to gain your attention. To determine this, use an A-B-C analysis.
2. Remember that when an ignoring intervention is successful, disruptive behavior will increase before decreasing. Do not give up.
3. Develop ways in which other adults present can distract you from the student who is being disruptive so that you do not find yourself giving the student attention. Let others present know that the student's disruptive behavior is to be ignored.
4. Be sure to praise the student for appropriate behaviors. Ignoring without praise will not work.

DIFFERENTIAL REINFORCEMENT OF OTHER BEHAVIORS

Differential Reinforcement of Other Behaviors, or DRO, is a strategy whereby you reinforce the nondisruptive behaviors when they occur during a specified time interval. One simple way to use the DRO approach is through a **timer game.** This intervention has proven successful in reducing disruptive behaviors of *groups* of students, making it valuable for regular education classes. Consider this example from a study by Allen, Gottselig, and Boylan (1982).

> A group contingency . . . allowed the class to earn free time, to be awarded at the end of the class period, contingent upon intervals in which behaviors other than the specified disruptive behaviors occurred. On the first session of intervention, the teacher posted, explained, and gave examples of new class rules that included the following: (a) We raise our hands to ask to leave our seats; (b) We raise our hands to get help; (c) We do not disturb others while working; (d) We do not argue with others; (e) We do assigned work only; and (f) We put our heads down between classes for quiet time. The rules were briefly reviewed at the beginning of each session and were permanently posted on a brightly colored, easily read sign located at the front of the classroom.
>
> Also during the first session the teacher explained the procedure that would be followed from that point forward. At the beginning of the session, a kitchen timer was set for five minutes. The timer continued running as long as disruptive behaviors were not emitted, and at the end of the five-minute interval, the bell rang. At this time, the teacher praised the class, told them that they had earned one minute of free time, and turned over a card located on a flip stand denoting the number one. Each time the five-minute interval passed with no disruptive behaviors noted by the teacher, this procedure was repeated. It was possible for the class to earn a total of eight minutes of free time during math and ten minutes during language arts. When a rule violation was observed by the teacher, she briefly stated which rule was broken and who broke it, told the class that they had lost the chance to earn a minute of free time, and then reset the timer for five minutes.
>
> The accumulated free time was awarded at the end of each session by terminating the class early by the allotted number of minutes earned.
>
> During the first session of this phase, the class also generated a list of possible free time activities and voted to select the four most preferred ones. These were rotated in random order across days so that one activity was presented each week. As this phase progressed, new activities were periodically substituted for the original four at the request of the students. (pp. 349-350)

Note how several approaches were combined successfully in this example: classroom rules, group contingency, student-selected reinforcement, and DRO. This study focused on a regular third-grade class. How might you modify the procedure for older students?

A good way to alter the timer game intervention is by awarding points or reinforcement on what is called a **variable reinforcement** schedule. This schedule calls for students to be observed or reinforced after *varying* (as opposed to fixed) time intervals, which *average* a designated time interval. Figure 3-5 in Chapter 3 shows a variable interval (VI) schedule form you can use for the timer game. You will see that the first column of numbers averages four minutes in length, but varies from one to seven minutes. Setting your timer by this schedule would allow you to observe or reinforce students about every four minutes. The practical advantage of a variable schedule is that students do not know when they will be observed, and they will tend to be more careful about their behavior.

DIFFERENTIAL REINFORCEMENT OF LOW RATES OF BEHAVIOR

Differential Reinforcement of Low Rates of Behavior has been applied to swearing (Epstein, Repp, & Cullinan, 1978), talking out (Dietz & Repp, 1973), inappropriate questioning, and negative verbal statements. Teasing and name-calling were targeted by Zwald and Gresham (1982). Here are the steps they took:

1. The teacher posted and discussed class rules, telling the group the maximum num-

ber of teasing/name-calling occurrences allowed to still obtain reinforcement for that day.

2. A mark was made on the blackboard for every teasing/name-calling verbalization. These verbalizations were not discussed or reprimanded: a mark was merely placed on the board.

3. Positive reinforcement was selected by each boy from a reinforcement menu mutually decided upon by the teacher and class members. The reinforcement menu for each day consisted of a hot drink (hot chocolate, tea, or coffee), free reading, or listening to radio.

4. In order to prevent the number of teasing remarks from getting out of hand if the students went beyond the limit set for the day (thereby losing that day's reinforcement), a larger reward was given at the end of the week if the group had five or fewer "extra" recorded teasing remarks for the week. The large reinforcer was twenty minutes of free time on Friday.

5. A line graph was posted so that class members could graphically see their progress. The extra teasing remarks (the number of remarks that exceeded the imposed limit) were recorded on a bar graph so the students could observe whether they would obtain free time at the end of the week. (p. 430)

Trice and Parker (1983) reduced obscene words in a resource room by using DRL and a response cost. Specific words were targeted, and each time a student said one of the six targeted words, he got a colored marker. At the end of the period, the markers were tallied and the students' behavior was posted on a graph. A five-minute detention (the response cost) was required for each marker. Under the DRL condition, students received praise each time the tally fell below the mean tally for the day before; students whose tallies were higher received no comment. The authors cited the re-

sponse cost procedure as more immediately effective than the DRL procedure.

PHYSICAL INTERACTIONS WITH STUDENTS

Most of your interactions with student problems will be, and certainly should be, verbal, not physical. However, we are often asked about physical interventions. Our advice is that you do not engage in any physical interactions that you would deem inappropriate with an unfamiliar adult. Whereas a handshake may be appropriate and courteous, touching a student in any other way may lead to problems, especially with students who have a history of acting-out behaviors. Naturally, there will be good exceptions to this rule, but a conservative stance is usually best. Adolescents who are developing their own sexual identities are often confused about physical affection. Hypersensitive to your initiations, they may misunderstand your intentions. This likelihood increases when the teenager is under stress, angered, or embarrassed.

Physical interventions for aggressive students create their own problems. Our advice is to avoid physical confrontations whenever possible, taking precautions to protect yourself and others.

CONTINGENCY CONTRACTING

A written explanation of contingencies to be used by a student's teacher or parents is termed a contingency contract (Homme, 1970). Contingency contracting is a useful procedure when there are only one or two disruptive students in a classroom. General guidelines for implementing a contingency contract would include the following:

1. Explain to the student what a contract is. Your explanation will depend upon the conversational level of the child, but it may

be helpful to use examples of contracts that the student will encounter.

2. Give the student an opportunity to discuss what a contract is by sharing examples.

3. Ask the student to suggest some tasks that might be included in a contract between student and teacher. Write these down.

4. Suggest some tasks that you would like to see the student accomplish, and write these down.

5. Decide on mutually agreeable tasks. If a third party is to be involved in the contract, be sure that the party also agrees on the tasks that you have selected.

6. Discuss with the student possible activities, items, or privileges that the student would like to earn. Write these down.

7. Negotiate how the student will earn the reinforcers by accomplishing portions or all of the tasks.

8. Identify the criteria for mastery of each task (time allotted, achievement level, how the task is to be evaluated).

9. Determine when the student will receive the reinforcers for completing tasks.

10. Determine when the contract will be reviewed to make necessary revisions or to note progress.

11. Make an extra copy of the contract. Give this copy to the student. If a third party is involved, give that party a copy of the contract also.

12. Sign the contract; get the student to sign the contract; and if there is a third party involved, also ask the third party to sign the contract.

Figure 6-5 provides an example of a contract for a disruptive child. Notice that it is a **home-based contract,** one in which the parents have agreed to participate. Involving parents (or other persons important to the child) is an excellent way to strengthen a contingency contract. At the bottom of the home-based contract is an important feature: the review date. This frequent review allows everyone in-

volved to offer suggestions (on how the procedure can be improved) before major problems arise. Did you also note that the reinforcers within the contract tend to be educational activities? By selecting special privileges that enhance your academic program, you move away from the tendency to "bribe" students into improved performance.

TOKEN ECONOMY PROGRAMS

Token economy programs have been used in numerous schools and clinics, including special education classrooms (Broden, Hall, Dunlap, & Clark, 1970), regular classrooms (McLaughlin & Malaby, 1972), and even the school cafeteria (Muller, Hasazi, Pierce, & Hasazi, 1975). Token economies have been successful in decreasing disruptive behavior such as jumping out-of-seat, and they have been successful in increasing attention and academic performance. Use the Strategy Selection Chart (Figure 6-14) to determine whether a token economy program will work in your situation. The resources you will need before initiating a token economy program are

1. Back-up reinforcers appropriate for your classroom group

2. Tokens appropriate for your group

3. A kitchen timer, if you plan to reinforce behaviors by measuring their duration

4. A monitoring sheet on which to record the tokens or points earned

5. Token dispensers, containers, or devices to denote the gain or loss of tokens

You will need a couple of hours to get materials together and to get the monitoring sheets duplicated. Once you have materials ready, plan to spend about thirty minutes a day for the first week of the program introducing the tokens and orienting students to the program. After the first week, the program should require no more than twenty minutes a day in addition to the time spent delivering tokens.

Figure 6-5.   Home-Based Report

I, _Randy_ _____ agree to do the following at school:
   (student)

1. _____
   Try not to interrupt the teacher

   on this schedule: _during social studies class_

2. _Try to work without disturbing other_
   kids

   on this schedule: _during math_

I, _Mr. Jamieson_ _____, agree to provide assistance as follows:
   (teacher)

   Arrange for Randy to take part in
   the social studies discussion, by
   calling on him daily.
   Move Randy away from the
   gerbils.

We, _the Bergers_ _____, agree to provide privileges as follows:
   (parents)

   provide Randy with ✓ marks on the
   chart posted in the kitchen. When Randy
   earns 50 ✓'s, he can buy a gerbil. We will also
   try to have conversations about the news at home.

We have read and discussed this contract in an after-school meeting on _2/16_,
and we hereby sign as a way of making our commitment to this arrangement.

We will all meet on _2/28_, to re-evaluate the contract.

Signed: _Randy Berger_
         (Student)
        J. Jamieson
         (teacher)
        Anita Berger
         (parent)
        George Berger
         (parent)

Date: _2/16_

(Note: programs may differ in the amount of time required.)

To begin the program, select target behaviors for your class. Some of the behaviors you list should be ones you take for granted presently. Select easy behaviors to be sure all students can earn a few tokens from the beginning of the program. Try to select target behaviors compatible with your classroom rules. Sample target behaviors developed for a primary classroom token economy could include the following:

1. Say hello to teachers when you arrive at school.
2. Hang up your coat when you come to school.
3. Put your lunch up when you arrive at school.
4. Pick up your work for the day and take your seat.
5. Eat lunch within the allotted time.
6. Line up for activities outside the room.

To ensure that the target behaviors selected are appropriate, ask yourself the following questions:

1. How can I describe this behavior in words the student(s) can understand?
2. How can I measure this behavior when it occurs? If the behavior is measured in terms of time (on-task for ten minutes, no outburst during a fifteen-minute period, solving a certain number of math problems within a specified amount of time) then assign the tokens or points on the basis of a token-to-time ratio. If the behavior is measured in terms of frequency (percent correct on a worksheet, number of positive verbal comments to a peer, number of independent steps in a self-care task) then award tokens or points on the basis of a token-to-frequency ratio.
3. How will I know when this behavior is exhibited?
4. How important is this behavior? You will not be able to initiate the program with *all* of the behaviors you identify, so you may have to rank them. Try to start with some behaviors that you can modify successfully.
5. Is the behavior one that you wish to reduce or eliminate? You can handle this behavior in two ways. First you can determine incompatible, desired behaviors for which the student will be rewarded. Second, you can apply a fine or a response cost to the student for engaging in this behavior.
6. Does this behavior occur in other settings? If so, you may want to extend the token economy program to include other classes or the home. To do this, you will need to monitor the behavior in those settings, so include space on your monitoring form or develop a different form for those settings.

As you present these target behaviors, or rules, to your students, remember that research has shown that a daily review of the rules strengthens the effectiveness of the token economy (Rosenberg, 1986). Use this supplemental activity by calling on students and asking them to state the rules and the tokens or points that the behaviors can earn. Rosenberg (1986) found that a mere two-minute review each day improved students' responses to the token economy intervention.

Selecting reinforcers and fines is the next step. If your students can help, let them develop a list of reinforcers. Think of items or events that will be enjoyable and that can be obtained within the school. Some ideas for involving students in identifying their own reinforcers might include the following:

1. Ask students to draw, write, or select from a set of pictures those items or events that appeal to them.
2. Allow students some free time, and observe what they choose to do.
3. Allow students to "sample" reinforcers by placing them in an accessible place and recording which items the students select frequently.

Selecting tokens is the next step in the token economy program. In considering the types of tokens to use, you must consider the following variables:

1. The age of the students
2. The skill level of the students
3. The likelihood that students will destroy, eat, or cheat with respect to the tokens

4. The expense of the tokens
5. The durability of the tokens
6. The convenience of using the tokens
7. Tokens that are being used in other programs within the same setting (Do not use these!)

Once you have chosen tokens for your program, select an appropriate container for them. Figure 6-6 shows various kinds of tokens and token containers for different age groups and skill levels. Counterfeiting may be prevented by using a special color marking pen, by awarding tokens at specified times, or by awarding bonus points for honesty and deducting points for cheating.

Next, we recommend that you design a **levels system** within your token economy in order to account for improvement that your students will exhibit as they respond to the economy. Bauer, Shea, and Keppler (1986) offer guidelines for developing a levels system. First, select the entry behaviors that you anticipate from your students. Second, pick the terminal behaviors, or the behaviors you hope your students will display as they leave your setting. Third, make two to four lists of "intermediate" behaviors that would fall between the entry and the terminal behaviors. Fourth, assign privileges or reinforcers to each of the lists, or levels.

To understand a levels system within a token economy, take a look at the three levels designed by Theroux (personal communication, 1987). This token economy is called "Money Makers" and is based on a "real" economy. Behaviors are classified either as money makers or as costly capers. To develop the first level, the teacher completes the student's name, the date for the present day, and the

Figure 6-6. Sample Tokens and Containers

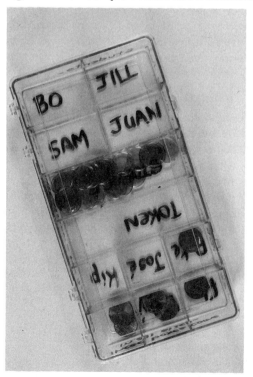

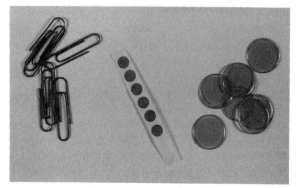

date the child began the level. (This date does *not* change until the child reaches the next level of the program).

Deposit Times

At Level 1, there are four deposit times. These are the only times tokens are exchanged. Each deposit time is associated with a list of behaviors that are to be observed. For example, the 9:15 deposit time is associated with behaviors

that would have occurred between the start of the day and 9:15.

Deposit Time Procedures

The teacher circles the number next to the behavior on each child's monitoring sheet if this behavior was demonstrated by the child. The class work is temporarily stopped so that the teacher can tell each child the points he has earned. A Level 1 chart displayed on the bulle-

Figure 6-7. Token Economy Monitoring Form, Level 1

```
                        Target Behaviors
                             Level 1

  Student: _____    Date: _____
  Date Level Started: _____

                      Money Makers (Deposits)

        9:15 Deposit Time                      11:00 Deposit Time
  Enter the room quietly      1         Ready to work              2 2 2
  Put coat and lunch away     2         Be helpful                 2 2
  Go directly to your seat    1 1       Sit straight               1 1 1
  Say good morning            1         Share with someone         2 2 2
                                        Line up quietly            1 1 1

        1:00 Deposit Time                      Dismissal Deposit Time
  Ready to work               2 2 2     Ready to work              2 2 2
  Sit straight                1 1 1     Sit straight               1 1 1
  Line up quietly             1 1 1     Line up quietly            1 1
  Be helpful                  2 2       Be helpful                 2 2
  Go directly to your seat    1         Say goodbye                1
  Share with someone          2 2 2     Share with someone         2 2 2

                     Costly Capers (Withdrawals)

               Talk in a loud voice            2 2 2 2
               Out of your seat                2 2 2 2
               Hit, kick, or push              6 6 6
               Laugh in a loud, silly voice    2 2 2
               Talk back                       4 4 4 4

  TOTAL DEPOSITS _____    TOTAL WITHDRAWALS _____    EARNING EFFORTS _____
```

Source: Denise Theroux, personal communication, 1987.

tin board may be used as a visual aid while the teacher is detailing the points earned. (The monitoring form and the level of chart are identical. See Figure 6-7.) If a student has demonstrated any of the costly caper behaviors, the appropriate number is circled. These withdrawals are also explained to each child. The same costly capers are used for each deposit time. During each deposit time, the child receives the tokens he has gained for those behaviors; he must make a withdrawal for his total of costly capers, and the remaining tokens are deposited in his account (e.g., a spice jar). The day's total

deposits, withdrawals, and final total efforts are calculated at the end of the day. By subtracting the withdrawals from the deposits, the total earning efforts are determined. This total reflects the number of token pennies the child deposited in his account (spice jar) for the day. The maximum total points a child can receive at Level 1 is seventy-three points (token pennies).

Moving on to Level 2

A child who receives an average daily score of fifty points for four consecutive weeks may

Figure 6-8.   Token Economy Monitoring Form, Level 2

Target Behaviors
Level 2

Student: _____   Date: _____
Date Level Started: _____

Money Makers (Deposits)

11:00 Deposit Time		Dismissal Deposit Time	
Raise your hand	2 2 2 2	Raise your hand	2 2 2 2
Pleasant voice	2 2 2 2	Pleasant voice	2 2 2 2
Neat papers	2 2 2	Neat papers	2 2 2 2
Answer questions	3 3 3 3	Answer questions	3 3 3 3
Finish homework	3	Good play at recess	3
Neat desk	2	Neat desk	2
Finish your work	3 3 3	Finish your work	3 3 3
Go to reading group when called	3	Go to math group when called	3
		Eat with good manners	3

Costly Capers (Withdrawals)

Not wait your turn	4 4 4 4
Get angry	6 6 6
Fight	6 6 6
Scream	4 4 4
Tease others	4 4 4
Argue	4 4 4 4

TOTAL DEPOSITS _____   TOTAL WITHDRAWALS _____   EARNING EFFORTS _____
(add 73 points to total deposit)

Source: Denise Theroux, personal communication, 1987.

move on to Level 2. At Level 2, there are only two deposit times; the 9:15 deposit time has been omitted, and children at Level 2 continue to work during the Level-1 9:15 deposit time. At 11:00, both Levels 1 and 2 receive the tally of their points. The procedures used are the same as those in Level 1. The second deposit time is prior to dismissal, and the final tally is completed at this time. Level-2 children are to continue working as other children at other levels receive their tokens. (See Figure 6-8.) Remember, there are only two deposit times in Level 2. The maximum total points a child can receive at Level 2 is 180 points. *Remember that Level-1 points are automatically added to the daily total of Level-2 points. Every Level-2 child adds seventy-three points each day to his total earning efforts.*

Moving on to Level 3

If a child receives an average of 160 points for four consecutive weeks he or she can move on to Level 3. The Level-3 monitoring form lists

Figure 6-9. Token Economy Monitoring Form, Level 3

Target Behaviors
Level 3

Student: _____   Week of: _____
Date Level Started: _____

Money Makers (Deposits)

	Follow directions	Score 90%	Ask good questions
A.M.	3 3 3 3 3	3 3 3 3 3	2 2 2 2 2
P.M.	3 3 3 3 3	3 3 3 3 3	2 2 2 2 2
	Tutor a friend	Good sport	Meet contract goal
	2 2 2 2 2	2 2 2 2 2	3 3 3 3 3
	Good gym report	Good music report	Good art report
	2 2	2 2	2 2

	Walk quietly in halls	Work without disturbing others
A.M.	2 2 2 2 2	3 3 3 3 3
P.M.	2 2 2 2 2	3 3 3 3 3

	No arguing all day	Show respect	Ignore trouble
A.M.	3 3 3 3 3	3 3 3 3 3	3 3 3 3 3
P.M.	3 3 3 3 3	3 3 3 3 3	3 3 3 3 3

Costly Capers (Withdrawals)

Foul language	4 4 4 4 4
Moan about tokens	4 4 4 4 4
Detention offense	6 6 6 6 6
Suspension offense	6 6 6 6 6

TOTAL DEPOSITS _____   TOTAL WITHDRAWALS _____   EARNING EFFORTS _____
(add 107 points to total deposit)

Source: Denise Theroux, personal communication, 1987.

behaviors that either earn or lose points. This form represents a week's worth of points that can be earned by the child. The concepts of money makers and costly capers are still retained. However, there are no deposit-time lists on the form. Instead, A.M. and P.M. are indicated for those behaviors that have two lines of points. There are five numbers in each line representing a point for each day.

Management

The child is now allowed to make a folder to hold the monitoring form; this folder is the child's own ledger to maintain. Each form is used for one week, and it should be kept in the ledger. (See Figure 6-9.)

Completing Form Information

The child fills in his name, the week, and the starting date for this level. Only one sheet is needed for the week. At the 11:00 deposit time, a child at Level 3 circles one number in the A.M. rows if he has demonstrated these behaviors. If these behaviors have not occurred in the morning, the second row of points provides the opportunity to gain a set of points in the afternoon. This would occur prior to dismissal. Some behavior squares have only one row of points. The number of points indicates the number of days in the week that these points can be earned. For example, "tutor a friend" can gain one set of points on one day. It is possible to gain all five sets if tutoring is done each day. The squares describing a good gym report contain only two sets of points because gym occurs only twice a week. Points in these squares are gained when they occur (A.M. or P.M.). The costly capers are circled if the teacher or aide instructs the student to circle a set of points because that behavior was demonstrated. At the end of the day, the student totals the deposits, subtracts any withdrawals, and adds 107 points to determine his earning efforts. The student is allowed to go to the safety de-

posit box (spice rack), obtain his account (spice jar), count out the amount earned, and deposit the coins in the spice jar. The jar is returned to the spice rack.

Moving Off Levels

To earn a certificate of extraordinary earning efforts, a child must achieve an average of 200 points for four consecutive weeks. The child has now earned the privilege of being taken off levels altogether. It is important that your token economy include levels and a provision for moving students away from the externally controlled reinforcement that prevails in many token economy systems. The self-monitoring component of Level 3 in this system is a good way to promote students' independence. Adjusting the reinforcers so that they move students from more immediate gratification to delayed rewards is important also. This token economy helped to promote this concept by reducing the number of deposit times as children moved through the levels. The kind and number of reinforcers should also shift as students develop better self-control. Consider these reinforcing activities for a Level-1 student:

- Color or draw for ten minutes
- Do a fun ditto
- Play with a toy for ten minutes
- Have a snack

Now review this list of reinforcing activities for a Level-2 student:

- Read with a friend for ten minutes
- Change your seating assignment
- Be in charge of the flash-card game
- Skip a homework assignment

Finally, examine this list of reinforcers for a student nearly ready to return to the mainstream:

- Go to the library to read magazines
- Correct today's homework papers
- Use the computer for thirty minutes
- Be the token economy "banker" all day
- Select the class filmstrip

As students learn to manage their behavior, their reinforcers should reflect their increasing ability to handle classroom freedom. Moreover, their reinforcers should provide them with a smooth transition to the less restrictive mainstream environment where frequent and tangible reinforcers are not common. After all, we cannot expect any child to leave a special education classroom willingly if that classroom resembles a toy department.

Another component of your token economy will facilitate the development of new—and unexpected—skills. "Bonus points" can be issued for spontaneous behaviors that you would like to recognize but did not include in your monitoring forms.

Finally, be sure that you review your token economy program with your students at least once a month. Remember that you will have students *at different levels at the same time,* so you will need to examine how each level is functioning. If you find that no students are moving from one level to another, then make the higher level a bit easier to reach, or reexamine your lower level to see *why* students are not succeeding. This review is similar to the strategy teachers use in assessing students' progress in academic curricula or materials. Through careful initial planning and regular monitoring, your token economy will be a success and will save you considerable time, compared to multiple, individual behavior management programs.

Here are some tips for making your token economy successful (Bicanich, 1986).

DO:

- include your students, whenever possible, in planning your token program
- deliver the reinforcement *only* as a consequence of the desired behavior
- let the student know why a reinforcer is being given
- give some free tokens at the beginning of your program
- gradually reduce tokens so that more work is done for each reinforcer

- review all rules frequently
- exchange tokens formally
- consider reinforcers that are controlled by the peer group
- change reinforcers whenever boredom sets in (If you become bored, your students have probably been bored for some time!)
- make the number of tokens needed consistent with the difficulty or effort required to perform the behavior
- keep reinforcers appropriate to your system's levels
- keep a record of tokens earned for everyone to see
- include behavior/reinforcers and response cost/fines on the same classroom poster but in separate columns
- combine praise with tokens so that social reinforcement can eventually be used alone
- gradually withdraw material reinforcers and let social reinforcement maintain the behaviors
- encourage students to compete with themselves to earn tokens as they improve their own behavior
- change the token system over the school year; target behaviors should change from September to June

DO NOT:

- use tokens that students can obtain outside your system
- give away the best reinforcers at the beginning; high-level reinforcers (the best ones) should cost more and be more appealing
- wait until you get to know your students before setting up your token economy; you will give the problem behaviors a chance to begin
- spend tokens for your students; let them choose for themselves
- let students stockpile tokens
- let students "go in the hole"

TIME-OUT FROM REINFORCEMENT

Time-out from reinforcement was introduced in Chapter 5. As you recall, this potentially

Table 6-4. Procedures for Use of Time-Out

1. Identify the situations that are reinforcing the child's inappropriate behavior.

2. Explicitly state those behaviors that will result in time-out before the contingency is implemented.

3. Attempt to control the inappropriate behavior through milder forms of time-out (ignoring, contingent observation, and exclusion time-out, respectively) prior to resorting to seclusionary time-out.

4. Provide documentation that milder forms of time-out have proved ineffective in suppressing the inappropriate behavior before resorting to seclusion time-out.

5. Avoid lengthy verbal explanations as to why the student is being placed in time-out. Behaviors resulting in time-out should be clearly explained prior to implementing the time-out program. If an explanation is provided, it should be brief but should adequately inform the student of the misbehavior involved. A standard explanation format such as, "Because you _____, you go to time-out for _____ minutes," is recommended. All other interaction should be avoided.

6. Identify those behaviors, if any, that will result in a warning before time-out is implemented. These generally are behaviors of low frequency and magnitude that have not previously been defined explicitly. (Other behavior normally will require no warning.)

7. To maximize opportunities to exercise self control, give students the opportunity to take their own time-out after receiving the instruction from the teacher. However, if students refuse to take their own time-out or if they fail to respond to the teacher's instruction within a reasonable time interval (five to ten seconds), the teacher should physically remove them to the time-out area. For high-intensity behavior (kicking, screaming), the student should be immediately escorted to time-out. It is important that teachers realistically evaluate their ability to physically remove a child to the time-out area. If a pupil is able to break away, requiring a teacher physically to remove the student would be inappropriate. Presumably, classrooms with such students would either have a teacher or teacher aide who could control such resistance. If such is not the case, an alternative strategy will be required. This may entail a reevaluation of the reinforcers in the classroom and the possible use of a response cost contingency in conjunction with a token economy. Other alternatives may include reinforcing other children for ignoring disruptive behaviors or reassigning of the uncontrollable student to a teacher who is capable of managing highly aggressive and resistant behavior.

---

powerful procedure takes away or reduces the reinforcers students might otherwise enjoy (Alberto & Troutman, 1982; Brantner & Doherty, 1983; Harris, 1985). Detention and in-school suspension, introduced earlier in this chapter, are school-wide interventions that build upon the concept of time-out from reinforcement. In a variation of the time-out ribbon procedure (discussed in Chapter 5), Salend and Gordon (1987) designed a group-oriented intervention to control the inappropriate verbalizations of a group of elementary-school resource-room students. The time-out ribbon was placed at the front of the classroom near the teacher's desk. As long as the group did not engage in the in-appropriate verbalizations, the ribbon remained up, and the students were reinforced through their token economy system. Whenever any student was verbally disruptive, however, the ribbon came down, and the group lost its token-earning privileges for one minute. One minute of "corrected" behavior reinstated both the ribbon and the privileges. This **group-contingency** procedure, in combination with the token economy, helped the students to decrease dramatically their problem behaviors. The teacher also reported that the students improved their academic performance. You might find this group intervention a bit more convenient than the individual time-out ribbon

Table 6-4. *continued*

8. Be sure that the duration of each time-out period is brief. One to five minutes generally is sufficient. It is doubtful that time-out periods exceeding fifteen minutes serve the purpose for which they are intended (temporary withholding of positive reinforcement).

9. Release from time-out should be contingent upon the student's behavior while in time-out. A contingency for release from time-out of one minute in which no inappropriate responses are emitted will avoid reinforcing a child's inappropriate behavior while in time-out. (Do *not* say, "Come out when you are ready.")

10. If a seclusion time-out is to be used, the time-out room should
    a. Be at least six by six feet in size.
    b. Be properly lighted (preferably recessed with the switch outside the room).
    c. Be properly ventilated.
    d. Be free of objects and fixtures with which children could harm themselves.
    e. Provide the means by which an adult could continuously monitor, visually and auditorily, the student's behavior.
    f. Not be locked. A latch on the door should be used only as needed, and only with careful monitoring.

11. Records should be kept of each occasion when time-out is implemented and should include the following information:
    a. The student's name.
    b. The episode resulting in student's placement in time-out (i.e., behavior, activity, other student involved, staff person).
    c. The time of day the student was placed in time-out.
    d. The time of day the student was released from time-out.
    e. The total time in time-out.
    f. The type of time-out (contingent observation, exclusion, or seclusion).
    g. The student's behavior in time-out.

12. Be sure that differential reinforcement of more appropriate social behavior always accompanies a time-out contingency.

Source: D. L. Gast & C. M. Nelson. Time-out in the classroom: Implications for special education. *Exceptional Children,* April 1977, 462–464.

if several students in your class are exhibiting disruptive behavior.

Serious forms of disruptive or aggressive behavior may require the use of seclusionary time-out (time-out room). Table 6-4 provides you with guidelines for the use of these time-out procedures. *Consult your supervisor before using seclusionary time-out; it is considered an aversive procedure by many school systems.* Whenever seclusionary time-out is used, each instance of time-out should be recorded. This is a requirement of most human rights committees (i.e., boards that oversee the use of unconventional behavior modification programs in schools and residential institutions).

Peer-Mediated Interventions

The entire class can be involved in changing a student's disruptive behavior or the disruptive behavior of the group in general. Behavior management interventions involving the entire class are explored in this section.

GROUP GOAL SETTING AND FEEDBACK

This intervention is based on a group discussion in which peers "vote" on a fellow student's behavior. Each student receives a behavioral goal. Either daily or twice a week, students meet in a highly structured twenty-minute group discussion to vote and give feedback under adult direction. Here are some target goals for your consideration:

• Rob will assist another student during recess.
• Mario will go from class to the library without getting a detention slip.
• Theresa will not swear during her morning classes.
• Alexa will stay awake in classes after lunch.
• Bruce will attend his last class.

The goals are very specific. You may wonder why they are not more ambitious; after all, would we not want Alexa awake all the time? Should Bruce attend all classes? Two rationales support these goals. First, the behavior may be specific to a particular class. Second, the goal should shape successive approximations. We will succeed in changing behavior if we break the goal into small, attainable target behaviors and reinforce students for mastering them.

Steps for directing group goal setting and feedback are outlined in Table 6-5.

PEER MONITORING

To give you an idea of the versatility of peer-mediated interventions — even with younger children — we now review a peer-monitoring procedure. Carden-Smith and Fowler (1984) taught kindergarten children to issue and withdraw points from their classmates. To introduce the strategy, a teacher-directed points program was begun. The eight children received or lost a point for obeying or disobeying each of these "rules": cleaning up after play, waiting appropriately, and going to and from the bathroom appropriately. After a few training sessions, the class was divided into two teams that changed membership each day. Each child on each team then earned (or lost) teacher-distributed points for the designated behaviors. In this system, the token exchange

was simple: children with three points each day could vote on and participate in play activities; children with two points could participate but not vote; children with one point were required to remain inside and complete clean-up chores.

The peer-mediated feature of the program built upon the introductory teacher-directed program. During the peer-intervention, the teacher appointed a team captain who issued and withdrew points from classmates. (The privilege of team captain was awarded students who had earned three points the previous day.) The program showed that even young children with learning and behavior problems could manage a basic token economy. Think about ways to "turn over" your token economy to the students in your classroom.

One way to incorporate the peer group into a token economy is to consider interactions and time with peers as privileges to be earned, not to be taken for granted. Too often, we allow students free access to their friends. Consider removing peer experiences from a student who misbehaves. For example, take away the privilege of changing classes with friends, and require the student to change classes alone.

GROUP CONTINGENCIES

The basic ingredient of a group contingency is group reinforcement. Litow and Pomroy (1975) described three types of group contingencies: dependent, independent, and interdependent.

In a **dependent group contingency** the peer performance of certain group members determines the consequence received by the entire group. This arrangement works best when the behavior of the large group is better than that of the target student or students (Hayes, 1976). This may not be the best plan for a group whose behavior is generally disruptive. To be sure that a group-oriented contin-

Table 6-5. Strategy for Conducting Group Goal Setting and Feedback

1. For each student in the group, develop a social behavior objective that is written in language the student can understand. Typical goals might be "To speak up in the class discussion times," "To share materials with others on the playground," "To play baseball without teasing my classmates," "To play with at least one other child at recess."

2. Write each student's name, goal, and the date on which the goal was announced on a separate sheet in the group notebook. Record the feedback of the student's peers each day during the group session.

3. Schedule a fifteen- to twenty-minute daily session for the group goalsetting and feedback session.

4. Ask everyone to sit in a circle for the group session. Instruct students that this is a time when everyone will speak and that no one is to speak out of turn. Explain further that each student has some behavior that warrants improvement and that the time will be spent talking about our behavior goals.

5. Explain to each student on the first day of the group goalsetting session what his or her goal is for the next week or two. It is recommended that individual goals be maintained for at least ten school days.

6. On subsequent days of the group goalsetting session, turn to the first student sitting next to you in the group, announce that student's goal, and state either "I think you made your goal today," or "I don't think you made your goal today." Then provide limited feedback in the form of a statement to support your evaluation. A typical evaluation statement might be, "I like the way you cooperated with Charlie on the playground," or "I don't like the way you took the baseball away from Jane."

7. Request that the student sitting next to the target individual now evaluate that individual's progress towards the goal. Reinforce eye contact with the target student and other constructive feedback. Be certain that each student in the group provides not only an evaluation but a feedback statement. Repeat this process until each student in the group has provided the target individual with an opinion and a feedback statement.

8. Tally the votes of making the goal or not making the goal and announce the result. If the student has made the goal, invite others in the group to give the student a handclap or other reinforcement you have chosen. If the student has not made the goal, there is no group response.

9. Repeat this process until all members of the group have received feedback on their goals.

10. If the group has developed a consistently productive performance, you may decide to allow one of the students to be the group leader. This student will then read each student's goals and request feedback from members of the group. These goals could still be teacher-assigned, or in the case of an advanced group, the goals could be self- or peer-assigned.

Source: From "PowWow: A Group Procedure for Reducing Classroom Behavior Problems" by M. M. Kerr and E. U. Ragland. *The Pointer*, 24, pp. 92-96. 1979. Reprinted with permission of the Helen Dwight Reid Educational Foundation. Published by Heldref Publications, 4000 Albemarle St., N.W., Washington, D.C. 20016. Copyright © 1986.

gency does not create negative peer pressure, follow these two rules: use a group reinforcement rather than a response cost, and be sure that the behavior target and criteria are within the students' reach. The primary characteristic of **independent group contingencies** is that the same consequence is applied to individual group members (Litow & Pomroy, 1975). Contingency contracting is an independent group contingency. In an **interdependent** **group contingency,** each student must reach a prescribed level of behavior before the entire group receives a consequence. Table 6-6 illustrates the three types of group contingencies. Pay special attention to each example.

One nice variation of a group contingency is the "Hero Procedure," in which one student earns reinforcers for the rest of the group. As one teacher described this intervention (Briand, personal communication, 1986):

Table 6-6. Group Contingency Arrangements

Type of Group Contingency	Examples
Interdependent	If each student meets his self-monitoring goal on Tuesday, the whole class can skip one homework.
	As soon as each student teaches his lab partner this week's vocabulary wordlist in earth science, we will launch our weather balloons.
	As soon as each student makes it through one home economics class without one reprimand for disruptive behavior, we will prepare lunch for the class and our guests (one per student).
Independent	Each student who finishes his homework on time during the allotted 15-minute homework drill time will receive a food coupon for a fast-food restaurant.
	Each student who meets her group goalsetting and feedback goal may have an extra gym period for the week she met her goal.
	Each student who goes for an entire English class without a reprimand will receive 5 extra grade points.
Dependent	If a student who returns to the regular classroom from the in-school suspension room has a good day (i.e., no warnings and classwork completed), all students will get to drop their lowest daily classwork grade. This recognizes the supportive role that classmates can play in a student's reentry.
	Three students in this class got detention last week for pushing in the class. If these three students do not get detention for two weeks, then the entire class will get popcorn during the Friday film.

Source: Reprinted with permission from Kerr, M. M., Nelson, C. M., & Lambert, D. L. (1987). *Helping adolescents with learning and behavior problems.* Columbus, Ohio: Merrill.

Not only does this procedure help to improve the target student's behavior, but it also stops other class members from reinforcing that behavior that you have deemed inappropriate — they want to get the reinforcers! With this type of procedure you will need to keep a sharp eye on peer interactions to keep class members from pressuring or bullying the target student. If you have set the initial contingency at a low level and made sure that the child can perform the desired behavior, your program should run fairly smoothly. To initiate this procedure, you should discuss the program with the target student first. The two of you should decide upon the goal or objective the child will be working toward, and tell him or her that you are thinking of having his classmates help him to reach that goal. Next you should explain that if he accomplishes the agreed upon task, the entire class will get a reward. Following this one-to-one discussion,

you should then meet with the class. The target student may or may not be present; it is up to your discretion. You should explain to the students what behavior is going to be worked on and why. They should be asked for their help by not encouraging the inappropriate behavior. You should then discuss the possible reinforcers the group can earn if the target student reaches his goal.

The **Good Behavior Game** is still another variation on a group contingency. This intervention involves teams of students competing on the basis of their behavior in the classroom (Barrish, Saunders, & Wolf, 1969; Saigh & Umar, 1983).

To help you understand how the Good Behavior Game works, Figure 6-10 is a consultant's description of the intervention for a group of "rowdy" sixth graders.

Our next section describes interventions in which the target student plays the major intervention role.

Self-Mediated Interventions

One of our goals with disruptive students is to promote self-control of their problem behaviors. In recent years, increasing attention has been focused on self-control procedures such as self-instruction and self-evaluation (Albion, 1983; Hallahan, Lloyd, & Stoller, 1982; Rueda, Rutherford, & Howell, 1980). In this section we focus on three procedures: self-recording, self-evaluation, and self-instruction. Use the Strategy Selection Checklist (Figure 6-14) to determine whether these procedures are suitable for your disruptive students.

Figure 6-10.   A Consultant's Description

October 2

Dear Mrs. Schaeffer,

I'm aware from our conversation that you are having a difficult time with your sixth graders. You told me that they can't seem to get to class on time, and that it takes them at least ten minutes to settle down.

I talked with you briefly about the possibility of trying out a game which requires team members to work toward a goal in order to win a reward. Here are some specifics about setting up this game:

1. It's been called the "Good Behavior Game," but your class can choose any name for it, e.g., PARTY!, PARTY POSSIBILITIES, etc.
2. If you have not yet established and posted conduct rules for your room, do so before you start the game.
3. To set up rules, talk with the students and allow them input. Suggest your own ideas and consider theirs. Agree upon a limited number of reasonable rules, and write them behaviorally in language the students understand. Examples:

   • Do not kick, hit, shove, or push other students.
   • Keep your hands and feet to yourself.
   • Raise your hand when you want to say something.
   • Talk when it's your turn.

   Set up contingencies (the relationships between behaviors and their consequences), and maintain consistent consequences when rules are broken.
4. Find out what might be powerful reinforcers for the students. Poll them, or offer them the possibility of free time for the last half of a Friday class each week. (I will use this as a sample reinforcer for the remainder of this program description.)
5. Divide the class into two teams.
6. Review rules and contingencies with the students.
7. State that 80% of each team's members will be required to reach or exceed this goal: to have at least one marker left out of three next to their names at the end of class each day. If 80% of a team reaches this goal, then team members will be rewarded with free time on Friday. The 80% criterion (as opposed to a higher percentage) is set to prevent the same one or two disruptive students from ruining a team's chances of winning free time. Unreasonably high criterion levels might lead to low morale and lack of motivation among team members. For students who have serious behavior problems, repeated failures to achieve the goal in a game where "all must achieve to receive" could lead to their being ridiculed, ostracized, or scapegoated. Prevent this by specifying a reasonable criterion, and by setting up individual problems and/or contingencies for the extremely disruptive students.

Fig. 6-10. *continued*

8. Explain to the students that the goal must be reached in one specified class period during the first week. During the second week, it must be achieved in two specified classes. Continue adding a period per week until you're at the point where the goal must be achieved during all periods the students are with you for instruction.

9. Hang a poster or use bulletin boards for each team, listing the members. At the beginning of each class, every student should have three markers next to his/her name. (For markers, use rock concert ticket stubs, small, laminated mock "record albums," or some other easily made or acquired items.)

10. Remove one marker from beside a student's name each time he/she breaks a rule, e.g., punches somebody, arrives late, etc.

11. At the end of the period, determine if 80% of each team's members have at least one marker next to their names. If 80% or more of one team achieved criterion, they win the privilege of receiving 20 minutes of free time during the last half of a Friday class. At this time, they will be free to go to the cafeteria for a "party." Enlist the aid of another staff member who can supervise the students as they talk, listen to radios or tape players, and drink cans of pop that they've brought or bought. The other team will be required to complete work in the classroom during the same period on Friday. If 80% of both teams achieve the goal, then all students will be awarded free "party" time.

12. Run the game for entire class periods. Even though most of this group's problems occur during the first 10 minutes, you don't want to operate it for 10 minutes and then leave 30 minutes open to possible disruptions. Set the rules and contingencies for the full 40 minutes. Self control will probably be hardest to demonstrate during the initial 10 minutes, but it may get easier once they get over that "hump" each day. And hopefully, it will increase throughout the course of the game.

13. Remember to provide lots of positive verbal reinforcement for both group and individual team improvements.

14. Again, severely disruptive students may be good candidates for individualized behavior management programs. You may want to consider what you'll do, though, when students occasionally lose all three markers in the same class. In order to prevent their getting completely out of control once they've broken three rules and lost all markers, perhaps you could arrange the following: If a student breaks four rules in one class period, he/she receives one day of detention. If he/she breaks five rules, he/she is assigned to two days of detention, etc.

Good luck with this game!

Mrs. Prisby

Source: Prisby, personal communication, 1987

Here are some tips to help you succeed with a self-management program (Albion, 1980):

1. Do display an optimistic attitude when explaining the program to students. You may benefit from the placebo effect!

2. Do encourage students to develop a visual image of the behaviors they are performing. This is called *imaginal training.*

3. Do use shaping of successive approximations when training students. In other words, teach and reinforce even small attempts to use the procedures.

4. Don't forget to use *fading* to reduce the number of teacher prompts and reinforcers to students after the program has been well under way and progress has been seen.

5. Do remember that self-instruction that includes statements of positive affect will be more productive than rote instructions.

6. Don't forget that you can use self-management with individuals or with a

classroom group. Do remember each student evaluates himself, not others.

7. Do see that students receive thorough training so they understand the procedures. The program is not a success unless it's used!

SELF-RECORDING

The first step in implementing a self-management program is to define the specific target behaviors. Consult the section on token economy programs for ideas about selecting appropriate target behaviors. Once you have selected an appropriate target behavior, decide how this behavior might be measured most easily by the student. Table 6-7 offers specific steps to follow in implementing a **self-recording** intervention for disruptive behavior.

One of your decisions in designing this intervention is to select a practical monitoring form. Figure 6-11 shows the monitoring form used by Keith, the student in this chapter's case study. Space is provided for tallies each day and period, although you might find that your student will at first need to monitor in only one or two periods a day. Printing the target behavior definition at the bottom of the form is a good idea; it helps the child remember what he is monitoring. For an older or more sophisticated student, the form could be modified.

Once you have trained a student to self-record, you can move to a behavior management program. During the first few days of the program (at least three days), ask the student to self-record disruptive behaviors without additional intervention. The data from these sessions will provide you with a baseline assessment of the student's performance. The next step in this program is to establish contingencies under which the student receives a reinforcer for reducing the number of disruptions per session. A student might use a contract form to record the reinforcement to be earned

Table 6-7. Guidelines for Training Students to Use Self-Monitoring

1. Identify target behaviors. Include behaviors to be increased as well as those to be decreased (e.g., on-task, off-task).

2. Discuss target behaviors with the student. Redefine target behaviors using the student's own words. For example, one teenager defined study behaviors as follows:
   On-task:
   —writing, or
   —reading, or
   —thinking about the content area.
   —conference with teacher, or other adult, about work.
   —charting data.
   Off-task:
   —anything else!

3. Select a practical way to measure the target behaviors.

4. Train the student to use the measurement system (e.g., to mark a three-by-five card with (/) marks for off-task behaviors) in the classroom. You may find it helpful to provide *external* monitoring (the teacher scores the student's performance and provides feedback) prior to moving to *self*-monitoring.

5. Once the student is self-recording behaviors, conduct an occasional reliability check to ensure that the evaluation was done accurately.

6. Provide reinforcement to students who reduce their disruptive behaviors. Consider using a response cost if disruptive behaviors continue above a designated level.

Note: The material for this table was taken from F. Albion. *Development and implementation of self-monitoring/self-instruction procedures in the classroom.* Paper presented at CEC's 58th Annual International Convention, Philadelphia, 1980.

Figure 6-11. Self-Monitoring Form

	Reading	Math	Language Arts	Science	Social Studies	Total
Monday	//		/	//	/	⑥
Tuesday	/	/	/		/	④
Wednesday	//		//		///	⑦
Thursday		/	///	/	//	⑦
Friday	/	/	///			⑤

I will put a tally mark in the box each time I get out of my seat without asking permission during class. I know I am out of my seat when my backside is not touching my chair and I have not asked permission to leave my seat.

Name: _Keith_   Date Begun: _2-22_   Teacher: _Covaleski_

by controlling problem behaviors. In still another approach, the student might self-reinforce without using tokens or contracts. For some students, self-recording alone may reduce disruptions.

Whether you use self-monitoring alone or as part of a larger behavior management system, encourage students to reduce disruptions and increase appropriate behavior relative to their own baseline performance. For example, a student whose baseline assessment indicates that he is off-task 80 percent of the period could be encouraged to improve his performance little by little until he reaches a mutually agreed-upon goal (e.g., on-task 80 percent of the period). By setting small but reasonable goals for students and gradually increasing expectations for their behavior, you help ensure that the self-monitoring program will be successful. This strategy is referred to as shaping of successive approximations (see Chapter 5).

SELF-EVALUATION

Self-evaluation requires a student to assess the quality of his behavior, unlike self-monitoring

in which the student simply counts his behavior. Rhode, Morgan, and Young (1983) conducted a study of self-evaluation in a resource room with behaviorally handicapped students from the first through the fifth grades. In this case, self-evaluation was used to facilitate the reentry of the students to regular education. The self-evaluation consisted of students' rating themselves on a 0-5 scale identical to the scale on which their mainstream teachers were rating them. Here are the criteria for the ratings:

5 = *excellent* — Followed all classroom rules entire interval; work 100% correct.

4 = *very good* — Minor infraction of rules (i.e., talk-out or out-of-seat occurrences), but followed rules rest of interval; worked almost entire interval; work at least 90% correct.

3 = *average* — Did not follow all rules for the entire time, but no serious offenses. Followed rules approximately 80% of the time (i.e., inappropriate behavior may have involved talking-out or out-of-seat occurrences).

2 = *below average* — Broke one or more rules to extent that behavior was not acceptable (e.g., aggressive, noisy, talking) but

followed rules part of the time. Work approximately 60 to 80% correct.

1 = *poor* — Broke one or more rules almost entire period or engaged in higher degree of inappropriate behavior most of the time. Work between 0 and 60% accurate.

0 = *totally unacceptable* — Broke one or more rules entire interval. Did not work at all or work all incorrect. (p. 174)

To facilitate reliability of ratings between the students and their teachers, student ratings were compared with teacher ratings. Initially, all students were checked for matched ratings; gradually, the checks were done on fewer and fewer students by "drawing names" to see which subgroup of students would be checked. Ultimately the matching was eliminated altogether.

Ratings directly corresponded with the points that each student could receive; points could be exchanged for reinforcers. We encourage you to consider a self-evaluation intervention for your mainstreamed students. In this case, even a six-year-old was successful in using the self-mediated intervention!

An interesting twist on self-management interventions is to train students to modify teacher behavior (e.g., praise). Hrydowy, Stokes, and Martin (1984) developed an intervention to teach fourth graders to elicit praise from their teacher when they completed a language arts or social studies assignment. A consultant worked with the children to train them how to (1) evaluate their written worksheet, (2) quietly and accurately correct their errors, and (3) cue the adult that they had finished their assignment. Cues suggested by the children were varied, and students were urged not to repeat cues to the teacher. A role-play training procedure combined with feedback and reinforcement from the consultant was successful in teaching the fourth graders these skills. Morever, these trained skills generalized spontaneously to the regular classroom setting in which the students effectively increased the praise they received from the teacher.

Table 6-8. Guidelines for Training Students to Use Self-Instruction

---

1. Analyze the task for the student, listing necessary steps. For example, the task might involve specific steps such as reading the problem, writing out the necessary information, and performing the operations. Or the task might be more generic, requiring steps such as getting out pencil and paper, opening the text to the correct page, not talking to others, signalling when help is needed.

   Consider including specific questions about task demands, planning statements, self-guiding instructions, coping statements for errors, and self-praise statements.

2. With help from the student, rewrite the steps in the student's conversational style. For example, one primary school student developed these self-instructions:

   "Okay, in order to be a good student I need to stay in my seat, not bother others, and complete my assignment. I have to take my time and do the work the way Mrs. Smith showed me. Good, I did it. Right on!"

3. Practice the self-instruction procedure with the student. Begin by saying the words together aloud. Then whisper as the student self-instructs aloud. Finally, have the student whisper alone.

4. Provide the student with the opportunity to use the self-instructions in the classroom. If possible, allow the student to whisper quietly, as this may be more effective (and easier to monitor!) than covert, or silent, rehearsal.

Note: The material for this table was taken from F. Albion. *Development and implementation of self-monitoring/self-instruction procedures in the classroom.* Paper presented at CEC's 58th Annual International Convention, Philadelphia, 1980.

SELF-INSTRUCTION

In a self-instruction program, the student is trained to whisper statements that will help accomplish the task. Table 6–8 provides guidelines for using a self-instruction procedure. Be sure to analyze the self-instructional task before attempting to use this procedure with a student.

Summary

This chapter offers you many suggestions for managing or preventing disruptive behavior.

School-wide strategies include detention and in-school suspension. In these, as in all approaches, we urge close communication among staff and with families. Our teacher-mediated strategies include the ever-popular token economy—an outstanding way to set up classroom-wide contingencies. To enhance your overall contingency management, we encourage you to plan group contingencies. Finally, the self-management strategies promote generalization of new behaviors to other settings. Our case study illustrates self-monitoring for a disruptive third grader, Keith.

Using Self-Monitoring and Home-Based Contracting to Reduce Disruptive Behaviors

Nancy Prisby

Keith, a third grade student, constantly got out of his seat. Although he sat down if verbally reprimanded by the teacher, he was typically out of his chair again within minutes. Keith was aware that his behavior was disruptive to his teacher and classmates. He understood that he was expected to sit in his seat, yet he seemed incapable of demonstrating the self-control necessary for remaining seated for extended periods of time.

A self-management program was initiated with Keith. Through instructions and demonstrations, he was taught to self-record his out-of-seat behaviors. He took baseline data for three days and then continued to self-record during a management program that involved a contingency contract.

Motivating reinforcers were provided by Keith's classroom teacher and parents, who also verbally praised him for accomplishments.

A classroom chart reflected achievement of daily goals, and home-based reports informed his parents that weekly goals had been met. A "hero procedure" was instituted, allowing Keith the privilege of rewarding his classmates with a treat provided by his teacher contingent upon his achieving five daily goals. This was intended to elicit positive peer support/reinforcement for Keith. At first, Keith received positive, external reinforcement. Our ultimate goal, however, was for Keith to identify his out-of-seat behaviors as disruptive and undesirable through the daily, visual tracking procedure. Moreover, we hoped that the challenge of trying to "beat" his last lowest score would motivate Keith to participate fully in this intervention to increase his in-seat behavior. Figure 6–12 is the letter I sent to Mrs. Covaleski, Keith's teacher, to explain the intervention.

Figure 6-12. Letter to Mrs. Covaleski

January 31

Dear Mrs. Covaleski,

This letter is a follow-up to our conversation concerning Keith's constant out-of-seat behavior. Because you told me that Keith seems to recognize his behavior as being disruptive to you and the other students, I suggested the possibility of using a self-management procedure to help him identify when and how often he gets out of his chair. In turn, this intervention might result in motivating him to improve his score each day.

Keith's parents have agreed to provide the reinforcing activities we discussed during our first meeting. Each of the privileges would be contingent upon his achieving a weekly goal. You have also agreed to provide a treat for the class each time Keith reaches five daily goals. This type of "hero procedure" might foster peer support and encouragement for Keith.

Follow these guidelines and use the attached form [Figure 6-13] in instituting Keith's self-management program:

1. Explain the self-monitoring form [Figure 6-11] to Keith and demonstrate the self-recording procedure for him. The form is an event record or tally sheet, and it is used to count occurrences of a behavior.
2. Have him tally along with you for a day or two, comparing totals. When his numbers match yours within plus-or-minus five behaviors, instruct him to take baseline for three days. You may chart along with him and provide verbal praise for accurate recording, but don't use any of the reinforcers. Use his lowest score as the first goal in his behavior management program.
3. Instruct Keith to self-record his out-of-seat behavior during five academic classes: reading, math, language arts, science, and social studies.
4. Show him the classroom chart and explain that he will receive a sticker each day his daily total number of out-of-seat behaviors is lower than his last lowest score. Hang this chart in the room.
5. Explain that when he achieves five stickers, he'll receive the opportunity to pass out a treat (that you'll provide) to the class.
6. Verbally praise Keith's daily accomplishments, including (1) decreases in out-of-seat behaviors, and (2) accuracy in recording them. Challenge him daily to "beat" his last lowest score.
7. Measure Keith's behaviors along with him some days (without him knowing) and check for accuracy. Stipulate that if you record five or more total behaviors over what he does on any given day, he will lose the opportunity to get a sticker that day. Stress the importance of counting his behaviors accurately—each time they occur.
8. Review the contingency contract we developed during the initial meeting [Figure 6-13]. Obtain signatures from Keith and his parents, and provide them with a copy. Remember to invite Keith and his parents for a review conference any time the contract is due to be revised (for example, when there is need for a change in criteria, reinforcement, etc.). Hold conferences over the phone if Keith's parents cannot come in to school.
9. If you note a decrease in out-of-seat behaviors by the second week, continue operating the program for one month. At that point, we will meet to discuss its results and possible adjustments. Contact me sooner if it does not seem to be working.

Good luck to all of you! Contact me at any time if you have questions or comments.

Mrs. Prisby

Figure 6-13.   Contingency Contract for Keith

I, Keith, will try to spend more time sitting in my seat. For the next month, I will count the number of times I get out of my chair without asking or without being told.

Each day that my total number is lower than my last lowest score, I'll get a sticker for my chart. When I get 5 stickers, I'll be allowed to pass out a treat to the class from me and my teacher. (My teacher will provide the treat.)

If I get 5 stickers in <u>one</u> week, I'll take home a report to my parents and they will let me invite a friend to go:
① bowling, or ② to a movie, or
③ to the park over the weekend.

Some days, my teacher may also keep count of how many times I get out my seat. If her number is bigger than mine by 5 or more, I won't be able to win a sticker for the day. I will try to keep track of <u>every</u> time I get out of my chair.

This contract is good for 1 month. Each of us understands our responsibilities listed in it.

Signed: Date:

(Keith)_____   (parent)_____

(teacher)_____   (parent)_____

Figure 6-14. Strategy Selection Chart for Disruptive Behaviors (pp. 207–208)

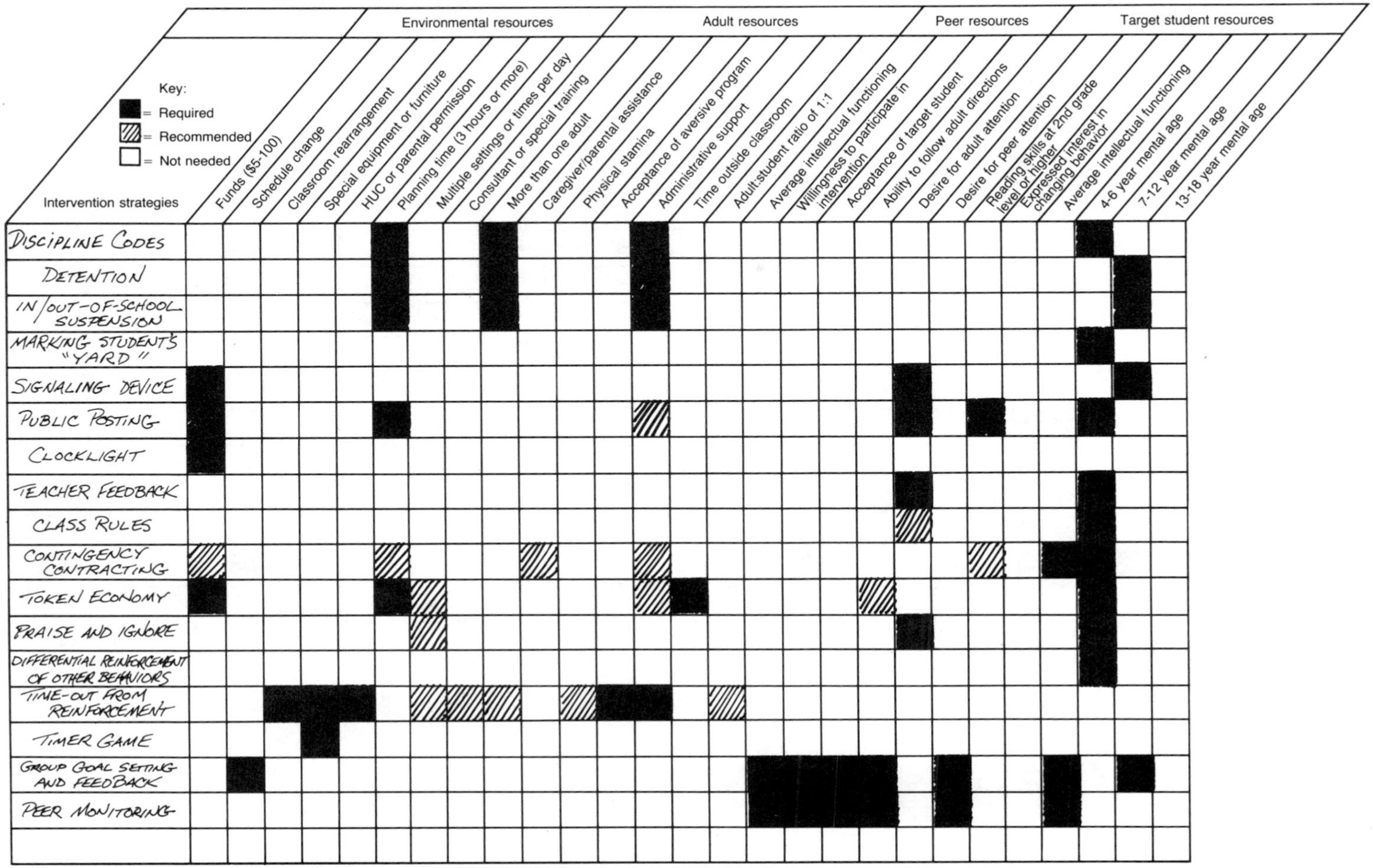

Figure 6-14. *Continued*

Key:
■ = Required
▨ = Recommended
□ = Not needed

	Environmental resources							Adult resources								Peer resources				Target student resources							
Intervention strategies	Funds ($5-100)	Schedule change	Classroom rearrangement	Special equipment or furniture	HUC or parental permission	Planning time (3 hours or more)	Multiple settings or times per day	Consultant or special training	More than one adult	Caregiver/parental assistance	Physical stamina	Acceptance of aversive program	Administrative support	Time outside classroom	Adult:student ratio of 1:1	Average intellectual functioning	Willingness to participate in intervention	Acceptance of target student	Ability to follow adult directions	Desire for adult attention	Desire for peer attention	Reading skills at 2nd grade level or higher	Expressed interest in changing behavior	Average intellectual functioning	4-6 year mental age	7-12 year mental age	13-18 year mental age
GROUP CONTINGENCY																					■		▨		■		
GOOD BEHAVIOR GAME		■														▨	■		■	▨	▨			■		■	
SELF-RECORDING																			■			▨	■	▨			
SELF-EVALUATION																			■			▨	■	▨			
SELF-INSTRUCTION																			■			▨	■	▨			
STUDENT PROMPTING OF TEACHER PRAISE																				■			■	■			

Discussion Questions

1. Which strategies are preferable for younger students? Older students?
2. When are peer-mediated strategies preferable to teacher-mediated approaches?
3. How can several strategies be combined to reduce disruptive behaviors?
4. What are some possible mistakes one might make in implementing a token economy?
5. For what disruptive behaviors is self-monitoring a good choice?
6. What is the importance of levels within a token economy?
7. Describe the hierarchy of time-out from reinforcement strategies.
8. How can parents be involved in interventions for disruptive behavior?
9. What can a teacher do to *prevent* disruptive behaviors?
10. Give three examples of ways we measure disruptive behaviors.

References

Adams, G. L. (1984). An inexpensive wireless, remote-controlled clocklight. *Education and Treatment of Children, 7*(1), 75-79.

Alberto, P. A., & Troutman, A. C. (1986). *Applied behavior analysis for teachers: Influencing Student Performance* (2nd ed.). Columbus, OH: Merrill.

Albion, F. M. (1980). *Development and implementation of self-monitoring/self-instruction procedures in the classroom.* Paper presented at CEC's 58th Annual International Convention, Philadelphia.

Albion, F. M. (1983). A methodological analysis of self-control in applied settings. *Behavioral Disorders, 8*(2), 87-102.

Allen, L. D., Gottselig, M., & Boylan, S. (1982). A practical mechanism for using free time as a reinforcer in classrooms. *Education and Treatment of Children, 5*(4), 347-353.

Barrish, H. H., Saunders, M., & Wolf, M. M. (1969). Good behavior game: Effects of individual contingencies for group consequences on disruptive behavior in a classroom. *Journal of Applied Behavior Analysis, 2,* 119-124.

Bauer, A. M., Shea, T. M., & Keppler, R. (1986). Levels systems: A framework for the individualization of behavior management. *Behavioral Disorders, 12*(1), 28-35.

Bicanich, P. (1986). *So you want to try a token economy.* Unpublished manuscript, University of Pittsburgh.

Brantner, J. P., & Doherty, M. A. (1983). A review of timeout: A conceptual and methodological analysis. In S. Axelrod & J. Apsche (Eds.), *The effects of punishment on human behavior* (pp. 87-132). New York: Academic.

Broden, M., Hall, R. B., Dunlap, A., & Clark, R. (1970). Effects of teacher attention and a token reinforcement system in a junior high special education class. *Exceptional Children, 36,* 341-349.

Carden-Smith, L. K., & Fowler, S. A. (1984). Positive peer pressure: The effects of peer monitoring on children's disruptive behavior. *Journal of Applied Behavior Analysis, 17*(2), 213-227.

Dietz, S. M., & Repp, A. C. (1973). Decreasing classroom misbehavior through the use of DRL schedules of reinforcement. *Journal of Applied Behavior Analysis, 6,* 457-464.

Epstein, M. H., Repp, A. C., & Cullinan, D. (1978). Decreasing obscene language of behaviorally disordered children through the use of a DRL schedule. *Psychology in the schools, 15,* 419-423.

Gast, D. L., & Nelson, C. M. (1977). Time out in the classroom: Implications for special education. *Exceptional Children, 44,* 461-464.

Gilliland, H. (1974). *A practical guide to remedial reading.* Columbus, OH: Merrill.

Greenwood, C. R., Hops, H., Delquadri, J., & Walker, H. M. (1977). *Program for academic survival skills (PASS): Manual for consultants.* Eugene, OR: Center at Oregon for Research in the Behavioral Education of the Handicapped, University of Oregon.

Hallahan, D. P., Lloyd, J. W., & Stoller, L. (1982). *Improving attention with self-monitoring: A manual for teachers.* Charlottesville, VA: University of Virginia Learning Disabilities Research Institute.

Harris, K. (1985). Definitional, parametric, and procedural considerations in timeout interventions and research. *Exceptional Children, 51,* 279-288.

Haubrich, P. A., & Shores, R. E. (1976). Attending behavior and academic performance of emotionally disturbed children. *Exceptional Children, 42,* 337-338.

Hayes, L. A. (1976). The use of group contingencies for behavioral control: A review. *Psychological Bulletin, 83,* 628-648.

Homme, L. (1970). *How to use contingency contracting in the classroom.* Champaign, IL: Research Press.

Hrydowy, E. R., Stokes, T. F., & Martin, G. L. (1984). Training elementary students to prompt teacher praise. *Education and Treatment of Children, 7*(2), 99-108.

Huguenin, N. H., & Mulick, J. A. (1981). Nonexclusionary timeout: Maintenance of appropriate behavior across settings. *Applied Research in Mental Retardation, 2,* 55-67.

Jones, D. B., & Van Houten, R. (1985). The use of daily quizzes and public posting to decrease the disruptive behavior of secondary school students. *Education and Treatment of Children, 8*(2), 91-106.

Kerr, M. M. (1986). *Report on adult interviews: Arsenal Middle School.* Unpublished manuscript, University of Pittsburgh.

Kerr, M. M., Nelson, C. M., & Lambert, D. L. (1987). *Helping adolescents with learning and behavior problems.* Columbus, OH: Merrill.

Kerr, M. M., & Ragland, E. U. (1979). Pow wow: A group procedure for reducing classroom behavior problems. *The Pointer, 24,* 92-96.

Kubany, E. S., & Slogett, B. B. (1973). Cod-

ing procedure for teachers. *Journal of Applied Behavior Analysis, 6,* 339-344.

Litow, L., & Pomroy, D. K. (1975). A brief review of classroom group-oriented contingencies. *Journal of Applied Behavior Analysis, 8,* 341-347.

McLaughlin, T. F., & Malaby, J. E. (1972). Intrinsic reinforcers in a classroom token economy. *Journal of Applied Behavior Analysis, 5,* 263-270.

Muller, A. J., Hasazi, S. E., Pierce, M. M., & Hasazi, J. E. (1975). Modification of disruptive behavior in a large group of elementary school students. In E. Ramp & G. Semb (Eds.), *Behavior analysis: Areas of research and application.* Englewood Cliffs, NJ: Prentice-Hall, 269-308.

O'Leary, K. D., Kaufman, K. F., Kass, R. E., & Drabman, R. S. (1970). The effects of loud and soft reprimands on the behavior of disruptive students. *Exceptional Children, 37,* 145-155.

Porterfield, J. K., Herbert-Jackson, E., & Risley, T. R. (1976). Contingent observation: An effective and acceptable procedure for reducing disruptive behavior of young children in a group setting. *Journal of Applied Behavior Analysis, 9,* 55-64.

Rhode, G., Morgan, D. P., & Young, K. R. (1983). Generalization and maintenance of treatment gains of behaviorally handicapped students from resource rooms to regular classrooms using self-evaluation procedures. *Journal of Applied Behavior Analysis, 16*(2), 171-188.,

Rosenberg, M. S. (1986). Maximizing the effectiveness of structured classroom management programs: Implementing rule-review procedures with disruptive and distractible students. *Behavioral Disorders, 11*(4), 239-247.

Rueda, R., Rutherford, R. B., & Howell, K. W. (1980). Review of self-control research with behaviorally disordered and mentally retarded children. In R. B. Rutherford, A. G. Priesto, & J. E. McGlothlin

(Eds.), *Severe behavior disorders of children and youth* (Vol. 3, pp. 188-197). Reston, VA: Council for Exceptional Children.

Saigh, P. A., & Umar, A. M. (1983). The effects of a good behavior game on the disruptive behavior of Sudanese elementary school students. *Journal of Applied Behavior Analysis, 16*(3), 339-344.

Salend, S. J., & Gordon, B. D. (1987). A group-oriented timeout ribbon procedure. *Behavioral Disorders, 12*(2), 131-137.

Salend, S. J., & Maragulia, D. M. (1983). The timeout ribbon: A procedure for the least restrictive environment. *Journal for Special Educators, 20*, 9-15.

Shores, R. E., & Haubrich, P. A. (1969). Effects of cubicles in educating emotionally disturbed children. *Exceptional Children, 36*, 21-24.

Staub, R. W. (1987). *The effects of publicly posted feedback on middle school students'*

disruptive hallway behavior. Unpublished doctoral dissertation, University of Pittsburgh.

Trice, A. D., & Parker, F. C. (1983). Decreasing adolescent swearing in an instructional setting. *Education and Treatment of Children, 6*, 29-35.

Van Houten, R., Nau, P. A., MacKenzie-Keating, S. E., Sameoto, D., & Colavecchia, B. (1982). An analysis of some variables influencing the effectiveness of reprimands. *Journal of Applied Behavior Analysis, 15*, 65-83.

Worell, J., & Nelson, C. M. (1974). *Managing instructional problems: A case study workbook.* New York: McGraw-Hill.

Zwald, L., & Gresham, F. (1982). Behavioral consultation in a secondary class: Using DRL to decrease negative verbal interactions. *The School Psychology Review, 11*(4), 428-432.

Aggressive Behaviors

Chapter 7

OUTLINE

Functional Analysis of Aggressive Behavior

Prevention Strategies

Environmental Modification Strategies

Teacher-Mediated Strategies

Peer-Mediated Strategies

Self-Mediated Strategies

Case Studies

OBJECTIVES

After completing this chapter, the reader should be able to

- Define verbal and nonverbal aggression.
- Offer four reasons children engage in aggressive behavior.
- Conduct a functional analysis of aggression.
- Name four ways to prevent aggression in the classroom.
- Implement three interventions for aggression.

This chapter focuses on behaviors classified under the general category of *aggression,* a concept that has evaded precise description despite years of research. As noted by Parke and Slaby (1983, p. 459), "an objective and unambiguous definition of aggression has yet to be satisfactorily formulated, despite numerous attempts." Aggression was defined as "the inflicting of harm, injury, or discomfort on persons, or damage to property" by the Surgeon General's Scientific Advisory Committee on Television and Social Behavior (1972, p. 9). This definition differs from that of Dollard, Dobb, Miller, Mowrer, and Sears (1939), who considered aggressive behavior to be *any* act that results in injury. Others have placed less emphasis on the consequences of aggressive behavior, preferring a definition such as "presentation of a painful stimulus" (Knutson, 1973, p. 262). Still others have cited the futility of trying to describe a general phenomenon such as aggression and have taken the position that specific behavioral descriptions should replace the general term, *aggression.*

The difficulties in reaching a universally accepted definition create a dilemma for teachers and counselors who need to describe and assess aggressive behaviors prior to intervention. To assist you, we provide illustrations of behaviors considered aggressive, although we recognize that these behaviors are subject to multiple interpretations depending on the setting and circumstances in which they occur. You will undoubtedly note here the inclusion of behaviors that may be suitable for another chapter of this book; moreover, the assessment and intervention procedures described may be used with behaviors that are not considered aggressive. To illustrate this overlap of behavioral categories, Patterson and Cobb (1973) stated:

> It seemed to us that if classes of aggressive-like responses existed, they would be comprised in large part of some combination of these thirteen responses. . . Command Negative, Dependency, Destructive, Disapproval, High Rate (hyperactive), Humiliate, Ignore, Negativism, Noncomply, Physical Negative, Tease, Whine, and Yell. (pp. 164-165)

You *can* get ideas for target behavior descriptions as you examine the research definitions in Table 7-1.

Functional Analysis of Aggressive Behavior

To prevent aggression, you must first understand the factors that influence or set the occasion for aggressive behavior. More precisely, one must discern the following (Caprara & Kerr, 1985):

- The influences of peers and adults in eliciting, modeling, and reinforcing aggression
- The influence of groups of norms in regulating aggression
- The consequences of aggression in terms of social acceptance or rejection
- Other responses more or less incompatible with aggression that would reach the goal or solve the problem for which aggression is used (p. 20)

This section tells how to analyze aspects of a student's aggressive behavior. Some of the direct observational and interview strategies you learned in Chapters 2 and 3 will help you. One of the first tools you can use is Antecedent-Response-Consequence (A-R-C) Analysis.

Because many aggressive acts take place suddenly and without warning, you are prevented from recording antecedent and consequent events in a systematic fashion. To treat this problem, we have developed an "after-the-fact" A-R-C checklist for recalling aggressive incidents, as shown in Figure 7-1. To use this form, describe the aggressive or destructive behavior in the far left-hand column, using as many specific terms as possible. Second, write the date and time (beginning and end) of the aggressive incident, if known. Next, describe the location and name all other participants or observers. State whether the aggression was directed toward property or persons or both and whether there was any personal injury or property damage. Then describe as accurately as possible what happened before and after the aggression. Note whether you directly observed the behavior or received the report of it. Finally, add any comments considered helpful in predicting future aggressive events.

Persons involved should fill out this form *independently;* they may have a tendency to "color" each other's account of what actually took place. Remember, you need the most objective retelling of the situation possible. Also, try to capture each person's recollection as soon after each incident as possible. By comparing facts and independent impressions, you may form useful hypotheses about the antecedents ("triggers") to a student's aggression. For example, you may notice that a student is aggressive toward younger children or only during unsupervised transitional activities. The checklist form may also reveal that aggressive behaviors are inadvertently reinforced or otherwise consistently rewarded by the actions of others. For example, a student cursed aloud to his easily embarrassed teacher because it resulted in expulsion from history, his most difficult subject. Can you detect any clues in Figure 7-1 that might explain Helen's actions?

The goal of the after-the-fact Antecedent-Response-Consequence Form is to *detect patterns in the aggression so that you and others can "see it coming" in the future.* Only through

Table 7-1. Definitions of Aggressive Behaviors

Behavior	Definition	Author(s)
Aggression	Striking, slapping, tripping, kicking, pushing, or pulling others; "karate" moves ending within one foot of another person; doing anything that ends with another child falling to the ground	Murphy, Hutchinson, & Bailey (1983)
Property abuse	Taking another person's property without permission; throwing school books, lunches, or anyone else's property; throwing any object at passing or parked cars; digging holes in the ground with one's feet or hands; breaking pencils or pens	Murphy, Hutchinson, & Bailey (1983)
Nonverbal	The person destroys, damages, or attempts to damage any (nonhuman) object; the damage need not actually occur, but the potential for damage must exist. A subject physically attacks or attempts to attack another person with sufficient intensity to potentially inflict pain. Teasing another person in such a way that the other person is likely to show displeasure and disapproval or when the person being teased is trying to do some other behavior, but is unable to because of the teasing.	Patterson, G. R. (1977)

this kind of prediction (and subsequent prevention strategies) can aggression be avoided. Remember: adults and peers will respond much more effectively to aggression in the classroom if they can feel more in control of the situation. To gain this control, however, they must be able to predict and plan for the aggression *before* it occurs. In other words, we want others in the environment to *act, not react.*

In attempting to reduce antisocial and aggressive behaviors, it is imperative that you consider thoughtfully the question, "When do I intervene?" We are often asked how teachers should deal with students who are out of control. We want to emphasize that *the best time to deal with aggressive behaviors is before, not after, the aggression takes place.* Physical restraint should be a last resort, when all other attempts at systematic programming have failed. Moreover, your attention should focus primarily on identifying and modifying behaviors that immediately *precede* acts of aggression, destruction, or theft. For example, the preferred time to intervene with a student who initiates

fights is not *after* the fight has begun but when that student first teases or picks the fight. Students who cannot express themselves verbally will not tease, but they may give a nonverbal indication of imminent trouble. Look again at Figure 7-1, and note that one column is devoted entirely to antecedent events. As you use the information in this column, remember that antecedents may be good target behaviors on which to intervene (teasing remarks, initial physical contact with another student, subvocal utterances, facial flush, movement of an arm to a fighting position).

As another consideration for managing aggression, think of the three functional explanations for this behavior. First, *the aggressive behavior may be under inappropriate stimulus control.* We know that certain forms of hurtful behavior are deemed appropriate under specific conditions (e.g., in self-defense, with mutual consent, for protection of others), but the student with a problem exhibits these hurtful behaviors in situations that *do not* warrant aggression. Consider a preschooler who has just

Figure 7-1. Checklist for Assessing Aggressive Behaviors

<u>Directions:</u> Complete this checklist for each <u>aggressive</u> behavior the student has exhibited.

Person Completing Form: _Mrs. Blonge_   Student: _Helen A._   Date: _November 6_

Description of the behavior	When did this behavior most recently occur?	Where did this behavior take place?	Who else was in the setting?	Was the aggression directed towards anyone, or towards property? Whom? What?	What was going on immediately (15 min.) before the aggressive behavior?	What happened immediately (15 min.) after the aggressive behavior?	Did you directly observe the behavior?	Comments: (Describe anything that was unusual about the schedule, setting, or student when the event took place, or anything you think would be helpful to consider.)
Came into room, threw book on desk, refused to open it.	Yesterday	Regular Reading Class	Other students (entire class)	More towards teacher	Was in art and came down the hall to reading class.	I told her again to open that book.	Yes	She seems to come to class already mad or upset.
Threw book on floor						Told her to pick it up.		
"Sassed" me						Told her to leave room.		
Refused to leave						Took her hand to lead her.		
Resisted, was verbally abusive, then hit me.						Buzzed the principal's office		

discovered the joy of rough and tumble play but attempts to play roughly with all playmates, willing or not. Or consider a seventh grader who has been taught to defend himself on the street but deals similarly with teachers. As Kozloff (1973) summarized in a textbook for parents:

> Before you decide which method to use to replace a target problem behavior . . . you must take *baseline* counts . . . [to] give you some clues as to the right [intervention] method to use. For example, *if the behavior happens only once in a while, there may be some special signal that starts it. So, you may be able to decrease the behavior by making sure that the signal does not happen. Or, you may teach the child something else to do when the signal happens.* (p. 388)

A second explanation for aggression, following a social learning theory approach, is that *the student's behavior has been, and continues to be, reinforced.* Reinforcement may take many forms. For example, a student may act tough because of reinforcement by the reactions of others (e.g., fear, avoidance, pain, surprise). We have often observed students whose aggressive behaviors controlled adults. By creating a crisis climate, these students stop all usual routines, gain abundant attention from peers, and essentially overwhelm the adults in authority. Throwing work materials at the teacher may serve this purpose for a student who wants to terminate a lesson. Aggressive behavior may be reinforced if, as in this example, it provides the student with a way of avoiding an unpleasant situation. When you suspect that aggressive behavior is being reinforced in one of these ways, consider changing the contingencies of reinforcement for those aggressive acts.

Aggressive behavior, to consider a third explanation, *may be imitated behavior,* particularly if a student is a member of a culture that places value on aggression and toughness. It has been suggested that students imitate aggressive behavior they observe on television

programs (see Nelson & Polsgrove, 1981). Aggression may be modeled and encouraged within a student's family, as illustrated by the mother of an aggressive teenager:

> They tell me at school that he is beating up on other kids. Well, I raised my kids to defend themselves . . . not to take anything off anyone. Just like when they try to hit me, I haul off and hit them back. It's the only way they'll ever learn. I don't raise any sissies.

In their behavioral analysis of a high crime community, Aiken, Stumphauzer, and Veloz (1977) found that nondelinquents had role models within their families who refused to support delinquent behavior. On the other hand, many delinquents were members of gangs and families that supported their illegal activities.

Thus, before intervening to correct aggressive behavior, try to answer the question, "What function does aggression serve for this student?" Then target a behavior that can be reasonably addressed, not an out-of-control behavior. Finally, select a suitable intervention, taking into account the following general guidelines:

1. *Do* conduct a thorough behavioral analysis before intervening.
2. *Do not* overextend your role—you may *not* be able to control all aggressive behaviors, but you *can* work on teaching social skills.
3. *Do* intervene as early as possible — *do not* wait until a student "blows."
4. *Do not* remove the aggressive student from his natural setting (school, vocational workshop) for intervention unless this is absolutely necessary (e.g., for legal reasons).
5. *Do* involve others (peers and adults) in the intervention effort.
6. *Do not* forget to monitor your own intervention program as well as the student's behavior.

Figure 7-2 presents an interview for aggressive behavior. As you consider the behavior

Figure 7-2. Interview for Aggressive Behavior

Interviewer: _Williams_   Interviewee: _Mrs. Blouze_

Date: _Nov. 7_   School: _Rockville_   Child: _Helen A._

1. First, can you describe exactly what this student does when s/he is aggressive?

    Throws books, sasses me, refuses to comply, hits me.

2. Has the student ever hurt anyone?

    Yes, she has hit me and other kids.

3. Is the student receiving any outside services at this time (e.g., mental health, medical, counseling, vocational, recreational)?

    _No._

    Where?

4. Has the student ever received any services in the past?

    Yes.

    Where?

    Community Mental Health Clinic, last summer.

5. Do you have a release of information so that we can contact those agencies?

    Yes.

    Can you get one?

6. Are the parents aware of these aggressive behaviors?

    Yes.

    How do you know?

    Mother has reported aggression at home.

7. I'd like to look at the causes for this aggression now. Let's begin with the possibility that others at school may inadvertently be encouraging the behavior. Tell me what you do when the aggression occurs.

    I tell her to calm down and physically stop her from hitting.

    I see. Can you tell me what the other adults in the building do?

    The principal paddles her, but it doesn't help.

    Do you have any idea how the student perceives these adult reactions?

    She seems to get more upset.

    What do the other children do?

    They look scared and come to me for help. Some older ones taunt her.

Figure 7-2. *Continued*

8. Now let's look at another possible cause for aggression. What would you say are the norms for aggression in this school? Is *any* aggression allowed?

No. The principal is very strict.

How about this student's peer group—what are their norms for aggression?

A few older kids seem to approve of fighting.

And the parental norms?

Her father has told her to fight back when others bother her.

9. Would you say this child is popular in the peer group?

Not really.

Is the child rejected by peers?

Yes, most in this class avoid her.

10. What alternatives does this student have to aggression in these circumstances?
Property or territory disputes:

By her age she should be able to share. She doesn't seem to know how.

Exclusion:

She does this to any kid who comes near her at play. She seems to know no alternative.

Precedence:

She can't take turns, although I tell her to.

Ordering about:

She usually bosses kids around – no alternatives.

Organization ordering:

This isn't a problem.

Criticism:

She doesn't usually do this in class.

Harrassment of others:

She does this a lot, just to be mean. She could try being nicer.

Game hostility:

She's never asked into games.

Defending him(her)self:

She fights back, but usually kids avoid her.

11. What interventions have you already tried?

Office referral, reprimands, conferences with mother.

described, keep in mind the crucial role of good planning. Next, we look at preventive steps you can take.

Prevention Strategies

Let us consider several prevention strategies a classroom teacher can use. But first, *what is it that we want to prevent?*

Our first task is *to prevent double messages to children by communicating clear norms for behavior.* Sometimes it helps a child to decipher a double standard for a behavior by delineating the setting differences for that behavior. Although most of us would prefer that a child never solve problems through aggression, we in schools may have to settle for a compromise solution: when the child is at home, the child can follow parental guidelines; at school the child must comply with the school's norms.

To convey a clear set of norms, we must ensure that all acts of aggression are treated similarly. The school-wide disciplinary practices described in the previous chapter are attempts to establish uniform and consistent policies for serious behaviors. These school-wide practices fail to prevent aggression, however, if the adults do not institute them consistently (Staub, 1987). Real teamwork is a vital component of prevention, and parents should be a part of the team whenever possible. By consistently enforcing the school policies, adults will reinforce the correct norms and prevent themselves from reinforcing aggression.

Our second prevention task is *to prevent the adults in the environment from inadvertently reinforcing, modeling, or encouraging aggressive acts.* To accomplish this prevention task, the adults must avoid aggressive solutions themselves; these actions may model the aggression for the child. For example, Helen's principal must abandon the ineffectual paddlings. The deleterious effects of aggressive

role models on children's behavior have been recognized by a number of researchers (Caprara & Kerr, 1985) and have led to the ban on corporal punishment in many school districts. The verbal monitoring skills for adults described later in this chapter will enhance your ability to recognize and curtail your reinforcement of students' confrontations.

Our third prevention task is *to prevent other children from reinforcing aggression.* Establishing school-wide norms and practicing to support them will help meet this goal. Furthermore, the classroom teacher can withhold reinforcement from students who "egg on" an aggressive student. The peer-mediated strategies discussed later in this chapter will give you some ideas. One important step in preventing the reinforcing reactions of other students—especially younger ones—is to have a well-established and rehearsed routine in the event that an aggressive student acts out. The guidelines in Table 7-2 will help you to prepare your students for this situation. In our experience, this "drill" also alleviates the anxiety of adults in the building. Just compare this readiness tactic with the way we approach other potentially upsetting events such as a fire.

Once again, consider the case of Helen. Her peers were either afraid of her or supportive of her aggression. Had her teacher been able to activate a routine, she might have been able to circumvent these peer reactions, neither of which was helpful to Helen. By calmly removing the other children from the environment, the teacher might have diminished their reinforcement or their anxiety. This prevention strategy will work best with younger children (i.e., those below the age of eleven). With older students, many of your confrontations may be verbal. The next section discusses ways to avoid unnecessary confrontations.

One prevention strategy is to avoid unnecessary confrontations. As students reach the adolescent stage of their development, they look for ways to prove their increasing autonomy and individuality. Some of these ways are

Table 7-2. Readiness Drill for Aggressive Events

1. With your principal and at least one other teacher whose room is nearby, develop a plan for how you will get help when the aggressive child loses control. This plan should include
   a. the transmission of a signal to the nearby adult or an alternate in the event that that person is not available.
   b. the kind of assistance you will need. For example, you might want the adult to come to your class and escort your other students out of the room so that they do not reinforce or taunt the target student.
   c. how you will notify the principal. You may want a second colleague to do this for you.
   d. how you will handle the aggressive student(s). This plan will depend in part on your school's policies. Interventions presented later in this chapter will help you.

2. Develop a "signal" that you can give to a dependable child in your classroom. This signal should be different from anything else the children may have encountered. For example, you might paint a wooden block a particular color. [If you also wish to notify the principal, then you might want two such signals given to two students or their alternates.]

3. Select an alternate in the event that the above-mentioned child is absent the day you need to use your procedure.

4. Tell the students that you have an important drill for them to practice, like the fire and other drills to which they are accustomed. You do not need to declare the circumstances under which you would activate your readiness plan. If the students can read, then give them a handout outlining the steps they are to take. If they are not capable readers, you might want to post an abbreviated set of steps on a poster.

5. Practice the drill, including the activities of the other adults. Begin with a weekly practice until the students and adults can complete the activities smoothly. Then have a monthly "surprise drill."

6. If at any time the drill does not proceed as you planned, revise the steps and inform everyone of the revision.

not much fun for adults! For example, teenagers often engage in verbal confrontations as if to prove to themselves that they can "win" with an adult. On the other hand, adults may be caught off guard and participate in these confrontations, making matters worse for everyone. How can you avoid unnecessary confrontations with your students? Here are a few ideas (Kerr, Nelson, & Lambert, 1987):

1. *Remember that adolescence is a time for many students to challenge authority figures.* Although you may not condone all of the expressions of a teenager's autonomy, you may *feel* better if you keep this important developmental milestone in mind.

2. *"Pick your battles."* An experienced middle school teacher once advised us that some confrontations can be avoided if you simply refuse to participate in them.

Most are not worth pursuit.

3. *Suggest a later, private conference to the student who is attempting to engage you in a public scene.* Often the passage of time will reduce the student's vehemence.

4. *Stay in control of your own emotions.* Teachers who get angry whenever confronted by a teenager are likely to experience repeated, unsuccessful confrontations. If you *are* angry then take some time for yourself, to cool off and collect your thoughts. Not all confrontations need to be dealt with immediately.

5. *Avoid needing the last word.* As one principal said, "these students need the last words a lot more than I do." We have witnessed many episodes of aggression exacerbated by an adult's insistence on getting the last word, rather than letting the student leave the interaction mumbling something under his or her breath. "I

heard what you said — now come back here and apologize!" can worsen an already tense situation.

6. *Listen!* Students often tell us that this is really what they want. By listening to the student's complaint (just as a well-trained customer service representative would listen as you provide a litany of problems with a service or product), you may reduce the student's hostility and negotiate a good conclusion.

7. *Avoid sarcasm.* This form of humor rarely helps in a confrontation.

8. *Offer the student a choice whenever possible.* Be sure that both options are acceptable to you! The following conversations illustrate this idea. No choice: "Janice, go to your civics class right now — the bell rang five minutes ago. This is no time for a phone call!" Two options: "Janice, it's time for sixth period. *Either* go on to class *or* make your call now and spend some of the afternoon break making up your work."

9. *Ignore minor rule infractions when you think you can.* Here is an example of ignoring: "Juan, sit down and open your book. [No response] Sarah, you're ready; go ahead with the story."

10. *Maintain your flexibility and your sense of humor.* Finally, we address a strategy you may not have considered: maintaining your own flexibility and sense of humor on the job. Studies have shown that teachers who are under stress become irritable, tired, bored, and even depressed. In the later stages, stress may lead teachers to resist change and to become inflexible (Weiskopf, 1980). Such traits would make interacting with disgruntled teenagers difficult. On the one hand, being flexible will increase your chances of managing and coping with problem behaviors on the job. On the other hand, not handling the stresses of your job may lead you to be irritable, short-tempered, and less able to

handle potentially difficult interactions with teenagers. Adolescents, especially those with a history of behavior problems, often provoke adults into conversations or interactions that lead to bigger problems such as aggressive behaviors (Strain & Ezzell, 1978). Learn to cope with the stresses of working with adolescents.

Weiskopf (1980) offered these suggestions for reducing the stress of your job:

a. Know in advance what the job requires in terms of emotional stress.

b. Set realistic goals for yourself and for your students.

c. Delegate routine work, such as paperwork, to aides or volunteers.

d. Avoid becoming isolated from other staff members.

e. Break up the amount of direct contact you have with students through team teaching, the use of learning centers, etc.

f. Remain intellectually active off the job.

g. Get physical exercise.

h. Interject newness and variety into your day to counterbalance the routine.

i. Participate in hobbies and activities not related to your job.

Now we turn to the role of the environment in preventing or reducing aggressive behaviors.

Environmental Modification Strategies

Altering the classroom or school rarely eliminates aggressive behavior, but such strategies may provide relief by lessening provocative situations. For example, security guards have been hired in many large city high schools to monitor hall traffic and to provide general surveillance of students as they move through traditionally unsupervised areas. Although the presence of security guards may reduce fighting or destruction of school property, it does not teach students new behaviors, nor does it prevent problems in other parts of the school. Or consider a severely handicapped child who may not be able to destroy work materials if the materials are placed out of his reach. Once again, the problem may be prevented but it has not been solved.

In other instances, minor environmental modifications may be prerequisite to successful programming. For example, a token-economy response cost for destroying school property will be ineffective unless damage can be documented accurately. This requires that school property be inventoried and that the classrooms be examined periodically in order to levy fines accurately. At one school, all classes share the fine when the property damage cannot be conclusively attributed to one person or group (West, F., personal communication, 1981).

Cheating, a problem behavior even though the "injury" caused is intangible, can be reduced by environmental modifications within the classroom. All of us are familiar, for example, with the rearrangements that take place on major achievement testing days in public schools: students must work with at least one desk (or adequate space) between them in order to prevent them looking on one another's answer sheets. Modification of the curriculum may be necessary, as explained by Millman, Schaefer, and Cohen (1980): "If students feel able to succeed in their school work, they will probably not risk cheating. If the work is extremely difficult, cheating and denial of cheating may be viewed as the only ways to succeed" (p. 16).

STIMULUS CONTROL

Rosen and Rosen (1983) designed a clever environmental modification to reduce stealing in a first grader who took things from other chil-

dren. To modify the behavior, the teachers marked all of the target child's possessions with green circles. Every fifteen minutes, the child's desk, person, and supply box were checked, and he was reprimanded and fined five points (under the token economy system) for every possession that did not have a green circle. If no stolen items were found, he received praise and points. Gradually, the teachers checked only once every two hours in order to reduce the level of intervention. During a later followup, the staff kept a list of the child's possessions and checked it whenever anyone reported a missing item. This simple procedure was very successful in eliminating the stealing both in the classroom and in other settings.

CONTROLLING ENVIRONMENTAL FACTORS CONTRIBUTING TO VANDALISM

In an attempt to understand some of the factors leading to school vandalism, Mayer, Nafpaktitis, Butterworth, and Hollingsworth (1987) collected data in twenty-eight schools. They found that a *punitive school environment was a major factor in promoting vandalism.* This finding confirmed earlier research showing that poor scholastic achievement was related to acts of vandalism (Gold & Mann, 1982). Mayer and his colleagues made three suggestions for altering the school environment, thereby reducing vandalism: (1) make the school environment reinforcing and individualized for students, (2) reduce the misuse of behavioral interventions, and (3) substitute positive behavioral management approaches for the more punishing interventions.

ALTERING CLASSROOM DENSITY

Classroom crowding has been examined as a factor in aggressive behavior by several researchers (Hood-Smith & Leffingwell, 1984; McAfee, 1987). McAfee studied behaviorally handicapped and mentally retarded students (ages ranged from seven to sixteen) and noted that the amount of floor space available to students had an impact on their disruptive and aggressive behaviors. *Densities of .90 square meters and .86 square meters significantly increased aggressive behaviors.* To calculate how much space your students have, use the formula prescribed by McAfee (1987): measure the perimeter of the classroom and calculate the total area. Subtract from this total the floor space that is not available to children "by virtue of its being occupied by objects such as cabinets, files, stacks of boxes, or any other objects that would preclude student work in that space" (p. 138). Include in *available work space* the students' desks and other furniture designed for their use.

ORGANIZED GAMES

Murphy et al. (1983) manipulated the play of primary school children in order to reduce the level of aggression during recess. Teachers read and explained a brief description of organized games (i.e., jumprope and foot races) and explained a two-minute contingent observation time-out procedure (See Chapter 6) to their students, who had been engaging in the aggressive behaviors described in Table 7-1. *The combination of the organized games and the "sit and watch" time-out procedure resulted in a 50 percent reduction in aggressive behaviors.*

Huber (1976) offered suggestions for the *types* of organized games that foster cooperation and diminish competition. He recommended that teachers avoid games in which players are eliminated as a part of the rules; elimination type games include "horse," "Simon says," and dodge ball. Suggestions for modifying group games, as outlined by Huber, are as follows:

Simon Says. This game can be played without the noxious elimination of players who miss a direction and thereby receive no further practice in the activity. By not being eliminated, the

competitive factor between children is reduced, as well as the competition between teacher and child. If the competitive element needs to be reintroduced, the primary competition can be between the teacher and the total group: seeing how many can or can't be caught at any one time. The teacher will invariably lose, which isn't necessarily bad for the children's morale.

Kickball and Softball. These games are usually organized by teams, with three outs indicating a team change from "at bat" to "field." Often one team is stronger and they remain at bat so long there's little time left for the other team. Futility and frustration galore! If each player has one time at bat in rotation, however, and then automatically the other team comes up to bat, every child has an equal turn at bat and the frustration of three outs is avoided. Runs may still be counted. Another variation allows all players three hits or kicks, running out only the last one. All players rotate through all positions, with the only competition being how far each player hits or kicks.

Volleyball. Volleyball can be a great cooperative game. With one team on either side of the net they can attempt to keep the ball in play as long as possible without it touching the ground; the challenge is to get higher and higher numerical counts. This form of volleyball is even more fun without a net. Three to ten players stand in relatively close proximity; one player taps the ball in the air with everyone attempting to maintain it there, but no player may tap the ball twice in succession. The higher the counts the more exciting the game gets. It's good for all age levels and gets everyone involved in a cooperative effort.

Dodgeball. This can be a very aggressive game for children — actually striking someone with a ball is overt aggression and repugnant to some children. To some extent, this can be controlled by the group's inability to get a few agile players remaining in the center "out." This complication can be easily remedied, however, by making the circle smaller or giving the participants one or two more balls to throw. This will get them "out" in a hurry. With unskilled players in the center, limit the action to one ball and keep the circle larger. This will result in better apparent performance by these children. These two factors — size of circle and number of balls—allow almost complete control of the game by the adult according to whatever intent he has in mind.

"It" Games. "It" games should always start with a strong runner as "It," rather than a slower child who is unable to catch anyone. Also, the cumulative version (all participants caught become "It" until the last child is caught) makes for a more exciting game, brings forth maximum participation, and enables the slower runners to catch the speedier players at times.

"I got it" is a good variation highlighting the fastest runners. Anyone tagging "It" becomes the one who's "got it" and is chased by the group. This game always involves the group against one individual and rarely is the group unsuccessful. Of primary importance in "It" games is the designation of a circumscribed area for play. Otherwise, "It" can run off with the game.

Soccer. Soccer is a good all-around game for the preadolescent age group. It has good running activity, some physical contact, beginnings of teamwork, low-focus and chance occurrences, and quick shifts in offensive and defensive situations that keep the excitement level high. In addition, all children can participate regardless of the level of skill, and all can contribute something to the team. In soccer it is almost impossible for any player to be regarded as a liability. The necessity for umpire services is paramount in this game because of the inherent tendency to use the hands to control the ball. This becomes the one drawback for players forced to get along without these services (Huber, 1976, pp. 270–271. Reprinted by permission of Franz Huber and Wadsworth Publishing Company).

REVIEW

This section has offered ideas for changing your school or classroom environment to support the preventive strategies outlined in the previous section. Recall the major environmental strategies: First, you want to be conscious of the density of your classroom, using the formula provided by McAfee (1987). Second, you can improve your school's individualized, positive "tone" to prevent vandalism, as men-

tioned by Mayer et al. (1987). Third, you can use organized games to reduce aggression during gym and recess times. Fourth, you can adopt special changes in the environment to reduce stealing or to prevent cheating. Keep in mind that these interventions are most effective in the context of a good overall contingency management plan, such as the token economy we discussed in the last chapter.

In our next section we address teacher-mediated interventions that work to reduce aggressive behaviors.

Teacher-Mediated Strategies

Two primary types of intervention enable teachers to manage aggressive behaviors: the rearrangement of reinforcement contingencies for aggression, and the teaching of appropriate, prosocial skills that are incompatible with acts of aggression. These two approaches are based on a social learning theory model that presumes that aggressive behaviors are learned and that incompatible, prosocial skills can likewise be taught (Bandura, 1971).

Contingency management for an aggressive individual requires that you pinpoint problem behaviors and provide negative consequences for them while providing positive consequences for behaviors incompatible with aggression. Contingency management has been discussed throughout this text in procedures such as token economies, contingency contracts, and time-out from reinforcement. Nevertheless, aggressive behaviors and antisocial behaviors (e.g., stealing and cheating) warrant special consideration when these general behavioral management procedures are implemented.

TOKEN REINFORCEMENT

When you develop a token economy to include management of aggressive behaviors, apply a response cost or fine to aggressive acts as well as to behaviors that predict aggression or destruction of property. The following lists display part of a teacher's classroom token economy for aggressive students:

Points may be earned for	*Points*
1. Walking away from a fight.	+ 10
2. Ignoring someone who teases.	+ 5
3. Accepting teacher feedback with a nonangry statement.	+ 5
4. Substituting a socially acceptable word for an opportunity to curse.	+ 5
5. Keeping hands off others for one period.	+ 10

Points will be lost for	*Points*
1. Fighting or hitting.	− 20
2. "Mouthing off" at a school visitor.	− 20
3. Teasing a classmate.	− 10
4. Threatening a classmate.	− 10

Note that the actions that *inhibit* aggression are listed for token *reinforcement*. Recall our discussion of the role that stimulus control plays in maintaining or reducing aggressive behaviors. By identifying behaviors that inhibit aggression as well as those that provoke hurtful behavior, this teacher controlled the *stimuli* preceding aggression through token reinforcement and response cost.

CONTRACTING

Contingency contracts have effectively reduced destructive behaviors, including fighting, property damage, fire-setting, and verbal aggression (Gershman, 1976; Mann, 1985). In the former study, an eight-year-old boy was taught to control his fire-setting behaviors through a home-based contingency contract program. He was rewarded first for completing homework then for controlling his use of matches. (The student was rewarded each time he returned to his mother matchbooks that she deliberately placed around the house.) This unusual example of contingency management for an individual child's behavior was closely supervised and

is not recommended for a classroom situation. However, you may decide that contingency contracting would be helpful for certain aggressive behaviors (cursing, teasing, destroying school property or work materials, and engaging in fights). In Figure 7–3 you see a contingency contract, with home-based reinforcement, developed for Helen, the sixth grader mentioned earlier.

Notice that the conditions of the contract apply across classrooms as well as transition activities. With an aggressive student, it is important that all adults advocate the same position: *aggressive behavior will not be tolerated.* Otherwise, aggression may be intermittently reinforced and thereby strengthened.

TIME-OUT FROM REINFORCEMENT

Time-out procedures can be effective in reducing aggressive behaviors, as evidenced in a study of a ten-year-old chronically aggressive boy (Webster, 1976). This student was sent to a time-out area for each incident of unprovoked aggression. Over time, he improved both his social and academic performance. Many aggressive students, like classroom disruptors, fail to complete academic tasks because they are expelled from the instructional setting at each outburst. As a result, aggressive students may develop a "double handicap" requiring remediation in both academic *and* social skills.

When using time-out with an aggressive student, remember that it is best (and easiest) to apply it *before* the child loses control or becomes assaultive (especially when going to seclusion time-out). For this reason, behaviors to be pinpointed for time-out should be those *antecedents* to aggression (teasing, threats, lifting arm to "deck" someone). Also provide reinforcement for incompatible, acceptable behaviors once the student returns to the ongoing classroom activities.

Occasionally a destructive student will attempt to destroy the time-out area. If possible,

Figure 7-3. Contract for an Aggressive Student

I, *Helen Alison*, understand that I have a problem with these behaviors:

1. Talking back to my teachers when they tell me to do something.
2. Refusing to do or finish my schoolwork.
3. Getting into fights with other kids at lunch and at recess.

This week I am going to work on these behaviors:

1. Talking back to my teachers.
2. Finishing my work in the resource reading room.

I know that if I do either one of these behaviors I will lose my shopping trip Saturday to the mall with my friends.

to remind me that what I did was not right.

But, if I control these behaviors and have a week without them, I will get to:

Go to a movie with Jeanie, or get an extra 50¢ allowance.

as a reward.

Signed: Helen Alison   Date: 11/20
    (Student)

Mrs. Blouze   Date: 11/20
    (Teacher)

Mr. Sider   Date: 11/20
    (Resource Teacher)

Mrs. P. Alison   Date: 11/20
    (Parent)

We have read and discussed this contract in an after-school meeting on 11/20. And we hereby sign as a way of making our commitment to this arrangement.

We will all meet on 11/28 to reevaluate the contract.

require the student to restore the area to its original condition before being allowed to leave it (i.e., use restitutional overcorrection). If the student is extremely destructive, within-school interventions may have to be supplemented with external penalties. Examples are a legally imposed fine for destruction of public property, the requirement that a student pay for damage while parents withhold his allowance for other spending purposes, the assignment of a student to a custodial job for a designated period, or "grounding" an institutionalized student to a more restrictive physical environment until better care of property can be demonstrated. In the case of time-out or punishment strategies, you must consult with your supervisor about institution or school policies.

Another form of time-out from reinforcement is the in-school suspension procedure you read about in Chapter 6. If the in-school suspension program is implemented properly and if the student is motivated by being with his friends in the regular school program, then the removal of friends through the in-school suspension assignment may reduce aggression. Unfortunately, very little research has been conducted on these school-wide interventions, so we cannot predict how effective they will be in deterring aggression (Staub, 1987). We do advise that you monitor these interventions (especially home suspension) to see whether you are remediating or worsening the problem.

OVERCORRECTION

One way to teach skills incompatible with problem behaviors is through *positive practice overcorrection,* a procedure in which the student is required to engage in a period of exaggerated alternative behaviors (e.g., exercises after an episode of an unwanted behavior). This procedure was applied to stealing, according to a report by Azrin and Wesolowski (1974). In this investigation, severely retarded persons who grabbed food from others' plates were reprimanded and prompted to return the stolen food. The thief was then told to obtain an identical item from a display area and to give it to the victim. This overcorrection procedure quickly eliminated all thefts. The authors cited four possible reasons for this procedure's success: in returning the stolen item, the thief no longer enjoyed its reinforcing qualities; securing another similar item was an unpleasant experience; the time spent in overcorrection lessened the amount of reinforcement available to the thief; and by returning items, the thief learned a new and incompatible behavior (Azrin & Wesolowski, 1974).

Luce, Delquadri, and Hall (1980) used contingent exercise (functional movement training) for two severely disturbed elementary school children who engaged in hitting and aggressive verbalizations. Whenever hitting or threats occurred, the student was prompted to do ten exercise sets. This procedure is detailed in Chapter 10.

You might consider overcorrection to reduce aggressive or stealing behavior if you are working with severely behaviorally handicapped or with young children. This strategy, when it involves contingent functional movement training, is not usually advised for an adolescent who is likely to be physically resistant.

TEACHING ALTERNATIVE BEHAVIORS

Perhaps your most important task with aggressive students is to teach them alternatives to their angry behavior (see Hazel, Schumaker, Sherman, & Sheldon-Wildgen, 1981; Hollin & Courtney, 1983; Feindler, Marriott, & Iwata, 1984; Long & Sherer, 1984). After all, the contingency management procedures we have reviewed will help manage the outbursts of an aggressive student but may fall short of offering the student new and better ways to solve problems with others.

When faced with the task of teaching alternative behaviors, educators often ask: Where should I begin? We think you might find

Table 7-3 helpful for targeting behaviors. In the left-hand column are behaviors that would lead to positive responses on the part of others, whereas the righthand column outlines angry or hostile behaviors. This table might be a good discussion handout for your older students; when you read the group case study for this chapter, you will see that the teacher did use this handout to help her students understand their own expressions.

STRUCTURED LEARNING

One of the most popular approaches to teaching alternative, prosocial behaviors to aggressive students is **structured learning** (Goldstein, 1987). Through this approach, students experience four training components: (1) modeling; (2) role-playing; (3) performance feedback; and, (4) transfer of learning (Goldstein, 1987). Let us examine this four-part intervention and see how you might benefit from adopting it in your classroom.

Goldstein described the structured learning groups as consisting of from six to twelve participants who are assessed as having similar skill deficits. (See Goldstein, 1987, for a listing of assessment procedures.) Problem situations are task-analyzed and modeled for the students by their teacher or through audiovisual aids. Table 7-4 offers you a list of these task-analyzed psychological skill areas.

Table 7-3. Appropriate versus Inappropriate Expressions of Anger and Their Effects

| Expression | Appropriate | | Inappropriate | |
	Action	Effect	Action	Effect
1. Eye contact	direct	people look back	glaring	people look away
2. Tone of voice	calm, polite, pleasant	people more likely to listen calmly, pleasantly	loud, screaming, cursing	people less likely to listen, may yell back
3. Facial expression	positive, relaxed, pleasant	people more likely to respond positively, look pleasant	frowning, scowling, snarling	people more likely to walk away or look unpleasant
4. Body movement	open position, relaxed stance, gestures not threatening	feelings more likely to be recognized, problems more likely to be resolved, people more open to suggestion	throwing, hitting, threatening, fist shaking	person may respond physically and someone may get hurt, could result in legal action, property damage

Note: This table was taken from D. Larkin, personal communication, 1986.

Table 7-4. Psychological Skill Areas for Aggressive Students (pp. 230-232)

Asking for help
1. Decide what the problem is.
2. Decide whether you want help with the problem.
3. Identify the people who might help you.
4. Make a choice of helper.
5. Tell the helper about your problem.

Giving instructions
1. Define what needs to be done and who should do it.
2. Tell the other person what you want him or her to do and why.
3. Tell the other person exactly how to do what you want done.
4. Ask for the other person's reaction.
5. Consider that reaction and change your direction if appropriate.

Expressing affection
1. Decide whether you have warm, caring feelings about another person.
2. Decide whether the other person would like to know about your feelings.
3. Decide how you might best express your feelings.
4. Choose the right time and place to express your feelings.
5. Express affection in a warm and caring manner.

Expressing a complaint
1. Define what the problem is and who is responsible.
2. Decide how the problem might be solved.
3. Tell that person what the problem is and how it might be solved.
4. Ask for a response.
5. Decide whether you want to try again.
6. If it is appropriate, try again, using your revised approach.

Responding to contradictory messages
1. Pay attention to those body signals that help you know you are feeling trapped or confused.
2. Consider the other person's words and actions that may have caused you to have these feelings.
3. Decide whether that person's words and actions are contradictory.
4. Decide whether it would be useful to point out any contradiction.
5. If appropriate, ask the other person to explain any contradiction.

Responding to anger
1. Listen openly to the other person's angry statement(s).
2. Show that you understand what the other person is feeling.
3. Ask the other person to explain anything you don't understand about what was said.
4. Show that you understand why the other person feels angry.
5. If it is appropriate, express your thoughts and feelings about the situation.

Preparing for a stressful conversation
1. Imagine yourself in the stressful situation.
2. Think about how you will feel and why you will feel that way.
3. Imagine the other person(s) in that stressful situation. Think about how that person(s) will feel and why they will feel that way.
4. Imagine yourself telling the other person(s) what you want to say.
5. Imagine the response that your statement will elicit.
6. Repeat the above steps, using as many approaches as you can think of.
7. Choose the best approach.

Table 7-4. *Continued*

Determining responsibility
1. Decide what the problem is.
2. Consider possible causes of the problem.
3. Decide which are the most likely causes of the problem.
4. Take actions to test which are the actual causes of the problem.

Setting problem priorities
1. List all the problems that are currently pressuring you.
2. Arrange this list in order, from most to least urgent.
3. Take steps (delegate, postpone, avoid) to temporarily decrease the urgency of all but the most pressing problem.
4. Concentrate on solving the most pressing problem.

Dealing with being left out
1. Decide whether you're being left out (ignored, rejected).
2. Think about why the other people might be leaving you out of something.
3. Consider how you might deal with the problem (wait, leave, tell the other people how their behavior affects you, talk with a friend about the problem).
4. Choose the best way and do it.
5. Show that you understand the other person's feelings.
6. Come to agreement on the steps to be taken by each of you.

Persuading others
1. Decide on your position and predict what the other person's is likely to be.
2. State your position clearly, completely, and in a way that is acceptable to the other person.
3. State what you think the other person's position is.
4. Restate your position, emphasizing why it is the better of the two.
5. Suggest that the other person consider your position for a while before making a decision.

Following instructions
1. Listen carefully while the instructions are being given.
2. Give your reactions to the instructor.
3. Repeat the instructions to yourself.
4. Imagine yourself following the instructions and then do it.

Responding to the feelings of others (Empathy)
1. Observe another person's words and actions.
2. Consider what the other person might be feeling and how strong the feelings are.
3. Decide whether it would be helpful to let the other person know that you understand his or her feelings.
4. If appropriate, tell the other person in a warm and sincere manner how you think he or she is feeling.

Responding to a complaint
1. Listen openly to the complaint.
2. Ask the person to explain anything you don't understand.
3. Show that you understand the other person's thoughts and feelings.
4. Tell the other person your thoughts and feelings, accepting responsibility if appropriate.
5. Summarize the steps to be taken by each of you.

Responding to persuasion
1. Listen openly to another person's position.
2. Consider the possible reasons for the other person's position.
3. Ask the other person to explain anything you don't understand about what was said.
4. Compare the other person's position with your own, identifying the pros and cons of each.
5. Decide what position to support, based on what will have the greatest long-term benefit.

Table 7-4. *Continued*

Responding to failure

1. Decide whether you have failed.
2. Think about both the personal reasons and the circumstances that have caused you to fail.
3. Decide how you might do things differently if you tried again.

Dealing with an accusation

1. Think about what the other person has accused you of (whether it is accurate, inaccurate, said in a mean way or in a constructive way).
2. Think about why the person might have accused you (have you infringed on that person's rights or property?).
3. Think about ways to answer the person's accusations (deny, explain your behavior, correct the other person's perceptions, assert, apologize, offer to make up for what has happened).
4. Choose the best way and do it.

Dealing with group pressure

1. Think about what the other people want you to do and why (listen to the other people, decide what their real intent is, try to understand what is being said).
2. Decide what you want to do (yield, resist, delay, negotiate).
3. Consider how to tell the other people what you want to do (give reasons, talk to one person only, delay, assert).
4. If appropriate, tell the group or other person what you have decided.

Source: Reprinted with permission from Goldstein, A. P. (1987). Teaching prosocial skills to antisocial adolescents. In C. M. Nelson, R. B. Rutherford, & B. I. Wolford (Eds.), *Special education in the criminal justice system.* Columbus, OH: Merrill, pp. 223–226.

After students have witnessed *good* ways to manage difficult situations, they get a chance to *role-play* these skills themselves. Goldstein (1987) described the role-play as follows:

A brief, spontaneous discussion almost invariably follows the presentation of a modeling display. Trainees comment on the steps, the actors, and often the occurrence of the situation or skill problem in their own lives. Because our primary goal in role-playing is to encourage realistic behavior rehearsal, a trainee's statements about individual difficulties using the skill can often develop into material for the first role-play. To enhance the realism of the portrayal, the main actor is asked to choose a second trainee (co-actor) to play the role of the significant other person in his or her life who is relevant to the skill problem. It is important that the main actor seeks to enact the steps just modeled.

The main actor is asked to briefly describe the real skill-problem situation and the real person(s) involved in it. The co-actor is called by the name of the main actor's significant other person during the role-play. The trainer then instructs the role-players to begin. It is the trainer's main responsibility, at this point, to be sure that the main actor keeps role-playing and attempts to follow the behavioral steps in so doing.

The role-playing is continued until all trainees in the group have had an opportunity to participate — even if all the same steps must be carried over to a second or third session. However, even though the framework (behavioral steps) of each role-play in the series remains the same, the actual content can and should change from role-play to role-play; the skill-deficiency problem as it actually occurs in each trainee's real-life environment should be the content of each role-play. When the role-plays are completed, each trainee should be better armed to act appropriately in real situations. (p. 220)

The next stage of training is **performance feedback,** in which the actors in the role-plays receive comments on how they enacted the skills. Goldstein stressed the importance of specific, encouraging comments here. Finally, students experience the **transfer of training,** a phase in which *overlearning is emphasized.* Students reexperience the modeling, role-plays, and performance feedback many times in order to ensure that they have really captured the important skills they lack. To help with this process, you might give students "behavioral homework assignments," writing assignments for their notebooks, "cue cards," and other learning aids. Moreover, try to link the skills with "real-life" situations by offering relevant teaching examples, role-plays, and discussion topics.

ANGER-CONTROL TRAINING

Feindler et al. (1984) researched a similar approach to helping juvenile delinquents manage their aggressive behavior. Small groups of high school students received self-control training in a ten-session workshop. (A training manual is available from Eva L. Feindler, Psychology Department, Adelphi University, Garden City, New York 11530.) Once again, the training offered modeling, role-plays, visual clues (e.g., flash cards), and homework assignments. A special feature of this training was the introduction of a "graduated presentation of specific provocations to the adolescents, with decreased warnings or prompts to prepare for them" (p. 305). Students also learned to recognize and analyze components of angry interactions; this recognition strategy is a feature of the case studies for this chapter. Two specific skills taught were called *time-out:* first, students learned to pause between the provocation and their response to it; second, students learned to ignore the provocation for a few seconds. Replacing aggressive verbal responses with assertive responses helped the students, too.

We hope that you have begun to detect the components of a successful skills training program for aggressive teenagers. The complete programs are too long to include here, but we urge you to read them on your own if you are working with aggressive teenagers. Now let us look at a similar program for younger students.

Elementary school students have also benefited from the kind of training we have just described (Lochman, Burch, Curry, & Lampron, 1984; Lochman & Curry, 1986). One of the best-known programs for teaching younger children prosocial skills is the *Getting Along With Others* program developed by Jackson, Jackson, and Monroe (1983). This curriculum offers lesson plans for teaching a number of important social skills, as well as relaxation exercises. Here are some of the topics covered (Jackson et al., 1983):

- Sending an ignoring message
- Handling name-calling and teasing
- Saying "no" to stay out of trouble

We have found this curriculum to be easy to teach and successful with aggressive students in elementary school. The format is similar to those mentioned earlier: students are shown a model of a correct response and then have a chance to role-play it with each other, before moving on to behavioral homework.

In summary, both contingency management and direct skills-training approaches are advised for teachers coping with aggressive behaviors. To promote maintenance of intervention gains and to increase generalization or transfer of these skills across settings and persons, we encourage you to involve as many other persons as possible in the intervention planning and implementation.

CRISIS INTERVENTION WITH PHYSICAL AGGRESSION

In spite of your best efforts to prevent behaviors that threaten the physical safety of an aggressive student or of others in the classroom, a situation may erupt into violence before you can intervene. We believe these instances will be rare if you employ the strategies described in this chapter. However, when violent behavior does occur, you should know what to do. Basically, two goals are paramount: (1) to physically manage the student, preventing him from harming himself or others until he has calmed down; and (2) to protect yourself from injury.

Methods for physically managing aggressive pupils and methods for self-protection are not easily presented in a textbook. It is imperative that training in such techniques be provided by a certified expert. Furthermore, such training involves assessing the nature of the aggressive behavior as well as the context in which it occurs. *We do not recommend that you employ any of these physical management techniques unless you have received appropriate training.* A training booklet, developed for use by staff in institutions for severely retarded clients, may be obtained by writing for *A better way: An illustrated guide to protective intervention techniques* (Staff Development Murdoch Center, Butner, North Carolina 27509).

Until you have received direct training in the physical management of physically aggressive confrontations, our advice is to avoid them unless you are attacked without warning. Remove yourself and others from the vicinity of a student displaying violent behavior; seek the assistance of qualified others (those who know how to restrain an out-of-control pupil without endangering anyone) if the pupil's behavior poses a serious threat to himself, others, or to expensive property. As with any other incident involving aggressive behavior, complete a checklist similar to that presented in Figure 7-1 immediately afterward. And finally, be sure that you are familiar with your school district's policies regarding the handling of crisis situations, establish procedures which are compatible with these policies, and inform parents of these policies and procedures (Gilliam, 1981).

Peer-Mediated Strategies

A student's peer group can play a major role in intervention programs to reduce aggressive and destructive behaviors. For example, the peers may take part in a group contingency or learn to ignore or respond in a new way to teasing or threats by the target student. These peer-mediated procedures have been described in the previous chapter, and only general guidelines and programming modifications specific to aggressive behavior are mentioned here.

GROUP CONTINGENCY MANAGEMENT

Patterson (1974) describes several studies involving a group contingency arrangement with a signaling work box placed on the target student's desk. (A consultant operated the work box signals to indicate the student was behaving appropriately.) As the student's behavior improved, time between signals was increased gradually from sixty seconds to longer intervals. Intervals of appropriate behavior, as signalled by the work box (or during subsequent phases, a "work card"), were rewarded by free time, special classroom events, or privileges, *all shared with the student's classmates.* This variation of the hero procedure (a program in which the target student earns reinforcers for his peers) helps a single student develop peer relationships with classmates who have been alienated by past hurtful behaviors.

Group contingencies have also been devised to control episodes of stealing (Brooks & Snow, 1972). Under this individual performance/group contingency arrangement, a student earned points for completing academic tasks and remaining in the classroom. Each time the student earned ten points, the class enjoyed free time. If the student violated a classroom rule, however, they all lost the free time. In this particular study, the target behavior, stealing, was not identified explicitly; rather, behaviors incompatible with stealing were highlighted and reinforced.

Before you try a group contingency such as the two described, read over the guidelines in Chapter 6, because an improperly managed group contingency may result in scapegoating and further alienation of the target student.

GROUP GOAL SETTING AND FEEDBACK

Group goal setting and feedback, a strategy explained in Chapter 6, has been applied to aggressive behaviors on the playground (Kerr, Strain, & Ragland, 1982). In this study, preadolescent students participated in daily group goal-setting and feedback sessions to improve their recess activities, originally described by their teacher as follows:

> The kids go outside for a thirty-minute recess and start right off arguing about what game to play. Once that's settled, they bicker about who will pick teams. After teams are finally chosen, a fight breaks out over unfair membership on the two teams. About ten minutes before the bell rings, they get down to playing baseball or something. By the time recess is over they've almost killed each other fighting about the rules . . . (Ragland, personal communication, 1981).

For ideas about establishing goals, look at the target behaviors listed in Table 7-1. Guidelines for using this activity are described in Chapter 6.

PEER REPORTING

Young children may improve their social interactions and reduce aggression through an activity designed by Kauffman, Grieger, and Grieger (1976):

1. Set aside approximately ten minutes per day for this activity. You will also need "happy face" badges (or a similar item) for each student. These should fit onto a hook or flannel board and should also be able to be attached to a child's clothing or desk.
2. At the designated time, assemble the group and ask that children take turns nominating someone who had been friendly and stating what the friendly act was.

3. A nominated child is eligible to receive a "friendly badge." Be sure the badge is received from a peer, not the teacher.
4. Discourage students from describing themselves.
5. Don't praise or otherwise recognize students who are not nominated. (This is a modification of the original method.)
6. If students cannot nominate a peer, encourage them to do so the next day (pp. 307–313).

Self-Mediated Strategies

Research has begun to address self-management of aggressive behaviors *in the classroom,* and a few reports offer suggestions that you may find practicable.

COLLABORATIVE APPROACHES

McCullough, Huntsinger, and Nay (1977) used a program for Larry, an adolescent who had a long history of aggressive outbursts. A case study on Larry is presented at the end of this chapter. The program consisted of these elements:

1. Obtaining Larry's cooperation for the program
2. Identifying feelings, thoughts, and reactions that he experienced prior to an outburst
3. Viewing a videotaped role-play in which Larry reacted to a frustrating situation (described earlier in this chapter)
4. Role-playing behaviors incompatible to the earlier identified reactions
5. Training in a specific sequence of incompatible responses (e.g., stop subvocal speech, relax tensed muscles, walk away momentarily to cool off)
6. Signing a contract that outlines implementation of these steps

The therapist who implemented these six steps also arranged a school-supported program for the student. As part of a multidisciplinary team approach, perhaps you can identify the program's components that could help you cope with an aggressive student.

SELF-INSTRUCTION

Some studies suggest that students who practice "coping statements" to themselves reduce their level of verbally and, to a lesser extent, physically aggressive behaviors (Camp, Bloom, Hebert, & VanDoorninck, 1977; Coats, 1979). Camp et al. developed the "Think Aloud" program for aggressive primary school students, in which children are taught to tell themselves to relax, a procedure familiar in its simplified, everyday versions:

> "Tell yourself to count to ten before you lose your temper."
>
> "Try to cool off before you confront somebody."
>
> "Walk around the block when you feel like blowing off steam."

Unfortunately, the research thus far on self-instruction training, or SIT, has not demonstrated that this procedure will definitely reduce aggressive behavior (Wilson, 1984). We encourage you to continue to scan your professional journals for new findings about this promising approach to serious behavior problems.

SELF-MANAGEMENT IN COMBINATION WITH OTHER STRATEGIES

At least two reports suggest combining self-management with other activities for aggressive students. Kendall and Finch (1976) success-fully used self-instructions with a token response cost for aggressive outbursts. Self-recording (described in Chapter 6) with points for accurate assessment of aggressive behaviors has been used with contingency contracting to reduce problem behaviors of early adolescent boys in a residential setting (Bardill, 1977).

Another successful approach combining self-management with other techniques is through *teaching students to monitor their own behaviors* (see Chapter 6), the approach taken in both our group and our individual case studies at the conclusion of this chapter. We believe that you will find self-control strategies especially helpful in supplementing the direct instruction, modeling, and role-play strategies included in your skills-teaching programs.

Summary

We hope you understand the importance of a thorough analysis of aggression, including direct observation and interview tools. Several environmental changes are available to solve specific problems. Most strategies, however, are teacher-mediated, requiring a high degree of control of your own reactions. Few studies have reported peer- or self-mediated strategies, although *teaching* self-control is a widely accepted solution to aggression.

Our chapter concludes with two case studies depicting approaches to aggressive behavior. In the first, a single student received self-control training from a behavioral therapist who collaborated closely with school staff. In the second case study, a teacher describes how she worked with a group of students to make them more aware of their aggressive behaviors. You will notice that both cases involve combined approaches to managing aggressive students, reflecting our belief that a *combination of interventions* offers the most hope for solving the serious problem of aggression in school.

CASE STUDY

Role-Playing Using Video Feedback and Self-Control Training Combined with a Teacher-Coordinated Intervention Program to Control the Aggressive School Behavior of a Sixteen-Year-Old Male

Dr. James P. McCullough[1]

Case Background

Larry was a sixteen-year-old male of average intelligence who had had temper problems throughout his eleven years of public schooling (he repeated the fourth grade because of this problem). Larry's school records showed that he lost his temper whenever a student or teacher questioned his behavior, when a peer did something he did not like, or when his behavior resulted in some penalty at school (e.g., having to stay after school; suspension; being taken to the principal's office). During such times he would lash out, either physically hitting or verbally abusing the other person.

Larry was a sophomore when the treatment program began. He had just been suspended from school due to loss of temper following arguments with a P.E. instructor and the school principal. During the previous month he had been expelled from the varsity football team due to frequent fights with his teammates. The primary goal of the therapy program was to reduce both the frequency and intensity of these destructive outbursts at school. I met with Larry

during mid-December 1973, immediately following his school suspension. During the therapy session, I combined role-playing with video feedback and training in self-control to help him learn temper control during periods of stress. Next, I contacted all of Larry's teachers to assist in carrying out an intervention program at school.

Therapist and Faculty Coordinated Training Program

Role-Playing Feedback and Self-Control Training. I wanted Larry to see how he looked when he lost his temper. In order to do this, I had him role-play the two recent conflicts while I videotaped the scenes. Then, we watched the replays together. Although Larry thought role-playing was a humorous exercise at first, he participated more energetically with prompting from me and finally, he played himself in a realistic fashion. He was mildly shocked to see how he looked when he became angry. He tilted his head to one side; he rolled his eyes back while talking out of one side of his mouth; then he placed his hands on his hips bending his upper torso to the right. The next thing I did was have him role-play these situations again only this time I instructed him to remain calm, avoid distorting his body, and to say what he wanted to. I took the roles of the instructor and the principal, respectively, and we videotaped the scenes again. Watching the replay produced some unexpected results for both of us. I angrily confronted him as the

[1]The case summary is based upon the following article: McCullough, J. P., Huntsinger, G. M., and Nay, W. R. Self-control treatment of aggression in a 16-year-old male. *Journal of Consulting and Clinical Psychology*, 1977, 45: 322-331. Copyright 1977 by the American Psychological Association. Adapted by permission of the publisher and author.

two faculty members had done. Larry remained calm and talked to me in a normal manner. My behavior had changed when these scenes were compared to the first ones we taped. I could not think of what to say and my speech style was noticeably affected. We both saw that it was difficult for me to act angry when he kept his composure. Larry had changed my behavior by controlling his anger. This obvious fact gave me the opportunity to talk to him about the changes he might bring about in others if he learned to control his anger. We ended this part of the therapy session with Larry gaining awareness of how his anger looked to others. An unexpected outcome of the role-playing trials was the insight into how he might positively affect others as he learned to control his temper.

The last part of the session was spent teaching Larry a self-control strategy to use in stress situations. I helped him pinpoint several internal, antecedent events that usually preceded his loss of temper. The antecedent events were subvocal cursing, progressive tensing of the body, and finally, a tenseness in his right arm that was usually followed by a temper outburst. Having pinpointed the internal events in the "sequential chain," we now had to focus on how Larry could interrupt the sequence before it ran its course. I taught him thought-stopping (Wolpe, 1969) to counter the subvocal cursing; then, I taught him a relaxation exercise he could use to inhibit the progressive tensing of his body. In the event these inhibitory strategies

did not work and Larry felt tension in his right arm he agreed to walk away from the interaction and to stay away until he calmed down. Then, he would come back and resume the conversation calmly. The goal of this phase of treatment was to teach Larry to avoid the temper outburst by providing him with several alternative self-control tactics.

The Teacher-Coordinated Treatment Program. Larry's teachers and I met at the school several days after the training session described above ended. The self-control strategy was explained to the group and all agreed that whenever Larry walked away they would await his return before pursuing the conversation. The teachers also agreed verbally to reinforce Larry whenever he handled a stressful event without losing control. He would be allowed to walk out of a classroom if the need arose and stand in the hall by the classroom door; when he calmed down, he could reenter the room.

The teachers also agreed to collect data on Larry's behavior throughout the entire spring semester. They used a daily log to record their observations. Once a week they turned in their observations to the school counselor who gave me the weekly data report every Friday after school. The behavioral log the teachers used is shown below in Figure 7-4.

Results of the Treatment Program

The results of the school coordinated program based on the observational data reported by

Figure 7-4. Data Form Collected from the Teachers Regarding Client's Weekly Behavior

	Monday	Tuesday	Wednesday	Thursday	Friday
Number of temper episodes					
Number of stress interactions handled successfully					

Teacher's Name _____

Figure 7-5. The Frequency of Temper Losses and Utilization of Self-Control During Stress Interactions

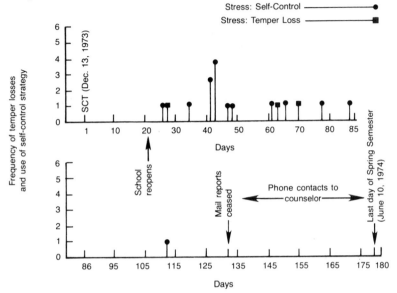

the teachers are shown in Figure 7-5. Stress situations handled successfully are represented in the figure as self-control responses. The teachers reported stress situations as interactions between themselves and Larry or Larry and his peers where conflict was involved. He lost his temper three times during the semester. I continued to see Larry once a week during the semester to review the teachers' data and to provide him with support and encouragement. The program ended on June 10, 1974, which was the end of the term. A follow-up contact one year later was made with the school counselor who mentioned that Larry had had only two reported temper outbursts during the year.

This successful program illustrates how teachers can assist in a behavior control program with minimal cost to themselves in time and energy. It should also be noted that the program was carried out at no financial cost to the school system. The teachers' commendable recordkeeping on Larry's behavior helped me to evaluate the efficacy of the program. The observational data provided another benefit. Using the weekly data reports, I was able to keep the teachers informed of Larry's progress. This had a positive effect on the faculty and made them feel that their efforts were producing a desirable effect.

CASE STUDY

A Self-Instruction Technique to Teach Appropriate Anger Control

Donna Larkin

Positive consequences for behaviors that are not compatible with aggression are essential to a successful program. You must teach an alternate way of behaving. Training in self-control can be used in combination with a contingency management program to help develop skills that are incompatible with the problem behavior. While you are externally controlling students' aggressive behavior through a contingency management system, you can teach them an internal system of control. Eventually, the external system and teacher assistance in developing the self-control strategy can be withdrawn. Skills in self-control, once internalized, will generalize across settings and ultimately bring their own reward.

I'd like to describe an anger-control-and-expression procedure that I use in combination with my existing behavior management system. In this procedure, students learn to self-instruct. Eventually, they can internalize a strategy to control their own behavior.

I. In teaching students to self-instruct using this procedure, first explain the technique to them in the context of their current behavioral program. (See Figure 7-6, "Anger Control and Expression Procedure.") Explain to students that this procedure can be used to help control aggressive behavior so that they can earn more points, fulfill their contracts, or feel better about themselves. Enlist their cooperation in learning to use the procedure or "plan." For this technique to be effective, the students must want to control their own behavior, or they must be motivated otherwise (e.g., use it to earn more points). Students must be good candidates for self-instruction as well. Once students are committed,

Figure 7-6. Anger Control and Expression Procedure

1. *Recognize*
   "I'm getting angry."
2. *Restrain*
   "I need to cool down."
3. *Relay*
   "I need to express my feelings appropriately."

   • "I feel _____ (emotion) _____

   • When you _____ (specific behavior of other) _____, and

   • I would like it if _____ (make request for behavior change) _____ "

4. *Reward*
   "I did a great job controlling my feelings!"
   "I get _____ (reinforcer) _____."

describe the four *R*s of anger control and expression in general terms: *recognize, restrain, relay, reward.* Students must first recognize when "I am getting angry." Once students are aware that they are getting angry, they can immediately engage in an alternate behavior to calm down, or "restrain," that anger. In this way, students avoid the potential negative consequences of inappropriate expression of anger, whatever it may be. In this second step, students realize that, "I need to calm down." After a cool down period of several minutes, students "relay" their anger appropriately in the third step of this strategy. Students learn to "express my feelings appropriately," by completing a series of statements to another individual when calm. Finally, in the fourth step, students are rewarded after successfully controlling their anger. In addition to a positive self-statement, "I did a good job controlling my anger," students can be reinforced according to the conditions of their contingency management system.

II. Once students clearly understand the procedure, the teacher can relate the strategy to them. I'd offer the following suggestions to help students relate the strategy to their own behaviors. I developed a handout to help students with these concepts. (See Figure 7-6.)

A. *Recognition* — Students can learn to distinguish appropriate versus inappropriate expressions of anger through analyzing facial expressions, tone of voice, body movement, and eye contact. Components of their expression are likely to produce certain effects. Students can learn to predict the cause and effect of their own behavior. Teachers can use a variety of techniques (i.e., modeling, role-playing, videotaping, etc.) to enable students to analyze the appropriateness, sequence, and effect of their own responses. For example, students may identify hands clenching as the first sign of anger. At this point, they recognize, "I am getting angry." Create a self-statement in the student's own language.

B. *Restrain* — Once an anger sequence begins, students can "restrain" themselves when they realize that, "I need to calm down," or an equivalent statement. Develop individual "cool down" techniques in accordance with classroom rules and contingencies. Students can select one technique or try a variety, including taking a walk, doing a deep breathing exercise, looking at a magazine, drawing a picture, sitting in a quiet room, standing outside the door, and doing physical exercise.

C. *Relay* — Students identify a self-statement when they feel calm enough to express their own feelings; for example, "I need to express my feelings appropriately." Students relay their anger to another individual by completing a series of statements in the following formula:

- I feel *angry*
- When you *don't call on me in science*
- I would like it if *you called on me next time*

D. *Reward* — When the procedure successfully interrupts the aggressive or angry response, the students reward themselves. Develop rewarding statements with each student. Reinforcers should be agreed upon in advance and may easily comply with token, point, or contract systems.

III. Practice the procedure with each student. You can begin by saying the statements together. Then, whisper as the student self-instructs out loud. Finally, the student whispers alone, or eventually, to himself. Practice the series with actual problem situations. Teacher and student can role play completing the anger expression formula with various sentence completions to match each situation.

IV. Provide the student with the opportunity to use the procedure in the classroom. If other teachers are involved, make sure that the procedure is understood and allowed (i.e., John should be allowed to stand outside the classroom for five minutes to cool down in all classes.)

The system should be closely monitored to prevent abuse and to ensure consistency. For example, if a verbal cue is used to prompt the self-instruction, then all should use the same cue at the appropriate time. As the student begins to use the system independently, decrease participation cues. Parent participation can also help generalize the strategy.

Figure 7-7. Strategy Selection Chart for Aggression

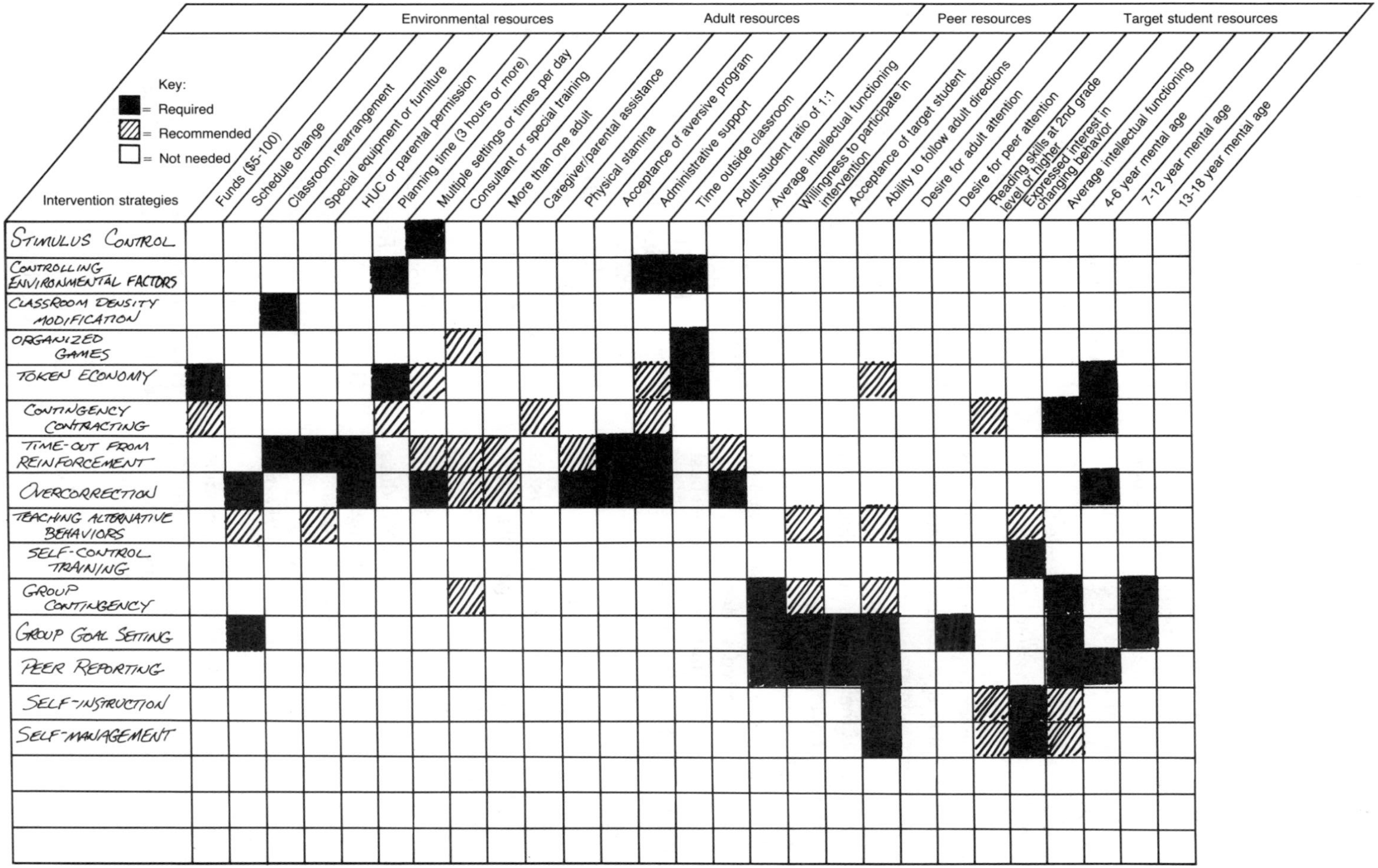

243

Discussion Questions

1. Why is it important to conduct a thorough analysis of aggressive behaviors, even after they take place?
2. Name four types of aggression that children may exhibit and give examples of each one.
3. Discuss the importance of *preventing* aggression and give five examples of how you might prevent aggression or confrontations at school.
4. Describe three environmental strategies for intervening on aggression or related behaviors.
5. How does teacher verbal behavior play a role in aggression and confrontation?
6. In using group contingencies for aggression, why should you exercise caution?
7. Name five skills that you would include in a prosocial, behavior-skill-training program for antisocial students.
8. What are the key features of a skills-training program for aggressive students?
9. How can self-management approaches best be used for aggressive behaviors?

References

Aiken, T. W., Stumphauzer, J. S., & Veloz, E. V. (1972). Behavioral analysis of nondelinquent brothers in a high juvenile crime community. *Behavioral Disorders, 2,* 212–222.

Azrin, N. H., & Wesolowski, M. D. (1974). Theft reversal: An overcorrection procedure for eliminating stealing by retarded persons. *Journal of Applied Behavior Analysis, 7,* 577–581.

Bandura, A. (1971). *Social learning theory.* New York: General Learning Press.

Bardill, D. R. (1977). A behavior-contracting program of group treatment for early adolescents in a residential treatment setting. *International Journal of Group Psychotherapy, 27,* 389–400.

Brooks, R. B., & Snow, O. L. (1972). Two case illustrations of the use of behavior modification techniques in the school setting. *Behavior Therapy, 3,* 100–103.

Camp, B. W., Bloom, G. E., Hebert, F., & VanDoorninck, W. J. (1977). "Think aloud": A program for developing self-control in young aggressive boys. *Journal of Abnormal Child Psychology, 5,* 157–169.

Caprara, G. V., & Kerr, M. M. (1985). Aggression in children. Unpublished manuscript, University of Rome, Italy.

Coats, K. I. (1979). Cognitive self-instructional approach for reducing disruptive behavior of young children. *Psychological Reports, 44,* 127–134.

Dollard, J., Dobb, L., Miller, N., Mowrer, O., & Sears, R. (1939). *Frustration and aggression.* New Haven: Yale University Press.

Feindler, E. L., Marriott, S. A., & Iwata, M. (1984). Group anger control training for junior high school delinquents. *Cognitive Therapy and Research, 8*(3), 299–311.

Gershman, L. (1976). Eliminating a fire-setting compulsion through contingency management. In J. D. Krumboltz & C. E. Thoresen (Eds.), *Consulting methods.* New York: Holt, Rinehart & Winston, 206–213.

Gilliam, J. E. (1981). *Crisis intervention project SED: The training program for teachers of the seriously emotionally disturbed.* Austin, TX: Education Service Center Region XIII.

Gold, M., & Mann, D. W. (1982). Alternative schools for troublesome secondary students. *The Urban Review, 14,* 305–316.

Goldstein, A. P. (1987). Teaching prosocial skills to antisocial adolescents. In C. M. Nelson, R. B. Rutherford, Jr., & B. I. Wolford (Eds.), *Special education in the criminal justice system* (pp. 215–250). Columbus: Merrill.

Hazel, J. S., Schumaker, J. B., Sherman, J. A., & Sheldon-Wildgen, J. (1981). *ASSET: A social skills program for adolescents.* Champaign, IL: Research Press.

Hollin, C. R., & Courtney, S. A. (1983). A skill training approach to the reduction of institutional offending. *Personality and Individual Differences, 4,* 257-264.

Hood-Smith, N. E., & Leffingwell, R. J. (1984). The impact of physical space alteration on disruptive classroom behavior: A case study. *Education, 104,* 224-230.

Huber, F. (1976). A strategy for teaching cooperative games: Let's put back the fun in games for disturbed children. In N. J. Long, W. C. Morse, & R. G. Newman (Eds.), *Conflict in the classroom: The education of emotionally disturbed children* (pp. 266-278). Belmont, CA: Wadsworth.

Jackson, N. F., Jackson, D. A., & Monroe, C. (1983). *Getting along with others: Teaching social effectiveness to children.* Champaign, IL: Research Press.

Kauffman, J. M., Grieger, T., & Grieger, R. M. (1976). Effects of peer reporting on cooperative play and aggression of kindergarten children. *Journal of School Psychology, 14,* 307-313.

Kendall, P. C., & Finch, A. J. (1976). A cognitive-behavioral treatment for impulse control: A case study. *Journal of Consulting and Clinical Psychology, 44,* 852-857.

Kerr, M. M., Nelson, C. M., & Lambert, D. L. (1987). *Helping adolescents with learning and behavior problems.* Columbus, OH: Merrill.

Kerr, M. M., Strain, P. S., & Ragland, E. U. (1982). Component analysis of a teacher-mediated peer-feedback treatment package: Effects on positive and negative interactions of behaviorally handicapped children. *Behavior Modification, 2,* 277-280.

Knutson, J. F. (1973). Aggression as manipulable behavior. In J. F. Knutson (Ed.), *The control of aggression.* Chicago: Aldine Publishing.

Kozloff, M. A. (1973). *Reaching the autistic child: A parent training program.* Champaign, IL: Research Press.

Lochman, J. E., Burch, P. R., Curry, J. F., & Lampron, L. B. (1984). Treatment and generalization effects of cognitive-behavioral and goal-setting interventions with aggressive boys. *Journal of Consulting and Clinical Psychology, 52*(5), 915-916.

Lochman, J. E., & Curry, J. F. (1986). Effects of social problem-solving training and self-instruction training with aggressive boys. *Journal of Clinical Child Psychology, 15*(2), 159-164.

Long, S. J., & Sherer, M. (1984). Social skills training with juvenile offenders. *Child and Family Behavior Therapy, 6,* 1-11.

Luce, S. C., Delquadri, J., & Hall, R. V. (1980). Contingent exercise: A mild but powerful procedure for suppressing inappropriate verbal and aggressive behavior. *Journal of Applied Behavior Analysis, 13,* 583-594.

Mann, R. A. (1985). Conduct disorder. In M. Hersen & C. G. Last (Eds.), *Behavior therapy casebook: Springer series on behavior therapy and behavioral medicine* (pp. 318-330). New York: Springer.

Mayer, G. R., Nafpaktitis, M., Butterworth, T., & Hollingsworth, P. (1987). A search for the elusive setting events of school vandalism: A correlational study. *Education and Treatment of Children, 10*(3), 259-270.

McAfee, J. K. (1987). Classroom density and the aggressive behavior of handicapped children. *Education and Treatment of Children, 10*(2), 134-145.

McCullough, J. P., Huntsinger, G. N., & Nay, W. R. (1977). Self-controlled treatment of aggression in a 16-year-old male: Case study. *Journal of Consulting and Clinical Psychology, 45,* 322-331.

Millman, H. L., Schaefer, C. E., & Cohen, J. J. (1980). *Therapies for school behavior problems.* San Francisco: Jossey-Bass Publishers.

Murphy, H. A., Hutchinson, J. M., & Bailey, J. S. (1983). Behavioral school psychology goes outdoors: The effects of organized games on playground aggression. *Journal of Applied Behavior Analysis, 16*(1), 29-36.

Nelson, C. M., & Polsgrove, L. (1981). The etiology of adolescent behavior disorders. In G. Brown, R. L. McDowell, & J. Smith, (Eds.), *Educating adolescents with behavior disorders.* Columbus, OH: Merrill.

Parke, R., & Slaby, R. (1983). The development of aggression. In P. Mussen (Ed.), *Handbook of child psychology* (Vol. 4), *Socialization, personality, and social development.* New York: Wiley.

Patterson, G. R. (1974). Interventions for boys with multiple conduct problems: Multiple settings, treatments, and criteria. *Journal of Consulting and Clinical Psychology, 42,* 471-481.

Patterson, G. R. (1977). Naturalistic observation in clinical assessment. *Journal of Abnormal Child Psychology, 5,* 309-322.

Patterson, G. R., & Cobb, J. A. (1973). Stimulus control for classes of noxious behaviors. In J. F. Knutson (Ed.), *The control of aggression.* Chicago: Aldine Publishing Co., 145-199.

Rosen, H. S., & Rosen, L. A. (1983). Eliminating stealing: Use of stimulus control with an elementary student. *Behavior Modification, 7*(1), 56-63.

Staub, R. W. (1987). *The effects of publicly posted feedback on middle school students' disruptive hallway behavior.* Unpublished doctoral dissertation, University of Pittsburgh.

Strain, P. S., & Ezzell, D. (1978). The sequence and distributional behavioral disordered adolescents' disruptive/inappropriate behaviors. *Behavior Modification, 2,* 403-425.

Surgeon General's Scientific Advisory Committee on Television and Social Behavior. (1972). *Television and growing up: The impact of televised violence.* Washington, DC: Government Printing Office.

Webster, R. E. (1976). A timeout procedure in a public school setting. *Psychology in the Schools, 13,* 72-76.

Weiskopf, P. E. (1980). Burnout among teachers of exceptional children. *Exceptional Children, 47,* 18-23.

Wilson, R. (1984). A review of self-control treatments for aggressive behavior. *Behavioral Disorders, 9*(2), 131-140.

Wolpe, J. (1969). *The practice of behavior therapy.* New York: Pergamon Press.

Chapter 8

OUTLINE

Assessing Deficits in School Survival Skills

School-Wide Strategies

Environmentally Mediated Strategies

Teacher-Mediated Strategies

Peer-Mediated Strategies

Self-Mediated Strategies

Case Study

OBJECTIVES

The reader who completes this chapter should be able to

- List the most important school survival skills and deficits.
- Describe three environmental modifications to improve school survival skills.
- Design a teacher-mediated intervention for students who arrive late to class.
- Use a group contingency procedure to modify the off-task behavior of secondary school students.
- Develop a self-monitoring procedure to improve students' academic productivity.

This chapter addresses an important group of problems that have been overlooked in many behaviorally handicapped students: **deficits in school survival skills,** those behaviors that enable a student to get the most from instructional interactions. Recent research has shown that many students simply do not learn how to adjust to the many demands of the school setting (Kerr & Zigmond, 1984). Consider these vignettes:

Andy was never really a troublemaker, but he just didn't seem to "get his act together" at school. His projects were always incomplete, and he often showed up late for classes. Frequent tardiness resulted in repeated detentions. Sometimes he forgot he had detention and wound up having to go to the in-school suspension room for a day or two. We never seemed to find the right intervention for Andy, and he developed a reputation as a "loser."

Yvonne just didn't seem to fit into any classroom. She wasn't exactly a behavior problem, but she

was no angel, either. For example, she would never answer the questions I asked, and I found myself repeating questions to her just because she was daydreaming during our discussions. Sometimes I actually wondered if she had a neurological problem, but her pediatrician said she was fine. Let's face it: Yvonne was a "space cadet."

How could I ever forget Corrado? I never could put my finger on his problem. He was a nice enough kid, but he was totally disorganized. His desk would have scared the Health Department, his assignments always looked like they had been run over, and his test papers were decorated with doodles. No amount of lecturing could ever change that kid. I wonder what ever happened to him?

I guess you would call Lila unmotivated or lazy. She really got under my skin, because she never did what I asked the first time. Every request turned into a battle—and all this struggling with a five-year-old! She was fine as long as you didn't ask her to do anything . . .

These recollections may sound familiar to you. Some researchers might call these children "socially immature," "socially inadequate," or attention deficit disordered (Kauffman, 1989; Kerr, Nelson, & Lambert, 1987; Quay & Werry, 1979). Regardless of the term you use, the *behaviors* will be your real concern. Table 8-1 lists definitions for some of the behaviors we discuss in this chapter.

Assessing Deficits in School Survival Skills

Many of the problems in Table 8-1 will be obvious to you and to the other teachers. In a large secondary school, however, you may not have a chance to compare notes with a student's other teachers. Consider using a pencil-and-paper checklist for assessing a student's specific skill deficits. Figure 8-1 (pp. 252-53) displays the School Survival Skills Scale, appropriate for middle and high school students.

As you read through the items of the School Survival Skills Scale, consider the skills and problems cited in a recent study as *most important for high school students* (Kerr, Zigmond, Schaeffer, & Brown, 1986):

Important Skills	*Problem Behaviors*
1. Meets due dates	1. Seldom completes assignments
2. Arrives at school on time	2. Cannot follow written directions
3. Attends class every day	3. Gives "back talk" to teacher
4. Exhibits interest in academic work	4. Falls asleep in class
5. Accepts consequences of behavior	5. Is quick to give up

Focus your intervention efforts on these skills and problems first. By the way, similar lists have resulted from work with elementary school children (Cobb, 1972; Kerr & Zigmond, 1984; McConnell et al., 1984; Walker & Rankin, 1983). Notice the emphasis on *compliance and academic productivity;* as you prepare children for mainstreaming at any grade level, be sure to give these skills special emphasis.

Here are a few questions to ask yourself as you analyze a student's classroom performance.

1. *Is the behavior developmentally appropriate for this student?* Reconsider the environment. Perhaps the environment or the social situation is too demanding for a student at this developmental level. Remember, the behavior may be a message that the student *cannot* handle a situation or setting. If so, alter your objectives and requests.

2. *Is there a clear expectation for an alternative, appropriate behavior in this setting?* Be sure the student has clear, appropriate expectations for performance. Are the rules posted or orally reviewed for the student? Is someone feeling sorry for the student and thereby not enforcing the rules for behavior?

3. *Has the student received training in alternative appropriate behaviors?* If you're unsure about a student's skills, it does not hurt to review these skills as a teaching assessment. Remember that some students require regular review and practice in order to maintain their self-help and social skills.

4. *Has the student* suddenly *lost the skills?* If so, then contact as many other persons involved with the student as possible. See if there is a health or family change that may be responsible for the sudden behavioral change. Remember, many of the problem behaviors described in this chapter may be the result of anxiety or depression, and this may reflect a serious problem.

5. *Has the problem occurred before?* See if you can identify any similarities between the episodes. Consider using an A-B-C analysis to determine what causes or maintains the behavior. Perhaps the behavior is being reinforced.

Table 8-1. Definitions of School Survival Skills and Deficits

Skill or Deficit	Definition	Author
On-task	. . . any time a student [has] his or her eyes focused on a book, paper, or self-monitoring question card, [has] eyes closed or word covered and lips moving, [is] writing words, or [is] checking words.	Harris (1986)
Preparation	The student is preparing to work or completing an activity or participating in the routine procedures of the class. The following are considered preparation. 1. Getting books or paper 2. Looking for materials 3. Sharpening a pencil 4. Flipping through pages of a book to find the correct page 5. Moving into a structured group 6. Putting materials away 7. Passing in homework or classwork 8. Waiting for teacher direction 9. Waiting for teacher's help	Kerr & Zigmond (1984)
Off-task	The student is off-task if she is not paying attention to or participating in a class activity or if she is not working on a class assignment or project. Examples of off-task behaviors are the following: 1. Student looks at fingernails. 2. Student reads a note from a friend. 3. Student puts head down on desk during math. 4. Student folds her paper into a small triangle. 5. Student stares at teacher during individual reading time. 6. Student stares at blank chalkboard. 7. Student draws faces on paper during math class. 8. Student reads a comic book during language arts. 9. Student wanders around room. 10. Student writes a letter (Note: you must be able to see this to know that it is off-task).	Kerr et al. (1987)
On-task	The student is on-task if he is working. Students engaged in one of the following are considered on-task or attending: 1. Looking at teacher in absence of inappropriate behavior 2. Looking or working at the chalkboard 3. Writing or taking notes 4. Reading book or assignment 5. Raising hand to ask or answer questions about classwork 6. Asking questions related to classwork 7. Questions or statements to the teacher regarding one's grades or performance on a test or paper 8. Talking to teacher if teacher initiates conversation 9. Peer-tutoring/working	Kerr et al. (1987)

6. *Are other students engaging in the same behavior?* There's a possibility that the student is imitating others. Reevaluate the contingencies for the other students. Are *they* being reinforced? How can you alter the contingencies for the target student *and* peers?

Once you have answered these questions, you will want to ensure that your school and classroom environment support your efforts to improve your students' on-task behavior. Let's look at a few school-wide interventions first.

School-Wide Strategies

Most of the school-wide interventions are designed to improve transitional behaviors of older students (e.g., changing classes, tardiness). Here are some possibilities.

Hall monitors are those nonprofessionals who check nonclassroom areas for unauthorized student "trespassers." Security guards serve this purpose in some schools; in others, parent volunteers monitor the halls. In any event, these individuals are not normally trained to recognize the special needs of handicapped youth. They do not attend in-service sessions tailored to their interactions with handicapped students. Consequently, they may dismiss the actions of a handicapped student who needs "regular" treatment with respect to enforcing rules, or they may unjustly penalize a mentally retarded student who has not understood school policy. We suggest that special educators review the operations of hall monitors to help these personnel individualize (when appropriate) their strategies for dealing with handicapped students. In turn, handicapped youth should receive (and review as often as necessary) a clear explication of class attendance and of hall-monitoring policies. In this explanation, teachers should make the

real-world link to individuals with whom students may have similar interactions:

- Ticket takers at athletic events, concerts, and movies
- Traffic police officers
- Airport security personnel
- Department store security agents and dressing-room monitors

Drawing these realistic analogies can reduce the feelings that only students are scrutinized in moving about an environment. Taking the illustrations one step further, you can talk about managing interactions (especially confrontations) with persons in these positions of authority.

Of course, it is important to discuss school-hall monitoring before the student develops problems (or a faulty reputation) with security people.

Hall passes, if they are to be effective, must be produced in a way that prevents counterfeiting. Like tokens in a token economy program, hall passes should be durable (if they are to be reused), unique (to avoid counterfeit), convenient to produce, and age-appropriate.

Random attendance checks may control absenteeism and tardiness. Each day (or check), a class period (not announced in advance) is chosen for monitoring. After attendance has been taken, the names of the late or absent students are announced for penalties. Alternatively, students who were on time might be recognized or reinforced for their behavior. Van Houten's (1981) research on public posting offers principles that warrant our consideration. His work on public posting involves publicly listing the names of persons who have (or have not) engaged in a target behavior. In one middle school, the problems of class cutting and tardiness are being applied as follows: when a student arrives late to class, he is assigned a detention for the next afternoon; the names of all students earning detention for tardiness or cuts are posted in visible areas throughout the school, such as in the cafeteria.

Figure 8-1.   School Survival Skills Scale

DATE: _____

STUDENT'S NAME: _____   TEACHER'S NAME: _____
(please print)   (please print)
Circle the appropriate response.
STUDENT'S GRADE: 9   10   11   12   THIS STUDENT IS IN YOUR CLASS FOR:
STUDENT'S SEX: M   F   Homeroom   Social Studies
STUDENT'S SPECIAL ED CLASSIFICATION: English   Science
SED   LD   EMR   VH   HI   PH   Math   Other _____

_____

DIRECTIONS: *Please read each statement and circle the corresponding letter that best describes this student's typical behavior. Be sure that you mark every item.*

THIS STUDENT:	NEVER	SOMETIMES	USUALLY	ALWAYS	NOT OBSERVED
1. . . . stays awake in class.	N	S	U	A	X
2. . . . gets to class on time.	N	S	U	A	X
3. . . . complies with requests of adults in authority.	N	S	U	A	X
4. . . . stays calm and in control of emotions.	N	S	U	A	X
5. . . . brings necessary materials to class.	N	S	U	A	X
6. . . . is persistent even when faced with a difficult task.	N	S	U	A	X
7. . . . asks for help with schoolwork when necessary.	N	S	U	A	X
8. . . . responds to others when they speak.	N	S	U	A	X
9. . . . arrives at school on time.	N	S	U	A	X
10. . . . completes assigned work.	N	S	U	A	X
11. . . . behaves appropriately in a variety of settings.	N	S	U	A	X

Figure 8-1. *Continued*

THIS STUDENT:	NEVER	SOMETIMES	USUALLY	ALWAYS	NOT OBSERVED
12. . . . manages conflict through nonaggressive means.	N	S	U	A	X
13. . . . organizes study time efficiently.	N	S	U	A	X
14. . . . can concentrate on work without being distracted by peers.	N	S	U	A	X
15. . . . works well independently.	N	S	U	A	X
16. . . . accepts the punishment if caught doing something wrong.	N	S	U	A	X
17. . . . turns in assignments when they are due.	N	S	U	A	X
18. . . . speaks appropriately to teachers.	N	S	U	A	X
19. . . . follows written directions.	N	S	U	A	X
20. . . . talks calmly to an adult when perceived to be unjustly accused.	N	S	U	A	X
21. . . . uses time productively while waiting for teacher.	N	S	U	A	X
22. . . . attends class.	N	S	U	A	X
23. . . . exhibits interest in improving academic performance.	N	S	U	A	X
24. . . . is good at taking tests.	N	S	U	A	X
25. . . . appropriately handles corrections on classwork.	N	S	U	A	X
26. . . . identifies the central theme of a lecture (demonstrates by stating or writing the main ideas and supporting facts).	N	S	U	A	X

PLEASE CHECK TO MAKE SURE ALL ITEMS ARE MARKED.

Source: From *The School Survival Skills Curriculum* by N. Zigmond, M. M. Kerr, A. Schaeffer, G. Brown, and H. Farra, 1986. Pittsburgh: University of Pittsburgh. Reprinted by permission.

Environmentally Mediated Strategies

Within your classroom, you can make changes to assist your students in learning better school survival skills. For example, you can adjust the curriculum, have clear expectations for class preparedness, and promote independence rather than teacher dependency. Let us take a look at some strategies.

SCHEDULING

Post a schedule of daily activities (for younger students) or classroom periods (for older students) that accounts for time within 30-minute intervals (younger students) or for class periods. The schedule should be specific about what the activity requires of the students, especially if a change of classes is required.

Many teachers have found it helpful to post a shorter schedule adjacent to the overall one for changeable aspects of the school day. For example, this "little" schedule might include weekly sessions with a speech therapist, special schoolwide events, or vacation days.

For junior high or high school students, provide an 8½-by-11-inch printed schedule for their notebooks. If you work with a student who has tantrums or seems easily upset when the school schedule changes, arrange a time to review the schedule with the student, and suggest that the student use a highlighter pen to mark special or important dates (when a term paper is due, when auditions for the school chorus are being held, when the deadline for ordering class rings is here).

Be sure your classroom has a large wall clock to help students who want to remain on schedule. It may also be useful in giving students some idea about how much time has elapsed during a work period and how much time remains for them to complete work. To assist elementary school students in becoming independent in time-management, announce that it is time to check the clock and ask one student to tell the group how much time remains in the period. Repeat this process until each student is able to use the clock independently.

PLACEMENT OF WORK

Each student should be given a designated place to pick up daily work. For a younger student, this might be a work tray with the student's name on it. In this work tray would be textbooks and work sheets, as well as a schedule of assignments. If you are working with very young children use the work tray to store each child's favorite toys, nametag for field trips, or art work to take home. For a secondary school student, work trays are not appropriate, but a businesslike in/out filing tray may be suitable. Be sure to provide trays for all students so that you do not call attention to the student needing extra support.

CURRICULAR MODIFICATIONS

You will need certain curricular modifications to support the student whose problem is temporary developmental regression or dependency. Assisting a student by modifying assignments does *not* mean, however, that you should prevent the student from *ever* experiencing failures, as emphasized by Seligman (1975):

> . . . creating short cuts around [all] difficulties for children is not kind — depression follows from helplessness.
>
> A sense of worth, mastery or self-esteem cannot be bestowed. It can only be earned. If it is given away, it ceases to be worth having, and it ceases to contribute to individual dignity. If we remove [all of] the obstacles, difficulties, anxiety, and competition from the lives of our young people, we may no longer see generations of young people who have a sense of dignity, power, and worth (pp. 158–159).

The following guidelines for curricular modifications include ways to prevent a child from experiencing the repeated failure or the unwarranted success that Seligman concludes can be demoralizing to a child's sense of self-worth and achievement. We see the necessity of making the environment demanding but predictable, allowing the child a sense of control and accomplishment.

1. Do schedule ample time for a student working at a typical pace to complete the assignment.
2. Do not give in to a student's complaints that a task is too long, if you have planned it carefully.
3. Do place work materials in a designated storage area — off your desk — so that the student must take responsibility for picking up work.
4. Do plan tasks that will challenge students but that will occasionally allow them to experience some failure so that they will learn how to handle frustration.
5. Do let students know when an assignment is difficult or encompasses new knowledge or skills.
6. Do not keep students from knowing how they are performing. Help students develop a sense of competence by sharing your evaluations with them.
7. Do provide specific feedback on students' papers so that they can modify their performances accordingly. Use descriptive praise, too.
8. Do not assist students any time they request help. Establish guidelines for requesting help (perhaps a signaling device on the student's desk) and follow these guidelines.
9. Do encourage students to help themselves by using the dictionary, reference books, or answer keys.
10. Do encourage students to assist one another through peer-monitoring or peer-tutoring.
11. Do give students lots of positive feedback on their performances. Encourage them to make positive statements about their own work by asking questions ("How did you do in algebra today?" "Did you organize your study time well for this exam?").

Think of ways in which you can translate these general guidelines into actual practice in your classroom or other school setting.

Teacher-Mediated Strategies

Being the teacher of students who have problems with school survival skills is not easy. On the one hand, you need to create a structured environment that helps students perform their best. On the other hand, you face the challenge of helping students become more independent and less needy of outside structure and support. In this section we cover some of the familiar teacher-mediated interventions (contingency contracting, token economies, public posting, verbal feedback) and a few that have just begun to emerge in the literature (teaching school survival skills instruction and combined interventions). We begin with contingency contracting.

CONTINGENCY CONTRACTING

Kelley and Stokes (1982) summarized the advantages of establishing a contracting procedure as follows (Kerr, Nelson, & Lambert, 1987):

- Goal setting permits both parties to negotiate the amount of behaviors required to earn a contingent reward.
- This procedure has all of the advantages of a self-management strategy, without all of the responsibilities.
- Academic productivity can be directly targeted.

• Defining and achieving goals give students a sense of accomplishment.

Figure 8-2 displays a contract between an adolescent, Jerry, and her teacher. The purpose of this intervention was to encourage Jerry to work independently. Figure 8-3 shows the self-recording sheet Jerry used. Contracting is especially valuable if one or two students in your class need help on school survival skills. If several students share a skills deficit, however, you may prefer the convenience of a token economy, which can be very simple or more complex.

TOKEN ECONOMIES

Figure 8-4 shows a token economy chart for a resource room. Each student has a place to mark his own progress. Each space of the box allows one day's check. In this program, no checking was done on Friday, the reinforcement day. This chart was designed for students who spend one period per day (the chart depicts names of students for one period) in the resource room.

As you develop the token economy levels for your classroom, remember to include school survival skills. Their inclusion is especially important in the levels that immediately precede a student's return to the mainstream where these skills are so highly valued by regular classroom teachers.

TEACHING SCHOOL SURVIVAL SKILLS

One of your best approaches to improving your students' time on task is to teach them the important skills they lack. One curriculum (Zigmond, Kerr, Schaeffer, Brown, & Farra, 1986) thus far has addressed these important skills. This curriculum was developed especially for students in middle and high schools; it addresses the important survival skills and problems through a series of lessons accompanied by handouts, discussions, and a self-monitoring/group contingency procedure.

Unfortunately, we have not yet seen a similar curriculum for younger students. Some of the social skills curricula discussed in the last chapter include skills that would promote good classroom deportment, so you might want to review them for ideas for your younger students.

Time management is one of the most helpful skills your students can learn — how to organize their time for school tasks. To prepare for this instruction, consult a good time-management book; we suggest *Doing It Now* or *Getting Things Done,* both by E. C. Bliss.

A handy tool for improving time-management skills is an assignment sheet or notebook (Zigmond et al., 1986). Even young children can begin thinking about the length of assignments and how they will plan to accomplish them. Figure 8-5 shows a planning form for a primary school child; Figure 8-6 is for high school students.

PUBLIC POSTING

Public posting is a strategy that can be easily implemented in your classroom. When performance feedback is publicly displayed on a daily or weekly basis, student productivity and academic behavior improve (Fink & Carnine, 1975; Van Houten, 1979; Van Houten & LaiFatt, 1981). Exhibit student quiz and test scores, or number of academic units completed in the curricula. For example, your students might be independently pacing themselves. You can exhibit visually the check-off points along the way to assure that students understand how they are moving through the lessons. You may, for example, decide that students must read a certain number of sections in their science book, take a test, pass at a pre-established level, and then move on to the next section. When they pass, give them a visible mark on the classroom poster. If they do not

Figure 8-2.   Contract to Promote Independent Classwork

Contract

This contract is between _____*Jerry*_____ and _*Mrs. Rothchild*_
                          (Student)   (Teacher)

and is effective on ____*4-8*____ .
                        (Date)

*I, Jerry*_____ agree to try these behaviors.

(1) to stop and think, "Do I really need help?", before calling
on the teacher.

(2) to use at least one other source of help before calling on
Mrs. Rothchild

These other sources are:

textbook
study partner
the blackboard

(3) to check off on my "help" sheet which kind of help I tried
to use.

My goal is to have at least three (v) per English period, showing
that I tried to use other kinds of help.

If ____*Jerry*____ meets her goal, I, *Mrs. Rothchild*, will
provide her with an extra 5 points on the assignment for that
period. If there was no graded assignment, she will be issued a 5
point credit to be used when she chooses.

Signed: _*Jerry Kudo*_____   Date: __*4/8*____
          (Student)

Signed: _*Mrs. G. Rothchild*_   Date: __*4/8*____
          (Teacher)

Signed: _*J.L. Morton*_____   Date: __*4/9*____
          (Principal)

We will review this contract on ___*4/15*_____
                                     (Date)

Figure 8-3.   Checklist for Using Classroom Resources

Alternate Source of Help	Date: 4/9	Date: 4/10	Date: 4/11	Date: 4/12	Date: 4/13
1. Reread the assignment on the board.	✓	✓	✓	✓	✓
2. Consult the index of the textbook for other information.	✓		✓	✓	✓
3. Reread the chapter material that's relevant.	✓	✓	✓	✓	✓
4. Use a reference book (thesaurus, dictionary, etc.)					
5. Ask my assigned study partner		✓			
6. Asked the librarian later (Other)					✓
Total:	3	3	3	3	~~3~~ 4

Name: _Jerry_

Week of: _4/9_

Rev'd by: _E. Rothschild._

Figure 8-4. Token Economy Monitoring Chart: Resource Room

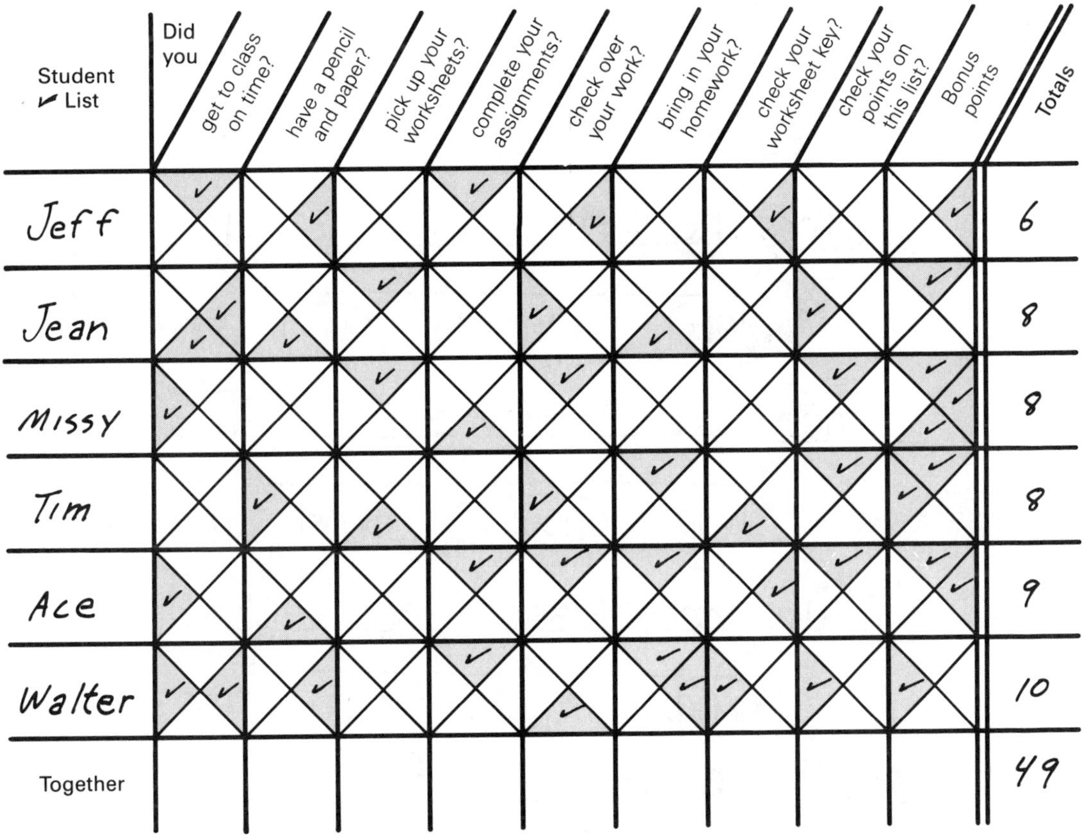

Student ✓ List	Did you get to class on time?	have a pencil and paper?	pick up your worksheets?	complete your assignments?	check over your work?	bring in your homework?	check your worksheet key?	check your points on this list?	Bonus points	Totals
Jeff	✓	✓		✓		✓	✓		✓	6
Jean	✓	✓	✓		✓	✓		✓	✓	8
Missy	✓		✓		✓			✓	✓	8
Tim		✓	✓	✓		✓	✓	✓	✓	8
Ace	✓	✓		✓	✓			✓	✓	9
Walter	✓ ✓	✓		✓		✓		✓	✓	10
Together										49

Source: Reprinted with permission from Kerr, M. M., Nelson, C. M., and Lambert, D. L. (1987). *Helping adolescents with learning and behavior problems.* Columbus, Ohio: Merrill (p. 129).

successfully reach the criterion level, give them remedial materials and later retest them. Task-analyzing the various assignments for the students can be monitoring in itself. According to Van Houten and Van Houten (1977), public posting promotes peer comments that are motivating. Public posting, with its elements of program charting, communicates to your students that you have multiple expectations of them that are to be achieved on a continuous basis.

COMBINING STRATEGIES

In a study by Smith, Schumaker, Schaefer, and Sherman (1982), students were trained to improve classroom participation. Positive changes were seen in a classroom previously troubled by disruptive behavior and poor group discussion. The key variables included teacher-posted rules for discussions, praise for student contributions, teacher restatement of the contribution, teacher-outlined discussion questions, graded student contributions, and public posting. An expanded version of the steps used to promote classroom discussion is displayed in Table 8-2 (p. 262).

This study was highlighted because it illustrates an excellent "combination intervention." Here students were given clear direction, feedback, reinforcement, praise, and public recognition. The teacher also assisted students with

Figure 8-5. Primary School Planning Form

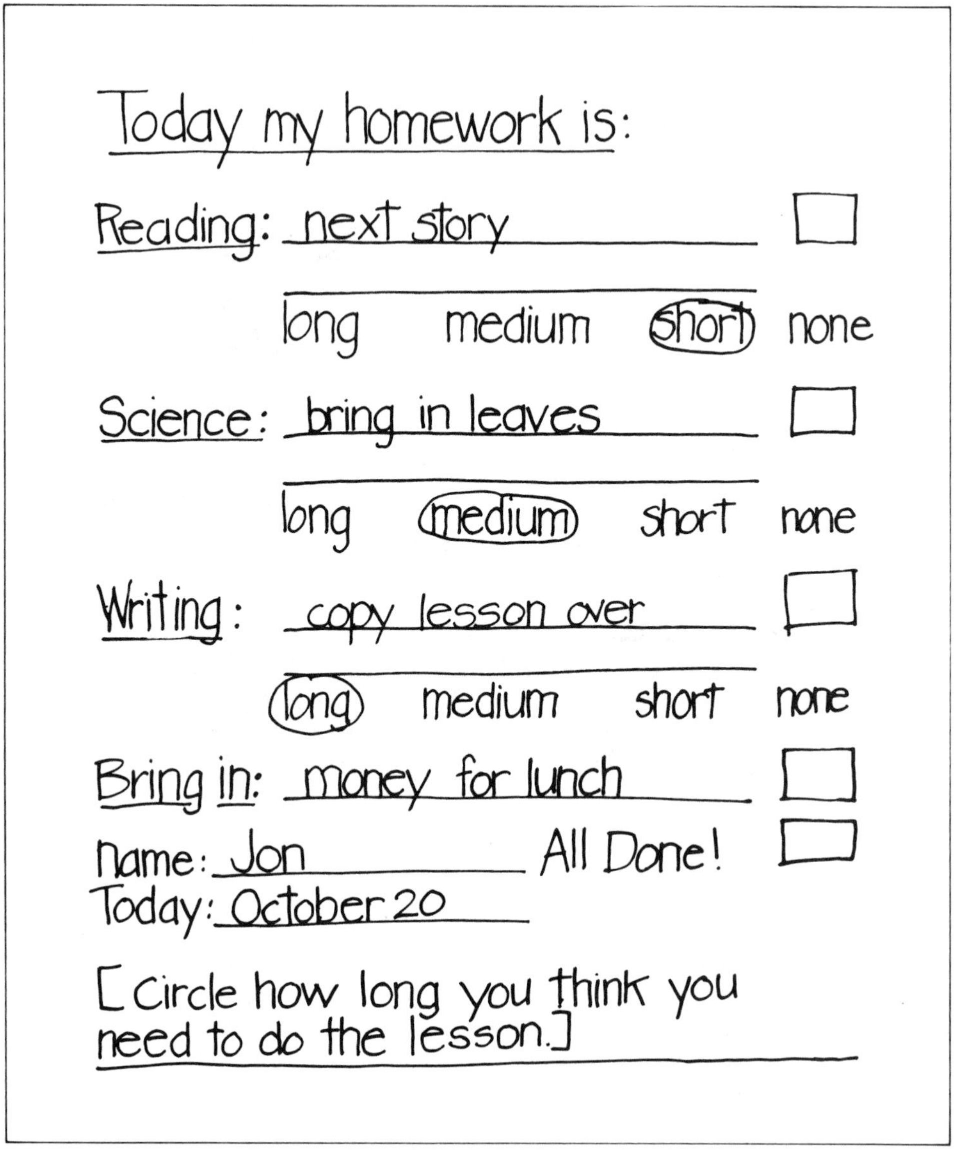

Today my homework is:

Reading: _next story_ ☐

  long   medium   (short)   none

Science: _bring in leaves_ ☐

  long   (medium)   short   none

Writing: _copy lesson over_ ☐

  (long)   medium   short   none

Bring in: _money for lunch_ ☐

name: _Jon_   All Done! ☐

Today: _October 20_

[Circle how long you think you
need to do the lesson.]

their note-taking methods by giving them out-lines or lists of questions before each discussion. Students took notes, previewed the material, and then prepared for relevant classroom discussion. We can assume that grades served as strong and effective reinforcers, because classroom discussion and participation im-proved. A response cost also was included in a clear hierarchy of expectations.

Another illustration of a combination strategy was offered by Kastelen, Nickel, and McLaughlin (1984), who used rapid teacher feedback, public posting, and teacher praise to improve the on-task and academic perfor-

Figure 8-6. High School Student's Grade and Progress Monitoring Form

As of Friday, Sept. 11

Course	Grade
French level three	70

comments _____ I was well prepared for the two small quizzes we had, one

on grammar and the other on vocabulary

American Literature Advanced .... —

comments _____ no grades thus far: working on a short paper due Monday—

will be our first grade

History 85

comments _____ This is the same as last week. I expect a test next week.

Elementary Physics 41

comments _____ I was barely able to grasp a simple principle and did poorly

on a quiz. Afterwards I went in for HELP. I understand it now.

Algebra and Trigonometry Advanced 90

comments _____ I am keeping up so it is not so bad as I might have expected.

Table 8-2.   Ten Steps to Promote Classroom Discussion

Step 1.   Hand out this list of rules pertaining to the discussion procedures. The rules for the students are as follows:
1. Raise your hand when you have something to say.
2. Speak only when you are called on.
3. If classmate is called on, put your hand down and listen quietly.
4. If you have something to add after your classmate is finished, raise your hand again.

Step 2.   Explain to the class why you think classroom discussion is important.

Step 3.   Designate a "recorder" to mark a point for student contributions that appear relevant. Contributions can be in the form of a question, answer, or comment.

Step 4.   Give examples of relevant statements.

Step 5.   Give examples of irrelevant statements.

Step 6.   Explain to the class and the classroom recorder that one point will be subtracted for irrelevant statements and disruptions (e.g., out of seat, talking out, or hand waving).

Step 7.   Discuss your discipline hierarchy. If anyone loses three points during one discussion period, she will be sent to the office and will have to attend an afternoon detention.

Step 8.   Let the students know that their total number of points earned or lost will determine their daily grade. Explain the point system as follows (the difference between the number of points earned and the number of points lost):

    Six or more = A
          Five = A−
          Four = B+
        Three = B
          Two = B−
          One = C+
    No points = C
    Minus One = C−
    Minus Two = D
  Minus Three = F

Step 9.   Post the weekly average of the discussion grades.

Step 10.   At the end of the semester, average the weekly grades, and convert them to 25% of their final grade.

Source: Reprinted with permission from Kerr, M. M., Nelson, C. M., and Lambert, D. L. (1987).
Helping adolescents with learning and behavior problems. Columbus, Ohio: Merrill (p. 130).

mance of an eighth-grade English class. Students received points for several school survival skills: bringing materials to class, starting to work promptly, reading as directed, and completing assignments correctly. Students' points were posted on a large display chart and were accompanied by teacher praise when a day's performance exceeded the previous one. The

students dramatically improved their academic productivity.

So far we have focused on academic-related behaviors. Now consider two teacher-mediated interventions for younger or more delayed children whose noncompliant behavior—like Lila's in the opening vignette—interferes with learning.

COMPLIANCE TRAINING

Severely handicapped or young students who ignore classroom rules and refuse to comply with teachers' requests may benefit from a procedure called compliance training (Schoen, 1986). The purpose of compliance training is to modify oppositional behavior and to train students to respond quickly to adult directions. In other words, **compliance training** is used when a student's behavior indicates he or she is not under the verbal stimulus control of an adult. The following steps can be used as guidelines in planning and implementing a compliance training program.

1. Write down at least ten behaviors that the student is capable of doing.
2. Select simple behaviors that can be done typically within fifteen seconds of your request.
3. Do not use commands to talk or to say a certain word or phrase.
4. Think of behaviors that the student perhaps will not do now but *can* do.
5. Examples of behaviors to use in compliance training are as follows: come here; sit down; pick up _____; give me _____; shake hands; stand up.
6. Once you have developed a list of behaviors, write these on a compliance training chart.
7. Plan a time during the day (usually about ten minutes) when you can work with the student.
8. Make the first request. If the student responds within fifteen seconds, give the student praise or the previously designated reinforcer.
9. If the student does not respond in fifteen seconds, physically prompt the response.
10. Praise the physically prompted response, but do not provide an additional reinforcer.
11. Do not use the verbal request at times during the day when you are unable physically to prompt the student's response.

12. Do not make repeated requests of the student for any response. One request is enough.
13. If necessary, schedule more than one session per day per student.

Once a student has mastered the requests in the initial compliance training program, add additional commands to the list. Gradually you should notice that the student complies promptly to most adult directions.

RESTITUTIONAL OVERCORRECTION

This intervention requires that students restore the environment that they mess up or destroy as a function of their noncompliant behavior (Foxx & Azrin, 1973). As restitutional overcorrection may be considered an aversive procedure, check with your supervisor before implementing this intervention. Specific guidelines for restitutional overcorrection are listed in Table 8-3.

Peer-Mediated Strategies

In the section describing environmentally mediated strategies, we suggest several ideas that could be implemented for an entire classroom. One reason for suggesting that activities be used for all students is to highlight the benefits of peer modeling. In some activities you do not select an individual as a peer model but emphasize the accumulated influence of all members of a student's peer group. For other activities, you designate a certain child to serve as a peer model.

You may want to choose peer models from a classroom of students older than your own group. In one school, for example, third graders had "accountant/advocates" in the fifth grade who helped the younger children tally their tokens and bid with these tokens at an annual white elephant sale.

Table 8-3. Guidelines for Using Restitutional Overcorrection for
Oppositional Behaviors

1. Define the problem behavior specifically.
2. Record baseline data on the rate or frequency of the problem behavior for at least three days. (Continue data collection during the program.)
3. Select a verbal cue to use when the student engages in the problem behavior, for example, "no spitting," "no throwing."
4. Select a restitutional activity that is relevant to the problem behavior. For example, have the student pick up the toys or work materials thrown then pick up all the trash on the classroom floor. Or have the student wipe up all spit then damp mop the classroom or hall floor and wipe all tables.
5. Decide when the program will be in effect each day; then arrange an adequate amount of time and staff assistance to implement the program. An adult must be available for at least forty-five minutes per problem behavior instance in the initial days of the program.
6. When student engages in the problem behavior, give the verbal cue and proceed with the restitutional activity.
7. Avoid eye contact, unnecessary physical contact, and unnecessary conversation during restitutional overcorrection. However, you will likely need to physically prompt the cleaning activities at first.
8. During the overcorrection procedure, if the student reengages in any of the designated problem behaviors, start the activities again.
9. Never use the verbal cue without the restitutional overcorrection activities until the problem behaviors are reduced to a low and stable rate.
10. Be sure to provide ample opportunity during the rest of the day for the student to receive attention for appropriate behaviors.
11. Remember, this program may require parental or guardian permission and should be implemented under the supervision of a professional competent in this aspect of behavior modification. Medical approval of this program should be obtained prior to the student's participation in it.

Note: The material in this table was adapted from R. M. Foxx & N. H. Azrin. The elimination of autistic self-stimulatory behavior by overcorrection. *Journal of Applied Behavior Analysis,* 1973, *1:* 13.

Peer tutoring, a successful way of structuring academic activities to involve peers, relies upon the principles of peer modeling and peer teaching (Scruggs & Osguthorpe, 1986). The peer tutor has to be a student who wants to do the tutoring, who may or may not have the skills in content area but who can follow teacher directions and learn from a model. Use your judgment when pairing up students for tutoring. Do not select a tutor who may embarrass the target student (e.g., a regular-class child who may criticize the special education student). When using a cross-age peer tutor (someone from another class), plan a schedule with the other that is mutually convenient and decide how to evaluate the tutor student's involvement.

The selection of the task for peer tutoring is an important step. Give first priority to the subject area in which the target student has difficulty. Choose academic tasks that are best taught through a "model or prompt + feedback or praise" format. Good choices could include spelling, vocabulary, sight words, and foreign language vocabulary; math facts; scientific formulas; and dates and names in social studies. Select academic tasks that require discrete responses and simple evaluation procedures (e.g., written tally of number correct and errors; sorting flashcards into mastered and nonmastered piles). Plan tasks that require relatively brief fifteen- to twenty-minute sessions. Guidelines for tutor training would include the following:

1. Pinpoint the task and analyze it before you begin.

2. Collect all needed materials.
3. Explain the goal of tutoring to the tutor.
4. Explain the task to the tutor, as much as you think is needed.
5. Instruct the tutor in the use of the materials.
6. Explain how the data are to be collected.
7. Role-play the actual tutoring procedures with the tutor.
   a. Model the teaching and the feedback/praise with the tutor and the target student.
   b. Ask the tutor to try being the student for a couple of steps.
   c. Provide feedback to the tutor.
   d. Role-play some problems the tutor may encounter.
   e. If needed, train the tutor to use particular phrases to reinforce the student.
   f. Provide the tutor with sample data and have him record them.
   g. Meet with the tutor before the first session to review the procedures.
   h. Meet daily after the tutoring session to answer questions.
   i. Reinforce the tutor for her efforts.

If you have questioned the usefulness of peer tutoring, consider the large body of research showing that peer tutors can be

- better instructional agents than teachers (Greenwood et al., 1984),
- trained to praise on-task behavior (Greer & Polirstok, 1982),
- effective in promoting academic behaviors that replace disruptions (Gable & Kerr, 1980),
- basic skills teachers (Ruffin, Lambert, & Kerr, 1985; Sindeler, 1982), and
- after-school sources of academic support and instruction.

We urge you to take advantage of this excellent peer-mediated intervention.

Group contingencies are powerful peer-mediated strategies that can be especially useful for older students whose poor academic skills are the result of having too much fun in the classroom. Our case study for this chapter highlights a group contingency for eighth grade students who arrived late to class and would not settle down and get to work. Notice how carefully the group contingency was planned (*with* the students) to avoid scapegoating or noncompliance with the intervention.

Self-Mediated Strategies

In this section we describe programs wherein the student serves as the primary agent of change. These strategies, introduced in Chapter 6, are strongly recommended for dependent students or students who are manipulative or oppositional when confronted with adult demands. Moreover, "such procedures are considered particularly appropriate for facilitating the educational success of handicapped students in mainstream environments, where resources for external management programs may be limited" (Sabatos, 1986, p. 23).

SELF-VERBALIZATION

Self-verbalization, sometimes termed **self-instruction,** has been used with socially immature and impulsive students to improve their academic performance. Figure 8-2 displays the contract of Jerry, a teacher-dependent girl who used self-verbalizations to remind herself of sources other than her teacher.

Shepp and Jensen (1983) used self-instruction with a seven-year-old hyperactive student to help him stay on-task and complete his work. Here are the self-verbalizations they taught the child:

What am I supposed to do?

How do I do it?

Do it!

Did I do it right?

Am I all done?

Hand it in!

Gradually the child learned to use simple one-word cues to remind him of these steps; then he was reminded by only a three-by-five card of happy faces, which he kept on his desk.

One commercially available program, *Think Aloud* (Camp & Bash, 1981), is designed for preschool and primary school children to self-instruct and learn to manage their impulsive behavior. This program can also be extended to include parents (Hughes, 1985). Perhaps your university or school district professional library has a copy you can review.

Although self-instruction seems to be a valuable tool for improving academic productivity, some studies have shown that this intervention alone is not necessarily effective (Shepp & Jensen, 1983). We recommend that you combine self-instruction with some form of external reinforcement and possibly response cost (Walker, 1983) for maximum effectiveness.

SELF-MONITORING

Recording one's own behavior is an effective way to increase academic productivity and on-task behavior (Sabatos, 1986). A question may arise in planning this intervention: What should the student monitor? Harris (1986) found that students fared about equally, whether they monitored academic task completion or on-task behavior. Perhaps you should choose the target behavior easiest for the child to understand and record.

REDUCING TEACHER ASSISTANCE IN SELF-MANAGEMENT PROGRAMS

A critical aspect of a successful self-management program is the reduction or fading out of teacher participation in the program. Once a student has shown consistent ability to self-monitor or self-instruct behavior, you should reduce your involvement in the program. Compare the student's self-monitoring data with your reliability checks on performance. If the student is reliably monitoring performance, consider the steps outlined in Table 8-4 for elementary school children. For adolescents, this "game" would not be appropriate. Rather,

Table 8-4. Guidelines for Reducing Teacher Input in Self-Management Programs

---

1. For self-management programs that involve a group of students, divide the group into two teams. List students' names, according to teams, on the chalkboard.

2. Announce that only one group will be lucky and have their self-management records checked each day. The same group will be eligible for bonus points.

3. Flip a coin each afternoon, designating one group heads and one group tails. The winning team has self-monitoring cards checked for reliability with teacher records. If each member of the team has a reliable score, team members then win bonus points or reinforcers.

4. Remember, promote the idea that being checked is a privilege.

5. Continue this procedure for at least seven school days.

6. During the next stage of the fading program, announce that a new game is beginning.

7. Place all students' names, written on paper strips, into a jar. Draw two names each day. These two lucky students receive the opportunity to earn bonus points or reinforcers.

8. After a period of at least seven school days, adjust the program so that you draw only one name. Maintain this stage of the program for at least one school week.

9. At the completion of the final phase, checking is discontinued.

Note: Material presented in this table was taken from F. Alford. *Self-management for teachers.* Nashville, Tenn.: George Peabody College for Teachers, 1980. Some of the ideas were based on Drabman, Spitnalnick, and O'Leary, 1973.

meet with the student to discuss termination of the self-evaluation activities and to recognize achievement of the student's goal.

Summary

This chapter offered remedies for students who lack school survival skills—those behaviors necessary to meet one's academic potential. School survival skills are crucial for students mainstreamed to least restrictive classrooms, and several strategies have proven effective in preparing students for this transition to regular education. We urge you to try one of these interventions—after you have determined through careful assessment what skills a student lacks.

Our case study for this chapter illustrates a group contingency solution to the problems of tardiness and poor class preparation.

CASE STUDY

A Group Contingency for Tardy Eighth Graders

Mary Elizabeth Nagy

As an eighth-grade teacher with a class experiencing transitional difficulties (specifically, late arrival and refusal to get on-task), I initially explored several possibilities before implementing a behavioral management program. First, I checked to see whether the students traveled as an entire group to my class. If they did, what class preceded mine? Were they coming from an area close to my classroom, or were they coming from another part of the building?

My eighth-grade class was ability-grouped, thus they traveled as a unit throughout the building. They traveled from areas within the building that were not in close proximity to my classroom. I teach fourth period English, preceded by the following classes throughout the course of the week: gym, industrial arts, home economics, and art. Directly following my class period is lunch for this group of students. Thus all activities before and after mine are generally less structured.

The data I collected showed that the students had been late eleven of the previous twelve days. The one day they arrived on time, they came directly from their homerooms because of an altered daily schedule. Further data demonstrated that the students failed to become on-task for ten minutes after class was scheduled to begin.

With data in hand, I asked for a meeting with the teachers whose classes came directly before mine. At this meeting I shared my dilemma, asking my peers to work with me to rectify the problem. They all shared my concern and agreed to help in solving the transition problem. After brainstorming, we decided to incorporate a group quiet time to deescalate the students' level of excitement and better prepare them for a more successful transition. Each professional stated she would require three minutes of quiet prior to the end of each class, during which time the students would be required to sit silently, doing absolutely nothing. This period of relaxation would be supplemented by each teacher's reminder to move quietly and quickly to my class.

Figure 8-7. Contingency Contract

We, the students of Ms. Nagy's fourth period English class, agree to do the following in order to earn a pizza party during our regularly scheduled fifth period lunch:

1. Arrive at English class on time daily. The time will be monitored by the school change-of-class bell and by Ms. Nagy.
2. Begin English class within three minutes of the sound of the school bell. These three minutes will be timed through the use of a timer set by Ms. Nagy.

We understand that for each time we arrive to class on time, our group will earn one piece of pizza. In addition, each time we are successful at beginning class on time, one piece of pepperoni will be added. Once we have accumulated eight pieces of both pizza and pepperoni, our group will have earned the privilege of planning the party, to be held two days after earning it.

I, Ms. Nagy, agree to assist my class in the following ways:

1. Set a kitchen timer at the conclusion of the class bell to prompt my class for three-minute readiness.
2. Post the pizza parts as they are earned.
3. Purchase all pizza supplies within two days of students' earning the party.

I, Ms. Jagus, as Home Economics teacher, agree to help Ms. Nagy's English class by

1. Monitoring the elected class representatives in the pizza preparation prior to the party.

We have read and understand this contract. We agree to the terms and will prompt each other to be successful in completing our contract. We will evaluate ourselves daily by either posting or not posting our earned pizza parts.

_____   _____   _____   _____   _____

Class signatures:

_____   _____   _____

_____   _____   _____

_____   _____   _____

_____   _____   _____

_____   _____   _____

_____   _____   _____

_____   _____   _____

Staff signatures:

_____   _____

Date:

_____

Strengthened by their support, I then addressed the problem with my students. I had already decided that a group contingency would help to solve the problem. I chose this intervention to demonstrate to the group the direct relationship between their behavior and the consequences that followed. Late arrival and disorderly conduct caused the group to get off to a disorderly start. The class went downhill from there. By having a more orderly beginning, our class could run more smoothly, and the students would actually enjoy the period more.

During the meeting with the class, we discussed the problem, and I shared the data I collected. We discussed the exact time they were

Figure 8-8. Progress Graph for Eighth Graders

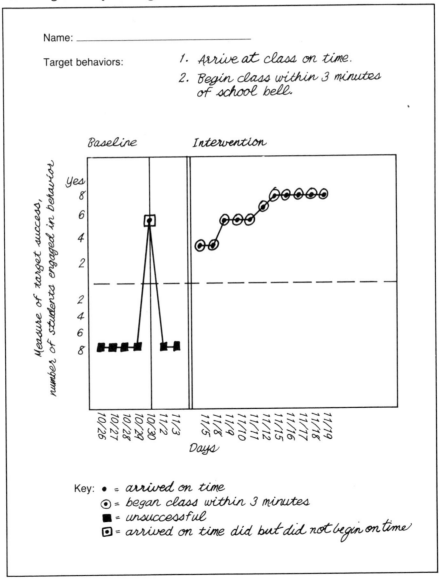

to enter my classroom and the time our class was to begin. I explained that to help the group reach these goals, we would enter into a contract. Our contract is shown in Figure 8-7.

The class chose to have a pizza party as a reinforcer for its success. This party would be held in my classroom during their regularly scheduled lunch time. The students chose toppings of cheese and pepperoni, agreeing that each student would receive two slices of pizza. They further agreed to invite the previously identified staff members. The pizza, the students decided, would be prepared by two peer-elected students within the group. All preparations would be completed in the home economics room under the supervision of that teacher, who agreed to this arrangement. The two students would be permitted to leave English the day of the party to go to her room.

The class chose to monitor its success using a large drawing of a pizza. Each day the group arrived on time, the class earned a slice of pizza. Pepperoni was earned by the class beginning on time. To check on this contingency, we used a kitchen timer set to ring three minutes after arrival to class. We set up the contract to extend over an eight-day period. The "monitoring pizza" was visible and permitted all of us to note group progress on a daily basis. The project was successful, as evidenced in Figure 8-8. We gradually stopped having the pizza parties on any regular basis, and the students maintained their new behaviors quite well.

Figure 8-9. Strategy Selection Chart for Deficits in School Survival Skills

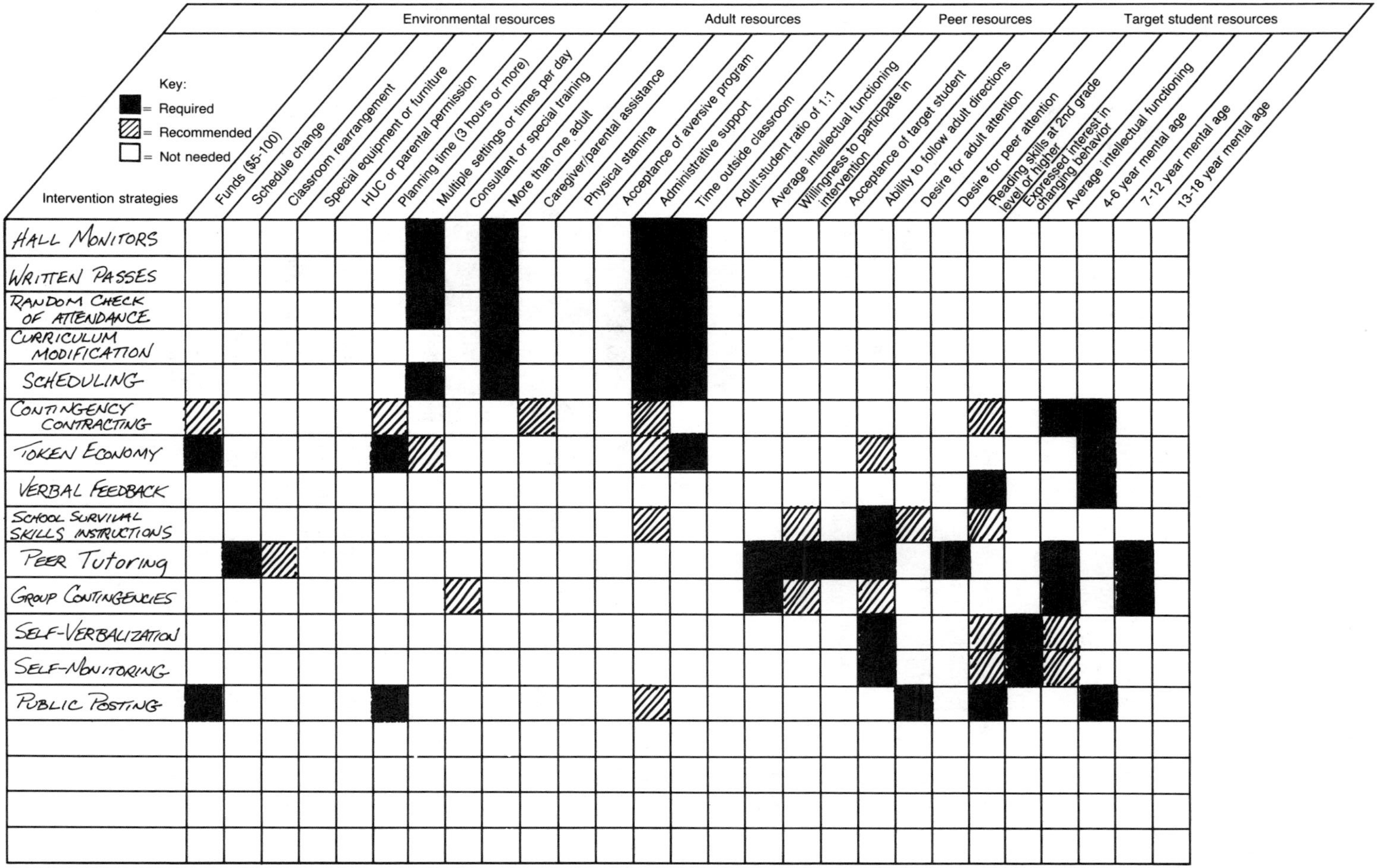

Discussion Questions

1. What are the most important school survival skills for mainstreamed students?
2. How can you assess school survival skills?
3. Name five ways you can increase the opportunities for your students' skills to generalize to other, less restrictive settings.
4. What environmental modifications can assist a student who is overly dependent on the teacher?
5. At what age can students begin learning time-management skills?
6. Describe a combined intervention for improving academic productivity.
7. What does research say about the benefits of peer tutoring?
8. How can a group contingency be used to improve students' school survival skills?
9. What is the most effective way of using self-instruction as an intervention for on-task behavior?

References

Alford, F. (1980). *Inservice on self-management for teachers.* Nashville, TN: George Peabody College for Teachers.

Bliss, E. C. (1983). *Getting things done.* New York: Scribner's.

Bliss, E. C. (1984). *Doing it now.* New York: Bantam.

Camp, B. W., & Bash, M. S. (1981). *Think Aloud.* Champaign, IL: Research Press.

Cobb, J. A. (1972). Relationship of discrete classroom behaviors to fourth grade academic achievement. *Journal of Educational Psychology, 63,* 74-80.

Drabman, R. S., Spitnalnick, R., & O'Leary, K. D. (1973). Teaching self-control to disruptive children. *Journal of Abnormal Psychology, 82,* 10-16.

Fink, W. T., & Carnine, D. W. (1975). Control of arithmetic errors using informational feedback. *Journal of Applied Behavior Analysis, 8,* 461.

Foxx, R. M., & Azrin, N. H. (1973). The elimination of autistic self-stimulatory behavior by overcorrection. *Journal of Applied Behavior Analysis, 6,* 1-14.

Gable, R. A., & Kerr, M. M. (1980). Behaviorally disordered adolescents as academic change agents. In R. B. Rutherford and A. G. Prieto (Eds.), *Severe behavior disorders of children and youth: CCBD monograph* (Vol. 4, pp. 117-124). Reston, VA: Council for Children with Behavioral Disorders.

Greenwood, C. R., Dinwiddie, G., Terry, B., Wade, L., Stanley, S. O., Thibadeau, S., & Delquadri, J. C. (1984). Teacher- versus peer-mediated instruction: An ecobehavioral analysis of achievement outcomes. *Journal of Applied Behavior Analysis, 17*(4), 521-538.

Greer, D. R., & Polirstok, S. R. (1982). Collateral gains and short term maintenance in reading and on-task responses by inner-city adolescents as a function of their use of social reinforcement while tutoring. *Journal of Applied Behavioral Analysis, 15,* 123-139.

Harris, K. R. (1986). Self-monitoring of attentional behavior versus self-monitoring of productivity: Effects on on-task behavior and academic response rate among learning disabled children. *Journal of Applied Behavior Analysis, 19*(4), 417-423.

Hughes, J. N. (1985). Parents as cotherapists in think aloud. *Psychology in the Schools, 22,* 436-443.

Kastelen, L., Nickel, M., & McLaughlin, T. F. (1984). A performance feedback system: Generalization of effects across tasks and time with eighth-grade English students. *Education and Treatment of Children, 1,* 141-155.

Kauffman, J. M. (1989). *Characteristics of children's behavior disorders* (3rd ed.). Columbus, OH: Merrill.

Kelley, M. L., & Stokes, T. F. (1982). Contingency contracting with disadvantaged youths: Improving classroom performance. *Journal of Applied Behavior Analysis, 15,* 447-454.

Kerr, M. M., Nelson, C. M., & Lambert, D. L. (1987). *Helping adolescents with learning and behavior problems.* Columbus, OH: Merrill.

Kerr, M. M., & Zigmond, N. (1984). *School Survival Skills: Grant Report for Year Three.* Unpublished document, University of Pittsburgh.

Kerr, M. M., Zigmond, N., Schaeffer, A. L., & Brown, G. (1986). An observational follow-up study of successful and unsuccessful high school students. *High School Journal, 71,* 20-32.

McConnell, S. R., Strain, P. S., Kerr, M. M., Stagg, V., Lenkner, D. A., & Lambert, D. L. (1984). An empirical definition of elementary school adjustment: Selection of target behaviors for a comprehensive treatment program. *Behavior Modification, 3*(4), 451-473.

Quay, H. C., & Werry, J. S. (Eds.). (1979). *Psychopathological disorders of childhood.* New York: Wiley.

Ruffin, C., Lambert, D., & Kerr, M. M. (1985). Volunteers: An extraordinary resource. *The Pointer, 29,* 30-38.

Sabatos, M. A. (1986). *Private cues in self-monitoring: Effects on learning-disabled students' on-task performance and reading productivity during sustained silent reading.* Unpublished doctoral dissertation, University of Pittsburgh.

Schoen, S. F. (1986). Decreasing noncompliance in the severely multihandicapped child. *Psychology in the Schools, 23*(1), 88-94.

Scruggs, T. E., & Osguthorpe, R. T. (1986). Tutoring interventions within special education settings: A comparison of cross-age and peer tutoring. *Psychology in the Schools, 23,* 187-193.

Seligman, M. E. P. (1975). *Helplessness: On depression, development, and death.* San Francisco, CA: W. H. Freeman.

Shepp, M. S., & Jensen, B. F. (1983). A comparison of the treatment effects of an operant strategy, a cognitive strategy, and a combined approach with a hyperactive boy. *School Psychology Review, 12*(2), 199-204.

Sindeler, P. (1982). The effects of cross-aged tutoring on the comprehension skills of remedial reading students. *Journal of Special Education, 16,* 199-206.

Smith, B. M., Schumaker, J. B., Schaefer, J., & Sherman, J. A. (1982). Increasing participation and improving the quality of discussions in seventh-grade social studies class. *Journal of Applied Behavior Analysis, 15,* 97-110.

Van Houten, R. (1979). The performance feedback system: Generalization of effects across time. *Child Behavior Therapy, 1,* 219-236.

Van Houten, R., & LaiFatt, D. (1981). The effects of public posting on high school biology test performance. *Education and Treatment of Children, 4,* 217-226.

Van Houten, R., & Van Houten, J. (1977). The performance feedback system in the special education classroom: An analysis of public posting and peer comments. *Behavior Therapy, 8,* 366-376.

Walker, H. M. (1983). Applications of response cost in school settings: Outcomes, issues and recommendations. *Exceptional Education Quarterly, 3*(4), 47-55.

Walker, H. M., & Rankin, R. (1983). Assessing the behavioral expectations and demands of less restrictive settings. *School Psychology Review, 12,* 274-284.

Zigmond, N., Kerr, M. M., Schaeffer, A. L., Brown, G. M., & Farra, H. E. (1986). *School Survival Skills Curriculum* (limited published circulation). Available from Department of Special Education, 5M30 Forbes Quadrangle, 230 Bouquet Street, University of Pittsburgh, Pittsburgh, PA 15260.

Stereotypic Behaviors

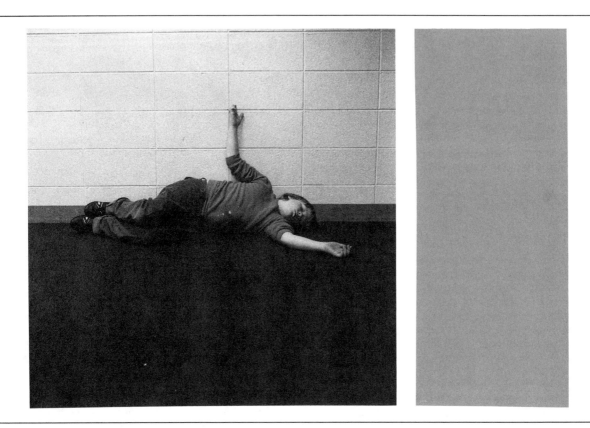

Chapter 9

OUTLINE

OBJECTIVES

The reader who completes this chapter should be able to

- Define the various types of self-injurious and self-stimulatory behaviors.
- Conduct a functional analysis of a stereotypic behavior.
- Discuss the theoretical concepts underlying self-stimulatory behavior.
- Choose an effective intervention for self-injurious behavior.
- Discuss the ethical issues in implementing aversive and restrictive interventions.
- Assist in conducting a sensory extinction intervention.

The behaviors described in this chapter may be the most complex that you will ever confront in teaching, and sadly, they are undoubtedly serious — if not life-threatening — to the students who exhibit them. Let's look first at what is meant by self-injurious behavior and self-stimulatory behavior and the terms associated with them.

Self-Injurious Behaviors

Self-injurious, self-mutilating, and *self-destructive* describe behaviors that hurt the person exhibiting them. These terms are commonly used for chronic, repetitive acts of severely handicapped individuals (e.g., retarded or autistic) (Baumeister & Rollings, 1976; Favell, 1982; Schroeder, Schroeder, Smith, & Dalldorf, 1978). In this chapter we use the term **self-injurious behavior,** or SIB, because it is the label you are most likely to hear and use. Note that although this term conceivably consists of all acts of self-injury, including suicide and substance abuse (Schroeder, Schroeder, Rojahn, & Mulick, 1981), we do not refer to these behaviors in this chapter.

Favell (1982) summarized into five categories the various kinds of SIB reported in research literature:

1. Striking oneself (e.g., face slapping, head banging against objects).
2. Biting or sucking various body parts (e.g., "mouthing").
3. Pinching, scratching, poking or pulling various body parts (e.g., eye-poking, hair-pulling).
4. Repeatedly vomiting, or vomiting and reingesting food (i.e., "rumination").
5. Consuming nonedible substances (e.g., eating objects, cigarettes: "pica"; eating feces: "coprophagia"). (p. 1)

These generic categories are reflected in the research definitions of SIB in Table 9-1. We excerpt these descriptions not only to illustrate problem behaviors, but to give you and your multidisciplinary IEP team ideas for writing target behavior descriptions. Also, note the measurement approaches used by the various authors. These may help you decide how to measure the SIB of your students.

The studies cited are attempts to resolve the serious problems of SIB individuals. This is a new area for researchers and classroom teachers, and you may find that your previous experience and training in the management of SIB are limited. Still, you must try to understand these often frightening behaviors because they can result in serious injury to a student, such as retinal detachment (Favell, 1982), loss of an appendage or of the use of a sensory modality, or a skull fracture (Dorsey, personal communication, 1981). We do not wish to scare you nor to overdramatize a behavioral disorder, but it is imperative that you recognize the significance of SIB and respect the highly systematic interventions designed to treat it.

To introduce you to the complex world of these bizarre behaviors, let's review some explanations for why they occur. Understanding the motivational conditions of SIB is a rapidly developing area for research, often called *functional analysis* (Carr, 1977; Carr & Durand, 1985; Durand & Carr, 1985).

Durand and Carr (1985) cited four motivational conditions for self-injury. The first, social attention, refers to the maintenance of the behaviors through the verbal or nonverbal feedback of others (See Carr & McDowell, 1980). Second, self-injury may be maintained through tangible consequences (e.g., access to play activities). Third, the student may exhibit self-injury to avoid a situation the student dislikes (e.g., a difficult self-help lesson). Finally, the sensory feedback a student receives from injuring himself may be reinforcing to him.

Durand and Crimmins (1987) have developed an assessment for determining the functional significance of self-injury, the Motivation Assessment Scale (MAS). You and your supervisor might use this instrument (available from V. Mark Durand, State University of New York at Albany) to gain a better understanding of a student's stereotypic behaviors.

A functional analysis of self-injury can be invaluable because it suggests the purpose for the behavior. Once we understand *why* a student injures himself, we can move to teaching the student alternative behaviors for achieving the same goals. Carr and Durand (1985) illustrated this approach in a communication training program for developmentally disabled children. Very carefully selected and trained phrases enabled the children to satisfy their needs without resorting to self-injury.

Another illustration helps us summarize this section (Durand & Carr, 1985):

> As we have seen, it is essential to match the consequences involved in alternative behaviors to the assessed motivating conditions. Problems may arise if such a match is not made. For example, if a teacher chose to stand up and walk away from a boy who hit himself for attention, then his self-injurious behavior may very well decrease in frequency over time. However, if his self-injurious behavior were escape motivated, having the teacher walk away might produce an increase in self-injurious behavior since the teacher's leaving would be associated with removal of task demands. That is, the teacher would be providing the child with what he wanted, namely, a cessation of the task. This contingency would strengthen self-injurious behavior. The case just discussed illustrates the extreme importance of designing treatment intervention based on the specific motivation of the self-injurious behavior. (p. 175)

Self-Stimulatory Behaviors

These actions, like SIB, are repetitive and frequent, but do not cause physical injury. **Ritualistic** and **stereotypic** are global terms also used to describe self-stimulatory behaviors. For purposes of this chapter, however, we adopt **self-stimulatory behavior** (SSB), the term most commonly used, to describe "behaviors that are stereotyped and performed repetitiously, and that fail to produce any apparent positive environmental consequences or physical injury" (O'Brien, 1981, p. 117). You should be aware, however, that controversy surrounds (and may eventually alter the usage of) the term self-stimulation because the term implies a questionable motivation for the behavior (Baumeister, 1978). For this reason usage of SSB may eventually be altered. Even

today, some authors prefer the term *stereotyped movements* because it is "without inference and purely descriptive" (O'Brien, 1981, p. 118).

Like SIB, self-stimulatory behaviors are seen most often in those with severe behavioral handicaps. Staff working with severely and profoundly handicapped individuals consider SSB a widespread, major problem (Whitman & Scibak, 1979; Lovaas, Newsom, & Hickman, 1987).

Recent research on the nature of SSB has revealed that this serious behavior problem may be maintained by the perceptual reinforcement that it provides to the self-stimulating individual (Lovaas et al., 1987). Let's review some of the important concepts put forth by these authors, to help you understand why SSB is so difficult to eliminate in most individuals (Lovaas et al., 1987).

Concept #1: Many self-stimulatory behaviors are "so elaborate and idiosyncratic" (p. 46) that children must have *learned* them somehow. It is simply inconceivable that a child could be born with such complex behavioral preferences.

Concept #2: Children exhibiting SSB show a wide range of different kinds of SSB. These self-stimulatory behaviors are nearly identical, regardless of the culture in which the children were reared.

Concept #3: Withdrawal of social reinforcers and attention has not reduced these behaviors, which leads us to believe that these self-stimulatory behaviors are not the result of a "common social reinforcement history" (p. 46).

Concept #4: While engaged in SSB, children seem to be totally absorbed in their behaviors and become very difficult to interact with socially or instructionally.

Concept #5: When children do receive behavioral treatment, they often respond

Table 9-1. Definitions of Self-Injurious Behaviors

Behavior	Definition	Measurement Procedure	Authors
Hair-pulling	—either hand touching hair. Response ended when hand dropped below shoulder level.	—response per minute of SIB behavior, measured with an event recorder. Duration was also measured during each 90-minute session.	Altman, Haavik & Cook (1978)
Eye-gouging	—finger contact with sclera.		
Self-hitting	—any blow delivered to the face or head with the closed fist or the palm of the hand.	—response per minute during 10-minute observations.	Carr, Newsom & Binkoff (1976)
Skin-tearing	—closure of the index finger and thumb in a pincerlike fashion while in contact with either the lip or forearm.		
Head-striking	—hitting both sides of head with fist.	—response per minute and elapsed time (in seconds) needed to accumulate 60 seconds without self-injurious activity. (A stopwatch was used to monitor total strikes per minute. A second stopwatch measured time spent in overcorrection procedure.)	Kelly & Drabman (1977)
Rubbing	—rapid rubbing of face with hands.	—3-minute observations during which the first occurrence of the type of behavior was scored in a 15-second interval recording sheet. (Observers watched for fifteen seconds, then scored for 5 seconds).	Luiselli, Pemberton & Helfen (1978)
Slapping	—slapping head with the open palm of one hand.		
Pica	—ingestion of or attempt to ingest nonnutritive items	—10-second continuous interval record	Rojahn, McGonigle, Curcio, & Dixon (1987)
Self-injurious behavior (SIB)	—behavior directed against own body, which causes physical damage or presents a health hazard. The following SIB types are likely to occur: head hitting (hit her head with her extremities); pinching; thigh slapping; hand pounding on hard surfaces; eye gouging with fingers		
Hand or arm biting	—insertion of the hand or arm into the mouth beyond the lips	—frequency, duration measures	Jenson, Rovner, Cameron, Peterson, & Kesler (1985)

Table 9-1. *Continued*

Behavior	Definition	Measurement Procedure	Authors
Hand-biting	—placing hands into mouth and biting down upon the skin with teeth	—frequency count	Luiselli (1984b)
Self-injurious behavior (SIB)	—a tantrum that involves hitting head against the wall or floor, scratching at face, or hitting in the head or upper chest with clenched fists	—frequency count	Rolinder & Van Houten (1985)
Mouthing objects	—placing any inappropriate objects such as rocks, napkins, cloth, part of toys, and dirt into his mouth		
Self-injurious behavior (SIB)	—striking the face, head, neck, throat, torso, or extremities with closed hand (fist), open hand (palm), or extended fingers —striking the face, head, neck, throat, torso, or extremities with any object held in the hand(s) —striking the head against any fixed surface such as a wall, floor, tabletop, or partition	—frequency count	Luiselli (1986)
Self-biting	—self-biting behavior was defined both in terms of frequency of daily occurrence and intensity of each occurrence and was scored when any part of the participant's body was pressed between her upper and lower teeth. The intensity of each occurrence was gauged according to the following five-point scale: 1. no teeth marks or lesions 2. teeth marks not breaking skin 3. scraping skin but no bleeding 4. breaking of skin and bleeding 5. breaking of skin, bleeding, and biting others attempting to restrain her	—frequency and intensity	Neufeld & Fantuzzo (1984)

by developing new versions of SSB in place of the targeted behaviors.

Concept #6: "The most reliable and inevitable consequences of self-stimulatory behaviors are the perceptual or sensory stimuli that these behaviors produce." (p. 46)

Concept #7: As SSB is a high probability behavior, we can argue that SSB itself is a reinforcing event. (Review Chapter 5 on this concept of reinforcement.)

To better understand the particular role of perceptual reinforcement in SSB, consider these points made by Lovaas et al. (1987):

1. The child controls the perceptual reinforcers; these reinforcers are not controlled by others or the environment.
2. Perceptual reinforcers are primary reinforcers. Also, they are quite durable and not as vulnerable to satiation as other reinforcers.

When does a child begin to exhibit self-stimulatory behaviors? Research has shown that these behaviors begin in infancy in some developmentally delayed individuals (normal infants engage in SSB until about eight months of age, according to Thelen, 1979) and before the age of two years in most cases (Berkson, McQuiston, Jacobson, Eyman, & Borthwick, 1985).

How does a child "learn" to engage in SSB? Consider this illustration (Lovaas et al., 1987):

An autistic child initially twirls a string in a variety of different ways. Sooner or later (through trial and error) a pattern of string movements is discovered that is particularly attractive to look at (i.e., that strongly reinforces twirling the string). With practice, he or she learns to perform exactly the right manipulation of the string to achieve the preferred pattern and tends to perform only that topography and closely related topographies most of the time. Consider another example: A child will retrieve and then skillfully manipulate a variety of objects (dishes, sink-stoppers, balls, etc.) to make them rotate or spin. Once the object comes to a resting position he or she will resume the behavioral sequence. In such an example, the child's spinning of various objects may be an acquired response, an operant, whose visual consequence (the spinning object) is the perceptual reinforcer that shapes and maintains the response. In the example of the child who repeatedly arranges (lines) objects such as toys, books, or shoes in neat rows across the living room floor, "objects in a line" may constitute a positively reinforcing perceptual consequence, shaping and maintaining the lining behavior. (p. 49)

How does the SSB persist? You probably already know the answer: SSB is highly reinforcing. Also, individuals engaged in SSB simply may not have other, alternative behaviors in which to engage.

As you study intervention possibilities later in this chapter, you will notice an emphasis on controlling the perceptual experiences of self-stimulating individuals. Also, you will learn how very carefully all assessments and interventions must be implemented if a program is to have any success with this difficult and durable set of behaviors. If you have worked with severely handicapped students, the behaviors listed in Table 9-2 are probably familiar. Only a few of the possible self-stimulatory behaviors are included; research has uncovered fifty types of SSB (LaGrow & Repp, 1984).

Self-stimulatory behaviors are not harmful in themselves but may, in time, change to self-injurious behaviors through a slight shift in topography (O'Brien, 1981). Furthermore, several researchers have reported that SSB dramatically limits an individual's attention to learning activities, thus reducing the potential skills repertoire of an already deficient learner (Foxx & Azrin, 1973). It would seem, then, that considerable effort should be expended toward the *reduction* of these troublesome behaviors. Indeed, this is now the generally accepted course of treatment.

How This Chapter Is Organized

The format used in our other chapters on problem behavior has been modified to accommodate the unusual issues presented in the management of SIB and SSB problems. The major difference between this chapter and others is that fewer procedures are outlined step-by-step for your use. We describe a few assessment and intervention procedures that you will be able to direct with little supervision or outside help.

Our exclusion of certain procedures here will not be popular with many educators, who argue that "we already have these students in our classrooms—why not go ahead and tell us how to use all of the interventions available?" We can only reiterate our concern, for both students and for you, that you may inadvertently misuse a procedure because of problems with time, support personnel, supervision, effectiveness data, and approvals. As Judith Favell (1981) stated in her monograph on self-injurious behavior for the American Association of Behavior Therapy,

> The apparent simplicity of these techniques may be misleading. They are complex procedures which require a high degree of competence to design and conduct. The improper use of *any* procedure may place a self-injurious client at severe risk. (p. 20)

Difficult to implement, many interventions are controversial because they create discomfort for the target student. **Aversive procedures** — always a last resort — are not universally condoned even for self-injurious behaviors. Legal and ethical questions always accompany aversive approaches.

A second consideration is the use of alternative, nonaversive procedures that might be suggested through a good functional analysis. For example, you might discover that SIB occurs primarily when instructional demands are placed on the child — a finding described by Carr, Newsom, and Binkoff (1976). By changing the instructional schedule or the environmental demands, you may affect SIB. Teaching preferred, nonstereotypic behaviors is another example of a nonaversive intervention.

We agree with Lovaas and Favell (1987), who stated that

> . . . if a program cannot conduct alternative interventions in a high quality fashion, then it should not employ aversive procedures. (p. 320)

> . . . the use of aversive and restrictive interventions should only be considered in the context of several issues surrounding their use. Such techniques are justified only when their effects are rigorously evaluated, caregivers are fully trained and adequately supervised in all dimensions of habilitative services, when a meaningful functional analysis of the child's problem has been conducted, alternative and benign treatments have been considered and are in place, parents and others are fully informed, and there is general agreement that the means justify the ends. (p. 324)

Furthermore, as Lovaas and Favell pointed out in their 1987 essay,

> These complexities illustrate the need for a "functional analysis" of what is reinforcing a particular client's problem behavior in order to prescribe an adequate treatment, whether that treatment contains aversive consequences or not. This requirement raises again the question of whether a facility or agency has adequately trained staff to conduct such a functional analysis before any kind of treatment is employed. It is a serious concern that because some programs do not have the expertise and resources to functionally analyze problem behavior, they employ aversive procedures in an attempt to override the reinforcers maintaining them. Quite the opposite should be true. Only programs that are capable of conducting an adequate analysis of problem behavior should be allowed to employ aversive and restrictive treatments. (p. 318)

Table 9-2. Definitions of Self-Stimulatory Behaviors

Behavior	Definition	Measurement Procedure	Authors
Scream	—vocalization above normal conversational level that contains no words.	—response rate per minute, using a stopwatch during a 10-minute session.	Bittle & Hake (1977)
Running and hopping	—normal running mixed with hops without any apparent attempt to move to a particular place.	—response rate per minute, using a stopwatch during a 10-minute session.	
Arm-waving	—extending arms at a 90° angle from one's side, moving them in a circular motion.	—response rate per minute, using a stopwatch during a 10-minute session.	
Finger-wiggling	—putting hands in front of face spreading fingers apart, then slowly flexing and extending them one at a time in sequence.	—response rate per minute, using a stopwatch during a 10-minute session.	
Looking out the corner of eyes	—turning head in one direction while moving eyes in the opposite direction without any apparent attempt to focus on an object.	—response rate per minute, using a stopwatch during a 10-minute session.	
Mouthing	—placing one or both hands, any fingers, or a toy in or on the mouth.	—scoring each 10-second interval in a 10-minute session as to whether self-stimulation or appropriate play occurred. (If both occurred, then only self-stimulation was scored.)	Coleman, Whitman, & Johnson (1979)
Head back	—tilting the head back at an angle of 45° to the normal upright position.		
Body motion	—any back and forth movement of the head and shoulders and the torso with the back moving away from and toward the chair back at least twice in a row.		

As in other chapters, we describe assessment procedures then interventions (environmental and teacher-mediated). First we present information on SIB, then a discussion of SSB. Two case studies illustrate the problems and interventions, and a Strategy Selection Chart (Figure 9-7) appears on page 306.

Assessment of SIB

The data you collect in performing multilevel assessments of SIB will help you accomplish the following:

Table 9-2. *Continued*

Behavior	Definition	Measurement Procedure	Authors
Bouncing	—bouncing up and down in the seat with up and down leg motion or kicking.		
Public masturbation	—putting either hand inside pants and directed toward penis. Hand was defined as in pants whenever one fingernail disappeared from view. Response ended when hand or fingers were removed from pants. Public masturbation meant that the behavior occurred anywhere outside of the child's bedroom or bathroom.	—rate of masturbation responses per day, measured during six 5-minute time samples.	Cook, Altman, Shaw, & Blaylock (1978)
Rubbing saliva	—placing fingers into mouth for 1–2 seconds, wetting them with saliva, and then rubbing the fingers together as student removed them from mouth.	—frequency count	Luiselli (1984a)
Tongue protrusion	—thrusting tongue out of mouth and exposing it for several seconds.		
Nonverbal self-stimulatory behavior	—any repetitive, nonfunctional movement of any body part or of the entire body	—10-second partial interval record	Rolinder & Van Houten (1985)
Self-stimulatory verbalizations	—any repetitive nonfunctional vocalizations, consisting of either words or noises		

recognize biological factors in SIB

analyze the interaction between SIB and the environment

summarize information so that you can get assistance from a behavioral consultant

learn procedures that will prove useful in monitoring progress of subsequent interventions

The last is especially critical because "it is not possible to predict in advance if a given procedure or set of procedures will be effective in an individual case" (Favell, 1982, p. 21).

The AABT monograph on self-injurious behavior recommends that thorough analysis of the behaviors precede *any* pinpointing of behaviors for intervention (Favell, 1982):

> A prior analysis of biological and environmental conditions and consequences which may be maintaining the client's self-injury, and the explicit inclusion of that information in the design of [the intervention should be conducted]. . . . Such an analysis must be done situation by situation, since different situations control different rates and intensities of self-injury, and because even in situations in which self-injury does occur, the behavior may serve very different functions. For example, at times the behavior may serve to escape demands, at others it may function to obtain attention. (p. 18)

You may want to get assistance in conducting a comprehensive behavioral analysis. Nevertheless, certain items of health-related information could be completed by the school nurse or physician with help from the student's parents. This medical history is critical in determining whether the student has recently had or now needs a comprehensive physical and neuropsychiatric examination. *We urge you to complete this step before proceeding with any intervention.* Questions regarding recent dental and physical examinations should offer information about the student's ongoing health care. A neuropsychological exam may be advised, as well as comprehensive testing for syndromes thought to cause SIB (Lesch-Nyan Syndrome, Cornelia de Lange's Syndrome). It is helpful in collaborating with medical professionals to keep a daily log of bruises, cuts, and other injuries that may appear, as well as of SIB such as pica, vomiting, and rumination. Be sure to record any oral or topical medications (e.g., lotion for chapped or scratched skin) administered.

An environmental analysis calls for several items of information gathered in various settings and demand-situations. In the following paragraphs we describe components of an **ecological approach,** which is outlined in Figure 9-1.

Naturally, the first item requests a specific *definition of the problem* behavior or behaviors. Since SIB is rarely confined to, say, school, we have included items that reflect different settings and different times of day. These variables are combined in question 4 when you are asked to provide information regarding possible alternative behaviors. Research on SIB individuals suggests that injurious behavior may be decreased by reinforcing alternative, noninjurious behaviors (Mulick, Hoyt, Rojahn, & Schroeder, 1978). Therefore, it is important for you to consider alternative behaviors to substitute for SIB.

Demands on the individual are described in question 5. Again, studies have indicated that levels of SIB may be altered by the presence of demands (Carr, Newsom, & Binkoff, 1976), or by activities the student finds particularly stressful. For example, a client studied by Schroeder and Humphrey (1977) engaged in more frequent SIB immediately following a daily weight check than after a quiet afternoon period.

Questions regarding consequation for SIB (7 and 8) reflect the need for a thorough understanding of what has maintained, reduced, or increased SIB in the past. Before designing and initiating a new intervention, your consultant and human rights committee should examine closely the data on prior attempts at intervention (see question 9).

A completed environmental analysis should provide your intervention team with specific settings, time, and adult actions for further examination. For a more complete review of SIB research on environmental variables, see Schroeder et al. (1981). This closer look at SIB might include a measure of the rate of the behavior. In Figure 9-2 you see a response-per-minute record for the student described in our SIB case study. The third column of Table 9-1 explores the measurement of SIBs in several research studies.

Figure 9-1. Environmental Analysis Form for SIB

Student: _____ Age: _____

Date: _____ Teacher: _____

1. What is (are) this student's self-injurious behavior(s)? Describe specifically. _____

2. List all the settings in which this behavior is exhibited. _____

3. At what times of day does the student engage in the SIB? _____

4. What activities could the student engage in, throughout the day, if he were not injuring himself?

Time	Alternative Activity
7–8 a.m.	
8–9	
9–10	
10–11	
11–12	
12–1 p.m.	
1–2	
2–3	
3–4	
4–5	
5–6	
6–7	
7–8	
8–9	
9–10	
10–11 p.m.	

5. What demands are made of the student immediately prior to episodes of SIB? (Use an A-B-C analysis to determine this.)

Demand	Setting	SIB

6. Are there particular antecedent events that you associate with this student's SIB? _____

7. When the student engages in SIB, what happens?

Setting   Consequence

8. List all the interventions you presently use to control the SIB (e.g., verbal statements, restraints, punishment, DRO). _____

9. Do you have data on these interventions: _____ Please provide, if yes.

Figure 9-2. Response per Minute Record for Self-Injurious Behaviors

Observer: _Mrs. Hanson, aide_   Student: _Paul_

Date: _February 15_   Observational Session 1 2③4 5 6

Setting: _classroom_   Activity: _prevocational_

Others present: _Mrs Lawson, teacher; data collector_

Time: _10:16_ _____ to _10:46_ / _____ to _____

Time to be excluded (e.g., minutes during which an intervention interrupted the behaviors.): _n. a._ _____ to _____

List of Behaviors* +	Frequency	Response per min.
1. striking head	⊥⊦⊦ ⊥⊦⊦ lll	13 ÷ 30 = .43
2. striking ears	⊥⊦⊦ ⊥⊦⊦	10 ÷ 33 = .33
3.		
4.		
5.		
6.		
7.		
8.		

* Use the behaviorial definitions established in the team conference.
+ Circle any behavior that is under intervention.

Response per minute calculation: $\dfrac{\text{No. of Behaviors}}{\text{No. of minutes elapsed} - \text{minutes excluded}}$

Intervention Strategies for SIB

This section presents strategies to decrease self-injurious behaviors. You will be able to implement some by yourself, whereas other programs require outside help.

ENVIRONMENTAL CHANGES

As mentioned earlier, your team or consultant may want to alter one or more of the following antecedent circumstances in order to determine their effects on SIB:

1. The demands placed on an individual during a specific part of the daily routine (or the reinforcement the student receives for compliance with that demand)

2. The available, reinforceable alternative activities that the student can engage in
3. The physical restraints used with a client, and the schedule for applying and removing them (see Favell, McGimsey, & Jones, 1978)
4. The student's daily routine, with the possibility of rearranging stressful events (see Schroeder & Humphrey, 1977).

We do not prescribe steps in conducting these environmental changes because any such alteration depends on a thorough analysis of each individual's behavior.

ENVIRONMENTAL SAFETY CONSIDERATIONS

To prevent a self-injurious student from further harm, take safety precautions in your classroom. Remove any chemicals that may be toxic (e.g., typewriter correction fluid; cleaning supplies; medications; and paint). Take the position that a self-injurious child or adolescent does not possess the judgment necessary to determine what might be dangerous. Remove sharp objects such as scissors, pens, needles, paper clips, and thumbtacks. It may be necessary to cushion objects having hard surfaces if the student pounds them with head or body.

RESTRAINT DEVICES

SIB is sometimes treated through the application of various kinds of restraints (Dorsey, Iwata, Reid, & Davis, 1982; Neufeld & Fantuzzo, 1984; Rincover & Devany, 1982). This intervention does not prevent self-injurious behaviors themselves, but it attempts to limit the harm of the stereotypic behavior. The disadvantages associated with restraints are (1) they do not teach new behaviors or eliminate the targeted ones, (2) they interfere with learning alternative behaviors (and may interfere with hearing and other senses), and (3) the appearance of a restraint may cause

others to ostracize the child (Baumeister & Rollings, 1976).

If your staff is considering a restraint procedure, you should consult the paper by Neufeld and Fantuzzo (1984) for the technical design of a "Bubble" restraint that does not interfere with other behaviors and that was successful in treating hand-biting.

DIFFERENTIAL REINFORCEMENT OF OTHER (DRO) BEHAVIORS PROGRAM

DRO is a term frequently cited in descriptions of programs for SIB (or SSB) individuals (Brawley, Harris, Allen, Fleming, & Peterson, 1969; Lovaas, Freitag, Gold, & Kassorla, 1965). DRO procedures often accompany the other interventions described in this chapter. Research has not proven DRO as successful as the "suppression interventions" in eliminating SIB (Dorsey, Iwata, Ong, & McSween, 1980), but we often rely on DRO to teach the student vitally needed alternative behaviors (Jenson, Rovner, Cameron, Peterson, & Kesler, 1985). The basic notion of a DRO program is *the reinforcement of intervals at a time during which the SIB* (or other undesirable behavior) *does not occur.* For example, students might be reinforced initially each time they engage in ten seconds of non-SIB behavior, then fifteen, then twenty seconds.

In some programs based on the DRO procedure, reinforcement is administered for intervals of time during which *certain* behaviors *incompatible* with SIB are exhibited (e.g., putting together a puzzle without biting one's hand). These programs are then termed *DRI, or Differential Reinforcement of Incompatible Behaviors.* Table 9–3 provides a step-by-step procedure for conducting a DRO or DRI program.

OVERCORRECTION

Overcorrection procedures are frequently used to modify the self-injurious behaviors of handi-

Table 9-3. Guidelines for Using a DRO or DRI Procedure

1. Set aside a block of time (e.g., fifteen minutes daily or several such times per day) to conduct the training.

2. Arrange for a staff member to spend time with (or near, in later stages) the student during these sessions.

3. Record rate-per-minute baseline data on the problem behaviors, and chart these. Continue recording data throughout the program.

4. Select an appropriate behavior for reinforcement (preferably one that is incompatible with the problem behavior). Be sure to choose a behavior that you can count easily by the frequency or interval method. If you cannot count it, you will have difficulty knowing when to reinforce it!

5. Select a powerful reinforcer for the student. Be sure the reinforcer is one you can remove from the student if response cost is to be incorporated into the procedure.

6. Gather the reinforcers, a container for them (e.g., clear plastic cup), and a data record sheet, and ask the student to sit across the table from you.

7. Say, "It's time to work (play)," and give the student the necessary items to engage in the appropriate (other) behavior (e.g., ballpoint pens to assemble and place in a tray, a toy car to roll towards you, a favorite stuffed animal to cuddle without self-stimulating).

8. Beginning with a "rich" schedule of reinforcement, provide the student with the reinforcer for each appropriate "other" behavior (each pen assembled) or for a brief interval of appropriate behavior (e.g., five to ten seconds of play with the teacher using a toy). If you use response cost, keep the reinforcers in the container until the end of the session.

9. If you desire, you can implement a response cost procedure at the same time. For this procedure, take away one (or two) of the reinforcers at each instance of the problem behavior after saying, "NO (*problem behavior*)!"

10. As the data indicate progress (e.g., a reduction in the response per minute of problem behaviors), you can "thin" the reinforcement schedule: you reinforce less frequently and require longer and longer intervals of time spent in the appropriate "other" behavior.

11. Be sure to praise the student at each time of reinforcement and to change the reinforcer if it seems no longer effective.

12. Do not use the verbal reprimand, "NO (*problem behavior*)" at times when you cannot remove the reinforcer until you see definite, stable behavior improvement.

---

capped individuals (Bierly & Billingsley, 1983; Carey & Bucher, 1986; Gibbs & Luyben, 1985; Luiselli, 1984a, 1984b). During an overcorrection procedure, the student engages in practice of nonstereotyped behaviors, while at the same time undergoing the removal of positive reinforcement for these problem behaviors. The goals of overcorrection programs, both restitutional and positive practice, have been described by their developers, Foxx and Azrin (1973).

In restitutional overcorrection, the self-injury is interrupted, and the student is required to *re-store his immediate environment to an improved condition* by practicing appropriate behaviors. To conduct a restitutional overcorrection procedure properly, you must first define the problem behaviors. Table 9-1 gives you well-specified target behavior statements. Restitutional overcorrection is used for self-injurious and oppositional behaviors, not for self-stimulatory behaviors because they do not upset the environment. For example, restitutional overcorrection might be recommended for a child who smears feces, injures the inside of his mouth, or in some other way harms himself or damages his environment. Table 9-4 displays examples of overcorrection activities that you might be asked to implement.

Correctly implementing overcorrection requires considerable staff time, so you will need help in conducting this program. Review the guidelines before working on an overcorrection program, and once again, *do not undertake this or any other SIB intervention without supervision* from someone who has been trained to use overcorrection. Also, remember that overcorrection programs may require approval from the review committee and the student's parents. Check with your supervisor about this. Table 9-5 provides guidelines for implementing restitutional overcorrection.

Positive practice overcorrection is similar to restitutional overcorrection (see Table 9-6). Unlike restitutional overcorrection, it does not require the learner to restore the environment. Positive practice overcorrection is used for behaviors that do not upset the environment or for behaviors for which no restitutional activity can be reasonably developed. Refer again to Table 9-4 for suggested positive practice activities. Positive practice overcorrection proce-

dures are frequently described as successfully reducing the level of self-stimulatory or self-injurious behaviors. However, there is evidence to suggest that new forms of injurious behaviors may appear if they are not also included in the overcorrection procedure (Epstein, Doke, Sajwaj, Sorrell, & Rimmer, 1974). To avoid this negative side effect of overcorrection, be sure that your overcorrection procedure is closely monitored by a trained behavioral program specialist and that more acceptable replacement behaviors are reinforced.

Gibbs and Luyben (1985) showed that time-out from reinforcement (i.e., preventing the individual from engaging in the preferred stereotypic behavior) was a critical feature of successful overcorrection. Accordingly, we classify positive practice overcorrection as an aversive or punishment procedure. This is in keeping with the advice of Foxx and Bechtel (1982) who have even suggested that the phrase *positive practice* be dropped from the term. (We have maintained the traditional title to assist readers who are acquainted with the two subtypes of overcorrection and who know of other, more purely educative uses of positive

Table 9-4. Suggested Restitutional and Positive Practice Activities for Self-Stimulatory and Self-Injurious Behaviors

Problem Behavior	Suggested Overcorrection Activity
Mouthing objects, injuring inside of mouth	Brush teeth with an oral antiseptic (mouthwash) and wipe lips with washcloth soaked in mouthwash. Periodically encourage student to spit out the rinse.[a]
Head weaving	Functional Movement Training for 5-7 minutes: Guide student to hold his head in each of three positions, up, down, and straight, for 15 seconds. (Give instructions in a random order.)[a]
Clapping	Guide student through a series of hand positions, or Functional Movement Training. For example, have the student hold hands out, above his head, together, and behind back, holding each position for 15 seconds.[a]
Hand flapping "airplaning"	Hold each of these positions for 15 seconds, repeating the entire series 15 times: hands on head, hands straight up, hands on shoulders, hands on hips.

[a]These activities were taken from R. M. Foxx & N. H. Azrin. The elimination of autistic self-stimulatory behavior by overcorrection. *Journal of Applied Behavior Analysis*, 1973, *6*, 1-14.

Table 9-5. Guidelines for Using Restitutional Overcorrection

1. Define the problem behavior or behaviors specifically.

2. Record baseline data on the rate or frequency of the problem behavior for at least three days. (Continue data collection during the program.)

3. Select a verbal cue to use when the student engages in the problem behavior. For example, "no throwing" or "no smearing."

4. Select a restitutional activity that is relevant to the problem behavior (see Table 9-4 for ideas). Be sure this activity sequence is long and extensive enough to have an impact on the student.

5. Decide when the program will be in effect each day, then arrange an adequate amount of time and staff assistance to implement the program. An adult must be available for at least 45 minutes per problem behavior instance in the initial days of the program.

6. When the student engages in the problem behavior, give the verbal cue and proceed with the restitutional activity. Be prepared to prompt the student physically to complete the activities.

7. Avoid eye contact, unnecessary physical contact, and unnecessary conversation during restitutional overcorrection.

8. If, during the overcorrection procedure, the student reengages in one of the designated problem behaviors, start the activities again.

9. *Never* use the verbal cue without the restitutional overcorrection activities until the problem behaviors are reduced to a low and stable rate.

10. Be sure to provide ample opportunity during the rest of the day for the student to receive attention for appropriate behaviors.

11. *Remember:* This program may require parental/guardian permission and should be implemented under the supervision of a professional competent in this aspect of behavior modification. Medical approval of this program should be obtained prior to the student's participation in it.

Note: The material in this table was taken from R. M. Foxx & N. H. Azrin. The elimination of autistic self-stimulatory behavior by overcorrection. *Journal of Applied Behavior Analysis*, 1973, 6, 1-14.

practice overcorrection.) However, one study has suggested that you can maintain the effectiveness of the overcorrection by reinforcing the students for correctly practicing the designated behavior (Carey & Bucher, 1986). Correct responses, performed without physical guidance from the adult, earned the child edibles and praise. The child received no feedback for approximate responses.

To review, positive practice overcorrection is considered a punishment procedure that must be applied contingently after an episode of the target behavior. This means that you, as a classroom teacher, cannot schedule the practice sessions but must interrupt your classroom activities to conduct the practice contingently (Gibbs & Luyben, 1985). Moreover, the time-out from the preferred stereotypic behavior is a valuable component of the intervention and strengthens the view that overcorrection is a restrictive intervention requiring approval.

Positive practice overcorrection can be applied if the student is physically smaller than the adult in charge. Some students, however, are too strong and resistant to complete a functional movement training series. Remember, in the initial days of an overcorrection program, a student may struggle with you in order to continue self-injurious behaviors instead of following the positive practice activities (Luiselli, 1984a, 1984b). If you are working with a student whose physical stature prevents you from conducting the typical overcorrection functional movement exercises, your consultant may suggest exercises that only partially involve the student's body. For example, De-

Table 9-6. Guidelines for Using Positive Practice Overcorrection

1. Define the problem behavior or behaviors specifically.

2. Record baseline data on the rate or percent of intervals of occurrence of each behavior. Continue collecting data throughout the overcorrection program.

3. Select a verbal cue to use whenever the student engages in the problem behavior.

4. Select a positive practice overcorrection activity, such as Functional Movement Training (see Table 9-4). Be sure the activity is sufficiently lengthy and intensive to modify the student's behavior.

5. Decide when the program will be in effect each day, then arrange an adequate amount of time and staff assistance to implement the program. An adult must be available for at least 45 minutes per problem behavior instance in the initial days of the program.

6. When the student engages in the problem behavior, give the verbal cue and proceed with the positive practice activity. Be prepared to physically prompt the student to complete the activities.

7. Avoid eye contact, unnecessary physical contact, and unnecessary conversation during positive practice overcorrection.

8. If, during the overcorrection procedure, the student reengages in one of the designated problem behaviors, start the activities over again.

9. *Never* use the verbal cue without the overcorrection activities, until the problem behaviors are reduced to a low and stable rate.

10. Be sure to provide ample opportunity during the rest of the day for the student to receive attention for appropriate behaviors.

11. *Remember:* This program may require parental/guardian permission and should be implemented under the supervision of a professional competent in this aspect of behavior modification. Medical approval of this program should be obtained prior to the student's participation in it.

Note: The material in this table was taken from R. M. Foxx & N. H. Azrin. The elimination of autistic self-stimulatory behavior by overcorrection. *Journal of Applied Behavior Analysis,* 1973, 6, 1-14.

Catanzaro and Baldwin (1978) used a forced arm exercise, relying only on the arm involved in self-injurious acts. In this procedure the teacher gently pumped the student's arm up and down once per second, repeating this action twenty-five times. Foxx (1978) offered the following guideline with regard to overcorrection with a counter-aggressive individual:

> . . . if the overcorrection requires the involvement of two trainers instead of one, the danger of physical injury is greatly increased, and the procedure will not be implemented correctly (Foxx, 1978, cited in Schroeder et al., 1981, p. 83).

Remember, *the student must receive positive attention at times other than during the overcorrection activities.* Conduct a daily DRO program to teach the student functional skills.

MOVEMENT SUPPRESSION PROCEDURE

The **Movement Suppression Procedure** is a variation of time-out from reinforcement in which the student is punished for any movement or verbalization while in a time-out area (Rolinder & Van Houten, 1985). In the Rolinder and Van Houten study, DRO alone (praise and candy every fifteen minutes of no targeted behavior) was compared with movement suppression time-out plus DRO. The movement suppression intervention consisted of the parents or school staff placing the child in the corner, restraining his movements manually, and directing him not to move or talk. This lasted for three minutes. This procedure was replicated with slight modifications across two other cases of SIB in two other children; all reports were successful.

If you are on a team that is deciding which of several related interventions to try, review the Rolinder and Van Houten studies; they also provide comparative information on movement suppression plus DRO versus other treatments (e.g., contingent restraint, exclusionary time-out, and corner time-out, respectively).

Assessment of SSB

In this section we address ways of assessing and analyzing self-stimulatory behaviors. Perhaps the first decision to be made with regard to referring a problem with SSB is whether it warrants treatment. In the event that a stereotypic behavior has become self-injurious, the decision is a quick "yes!" And there are types of SSB that, repeated over time, are self-injurious, as pointed out by O'Brien (1981): "tapping knuckles on hard surfaces . . . flipping fingers in front of eyes focused on the sun, keeping hands in a tight fist around the collar of a shirt" (page 143).

Also, an SSB individual may not gain access to less restrictive environments or to training programs within the present environment until the "annoying" SSB is reduced or eliminated (Baumeister, 1978; O'Brien, 1981). O'Brien (1981) illustrated this situation:

> Decreasing annoyance is a reason for treating self-stimulation. If parents, teachers, or peers reprimand, berate, or tease a client for self-stimulation it should be treated. Similarly, treatment should be provided if clients are regularly required to accept less preferred sitting or sleeping arrangements because they self-stimulate. Requiring clients to sit in a position farthest from the television set, sit at the least preferred table in the dining room, sleep in a less-preferred bed, or sit in a less-preferred seat on the bus are examples of this. When these types of annoyance can be reduced, it seems reasonable to treat self-stimulation. (p. 143)

In classroom situations, you may choose to pursue the assessment of the problem because SSB interferes with a student's ability to attend to appropriate instructional or adaptive behavior tasks (Foxx & Azrin, 1973; Lovaas et al., 1987). To define an SSB problem, use the questions in Figure 9-3 to assemble information gathered from all of the student's teachers and the student's family. The information listed on this form will help you complete your functional analysis of the student's SSB.

As you read about interventions for SSB, you will understand why certain items of information are important to a thorough definition and analysis of SSB. For example, questions regarding the type of sensory stimulation a student appears to gain from SSB (questions 3 and 4) provide initial information for a sensory extinction program, whereas questions 7, 8, and 9 target information for a DRO or punishment program. You should also complete a health history form or ask the student's parents to do this.

You need to record specific samples of SSB in preparation for (or to monitor the effects of) an intervention program. Review Table 9-2; the third column describes measurement procedures used for SSB. Notice that interval-based measurements are often used. We suggest you record SSB using an interval record such as the one in Figure 9-4, completed for Joey, the student in our case study.

If you have questions about designing or using an interval record, reread Chapter 3.

In summary, these assessment activities should provide information to facilitate the design of an appropriate intervention, although the task is still *not* simple. O'Brien (1981) offers these guidelines:

> Should a decision be made to treat self-stimulation, a behavioral evaluation must be completed. The evaluation should determine the situations in which self-stimulation occurs, its topography, frequency, and duration, and its consequences. If during the evaluation it is found the self-stimulation occurred only under one condition (e.g., in front of a particular

Figure 9-3.   Information-Gathering Form for SSB

Student: _____   Date: _____

1. What are the precise behaviors of concern?

2. Do these behaviors occur interchangeably, simultaneously, or separately?

3. Is any kind of sensory stimulation apparent (e.g., visual flickering, repetitive auditory signal)? In other words, what kind of *perceptual reinforcement* does the SSB provide the child?

4. Does the behavior appear only in selected settings (e.g., areas where there is a hard, smooth surface, well-lit areas)?

5. Do the behaviors prevent the student from engaging in an instructional activity? How?

6. Do the behaviors gain attention for the student from adults or peers? If so, what kind of attention? (Use an A-B-C analysis.)

7. Does the student cease self-stimulation when asked? For how long? When asked by whom? In what tone of voice?

8. Does the student stop these behaviors when alone? In the presence of whom?

9. Does the student stop the behaviors when engaged in certain activities? Specify these activities.

10. Could the self-stimulatory behaviors be considered developmentally age-appropriate for this student (e.g., masturbation)?

11. Is the student injuring himself?

12. Is the student presently involved in an intervention program? What is it? Where are the data on this program?

Name of person completing this form: _____

---

mirror, when wearing turtleneck sweaters), and it was reasonable to restrict the client from this condition, that might be the preferred treatment. Should it seem unreasonable to restrict the client from a particular situation in which self-stimulation occurred, it might be reasonable to apply sensory extinction (e.g., if self-stimulation occurs only at a wooden desk, the client should be seated in a soft-fabric chair).

Should a behavioral evaluation determine that people regularly provide a consequence for the self-stimulation, that consequence should be reviewed as a possible reinforcer. Should the behavior evaluation determine that self-stimulation occurs in many different situations, that the sensory consequences would be difficult to modify, and that no other consequences are regularly provided, a program should be designed along the recommendations presented by Foxx and Azrin (1973), including teaching and reinforcing adaptive behaviors, interrupting self-stimulation, and scheduling an annoying consequence to follow such.

When designing a treatment based on these recommendations, planners must address themselves to two treatment concerns: providing the

Figure 9-4. Interval Record for Self-Stimulatory Behaviors

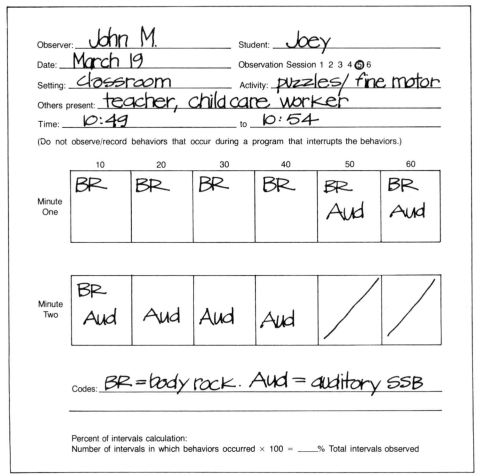

least restrictive (less intrusive) plan and providing treatment that is effective (pp. 144-145).

Intervention Strategies for SSB

GENERAL CONSIDERATIONS

Recent work in the area of self-stimulatory behavior has important implications for your

work as a classroom teacher. We review here some of the findings about interventions that are—and are not—effective with self-stimulatory behaviors.

Social Reinforcement Approaches

Evidence has shown that self-stimulatory behavior does not extinguish with the withdrawal of social reinforcement (Berkson & Mason, 1963; Lovaas et al., 1987; Newsom, 1974; Ritvo, Ornitz, & LaFranchi, 1968). In other words, ignoring a self-stimulating child will not affect his problem behavior. The attention of others is simply not powerful enough to compete successfully with the perceptual reinforcement the child receives from the SSB. Interestingly, a child whose *SSB* does not lessen with the withdrawal of social attention may still improve other behaviors when a social extinction approach is taken, so you do not want to eliminate this strategy altogether for a self-injurious child.

Sensory Preferences

Children engaged in SSB appear to have strong preferences for particular sensory experiences (e.g., either auditory or visual) (Lovaas et al., 1987). This finding underscores the importance of a thorough — and often tedious — analysis of the student's behaviors and the circumstances that maintain them.

Reinforcing Alternative Behaviors

The DRO approach described earlier might prove helpful in teaching the child alternative behaviors, but it does not seem fruitful as an intervention to eliminate SSB. This is a bit confusing for you as a classroom teacher because you may notice that the stereotypic behaviors do lessen when the DRO is implemented. This problem arises when — as has been observed — the self-stimulatory behaviors return once the DRO is terminated (Lovaas et al., 1987).

Enriching The Environment

Although you will surely want the most interesting environment possible in your classroom, this environmental manipulation alone will not reduce self-stimulatory behaviors (Favell, Mc-Gimsey, & Schell, 1982; Murphy, Carr, & Callias, 1986). However, there is evidence to show that self-stimulating individuals prefer objects (e.g., toys) that give them their preferred mode of perceptual feedback (Favell *et al.*, 1982), so you might want to consider this variable as you plan your classroom activities.

Perceptual Reinforcement

As you will recall from the introduction to this chapter, the key to understanding SSB is to view it as a form of perceptual reinforcement to the individual. Therefore, we believe that forthcoming research will prove the sensory manipulation strategies to be the most effective. In the section on teacher-mediated interventions, we highlight *sensory extinction,* one of these interventions.

In this section we describe interventions (both environmental modifications and teacher-mediated programs) for reducing SSB. Some require outside behavior change agents, but in many you may play a major role. Some of these procedures are described in the section Intervention Strategies for SIB, so we will only mention them here.

ENVIRONMENTAL SAFETY CONSIDERATIONS

In the discussion of SIB we mentioned safety precautions to be taken in the classroom, unless an individual is to be restrained (a last resort). For ethical reasons, restraints usually are not recommended for SSB students. It is difficult to justify the deliberate restraint of an individual whose behavior is hurting no one. Nevertheless, students who engage in self-stimulatory behaviors may incorporate some aspect of the environment as a part of their behavioral syndrome, thus creating a safety risk. Do not permit self-stimulatory students to use sharp objects, breakable items, or damaged toys as a part of a self-stimulatory sequence, for example. Toys that are safe for normal youngsters may present a hazard for a student who will use them inappropriately.

SENSORY EXTINCTION PROCEDURE

A recent development in the alteration of self-stimulatory behaviors, sensory extinction, is based on the notion that certain individuals have a strong preference for one aspect of sensory input (e.g., tactile, proprioceptive, visual, or auditory) and engage in self-stimulatory behaviors to increase this sensory input (Aiken & Salzberg, 1984; Rincover, Cook, Peoples, & Packard, 1979; Rincover & Devany, 1982; Rincover, Newsom, & Carr, 1979). For example, a child may spin objects for the auditory feedback (the sound of the plate spinning), may finger-flap (for the visual feedback of watching his finger movements), or tap his fingers (for the proprioceptive stimulation).

The first step in a sensory extinction program is to determine the sensory input the student receives while engaged in the behavior. The student may exhibit a behavior that provides more than one type of sensory feedback; in this case, additional sensory analyses must be completed. One study described such an assessment procedure (Rincover, 1978):

> We observed each child throughout the day and consulted with the teachers in an attempt to identify possible sensory consequences of their self-stimulatory behavior. We found that Reggie would incessantly spin objects, particularly a plate, in a stereotyped, repetitive manner. However, when he twirled the plate, he would also cock his head to the side and lean toward it, seeming to listen to the plate as it was spinning. This suggested that the auditory feedback may have been an important consequence of Reggie's self-stimulation. Robert engaged in excessive finger-flapping, in which he had one or both hands in front of his face and vigorously moved the fingers (but not the arms) back and forth. In this case, two sensory consequences were identified for testing: the visual feedback from watching the finger movements, and the proprioceptive stimulation from the finger movement itself. Brenda's self-stimulatory behavior consisted of twirling objects such as a feather or string of beads in front of her eyes. For Brenda, as with Robert, both the visual and the proprioceptive components were targeted for testing.
> During sensory extinction sessions we attempted to eliminate a particular sensory consequence of a given self-stimulatory behavior. First, in order to eliminate the

auditory feedback from Reggie's plate spinning, carpeting was installed atop the table in the classroom. The carpeting was .6 cm thick and completely covered the surface of the table. The surface of the carpet was hard and flat so as not to restrict the plate from spinning . . . no sound was audible from spinning the plate on the carpeted table. A second sensory extinction procedure was designed to mask the proprioceptive stimulation from finger-flapping (Robert) and object manipulation (Brenda). A small vibratory mechanism was taped to the back of each child's hand, generating a repetitive low-intensity, high-frequency pulsation. Significantly, the vibrator did not physically restrict self-stimulatory behavior. The final sensory extinction procedure involved removing the visual consequences for each of the three children. For this purpose a blindfold was introduced consisting of a handkerchief, once folded, snugly placed over each child's eyes and tied behind the head (pp. 302-303).

If you think an individual's self-stimulatory behavior reflects a strong preference for one aspect of sensory feedback, talk with a behavioral consultant who is trained in this procedure. In the study just cited (Rincover, 1978), daily twenty-minute sessions were conducted in which the child sat in a separate room with an adult. The child's preferred self-stimulation object was placed on a table before him or her. These sessions provided the children with experiences in which the preferred sensory feedback was eliminated. An additional benefit in using the sensory extinction procedure is that you may identify *appropriate* activities involving the preferred sensory input as potential reinforcers. For example, if a student prefers auditory input, you might try music or noise-making toys to reinforce appropriate responses during teaching sessions.

OVERCORRECTION

Overcorrection has been successful in some cases of SSB, as evidenced by a study by Luiselli (1984a) who targeted tongue thrusting and saliva rubbing (*see* Table 9-2). The type of overcorrection used was positive practice, and the time period for each practice session was thirty to forty seconds. If you decide to try overcorrection, refer to Table 9-5 and remember to monitor for the possibility that other SSB may emerge. (This was not the case in the Luiselli study.)

FACIAL SCREENING

This procedure has reduced stereotypic behaviors in a couple of studies (McGonigle, Duncan, Cordisco, & Barrett, 1982; Horton, 1987). To implement **facial screening,** you briefly (e.g., one minute) cover the student's face with either your hand or a cloth bib (Van Hasselt, 1983) when the student engages in the target behavior. The screen is removed when the student stops the stereotypic behavior. The positive features of this intervention, as cited by Van Hasselt (1983), are (1) it requires minimal training, (2) it appears to work effectively and rapidly, and (3) the improvements have been observed across settings and over time. Also, the procedure is only mildly aversive. The procedure may *not* be effective with physically strong and resistant children who struggle with the "screener." Our case study for this chapter illustrates the facial screening (**visual screening**) intervention.

The next four interventions are useful for teaching SSB individuals alternative behaviors, although they will probably not suppress the self-stimulatory behaviors themselves.

STIMULUS VARIATION

The purpose of **stimulus variation** is to increase the level of motivation and responsiveness exhibited by a student engaged in SSB. Although little research on this intervention has been conducted thus far, there is evidence to suggest that bored students may engage in SSB (Dunlap & Koegel, 1980). Review carefully the sequence and length of activities you present to students. Try to intersperse two or three target tasks among other tasks rather than focusing on fifteen minutes of one task followed by fifteen minutes of another.

RESPONSE-REINFORCER PROCEDURE

In a **response-reinforcer procedure,** the immediate environment is manipulated so that the student, as a result of completing a task, has immediate access to a reinforcer physically imbedded within the task. The following description of a manual task is an example of a response-reinforcer (Bittle & Hake, 1977):

> The manual task involved removing eight wing nuts that secured the transparent side of each of six boxes mounted on a wall at the child's eye level. Each box contained a small piece of bologna sausage and a cup with .25 ounces of Coke, known reinforcers for this child. Because the child averaged eleven seconds to remove a single wing nut, approximately ninety seconds was required to open one box and about nine minutes was required to open all boxes. The child was shown how to open the boxes prior to the study (p. 909).

Why might a response-reinforcer procedure result in rapid learning acquisition for severely behaviorally handicapped children? Perhaps it is because the reinforcer becomes immediately available as soon as the student engages in the correct response (completes the task). In other words, ". . . a functional response-reinforcer relationship may serve to highlight the contingency between the reinforcer and the intended target behavior" (Williams, Koegel, & Egel, 1981, p. 59).

SENSORY REINFORCEMENT

In contrast to the response-reinforcer intervention, a **sensory reinforcement** strategy provides the child with one or more sensory experiences that are deemed desirable to the child. Rincover and Newsom (1985) found that multiple sensory reinforcers were more effective than multiple edible reinforcers in increasing correct responses. When a single sensory reinforcer was compared with a single edible reinforcer, the results were about the same. The authors pointed out that "children may work longer and learn more when multiple-sensory events are used" (p. 245). Some of the sensory reinforcers used by Rincover and Newsom (1985) include tickling, hand clapping, finger tapping or drumming with sticks by the adult on a surface near the child, singing (by the adult), playing music very briefly, and caressing. To create the multiple-sensory reinforcement arrangement, the adult varied the reinforcers given for correct trials.

DIFFERENTIAL REINFORCEMENT OF OTHER BEHAVIORS (DRO)

This procedure, described in an earlier section, is frequently applied to SSB as an accompaniment to behavior reduction procedures. Refer to Table 9-3 for steps in using DRO.

Summary

Self-injurious and self-stimulatory behaviors are bizarre and complex problems facing the teacher of the developmentally disabled. Fortunately, new insights from research studies can provide relief to the classroom teacher seeking an end to stereotypic behavioral patterns. We urge you to consider the research-based interventions for self-injury and self-stimulation, fully respecting the complexity and intensity of some of these interventions and the assessments that must precede them. Our chapter closes with a case study about removing SIB and a case study illustrating facial screening.

CASE STUDY

A Positive Approach to Removal of Restraints for Self-Injurious Behavior

Howard C. Schneider
Charles L. Salzberg[1]

The occurrence of self-injurious behavior is common among mentally retarded children (Baumeister & Rollings, 1976). When it occurs with severe intensity and durability, self-

[1]This case study is reprinted with permission from H. C. Schneider & C. L. Salzberg. A positive approach to removal of restraints for self-injurious behavior. *Teaching Exceptional Children,* Summer 1981, *13*(4): 143-144.

injurious behavior presents dangerous health hazards for the child. Smolev (1971) and Johnson and Baumeister (1978) reviewed a variety of alternative treatments that have been used with some success. Choice of treatment procedure often depends on ethical and practical considerations that vary from setting to setting and from subject to subject (Schneider, Ross, & Dubin, 1979).

Occurrence of self-injurious behavior in the classroom presents a particularly difficult problem. In addition to the immediate danger to the child, the occurrence of frequent self-injurious episodes disrupts the ongoing educational programs for the target child as well as for other children. The child is often encumbered at school with restraining devices that do not eliminate self-injurious behavior, but are intended to reduce its physical damage. Among the most common restraining devices are heavy cardboard arm sleeves and protective headgear similar to a football helmet. Unfortunately, they limit the child's mobility and his or her subsequent ability to perform appropriately in many situations. A teacher is then presented with two alternatives: to circumvent the educational problems created by these restraining devices or to develop procedures to eliminate the self-injurious behavior and the accompanying protective restraints.

The child who has worn protective restraints for a long time is often subdued while the restraints are on. Indeed, the child sometimes appears to prefer to wear them. Their abrupt removal frequently results in high rate bursts of self-injurious behavior. In order to protect the child from physical harm, the restraints are usually immediately reapplied with the consequent problem that the child has then been inadvertently reinforced for the behavior. He or she has learned that the occurrence of self-injurious behavior results in regaining the restraints. Thus, removal of restraints by the teacher may have a negative effect. The program for removal of restraints described is presented as one practical alternative in a classroom situation. It is based on positive reinforcement, and puts control for removal of the restraints in the hands of the child. In a relatively brief time, the child is systematically taught to remove his or her own restraints.

Program to Remove Protective Restraints

The following program was used with Paul, an 18 year old Down's syndrome youth and a student in a self-contained special education class for the severely retarded in a large metropolitan public school system. Paul had been seriously self-injurious for many years. A variety of techniques to reduce self-injurious behavior had been tried, but reliable and durable results were not achieved. At the initiation of the present program, there were bruises, reddened skin, and scar tissue on his face, arms, and hands. Paul's ears were severely scarred and swollen, and he was in danger of losing his hearing. Heavy cardboard arm sleeves and headgear with hard plastic ear coverings were being used with Paul to prevent him from striking his head and ears with his hands. The following procedures were used to eliminate both these behaviors and the protective restraints.

Step 1: Reduce Self-Injurious Behavior in Restraints. The initial step was to reduce Paul's rate of self-injurious behavior while he was wearing his restraints. Through observation, the situations in which there were high rates of self-injurious behavior were identified. For Paul, it was discovered that such behavior was exhibited primarily when one particular teacher's aide was not attending to him and when he was asked to do tasks that displeased him. On the basis of this information, the teacher and aide were instructed to lavishly reinforce Paul with social praise for the absence of self-injurious behavior in those situations. The teacher and aide recorded all occurrences of self-injurious behavior on a simple record sheet which they kept conveniently available. This provided information showing the trends in Paul's self-injurious behavior. After a consistently low rate for self-injurious behavior was maintained, Step 2 was begun.

Step 2: Implement Token Reinforcement System. The purpose of this step was to shift from social praise to a more durable reinforcement system while maintaining a low rate of self-injurious behavior with all restraints still in place. A simple token system, as used in many classrooms with mentally retarded children, was implemented with Paul. Paul received tokens, paired with praise, for the absence of self-injurious behavior. Tokens were exchanged approximately every 30 minutes for the opportunity to engage in what were preferred activities for Paul (i.e., playing with water or the attention of the aide).

At exchange time, Paul was taken to a board where he could stack the tokens he had received. If his stack was high enough, as indicated by a red line on the board, he was permitted to choose a reinforcer. He made his selection by pointing to one of several pictures of different activities. The pictures were taped above the red line on the board. The picture selected was removed and served as a pass which Paul carried to permit access to the activity. Paul quickly came to understand the token system and, within two weeks after implementation, self-injurious behavior was being maintained at a near zero rate. Consequently, the process of removing his protective restraints was begun.

Step 3: Gradually Remove Arm Restraints. In this step, a gradual shaping program was used to remove Paul's arm restraints. Initially, the restraint was loosened and jiggled about his arm by the teacher or aide. Paul was reinforced with a token for the absence of self-injurious behavior. The teacher or aide then began to slide the restraint down his arm while continuing to reinforce the absence of self-injurious behavior with tokens. In a step by step procedure, the restraint was moved down Paul's arm until it was removed, at which time Paul immediately received token reinforcement if no self-injurious behavior occurred. Subsequently, the arm restraints were removed for progressively longer periods of time. Tokens were awarded to Paul for various appropriate behaviors while the restraints were removed.

On the infrequent occasions when self-injurious behavior did occur, Paul's arms were held still and he was admonished with a firm "No!" and a light tap on the hand. Throughout the program, arm sleeves were never immediately reapplied after an incident of self-injurious behavior but only after a minimum of 30 seconds had passed and some appropriate behavior had occurred since the last incident. Paul

was soon able to have his restraints off much of the school day while in the classroom with only an occasional incident of self-injurious behavior. It appeared that Paul understood that he received tokens for having the arm restraints off.

Step 4: Teach Paul to Remove His Own Restraints. The purpose of this step was to teach Paul to remove his own arm restraints. Using a combination of physical prompting and reinforcement, Paul's behavior was gradually shaped so that he could remove his own restraints. Administration of the token system, increasing the time of restraint removal, and token reinforcement for the absence of self-injurious behavior, were analogous to those used in the third step of the program. After he learned to remove his own restraints, while controlling his self-injurious behavior, Paul was taught to leave the restraints in the back of the classroom. He was soon treating the arm restraints as an article of clothing. He would remove them with his outerwear when arriving at school and retrieve them upon leaving. Subsequently, a similar program was introduced for use with Paul's protective headgear.

Program Benefits

At the conclusion of the program, Paul's incidents of self-injurious behavior during the school day occurred infrequently, and his activity was not impeded by awkward physical restraints. The use of positive reinforcement in a program such as this, which teaches the child to remove his or her own physical restraints, also has several other general benefits. First, the excitable behavior and increased incidents of self-injurious behavior that occur when the teacher abruptly removes the restraints are avoided. Second, the teacher does not have to use maximum physical force to restrain the child's self-injurious behavior. This avoids a potentially dangerous situation for the child, and legal and ethical problems for the teacher. A third benefit of the program is its ease of application and relative brevity. It can be administered by the teacher or aide and completed within a reasonably short time. The present program was conducted primarily by an aide over a period of approximately six weeks. Further, due to the low rate of self-injurious behavior maintained throughout the program, the teacher did not have to divert her attention from other students in order to focus exclusively on the problem child. A fourth benefit of the program is its applicability to varied settings. Replication of the program in the residential setting, or in other settings within the school, could be accomplished with relative ease and without undue risk.

The final, but perhaps most important, benefit of this program is that it begins to teach the child the important skill of controlling his or her own behavior. The child learns self control. Whereas prior to the program Paul's behavior was controlled externally through restraints, he now manages not only his own self-injurious behavior but the external controls of that behavior as well.

References

Baumeister, A. A., & Rollings, J. P. (1976). Self-injurious behavior. *International Review of Research in Mental Retardation, 8,* 1–34.

Johnson, W. L., & Baumeister, A. A. (1978). Self-injurious behavior, a review and analysis of methodological details of published studies. *Behavior Modification, 2,* 465–487.

Schneider, H. C., Ross, J. S. G., & Dubin, W. J. (1979). A practical alternative for the treatment of tantrum and self-injurious behavior. *Journal of Behavior Therapy and Experimental Psychiatry, 10,* 73–75.

Smolev, S. R. (1971). Use of operant techniques for the modification of self-injurious behavior. *American Journal of Mental Deficiency, 76,* 295–305.

Visual Screening: A Novel Procedure Used to Reduce Self-Stimulatory Behaviors

John J. McGonigle

An Alternative Procedure to Reduce Stereotypic Behaviors

The present case study was designed to evaluate the effectiveness of a novel procedure called visual screening on the reduction and elimination of stereotypic behaviors. Visual screening involved briefly covering the student's eyes (with the trainer's hand) whenever the target behavior was observed. A study was conducted to test the effectiveness of the visual screening treatment in a multiple baseline design on self-stimulatory behaviors that were topographically different.

Method

Student. Joey, a seven-year-old boy, is a student in an MR/SED classroom housed in a psychiatric hospital. Psychological testing, using the Stanford Binet (L-M), found Joey to be functioning intellectually at the four-year level with an I.Q. of 46. His score on the Vineland Social Maturity Scale cited a social age

(SA) of four years five months. A review of the records from Joey's previous school revealed that he displayed a very high rate of self-stimulatory behavior.

Procedure. A multiple baseline design across three self-stimulatory behaviors was used to evaluate the effectiveness of the visual screening procedure. The classroom staff had observed Joey exhibiting three modes of self-stimulatory behavior: body rocking, auditory self-stimulation, visual self-stimulation. Baseline and treatment sessions were conducted daily in the classroom for a twenty-minute free play period with the teacher and a classroom aide implementing the visual screening procedure.

Definition of Behaviors

1. Body rocking — a repetitive back and forth motion usually while standing or sitting.
2. Visual hand stereotypy — gazing fixedly at either hand while held approximately 12 inches from his eyes.
3. Auditory self-stimulation — any self-generated vocalizations or noises (e.g., humming, singing) usually occurred while body rocking.

Treatment

Figure 9-5 displays a portion of Joey's total Individualized Educational Program. A multiple baseline across the three self-stimulatory behaviors was used to evaluate the effectiveness of the visual screening. Treatment procedures were initiated on the eleventh session for body rocking. The teacher, upon observing the student engage in body rocking, would approach the student and interrupt the behavior by covering (visual screening) the student's eyes with one hand while placing the other hand on the back of the student's head for a ten-second period. Despite having his eyes covered Joey was still able to move about the room.

Recording and Reliability

A noncontinuous recording tape with ten-second observe/record intervals was used throughout the study. Interobserver agreement was measured by two independent observers and reliability was obtained during 32 percent of the sessions.

Effects of Visual Screening

Figure 9-6 illustrates the effects of the visual screening procedure on the three topographically dissimilar self-stimulatory behaviors. The data show that the three behaviors appeared to be dependent upon one another. When visual screening was applied to body rocking, there was not only an immediate reduction in the target behavior, but also in auditory and visual self-stimulation. Observations made outside of class noted that Joey would start body rocking and would raise either hand in front of his eyes and start to hum or chant. It appeared that the rocking behavior was the first link in the chain. During the follow-up period in session 23, there was a gradual increase in visual self-stimulation. On session 28 the screening procedure was applied to visual self-stimulation and immediately reduced it to a near zero level. The arrow indicates the visual screening procedure was implemented throughout the entire day.

Follow-up

Follow-up data were collected two months after the termination of visual screening, and the treatment gains were maintained.

Results and Summary

The results of this case study indicate that visual screening was an effective procedure for reducing and eliminating three self-stimulatory behaviors in a seven-year-old retarded/disturbed child with autisticlike behaviors. The design was a multiple baseline across three dissimilar

Figure 9-5. Joey's Individualized Educational Program

Name:

Date:

Instructional Area:

Annual Goal: To eliminate self-stimulatory behavior during independent and group work sessions.

Short-Term Objective	Instructional Methods Media/Material Title(s) (Optional)	Evaluation of Instructional Objectives		Date Completed
		Tests, Materials Evaluation Procedures To be Used	Criteria of Successful Performance	
To reduce body rocking by 20% during group activities.	Visual screening	Interval recording	Participate in group activities with body rocking 20% of the time over one week.	
To eliminate auditory and visual self-stimulation during a 20-minute free play period.	Visual screening	Interval recording	Participate in classroom free play without visual or auditory self-stimulation.	
To increase hand raising upon task completion during individual work sessions.	Positive reinforcement program (social praise)	Frequency count	Raise hand 80% when tasks are completed over one week.	
To eliminate out-of-seat behavior during classtime.	Ignore/Positive reinforcement (social praise)	Frequency count	100% throughout classtime.	

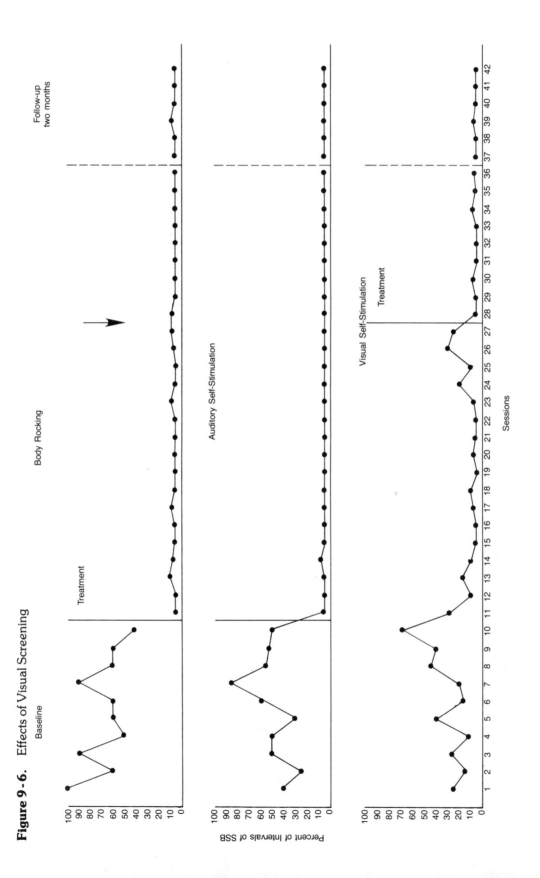

Figure 9-6. Effects of Visual Screening

self-stimulatory behaviors. When the visual screening procedure was applied to body rocking Joey's auditory and visual self-stimulatory behaviors decreased significantly. Clinical observations noted no negative collateral behaviors; however, observers noted an increase in physical interactions between the teacher and the student.

Visual screening appears to be an easily administered, quick procedure for controlling self-stimulatory behaviors. It requires minimal training and can be administered without props in a classroom or group setting. Visual screening is a mildly aversive procedure that imposes no risk to the student and no adverse side effects have been noted.

Figure 9-7. Strategy Selection Chart for Stereotypic Behavior

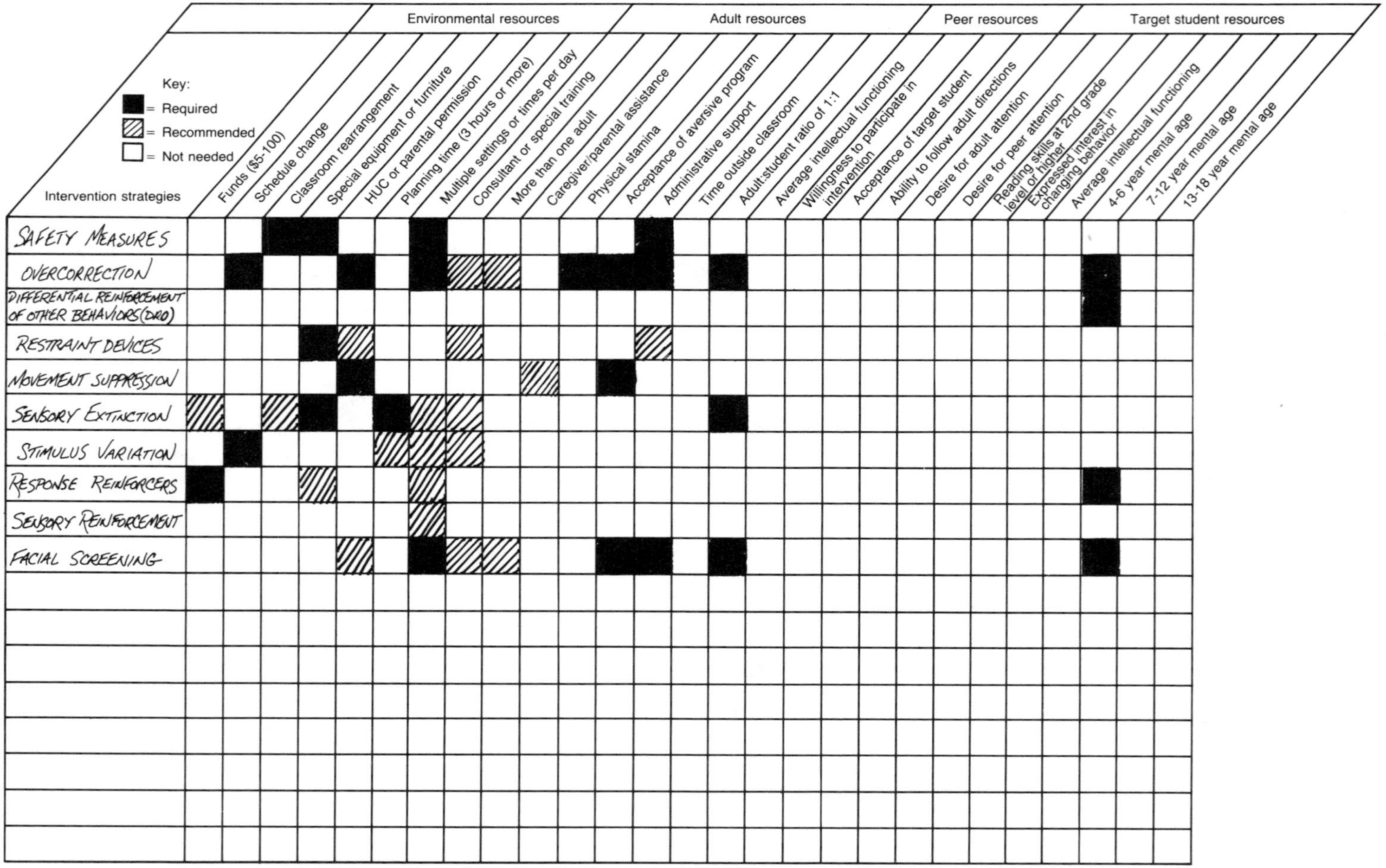

Discussion Questions

1. Discuss the major concepts explaining a perceptual reinforcement theory of self-stimulatory behavior.
2. Describe the steps in conducting a functional analysis for self-injurious behavior and on self-stimulatory behavior.
3. Describe how you would use sensory extinction to reduce the auditory SSB of a developmentally delayed child.
4. Discuss the importance of contingent practice and time-out in an overcorrection procedure for self-injurious behavior.
5. How is DRO best used for individuals with stereotypic behaviors? Will it suppress the stereotypic behaviors?
6. What criteria should you meet before trying an aversive or restrictive intervention?
7. What interventions have *not* proven effective in suppressing SSB? Why?
8. What are the advantages of facial screening?
9. What seems to be the most effective reinforcer for a child who engages in SSB?

References

Aiken, J. M., & Salzberg, C. L. (1984). The effects of a sensory extinction procedure on stereotypic sounds of two autistic children. *Journal of Autism and Developmental Disorders, 14*(3), 291-299.

Altman, K., Haavik, S., & Cook, J. A. (1978). Punishment of self-injurious behavior in natural settings using contingent aromatic ammonia. *Behavior Research and Therapy, 16,* 85-96.

Baumeister, A. A. (1978). Origins and control of stereotyped movements. In C. E. Meyers (Ed.), *Quality of life in severely and profoundly mentally retarded people: Research foundations for improvement.* Washington, D.C.: AAMD Monograph, No. 3, American Association on Mental Deficiency.

Baumeister, A. A., & Rollings, P. (1976). Self-injurious behavior. In N. R. Ellis (Ed.), *International review of research in mental retardation* (vol. 9). New York: Academic Press.

Berkson, G., & Mason, W. A. (1963). Stereotyped movements of mental defectives: III. Situation effects. *American Journal of Mental Deficiency, 68,* 409-412.

Berkson, G., McQuiston, S., Jacobson, J. W., Eyman, R, & Borthwick, S. (1985). The relationship between age and stereotyped behaviors. *Mental Retardation, 23,* 31-33.

Bierly, C., & Billingsley, F. F. (1983). An investigation of the educative effects of over-correction on the behavior of an autistic child. *Behavioral Disorders, 9*(1), 11-21.

Bittle, R., & Hake, D. F. (1977). A multielement design model for component analysis and cross-setting assessment of a treatment package. *Behavior Therapy, 8,* 906-914.

Brawley, E. R., Harris, F. R., Allen, K. E., Fleming, R. S., & Peterson, R. F. (1969). Behavior modification of an autistic child. *Behavior Science, 14,* 87-97.

Carey, R. G., & Bucher, B. D. (1986). Positive practice overcorrection: Effects of reinforcing correct performance. *Behavior Modification, 10*(1), 73-92.

Carr, E. G. (1977). The motivation of self-injurious behavior: A review of some hypotheses. *Psychological Bulletin, 84*(4), 800-816.

Carr, E. G., & Durand, V. M. (1985). Reducing behavior problems through functional communication training. *Journal of Applied Behavior Analysis, 18*(2), 111-126.

Carr, E. G., & McDowell, J. J. (1980). Social control of self-injurious behavior of organic etiology. *Behavior Therapy, 11,* 402-409.

Carr, E. G., Newsom, C. D., & Binkoff, J. A. (1976). Stimulus control of self-destructive behavior in a psychotic child. *Journal of Abnormal Child Psychology, 4,* 139-152.

Coleman, R. S., Whitman, T. L., & Johnson, M. R. (1979). Suppression of self-stimulatory behavior of a profoundly retarded boy across staff and settings: An assessment of situational generalization. *Behavior Therapy, 10,* 266-280.

Cook, J. W., Altman, K., Shaw, J., & Blaylock, M. (1978). Use of contingent lemon juice to eliminate public masturbation by a severely retarded boy. *Behavior Research and Therapy, 16,* 131-134.

DeCatanzaro, D. A., & Baldwin, G. (1978). Effective treatment of self-injurious behavior through a forced arm exercise. *American Journal of Mental Deficiency, 82,* 433-439.

Dorsey, M. F., Iwata, B. A., Ong, P., & McSween, T. E. (1980). Treatment of self-injurious behavior using a water mist: Initial response suppression and generalization. *Journal of Applied Behavior Analysis, 13,* 324-333.

Dorsey, M. F., Iwata, B. A., Reid, D. H., & Davis, P. A. (1982). Protective equipment: Continuous and contingent application in the treatment of self-injurious behavior. *Journal of Applied Behavior Analysis, 15,* 217-230.

Dunlap, G., & Koegel, R. L. (1980). Motivation of autistic children through stimulus variation. *Journal of Applied Behavior Analysis, 13,* 619-627.

Durand, V. M., & Carr, E. G. (1985). Self-injurious behavior: Motivating conditions and guidelines for treatment. *School Psychology Review, 14*(2), 171-176.

Durand, V. M., & Crimmins, D. B. (1987). Assessment and treatment of psychotic speech in an autistic child. *Journal of Autism and Developmental Disorders, 17*(1), 17-28.

Epstein, L. H., Doke, L. A., Sajwaj, T. E., Sorrell, S., & Rimmer, B. (1974). Generality and side effects of overcorrection. *Journal of Applied Behavior Analysis, 6,* 1-14.

Favell, J. (1982). *The treatment of self-injurious behavior.* New York: American Association for Behavior Therapy.

Favell, J. E., McGimsey, J. F., & Jones, M. L. (1978). The use of physical restraint in the treatment of self-injury and as positive reinforcement. *Journal of Applied Behavior Analysis, 11,* 225-241.

Favell, J. E., McGimsey, J. F., & Schell, R. M. (1982). Treatment of self-injury by providing alternate sensory activities. *Analysis and Intervention in Developmental Disabilities, 2,* 83-104.

Foxx, R. (1978). An overview of overcorrection. *Journal of Pediatric Psychology, 3,* 97-101.

Foxx, R. M., & Azrin, N. H. (1973). The elimination of autistic self-stimulatory behavior by overcorrection. *Journal of Applied Behavior Analysis, 6,* 1-14.

Foxx, R. M., & Bechtel, D. R. (1982). Overcorrection. In M. Hersen, R. M. Eisler, & P. M. Miller (Eds.), *Progress in behavior modification* (Vol. 13). New York: Academic Press.

Gibbs, J. W., & Luyben, P. D. (1985). Treatment of self-injurious behavior: Contingent versus noncontingent positive practice overcorrection. *Behavior Modification, 9*(1), 3-21.

Horton, S. V. (1987). Reduction of disruptive mealtime behavior by facial screening: A case study of a mentally retarded girl with long-term follow-up. *Behavior Modification, 11*(1), 53-64.

Jenson, W. R., Rovner, L., Cameron, S., Peterson, B. P., & Kesler, J. (1985). Reduction of self-injurious behavior in an autistic girl using a multifaceted treatment program. *Journal of Behavior Therapy and Experimental Psychiatry, 16,* 77-80.

Kelly, J. A., & Drabman, R. S. (1977). Overcorrection: An effective procedure that failed. *Journal of Clinical Child Psychology,* 38-40.

LaGrow, S. J., & Repp, A. C. (1984). Stereotypic responding: A review of intervention research. *American Journal of Mental Deficiency, 88,* 595-609.

Lovaas, O. I., & Favell, J. E. (1987). Protection for clients undergoing aversive/restrictive interventions. *Education and Treatment of Children, 10*(4), 311-325.

Lovaas, O. I., Freitag, G., Gold, V. J., & Kassorla, I. C. (1965). Experimental studies in childhood schizophrenia: Analysis of self-destructive behavior. *Journal of Experimental Child Psychology, 2,* 67-84.

Lovaas, O. I., Newsom, C., & Hickman, C. (1987). Self-stimulatory behavior and perceptual reinforcement. *Journal of Applied Behavior Analysis, 20*(1), 45-68.

Luiselli, J. K. (1984a). Therapeutic effects of brief contingent effort on severe behavior disorders in children with developmental disabilities. *Journal of Clinical Child Psychology, 13*(3), 257-262.

Luiselli, J. K. (1984b). Effects of brief overcorrection on stereotypic behavior of mentally retarded students. *Education and Treatment of Children, 7*(2), 125-138.

Luiselli, J. K. (1986). Modification of self-injurious behavior: An analysis of the use of contingently applied protective equipment. *Behavior Modification, 10*(2), 191-204.

Luiselli, J. K., Pemberton, B. W., & Helfen, C. S. (1978). Effects and side-effects of a brief overcorrection procedure in reducing multiple self-stimulatory behavior: A single case analysis. *American Journal of Mental Deficiency, 22,* 287-293.

McGonigle, J. J., Duncan, D., Cordisco, L., & Barrett, R. P. (1982). Visual screening: An alternative method for reducing stereotypic behavior. *Journal of Applied Behavior Analysis, 3,* 461-467.

Mulick, J., Hoyt, R., Rojahn, J., & Schroeder, S. (1978). Reduction of a "nervous habit" in a profoundly retarded youth by increasing toy play: A case study. *Journal of Behavior Therapy and Experimental Psychiatry, 9,* 381-385.

Murphy, G., Carr, J., & Callias, M. (1986). Increasing simple toy play in profoundly mentally handicapped children: II. Designing special toys. *Journal of Autism and Developmental Disorders, 16,* 45-58.

Neufeld, A., & Fantuzzo, J. W. (1984). Contingent application of a protective device to treat the severe self-biting behavior of a dis-turbed autistic child. *Journal of Behavior Therapy and Experimental Psychiatry, 15*(1), 79-83.

Newsom, C. D. (1974). The role of sensory reinforcement in self-stimulatory behavior. Unpublished doctoral dissertation, University of California, Los Angeles.

O'Brien, F. (1981). Treating self-stimulatory behavior. In J. L. Matson & J. R. McCartney (Eds.), *Handbook of behavior modification with the mentally retarded.* New York: Plenum Press.

Rincover, A. (1978). Sensory extinction: A procedure for eliminating self-stimulatory behavior in developmentally disabled children. *Journal of Abnormal Child Psychology, 6,* 299-310.

Rincover, A., Cook, R., Peoples, A., & Packard, D. (1979). Sensory extinction and sensory reinforcement principles for programming multiple adaptive behavior change. *Journal of Applied Behavior Analysis, 12,* 221-233.

Rincover, A., & Devany, J. (1982). The application of sensory extinction procedures to self-injury. *Analysis and Intervention in Developmental Disabilities, 2,* 67-81.

Rincover, A., & Newsom, C. D. (1985). The relative motivational properties of sensory and edible reinforcers in teaching autistic children. *Journal of Applied Behavior Analysis, 18*(3), 237-248.

Rincover, A., Newsom, C. D., & Carr, E. G. (1979). Using sensory extinction procedures in the treatment of compulsive-like behavior of developmentally disabled children. *Journal of Consulting and Clinical Psychology, 47,* 695-701.

Ritvo, E. R., Ornitz, E. M., & LaFranchi, S. (1968). Frequency of repetitive behaviors in early infantile autism and its variants. *Archives of General Psychiatry, 19,* 341-347.

Rojahn, J., McGonigle, J. J., Curcio, C., & Dixon, M. J. (1987). Suppression of pica by water mist and aromatic ammonia: A comparative analysis. *Behavior Modification,*

11(1), 65-74.

Rolinder, A., & Van Houten, R. (1985). Movement suppression time-out for undesirable behavior in psychotic and severely developmentally delayed children. *Journal of Applied Behavior Analysis, 18*(4), 275-288.

Schneider, H. C., & Salzberg, C. L. (1981, summer). A positive approach to removal of restraints for self-injurious behavior. *Teaching Exceptional Children,* 143-144.

Schroeder, S. R., & Humphrey, R. H. (1977). Environmental context effects and contingent restraint time-out of self-injurious behavior in a deaf-blind profoundly retarded woman. Paper presented at the 101st Annual Meeting of the American Association on Mental Deficiency, New Orleans.

Schroeder, S. R., Schroeder, C. S., Rojahn, J., & Mulick, J. A. (1981). Self-injurious behavior: An analysis of behavior management techniques. In J. L. Matson & J. R. McCartney (Eds.), *Handbook of behavior modification with the mentally re-*

tarded. New York: Plenum Press.

Schroeder, S. R., Schroeder, C., Smith, B., & Dalldorf, J. (1978). Prevalence of self-injurious behavior in a large state facility for the retarded. *Journal of Autism and Childhood Schizophrenia, 8,* 261-269.

Thelen, E. (1979). Rhythmical stereotypes in normal human infants. *Animal Behaviour, 27,* 699-715.

Van Hasselt, V. B. (1983). Facial screening. In A. S. Bellack & M. Hersen (Eds.), *Dictionary of behavior therapy techniques.* New York: Pergamon Press.

Whitman, T. L., & Scibak, J. W. (1979). Behavior modification research with the severely and profoundly retarded. In N. R. Ellis (Ed.), *Handbook of mental deficiency, psychological theory and research* (2nd ed.). Hillsdale, NJ: Eribaum.

Williams, J. A., Koegel, R. L., & Egel, A. L. (1981). Response-reinforcer relationships and improved learning in autistic children. *Journal of Applied Behavior Analysis, 14,* 53-59.

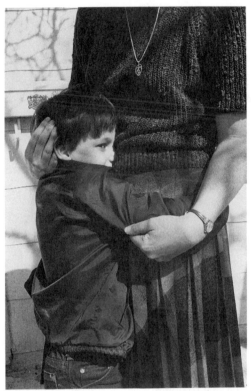

Chapter 10

OUTLINE

Assessment of Deficits in Social Skills

Intervention Strategies: General Considerations

Environmental Modification Strategies

Teacher-Mediated Strategies

Peer-Mediated Strategies

Self-Mediated Strategies

Case Study

OBJECTIVES

After completing this chapter, the reader should be able to

- Describe three assessment approaches for deficits in social skills.
- Name two environmental interventions for young socially isolate children.
- Plan a teacher-mediated intervention for an adolescent with poor social skills.
- Plan a comprehensive sequence of peer-mediated interventions for a socially withdrawn child.
- Select a social skills curriculum for a particular class group.

This chapter will help you work with students who do not get along well with others. Many behaviorally disordered children and adolescents have very poor social skills (Simpson, 1987). Fortunately, recent research has enabled us to remediate many of these problems.

To introduce you to this rapidly growing field of research and teaching, let us begin with a review of important terms. **Social skills** refers to specific social behaviors (e.g., a greeting, a nod during a conversation, a handshake) that facilitate interpersonal interactions. **Social competence** refers to an individual's ability to use these skills at the right time and place, showing social judgment or perception about how to act.

According to Putallaz and Gottman (1982), the major dimensions of social competence are (1) overall positiveness, (2) the ability to resolve conflicts, (3) awareness of group norms, (4) the ability to communicate accurately, (5) the ability to establish a common bond between oneself and another, and (6) positive self-perception. Additionally, Asher (1983)

suggests that social competence is characterized by (1) the ability to "read" the social situation so that one's behavior is relevant; (2) responsiveness, or the ability to initiate positive interaction as well as to respond positively to others' initiations; and (3) a "process view," or an understanding that relationships require time to develop. These characteristics broadly define social competence as the ability to accomplish appropriate goals in social situations (Parkhurst & Asher, 1985, cited in Hollinger, 1987, p. 18).

The inability to respond in social situations can lead to the disruptive, aggressive, or offensive behaviors you have read about in earlier chapters. To counteract these problem behaviors, a child may need instruction in the preferred, incompatible behavior. Consider these examples of problem behaviors and "replacement" social skills (Reprinted with permission from G. Cartledge & J. F. Milburn, *Teaching Social Skills to Children*, Copyright 1980, Pergamon Books Ltd.):

Problem Behaviors	*Social Skills*
1. The child calls others by uncomplimentary names	1. The child makes positive remarks to others
2. The child frequently interrupts the conversation of others	2. The child waits for pauses in the conversation before speaking
3. The child makes negative statements about his/her ability	3. The child identifies something (s)he does well
4. The child cheats when playing games with peers	4. The child plays games according to rules
5. The child tantrums when teased by peers	5. The child responds to peer teasing by ignoring or some other appropriate response
6. The child laughs at or ignores individual in need of help	6. The child assists individual in need of help

Social withdrawal refers to a cluster of behaviors that result in an individual escaping or avoiding social contact. This may be intentional, as in extreme cases of **elective mutism** (an uncommon syndrome involving a refusal to speak by someone who can talk), or it may reflect a broader lack of social competence, as often found in children or adults considered retarded, psychotic, or autistic. Social withdrawal may result from a lack of specific social skills, or it may have its origins in a history of rejection and punishment associated with social interaction.

In many cases, social withdrawal may be maintained by negative reinforcement: the specific form of withdrawn behavior is continued because it escapes or avoids social contact, which apparently constitutes an aversive stimulus for the individual. In other cases, behaviors incompatible with social interaction, such as self-stimulation, may be maintained by self-produced reinforcement. Thus, social withdrawal covers a broad and complex range of problem behaviors.

For a long time, social withdrawal was not considered a serious problem in the field of special education or in related disciplines. Even today, an extremely quiet child, seldom enjoying the benefits of positive relationships with others but creating no observable problems for his teachers, may drift unnoticed from one school year to the next. Yet, the consequences of untreated social withdrawal can be extremely serious. For example, some authors have suggested that withdrawn children are at greater risk for juvenile delinquency (Roff, Sells, & Golden, 1972) and adult mental health problems (Robins, 1966).

Unless a child can learn to interact with others at a reasonably competent level, access to the environment and subsequent learning and adjustment may be seriously curtailed. For instance, Cobb (1972) found that socially withdrawn children demonstrated major deficits in three behaviors—attending, talking with peers about assignments, and compliance—when compared with their normally achieving peers. It would seem, then, that social withdrawal could result in serious informational deficits in learning academic material and in restriction of a child's social development, problems that might even escalate in later years.

Assessment of Deficits in Social Skills

In this section we review some of the assessment and monitoring techniques you learned in the first part of this book. Let us begin with the most global assessments, rating scales, often used to screen for social behavior problems.

RATING SCALES AND CHECKLISTS

As stated in earlier chapters, rating scales and checklists are useful for an initial look at a student's problem behaviors. For example, you might use a problem behavior checklist or the evaluation checklists taken from *Getting Along With Others Curriculum* (Jackson, Jackson, & Monroe, 1983) to get a general picture of the social skill problems that one of your students is experiencing. To make this assessment especially helpful, solicit the ratings from as many significant others as possible, including the parents, teachers, and other professionals who know the child. Do not overlook the student's previous teacher, who might be a valuable source of information.

The information you gather from checklists and ratings can give you a starting place for further, more finely-grained assessments, including sociometric measures, behavioral interviews, and direct observations. Moreover, a curriculum-based checklist can clue you in on where to begin in the sequence of skills taught in that particular instructional program. Finally, a checklist or rating scale allows you quickly to compare the views of several individuals about the student's behavior.

SOCIOMETRIC MEASURES

Sociometric measures are discussed in an earlier chapter. They are used exclusively to assess a student's social problems as reflected by his popularity among his classmates or friends, who nominate or rate the student according to the format of the measure used. While sociometric measures have been reported with elementary-school-aged children, Cartledge and Milburn (1983) view this assessment as most useful for older students (Hops & Green-

wood, 1981). Available for this purpose is the Adjustment Scales for Sociometric Evaluation of Secondary School Students (ASSESS), authored by Prinz, Swan, Liebert, Weintraub, and Neale (1978). Teenagers taking this sociometric assessment report on their peers in five categories: social competence, academic difficulty, aggression-disruption, withdrawal, and anxiety.

As Gershman (1976) pointed out, sociometric measures may lack the specific information needed to plan social skills teaching. Perhaps the best use of sociometric measures is for screening and for progress monitoring, as suggested by Michelson, Foster, and Ritchey (1981). McConnell and Odom (1986) suggest that sociometric measure should be only one of *several* measures of social competence.

BEHAVIORAL INTERVIEWS

In Chapter 2 we suggested that you rely on interviews with students, their parents, and their teachers to gather information about a student's strengths and weaknesses. Although an interview cannot function as a *sole* source of information on social skills, it is a good place to begin the assessment process. Interviews are especially important in the assessment of social skills because others in the child's life are apt to have strong convictions about the student's social relationships and functioning. Some questions you might ask in a social assessment interview include the following:

1. Who are this student's friends?
2. What social situations are difficult for this student?
3. What "social mistakes" does this student make?
4. Does this student initiate social interactions?
5. What social skills does this student have?
6. What do others say about this student's social behavior?
7. What skills does this student need to be more socially successful?

8. Can this student maintain a social interaction?
9. In what situations is this student socially successful?
10. What behavior does this student exhibit in these situations?

ANALOGUE MEASURES

You have probably used **analogue measures** and not even realized it. For example, you may have asked a student to describe how he would respond to a certain social situation. Analogue assessment refers to a role-play or behavioral rehearsal in which an individual demonstrates how he would respond in a given social interaction (Cartledge & Milburn, 1983). Analogue procedures may help you understand a student's social perception and the skills the student needs to learn in order to respond successfully to a given social situation. In the ASSET Curriculum (Hazel, Schumaker, Sherman, & Sheldon-Wildgen, 1982) students respond to several videotaped social situations.

DIRECT OBSERVATIONS

Direct observations allow you to look at social skills and related problem behaviors. These skills and problems will be the focus of your planning and teaching activities. Table 10-1 offers you some examples, taken from research studies.

The observational strategies discussed in earlier chapters can be used to monitor social interactions. Review the section on interval recording for specific guidelines.

One special application of direct observations to social skills is the assessment of a student's group participation skills. How well does a student contribute to the instructional or discussion group, the class project or brainstorming session, or the peer tutoring activities? Our next section offers a model for learning more about your students in groups.

ASSESSING GROUP PARTICIPATION SKILLS

Many special education programs emphasize individualized instruction to the exclusion of group learning activities. This serves to further handicap students who must learn to share adult attention, wait their turns for participating, and accept the contributions of other children. In this section we offer an informal assessment process for determining your student's group participation skills and deficits. This model was developed by one of us with the help of several groups of classroom teachers who field-tested it. Figure 10-1 displays the hierarchy of skills to assess; you may think of others to add.

As you can tell from Figure 10-1, Level I describes students who lack basic skills to interact in an instructional setting. These students demand intensive teacher supervision and cannot manage with less structure. A group discussion, a social skills role-play, or a cooperative class project would be unmanageable with a group of Level-I students.

Level-II students, on the other hand, have beginning group skills and can succeed in highly structured, didactic activities led by the teacher. For example, these students function best when called on in group discussions.

Enjoyment of some unsupervised group activities is characteristic of students at Level III. Peer tutoring, well-planned group projects, and focused discussions suit these students well. Although they may not be popular in their groups, their interpersonal styles are tolerable, not obnoxious.

Level-IV students succeed in groups and seek out these experiences. They can help one another make group decisions and are good candidates for group goal setting and feedback, peer tutoring, and brainstorm sessions. They evidence self-evaluation and self-control.

Level V describes students who enjoy leading and designing their own groups. These students may tire of adult-directed activities and yearn to "do their own thing with their class-

Table 10-1. Sample Definitions of Social Behaviors

Behavior Category	Definitions	Authors
Motor-gestural	This included all positive physical contacts such as brushing another person's arm while reaching for something; cooperative use of an object such as looking at a book with another person, exchanging pens, taking turns placing puzzle pieces; touching and/or manipulating the same object or parts of the same object; all other gestural movement directed to another person such as handling an object, pointing, motioning to "Come" or "Go away," shaking head to indicate "Yes" or "No," and waving.	Dy, Strain, Fullerton, & Stowitschek (1981)
Vocal-verbal	This included all positive vocal expressions or verbalizations which by virtue of content, e.g., "Hey you," "Uh-huh" (while nodding), clearly indicated that the person was directing the utterance to another individual.	
Approach gestures	. . . consisted of any deliberate behavior of the child which involves the hand(s), arm(s), or other body parts in a motion directed to another child, e.g., an inward circular hand and arm motion, repeated bending and straightening of forefinger while arm extended towards a peer.	Gable, Hendrickson, & Strain (1978)
Play organizer	Verbalizations or responses to verbalizations wherein a child specifies an activity, suggests an idea for play, or directs a child to engage in a play behavior.	Odom, Hoyson, Jamieson, & Strain (1985)
Share	Offers or gives an object to another child or accepts an object from another child by taking the object in hand or using it in play.	
Share request	Asks a child to give an object to the speaker.	
Assistance	Helps another child complete a task or desired action which he or she could not complete or do alone.	
Complimentary statement	Verbal statement indicating affection, attraction, or praise.	
Affection	Patting, hugging, kissing, or holding hands with another child.	Odom, Hoyson, Jamieson, & Strain (1985)
Negative motor-gestural	Hitting, pushing, sticking out tongue, taking unoffered objects, or destroying others' constructions.	
Negative vocal-verbal	Crying, shouting, calling another child an ugly name, and refusal to engage in a requested behavior or corrections.	

Figure 10-1. Assessment of the Teenager for Groups and Dyads

Level I Skills/Problems:
1. Will answer specific teacher-directed questions.
2. Has minimal listening skills.
3. Needs lots of attention (e.g., must be called on).
4. Refuses other than highly directed responses.
5. Has poor self-disclosure skills.
6. Has few prior group experiences that were successful.
7. Generally does not get along well with others.
8. Has poor self-evaluation skills for group participation.

Level II Skills/Problems:
1. All of Level I Skills exhibited consistently.
2. Can make appropriate contributions with teacher calling on him/her.
3. Has a few classmate friends or can interact singly with others (e.g., converse).
4. Occasionally volunteers personal information.
5. Has high attention needs but can give others attention, also (e.g., can conduct short interview).
6. Requires adult direction; does not function well without supervision (e.g., engages in problem behaviors if activity is not teacher-directed and involves a group).
7. Responds well only in groups that practice previously learned skills.
8. Weak but improving self-evaluation skills.

Level III Skills/Problems:
1. All Level I and II Skills shown consistently.
2. Can interact in structured activity with one or two other students, without adult supervision and direction (e.g., structured peer tutoring).
3. Shows beginning leadership skills in a group activity (e.g., makes suggestions for projects, assists others in articulating their ideas).
4. May still require help with personal style in group (e.g., drones on and on, dominates conversation); can self-evaluate with help.
5. Exhibits irritating style, perhaps, but is not essentially disruptive to group.
6. Can learn new content or adjust to a *slight* change of format or topic within a group (e.g., structured lessons on different topics).

Level IV Skills/Problems:
1. All above skills are exhibited.
2. Can function successfully in peer-run groups with minimal adult direction (e.g., half-hour brainstorm with peers).
3. Can disclose personal information with relative ease.
4. Can peer tutor, peer monitor without adult supervision.
5. Can participate in group decision-making.
6. May still require contingent reinforcement.
7. Can self-evaluate in certain activities, without help.

Level V Skills/Problems:
1. Can serve as a group leader or co-leader.
2. Makes useful suggestions to others in the group regarding their participation (e.g., complimenting, revising, using their ideas).
3. Can succeed in a spontaneous, unstructured group.
4. May tire of structured groups or lessons.
5. Devises own peer tutoring strategies to enhance existing program.
6. Can accurately self-monitor own group participation skills.

Source: Reprinted with permission from Kerr, M. M., Nelson, C. M., & Lambert, D. L. (1987), *Helping adolescents with learning and behavior problems.* Columbus, OH: Merrill, p. 195.

mates." An overly controlling teacher may mis-read these students' desires to initiate and man-age their own group activities.

With these levels in mind, you can infor-mally "place" your students according to their group skills and plan group activities at their levels to enhance their skills. The classification also offers you objectives for the individualized education program.

Once you have assessed your students' skills, you should consider the match between your classroom group activities and the skills of your students. In many cases, teachers over-estimate the skills of their students. The check-list in Figure 10-2 will help you assess the group activity to see whether it is a good match with your student's skills.

Let us review the variables that predict how difficult a group experience might be.

Direction/adult involvement refers to how much structure you or your classroom as-sistants provide. To make an activity "easier" for students, change this variable by (Kerr, Nel-son, & Lambert, 1987)

- having the goals selected by the teacher, not the students
- having an adult direct the group activity
- increasing the ratio of adults to students
- relying on a familiar adult to lead the group

Predictability describes the amount of newness in a group experience. For added pre-dictability, try these strategies (Kerr et al., 1987, p. 197):

- offer a firm structure for each session
- have the same format each time
- keep the same topic for each session
- incorporate a number of skills students have learned previously (the last two items on the checklist allow you to list skills that serve as prerequisites for participants)
- do not require students to disclose highly personal information
- call on students, and
- hold the activity in a familiar environment

Intervention Strategies: General Considerations

A Strategy Selection Chart (Figure 10-3) ap-pears near the end of this chapter (see p. 335). As mentioned before, this chart is designed to assist you in using the intervention strategies described in the rest of this chapter. Notice that some of these interventions are designed for mildly handicapped individuals; others are de-signed specifically to help those with a severe social handicap.

There are some strategies that you should always avoid when dealing with the problem of social withdrawal. One of these is coercion, or punishment, designed to "make the child come out of himself." Unfortunately, classmates often ridicule and tease their withdrawn peers, making simple interactions even more difficult for the student to initiate. Try to help class-mates recognize that social withdrawal is a problem for that student, and consider using one of the peer-mediated interventions to assist the student.

Another strategy to be avoided is leaving the isolate individual alone. Isolate children who are left alone for long periods may develop ad-ditional serious problems, rather than learning skills that improve their social interactions. Time-out procedures are thus inappropriate in-terventions for the socially withdrawn.

A third approach to socially withdrawn stu-dents—one that has not proven effective—is to accept their social isolation as a developmental phase and simply to await their decision to ap-proach their classmates. Unfortunately, many withdrawn children have not learned the social skills required to develop social relationships with their classmates and cannot learn them without help. Maturation as a singular interven-tion on social withdrawal is not effective; chil-dren do not simply outgrow this problem because the more they avoid people, the less opportunity they have to develop personally reinforcing situations.

Figure 10-2. Analysis Checklist for Group Activities

Name of Activity _____

Purpose _____
_____

Time Required (per school day) _____

Proposed Level pre-I   I   II   III   IV   V

Direction/Adult Involvement

Adult:student ratio _____ Number of students _____

Adult directed _____ Peer-mediated _____ Both _____

Who selects the goals? _____

Is the adult leader a familiar classroom figure? _____

For what portion of the activity is the adult involved?   100%   60%   40%   0%

Level of Predictability/Structure

Is activity highly structured _____   Structured _____

  Somewhat structured _____   Without structure _____

Is the activity a peer tutoring activity? _____

Does the activity follow the same format every session? _____ Or does the format change? _____

Does the topic change with every session? _____

Does the activity allow students to practice old skills? _____

  Learn new skills? _____ Both? _____

Do students know the topic in advance? _____

Are students asked to disclose personal information? _____

Do students volunteer for the activity? _____ Or, are students called on? _____

Is the activity in a familiar environment? _____

Does it take place in the classroom? _____ In the community? _____

Name the academic skills this activity requires _____
_____
_____
_____

Name the social skills this activity requires _____
_____
_____
_____
_____
_____
_____

Comments _____
_____
_____
_____
_____

Source: Reprinted with permission from Kerr, M. M., Nelson, C. M., & Lambert, D. L. (1987), *Helping adolescents with learning and behavior problems.* Columbus, OH: Merrill, p. 196.

It is important that you understand that this chapter describes social withdrawal that is serious enough to warrant intervention. We are not talking about shy individuals whose personal style is simply more reticent than others, nor have we focused on unassertive students here.

It is encouraging to note that when social skills are acted upon, other problem behaviors improve as well. The effect of one intervention affecting several target behaviors is referred to as a **collateral effect** in research literature.

Environmental Modification Strategies

The environment of the classroom, playground, or free-play room can be altered to facilitate cooperative interactions. They may also help both isolate and nonisolate students enjoy their time and activities with each other.

One of the primary objectives of preschool and primary school training is to enhance students' ability to play with one another in an unstructured situation. For this reason much of the research on children's social skills has focused on play behaviors in the child's early years. Some of this work has addressed the question of what toys and play equipment should be included in a free-play area.

Stoneman, Cantrell, and Hoover-Dempsey (1983) named items that promoted social interaction: blocks, vehicles, and water. Inhibiting social interaction were fine motor, library, and art activities (McEvoy & Odom, 1987). There are other guidelines for selecting and using young children's toys. First, place toys together if they are to be used together (toy telephones placed next to each other, dolls placed near the dollhouse, and blocks stacked up in the block area). A second suggestion is that you try to select toys that are durable, nontoxic, and too large to be swallowed. A good rule of thumb is to select toys whose shortest side is at least two inches. Also, you may want to avoid purchasing toys equipped with pins or screws that can be loosened easily. If aggressive behavior is of real concern to you, think about selecting toys whose largest side is no more than fifteen inches. Remember that toys wear out and so does a child's interest in them. Check your inventory from time to time for toys that are broken or otherwise damaged and toys that are no longer of interest to the students. Some teachers prefer to have a large inventory of toys from which they select only a few at a time for the classroom. Neither normal nor withdrawn children need an endless supply of play materials. A study conducted by Doke and Risley (1972) showed that children in a day care center did not play with a certain toy frequently because several others like it were available.

Doke and Risley (1972) had some good suggestions concerning the choice and scheduling of activities, including nonplay activities. They found that children were most likely to participate in a typical day-care activity when (1) they were dismissed from that activity individually and did not have to wait for the entire group to finish, (2) there were enough materials to enable children to participate in the activity, and (3) enough adults were available to assist children in starting and in completing the activities. By meeting these three conditions, you increase the likelihood that young children will participate with each other in the activity you have planned for them.

One study has examined the effects of *proximity* on severely and profoundly multiply handicapped students' social interactions (Speigel-McGill, Bambara, Shores, & Fox, 1984). This investigation suggested that placing the students close to one another in pairs improved their social interactions, which consisted of head orientation, vocalizations, and gestures. More social interchanges were observed at one foot than at five or ten feet.

Teacher-Mediated Strategies

There are several interventions for social skills deficits that rely on a teacher as the principal change agent. A school counselor, a residential program child-care worker, a paraprofessional, or a volunteer could also use these strategies. If you are focusing your interventions on social or free-play activities, please read carefully the section on environmental modifications so that you will be able to select the most appropriate toys and play materials for the student. If, on the other hand, you want to focus on nonsocial activities, try to select projects and activities that require the involvement of more than one pupil. For example, in the self-help area, two students are more likely to interact if they are assembling something that requires both of their materials.

TEACHER PROMPTING AND REINFORCEMENT

One intervention procedure available to you as a teacher is reinforcement and prompting. As the name suggests, this procedure requires you to prompt and reinforce an isolate pupil's peer interactions. Even though this procedure is fairly simple, research studies conducted over a number of years have indicated that it is successful, particularly with young children (Bryant & Budd, 1984; Strain, Shores, & Kerr, 1976; Strain & Timm, 1974). The following suggestions outline a teacher prompting and reinforcement procedure.

1. Arrange the free-play area as directed in the section on environmental modification. Invite the target individual and the nontarget students to play in the free-play area for a period of at least fifteen minutes.
2. Prompt a nonhandicapped student to initiate play with the target individual by using a phrase such as, "Why don't you ask Jamie if she would like to play with the blocks?" This type of prompt is a play organizer.
3. Try also to use a prompt to share a material. You may do this by using a phrase such as, "Hand Tommy the truck."
4. Use a prompt such as asking the child to assist another student. You may do this by using a phrase such as, "Help Kathy roll the truck into the blocks."
5. Reinforce any attempt on the part of the student to interact with the target individual. You may do this by using a simple statement of praise (e.g., "That's good! I like the way you rolled the truck to Tommy."). With a severely behaviorally handicapped child, you may wish to use a tangible reinforcer.
6. Make your reinforcement as brief as possible; research has shown that teacher reinforcement tends to interrupt the ongoing social interaction of two children.
7. Once the students have established a fairly steady rate of interacting with one another during free-play times, try to reduce the number of prompts and reinforcement instances that you provide. For example, if you have been prompting the students on an average of once every thirty seconds or once every minute, try to reduce the number of prompts to one every three to five minutes.
8. Remember that a peer trainer can be used to provide prompting and reinforcement. If you feel that you have gotten the intervention off to a good start, consider using a peer to maintain it.

SOCIAL SKILLS TRAINING

Several social skills teaching packages have appeared recently in the commercial marketplace. Table 10-2 lists good social skills curricula and supplementary activities.

Table 10-2. Annotated Bibliography of Social Skills Curricula (pp. 322-324)

---

a. Goldstein, A. P.; Sprafkin, R. P.; Gershaw, N. J.; and Klein, P. *Skillstreaming the adolescent*. Champaign, Illinois: Research Press, 1980.
   Target population. This program was developed for adolescents, and can be utilized with intermediate level elementary students.
   Description of materials. The text provides the educator with 50 lesson plans for 50 social skills, two different homework report forms and instructions for implementing the program.
   Format. The teacher selects one of the 50 skills to be taught. Each lesson follows the same format: (1) define and discuss the skill to be learned, (2) distribute skill cards containing the steps for the skill, (3) model appropriate use of the skill, (4) organize role-plays during which students practice the skill, (5) give and invite feedback, (6) provide social reinforcement, and (7) assist students in planning homework assignments.

b. Hazel, J. S.; Schumaker, J. B.; Sherman, J. A.; and Sheldon-Wildgen, J. *Asset: A social skills program for adolescents*. Champaign, Illinois: Research Press, 1982.
   Target population. Designed for adolescents grades six through 12, this program functions best when used with groups of five to eight members.
   Description of materials. The Asset manual provides the leader with training procedures, nine lesson plans, skill sheets outlining the steps for each skill, home notes, checklists, consent forms and various questionnaires. The program includes nine video taped sequences modeling appropriate and inappropriate social interaction skills. The leader is encouraged to utilize appropriate props for role-plays.
   Format. Each session follows the same format: (1) review of home notes, (2) review of previously learned skills, (3) presentation and discussion of positive and negative examples of the target skill on video tape, (4) distribution and examination of skill sheets containing the steps in the target skill, (5) verbal rehearsal, (6) role-play or behavioral rehearsal, (7) feedback, (8) criterion role-plays and (9) home notes assigned.

c. *MARC: Model affective resource curriculum*. Orlando, Florida: Orange County Public Schools.
   Target population. This program is designed for adolescents.
   Description of materials. The manual provides the teacher with lessons for skills in four areas: self-control, interpersonal problem solving, communications and behavioral interactions.
   Format. Each lesson teaches a specific skill or component of a skill. The leader (1) facilitates discussion, (2) models appropriate behavior, (3) assists students in practicing the skill through role-plays, (4) provides feedback, (5) summarizes the lesson and (6) gives a practice assignment. Several lessons involve practicing the skills in natural environments, as well as simulation.

d. Stephens, T. M. *Social skills in the classroom*. Columbus, Ohio: Cedars Press, Inc., 1978.
   Target population. This program can be used with student groups of all ages.
   Description of materials. The manual provides the educator with instruction in a variety of directive teaching techniques: social modeling, social reinforcement and contingency management. The manual also provides three lesson plans (one for each teaching technique) for each of the 136 skills. The teacher selects the skill to be taught and the teaching technique most applicable to the student's needs.
   Format. When teaching a new skill, the educator uses the social modeling strategy: (1) set the stage through discussion, a story, a film, etc., indicating the value of learning the skill, (2) draw out of discussion the specific steps which make up the skill, (3) model correct behavior, (4) set up role-plays in which the students practice correct behavior, and (5) plan and implement reinforcement strategies for the skill throughout the day. The teacher may use social reinforcement or contingency management techniques if needed to continue to maintain the skill once learned.

Table 10-2. *Continued*

e. Ball, G. *Interchange*. San Diego, California: Human Development Training Institute, 1977.
   Target population. Separate kits are available for junior high and senior high students.
   Description of materials. Each kit is packaged in a storage box for easy access to leader's manual and cards for discussion sessions. The discussion topic cards are organized into approximately 40 units, each with six to 10 discussion lessons outlined.
   Format. The leader facilitates a supportive, open-ended style discussion session which focuses on one of the discussion topics.

f. *Project Transition*. Seattle, Washington: Seattle Public Schools, Dept. of Student Services, 1981.
   Target population. This comprehensive program is designed for use by counselors at the senior high level. Use by classroom teachers is encouraged as well.
   Description of materials. The materials are organized into six booklets, each one a separate unit. The six content areas are introduction, communication, self-assessment, goal setting/decision-making, career exploration and long-range planning.
   Format. The leader follows the manual for each discussion session or activity lesson. Activities include paper-pencil tasks, group tasks, art, etc. Discussion following the activity is directed by the leader.

g. Jackson, N. F., Jackson, D. A., and Monroe, C. *Getting Along with Others: Teaching Social Effectiveness to Children*. Champaign, Illinois: Research Press, 1983.
   Target population. This program was developed for use with elementary-aged children. With some modifications, it can be utilized with middle school students, by teachers, psychologists, counselors and others.
   Description of materials. There are two books provided in each set. *The Program Guide* provides a step-by-step training procedure which describes the program, the teaching strategies, and the utilization of the program components. The other part of the set is a spiral bound *Skill Lessons and Activities* book, which provides 17 scripted skill lessons, each of which includes homework sheets, homenotes, sample role play situations, relaxation exercises and activities. The leader is encouraged to utilize role-playing as a significant part of the program.
   Format. Each lesson follows the same format: (1) Review of homenotes and homework, (2) Relaxation Training, (3) Introduction of skill components, (4) Role play appropriate and inappropriate examples, (5) Give and invite positive feedback, (6) Reality check, (7) Activity reinforcing acquired skills.

h. *Social Solutions*. Professional Associated Resources, Burlingame, California. (no date given)
   Target population. This program was developed for mildly delayed adolescents, and is written at a 4th-6th grade reading level. It can be used effectively with upper elementary students as well as delayed adolescents.
   Description of materials. Components of this program are presented in several media, including a Mentor's Manual for explanation of program, Individual and Group Study Units, two audiotapes, a videotape, and individual study and record-keeping sheets.
   Format. There are eleven areas of study, among them: Handling Stress and Conflict, Taking Responsibility for Actions and Decisions, Communicating Effectively, Developing Close, Caring Relationships, and Respecting the Rights of Others. These areas are then divided into 85 learning points. Each of the learning points skill sheets is presented at both 4th and 6th grade reading levels. Activities are presented for individuals, small groups, involving role plays, giving and receiving feedback, problem solving and individual writing activities. Progress can be monitored by individual students or groups.

Table 10-2.   *Continued*

___

i.   Walker, H. M., McConnell, S., Holmes, D., Todis, B., Walker, J., and Golden, N. *The Walker Social Skills Curriculum: The ACCEPTS Program.* Austin, Texas: Pro-Ed, 1983.

Target population. The ACCEPTS curriculum (A Curriculum for Children's Effective Peer and Teacher Skills) is designed for use with mildly and moderately handicapped children in the primary and intermediate grades. It can be used by teachers and other school professionals concerned with students' social-behavioral competencies, as well as other mainstreaming issues.

Description of materials. The ACCEPTS curriculum is a spiral bound guide including research as well as the program itself. An optional videotape illustrates positive and negative modeling of target skills, for use with students.

Format. Included in the program are a pre-test, guidelines for teaching the program, scripts for teaching in each of the five areas: Classroom Skills, Basic Interaction Skills, Getting Along, Making Friends, and Coping Skills. A behavior management procedure is also included. This is an interactive program, using role playing as a main learning and evaluation activity.

j.   Walker, H. M., Todis, B., Holmes D., and Horton, G. *The Walker Social Skills Curriculum: The ACCESS Program.* Austin, Texas: Pro-Ed, 1988.

Target population. The ACCESS program (Adolescent Curriculum for Communication and Effective Social Skills) is designed to improve the social competence of adolescent students in middle and high school settings.

Description of materials. The curriculum guide is spiral bound, and includes a placement test, scripted lessons, skills list and situational role play cards for the 31 lessons. A Student Study Guide provides contracts and short exercises for students participating in the program. The main areas of study are: Peer-related skills, Adult-related skills and Self-related skills.

Format. The program involves placement, scripted lessons in which role playing is a major component, and homework assignments. The Student Study Guide provides student contracts and brief written exercises for each lesson.

___

Source: Items a–f from Neel, R. (1984). Teaching social routines to behaviorally disordered youth. In J. Grosenick, S. Huntze, E. McGinnis, and C. Smith (Eds.), *Social/Affective Interventions in Behavioral Disorders.* Washington, DC: U.S. Department of Education. Remainder of material from Lynne Cummings, personal communication, 1988.

___

Let's look at the key features of social skills curricula:

1. *Modeling.* The first step in most social skills teaching programs is to introduce students to examples of the social skill through live, audio, or video modeling. Usually, one skill, broken down as much as possible, is the focus of each vignette or lesson. To incorporate peers, you might call on various students in your class to demonstrate social skills during a lesson. To prepare for this activity, review the guidelines in Chapter 5 for selecting and using peer models.

2. *Role-Playing.* After an initial demonstration, the social skills program may call for a role play of the targeted skill. To facilitate this component, encourage students first to discuss the demonstration and to think of real-life situations in which they might use the skill. Following this discussion, you can arrange student-designed role-playing or follow a scripted role-play from the curricular materials. (Before teaching a lesson, be sure that you would feel comfortable role-playing the social skill yourself!) This strategy has proven very successful with various handicapped populations (Hazel, Schumaker, Sherman, & Sheldon, 1982; Schumaker, Hazel, Sherman, & Sheldon, 1982).

3. *Performance Feedback.* Letting students

know how they performed the skill during the role-play is crucial. Some of the most helpful (and candid!) feedback (e.g., approval, praise, constructive criticism) will come from the other group members. A good rule of thumb is to encourage positive, supportive feedback while indicating aspects of the behavior that the student could improve. *Adult supervision is very important during this phase.* A helpful strategy is to have the student immediately *replay* the scene so that the group can give feedback on the improved performance.

4. *Generalization and Maintenance.* By now these terms are familiar to you. The chance to "overlearn" and repeatedly practice the social skills in other settings is vital to a youngster's social development, as demonstrated by Schumaker and Ellis (1982). Self-monitoring can be an essential feature of this transfer-of-learning phase (Kelly et al., 1983). Many social skills programs include "behavioral homework" and notes sent home to reinforce the skills outside of the classroom. One way to increase the generalization of social skills out of school is first to ask parents which social skills are important to them. Also, try to incorporate different "trainers." In one consultation experience we had, a teacher of moderately handicapped junior high school students had various faculty colleagues "primed" to enter her classroom and initiate certain social interactions, including gentle teasing for a student having trouble with this kind of interaction. She simply posted her "social skills needs list" in the teachers' lounge each Monday.

In reviewing various social skills programs, check to see that the essential components are included. (You may find that they are titled differently.) Once you have selected a social skills curriculum, remember that not all students will need to begin with Lesson One. Social skills instruction, like academics, must be individualized. Most curricula have "placement tests" to

help you tailor your instruction to a student's needs.

TOKEN REINFORCEMENT

We have described token reinforcement in detail in Chapter 6. Here, we call your attention to a study of token reinforcement to improve the social interactions of preschool children. Wolfe, Boyd, and Wolfe (1983) devised a system whereby targeted socially withdrawn children wore bright yellow "happy face" charts with boxes marked to indicate the intervals during which they played cooperatively. Happy face stickers placed on (or removed from) the charts constituted the tokens. Here is a description of the intervention (Wolfe et al., 1983):

> Training the target children to play in a cooperative, nonaggressive manner consisted of the following procedures. All children in the classroom were told that sharing time was about to begin, and the target children were given their "happy face" charts to wear. All of the children in the class were then encouraged to find a play activity and a friend with whom to share the activity. Once the target children had found an activity and friend a bell signaled that the play program had begun. During the next minute, general praise was given to the group of children for cooperative play (e.g., "I like the way everyone is playing") and specific praise was administered to the target children contingent upon appropriate play (e.g., "I like the way Jimmy is playing with Billy"). At the end of 1 minute, the bell rang and the teacher placed happy face stickers on the charts of target children who had engaged in cooperative play for the entire minute. Target children who had not earned a happy face were prompted to engage in cooperative play by the teacher and were reminded of the backup reinforcers they could earn (i.e., outside play time). In the event a target child did not engage in play following this prompt, a gentle physical prompt was used to lead the child to a play activity. This prompt was repeated every 3 to 5 minutes for any target child who did not engage in cooperative play. The cycle of 1-minute play

periods, signaled by the bell, was repeated 15 times during each session.

At the end of the session the teacher counted the happy faces on each child's card and praised the child for his/her efforts to share with others. Initially, the backup reinforcer (10 minutes of outside play) was administered for earning eight or more stickers. This criterion was gradually increased over several sessions to 12 stickers. Children who did not earn enough tokens to go outside were allowed to look at books and play with toys inside the classroom while the other children went outside. Subsequently, they were reminded of this missed opportunity the following day before the training session was begun. The token reinforcement program continued in the morning for 20 sessions, and then was extended to include the afternoon sessions as well. Once a target child displayed an 80% rate of cooperative play on three consecutive sessions in either the morning or afternoon setting, a fading procedure was implemented that involved a gradual lengthening (over several sessions) of the required interval of cooperative play from 1 minute to 5 minutes. When the child was able to play for a 5-minute duration before reinforcement with an overall rate of cooperative play exceeding 80%, the happy face chart was discontinued. Intermittent verbal praise was used in the classroom, and outside play was continued as a reward at the end of each session contingent upon an 80% rate of cooperative play. (pp. 4-5)

You will notice that this intervention actually combined several of the teacher-mediated strategies we have recommended in this section: prompting, praise, and feedback. This approach also incorporated *peers* as interventionists. Our next section details peer-mediated interventions.

Peer-Mediated Strategies

In a peer-mediated intervention, a member of the individual's peer group, rather than an adult, is the primary agent of change in behavior. Why should you consider peer involvement in social skills training? Consider the response offered by Hollinger (1987):

> To date, social skills training interventions consistently focus exclusively on the children who are identified as those with the behavior problems or low social status. Yet social behavior and status are defined in part by other persons in the target child's life. Consequently, it may be important to consider peers' perceptions in social skills training, thus focusing on interactive exchanges rather than discrete behaviors (Strain et al., 1984). It seems especially important to address negative social perception biases among peers in their interactions with behaviorally disordered children. (p. 22)

By including peers in the intervention, you increase the likelihood that they will alter their attitudes towards the socially handicapped child.

Few aspects of behavioral change have witnessed such growth as the peer-mediated interventions for socially handicapped children and adolescents. Entire volumes now offer suggestions for incorporating peers in social skills training (e.g., Strain et al., 1986). Naturally, we can highlight only the more basic, classroom-tested approaches here. We begin with peer-mediated strategies for young or more severely disturbed children: peer imitation training, peer social initiation, and peer prompting and reinforcement. Then we consider strategies for older or mildly handicapped students: a peer manager intervention, peer coaching, and peer tutoring.

PEER IMITATION TRAINING

This intervention requires a classmate of the isolated child to model appropriate social behaviors for the student to learn. **Peer imitation training** is particularly well suited for students with severe behavioral handicaps who do not exhibit appropriate social behaviors. This training is the most intensive peer-mediated in-

Table 10-3. Peer Imitation Training: Selection of Peer Behavior Model

1. Select a student who attends school regularly in order to promote continuity of the intervention.
2. Select a student who exhibits frequent appropriate social skills with other students.
3. Select a student who can follow a teacher's verbal instructions reliably and can imitate a teacher model.
4. Select a student who can concentrate on the training task for at least ten minutes per target individual.

Note: Material was taken from M. M. Kerr and P. S. Strain. The use of peer social initiation strategies to improve the social skills of withdrawn children. In A. H. Fink (Ed.), *International perspectives on future special education.* Reston, VA: Council for Exceptional Children, 1979.

tervention we describe, for it involves not only the peer model, but an adult who prompts and reinforces the isolate student. Table 10-3 gives you some ideas about how to select a good peer behavior model.

Once you have selected a peer model, you should begin the program. Table 10-4 provides general guidelines for conducting a peer imitation session. You may want to modify them according to the chronological and intellectual level of the peer model selected.

In Table 10-4 the peer model is cued to demonstrate *target behaviors.* This means that the peer model should demonstrate social behaviors from a predesignated list, repeating them until the withdrawn student consistently imitates them. One source for generating a list of target behaviors is the IEP for the isolate student. For example, you may want the student to learn how to ask other children to play. In this case, you might have the peer model say a standard phrase such as, "I want to play with you. Here is a toy." This is a *verbal* target behavior. You might also want the student to learn *motor* skills such as how to hand a toy to another child without throwing it. You would direct the model to offer a toy gently so that the isolate child could observe this and learn to do it. Other examples of suitable target behaviors are these: smile, push a toy, add a block to a tower, throw a ball, offer a verbal compliment, share, hug, pat. Remember that target behav-

Table 10-4. Steps in Conducting a Peer Imitation Training Session

1. Seat the children about two feet apart and facing one another.
2. Station a trainer behind each child in a "shadowing" style.
3. The trainer behind the peer model whispers in the child's ear to cue the target behavior, e.g., "Kevin, drink from your cup."
4. The model child drinks from his cup.
5. The trainer behind the target child says, "See what Kevin's doing? You do it too!"
6. If the target imitates the modeled behavior, the trainer offers verbal praises and affectionate pats.
7. If the target does not imitate the modeled behavior, the trainer behind the target physically guides (handshapes) the desired behavior (e.g., guides the hand-held cup to the mouth of the child).
8. The trainer gradually fades physical guidance and continues to reinforce successive approximations.
9. When the target can successfully imitate the peer model while seated across from each other, move the training to a less structured setting, e.g., a free-play situation.
10. When the peer model exhibits an appropriate behavior, approach the target and say, "See what Kevin's doing? You do it too!"
11. Provide physical guidance if the target fails to imitate.
12. Fade physical guidance and reinforce successive approximations.

Note: This table was contributed by Thomas P. Cooke.

iors are not always selected from play activities but might be behaviors from a self-help or pre-vocational activity as illustrated in Table 10-4.

It is important that you think about where you would like the peer imitation to take place. Cooke, Cooke, and Apolloni (1978) suggest that peer imitation training take place in the most natural setting possible. In research conducted on young children, they found that the pupils performed better when training was conducted in their classroom instead of an individual session room. If your peer imitation intervention relates to play behaviors, plan training in a free-play area of the classroom or during an outside recess period. If you are attempting to use peer imitation training for, say, self-help or preacademic skills, then shift the intervention session to a setting that has the materials for these activities. You may find it helpful in the initial sessions to conduct the training when other students are not present. This enables a handicapped student to pay close attention to the peer model. The private peer training also allows you to give more attention to the intervention sessions.

PEER SOCIAL INITIATION

In this intervention, the peer trainer is required to make social bids to a withdrawn child or children. These bids may be vocal-verbal or motor-gestural ones (asking the isolate child to play, giving the isolate child a toy, or helping the child to use a particular material). The peer social initiation procedure has been used successfully with both severely behaviorally disordered children and normal to mildly handicapped children (James & Egel, 1986; Ragland, Kerr, & Strain, 1978; Strain, Shores, & Timm, 1977).

In addition to the general resources listed for peer interventions, you may want to make a set of cue cards to assist the peer trainer in carrying out his role. Each cue card should display a picture of a toy or play activity that the isolate child enjoys. Peer trainers need a little reminder to

move from one play material to another during the training session, which the cue cards accomplish when displayed in the play area.

Select a peer trainer for this intervention according to the criteria listed in Table 10-3. Research studies reveal the ability of even very young children (three years old) or developmentally delayed children (moderately retarded) to carry out this simple intervention (Young & Kerr, 1979).

Table 10-5 outlines the basic steps of preparing a peer trainer for intervention sessions. If you are working with a developmentally delayed peer trainer, this training may take longer than the four twenty-minute sessions suggested. In addition, you may find it helpful to provide frequent, tangible reinforcers to a developmentally delayed trainer.

When you are ready to schedule intervention sessions on a daily basis, allow enough time to enable the peer trainer to work with one isolate student at a time for a ten-minute interval. Do not plan to ask the trainer to work with several students at one time, because it becomes too difficult a role for the peer trainer and is not sufficiently intensive an intervention for the withdrawn pupils. Rather, "taking turns" is preferred. You may notice, however, that while the peer trainer is working with one student, others in the group play more cooperatively and frequently with each other.

The first few days of a peer social initiation intervention may leave you with the discouraging feeling that this intervention will not work at all. This is because isolate children, when first approached by the peer trainer, have a natural tendency to ward off these approaches through temper tantrums and other oppositional behaviors. You and the peer trainer must not give up at this point. Rather, the peer trainer should continue to make initiations toward the children, and you should reinforce these efforts. You may find that in the initial session, you will also need to prompt, either physically or verbally, the isolate student's responding to the peer trainer. This initial difficult period gener-

Table 10-5. Peer-Mediated Social Initiation Procedure: Preparing the Peer Trainer

1. Explain to the peer trainer what is expected during the training sessions. Modify the explanation to suit the conversational level of the individual. Examples of this brief explanation are, "Try your best to get other children to play with you," "To get others to play with you, give them a toy."
2. Train the peer trainer to expect rejection. This is accomplished by the adult's taking the role of an isolated individual. In every other instance of the peer trainer making a social initiation towards the adult, ignore the initiation. Pause for ten seconds or more, then explain to the child that your ignoring the initiation is a behavior the trainer is likely to encounter with the isolate student. Explain this in a manner that encourages the trainer to continue trying. For example, you can say something like, "Children will not always want to play, but you need to keep trying very hard."
3. Repeat the role play, first training the peer to hand you a toy or to otherwise make a motor-gestural initiation. Then train the student to make vocal-verbal initiations.
4. Carry out the role play using each of the toys or play materials that are in the free-play setting. Cue the peer trainer about any toys that have a particular appeal to the isolate individual. Introduce cue cards depicting each toy at this time, if necessary.
5. Continue practicing the role plays during daily twenty-minute practice sessions until the peer trainer can reliably make repeated social initiations towards you. Keep in mind that peer training in the research reported has typically required at least four sessions, with additional sessions needed for a severely handicapped peer trainer.
6. Be sure to reinforce the peer trainer's participation during each training session.

Note: Material was taken from M. M. Kerr and P. S. Strain. The use of peer social initiation strategies to improve the social skills of withdrawn children. In A. H. Fink (Ed.), *International perspectives on future special education.* Reston, Virginia: Council for Exceptional Children, 1979.

ally lasts no more than four or five sessions, after which pupils cooperate and begin to enjoy their interactions. Table 10-6 displays the basic steps in conducting the intervention sessions.

PEER PROMPTING AND REINFORCEMENT

Peer prompting and reinforcement, like teacher prompting and reinforcement, refers to the use of a trainer to assist withdrawn children in playing with each other. Again, verbal and physical prompts and frequent reinforcers are used. Research on this procedure has not been extensive, but the initial work has shown that a peer trainer could successfully use the procedure to increase the cooperative play behavior of two severely behaviorally disordered children (Strain, Kerr, & Ragland, 1979). Consider the peer prompting and reinforcement strategy as a follow-up to peer social initiations.

Once an isolate student begins reliably to respond to the peer trainer, a different playmate can be introduced by using the peer prompting and reinforcement strategies described in Table 10-7. We do not suggest that you train a peer to carry out both interventions (peer social initiations; prompting/reinforcement) at once; this would be too complex a task.

PEER MANAGER STRATEGY

Young socially withdrawn students may benefit from playing "class manager," a role studied by Sainato, Maheady, and Shook (1986). In their study, the withdrawn kindergarteners took turns directing pleasurable classroom activities: feeding the class pet, ringing the "clean-up bell," collecting milk money, and opening two play areas. This effort succeeded in improving social interactions and sociometric ratings.

Table 10-6. Peer-Mediated Social Initiation Procedure: Conducting the Intervention Sessions

1. Set aside at least six minutes for each target individual during the play session.
2. Try to use the same free-play area with the play materials suggested each day.
3. Before each intervention session, review with the peer trainer those activities that are most likely to be successful.
4. Remind the peer trainer before each session that the pupils may not be responsive at first, but to keep trying.
5. Remind the peer trainer to play with only one target individual at a time. It helps if the adult in the session reminds the peer trainer when to change toys and when to begin play with another student.
6. Reinforce the peer trainer for attempting to play with the withdrawn individuals. If the session is going slowly, you may wish to reinforce the peer trainer during the session. Otherwise, provide the peer trainer with some form of reinforcement at the end of the session.

PEER COACHING

Peer coaching, like peer imitation, involves students and adults who provide instruction. The purpose of this intervention is to teach withdrawn pupils social skills to gain them peer acceptance. Socially withdrawn children realize more opportunity to engage in social learning if they are trained to increase their acceptance by peers. In a study by Oden and Asher (1977), third- and fourth-grade socially isolated children were coached in skills for making friends. The coaching procedure was designed to be used in schools. This intervention requires the adult to train children verbally in social skills. Next, they are given the opportunity to practice their social skills by playing with a peer. Finally, they review the training procedure with their teacher/coach. (See Oden, 1980, for a detailed description of the coaching procedure.)

PEER TUTORING

Recent evidence (Franca, 1983; Maher, 1982) has convinced us that academic peer tutoring can have a positive influence on peer social interactions, although researchers cannot always document how and why (Cook, Scruggs, Mastropieri, & Casto, in press; Scruggs, Mastropieri, Veit, & Osguthorpe, 1986). Franca (1983) found that behaviorally disordered ado-

Table 10-7. Peer-Mediated Prompting and Reinforcement Strategy

1. Select a peer as suggested in the previous intervention strategies.
2. Plan at least four twenty-minute training sessions to prepare the individual for his role as peer trainer.
3. Explain to the peer trainer that you want assistance in helping other children to learn to play. Explain further that the role of peer trainer will be helping children play with each other and letting them know they are doing a good job.
4. Train the peer trainer by inviting two children into the play session, and practice with the trainer prompting and reinforcing them for playing together. Unlike other peer-mediated procedures, training for peer prompting and reinforcement should take place "on the job," using the isolate students from the beginning.
5. By modeling the strategies with the isolate children present, assist the peer trainer to think of ways to prompt and reinforce the isolate children.
6. Remind the peer trainer before each intervention session to try to get the two children to play with each other rather than directly with the peer trainer.
7. Set aside the time and materials and location described in the previous peer training intervention for the actual training sessions.
8. Remember to reinforce the peer trainer for efforts after each session.

lescents who tutored one another in fractions played more cooperatively in a physical education class. In this study, students were assigned to pairs and given specific tutoring scripts.

Peer-tutoring guidelines, as presented in Chapter 8, may help your students expand their opportunities to practice both social and academic skills. We suggest that you consider peer tutoring as a supplementary social skills training activity, relying on more direct interventions to teach new social skills (cf. Scruggs et al., 1986; Scruggs, Mastropieri, & Richter, 1985).

Another goal for peer tutoring may be a *shift in attitudes toward the behaviorally handicapped.* Shisler, Osguthorpe, and Eiserman (1987) found that nonhandicapped sixth graders rated their behaviorally disordered tutors more positively after their tutoring experience. According to Johnson and Johnson (1984), the tutoring may allow nonhandicapped students to view their handicapped peers in a different, less stereotyped role (Shisler et al., 1987).

Self-Mediated Strategies

Self-management strategies for the remediation of social withdrawal have not been explored extensively in research literature. However, newly emerging self-management strategies offer promise for an isolate student who is aware of his difficulty and wishes to have a role in remedying it. For example, this intervention might be very useful in a regular classroom for adolescents or in a classroom of behaviorally disordered youngsters who are returning to a regular classroom. The self-management strategies discussed here are similar to those discussed in other chapters; the primary difference is in the target behavior selected. In choosing target behaviors for self-management procedures, it is a good idea to get the student to participate.

The primary resource that you need to help students carry out a self-managed intervention for social withdrawal is a self-recording data sheet. Students should record their own performances to show visibly their progress towards meeting the goal of increased social interactions. Information on how to develop a self-recording sheet is described in Chapter 6.

The purpose of self-recording is to make the student aware of positive interactions with others and how to increase them. Thus the intervention is twofold: first, the teacher or counselor describes to students examples of social initiations and responses. Second, students collect data on their own interactions. A third component, self-reinforcement, may supplement the intervention, or the teacher or counselor may provide the reinforcement to the student. Here are examples of target behaviors for a student to record:

1. Raising my hand in classroom discussions to say something
2. Asking a question during the class meeting
3. Helping another student in my class on an assignment
4. Answering a question when another student asks me something
5. Saying "hello" to one of my classmates
6. Asking my classmate to eat lunch next to me
7. Asking someone in my class to play with me at recess
8. At recess, telling others they are doing a good job
9. Lending someone a pencil or paper during class
10. Sitting next to one of my friends during lunch
11. Bringing a toy for someone else to play with in school
12. Telling someone what I did after school yesterday
13. Signing up to tutor another person in my class
14. Asking someone else to help me with my self-recording project

Self-monitoring is a good way to extend your social skills training program, as suggested by Kelly et al. (1983), who found that self-monitoring improved the social interactions of behaviorally disordered adolescents with their vocational supervisors. In this case, self-monitoring was combined with role-playing and didactic training. Students rated themselves and then discussed their ratings with their teacher. When students monitored their interactions, their social skills showed greater generalization to a setting they were not trained for. A second study (Kiburz, Miller, & Morrow, 1984) achieved similar results with an eighteen-year-old learning to greet others and initiate conversations in a residential setting.

Summary

This chapter opened with suggestions for assessing the social skill problems of your students. Beginning with checklists to gather global opinions about students' functioning, we moved to the more precise assessments, sociometric measures and direct observations. In addition to measuring a student's one-to-one interactions, we recommend that you consider how well a student functions within a group context. Moreover, group activities within the classroom must be adapted to the individual strengths and weaknesses of the students while challenging them to improve their ability to work with others. The capacity to function within small and large groups is crucial to mainstreaming.

Many strategies were highlighted in this chapter, from environmental modifications for young children, to social skills curricula for adolescents. In general, the more didactic, curriculum-based approaches are well-suited to the students whose social skills are mildly impaired or who have the skills but lack consistency and judgment about when and how to use them. The prompting and reinforcement strategies, conducted by the teacher or by a trained peer, meet the needs of young or more severely handicapped students whose social interactions are still rudimentary in most instances.

To further your knowledge of social skills and of social development in general, we recommend Strain, Guralnick, and Walker (1986), a comprehensive review of research on the social development of handicapped children.

CASE STUDY

Assessing a Social Skills Problem

F. M. Gresham and T. A. Cavell

The following case study illustrates many of the issues and methods of assessing adolescent social skills. This particular case was seen as representative in that the methods chosen provide reliable and valid information within the constraints of practicality. Also, the evaluation process reflects an attempt to individualize assessment and link assessment findings with treatment targets. Finally, this case study demonstrates possible areas where newly developed instruments may be of some use.

Reason for Referral

Mike D. is a 14-year-old black male referred to our clinic because of a recent suicide attempt. He lives with his mother and a 9-year-old half-brother, Jake. Mike's natural father never lived with the family, whereas Jake's father left home approximately four years after Jake's birth. The boys' mother, Ms. D., reported that Jake's father often abused her and she often would call to Mike for help in such instances. It was during this period that Mike complained of frequent stomachaches.

Approximately one year ago, Ms. D. began seeing another man, Larry, who now visits three to four times per week. Because Ms. D. reported feeling guilty and anxious when disciplining her sons, she has allowed Larry to assume a prominent role as disciplinarian. His approach to handling conflicts with the boys tends to be fairly authoritative and characterized by loud demands and physical punishment.

Recently, Mike's behavior at school resulted in a temporary suspension. The school's guidance counselor (supported by documentation in Mike's school folder) reported that on separate occasions Mike had become quite upset with one of his teachers and with the school-bus driver. In both situations, he angrily cursed the adults when accused of "offenses" he had not committed. Immediately after the suspension ended, Mike was incorrectly prohibited by the driver from once again riding the school bus. Mike became upset and angrily cursed the bus driver. This behavior resulted in a second suspension, the news of which greatly upset his mother and his mother's boyfriend. As a result, Larry harshly disciplined Mike. Later that evening, Mike ingested 20 Tylenol capsules in an attempt to commit suicide.

Assessment Procedures

One part of the assessment and treatment focus in Mike's case was his interaction with school personnel. Behavioral interviews and school records had adequately identified several characteristics of the situations that resulted in Mike's angry outbursts. Based on interview data, the decision was made to have Mike initially self-monitor all interactions he had with the school-bus driver and his science teacher. An interaction was defined as any verbal response made by these two school personnel to

him and vice versa. Specifically, Mike was asked to record a one- to two-sentence description of the event and to rate on a 9-point scale (where 1 = not at all and 9 = extremely) the degree of anger he experienced. A small spiral-bound note pad was used as a record form, with Mike instructed to make his entries at the first convenient opportunity after the interaction.

Self-monitoring information suggested Mike was capable of engaging in positive exchanges with these adults except when the situations involved Mike's receiving negative feedback from them, especially in the presence of his peers. Two weeks of self-monitoring data indicated Mike had two negative (i.e., anger ratings of 5 or greater) interactions with the bus driver and one with his science teacher. Contrary to previous negative interactions, however, on these occasions Mike simply said nothing. The interaction with his science teacher was particularly noteworthy in that she had accused him of not studying for a test he had failed. For this interaction, Mike rated his anger as a "9" because he felt he had studied for the test and the teacher was simply picking on him.

When this particular scene was role-played with Mike given instructions to respond, not as he had, but as best he could, he was unable to generate appropriate alternative responses. When asked to relate what self-statements and emotional responses occurred when unjustifiably accused by the teacher, Mike pointed out that he could feel himself "heating up" but was trying not to curse at her. From the information collected, it appeared as though Mike's poor performance in these situations was a result of self-control skill deficits. In other words, he was unable to perform the skills required (i.e., appropriate assertive responses) and his anger and impulsivity were interfering with his ability to acquire these skills.

Though not particularly germane to changing his interactions with school personnel, Mike's tendency to respond with angry verbal outbursts may have been shaped through interactions with his mother. She had reported that she was ineffectual in disciplining Mike, especially when he would "blow up" at her; thus, Mike's angry outbursts had a history of negative reinforcement at home, which may have generalized to school situations.

The immediate impact of social skills training (consisting primarily of instructions, modeling, coaching, and feedback for assertive responses, coupled with techniques for reducing interfering emotional arousal) was evaluated through continued self-monitoring and behavior role-playing. Frequent phone contact also was made with the school's guidance counselor in order to corroborate Mike's self-monitoring data.

Assessment Results

The significance of changes associated with social skills training was evaluated in two ways. First, with Mike's consent, two different teachers were asked to participate in an assessment of the generalization of his newly acquired skills to novel situations. Without Mike knowing which teachers were contacted, two were asked to engage Mike in a potentially anger-provoking interaction (e.g., accusing him of making disruptive noises in class). Afterward, these teachers rated Mike's performance on certain aspects (e.g., appropriateness of verbal content) and reported these to us. The second method in which the significance of treatment's impact was assessed involved asking the bus driver and science teacher to report to the guidance counselor any incident in which Mike exhibited angry verbal outbursts. In this way, inquiries made to the counselor represented both a simple way to monitor Mike's performance over time and a return to very global, yet socially valid, information.

Source: Reprinted with permission from Gresham, F. M., & Cavell, T. A. (1986), Assessing adolescent social skills. In R. G. Harrington (Ed.), *Testing adolescents.* Kansas City: Test Corporation of America.

Figure 10-3. Strategy Selection Chart for Social Skills Deficits

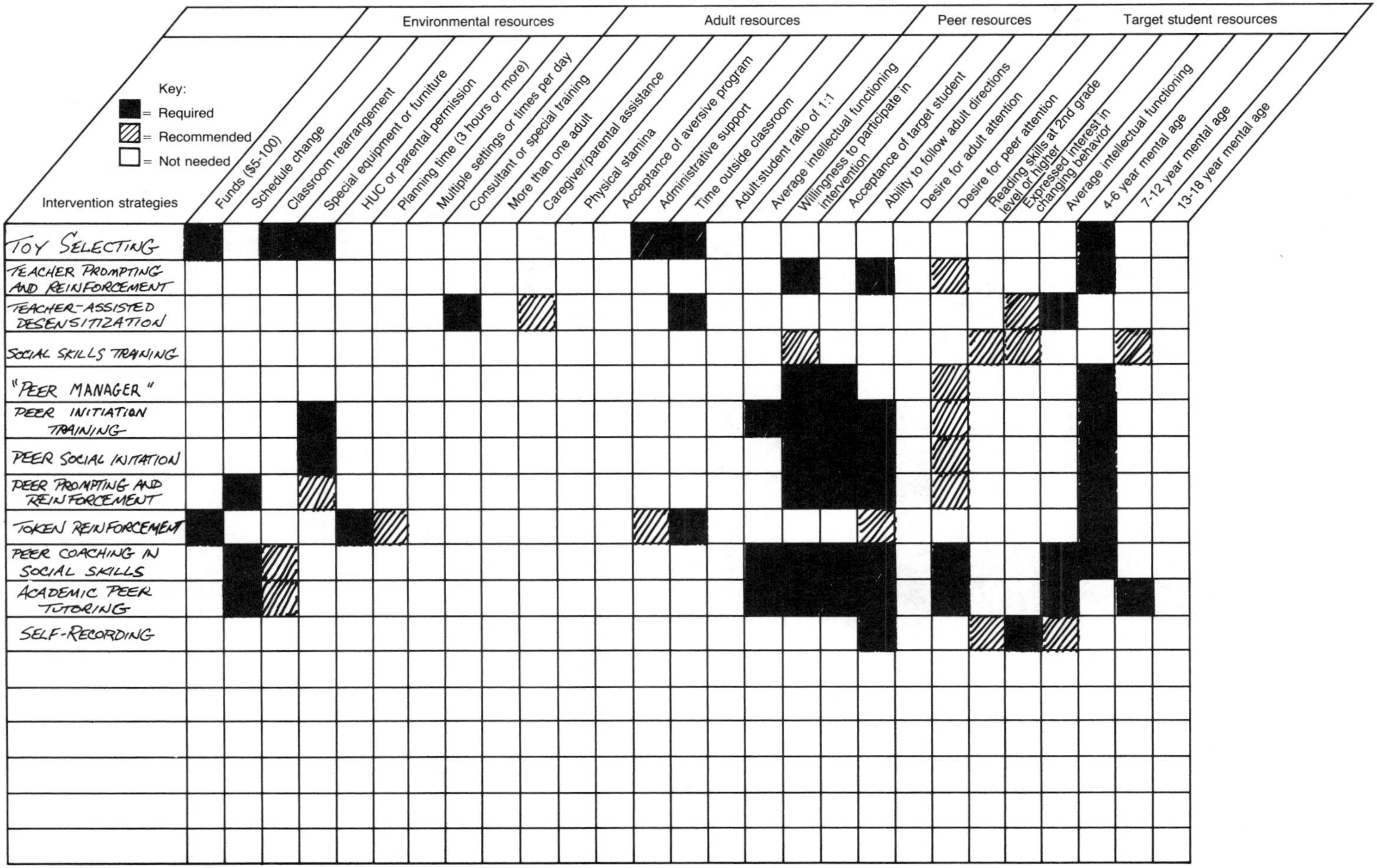

Discussion Questions

1. Discuss the do's and don'ts of social skills interventions.
2. Discuss the difference between social skills and social competence.
3. When are sociometric measures useful, and why?
4. Why is there such emphasis on *peer-mediated* interventions?
5. What does research suggest about environmental modifications for improving social skills?
6. Illustrate how a token economy can be used to improve social skills.
7. Will peer tutoring lead to improved social skills? Why or why not?
8. Name and illustrate the essential components of a social skills intervention.

References

Asher, S. R. (1983). Social competence and peer status: Recent advances and future directions. *Child Development, 54,* 1427-1434.

Bryant, L. E., & Budd, K. S. (1984). Teaching behaviorally handicapped preschool children to share. *Journal of Applied Behavior Analysis, 17*(1), 45-56.

Cartledge, G., & Milburn, J. F. (1980). *Teaching social skills to children.* Elmsford, NY: Pergamon Press.

Cartledge, G., & Milburn, J. (1983). Social skills assessment and teaching in the schools. In T. R. Kratochwill (Ed.), *Advances in school psychology* (Vol. 3, pp. 175-236). Hillsdale, NJ: Lawrence Erlbaum Associates.

Cobb, J. A. (1972). Relationship of discrete classroom behaviors to fourth grade academic achievement. *Journal of Educational Psychology, 63,* 74-80.

Cook, S., Scruggs, T. E., Mastropieri, M. A., & Casto, G. W. (in press). Handicapped students as tutors. *Journal of Special Education.*

Cooke, S. A., Cooke, T. P., & Apolloni, T. (1978). Developing nonretarded toddlers as verbal models for retarded classmates. *Child Study Journal, 8,* 1-8.

Doke, L. A., & Risley, T. R. (1972). The organization of day-care environments: Required vs. optional activities. *Journal of Applied Behavior Analysis, 5,* 405-420.

Dy, E. B., Strain, P. S., Fullerton, A., & Stowitschek, J. J. (1981). Training institutionalized, elderly mentally retarded persons as intervention agents for socially isolate peers. *Analysis and Intervention in Developmental Disabilities, 1,* 199-215.

Franca, V. M. (1983). *Peer tutoring among behaviorally disordered students: Academic and social benefits to tutor and tutee.* Unpublished doctoral dissertation, George Peabody College of Vanderbilt University, Nashville, TN.

Gable, R. A., Hendrickson, J. M., & Strain, P. S. Assessment, modification, and generalization of social interaction among multihandicapped children. *Education and Training of the Mentally Retarded, 13,* 279-286.

Gershman, L. (1976). Eliminating a fire-setting compulsion through contingency management. In J. D. Krumboltz & C. E. Thoresen (Eds.), *Counseling methods* (pp. 206-213). New York: Holt, Rinehart, & Winston.

Gresham, F. M., & Cavell, T. A. (1986). Assessing adolescent social skills. In R. G. Harrington (Ed.), *Testing Adolescents* (pp. 93-123). Kansas City: Test Corporation of America.

Hazel, J. S., Schumaker, J. B., Sherman, J. A., & Sheldon-Wildgen, J. (1982). Application of a group training program in social skills and problem solving to learning disabled and non-learning disabled youth. *Learning Disability Quarterly, 5,* 398-408.

Hollinger, J. D. (1987). Social skills for behaviorally disordered children as preparation for mainstreaming: Theory, practice, and new directions. *Recent Advances in Special Education, 8*(4), 17-27.

Hops, H., & Greenwood, C. R. (1981). Social skills deficits. In E. J. Mash & L. G. Terdal (Eds.), *Behavioral assessment of childhood disorders.* New York: Guilford Press, 347-394.

Jackson, N. F., Jackson, D. A., & Monroe, C. (1983). *Getting along with others: Teaching social effectiveness to children.* Champaign, IL: Research Press.

James, S. D., & Egel, A. L. (1986). A direct prompting strategy for increasing reciprocal interactions between handicapped and non-handicapped siblings. *Journal of Applied Behavior Analysis, 19*(2), 173-186.

Johnson, D. W., & Johnson, R. T. (1984). Classroom learning structure and attitudes toward handicapped students in mainstream settings: A theoretical model and research evidence. In R. L. Jones (Ed.), *Attitudes and attitude change in special education: Theory and practice* (pp. 118-142). Reston, VA: Council for Exceptional Children.

Kelly, W. J., Salzberg, C. L., Levy, S. M., Warrenfeltz, R. B., Adams, T. W., Crouse, T. R., & Beegle, G. P. (1983). The effects of role-playing and self-monitoring on the generalization of vocational social skills by behaviorally disordered adolescents. *Behavioral Disorders, 9*(1), 27-35.

Kerr, M. M., Nelson, C. M., & Lambert, D. L. (1987). *Helping adolescents with learning and behavior problems.* Columbus, OH: Merrill.

Kerr, M. M., & Strain, P. S. (1979). The use of peer social initiation strategies to improve the social skills of withdrawn children. In A. H. Fink (Ed.), *International perspectives on future special education (pp. 185-188).* Reston, VA: Council for Exceptional Children.

Kiburz, C. S., Miller, S. R., & Morrow, L. W. (1984). Structured learning using self-monitoring to promote maintenance and generalization of social skills across settings for a behaviorally disordered adolescent. *Behavioral Disorders, 10*(1), 47-55.

Maher, C. A. (1982). Behavioral effects of using conduct problem adolescents as cross-age tutors. *Psychology in the Schools, 19,* 360-364.

McConnell, S. R., & Odom, S. L. (1986). Sociometrics: Peer-referenced measures and the assessment of social competence. In P. S. Strain, M. J. Guralnick, & H. M. Walker (Eds.), *Children's social behaviors: Development, assessment, and modification* (pp. 215-284). New York: Academic Press.

McEvoy, M. A., & Odom, S. L. (1987). Social interaction training for preschool children with behavioral disorders. *Behavioral Disorders, 2*(3), 242-251.

Michelson, L., Foster, S. L., & Ritchey, W. L. (1981). Social skills assessment of children. In B. B. Lahey & A. E. Kazdin (Eds.), *Advances in clinical child psychology (pp. 119-165).* New York: Plenum Press.

Neel, R. (1984). Teaching school routines to behaviorally disorderd youth. In J. Grosenick, S. Hunter, E. McGinniss, and C. Smith (Eds.), *Social/affective intervention in behavioral disorders.* Washington, DC: U.S. Department of Education.

Oden, S. (1980). A child's social isolation: Origins, prevention, intervention. In G. Cartledge & J. F. Milburn (Eds.), *Teaching social skills to children: Innovative approaches (179-202).* New York: Pergamon.

Oden, S., & Asher, S. R. (1977). Coaching children in social skills for friendship making. *Child Development, 48,* 495-506.

Odom, S. L., Hoyson, M., Jamieson, B., & Strain, P. S. (1985). Increasing handicapped preschoolers' peer social interactions: Cross-setting and component analysis. *Journal of Applied Behavior Analysis, 18*(1), 3-16.

Parkhurst, J. T., & Asher, S. T. (1985). Goals and concerns: Implications for the study of children's social competence. In B. B. Lahey & A. E. Kazdin (Eds.), *Advances in clinical child psychology* (Vol. 8, pp. 199-228). New York: Plenum Press.

Prinz, R., Swan, G., Liebert, D., Weintraub, S., & Neale, J. (1978). ASSESS: Adjustment Scales for Sociometric Evaluation of Secondary School Students. *Journal of Abnormal Child Psychology, 6,* 493-501.

Putallaz, M., & Gottman, J. (1982). Conceptualizing social competence in children. In P. Karoly & J. J. Steffan (Eds.), *Improving children's competence: Advances in child behavioral analysis and therapy* (Vol. 1, pp. 1-33). Lexington, MA: Lexington Books.

Ragland, E. U., Kerr, M. M., & Strain, P. S. (1978). Effects of social initiations on the behavior of withdrawn autistic children. *Behavior Modification, 2,* 565-578.

Robins, L. N. (1966). *Deviant children grow up: A sociological and psychiatric study of sociopathic personality.* Baltimore: Williams and Wilkins.

Roff, M., Sells, S. B., & Golden, M. M. (1972). *Social adjustment and personality development in children.* Minneapolis: University of Minnesota Press.

Sainato, D. M., Maheady, L., & Shook, G. L. (1986). The effects of a classroom manager role on the social interaction patterns and social status of withdrawn kindergarten students. *Journal of Applied Behavior Analysis, 19*(2), 187-195.

Schumaker, J. B., & Ellis, E. (1982). Social skills training of LD adolescents: A generalization study. *Learning Disability Quarterly, 5,* 409-414.

Schumaker, J. B., Hazel, J. S., Sherman, J. A., & Sheldon, J. (1982). Social skill performances of learning disabled, non-learning disabled, and delinquent adolescents. *Learning Disability Quarterly, 5,* 388-397.

Scruggs, T. E., Mastropieri, M. A., & Richter, L. (1985). Peer tutoring with behaviorally disordered students: Social and academic benefits. *Behavioral Disorders, 11*(1), 283-294.

Scruggs, T. E., Mastropieri, M., Veit, D. T., & Osguthorpe, R. T. (1986). Behaviorally dis-

ordered students as tutors: Effects on social behavior. *Behavioral Disorders, 12*(1), 36-44.

Shisler, L., Osguthorpe, R. T., & Eiserman, W. D. (1987). The effects of reverse-role tutoring on the social acceptance of students with behavioral disorders. *Behavioral Disorders, 13*(1), 35-44.

Simpson, R. L. (1987). Social interactions of behaviorally disordered children and youth: Where are we and where do we need to go? *Behavioral Disorders, 12*(3), 292-298.

Speigel-McGill, P., Bambara, L. M., Shores, R. E., & Fox, J. J. (1984). The effects of proximity on socially oriented behaviors of severely multiply handicapped children. *Education and Treatment of Children, 7*(4), 365-378.

Stoneman, Z., Cantrell, M. L., & Hoover-Dempsey, K. (1983). The association between play materials and social behavior in a mainstreamed preschool: A naturalistic investigation. *Journal of Applied Developmental Psychology, 4,* 163-174.

Strain, P. S., Guralnick, M. J., & Walker, H. M. (Eds.). (1986). *Children's social behavior: Development, assessment, and modification.* New York: Academic Press.

Strain, P. S., Kerr, M. M., & Ragland, E. U. (1979). Effects of peer mediated social initiations and prompting/reinforcement procedures on the social behavior of autistic children. *Journal of Autism and Developmental Disabilities, 9,* 41-54.

Strain, P. S., Odom, S. L., & McConnell, S. (1984). Promoting social reciprocity of exceptional children: Identification, target behavior selection, and intervention. *Remedial and Special Education, 5,* 21-28.

Strain, P. S., Shores, R. E., & Kerr, M. M. (1976). An experimental analysis of "spillover" effects on the social interaction of behaviorally handicapped preschool children. *Journal of Applied Behavior Analysis, 9,* 31-40.

Strain, P. S., Shores, R. E., & Timm, M. A. (1977). Effects of peer initiations on the social behavior of withdrawn preschool children. *Journal of Applied Behavior Analysis, 10,* 289-298.

Strain, P. S., & Timm, M. A. (1974). An experimental analysis of social interaction between a behaviorally disordered preschool child and her classroom peers. *Journal of Applied Behavior Analysis, 7,* 583-590.

Wolfe, V. V., Boyd, L. A., & Wolfe, D. A. (1983). Teaching cooperative play to behavior-problem preschool children. *Education and Treatment of Children, 6*(1), 1-9.

Young, C. C., & Kerr, M. M. (1979). The effects of a retarded child's social initiations on the behavior of severely retarded school-aged peers. *Education and Training of the Mentally Retarded, 14,* 185-190.

Psychiatric Problems

Chapter 11

OUTLINE

Identifying Psychological Problems

Depression

Suicide

Drug and Alcohol Abuse

Eating Disorders

Enuresis and Encopresis

Anxiety Disorders

Phobias and Extreme Fears

OBJECTIVES

The reader who completes this chapter should be able to

- Describe the steps one takes when interviewing a student who may have an emotional problem.
- Define each of the following terms: enuresis, encopresis, anorexia nervosa, bulimia nervosa, suicide, depression, drug and alcohol abuse, pervasive developmental disorder, school and other phobias, anxiety disorder.
- Identify a student who is showing signs of a psychiatric problem.
- Make an informed referral for a student showing signs of a psychiatric problem.

This chapter deals with psychiatric, or emotional, problems that require treatment outside of school. Your role with respect to these problems is one of collaborator, usually with professionals from a mental health agency. Although we do not cover all of the possible psychiatric problems of children and adolescents, we hope to make you aware of those you are likely to identify in school-aged children. The problems covered in this chapter include: depression, suicide, drug and alcohol abuse, eating disorders, enuresis and encopresis, anxiety disorders, and phobias and extreme fears.

Within this chapter we highlight some of the signs of psychiatric problems and offer you guidelines in recognizing and referring these disorders. Classroom teachers are good observers of children's normal and abnormal behaviors (Kerr & Schaeffer, 1987; Hoier & Kerr, 1987). After all, educators are the one professional group constantly in touch with normal child and adolescent behavior. You can decipher when a student's actions fall outside these norms.

Therefore, your primary role in helping children with serious emotional or psychiatric problems is to *identify and refer them* for more intensive services. Moreover, you may be called on to collaborate in the student's subsequent treatment, especially if you are a special educator, school counselor, psychologist, or social worker.

First let us look at approaches to identifying students at risk for psychiatric problems.

Identifying Psychological Problems

Consider these general warning signs of a psychological problem:

1. a sudden change in behavior or mood
2. a prolonged sad, unhappy mood
3. fatigue and lethargy, or excessive energy and euphoria
4. a disinterest in activities that once were enjoyable
5. a change in sleep (being sleepier or having difficulty sleeping)
6. a change in appetite or a remarkable weight loss
7. making statements about hurting oneself
8. a sense of worthlessness or hopelessness
9. a decline in grades

We review these signs in our discussion of specific disorders. But first, we offer some assessment strategies. Interviewing is a good way to learn about a student's psychological problems.

INTERVIEW STRATEGY

To identify some of these warning signs, have a conversation with the student. See the student privately and allow enough time (no less than thirty minutes). Let the student know that you are concerned and want to help.

1. If the student hesitates, gently offer an example of the worrisome behavior.
   "You seemed to have lost your interest in the track meet."
   "I've noticed that you seem more excited than usual . . ."
   "You seem thin."
   "I notice you've been sleepy a lot lately."
2. Resist the urge to explain the symptom.
   "I guess the science class hasn't been too interesting after all."
   "Maybe you should eat more."
   "Are you sleeping enough?"
3. Be a good listener so that the student can feel comfortable talking. After all, you may guess incorrectly and throw the conversation off the track.
4. Do not badger! Here are some ways we badger.
   "I took time to talk with you and you're just going to clam up?"
   "Why don't you face facts, something is wrong with you!"
   "If you don't want help now, then don't come to me later."
   "Snap out of it and get your work done."
5. If the student does not want to talk, try another option.
   "Maybe this isn't a good time. We could meet after school."
   "I know you and Dr. Robb are rather close — do you feel you might want to talk with him? I could check to see when he is available."
   "If you ever want to talk, just let me know."
6. Listen! Students with problems are not always articulate. It may take a little while for them to explain how they feel. Be patient; do not interrupt. Show the student that you are interested by looking at him and nodding your head.
7. Avoid judgments. This is no time to evaluate the student's perceptions.
   "Well, that is nothing to worry about."
   "How did you ever get into such a mess anyway?"
   "I hope you've learned your lesson."
8. Next, name some action that you can take with the student. If you cannot immediately think of a plan, at least show your ac-

ceptance and willingness to help.

"I am not sure how we will solve this problem, but we can think it through tomorrow."

"Gee, this is a real problem. Let me give this some thought. We'll talk Wednesday, okay?"

"Now I see. How about if I share some of this with the counselor? I think he could help."

"I'd like to help you through this. How would you like to proceed?"

9. Close the conversation with some reassurance (even if you cannot genuinely show acceptance of the student's views). Some students really need information to help them view their situations more hopefully. If this is the case, offer it.

"I see why you were so worried about the quiz. You did not realize that everyone did poorly. I have decided to adjust everyone's grades."

"Suspension is serious; but no, it does not mean you fail the course."

"I know the seniors said they could vote you off the team. But that decision is made only by the coach."

10. Follow up on your commitment. Even if you have promised only to talk again, be sure you do. If you offered specific help, get it quickly.

11. Know *how* to help. Your work obligates you to know child and adolescent referral procedures, to understand the mental health services in your community, to know warning signs, and so forth.

12. Know how to handle confidentiality. Do not promise total confidentiality to a student; you may not be able to keep your word. You should not promise confidentiality, for example, in the case of suicide threats.

For very young children, you will need to interview the parents. Your school social worker or guidance counselor can assist you, or you can informally ask questions based on your concerns. One helpful strategy is to share your concerns with the parent and ask if the same or other problems have been apparent at home. Sometimes this approach cues the parents to recall events that may not have seemed problematic to them at the time. Just remember: follow the same guidelines in talking with a parent that you follow in talking with a student. Do not badger, explain the symptom, or pass judgment!

ASSESSMENT INSTRUMENTS

Teacher Interview for Psychiatric Symptoms

A new instrument for identifying psychiatric problems in children is the *Teacher Interview for Psychiatric Symptoms* (TIPS), developed by Kerr and Schaeffer (1987). Figure 11–1 displays some questions from this interview and was designed for counselors to ask teachers about worrisome students. The interview lasts approximately forty-five minutes and can be conducted by telephone.

Teacher's Report Form of the Child Behavior Checklist

Developed by Achenbach and Edelbrock (1980), this checklist is commonly used in this country and abroad for screening children for psychiatric problems. The teacher completes the checklist in about thirty minutes, rating each problem statement as *not true, somewhat or sometimes true,* or *very true or often true* for the target student within the past two months. Here are some sample items:

- clings to adults or too dependent
- not liked by other pupils
- gets hurt a lot, accident-prone
- feels or complains that no one loves him/her
- unhappy, sad, or depressed
- is afraid of making mistakes
- worrying

Figure 11-1.   Excerpts from the Teacher Interview for Psychiatric Symptoms

1. One of the feelings I'd like to know about is sadness. (This item refers to a mood of depression, sadness, "feeling bad.") Has (student's name) been feeling sad, unhappy, or miserable in school?
2. Does (student's name) appear to worry about things? Do you know of any current stressors that the student may be experiencing (at home or at school) that may be the reason for his/her worrying (e.g., parental divorce, boy/girlfriend problems, pending disciplinary action)?
3. Do you have a sense that (student's name) feels hopeless or pessimistic? Does s/he ever indicate that s/he has things to look forward to (e.g., movies, outings with family, basketball games, weekends)?
4. Does (student's name) have several friends with whom s/he plays or associates? If *no*, ask . . . does the student have a special friend with whom s/he plays or associates? When was the last time you noticed this student with (a) friend(s)?
5. When students are upset, sad, or angry, sometimes they think about hurting or killing themselves. Has (student's name) ever made a statement about wanting to hurt or kill her/himself? Has s/he ever made a statement about not wanting to live?

If you have referred students to a mental health clinic, you probably have completed this instrument.

The TIPS and the Child Behavior Checklist are only two of many available psychiatric screening instruments. Chapter 1 describes a screening procedure (Walker, Severson, Haring, & Williams, 1986) for problem behaviors. Refer to this chapter for additional assessment information.

DIRECT OBSERVATIONS

For some of the problems described in this chapter, you will be able to use a direct observation approach—or at least rely on your informal observations and impressions of a student. As we describe the disorders, we alert you to these warning signs.

Depression

Childhood depression is extremely difficult to diagnose, but it is included here because it may

also be a warning of a serious psychiatric disorder. *Depressed students do not always appear sad or unhappy; rather, you should pay attention to any sudden, unexplained change in behavior, even if it is acting-out or aggressive behavior.* As an illustration of the complex and apparently paradoxical nature of childhood depression, here is an excerpt from a seven-year-old boy's hospital file.

Eli returned to school after the death of his grandparents, his mother complaining that in addition to becoming more withdrawn he had been engaging in self-destructive and aggressive behavior. He had been running in front of automobiles and jumping down long flights of stairs in the apartment building where they live. He had been increasingly aggressive toward his mother to the point that she had become quite fearful of him. She noted that for no reason he would come up to her and slap her. He would often call her a pig or a liar and have frequent tantrums. Other times, he would ignore his mother and refuse to eat . . .

Eli's affect is depressed, and he will admit to feeling sad. He spent his entire physical examination and first two therapy sessions sitting in a constricted manner, sobbing throughout. Eli related that sometimes in the (psychiatric) hospital he wakes up crying because he misses his mom so much (Mendelsohn, personal communication, 1981).

Depression in children and adolescents is marked by these warning signs: sadness (sometimes called **dysphoria**), low self-esteem, irritability, changes in appetite or sleep, impaired concentration, anhedonia (loss of pleasure in activities the child previously enjoyed), somatic complaints, and antisocial behaviors. If you observe any of the warning signs for two weeks or more, then you should be concerned about the possibility of depression (American Psychiatric Association, 1980; Shaffer, 1985).

How does a depressed student *appear* at school? What should you look for? Here are some examples of teacher-reported behaviors from a study by Kerr and Schaeffer (1987):

1. Dejected/Dysphoric Mood

   "Susan has been very depressed since she learned that her mother has cancer. She cries often and has difficulty completing school work."

   "Bill repeatedly has stated that he is never happy, but does not give a reason for his unhappiness. He lays his head down in class and does not complete his work."

2. Irritability/Temper

   "Cindy's defiant and irritable moods have become more severe as the year has progressed. She becomes angry at her classmates over the littlest thing. Although she does not harm other students, her behavior has warranted her removal from the classroom. This disciplinary action usually provokes more anger; she frequently slams her books down on a desk."

   "Michelle is easily irritated by many things, and displays her temper by slamming a locker door or throwing books down on her desk."

3. Low Self-Esteem

   "After receiving a compliment about her appearance, Mary responded, 'I am not pretty at all.' She does not express pride in her academic accomplishments. Mary sees herself as unimportant and not worthy of attention."

4. Hopelessness

   "During a discussion of future plans, Ellen said, 'What is the future? Who knows if we have one?' She frequently comments 'What does it matter?' or 'What's the use?' "

5. Anhedonia

   "Mark no longer seems to be interested in his favorite activities. He used to enjoy listening to music and being on the swim team, but now avoids participating in those activities."

Suicide

The teenage suicide rate in the United States has increased by 226 percent since the 1960s (Brent, Perper, & Allman, 1987), making it the second leading cause of death in fifteen- to nineteen-year-olds (Pennsylvania Statistical Abstract, 28th edition, 1986). Moreover, research has shown that one in every twelve high school students has made a suicide attempt (Smith & Crawford, 1986). As you can see from these statistics, suicide is a problem you must be prepared to deal with if you work with adolescents.

What are the risk factors for suicide? A previous suicide attempt is a serious risk factor (Shaffer, 1986), as is threatening to take one's life. *You should immediately seek professional help for any student who talks about suicide or makes an attempt, regardless of how "serious" you think the student is.* **Drug and alcohol abuse** are often implicated in a suicide (Brent et al., 1987). Under the influence of drugs or alcohol, a vulnerable student may engage in risk-taking behaviors that he would otherwise avoid; these risks can include the fatal use of firearms (Brent et al., 1987). Access to firearms greatly increases the likelihood of suicide in adolescents who are already vulnerable (Lester & Murrell, 1982). Exposure to a suicide or suicide attempt is another risk factor, sometimes referred to as "contagion" (Davidson & Gould, 1986). This contagion effect is the basis for schools adopting carefully planned postvention efforts when a suicide takes place among the student body. **Postvention** (as compared with *prevention* taking place beforehand) refers to a set of actions that we take to prevent contagion after a suicide. Your school may have a postvention policy designed to lessen the risk of cluster suicides. Family variables in suicide include family conflict and a history of family psychiatric problems (including alcoholism). Indeed, a high percentage of suicide completers themselves had psychiatric problems, usually depression. This finding underscores the importance of your early recognition of the signs of depression.

What does this mean to you? First, increase your understanding of each risk factor. Try to learn about the families of your students. Second, know how to use your community mental health resources and drug rehabilitation agencies. Remember the warning signs for suicide.

- Hopelessness
- Chemical abuse
- Changes in eating or sleeping
- Isolation from friends and family
- A drop in academic achievement
- Giving away valued possessions
- Talking or writing about suicide, or not wanting to live
- A recent loss, such as divorce or death in the family, or a close friend moving away.

Reinforce the teenager's support network — family members, friends, and adults whom the student views as supportive. "Help in strengthening the [individual's] support system will be beneficial, as it is with all other psychiatric problems: with suicidal [individuals] it may be lifesaving." (Strayhorn, 1982, p. 480).

The following are specific steps to take with a teenager who discusses or threatens suicide:
1. Listen!
2. Help the student reach a mental health service, even if you must accompany the student there.
3. Contact the student's family.
4. Do not leave the student alone!
5. Do not underestimate the student's situation or expressed intent to end his life or hurt himself.

Drug and Alcohol Abuse

A 1984 survey of U.S. students revealed that 62 percent try some illicit drug before leaving high school (Johnston, O'Malley, & Bauchman, 1985; Miksic, 1987). Recognizing this widespread problem, most school districts have undertaken in-service training on drug and alcohol abuse for their teachers. This section merely highlights some important aspects of identifying and referring students at risk for drug and alcohol abuse. We begin with a review of the behaviors you might see in students who are engaged in substance abuse.

1. *Alcohol and Other Depressants.* A student who is intoxicated or in any identifiable stage of withdrawal should be removed from class. Do not confront the student with an accusation of drug use in front of peers. This may lead to opposition, resistance, or combativeness. When the student has been removed from the class explain why and ask if you can be of aid. School authorities and parents should be notified — and medical agencies if intoxication or withdrawal is severe. Referral to a counseling or rehabilitation program should be made as soon as possible.
2. *Marijuana.* It is the responsibility of front-line school personnel to provide adequate

supervision to prevent marijuana use during school hours. Teachers, counselors, school psychologists — all of the individuals who have regular direct personal contact with the student — share this responsibility.

The most effective means of prevention of marijuana-related problems is the creation of a system of peer control based on education of students and families, the ability to convey an attitude of openness to communicate about drug and personal problems, and the appropriate structure in planning daily activities. An important goal is to demonstrate to the young person that you are concerned with his or her academic and social success, and are not trying to control him/her unreasonably or remove his/her freedom in any other way. It is important to note that those who use marijuana most frequently are the individuals most interested in obtaining more specific information about it (Steffenhagen, Polich, & Lash, 1978).

Identification of an acute marijuana episode can be accomplished by closely observing student behavior. A sudden uncharacteristic change in appearance, academic performance, or social functioning may be indicative. Apathy, drowsiness, and taking on drug culture mannerisms also help to alert that marijuana use is being initiated or has become a significant problem.

3. *Stimulants.* Intense agitation, unreasonable suspiciousness, and bizarre behavior may be indicators of stimulant use. Hostility and aggression may result. Extreme talkativeness and flushed skin that are uncharacteristic of a student may also indicate stimulant use. Avoid physical confrontation if possible.

4. *Hallucinogens and Inhalants.* These chemicals usually severely disorganize behaviors so that medical or law enforcement intervention is necessary.

5. *Narcotics.* Overt intoxication or narcotic withdrawal can be identified through close observation. Drowsiness and slurred speech may appear to be simple fatigue, except that the person cannot become fully alert and awake when confronted and retains constricted pupils. Aggressiveness is unlikely to be a reaction of an individual under the influence of narcotics. However, agitation and impulsiveness are likely to accompany narcotic withdrawal. Significant withdrawal episodes require proper medical management, and such intervention should not be ruled out.

6. *General.* Do not attempt a power struggle with a student who appears to be under the influence of a drug. Certain drugs elicit combative behavior that can often be avoided if you do not respond impulsively to a physical threat.

Do not hesitate to seek emergency medical treatment for a student who appears to be experiencing a physical or emotional crisis. Sources of emergency care services are often listed in the human services section of the telephone directory and include poison control, crisis intervention, and the police department.

The classroom is not a place in which to attempt treatment of drug abuse. Prevention and identification are important activities for educators. It is appropriate to make individual referrals to proper agencies once drug use has been established, especially if it is the basis for disruptive behavior or poor academic performance. Table 11-1 summarizes the major drugs of abuse and their effects.

Eating Disorders

Professionals who work with adolescent girls should know of the two major eating disorders: **anorexia nervosa** and **bulimia**. The following vignette describes an anorectic teenager:

Table 11-1. Major Drugs of Abuse and Their Prominent Effects

Drug Class	Representative Drugs	Prominent Effects	
		Intoxication	Withdrawal
Depressants	alcohol phenobarbital Valium quaalude	relaxation sedation drowsiness irritability	tremulousness fever hallucinations psychological dependence
Marijuana	cigarettes (joints) hashish (resin)	relaxation sleepiness poor concentration confusion anxiety distortion of perception	psychological distress
Stimulants	amphetamines cocaine nicotine caffeine phencyclidine (PCP)	pupil dilation restlessness loss of appetite paranoia hallucinations	mental & physical depression fatigue

Hallucinogens	lysergic-acid-diethylamide
	   (LSD)
	mescaline
	psilocybin
	cannabis (marijuana)
	scopolamine
		pupil dilation
		disturbed attention
		hallucinations
		altered body concept
		distortions of time
		   perception
		emotional fluctuations
			inconsistent evidence —
			   little or none noted

Inhalants	aerosols glue paint thinner cleaning fluid	exhilaration confusion loss of balance drowsiness depression hallucinations frequent coughing	inconsistent
Narcotics	morphine Darvon methadone codeine Dilaudid	analgesia slurred speech drowsiness constricted pupils poor coordination	fever vomiting cramps sweating "goose flesh" chills irritability running nose tearing

Katherine states that in February she went on a diet. At that time she was 127 pounds and five feet eight inches tall. She decided to cut down because she felt she didn't look good at that weight. She was surprised that she had so much willpower, and she was able to get down to 100 pounds. Katherine reports that her mother became uncomfortable with her dieting around April. By the end of April, her mother was really getting angry about her diet. She said that she exercised about half an hour each night, and she would not eat sweets. She did find herself being too occupied with counting calories. Katherine does not currently see herself as being too thin, so she does have a distorted body image. Katherine has always felt herself to be different from the other kids. She has always been tall and was especially bothered by this in the seventh and eighth grades. When she was in ninth grade, her periods began. Her mother told her about periods and talked to her about sex. She also viewed some informational movies at school. Katherine was somewhat uncomfortable talking about this area. She reports that her periods stopped several months ago. Katherine reports a change in her personality since going on the diet. Before February she would become depressed only if her mother yelled at her, and her mother often became angry and upset. Now she becomes depressed over nothing, or so she feels, and just wants to be by herself. However, she does no excessive crying. She does not feel that her current problems have had any effects on her friendships, though she has only one close friend, Natalie.

Russell (1985) cited criteria for anorexia nervosa.

1. Marked loss of weight that is self-induced, usually through a systematic avoidance of "fattening" foods (e.g., high-carbohydrate foods) and excessive exercise. Self-induced vomiting and purging are less frequent (cf. bulimia nervosa).
2. A specific psychopathology: an overvalued idea that fatness is a dreadful state to be avoided at all costs.

3. A specific endocrine disorder. In the female: amenorrhea is an early symptom. In the male: there is loss of sexual interest and potency. (pp. 629–30)

Bulimia, which often follows anorexia nervosa, is evidenced by these criteria (Russell, 1985):

1. Preoccupations with food associated with episodes of gross overeating.
2. Devices aimed at counteracting the "fattening" effects of the food ingested: especially self-induced vomiting or purging or alternation with periods of starvation.
3. The psychopathology of anorexia nervosa: fatness is so dreadful as to be avoided at all costs.
4. In "true" bulimia nervosa there is a history of a previous episode of anorexia nervosa, possibly of minor severity. However, other forms of bulimic disorder may arise de novo. (p. 631)

Remember that "the very nature of the illness [is] that the [individual] tries to avoid measures that are aimed at inducing a gain in weight" (Russell, 1985, p. 632). Therefore, you will probably not succeed by encouraging or admonishing the student to eat better. Rather, your role is to inform parents and mental health professionals of your concerns. Above all, do not ignore the problem; the mortality rate for eating disorders can be as high as 25 percent (American Psychiatric Association, 1980).

Enuresis and Encopresis

Enuresis refers to uncontrolled urination, during the day or night, beyond the age when one is considered to be toilet-trained or continent. A child is generally not diagnosed as enuretic below the developmental age of five years. **En-**

copresis refers to the soiling or passing of feces into inappropriate places and is usually not diagnosed before the age of four years. To be termed enuresis, the act must take place twice within a month for children five to six years old or once per month for an older student. Encopresis is considered if the event takes place at least once per month after the age of four years (American Psychiatric Association, 1980). Note that in neither case can the cause be due to a physical illness or medication.

Treatment of enuresis or encopresis may involve your implementation of an overcorrec-

Figure 11-2. Restitutional Overcorrection/DRO Program for an Encopretic Child in a Residential Treatment Center

---

Goal:
   Short-term: Jeff will go for seven consecutive days without soiling.
   Long-term: Jeff will go for thirty consecutive days without soiling.

Recording:
   Each day is blocked into six time periods: 7:00-8:30, 8:30-12:00, 12:00-2:00, 2:00-6:00, and 6:00-9:00 (or bedtime). Jeff's cottage counselors will keep a chart, indicating whether Jeff has soiled during any of these time periods on a particular day. When the counselors are away, the chart will be kept by the relief counselors.
   In addition, Jeff will keep a weekly chart, blocked into the same time periods. This chart will resemble a stamp book. For each block of time in which Jeff does not soil, he may put a green stamp in the book.

Intervention Program
   I. Overcorrection
      When soiling occurs:
      1. Jeff reports to staff person that he needs to go to his cottage.
      2. Jeff cleans himself up (finishes going to toilet, takes a shower, dries off).
      3. Jeff puts on clean clothes.
      4. Jeff washes his dirty clothes, hangs them up to dry.
      5. Jeff reports to the cottage counselors (or relief counselors) who check to make sure he is clean.
      6. Jeff returns to the activity in which he was engaged when soiling occurred.
      7. If Jeff was working when soiling occurred, he must make up the work during his next free period.
   II. DRO (Nonsoiling)
      1. Daily: Each day he does not soil, Jeff may stay up until 10:00 P.M. Also, he will earn fifteen bonus points for each occasion in which he uses the toilet for a bowel movement.
      2. Weekly: Jeff and his social worker will set a weekly goal, in terms of the number of stamps Jeff earns in a given week. This goal will be based upon the number of stamps earned during the previous week. (The first goal should be set after the stamp book has been in use one week.) Each week, the goal is systematically increased, depending upon Jeff's accomplishments during the previous week. Jeff and his social worker will write out a weekly contract, setting the goal and the reinforcement for reaching it.
      3. Additional: The teachers, social worker, and cottage counselors will praise Jeff specifically for not soiling in a given block of time. Jeff will take his stamp book to show his social worker every day.

tion program (see Chapter 9). *Do not undertake such a program without assistance and supervision of a qualified professional, however.* These disorders may also involve medical treatment under the direction of a physician or child psychiatrist. Often the problem involves family participation since the child is encopretic or enuretic at home, too. Figures 11-2 and 11-3 depict an intervention program for Jeff, an encopretic child, with data on his progress.

Treatment for encopresis or enuresis may depend on the motivation perceived for the student's behaviors. If a child is oppositional (exhibits a persistent "oppositional attitude even when it is destructive to the interests and well-being of the child or adolescent," American Psychiatric Association, 1980, p. 63) and smears feces accordingly, his treatment will differ from that of an encopretic child who is anxious and fearful of adults. Here is a description of an oppositional encopretic child, excerpted from his file in a psychiatric clinic:

Larry is still not toilet-trained. There are times when he will go to the bathroom, but not always. . . . At one time when (his) mother was trying to train him to go to the potty, he did not have a bowel movement for three days. She then decided not to talk about it and Larry did have a (bowel movement) in his pants. Recently it has become a pattern that after (his) father bathes Larry and dresses him for bed he will then soil in his pants. There are times when he will soil his pants and then look at (his) mother and say "shame on me." He does not do this at school but controls it until home. . . . Recently he has smeared his feces on his toys (Cofsky, personal communication, 1979).

To assist a consultant, you should assess the antecedent and consequent events to encopresis and enuresis, using an A-B-C analysis. You can also help by establishing on what schedule, if any, these behaviors occur. Remember, a child may be afraid to ask for permission to go to the toilet; in this case, allow the student a dif-

Figure 11-3. Progress Data for Encopretic Student

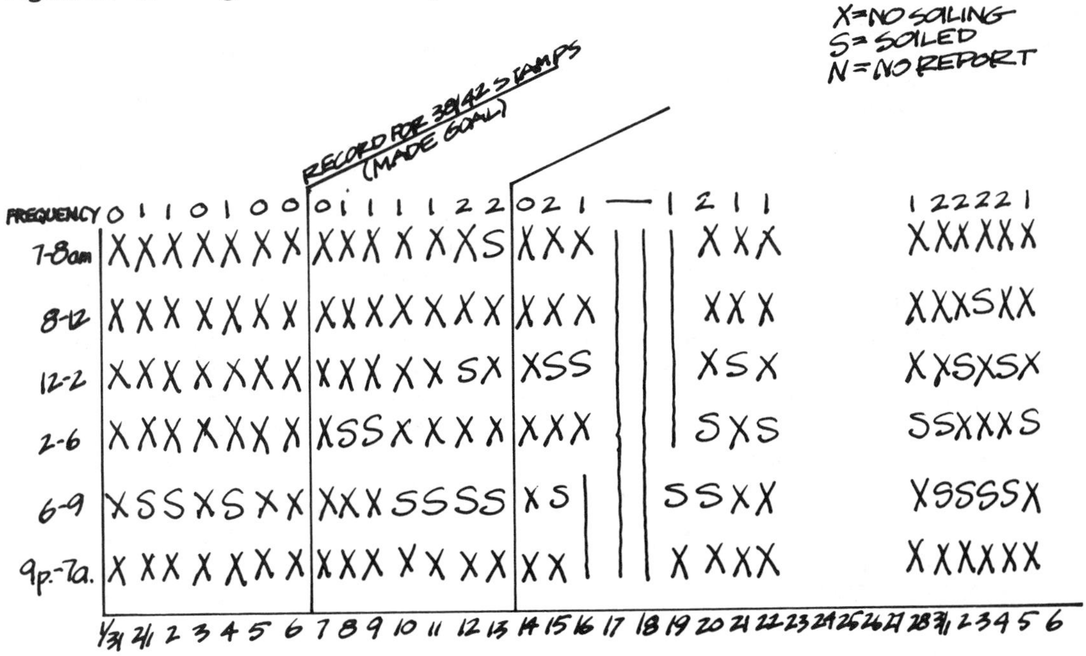

ferent, less public means of communicating his needs (e.g., a hall pass).

sure to keep the person informed about the student's progress and problems.

Anxiety Disorders

This term refers to three types of anxiety states that children may experience: separation anxiety, avoidant disorder, and overanxious disorder (Hersov, 1985; American Psychiatric Association, 1980). **Separation anxiety** describes the problem of a child who has great difficulty when separated from significant others or familiar surroundings. **Avoidant disorder** is experienced by children who go to great lengths to avoid contact with any strangers. **Overanxious disorder** refers to children who are chronically fearful or worried about future events, demands made of them, their health, or their social and academic skills (Hersov, 1985).

Children may become anxious in response to a specific, stressful event (e.g., hospitalization, prolonged separation from parent, car accident). On the other hand, some children seem to have a general temperamental tendency to be worried and fearful (Thomas, Chess, & Birch, 1968). When a child's anxiety interferes with normal school and social functioning, you should consider a referral to a mental health professional.

Treatment for anxiety disorders can be multi-faceted, including individual psychotherapy, behavioral relaxation, or desensitization techniques. Some children respond favorably to psychopharmacological interventions (Hersov, 1985).

In terms of classroom interventions, you may find the school survival skills described in Chapter 8 helpful in alleviating children's anxieties about school demands and deadlines. Time management can be especially helpful for an overanxious child. Other classroom suggestions will come from the child's therapist. Be

Phobias and Extreme Fears

"Phobias are emotional disorders in which there is an abnormally intense dread of certain objects, or specific situations that normally do not have that effect" (Marks, 1969, cited in Hersov, 1985). Children's phobias may include fears of animals, death, insects, the dark, noise, and school (Rutter, Tizard, & Whitmore, 1970). Consider this illustration of a phobic child:

> The presenting complaints at the time of the initial visit centered on Brenda's multiple fears. She is afraid of rain and lightning, and is fearful of leaving the house without . . . one of her parents. While Brenda does attend school, she expresses discomfort at being there. Furthermore, her school performance is poor, with Brenda having considerable difficulty with all school subjects.
>
> Brenda acknowledged the first two fears—her being afraid of lightning and of leaving the house alone—but she would not expand on either. However . . . Brenda's fear of being alone became evident. So that she would not have to be without her parents in the waiting room, Brenda instructed her mother to request that the social worker finish talking with the mother prior to Brenda's completing her session with me.
>
> With regard to school, Brenda did say that she disliked going to school. Brenda does not like her teacher, saying that her teacher is mean and always yells (Mendelsohn, personal communication, 1981).

Psychotherapeutic treatment of phobias may be categorized into four components described by Miller, Barrett, and Hampe (1974): development of a helping relationship with the therapist, clarifying what the feared object or situation is, helping the child become desensitized to the feared object or situation, and helping the child face the feared object or situation. Your role as an educator would be defined by the child's therapist.

In the case of school refusal, sometimes called **school phobia,** your role could be extensive. First, let's differentiate between school refusal and truancy. Truant students are not fearful of the school situation, whereas a school refuser may show fearfulness and anxiety such as somatic complaints, withdrawal from social interactions with other children, and a general inability to cope with demands to be independent of the family (Hersov, 1985). To give you an idea of the role you might play in assisting a school refuser, consider this description by Hersov (1985):

> Once back to school, on the first day contact must be maintained with child and parents by means of telephone calls to or from parents to gauge their own and the child's reactions to this first school attendance. Suggestions are made on how to deal with any new anxieties or attempts to manipulate parents to avoid school. If parents can manage unaided on successive mornings, they are praised and encouraged to take total responsibility for this, but support from clinic or school must be available if there are signs of faltering or loss of resolve in either child or parents. The child should be interviewed again after one week at school to sort out any existing or potential sources of stress and anxiety in the school or home situation which can then be discussed with teachers and parents. All concerned should be warned that the times of potential danger of breakdown of school attendance are after a weekend, after an illness requiring more than a day or two at home, the beginning of a new term, family illness or bereavement, and change to a new class or school. (Hersov, 1985, p. 395)

Summary

We hope that you have gathered information from the clinical vignettes and guidelines to help you identify and refer students at risk for psychiatric disorders. Do not hesitate to discuss a worrisome child with a colleague; you do not need to be absolutely sure about your concerns to make this inquiry on behalf of a child. Moreover, you may be the child's only advocate if the family is also impaired. Be sure to document your concerns so that future professionals working with the child will have a better understanding of the child's history. Evaluation of results is discussed in Chapter 4; you might want to review this material before making notes in a child's record.

Discussion Questions

1. Describe how you would talk with a student who appears to be depressed.
2. Why is a medical evaluation important to the treatment of enuresis and encopresis?
3. What are the warning signs for suicide?
4. What are the psychotherapeutic treatments for phobias?
5. How do truancy and school refusal differ?
6. What is an anxiety disorder?
7. What behavioral indicators might alert you to a student's use of alcohol, marijuana, cocaine, stimulants, narcotics, hallucinogens, or inhalants?
8. What are the warning signs for anorexia nervosa and bulimia nervosa?

References

Achenbach, T. M., & Edelbrock, C. S. (1980). The child behavior profile: II. Boys aged 12-16 and girls aged 6-11 and 12-16. *Journal of Consulting and Clinical Psychology,*

American Psychiatric Association. (1980). *Diagnostic and statistical manual of mental disorders* (3rd ed.). Washington, DC: Author.

Brent, D. A., Perper, J. A., & Allman, C. J. (1987). Alcohol, firearms, and suicide among youth — Temporal trends in Allegheny County, Pennsylvania, 1960 to 1983.

Journal of the American Medical Association, 257, 3369-3372.

Davidson, L., & Gould, M. S. (1986). *Contagion as a risk factor for youth suicide.* Unpublished Manuscript.

Hersov, L. (1985). School refusal. In M. Rutter & L. Hersov (Eds.), *Child and adolescent psychiatry: Modern approaches* (2nd ed.) pp. 382-399. Oxford, England: Blackwell Scientific Publications.

Hoier, T., & Kerr, M. M. (1987). Extrafamilial information sources in the study of childhood depression. *Journal of the American Academy of Child Psychiatry, 27,* 21-33.

Johnston, L., O'Malley, P., & Bauchman, J. (1985). Use of licit and illicit drugs by America's high school students, 1975-1984. *NIDA Monograph, 14,* 85-1394.

Kerr, M. M., Nelson, C. M., & Lambert, D. L. (1987). *Helping adolescents with learning and behavior problems.* Columbus, OH: Merrill.

Kerr, M. M., & Schaeffer, A. L. (1987). *Teacher interview for psychiatric symptoms (TIPS).* (Available from Mary Margaret Kerr, Ed.D., or Alice L. Schaeffer, M.Ed., at Western Psychiatric Institute and Clinic, 121 University Place, University of Pittsburgh, 3811 O'Hara Street, Pittsburgh, PA 15213.)

Lester, D., & Murrell, M. E. (1982). The preventive effect of strict gun control laws on suicide and homicide. *Suicide and Life-Threatening Behavior, 12,* 131-139.

Miksic, S. (1987). Drug abuse management in adolescent special education. In M. M. Kerr, C. M. Nelson, & D. L. Lambert (Eds.), *Helping adolescents with learning and behavior problems* (pp. 225-253). Columbus, OH: Merrill.

Miller, L. C., Barrett, C. L., & Hampe, E. (1974). Phobias of childhood in a prescientific era. In A. Davids (Ed.), *Child personality and psychopathology: Current topics.* New York: Wiley.

The Pennsylvania Statistical Abstract (28th Ed.). (1986). Prepared by Department of Commerce. Bureau of Statistics, Research and Planning.

Russell, G. F. M. (1985). Anorexia and bulimia. In M. Rutter & L. Hersov (Eds.), *Child and adolescent psychiatry: Modern approaches* (2nd ed.) (pp. 625-637). Oxford, England: Blackwell Scientific Publications.

Rutter, M., Tizard, J., & Whitmore, K. (Eds.). (1970). *Education, health and behavior.* London: Longman. (Reprinted, 1981, Huntingdon, NY: Krieger.)

Shaffer, D. (1985). Depression, mania, and suicidal acts. In M. Rutter & L. Hersov (Eds.), *Child and adolescent psychiatry* (2nd ed.) (pp. 698-719). Oxford: Blackwell Scientific Publications.

Shaffer, D. (1986). Developmental factors in child and adolescent suicide. In M. Rutter, C. E. Izard, & P. B. Read (Eds.), *Depression in young people: Clinical and developmental perspectives* (pp. 383-396). New York: Guilford Press.

Smith, K., & Crawford, S. (1986). Suicidal behavior among "normal" high school students. *Suicide and Life-threatening Behavior, 16*(3), 313-325.

Steffenhagen, R., Polich, J., & Lash, S. (1978). Alienation, delinquency, and patterns of drug use. In G. Beschner & A. Friedman (Eds.), *Youth drug abuse.* Lexington, MA: D. C. Heath.

Strayhorn, J. M., Jr. (1982). *Foundations of clinical psychiatry.* Chicago: Year Book Medical Publishers.

Thomas, A., Chess, S., & Birch, H. G. (1968). *Temperament and behavior disorders in children.* New York: Universities Press.

Walker, H. M., Severson, H., Haring, N., & Williams, G. (1986). Standardized screening and identification of behavior disordered pupils in the elementary age range: A multiple gating approach. *Direct Instruction News, 5*(3), 15-18.

Part Three

Extending Intervention Effects

Chapter 12

OUTLINE

Maintenance and Generalization Procedures

Programming for the Transition of Students to Less Restrictive Environments

Working Outside the Classroom

Case Study

OBJECTIVES

After completing this chapter, the reader should be able to

- Describe the relationship between the restrictiveness of treatment settings and the extent to which intervention effects generalize to other environments.

- Identify and describe obstacles to the maintenance and generalization of treatment effects.

- Describe strategies for achieving the maintenance and generalization of specific target behaviors.

- Describe procedures for assessing the expectations and tolerances of less restrictive settings for desired and maladaptive behaviors.

- Indicate factors to consider when planning for the transition of students to less restrictive school or postschool environments.

- Suggest strategies for accomplishing the successful transition of students to less restrictive environments.

Up to now, the major focus of this text has been on accomplishing changes in students' problem behaviors in settings where the primary intervention agent directly implements or supervises intervention procedures. In many cases, these **primary treatment settings** are individual classrooms that afford a high degree of stimulus control over pupils' behavior. As previous chapters have documented, there is a varied and powerful technology for accomplishing desired behavioral changes in settings in which intensive treatment may be applied. However, as we emphasized in Chapter 1, problem behaviors often occur in multiple settings. Furthermore, the effects of carefully designed and implemented interventions often do not generalize to other settings, nor do they tend to persist in primary treatment settings once intervention procedures are withdrawn. The failure of intervention effects to maintain and generalize is a significant problem, especially for pupils who are seriously handicapped by their behavior.

The failure of treatments applied in restrictive settings to generalize to less restrictive settings in which treatment variables are not in effect has been observed across many populations and age levels. For instance, Lane and

Burchard (1983) conducted an extensive review of behavioral interventions with delinquent youth and observed an apparent relationship between recidivism and the restrictiveness of the treatment setting. Their conclusion is relevant to all professionals who attempt to serve children and youth in restrictive environments: "To the extent that delinquents and criminals are locked up in institutions, the rationale for doing so should be to punish, and/or to temporarily protect the community, not to rehabilitate. *Very restrictive environments make rehabilitation less likely to happen*" (p. 273, emphasis added). Although the task of educators is habilitative rather than rehabilitative, research concerning the maintenance and generalization of behavioral changes accomplished in single settings (e.g., special classrooms, residential treatment programs) indicates that the "albatross of generalization" (O'Leary & O'Leary, 1976) also plagues those who attempt to modify the behaviors of school-age children and youth in restrictive environments.

Thus, extending intervention effects beyond individual classrooms is a critical task. There are several practical reasons for attempting to generalize behavioral changes across settings and over time. First, as we have just suggested, many pupils with behavior disorders have problems in other settings as well (e.g., other classrooms, halls, school buses, playgrounds, as well as their homes and neighborhoods). They clearly need help in these environments too, and persons in these settings need assistance in dealing with them constructively. Second, the school environment is actually composed of many different settings, such as those just mentioned. This is obvious in secondary schools where pupils move from classroom to classroom and may participate in a variety of extracurricular activities. But even in elementary schools composed of self-contained classrooms, pupils function in a variety of settings. It is important both to assess these environments to determine what problems, if any, the target student is having there and to generalize behavior changes accomplished in the primary treatment setting to these environments as well.

Third, from an ecological view, a behavioral problem is not "owned" exclusively by the target pupil. Thus, it is inappropriate to expect all the change to occur in the student alone. Frequently, those who interact with behavior problem students share ownership of the problem. In order for the pupil's behavior to change in the presence of these persons, their behavior must change as well. This is particularly important for generalizing behavioral changes to other settings. A fourth reason for extending treatment effects is to achieve social validation of important changes that have occurred in other settings. For example, if you successfully eliminate a pupil's stealing in your classroom, but her parents still find her stealing at home, the problem is not solved.

Finally, if you teach in a restrictive setting, we hope that you plan to move your pupils into more natural environments. And if you are working with secondary-level pupils, you must think about their successful transition to adult living and working environments. To accomplish these goals, you must involve a variety of other persons (e.g., other teachers, school administrators, bus drivers, parents, human services agency representatives, employers) in planning and implementing transition procedures.

This chapter describes strategies for extending the effects of interventions to other settings in which behavior changes are also needed, and these interventions are discussed in three sections. The first describes maintenance and generalization procedures that have been developed through the research of applied behavior analysts. The second section presents educational strategies for accomplishing the successful transition of pupils to less restrictive school and adult environments. Strategies for working with parents and professionals outside of primary treatment settings are discussed in the third section. Obviously, these sets of procedures overlap considerably. Throughout our discussion we emphasize issues that affect attempts to work across educational and non-educational settings.

Maintenance and Generalization Procedures

The question of whether desired behavior changes extend across settings is one of generality. As Baer, Wolf, and Risley (1968) explain, "a behavior change may be said to have generality if it proves durable over time, if it appears in a wide variety of possible environments, or if it spreads to a wide variety of related behaviors" (p. 96). Generality therefore may be defined in terms of three effects. **Response maintenance** is the continuation or durability of behavior in treatment settings after the intervention has been withdrawn. Thus, if improvement in a pupil's targeted social skills persists in the special classroom after social skills training procedures are discontinued, response maintenance has occurred. **Stimulus generalization** refers to the transfer of behaviors that have been trained in one setting or in the presence of specific *discriminative stimuli* to new settings or discriminative stimuli in the presence of which they have not been taught. An analogous term, *transfer of training,* is a better description of the process of transferring behavior changes accomplished in training to new settings or in the presence of new discriminative stimuli (e.g., cues, persons, physical objects). For example, a student may use a social skill taught in the classroom with her peers in the cafeteria. **Response generalization** involves changes in untreated behaviors related to those behaviors targeted for intervention. For example, if a pupil is taught to suppress his physical attacks on other students, and his rate of verbal aggression also decreases (even though this behavior was not treated), response generalization has occurred. Such generalization across behaviors is more likely in responses that serve the same function (i.e., are followed by the same reinforcers) as the target behavior.

For educators, the critical questions regarding the maintenance and generalization of intervention effects include the following (Rutherford & Nelson, 1988):

1. Will desired behavior changes persist when students leave structured, highly controlled training settings?
2. Will pupils exhibit newly learned behaviors in non-training settings, in the presence of other teachers or peers, and over time?
3. Will learning new skills facilitate the acquisition of similar behaviors which were not targeted for training in the original setting?

In this section, we examine the research concerning maintenance and generalization and describe specific procedures used to accomplish behavior changes across time, settings, and responses.

MAINTENANCE AND GENERALIZATION RESEARCH

Over two decades ago, Baer, Wolf, and Risley (1968) described the parameters of applied behavior analysis. Their discussion of this new field clearly expressed a concern for the generality of the effects of behavioral interventions. Nearly ten years later, Stokes and Baer (1977) reviewed 270 behavior analysis studies addressing generality, and they found that in over half of these investigations, maintenance and generalization were only assessed, not actually pursued or programmed. Rutherford and Nelson (1988) reviewed this literature another decade later and found that less than 2 percent of the approximately 5,300 applied research articles published between 1977 and 1986 addressed the maintenance and generalization of educational treatment effects, and less than 1 percent described studies in which maintenance and generalization were systematically programmed. Their analysis of this research was based on the nine procedures identified by Stokes and Baer (1977) as the major strategies for assessing or promoting generalization and maintenance of behavioral changes: Train and hope, sequential modification, introducing subjects to naturally maintaining contingencies, training sufficient exemplars, training loosely, programming indiscriminable contingencies, programming common stimuli, mediating generalization, and training to generalize. They concluded that although more researchers are addressing the generality of behavior changes, the "technology of generalization" called for by Stokes and Baer (1977) is still scattered and insufficient.

Rutherford and Nelson (1988) also noted that the complexity of intervention procedures, research designs, and methods of data collection required by such research contribute to the reluctance of investigators to study maintenance and generalization effects. For example, in designing procedures to manage inappropriate social behaviors, a high level of stimulus control is usually imposed. Target behaviors are carefully defined, specific environmental variables that affect these behaviors are identified, controlled, systematically manipulated, and reinforcement or punishment contingencies (often intrusive and artificial) are set. On the other hand, programming for maintenance and generalization requires transferring stimulus control so that target behaviors come under the control of less precise and systematic variables. This "loosening" of stimulus control interferes with the demonstration of experimental control over treatment variables that affect target behavior. Therefore, maintenance and generalization research places unusual demands on researchers (e.g., for more time, more data collectors, more training for more persons, more extensive and elaborate data analysis), which increase the cost and effort of such research. These same obstacles also impede the ability of practitioners to conduct training for generality. Educators face additional barriers imposed by the educational system: most teachers are isolated from their colleagues when in direct contact with pupils, and they develop a sense of autonomy and independence from others, even resenting intrusion into their classroom "domain."

Fortunately, maintenance and generalization training may be approached on two fronts: one focusing on procedures that influence the student's behavior during intervention so that it will maintain in other settings, and the other focusing on preparing other settings to support the pupil's new behaviors. If a teacher is unable to influence what goes on in other classrooms, for example, she can still select strategies that can be used in her own classroom. However, it is clear that maintenance and generalization programming is most effective when employed on both fronts, especially with students who are more severely handicapped (Nelson & Rutherford, 1988). One such strategy is **transenvironmental programming** (Anderson-Inman, Walker, & Purcell, 1984), which consists of four components: (1) assessing the behavioral expectations of specific generalization settings, (2) competency training in the special education environment, (3) selection and use of techniques for promoting the transfer of skills across settings, and (4) monitoring and evaluating student performance in generalization settings. Only the second component can be accomplished entirely in the primary treatment setting. Anderson-Inman et al. (1984) observed that the monitoring and evaluation of pupil behavior in targeted generalization settings is the most difficult aspect of transenvironmental programming because of the lack of training and support for regular education personnel to monitor and implement generalization procedures. You should consider these issues when reviewing the maintenance and generalization strategies presented below.

PROGRAMMING FOR MAINTENANCE AND GENERALIZATION

Stokes and Baer (1977) did not consider two of the nine strategies they described — namely, train and hope and sequential modification—to be techniques for programming generality of behavior across time, settings, or trainers. In *train and hope,* assessment probes are conducted in generalization settings, but generalization is not specifically programmed. Yet, in their review, this category accounted for over half of the studies addressing maintenance and generalization. Of the 103 studies specifically reviewed by Rutherford and Nelson (1988), train and hope accounted for 39 of them, or 38 percent of the total. *Sequential modification* was not considered a true generalization strategy because the procedure involves merely replicating the intervention procedures in other settings, without systematically programming for the durability of treatment effects once intervention is withdrawn. Procedures in this category accounted for nine of the studies reviewed by Rutherford and Nelson, or 9 percent. Stokes and Osnes (1986) revised Stokes and Baer's (1977) remaining categories into eleven tactics grouped into three categories that emphasize the general principles underlying the classification.

1. Take advantage of natural communities of reinforcement
   a. Teach relevant behaviors
   b. Modify environments supporting maladaptive behaviors
   c. Recruit natural communities of reinforcement
2. Train diversely
   a. Use sufficient stimulus exemplars
   b. Use sufficient response exemplars
   c. Train loosely
   d. Use indiscriminable contingencies
   e. Reinforce unprompted generalization
3. Incorporate functional mediators
   a. Use common physical stimuli
   b. Use common social stimuli
   c. Use self-mediated stimuli (pp. 417-418)

Take Advantage of Natural Communities of Reinforcement

The strategies included in this category emphasize using reinforcement that is normally available in the natural environment. For instance, appropriate social behaviors are usually followed by pleasant social responses from other persons, which most individuals experience as reinforcing. Thus, the first strategy, *teach relevant behaviors,* involves adding to the pupil's social repertoire behaviors that are likely to set up reciprocal social interactions that strengthen further social initiations on the student's part; for example, greetings and other positive social initiations, and effective language, communication, and interpersonal skills (Stokes & Osnes, 1986). Behaviors that are useful in generalization settings for gaining attention, inviting interactions, or generating praise effectively "trap" reinforcement; thus, the term **trapping effect** is used to describe the tactic of increasing behaviors that effectively capture naturally contingent reinforcement. When using this strategy, however, you should follow these suggestions. First, assess generalization settings to determine what skills and behaviors are required or are likely to result in reinforcement. A skill that is taught in your classroom (e.g., greeting every pupil in the class with a handshake) may not be necessary or even desirable in another setting. Although this strategy is implemented in the primary treatment setting, the trainer must obviously assess the generalization setting to identify relevant behaviors. A procedure that may be used for this purpose is described in the next section.

Our second recommendation involving teaching behaviors that trap reinforcement in generalization environments is to make sure that the student acquires sufficient proficiency in the skill. If the pupil does not use the skill fluently (i.e., as well as other students in the generalization setting) he is less likely to be reinforced when he does use it. One way to increase the probability of reinforcement in generalization settings is to prompt it. For example, in one study teachers had to prompt preschool children to interact with a withdrawn child in order to increase her social initiations enough to occasion their responses naturally (Baer & Wolf, 1970). Some pupils' social behaviors may not come under the control of peer responses without considerable training (e.g., see Gunter, Fox, Brady, Shores, & Cavanaugh, 1988). This points out the need to carefully monitor settings in which generalization is desired. It is also important *not* to provide training in only the primary treatment setting and simply hope that the target behavior occurs in generalization environments (e.g., the train and hope strategy). In fact, it is much more efficient and logical to train social skills in the settings where they are needed from the start (Nelson, 1988). Third, you should not assume that the apparent existence of a natural community of reinforcement for one student's behavior assures that the same naturally occurring consequences will be reinforcing to another pupil (Stokes & Osnes, 1986).

As most teachers and parents know, peers sometimes provide consistent reinforcement of undesired student behaviors. Also, adults and peers in generalization settings may not adequately reinforce desired target behaviors. In such cases, it may be necessary to *modify environments supporting maladaptive behavior.* If the peer group is supporting undesired behavior, this tactic entails controlling the consequences that peers provide for undesired behavior. Managing peer reactions can be extremely difficult, given the number of students and settings that may be involved. Peer-mediated procedures, such as dependent group-oriented contingencies and peer feedback, can be used to shift reinforcement contingencies to supporting desired behaviors. You may also need to prevent reinforcement of undesired behavior from occurring. This may be accomplished by training peers, other staff, or parents to ignore maladaptive behavior and to

attend systematically to desired replacement behavior (Stokes & Osnes, 1986). Obviously, this strategy requires intervention in generalization settings.

Another strategy that can be used when generalization settings fail to reinforce desired behavior is to teach the target pupil to *recruit natural communities of reinforcement.* This consists of training the student not only to emit behaviors desired in the generalization setting but also to draw positive adult or peer attention to these behaviors. This strategy has been effective in recruiting adult attention (e.g., see Graubard, Rosenberg, & Miller, 1971; Hrydowy, Stokes, & Martin, 1984), but its success with peers has not been as well documented. However, Gaylord-Ross, Haring, Breen, and Pitts-Conway (1984) taught autistic adolescent boys to use desirable objects (e.g., PacMan video game, Walkman tape player) and then to use them in social interactions with nonhandicapped peers. Generalized maintenance of those autistic students' social interactions with nonhandicapped pupils was observed. Dependent, group-oriented contingencies, in which the target pupil's desired behavior earns reinforcers desired by peers, have also been observed to increase peers' positive attention to the targeted student (Shores, Apolloni, & Norman, 1976). Initial training may be provided only in the primary treatment setting, but the trainer must be able, at least, to assess the pupil's skill in recruiting reinforcement in the generalization setting in order to adjust training procedures as needed.

Train Diversely

The objective of this group of strategies is to arrange training conditions and response and reinforcement criteria to cover a range of possible circumstances that occur in generalization settings. As with other strategies, those in this category (except (e) reinforce unprompted generalization) may be applied in the primary treatment setting, but they are much more effective when training occurs in generalization settings as well. The first strategy, *use sufficient stimulus exemplars,* means to arrange for more than one or for a small set of discriminative stimuli to control the target behavior. Thus, training should be conducted in more than one setting or under more than one set of training circumstances (Stokes & Osnes, 1986). An application of this strategy that has been used successfully with autistic pupils involves nonhandicapped peers as discriminative stimuli for targeted social behaviors (Simpson, 1987); however, this tactic is much more effective with trained, as opposed to untrained, peer confederates (Hollinger, 1987; McEvoy & Odom, 1987). Teachers should also augment peer-mediated strategies with direct instruction in generalization settings (Shores, 1987). Stokes and Osnes (1986) stress the importance of having a generalization plan to guide training across stimulus examples. You should decide where and with whom generalization is desired and tailor your strategy according to the characteristics of these persons, stimuli, and settings.

The response analogue of the above strategy is to *use sufficient response exemplars,* which involves including more than one example of the target behavior(s) in the training. Using multiple response examples is particularly important when attempting to generalize a complex behavior such as holding a conversation (Stokes & Osnes, 1986). In applying this strategy, the pupil is taught a range of correct responses that are appropriate in given situations and is reinforced for using them. Teaching several acceptable response variations is also useful for situations in which students may be required to exhibit different response topographies in different stimulus settings. For example, various greeting behaviors are appropriate for a male coming up on a group of adolescent boys (e.g., "How's it going?" or "Hey, what's happening?") than for greeting members of the opposite sex (e.g., "Hi!" or "Hello, Sandy."). Getting a drink of water requires different response topographies when at a drinking fountain, a restaurant, or a sink.

Train loosely is closely related to the previous two strategies. Control over the training conditions and acceptable responses is intentionally loosened to permit greater flexibility in the stimuli occasioning target behaviors as well as in the behaviors that are reinforced. More tightly controlled initial training conditions will require proportionately greater attention to loosening stimulus control. Consequently, Stokes and Osnes (1986) recommend that the least tightly controlled yet effective initial training environment be used. Therefore, teachers who have students work in study carrels, who provide daily work in folders, who time seatwork assignments, and who have very specific response requirements for reinforcement may not be facilitating their pupils' success in less structured environments.

The objective of the strategy *use indiscriminable contingencies* is to loosen control over the consequences of behavior. The most common application is to use intermittent schedules of reinforcement to lessen the predictability of reinforcement while at the same time increasing the durability of target behaviors. Koegel and Rincover (1977) demonstrated that even noncontingent reinforcement maintained autistic children's imitation and direction following after systematic treatment contingencies were withdrawn. However, we do not recommend this approach unless you are able to supervise pupils continuously in generalization settings. Another application is to use **vicarious reinforcement,** for example, by praising one student for appropriate behavior. Other pupils who observe this model are more likely to imitate the desired behavior (Kazdin, 1977; Strain, Shores, & Kerr, 1976). This has been referred to as a **ripple** or **spillover effect.** Another way of making reinforcement less predictable is to delay its delivery until some time after the target behavior has occurred or to reinforce the behavior when it occurs simultaneously with other nontarget responses

(Stokes & Osnes, 1986). One note of caution, however: you should be certain that desired responses are well-established under systematic and plentiful schedules of reinforcement before making such reinforcement less discriminable.

The last strategy in this category, *reinforce unprompted generalization,* involves monitoring in generalization settings and reinforcing spontaneous generalization of desired target behaviors when they occur or reinforcing the absence of maladaptive behaviors (Stokes & Osnes, 1986). Obviously, this strategy requires that persons in generalization settings be aware of target behaviors, monitor their occurrence, and apply the appropriate reinforcers contingently.

Incorporate Functional Mediators

The strategies included in this group attempt to take advantage of potential discriminative stimuli that are common to training and generalization settings. Again, assessment and training in generalization settings are critical to the success of these strategies. *Use common physical stimuli* means to ensure that physical discriminative stimuli are present in all settings in which target behavior is desired. Common work or play materials may be used to facilitate generalization. Marholin and Steinman (1977) found that by reinforcing the academic response rate and accuracy of special education pupils when the teacher was present, the academic materials became discriminative stimuli that occasioned working even when the teacher was not present. On the other hand, when the teacher merely reinforced on-task behavior, work productivity dropped when the teacher was out of the room, apparently because the teacher was the discriminative stimulus for academic responses in this condition. Peers are logical common stimuli when the next strategy, *use common social stimuli,* is selected. Significant peers and adults present in generalization settings may participate in training sessions in the primary treatment setting, either early in train-

ing or later, when transfer of training is contemplated (Stokes & Osnes, 1986). For example, Gunter et al. (1988) used nonhandicapped peers who were present in generalization settings as discriminative stimuli in the training environment for severely handicapped students' appropriate social initiations. This tactic is an option when trainers cannot work in generalization settings, but assessment in these environments is necessary to ensure that interactions in these settings are consistent with the generalization plan.

A readily available source of common stimuli is the pupils themselves. Thus the final strategy, *use self-mediated stimuli,* involves having the student carry or deliver stimuli that are discriminative of appropriate responses. Instructions, prompts, reminders written on a card, or a string on a finger, are tangible discriminative stimuli, whereas teaching the student to self-administer a verbal instruction or cue is intangible but more natural to generalization settings. Self-recording, self-assessment, and self-reinforcement are procedures that also employ self-mediated stimuli. This strategy is potentially one of the most useful and least intrusive for promoting transfer of training, but it is also difficult for researchers to evaluate the extent to which self-mediated procedures are used by subjects. Consequently, we are less confident in stating unequivocally that these procedures are responsible for some of the gains attributed to them. It also is important to realize that prior training in using self-mediated strategies is critical to ensuring their effectiveness in generalization environments (Polsgrove, 1979).

Cognitive behavior modification is a relatively new approach that involves teaching students cognitive strategies to help them solve problems. These strategies incorporate an analysis of the tasks to be performed (or the social problems to be solved) and teaching the strategy through modeling, self-instruction, and self-evaluation (Meichenbaum, 1977). For example, if a student needed to learn how to control his temper, the teacher might teach him—

through modeling, role-playing, and individual or group discussions—a set of steps to rehearse when he finds himself losing control (e.g., count to ten, leave the situation, repeat to himself that the other person is not trying to "get" him).

The strategies that you design to extend treatment effects to other settings, to other persons, to other specific discriminative stimuli, or over time will of course depend on your objectives for the student and situation. It is likely that a combination of strategies will be more appropriate to specific circumstances than a single procedure. We strongly recommend that you develop a generalization plan to guide your efforts and facilitate your evaluation of its effects. A format for this purpose is provided in Figure 12-1. Checklists like that illustrated in Figure 12-2 can be used to identify resource persons to assist in generalization programming. Once you have gained fluency in writing intervention and generalization plans, you may

Figure 12-1. Sample Generalization Plan Format

Student: _____ Target behavior: _____
Primary treatment setting: _____

Intervention Plan: (Include objective, procedures, data decision rules, review
                dates, etc.)

Outcome: (Narrative description, dates plan reviewed/revised, data summaries or
           graphs, etc.)

Generalization Plan
  Objective:
    Terminal Behavior:

      Conditions: (Settings, persons, reinforcers, schedule, etc.)

      Criteria:

    Strategy: (Procedures used, resources needed, etc.)

    Evaluation Plan: (Data to be collected, when it will be collected, who will collect
                  it, who will summarize/evaluate data, data decision rule, etc.)

    Outcome: (Narrative description, dates plan reviewed/revised, data summaries
            or graphs, etc.)

find it more convenient to incorporate the latter into your intervention plan from the beginning.

In discussing maintenance and generalization training strategies, we have emphasized the importance of assessment and training in the environments where skills are expected or needed. Interventions that fail to address the demands and idiosyncrasies of generalization settings are not likely to produce effects that persist in these environments. Thus, severe limitations are imposed on intervention agents who are unable to gain access to these settings because their direct teaching responsibilities prohibit it, because other teachers will not tolerate observers in their classrooms, or because staff members will not cooperate with training procedures. The organization of most public school environments is a significant obstacle to effective maintenance and generalization of treatment effects. Although you may have no authority to change factors such as teaching loads or released time from direct instruction, you may be able to identify resources in the school in order to accomplish generalization objectives. Your own enthusiasm and dedication to helping your pupils will assist in recruiting reinforcement and support for your efforts. We have known educators who, through modeling hard work and determination, evoked similar efforts by their colleagues. As more school districts adopt teacher assistance teams or **collaborative consultation** models (Idol, Paolucci-Whitcomb, & Nevin, 1986), better mobilization of the many resources available in schools (and communities) will follow.

Programming for the Transition of Students to Less Restrictive Environments

This section describes strategies directed toward the educational goal of moving students to less restrictive educational settings or to postsecondary school environments. The maintenance and generalization procedures just presented may be applied to this goal, of course. Our rationale for presenting **transition strategies** in a separate section is that movement of pupils to less restrictive environments is a common educational goal, and it involves transferring students and their entire repertoires of behavior to new settings. Thus, it is a broader task than that of programming for the maintenance and generalization of specific target behaviors. In addition, the movement of students among instructional settings is an activity peculiar to schools. Although it is desirable to generalize changes in those behaviors targeted in the primary treatment setting to these environments, each classroom teacher also has individual expectations regarding the behaviors required in his or her setting. Transition planning must take these expectations into account, and strategies for accomplishing the movement of pupils into less restrictive settings must involve a broad range of activities. Procedures have been developed for the specific purpose of facilitating this movement, especially in the case of handicapped students. We describe strategies to facilitate transitions to less restrictive educational settings and to adult environments separately, although many procedures, including those discussed in the previous section, are appropriate for either goal. We also consider follow-up assessment procedures because these are important for evaluating both pupils' status after leaving treatment settings and the effectiveness of the programs they received.

TRANSITIONS TO LESS RESTRICTIVE EDUCATIONAL SETTINGS

Successfully reintegrating your students into the mainstream of school life constitutes one of your most complex and difficult tasks. You must not only evaluate and develop appropriate pupil behaviors, you must also coordinate a number of environmental variables: schedules, curricula, materials, school staff, and other pu-

Figure 12-2. In-School Resource Checklist

PERSONNEL/AGENCIES	Willing to work with pupils?	Supportive of your program?	Have cooperated with you previously?	Willing to collect data?	Will require supervision?	Will require training?	Willing to devote time above normal duties?	Have reliably carried out procedures with pupils before?	COMMENTS (Phone numbers, etc.)
Teachers:									
Aides & Volunteers:									
Speech Clinician:									
Guidance Counselor:									
School Psychologist:									
Vice Principal:									
Principal:									
Secretaries:									
School Nurse:									
Custodian:									
Bus Driver:									
Cafeteria Workers:									
Others:									

pils, to name but a few. A technology for achieving this change is sorely lacking; however, we can offer suggestions and guidelines based upon our experiences and those re-ported by others. We begin with an assumption: you have improved the student's academic and social functioning to the point where he or she is able to profit from a less restrictive environment. If this assumption is met, the issue is one of generalization and maintenance of behavior change, which of necessity, involves arrangements with other persons.

The probability that critical behaviors will be maintained and generalized outside restrictive settings is enhanced by having a complete continuum of services available in the building. That is, rather than going directly from a self-contained, highly individualized program into a group-oriented regular classroom, students enter a resource room and are phased into regular classrooms from there. It is also helpful to specify entry and exit competencies for each level. For example, Taylor and Soloway (1973) devised a service delivery system consisting of four levels. *Preacademic competencies* include such skills as paying attention, starting an assignment immediately, working continuously without interruption, following task directions, doing what one is told, taking part verbally in discussions, getting along with others, and demonstrating adequacy in perceptual-motor and language skills. *Academic competencies* include proficiency in all core subjects, as well as being accurate, being neat, efficient, and well organized. *Setting competencies* involve learning to profit from instruction provided in settings found in regular classrooms (independent work, large and small group work, etc.), and *reward competencies* range from responding to tangible reinforcers, at the most basic level, to being reinforced by social recognition and the acquisition of new knowledge and skills. Pupils in the classroom are grouped according to their level of competence with regard to these skill categories. They move up through the levels as they demonstrate more advanced competencies. The environments corresponding to each level consist of a self-contained setting, a resource room (with increasingly greater time spent in regular classrooms), and the regular classroom. Table 12-1 illustrates a level system of student competencies leading to functioning in a regular classroom. This system was designed by Taylor and Soloway (1973).

Similar level or phase systems have been developed for secondary programs (e.g., Braaten, 1979) and for children with severe behavior disorders in an institutional program (Hewett & Taylor, 1980). The primary advantage of a level system is the specification of a hierarchy of competencies that are necessary for successful integration into less restrictive environments. Placement in a given level is based on performance, rather than on a diagnostic label. Within a given level, progress upward is maximized by a curricular emphasis on those competencies needed for the next higher level. The case study at the end of this chapter describes one teacher's level system.

You may not have the prerogative of developing a complete delivery system. However, you can arrange your own curriculum in terms of a hierarchy of competencies. If progress through the levels is associated with increasing independence and powerful (and naturalistic) reinforcers, student motivation to advance will pose few problems. However, your system will work only if it is based on skills your pupils actually need for success in the less restrictive environments within your school or institution. Therefore, you should begin by determining the minimum requirements of each environment. For example, what skills do pupils need to be manageable in regular classes in your building (e.g., which behaviors are more likely to be reinforced in the less-restrictive environment)? In general, we believe these consist of appropriate social behavior, compliance with teacher requests and directions, and basic language proficiency.

These general skills, as well as the school survival skills described in Chapter 8, suggest some target behaviors for students you are considering for movement to less restrictive settings. However, specific skill requirements will vary for each classroom teacher; therefore, you must assess each environment separately. The AIMS assessment system (Walker, 1986) presented in Chapter 2 consists of five assessment procedures and is designed to identify the behavioral standards and expectations of individ-

Table 12-1. A Level System of Student Competencies Leading to Regular Classroom Functioning

Continuum of Settings and Competencies Required →

Levels	Preacademic I Self-Contained Setting →	Preacademic II Resource Setting →	Academic I Resource Setting →	Academic II Regular Class Setting
Preacademic	*Major emphasis:* —Paying attention —Beginning work immediately —Working continuously —Following directions —Doing what one is told	*Minor emphasis:* —Behaviors stressed in preacademic *Major emphasis:* —Taking part in discussion —Getting along with others	*Minor emphasis:* —Preacademic behaviors stated in preacademic I & II	Regular classroom
Academic	*Minor emphasis:* —Academic assignments —Being accurate —Being neat	*Major emphasis:* —Basic school subjects —Remediation is supplemented by special materials and resources	*Major emphasis:* —School subjects —Some remedial —Some grade-level curriculum	Regular classroom
Setting	—Student works independently at desk or booth —1:1 relationship with teacher	—Student works in teacher/small-group setting —Students work independently in shared desk space —Group interaction and cooperation emphasized	—Simulates regular classroom —Large group receiving instruction from teacher —Opportunities to function independently	Regular classroom
Reward	—Checkmark system linked to tangible rewards for appropriate social and academic behaviors —Any incentive considered that will motivate child	—Checkmark system linked to free time —Greater emphasis on social approval	—Numerical grading system for effort, quality of work, and citizenship	Regular classroom

Note: This information is taken from F. D. Taylor & M. M. Soloway. The Madison School Plan: A functional model for merging the regular and special classrooms. In E. N. Deno (Ed.), *Instructional alternational alternatives for exceptional children.* Reston, VA: Council for Exceptional Children, 1973, pp. 147–149.

ual classroom settings, to assess the target pupil's behavior with respect to these expectations, to evaluate mainstream teachers' resistance to placement of handicapped students in their classrooms based on correlates of handicapping conditions, and to conduct follow-up observations of pupils after placement. The *SBS Inventory of Teacher Social Behavior Standards and Expectations* (Walker & Rankin, 1980b) is a 107-item rating scale, divided into three sections, describing adaptive and maladaptive student classroom behavior. The first section consists of fifty-six items describing adaptive student behavior, which the mainstream teacher rates as *critical, desirable,* or *unimportant* to a successful adjustment in her classroom. The fifty-one items in Section II describe maladaptive behaviors that the teacher rates as *unacceptable, tolerated,* or *acceptable.* Section III asks the teacher to reevaluate the items she rated as critical and unacceptable in terms of (1) whether the behavior of a pupil rated as deviant on these items would have to occur at "normal" rates prior to the student being integrated into her classroom, or (2) whether she would require technical assistance for these behaviors following the student's placement. The *SBS Checklist of Correlates of Child Handicapping Conditions* (Walker & Rankin, 1980a) is a twenty-four-item checklist describing conditions and characteristics commonly associated with handicapping conditions that, if manifested by target pupils, often cause teachers to resist placement. The **Walker-Rankin Child Behavior Rating Scale** is a criterion-referenced scale on which the teacher in the sending setting assesses the target pupil's behavioral status on the items the potential receiving teacher designates as critical or unacceptable (Walker, 1986). Thus, these three instruments allow the sending teacher to directly compare the receiving teacher's expectations with the student's current behavior. Discrepancies identify target behaviors for intervention prior to placement. The remaining instruments in the AIMS system are used to assess the adequacy of the pupil's

classroom and peer social adjustment following placement (Walker, 1986), and these are discussed in the section describing follow-up evaluation procedures.

Of course, students should also be prepared to meet the academic expectations of less restrictive environments if they are to have successful experiences in these settings. The delineation of academic instructional strategies is beyond the scope of this book, and we refer you to other sources for these (e.g., Mercer & Mercer, 1985). However, the general approach should be the same as for preparing students to meet the social demands of less restrictive settings: identify the behavioral expectations, assess the student with regard to these expectations, teach the pupil in the more restrictive setting up to the criterion levels expected in the less restrictive environment, provide generalization training in the new setting, and follow-up to determine whether the student is meeting expectations. It also helps to plan the student's academic program with the receiving teacher. In view of the likely possibility that the pupil may need special support and assistance not available to other students in the setting, you may need to help the teacher adapt instruction by providing special materials, tutoring the pupil, or training the teacher in errorless or mastery learning procedures. If your school has formed teacher assistance teams, staff may be available to assist teachers in adapting instruction and management practices.

We encourage you to use such teacher support services to facilitate the transition of your pupils to less restrictive settings. The more that dealing with behavior problem students is seen as a responsibility shared by all professional educators and not just by those who are certified as "special," the more quickly professionals will learn the necessary skills and accept responsibility for guaranteeing these students their educational rights.

In selecting target behaviors for intervention, with the goal of mainstreaming handicapped pupils in mind, appropriate social skills should be assigned a high priority. The social skill deficits of handicapped students are well documented. For example, Gresham, Elliott, and Black (1987) found that teacher ratings of social skills alone could be used to classify accurately 75 percent of a sample of mainstreamed, mildly handicapped pupils. In other words, lack of social skills appears to be a factor that discriminates between handicapped and nonhandicapped children. Social skills rating scales, such as those discussed in Chapter 2, may be used to evaluate pupils' social skills relative to normative standards and to select target behaviors for training prior to mainstreaming placement.

The settings in which training is conducted are an important consideration. Whereas it is desirable to provide initial social skills training in settings where a high level of stimulus control over instructional and response variables can be ensured, the most effective maintenance and generalization strategies involve training in generalization settings. For instance, the use of multiple peer exemplars is a critical social skill generalization strategy, and research clearly supports using nonhandicapped peers as confederates (Simpson, 1987). Further, although social skills are logical targets for trapping reinforcement, handicapped pupils acquire these responses more efficiently when peer confederates are trained to interact with them rather than when handicapped students are simply taught appropriate social responses and then placed in mainstream settings (Hollinger, 1987; McEvoy & Odom, 1987). More durable patterns of confederate interactions, in turn, occur when handicapped students are taught to make social initiations toward these peers (Gaylord-Ross & Haring, 1987). These strategies require that reciprocal social interactions between handicapped and nonhandicapped students be trained in generalization (i.e., mainstream) settings. This requirement is difficult for many school districts to implement because the staff members with expertise in social skills training (e.g., special education teachers) are restricted from working in settings with non-

handicapped students by their instructional responsibilities in special education environments. The most economical solution to this dilemma is to make social skills training the responsibility of regular education staff, but given the current pressures on general educators, this is not likely to happen (Braaten, Kauffman, Braaten, Polsgrove, & Nelson, 1988).

TRANSITIONS TO POST-SECONDARY SCHOOL ENVIRONMENTS

Concern regarding the adjustment of students to adult living has primarily focused on the handicapped. PL 94-142 mandated that schools serve handicapped youth through age 21, and subsequent amendments (PL 98-199, PL 99-457) have added specific emphasis to the provision of **transition services** to accomplish this objective. Follow-up studies of the postschool status of handicapped youth indicate that the special education enterprise has not been overwhelmingly successful in terms of preparing these young persons for successful postschool adjustment (see Kerr, Nelson, & Lambert, 1987). The *criterion of ultimate functioning* (Brown, Nietupski, & Hamre-Nietupski, 1976) has influenced curriculum planning for severely handicapped pupils for a decade. As we explained in Chapter 2, this top-down approach to curriculum design begins with the assessment of the skill demands of the least restrictive adult environments in which the student is likely to function, and the curriculum is developed around pupils' skill deficiencies with regard to these expectations. However, determining which adult environments are least restrictive for students exhibiting widely varying levels of cognitive, academic, and social functioning is complex in itself and must be accomplished before the expectations of these settings can be assessed. Therefore, specific postschool objectives for students with less severe disabilities, based on assumptions about the limits of their future capabilities, are more difficult to develop while they are still in school; however, we are not suggesting that objectives relevant to postschool living cannot be developed for these students. Appropriate social behaviors are useful in all adult settings, and are needed by persons at all levels of cognitive functioning. Students who interview for jobs or admission to post-secondary schools, who go out on dates, or who visit their local hair salon need to employ these skills every day.

Unfortunately, it is apparent that the lack of such skills is a common denominator among individuals who are chronically maladjusted. For example, Walker and his colleagues (Shinn, Ramsey, Walker, Stieber, & O'Neill, 1987; Walker, Shinn, O'Neill, & Ramsey, 1987) identified behavioral differences between fifth-grade boys who were designated "at risk" for engaging in antisocial behavior (on the basis of familial variables) and a control group of boys who were not designated "at risk." The behavior patterns that differentiated the "at risk" group included less time engaged in academics, higher rates of negative interactions with peers, more school discipline contacts, and lower teacher ratings of social skills. The behavioral characteristics of older youth and adults who are "at risk" for criminal behavior or who are incarcerated reveal similar patterns (see Nelson, Rutherford, & Wolford, 1987). Thus, early maladaptive social behavior patterns appear to be predictive of lifelong patterns of social failure (Robbins, 1966; Van Hasselt, Hersen, Whitehill, & Bellack, 1979). We agree with the authorities on social skills training, whose work we have cited, that early identification and remediation of social skills deficits in children who are at risk should be a major educational priority.

Planning for transitions to adulthood may not prevent the failure of all, or even many, students with behavior problems, but neither should it be assumed that the existence of problem behaviors condemns pupils to lives of crime or institutionalization. Transition programs for adolescents are useful for bridging the gap between school and productive adult experiences. They are based on a **transition plan,** which includes specified goals, objectives, and procedures for their implementation. If such a plan is to be meaningfully linked to the student's postschool life, it should be initiated well before graduation. Transition plans *must* be developed with persons who have a stake in the pupil's postschool adjustment (e.g., parents, the student herself) and they should take into account the full range of options the student may consider as an adult. Therefore, alternatives such as college, military service, and independent living should be considered in addition to employment. Support services likely to be needed (e.g., community mental health, developmental disabilities, vocational rehabilitation) should be indicated, and representatives from agencies that provide these services should participate in drafting the transition plan. Implementation of the plan should begin during the pupil's secondary school experience and should continue until the structure and support provided by the plan are no longer needed. If you are in a position to be involved in post-secondary school transition planning, consult Kerr et al. (1987).

It would be naive to assume that school-based interventions alone are sufficient to enable adolescents with behavior problems to successfully enter adult living and working environments. Ideally, they should also have the benefit of community-based training during their public school years. Community-based instruction has played an important role in the curriculum of severely handicapped pupils, and many good models are available (e.g., see Goetz, Guess, & Stremel-Campbell, 1987; Taylor, Bilken, & Knoll, 1987). Much less attention has been paid to teaching social skills to mildly handicapped students in the community settings where these skills are critical to their successful adjustment. Given the recent data indicating that many mildly handicapped adolescents fail to make adequate adjustments to adult life (e.g., see Edgar, 1987), appropriate changes in secondary school curriculum for these students clearly are needed.

FOLLOW-UP ASSESSMENT

The purposes of follow-up assessments are to evaluate the student's current status with regard to IEP or intervention objectives, to evaluate the effectiveness of the educational program or intervention for a pupil, or to evaluate the accuracy with which other staff members implement intervention procedures. Follow-up data thus serve three functions: to certify that objectives have been reached; to provide feedback to use in revising programs for future students; and to determine whether interventions are being properly implemented.

If the student in question has been certified as handicapped, follow-up data regarding IEP goals and objectives may be used as a basis for deciding that special education classification is no longer needed. In Chapter 1 we recommended that IEP committees specify criteria for *decertification* of pupils once the conditions that caused them to be labeled and certified are remediated. IEPs should contain goals and objectives related to successful integration or reintegration into the educational mainstream; therefore, follow-up assessment in mainstream settings will be needed for making decertification decisions. Follow-up evaluation of the maintenance and generalization of intervention effects is more specific and precise because the focus of assessment is on targeted behaviors. These assessments may or may not occur in other settings.

The specific follow-up assessment procedures used depend upon the student's current educational placement. If the pupil is in your classroom, follow-up may involve conducting measurement probes of targeted behaviors after an educational program or intervention strategy has been terminated. If the student has been moved to a less restrictive setting, the same behaviors should be assessed, but the measurement strategy used will be influenced by the setting and the person conducting the assessment. For example, if you must rely on a regular classroom teacher to do the assessment, you will probably select a less technically demanding procedure than you would if you were conducting the assessment yourself. In such circumstances you may elect to have the teacher complete a behavior rating scale, evaluate the student against criteria for behaviors in her classroom (e.g., Is the target pupil's frequency of disruptive behavior higher than, about the same as, or lower than that of the average student?). Frequency counts of discrete behaviors of course are preferable, and these data are even better when rates of similar behaviors collected on nontarget peers are available for comparison (see Chapter 2). However, such procedures require trained observers.

Two of the instruments in the AIMS system (Walker, 1986) may be used to evaluate the adequacy of students' classroom and peer social adjustments in less restrictive settings. The Classroom Adjustment Code (CAC) is a five-second interval recording system that measures three categories of pupil and teacher behavior. The pupil behavior codes are *on-task, off-task,* and *unacceptable* behaviors. The teacher codes include *approval/feedback, providing instruction/command,* and *reprimand.* Thus, the CAC can be used to assess interactions occurring between teachers and target students. For example, CAC observations may reveal that a mainstream teacher consistently attends to undesired pupil behavior with punitive consequences, while at the same time ignoring desired behaviors. The second instrument, the Social Interaction Code (SIC) assesses three major classes of events associated with the pupil's social interactions with peers. These include the structure or activity context in which such interactions occur (five categories are used to assess whether the target student is alone or engaged in structured versus unstructured activities), the type and quality of the pupil's interactive behavior (assessed with five appropriate and five inappropriate behavior code categories), and negative peer reactions to the student's social behavior. The CAC and the SIC are designed to evaluate general interaction patterns rather than specific target behaviors, and observer training is required to use them properly. Of course, they could be used to measure adult-to-student or student-to-student interactions in other settings as well (e.g., work environments). The AIMS System is a useful package for planning and evaluating the transition of students to less restrictive educational environments.

Although data obtained from the procedures just described cannot be compared to the graphs and charts used to analyze the student and his program while in your classroom, they can serve to *socially validate* that behavioral changes have taken place. Because how the student is perceived by others in his or her natural environment is the ultimate test of success in readjusting, these data should not be treated lightly. However, if you can obtain measures that are more comparable to the data you collected during intervention phases, a more specific analysis of the student's current status is possible. This can be important if target behaviors are once again problematic and you need to assess their occurrence in the new environment. If you are unable to collect these data, or if your presence in the environment influences the pupil's behavior, you can follow the guidelines presented in Chapter 3 for training other observers.

Finally, the length and schedule of follow-up assessments should be geared to the student, the behaviors, and the settings in which assessments are conducted. If you follow the suggestions offered in Chapter 3 (collect data that are sensitive to the changes you want to occur; measure only behaviors to which you will respond) follow-up data collection should not be unduly time-consuming. You may want to monitor some behaviors closely (e.g., verbal threats having a history of leading to physical aggression); others may require less regular

scrutiny because they are less important to the pupil's success in the new setting. Some data are easy to collect (e.g., number of assignments completed), whereas other data require more time and effort (e.g., time off-task). In general, you should attempt to use data that are readily available and that the classroom teacher or caregiver keeps and uses anyway.

If the student has been transferred out of your building or even further away, follow-up will be sporadic, at best. Few agencies are interested in the status of clients once their direct service responsibilities have ended. Still, you may make telephone or mail contacts to assess your former pupils' present status. No matter where former students are located, we recommend that you schedule follow-up contacts on your calendar so you will not forget. Initially, follow-up intervals should be brief (one to two or three weeks). The schedule may be thinned as time passes (one, six, and eighteen months). At some point, you will be able to decide to discontinue evaluation. As with other phases of assessment, your data will suggest when this point is reached.

Another reason for conducting follow-up assessments is to evaluate the implementation of maintenance and generalization training procedures. These evaluations address the question of **procedural reliability** (Tawney & Gast, 1984), or the extent to which intervention procedures are being followed. The recommended format for such assessments is a behavioral checklist containing a list of intervention procedures that are checked (by an observer familiar with the intervention) according to whether they are properly implemented. Figure 12–3 illustrates a procedural reliability checklist for a DRO intervention. Intervention steps that are not being properly implemented indicate a need for feedback or retraining of the responsible persons. Assessment of procedural reliability is especially important for identifying implementation failures when staff members report that a procedure "is not working."

Figure 12-3. DRO Procedural Reliability Checklist

	Observations		
Observer: _____ Observation Dates: _____			
	1	2	3
1. Length of DRO interval is set (Interval length _____ secs/mins)	_____	_____	_____
2. Teacher accurately observes occurrence/ nonoccurrence of target behavior during interval	_____	_____	_____
3. Behavior *does not* occur during interval	_____	_____	_____
3.1. Teacher delivers reinforcer immediately upon end of interval	_____	_____	_____
3.2. Teacher resets interval timer	_____	_____	_____
4. Behavior *does* occur during interval	_____	_____	_____
4.1. Teacher does not respond to behavior	_____	_____	_____
4.2. Teacher resets interval timer	_____	_____	_____

Working Outside the Classroom

The title of this section suggests that we consider individual classrooms to be the primary treatment setting for most students exhibiting problematic social behaviors. This is probably true in the majority of cases. However, remember that we began this chapter with a rationale for working in other settings based on the observation that undesired or maladaptive social behaviors may occur in many settings and that the successful management of a problem in one setting may not affect the same problem, or other problems, in other settings. Consequently, even if you serve behavior problem students in a single classroom setting, your work will lead you into other settings, both within and outside the school. In this section

we present a number of suggestions and strategies to increase your effectiveness with other professionals and lay persons in these settings. These suggestions are organized into three categories: working with school personnel, working with parents, and working with community persons and agencies.

WORKING WITH SCHOOL PERSONNEL

In a typical school building (or institution), there are a number of persons you can use as resources for your students. The extent of their involvement may range from delivering social praise to taking pupils on after-school trips, from simply rating performance as acceptable or unacceptable to taking frequency data, and from following a plan worked out by you to collaborating in the development of a complete intervention strategy. Different persons may prove useful for different functions, and we hope the checklist illustrated in Figure 12-2 helps you develop a profile of your various personnel resources.

Before you approach *anyone* to assist you with a pupil or program, get your objective clearly in mind. Do you want to assess the generalization of change in a target behavior? Do you want to evaluate a trial mainstream placement? Do you want to establish other persons as social reinforcers? Do you want to maximize reinforcement by using stronger reinforcers outside your classroom? Do you need physical assistance handling an aggressive student in emergency situations? Each objective dictates a different tactic. When you enlist the cooperation of other people, you should clearly explain what you want them to do, as well as when and how they are to communicate to you regarding their work with the pupil or pupils.

Once again, a written contract or agreement is the best approach if the program is complex. Remember that the student is your client (the one who is to benefit from the program). We emphasize this because conflicts may arise between involved parties, such as parents and school officials or child welfare workers. Each party may want to impose its agenda on your program (the parents want their child to pick up his clothes; the probation officer wants him to obey a curfew). This focus is somewhat different from the one you use when you are serving as a consultant, for in the latter case, while you are trying to relieve difficulties involving the student, your client is the person who comes to you with the problem. Many a good teacher has been rendered ineffective by trying to serve too many clients with conflicting demands. A written contract can specify objectives and roles at the outset, thereby preventing many such episodes.

Also remember that adult behavior needs to be reinforced too; therefore, be sure to show your appreciation for someone's assistance, and make your acknowledgement specific to the behavior you are reinforcing ("Your data on Alice's talking-out are very good"; "Thank you for the reports of Tommy's performance on his daily algebra quizzes"). You can increase the likelihood of a plan being followed by providing the structure or materials yourself: a checklist for regular classroom teachers to complete, a roll of smiley-face stickers for the cafeteria cashier or bus driver to put on the shirts of well-behaved students, a wrist counter for the librarian to use in counting talk-outs.

The school principal is traditionally regarded by pupils (and teachers) as the major disciplinarian for a building. In view of this, having the principal deliver reinforcement can be a potent tactic, as has been demonstrated in several studies. Copeland, Brown and Hall (1974) found in three separate studies that contingent principal recognition and praise increased attendance and academic performance. Brown, Copeland, and Hall (1972) involved a principal in administering tokens, playing basketball with pupils, and providing the opportunity to work on bicycles in the school basement, contingent upon appropriate school behaviors.

The school counselor can similarly provide reinforcement or other services. Clore (1974) had a school-phobic child report to the counselor's office each morning, and the counselor assisted in successfully phasing the child back into his classroom.

The school administrative staff may be helpful in other ways as well. For example, many reinforcing activities occur around the school office: pupils can be allowed to deliver attendance slips or notes, answer the telephone, run the ditto machine, file, or perform other office tasks as reinforcement for desired behaviors. The main reason such opportunities are not exploited is that teachers seldom think of them. Few persons will refuse to provide such experiences if you ask them (and remember to follow up with reinforcement).

Involving yourself has the further advantage of increasing your visibility to, and interaction with, school staff, which lessens the stigma attached to both teachers and students in segregated special classrooms. Volunteering to sponsor all-school activities such as clubs and social events will improve your standing with pupils outside your classroom. Also, you should not shirk cafeteria or bus duty, nor should you do all your work in the classroom where you are isolated from your colleagues. Instead, spend some of your time working in the teachers' lounge. In our experience, the more successful special education programs are run by teachers who are actively involved in the total school environment. When you are working with behaviorally disordered pupils, visibility and involvement are especially important because of the fear and misconceptions regarding persons having mental health problems.

WORKING WITH PARENTS

The two general objectives of working with parents are (1) training parents to manage problem behavior in their home or neighborhood, and (2) getting parents to support classroom objectives. Each goal calls for a slightly different approach.

Parent Training

If your objective is to train parents to deal with behavior problems at home, you are putting yourself in a consultative relationship. Because parents have learned to expect teachers to deal directly with their children and, consequently, may be less prone to let you help them, this relationship can be a difficult one. Also, parents of children with behavior problems (especially children who have been labeled emotionally disturbed or behaviorally disordered) may be defensive about admitting their problems because it is fairly common to attribute children's behavior disorders to faulty parenting. One way around this problem is to treat it as an educational issue, rather than as a problem requiring psychotherapy or analysis. We have found that presenting home management training as

an educational program overcomes many resistances. It helps, of course, for the parents to realize they have a problem and for them to ask for assistance. Another suggestion is to maintain your focus on the child. Presenting ideas and techniques to help the parents manage present problems is likely to meet with less resistance than giving them the impression that their parenting skills need a major overhaul.

When parents do recognize a problem and request your help, you have several options. One is to set up a specific program, following the consultation steps outlined above. Table 12-2 presents specific procedures for setting up a management program in the home. Note that these procedures are identical to those we recommend for use in the classroom for dealing with problem behavior. There is evidence that parents can successfully implement such procedures with a minimum of professional guidance. For example, Christophersen, Arnold, Hill, and Quilitch (1972) taught two sets of parents, who had five children between them, to administer a token economy in their homes. The parents successfully altered twenty-one problem behaviors, including performing chores, bickering, teasing, whining, and refusing to go to bed. However, as the authors observed, these were not severe behavior disorders. We might also question how well the techniques that the parents learned would apply to their handling of other problem situations.

Training parents in the principles of applied behavior analysis or social learning theory constitutes one alternative to specific problem-solving consultation. There are a number of books designed to teach these principles to parents (e.g., Becker, 1971; Patterson, 1975; Patterson & Gullion, 1971). Although these books have been given to parents to read on their own, we recommend that you provide specific instruction along with the reading. A combination of training in behavioral principles and techniques and in specific problem-solving consultation has been found to be more effec-

Table 12-2. Specific Procedures for Establishing a Home Management Program

Objectives	Activities
1. Pinpoint and define behavior (operationally).	List and objectively define the family's major concerns about child's behavior.
	Rank those concerns from highest to lowest priority.
	List and objectively define the child's positive, adaptive, and desirable behaviors.
	Select one behavior of critical importance to the family. *Caution: Probability of success is a prime factor in selecting a behavior to change.*
2. Evaluate situations and environments in which the behavior occurs.	Evaluate the situations, environments, and circumstances under which the target behavior usually occurs.
3. Specify contingencies.	Evaluate the reactions of the parents and others after the problem behavior occurs.
4. Observe and record target behavior daily.	Describe simple recording system and corresponding recording sheet.
	Observe and record target behavior using system and appropriate data sheet on a daily basis.
	Check on reliability between parents and parent counselor in defining target behavior.
	Make necessary adjustments in behavior definition or recording procedures.
5. Chart and inspect target behavior data.	Devise simple visual displays (charts) for target behavior.
	Record daily observations on charts.
	Inspect data for variability and trend before ending baseline period.
6. Devise intervention plans and establish performance expectations.	Develop appropriate reinforcing and punishing contingencies for specific target behavior.
	Ask parents what consequences have been effective or are likely to be effective with their child.
	Ask parents to describe techniques they have used before and to describe their effects.

	Interventions must be
	    practical
	    economical
	    feasible
	    realistic
	    applicable
	    effective

	Establish a desired rate (frequency/day) for target behavior.
	Establish a desired target date for the behavior and the respective desired rates.
	Establish sequentially placed interim rates and dates for the target behavior.

Table 12-2. *continued*

Objectives	Activities

7. Implement plans.	Apply contingencies to target behavior using
	    consistency
	    constancy
	    immediacy

	Observe and record target behavior daily.
	Chart target behavior daily.
8. Analyze data.	Inspect target behavior with respect to desired rates and dates.
9. Maintain or change intervention plans.	Suggest appropriate modifications for program maintenance or change.

tive than training in general principles and procedures alone (Glogowger & Sloop, 1976). The disadvantage of this approach is that it requires after-school time.

If you have several parents in training, a parent training group may be a useful strategy (Rinn, Vernon, & Wise, 1975). Several formats have been used. The format we prefer combines instruction in behavioral principles and procedures with specific problem-solving consultation. Parents show more interest in learning principles when they can immediately apply them to their children's behaviors. However, as Ferber, Keeley, and Shemberg (1974) found, a short-term parent course may be insufficient without long-term follow-up and retraining for other problem behaviors. Also, aggressive children who are community problems may not be helped at all through parent training (Ferber et al., 1974). For these individuals, more extensive community-based intervention may be required. If you need to go this far, consider referring the problem to another agency (see Chapter 13).

Parental Support of Classroom Goals

The goal of getting parents to support classroom objectives first involves some type of school-home communication system, for parents can hardly be expected to support the objectives of a behavior change program if they do not understand them or have little access to information regarding their child's progress.[1] Traditional reporting systems (grade cards, notes to parents, etc.) are unsuitable for this type of communication because they are infrequent and unsystematic, and they tend to communicate little useful information. Parental response to an unsatisfactory report card may be inappropriate, or parents may fail to respond at all to good reports. Therefore, we suggest a frequent (daily or weekly) reporting system that conveys meaningful information to parents, and to which they may respond in a systematic manner. This implies that you have worked out a plan with the parents beforehand. Tell them what to expect (e.g., a daily or weekly report containing points their child has earned for academic work and for social behavior each day), when to expect it (e.g., every day after school), and how to respond to each report (e.g., praise when the point total is above thirty-five, and for each subject or area for which four or more points are awarded).

In cases where you need more solid home support, work with parents to set up more explicit home contingencies based on their child's school performance. For example, they may

---

[1]PL 94-142 requires that individual program objectives be developed in collaboration with parents and guarantees parents access to their child's school records.

Figure 12-4. Daily Report Cards

Date _____

Classroom Work

☐ Good 😊

☐ Bad ☹

_____
Teacher's Signature
A

Date _____

Classroom Behavior

☐ Good 😊

☐ Bad ☹

_____
Teacher's Signature
B

Date _____

Social Behavior
☐ Acceptable
☐ Unacceptable

Academic Work
☐ Completed on time
☐ Not completed
☐ Accuracy acceptable
☐ Accuracy unacceptable

_____
Teacher's Signature
C

Date _____

Reading   _____
Math   _____
Spelling   _____
Science   _____
P.E.   _____
Lunchroom   _____
Playground   _____
Social Behavior _____
Bonus Points   _____
Fines   _____ Total
Total Points   _____ Possible _____

_____
Teacher's Signature
D

Subject _____   Date _____

_____ Is doing acceptable work and is keeping up with assignments
_____ Work is not acceptable
_____ Is behind on assignments
_____ Social behavior is acceptable
_____ Social behavior is unacceptable

Comments:

_____
                         E   Teacher's Signature

provide extra privileges (e.g., stay up thirty minutes later, extra TV time, special dessert) for good reports (specify the criteria for a "good" report) or lose privileges for a poor re-port. If required, you may even work out a menu of back-up home consequences similar to the classroom menu presented in Chapter 6. This provides for differential reinforcement and long-term savings for special privileges or treats (e.g., a movie, a fishing trip). It is preferable to work out the details of more elaborate systems with a simple contract among the pupil, parents, and you. All parties should sign and receive copies of the contract.

Figure 12–4 shows a variety of daily report cards (these could also be weekly reports). Panels A and B present forms useful for primary-age students. Panel C is a simple checklist for middle-grade students, and Panel D shows a form for reporting daily points. Panel E is a checklist for mainstreamed, upper-level or secondary pupils. One problem with daily report cards is that students may lose them. If you advise parents to respond to a missing report as though it were poor or below criterion, this problem seldom persists. If you are concerned that parents fail to read the report, include in the contract an agreement that reports are to be signed by them and returned the next day. Graphs and charts, such as those presented in Chapter 3, may also be sent home on a daily or weekly basis.

Home-school communication systems that use back-up home contingencies offer several advantages. First, they provide contingent consequences at home for performance in school. This can be a great help for students who do not respond well to school consequences (e.g., pupils who "do not care" if they miss recess or backup reinforcers available at school). Second, they keep parents informed of their child's progress and get them involved in what is going on at school. Third, by emphasizing reinforcing consequences for good performance, they break down the common expectation among parents of behavior-problem children that all school reports are bad reports. Furthermore, by teaching parents to reinforce their children, you may help break the criticism-punishment cycle that is prevalent in families with problem children.

School-home communication systems need not be elaborate, and if properly used, they can be effective. Ayllon, Garber, and Pisor (1975), for instance, sent a good behavior letter home with students in a third-grade class for meeting criteria for good conduct. Receipt or nonreceipt of these letters was followed by differential consequences by the parents. Disruptive behavior, which averaged 90 percent during the baseline period and did not appreciably decrease in response to a school-based contingency system, dropped to 10 percent when the letter was instituted.

Your strategies for working with parents can be as varied as the students and parents themselves. Each situation calls for different measures, but you should be able to adopt a general strategy for all parents and children in your class. There are several excellent texts on working with parents of exceptional children (e.g., Kroth, 1975; Kroth & Simpson, 1977; Rutherford & Edgar, 1979; Wagonseller & Mc-Dowell, 1979), and we suggest you consult these for additional ideas and information.

WORKING WITH COMMUNITY PERSONS AND AGENCIES

Your work with children and youth exhibiting behavior problems will lead you into the domain of other professionals and agencies. Recent amendments to PL 94-142 (e.g., PL 99-457) emphasize the need for interagency planning and cooperation on behalf of handicapped pupils, especially for those at the preschool or secondary school levels. The lack of interagency collaboration has been a major obstacle to achieving continuity of programming between public schools and other human service agencies. As we have stressed in this chapter, discontinuity in services contributes to the failure of treatment effects achieved in one setting to be generalized and maintained in other settings where these effects are expected and needed. As a professional attempting to extend the effects of interventions applied in educational settings or attempting to plan interventions across settings, you may work with a number of professional agencies such as the juvenile court, child welfare agencies, mental health centers, organizations serving the developmentally disabled, vocational rehabilitation agencies, medical clinics, and service organizations such as Big Brothers or Big Sisters, in addition to working with parent groups. The professionals working in these agencies (or in private practice) include social workers, psychologists, psychiatrists, physicians, dentists, and lawyers. It is well beyond the scope of this book to acquaint you with the workings of these professions and agencies. However, we can provide a few guidelines.

First, you should be aware of political realities. One of the foremost of these is that outside the school, special education is not viewed as the salvation of children with behavior problems. Do not expect other professionals to greet your suggestions and views with respect and admiration. Your credibility with these people will come from your record with their clients. If you succeed in accomplishing goals with students and parents that are in accord with the agency's goals, or if you have solved problems addressed by the agency or professional, you are more likely to be viewed as effective. However, it is foolhardy to set up programs that are in opposition to those established by another agency if you want to enjoy credibility with that agency. For example, if you set up a behavioral program with parents to deal with their child's enuresis while a psychiatrist is using psychoanalysis to treat the same problem, you are not likely to establish a good working relationship with that psychiatrist. A better tactic would involve demonstrating the effectiveness of your programs with other behaviors or students, and to offer suggestions as requested.

Second, learn to channel credit away from yourself toward the other professional whenever appropriate. However, do not suggest that the other professionals possess qualities or powers they do not have, and do not give credit where credit is not due. A good practice involves following the principle of contingently reinforcing practices with which you concur. For instance, if you approve of a psychologist's

plan for dealing with school phobia, say, "I like this plan," not "You're a terrific psychologist" or "You have so much insight into this client." At times you need to overlook that it was you who suggested a particular plan in the first place.

Third, you should recognize that other professionals may not speak your language. You must be tolerant of the jargon of other professions while minimizing the use of your own. This is particularly important in the case of behavior analysis terminology. By selecting nontechnical but meaningful words (e.g., reward instead of positive reinforcement), you can avoid both semantic confusion and value clashes (Reppucci & Saunders, 1974).

Fourth, you should realize that most human service agencies often do not communicate well with one another. That is, juvenile court personnel may seldom contact the school, and there may not be an automatic communication link between the school and the local mental health clinic. Communication among agencies requires someone who will initiate it and maintain it. Generally, such communication results from a dynamic individual rather than from agency policy. So, if you desire communication with other agencies, you should be prepared to take the initiative and follow through. Also, remember that communication will continue only as long as it is reinforced. You, therefore, need to acknowledge your appreciation of others' attempts to communicate and to make use of the communicated information. Further, you should be sure to communicate information that is useful to the treatment program being followed by the other agency. Irrelevant comments about a child's social history, or regarding the criminal record of his brother, only serve to cloud issues and professional judgment.

Finally, whether you approach another agency or professional or they approach you, clarify the purposes of the involvement and your mutual responsibilities. A major advantage of a written collaboration agreement is its clear delineation of roles and responsibilities. If an agreement is plainly spelled out and understood by all (you are to count the frequency of Ronnie's pants-wetting during school hours, his parents are to record it at home, and both parties are to call in their data to the psychologist every Friday) there is a greater likelihood that interactions will be efficient, productive, and mutually reinforcing.

As you work with other professionals and human service agencies, you will learn which are most useful for specific purposes. You may find it helpful to maintain a checklist, using the format presented in Figure 12-5, to keep track of your contacts and of the outcomes of your involvement. When working outside the school, keep in mind the limitations of your role. If you overextend yourself, or intrude too far into another's territory, you may experience unpleasant consequences. At the least, you are not apt to find that your efforts produce the effects you desire. Some limitations of the educator's role are discussed in Chapter 13. The range of persons and professional or volunteer agencies in the local community that you can use to assist your students is virtually endless. Each community has its own array of resources. These may be used in the same manner as parents or in-school resources, and the guidelines we presented for working in those settings apply here as well. Particularly when working with professional agencies, make your requests consistent with the functions and philosophy of those within the agency (do not ask a psychoanalytically inclined social case worker to put a child in time-out) unless you are able to provide sufficient training and supervision to ensure reliable performance.

A study by MacDonald, Gallimore, and MacDonald (1970) illustrates how a variety of persons may be used. They trained a parent and two school staff members (a counselor and a registrar) to contact persons in the communities of chronic school nonattenders. These community contacts (mediators) controlled reinforcers for the target pupils. The trained at-

tendance counselors arranged contracts between pupils and the mediators, making reinforcement contingent upon school attendance. The mediators included relatives, a girl friend, the guidance counselors themselves, and a pool hall proprietor. The reinforcers included privileges, money, and access to persons or places (time with a girl friend, permission to enter a pool hall). This arrangement improved the school attendance of twenty-six nonattenders, whereas a control group of fifteen pupils who received personal counseling by a trained school counselor did not improve their attendance records.

Summary

Extending the effects of interventions that have been successfully applied in primary treatment settings is a complex task requiring intensive programming within these settings as well as assessment and intervention in those settings where these behavior changes are also needed and desired. We have described a variety of strategies addressing the goals of achieving the maintenance and generalization of treatment effects and the transition of students to less restrictive environments. Although the technology for achieving these goals has advanced, helping students achieve desired behavior changes that endure over time and across settings continues to be difficult. A major factor seems to be the tendency to provide educational treatments, especially with certified handicapped pupils, in restrictive settings. Extending effects beyond the school environment is further complicated by problems of communication and the lack of collaborative relationships among educators, parents, and other professionals. However, research has demonstrated that generalization of desired intervention outcomes can occur when it is systematically planned and implemented. The challenge of the future is to alter the ways in which human service programs work to achieve better coordination and greater consistency on behalf of students and clients.

Figure 12-5. Outside School Resource Checklist

PERSONNEL/AGENCIES	Willing to work with pupils?	Supportive of your program?	Have cooperated with you previously?	Willing to collect data?	Will require supervision?	Will require training?	Willing to devote time above normal duties?	Have reliably carried out procedures with pupils before?	COMMENTS (Phone numbers, etc.)
Mental Health									
Child Welfare									
Juvenile Court									
Other Social Service Agencies									
Physicians									
Dentists									
Scout/Club Leaders									
Local Merchants									
Parents									
Volunteers									

CASE STUDY

I: The Garden Springs Phase System

Laura L. McCullough

The phase system I developed at my school is for a self-contained behavior disorders unit. Its objective is to provide a consistent guide for bridging the gap between the rigidly structured environment of a self-contained special education classroom and regular complex-style classrooms of an elementary (K–6) open school. The ultimate goal of my program is to provide the maximum mainstream experience appropriate for each student, and whenever possible, to return that student permanently to the regular public education system.

I believe that, while there appears a wide range of difference in specific behavioral deficits for which children are labeled behaviorally disordered or emotionally disturbed and therefore are excluded from regular education classrooms, the most obvious common denominator for referral is an apparent lack of self-control. If, then, our task as special educators is to develop self-control abilities, what do we teach? Answers to this question have not come easily. However, I feel that we must do more than just make students quieter and smarter. My phase system is designed to teach a cognitive set of self-control principles while simultaneously providing a framework in which my students may learn to make choices based upon public consequences, privileges, and responsibilities. Since feedback is so essential to the monitoring and maintenance of behavioral progress, my phase system continuum includes a set of criteria for evaluating specific behaviors at regular intervals.

The phase steps account for receiving a student who is exhibiting problematic behavior (entry level behavior); placing a student back in a regular program (exit level behavior); and a hierarchy of skills between. After determining the specific behavioral expectations important to survival in the environment to which my students are to return, I task-analyzed the behaviors into five component steps. Phase I consists of minimal student behaviors (what must the student do to maintain himself in a special class?). Phase V lists the desired outcome behaviors which appear necessary for integration into regular classrooms in my school. Phases II, III, and IV provide intermediate goals or benchmarks for measuring progress toward that integration. Tables 12–3 and 12–4 summarize student responsibilities and privileges, as well as some of the considerations used in making decisions about student progress through the phases.

Students are provided a list (phase sheet) of specific behaviors for which they are responsible. At the end of the day, I review any behavioral observation data that I have collected. At this time, I also encourage the pupil to recall his day in reference to the phase requirements. I (and later the student) assign a + or − to each specific goal or behavior to indicate whether desired behaviors were demonstrated or lacking. Seven out of ten consecutive + days would, for example, constitute criterion (70 percent) for movement from Phase I to Phase II. Similarly, a Phase II student who receives only six out of ten consecutive + days has failed to maintain criterion at 70 percent and drops to Phase I the following day. I keep a public chart of students' location in the phase system, in addition to charting their daily point totals.

I maintain greater stimulus control at the lower phase levels to minimize maladaptive behaviors and noncontingent reinforcement. Students who do not advance through phase steps

Table 12-3. Garden Springs Phase System: Student Responsibilities

Phase I	Phase II	Phase III	Phase IV	Phase V Regular Class
		Academic		
State basic information Procedure Rules Points Names				
Start assignments →	Start immediately →	Start and finish →	Finish all work →	Finish all on time
Attempt all work →	Stay on task →	Complete: 80% accuracy →	Complete: 90% accuracy →	Complete: 95% accuracy
Use help sign →	Wait for help quietly →	Do other work (waiting) →	Work independently →	Work in small group
Explain homework assignment →	Take homework folder home →	Homework folder signed/returned →	Complete all homework →	All homework is on time
Listen/repeat instructions →	Remember instructions (restate later) →	Follow short-range instructions →	Follow long-range instruction	
Attend class →	Be punctual →	Bring materials →	Organize materials →	Show responsibility for all: Materials Assignments Instructions

Social

Enter	70%	80% Mainstreaming	87%	93% exit
State individual goal →	State two goals →	State three goals →	State all individual goals →	State all individual goals
	Begin daily evaluation of behavior with special education teacher →		Regular teacher →	Self evaluate (weekly journal)
Try to follow class rules →	State P.E./music/library rules →	State regular class rules →	Respond to regular class rules/consequences →	Follow all regular class rules/consequences
Take time-out when told →	Take time-out immediately when told (put head on desk) →	Time yourself out if necessary →	Take time-out without putting head on desk →	Time yourself out internally (maintain cool)
Define self-control communication →	Try to avoid fights, control verbal aggression →	Talk calmly to staff and group session when angry/upset →	Defer discussion until later time →	Problems presented at convenience of regular class teacher/schedule
			Ignore inappropriate behavior of others	

Daily Criterion

Enter	70%	80% Mainstreaming	87%	93% exit
No mainstream access →	P.E./music/library access →	Homeroom/lunch/recess access →	Academic class access →	All day! (as appropriate)

Table 12-4. Garden Springs Phase System: Student Privileges

	Phase I	Phase II	Phase III	Phase IV	Phase V
Example Items					
Seat location:	Assigned	Request considered	Variable	Any area by request	Regular class
Silent reading	In seat only	At group table	In reading pillow corner	Anywhere including floor (with pillows)	Regular class
Creative writing	Work in seat	Work at group table	With headphone music	Music and snack	Regular class
Free time:					
Materials	Art, games, lagos	Plus records, tapes	Plus radio	Request by contract	
Area Time	In seat only	Free-time area	In room	Check out materials to regular class	Check out materials overnight— take home
Cost	25 points	20 points	10 points	Free	
Class trips	Pay full cost	Pay self/parent	Pay self/guest	Pay self/2 guests	Free/contract agreement
Homework	Assigned	Request sequence	Request type task	Contract homework	Regular class

Mobility:

Restroom	Group supervision only	→ Paid escort for special trip	→ Alone with permission/time limit	→ Inform teacher	→ Regular class
In building transit	No unsupervised mobility	→ Trial basis free to music/P.E.	→ Free to all scheduled classes (trial basis)	→ Free	→ Regular class
Classroom	In seat all times	→ Free access to trash, tissues, sharpener	→ Free access to materials, needs	→ Free	→ Regular class
Jobs	In class routine	→ Class/building routine	→ Messages, flexible transit, class helper	→ Special jobs/by contract Class leadership	→ Regular class Unlimited special contract

Feedback:

	Immediate	→ Frequent	→ Deferred by necessity	→ Intermittent	→ Regular class/weekly
Artificial reinforcers	Points: continuous	→ Points: end of task	→ Points: twice daily	→ Points: once daily	→ Off points!
Intolerable behavior	Place on homebound (start over)	→ Homebound (two homebounds = drop to Phase I)	→ One homebound = drop to Phase II	→ One homebound = drop to Phase III	→ One homebound = drop to Phase III or suspension

Note: Homebound consists of a one- to two-day school suspension. Student is sent home with specific academic assignments to complete, and parents are to supervise and restrict access to privileges (e.g., TV, playing outside).

find themselves with little mobility, close supervision, and less choice. Once my authority has been established I can begin to turn some of the control over to the student. As the requirements and expectations for desired behaviors expand at each level, the number of pupil choices is widened and flexibility increases. As students advance through the phases, they are permitted greater mobility in the classroom and school building, in addition to the opportunity for participation in regular classes. Consequently, students at upper levels provide peer models to lower phase students who are more restricted.

The phase system is also a useful tool for communicating with school personnel and parents. Often alarmed by a student's label, they are more comfortable discussing specific behaviors students presently are exhibiting. The sequence of pupil responsibilities is also helpful for outlining a sequence of behaviors that should be expected or required in the home or the educational mainstream. I urge parents to ask their children every day about their phase levels and to provide social reinforcement for advancement. Given consistent implementation over time, the regular classroom teachers seem to have more respect for, and confidence in, mainstreaming requests. In addition, regular classroom teachers find the phase system supportive. For example, they know they will not be stuck with a child whose behavior has seriously deteriorated, as the system provides for dropping students back to lower levels if percentage criteria are not maintained.

Another advantage to phase mainstreaming is that generalization can be monitored and evaluated on the spot in the regular classroom. Students are exposed to a gradual transition from the rules and authority of a single special teacher to the rules and personal biases found in numerous settings. For instance, students reporting to regular P.E. class are aware that the arrangement is made on a trial basis. Continued access is contingent upon conformity to the gym rules and appropriate response to the P.E. teacher.

As students approach the upper phase steps (IV and V), artificial reinforcers (points) are withdrawn or transferred in favor of long-term natural reinforcement. Feedback is given less often and rewards are put on a more intermittent schedule. Token reinforcers (points) are faded and discontinued. If real academic or social progress has been met with consistent systematic praise and peer encouragement, conversion to these natural reinforcers is smoothly accomplished. Regular staff personnel (principal, teachers, custodians, etc.) and parents who have learned to recognize and selectively attend to student improvements have tremendous positive influence on maintaining desired behavior at acceptable levels. They may also see an enormous sense of pride develop and spill over a student who just couldn't make it before.

Discussion Questions

1. Given that the generalization of treatment effects is much more difficult when interventions occur in restrictive settings, how could treatment procedures be designed to facilitate generalization within school environments? How might educational services be reorganized to make generalization of intervention outcomes more accomplishable?

2. Assume that you have reduced a student's aggressive behavior to an acceptable level in a special classroom environment, but he still exhibits verbal and physical aggression in other school settings. How would you assess these behaviors in other settings, and what strategies would you use to accomplish a generalized suppression of his aggression?

3. How would you prepare a behaviorally disordered student to be mainstreamed in a regular classroom? Describe the procedures you would use in the special education setting and the strategies you would apply in the mainstream environment.

4. A parent of one of your students complains that her child is "unmanageable" at home (refuses to do chores, disobeys rules and direct requests, and fights with siblings). As a classroom teacher, what would you do?

References

Ayllon, T., Garber, S., & Pisor, K. (1975). The elimination of discipline problems through a combined school-home motivation system. *Behavior Therapy, 6,* 616-626.

Anderson-Inman, L., Walker, H. M., & Purcell, J. (1984). Promoting the transfer of skills across settings: Transenvironmental programming for handicapped students in the mainstream. In W. R. Heward, T. E. Heron, D. S. Hill, & J. Trap-Porter (Eds.), *Focus on behavior analysis in education* (pp. 17-39). Columbus, OH: Merrill.

Baer, D. M., & Wolf, M. M. (1970). The entry into natural communities of reinforcement. In R. Ulrich, T. Stachnik, & J. Mabry (Eds.), *Control of human behavior: Vol. II. From cure to prevention* (pp. 319-324). Glenview, IL: Scott, Foresman.

Baer, D. M., Wolf, M. M., & Risley, T. R. (1968). Some current dimensions of applied behavior analysis. *Journal of Applied Behavior Analysis, 1,* 91-97.

Becker, W. C. (1971). *Parents are teachers.* Champaign, IL: Research Press.

Braaten, S. (1979). The Madison School program: Programming for secondary level emotionally disturbed youth. *Behavioral Disorders, 4,* 153-162.

Braaten, S., Kauffman, J. M., Braaten, B., Polsgrove, L., & Nelson, C. M. (1988). The regular education initiative: Patent medicine for behavioral disorders? *Exceptional Children, 55,* 21-27.

Brown, L., Nietupski, J., & Hamre-Nietupski, S. (1976). The criterion of ultimate functioning and public school services for severely handicapped students. In A. Thomas (Ed.), *Hey, don't forget about me: New directions for serving the severely handicapped* (pp. 2-15). Reston, VA: Council for Exceptional Children.

Brown, R. E., Copeland, R. E., & Hall, R. V. (1972). The school principal as a behavior modifier. *Journal of Educational Research, 66,* 175-180.

Christophersen, E. R., Arnold, C. M., Hill, D. W., & Quilitch, H. R. (1972). The home point system: Token reinforcement procedures for application by parents of children with behavior problems. *Journal of Applied Behavior Analysis, 5,* 485-497.

Clore, P. (1974). Chris: "School phobia." In J. Worell & C. M. Nelson (Eds.), *Managing instructional problems: A case study workbook* (pp. 212-217). New York: McGraw-Hill.

Copeland, R. E., Brown, R. E., & Hall, R. V. (1974). The effects of principal-implemented techniques on the behavior of pupils. *Journal of Applied Behavior Analysis, 7,* 77-86.

Edgar, E. (1987). Secondary programs in special education: Are many of them justifiable? *Exceptional Children, 53,* 555-561.

Ferber, H., Keeley, S. M., & Shemberg, K. M. (1974). Training parents in behavior modification: Outcomes of and problems encountered in a program after Patterson's work. *Behavior Therapy, 5,* 415-419.

Gaylord-Ross, R., & Haring, T. (1987). Social interaction research for adolescents with severe handicaps. *Behavioral Disorders, 12,* 264-275.

Gaylord-Ross, R. J., Haring, T. G., Breen, C., & Pitts-Conway, V. (1984). The training and generalization of social interaction skills with autistic youth. *Journal of Applied Behavior Analysis, 17,* 229-247.

Glogowger, F., & Sloop, E. W. (1976). Two strategies of group training of parents as effective behavior modifiers. *Behavior Therapy, 7,* 177-184.

Goetz, L., Guess, D., & Stremel-Campbell, K. (Eds.). (1987). *Innovative program design for individuals with dual sensory impairments.* Boston: Paul H. Brookes.

Graubard, P. S., Rosenberg H., & Miller, M. B. (1971). Student applications of behavior modification to teachers and environments or ecological approaches to social deviancy. In E. A. Ramp & B. L. Hopkins (Eds.), *A new direction for education: Behavior analysis: 1971* (pp. 80-101). Lawrence, KS: University of Kansas Support and Development Center for Follow Through.

Gresham, F. M., Elliott, S. N., & Black, F. L. (1987). Teacher-rated social skills of mainstreamed mildly handicapped and nonhandicapped children. *School Psychology Review, 16,* 78-88.

Gunter, P., Fox, J. J., Brady, M. P., Shores, R. E., & Cavanaugh, K. (1988). Nonhandicapped peers as multiple exemplars: A generalization tactic for promoting autistic students' social skills. *Behavioral Disorders, 13,* 116-126.

Hewett, F. M., & Taylor, F. D. (1980). *The emotionally disturbed child in the classroom: The orchestration of success* (2nd ed.). Boston: Allyn & Bacon.

Hollinger, J. D. (1987). Social skills for behaviorally disordered children as preparation for mainstreaming: Theory, practice, and new directions. *Remedial and Special Education, 8*(4), 17-27.

Hrydowy, E. R., Stokes, T. F., & Martin, G. L. (1984). Training elementary students to prompt teacher praise. *Education and Treatment of Children, 7,* 99-108.

Idol, L., Paolucci-Whitcomb, P., & Nevin, A. (1986). *Collaborative consultation.* Rockville, MD: Aspen.

Kazdin, A. E. (1977). Vicarious reinforcement and direction of behavior change in the classroom. *Behavior Therapy, 8,* 57-63.

Kerr, M. M., Nelson, C. M., & Lambert, D. L. (1987). *Helping adolescents with learning and behavior problems.* Columbus, OH: Merrill.

Koegel, R. L., & Rincover, A. (1977). Research on the difference between generalization and maintenance in extra-therapy responding. *Journal of Applied Behavior Analysis, 10,* 1-12.

Kroth, R. L. (1975). *Communicating with parents of exceptional children: Improving parent-teacher relationships.* Denver, Co.: Love.

Kroth, R. L., & Simpson, R. L. (1977). *Parent conferences as a teaching strategy.* Denver, CO: Love.

Lane, T. W., & Burchard, J. D. (1983). Failure to modify delinquent behavior: A constructive analysis. In E. B. Foa & P. M. G. Emmelkamp (Eds.), *Failures in behavior therapy* (pp. 355-377). New York: Wiley.

MacDonald, W. S., Gallimore, R., & MacDonald, G. (1970). Contingency counseling by school personnel: An economical model of intervention. *Journal of Applied Behavior Analysis, 3,* 175-182.

Marholin, D., & Steinman, W. (1977). Stimulus control in the classroom as a function of the behavior reinforced. *Journal of Applied Behavior Analysis, 10,* 465-478.

McEvoy, M. A., & Odom, S. L. (1987). Social interaction training for preschool children with behavioral disorders. *Behavioral Disorders, 12,* 242-251.

Meichenbaum, D. (1977). *Cognitive-behavior modification: An integrative approach.* New York: Plenum.

Mercer, C. D., & Mercer, A. R. (1985). *Teaching students with learning problems* (2nd ed.). Columbus, OH: Merrill.

Nelson, C. M. (1988). Social skills training for handicapped students. *Teaching Exceptional Children, 20*(4), 19-23.

Nelson, C. M., & Rutherford, R. B., Jr. (1988). Behavioral interventions with behaviorally disordered students. In M. C. Wang, H. J. Walberg, & M. C. Reynolds (Eds.), *The handbook of special education: Research and practice* (Vol. 2, pp. 125-153). Oxford, England: Pergamon.

Nelson, C. M., Rutherford, R. B., Jr., & Wolford, B. I. (Eds.). (1987). *Special education and the criminal justice system.* Columbus, OH: Merrill.

O'Leary, S. G., & O'Leary, K. D. (1976). Behavior modification in the school. In H. Leitenberg (Ed.), *Handbook of behavior modification and behavior therapy* (pp. 475-515). Englewood Cliffs, NJ: Prentice-Hall.

Patterson, G. R. (1975). *Families: Applications of social learning to family life.* Champaign, IL: Research Press.

Patterson, G. R., & Gullion, M. E. (1971). *Living with children.* Champaign, IL: Research Press.

Polsgrove, L. (1979). Self-control: Methods for child training. *Behavioral Disorders, 4,* 116-130.

Reppucci, N. D., & Saunders, J. T. (1974). Social psychology of behavior modification: Problems of implementation in natural settings. *American Psychologist, 29,* 649-660.

Rinn, R. C., Vernon, J. C., & Wise, M. J. (1975). Training parents of behaviorally disordered children in groups: A three years' program evaluation. *Behavior Therapy, 6,* 378-387.

Robbins, L. N. (1966). *Deviant children grown up: A sociological and psychiatric study of sociopathic personality.* Baltimore: Williams & Wilkins.

Rutherford, R. B., Jr., & Edgar, E. (1979). *Teachers and parents: A guide to interaction and cooperation.* Boston: Allyn & Bacon.

Rutherford, R. B., Jr., & Nelson, C. M. (1988). Generalization and maintenance of treatment effects. In J. C. Witt, S. N. Elliott, & F. M. Gresham (Eds.), *Handbook of behavior therapy in education* (pp. 277-324). New York: Plenum.

Shinn, M. R., Ramsey, E., Walker, H. M., Stieber, S., & O'Neill, R. E. (1987). Antisocial behavior in school settings: Initial differences in an at risk and normal population. *Journal of Special Education, 21,* 69-84.,

Shores, R. E. (1987). Overview of research on social interaction: A historical and personal perspective. *Behavioral Disorders, 12,* 233-241.

Shores, R. E., Apolloni, T., & Norman, C. W. (1976). Changes in peer verbalizations accompanying individual and group contingencies. *Perceptual and Motor Skills, 43,* 1155-1162.

Simpson, R. L. (1987). Social interaction of behaviorally disordered children and youth: Where are we and where do we need to go? *Behavioral Disorders, 12,* 292-298.

Stokes, T. F., & Baer, D. M. (1977). An implicit technology of generalization. *Journal of Applied Behavior Analysis, 10,* 349-367.

Stokes, T. F., & Osnes, P. G. (1986). Programming the generalization of children's social behavior. In P. S. Strain, M. J. Guralnick, & H. M. Walker (Eds.), *Children's social behavior: Development, assessment,* and modification (pp. 407–443). Orlando, FL: Academic Press.

Strain, P. S., Shores, R. E., & Kerr, M. M. (1976). An experimental analysis of "spillover" effects on the social interaction of behaviorally handicapped preschool children. *Journal of Applied Behavior Analysis, 9,* 31–40.

Tawney, J. W., & Gast, D. L. (1984). *Single subject research in special education.* Columbus, OH: Merrill.

Taylor, F. D., & Soloway, M. M. (1973). The Madison School plan: A functional model for merging the regular and special classrooms. In E. Deno (Ed.), *Instructional alternatives for exceptional children* (pp. 145–155). Reston, VA: Council for Exceptional Children.

Taylor, S. J., Bilken, D., & Knoll, J. (1987). (Eds.). *Community integration for people with severe disabilities.* New York: Teachers College Press, Columbia University.

Van Hasselt, B. B., Hersen, M., Whitehill, M. B., & Bellack, A. S. (1979). Social skills assessment and training for children: An evaluative review. *Behavior Research and Therapy, 17,* 413–437.

Wagonseller, B. R., & McDowell, R. L. (1979). *You and your child: A common sense approach to successful parenting.* Champaign, IL: Research Press.

Walker, H. M. (1986). The assessment for integration into mainstream settings (AIMS) assessment system: Rationale, instruments, procedures, and outcomes. *Journal of Clinical Child Psychology, 15,* 55–63.

Walker, H. M., & Rankin, R. (1980a). *The SBS Checklist: Correlates of child handicapping conditions* (Available from Hill Walker, Center on Human Development, Clinical Services Building, University of Oregon, Eugene, OR 97403).

Walker, H. M., & Rankin, R. (1980b). *The SBS Inventory of Teacher Social Behavior Standards and Expectations.* (Available from Hill Walker, Center on Human Development, Clinical Services Building, University of Oregon, Eugene, OR 97403).

Walker, H. M., Shinn, M. R., O'Neill, R. E., & Ramsey, E. (1987). A longitudinal assessment of the development of antisocial behavior in boys: Rationale, methodology, and first year results. *Remedial and Special Education, 8*(4), 7–16 & 27.

Limitations on the Educational Role

Chapter 13

OBJECTIVES

After completing this chapter, the reader should be able to

- Identify the major limitations that apply to educators working in school settings and describe the consequences of exceeding these limitations.
- Identify potential sources of conflict for educators working on behalf of students exhibiting behavioral disorders.
- Discuss strategies for working effectively within professional role boundaries.
- Identify signs of stress and burnout and suggest appropriate strategies for their reduction.

In previous chapters we have considered a broad range of intervention strategies for dealing with an equally wide range of behavioral problems. Chapters 2 and 12 have indicated that problem behaviors may be present in non-educational settings, and procedures for assessing and intervening in these settings were discussed. The present chapter provides a context for evaluating the extent to which educators can realistically operate outside of the settings that are their responsibility. Specifically, in this concluding chapter we describe some of the limits imposed on educational personnel by various factors. Learning which limits apply to the roles occupied by professional educators, and functioning within them, is both important and complex. The consequences of overstepping one's professional boundaries can be devastating. Therefore, we provide you with guidelines derived from research, litigation, authoritative discourse, and experience. Our belief is that recognizing the limits of the educational role not only helps you avoid aversive personal and professional consequences but also benefits you in two ways. First, you avoid overextending yourself in areas beyond your scope, which helps reduce stress and potential

teacher burnout. Second, you function more effectively and more flexibly in your work as a student advocate and as a member of a professional team.

Our discussion of limitations is organized into three categories: ecological constraints, role constraints, and legal constraints. This division is strictly arbitrary; in practical situations, the categories overlap considerably. This chapter concludes with a discussion of stress and burnout.

Ecological Constraints

OVEREXTENSION AND INTRUSION

We have emphasized that problem behaviors do not occur only in educational settings. In particular, students who are handicapped by their behavioral disorders display maladaptive behaviors or deficits in appropriate social skills across many settings. Caregivers and other persons who must deal with these individuals may very well lack the skills to design and implement sophisticated and effective intervention procedures. As a professional educator, you are constrained by the practical limits of your role. This means that you are sure to encounter circumstances in which you cannot manage all the student's environmental contingencies and reinforcers, nor can you train all those who do. It is important that you recognize this fact, *even though you may have the expertise to deal with the student's problems.* For example, there may be serious difficulties in the pupil's family interactions, or the student may be involved in gang delinquency. If you know, or think you know, how to attack such problems it may be tempting to try to manage them. However, this tactic presents several dangers. First, you may be overextending yourself. Your official responsibility, remember, is to the student's educational program, unless you are acting in another professional role. Attempting to resolve family or community problems, for example, may interfere with planning and implementing educational programs. If you are in a consulting role or have released time for parent training or community work, there is less conflict; nevertheless one can easily become overextended when working with multiple-problem situations.

There also is the risk of intruding upon another professional's domain. If a family receives counseling from a mental health agency, or if a probation officer is working on the pupil's delinquent behavior, you should not initiate interventions without the prior consent of the other professional or agency. Then too, you may risk providing ineffective treatment: your involvement outside the school may detract from your performance here, or you may find yourself working in areas or on problems for which you are not adequately trained. The dangers of overextension are increased by your own effectiveness. That is, the better you are at your job, the more you may be called upon to help in other areas. It is very tempting to respond to the social reinforcement offered by your clients and other professionals by increasing your participation in areas beyond your jurisdiction. However, this pattern may lead to undesired consequences for you or your pupil. For this reason you should recognize this as a limitation on your role.

Extending yourself beyond your limitations may be more likely if you are the only resource in the geographic area for a pupil or a family, as in rural locales. In more urban areas, where other professionals are available, you may be the only one the student or family trusts. Whether you provide assistance in these instances may indeed represent difficulty.

You can pursue several options when confronted with any of the problem situations mentioned thus far. As a first step, we recommend that you assess the pupil's ecology. This task sounds more imposing than it actually is. You can initiate an ecological assessment by interviewing the student or his caregivers. Wahler and Cormier (1970) developed three behavior checklists, reproduced here in Figures 13-1, 13-2, and 13-3 (pp. 398-400), that can be used to map student ecological settings. Neither the problem behaviors nor the situations listed here are exhaustive, but you can use these checklists as models to develop your own. To use the checklists, focus on specific behaviors and ask the interviewee in which of the settings they occur, or ask which behaviors present problems in the student's ecological settings. By entering checks in the appropriate rows and columns, you can develop a map of the student's problem behaviors in various settings and thereby gain a general understanding of the extent of such problems, as well as which behaviors the student displays in specific settings. Further questioning may reveal specific persons in whose presence problems occur, typical reactions or approaches to handling problem behaviors, and so forth.

Following the interview (or series of interviews), you can make a decision whether to approach the problem situation yourself or refer the student or caregiver elsewhere. Referring students and caregivers to other agencies

Figure 13-1. Child Home Behavior Checklist

The following checklist allows you to describe your child's problems in various home situations. The situations are listed in the column at left and common problem behaviors are listed in the row at the top. Examine *each* situation in the column and decide if one or more of the problem behaviors in the row fits your child. Check those that fit the best—if any.

	Always has to be told	Doesn't pay attention	Forgets	Dawdles	Refuses	Argues	Complains	Demands	Fights	Selfish	Destroys toys or property	Steals	Lies	Cries	Whines	Hangs on or stays close to adult	Acts silly	Mopes around	Stays alone	Has to keep things in order	Sexual play
Morning: Awakening																					
Dressing																					
Breakfast																					
Bathroom																					
Leave for school																					
Play in house																					
Chores																					
Television																					
Afternoon: Lunch																					
Bathroom																					
Play in house																					
Chores and homework																					
Television																					
When company comes																					
Evening: Father comes home																					
Dinner																					
Bathroom																					
Play in house																					
Chores and homework																					
Television																					
Undressing																					
When company comes																					
Bedtime																					

Source: Reprinted with permission from the *Journal of Behavior Therapy and Experimental Psychiatry, 1*: 279–289. R. G. Wahler & W. H. Cormier, The ecological interview: A first step in outpatient therapy. Copyright 1970, Pergamon Press, Ltd.

Figure 13-2. Child Community Behavior Checklist

The following checklist allows you to describe your child's problems in various situations outside the house. The situations are listed in the column at left and common problem behaviors are listed in the row at the top. Examine *each situation* in the column and decide if one or more of the problem behaviors in the row fits your child. Check those that fit the best—if any.

	Always has to be told	Doesn't pay attention	Forgets	Dawdles	Refuses	Argues	Complains	Demands	Fights	Selfish	Destroys toys or property	Steals	Lies	Cries	Whines	Hangs on or stays close to adult	Acts silly	Mopes around	Stays alone	Has to keep things in order	Sexual play
In own yard																					
In neighbor's yard or home																					
In stores																					
Public park																					
Downtown in general																					
Church or Sunday school																					
Community swimming pool																					
In family car																					

Source: Reprinted with permission from the *Journal of Behavior Therapy and Experimental Psychiatry, 1*: 279–289. R. G. Wahler & W. H. Cormier, The ecological interview: A first step in outpatient therapy. Copyright 1970, Pergamon Press, Ltd.

and professionals is another practical solution to problems that may be beyond your scope. You should not be embarrassed or concerned that making a referral indicates failure on your part. On the contrary, as we suggested in Chapter 12, collaboration with other professionals represents an important part of your role, and you should view yourself as a team member. In the interest of your pupils and your own credibility, however, it behooves you to make certain the professionals or agencies to whom you make referrals render high-quality service. Therefore, we recommend that you maintain a list of agencies and persons who have proven their worth to you and to your students. This list should include a variety of human service agencies to enable you to make

the most appropriate referral possible. For example, your local Agricultural Extension Office may employ a consultant home economist or family nutritionist who can help families with such diverse problems as budgeting income or providing a diet free of food additives; these have been linked to hyperactivity in some children (Kauffman, 1985).

In several instances we have referred clients to field nursing services for help with such problems as hygiene, diet, and general health care. Even sparsely populated areas may be served by a variety of such professionals, and you may begin to develop a community resource guide by contacting your county courthouse or your state's department of human services to find out what services are locally available. As sug-

Figure 13-3. Child School Behavior Checklist

The following checklist allows you to describe your student's problems in various situations. The situations are listed in the column at left and common problem behaviors are listed in the row at the top. Examine *each* situation in the column and decide if one or more of the problem behaviors in the row fit your student. Check those that fit the best—if any.

Situation	Out of seat	Talks to others	Always has to be told	Doesn't pay attention	Forgets	Dawdles	Refuses	Argues	Complains	Demands	Fights	Selfish	Destroys toys or property	Steals	Lies	Cries	Whines	Hangs on or stays close to adult	Acts silly	Mopes around	Stays alone	Has to keep things in order	Sexual play
Morning: Teacher explains lesson																							
Teacher discusses with group																							
Silent work time																							
Cooperative work with other students																							
Oral reading or class presentation																							
Line up for lunch or recess																							
Hall																							
Playground																							
Lunch																							
Afternoon: Teacher explains lesson																							
Teacher discusses with group																							
Silent work time																							
Cooperative work with other students																							
Oral reading or class presentation																							
Line up for recess or dismissal																							
Hall																							
Playground																							

Source: Reprinted with permission from the *Journal of Behavior Therapy and Experimental Psychiatry, 1*: 279-289. R. G. Wahler & W. H. Cormier, The ecological interview: A first step in outpatient therapy. Copyright 1970, Pergamon Press, Ltd.

gested in the previous chapter, whenever you make a referral for a service, you should clearly communicate your goals and objectives to the appropriate agency or professional.

One of the most difficult solutions to the problem of being overwhelmed or overextended is saying "no." If you or your school board have carefully defined and explained the limits of your services to your clientele initially, this should not alarm you. Nevertheless, there are tactful ways of turning people down, and there are ways that reinforce their coming to

you without building up false hopes that you will take on their case. Ideally, when you must say no, you will be able to refer the person or family to an appropriate service. If there are no referral options, you may need to advocate for the needed services in your community, which is the alternative we take up next.

ADVOCACY

In your role as an advocate for students exhibiting problem behavior, you will undoubtedly find many shortcomings in the system. These may include gaps in special educational provisions, or the lack of needed related services. When confronted by these problems, you have two choices: to campaign for the services your pupils require or to make do with what you have. The first option poses several questions: What educational or related services are most critical? Is the school or another agency responsible for providing these? What are the consequences to you of advocating for these services?

Figure 13-4 presents the service continuum originally described in Chapter 1. However, here we have indicated for each level whether related services are likely to be needed, as well as which agency will probably have primary administrative responsibility for the educational program. These are important considerations because PL 94-142 obligates the agency responsible for each pupil's educational program to provide a free and appropriate educational program in the least restrictive environment. In addition, the agency must obtain the necessary related services, which include "transportation . . . and such developmental, corrective, and other supportive services as may be required to assist a handicapped child to benefit from special education" (Federal Register, 1977, p. 42479). The Education of the Handicapped Act lists the following related services: "transportation, speech pathology, audiology, psychological services, physical therapy, occupational therapy, recreation, early identification and assessment of disabilities, counseling, medical services (for diagnostic and evaluation purposes), and parent counseling and training" (Rosenfield, 1980, p. 6). The Act cautions that this list is not exhaustive. For example, psychotherapy may be considered a related service because of the precedent set by litigation on behalf of a severely disturbed schizophrenic child. Other courts have suggested that psychotherapy must be provided (Rosenfield, 1980).

The point to keep in mind is that additional educational and related services cost money, and the law requires the education agency

(e.g., local school district) to be accountable for these services. By advocating for such services, you may be causing embarrassment or the threat of legal sanction to your employers. Therefore, you are placing yourself in jeopardy. As Frith (1981) observes, "It is becoming increasingly difficult for professionals in the field to assume the role of child advocate, while simultaneously attempting to support their employing agency" (p. 487). So, do you risk your job by pressing the issue, or do you take the safe course and let the student go on being inadequately served? A practical compromise is to inform the parents of their rights and let them handle the matter; but even here, there is no small risk of your participation in the plot being discovered. It is unfortunate that, except for the National Society for Autistic Children, no strong parent group exists to lobby for the rights of behaviorally disordered children and youth. Consequently, the best advice we can offer in such cases is to work cautiously through existing channels, unless you are willing to put your job on the line.

Role Constraints

The limitations we include in this category overlap considerably with ecological constraints, for *role constraints* means that the required intervention is not suited to a person in your professional role. Related services such as psychotherapy or family counseling fit this category. Although you may *feel* qualified to provide informal counseling, and the service you provide may *be* effective, you do not possess the professional authority (credentials or training) to render the service.

Another constraint exists if you are working in a residential setting where the treatment program is prescribed and supervised by another professional. For example, a pupil may be institutionalized for treatment of a severe behavior disorder or delinquency. In such a case, the

Figure 13-4. Continuum of Services for Behaviorally Disordered Children and Youth

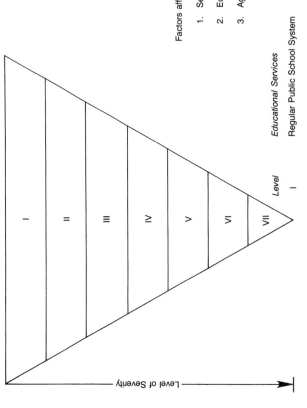

Factors affecting placement in the continuum

1. Severity of behavior disorder
2. Ecological factors (strengths and weaknesses of child's ecological settings)
3. Age of pupil (older pupils are more likely to receive related services)

Level	Educational Services	Related Services	Primary Administrative Jurisdiction
I	Regular Public School System	None	Public School
II	Regular Class, plus Consultation to Teacher	Possible (e.g., Family Counseling, Juvenile Court)	Public School
III	Resource Room (Part-Time Special Education)	Possible	Public School
IV	Self-Contained Special Class (Full-Time Special Education)	Possible to Likely (e.g., Alternative Living Arrangement)	Public School
V	Segregated Public Day School	Possible to Likely	Public School
VI	Residential Education Program	Possible to Likely	Public or Private Treatment Agency
VII	Residential Treatment Program	Likely (e.g., Chemotherapy, Psychotherapy)	Public or Private Treatment Agency

treatment program will probably be developed and supervised by a psychologist or correctional worker, and the education program will be just part of the total treatment package. In these situations, you are not free to make unilateral treatment decisions or to implement programs that affect the student outside the school program.

Failure to recognize role constraints can result in wasteful duplication of effort. This often happens with behaviorally disordered children and youth because they come to the attention of several agencies. Another undesirable consequence results in the provision of conflicting treatment programs. For example, a pupil could receive cathartic play therapy for aggressive behavior from a psychiatrist while you use contingency management for the same problem. If you assume too much of another professional's treatment responsibility, you may face professional sanction or at least suffer bad public relations in certain quarters. In our view, however, the most harmful consequence of overstepping role boundaries is that it erodes the effectiveness of all treatment or educational programs through professional conflict and disharmony. Students exhibiting severe behavior problems need consistency in their environment, and this is impossible when different agencies or professionals pull in different directions or haggle with each other over territorial issues.

Several of the reactions to the ecological limitations we discussed in the previous section will also help you deal with role constraints. For example, you can clarify the goals and purposes of your program and concentrate on doing a credible job within your specific role. This point is well illustrated in the history of education programs for children and youth with behavior disorders. Many early educational programs were established in residential treatment or psychiatric settings. Initially, these educational programs were regarded as little more than day care or as an adjunct to medically oriented treatment. However, such professional leaders as Bettelheim, Berkowitz, Rothman, Fenichel, Hobbs, Haring, Phillips, Whelan, and Hewett have been instrumental in the development of a uniquely educational perspective and have helped establish credibility for the educator's role in treatment programs (see Kauffman & Lewis, 1974).

Hewett and Taylor's (1980) description of the experience of opening an educational program at the University of California at Los Angeles' Neuropsychiatric Institute (NPI) illustrates how educators have had to reconceptualize their role as distinct from that of other professionals. The school program was originally viewed as a baby-sitting service by the psychodynamically oriented staff. The teachers were not considered part of the powerful triumvirate, composed of the psychiatrist, clinical psychologist, and psychiatric social worker. In time, the educational staff began to see that their low status was caused by their failure to conceptualize the role of their program in terms of its unique contribution to the overall treatment program. When they formulated their concept of an educational program in this setting in terms of teaching the skills pupils needed in order to function in less restrictive environments, the school staff were better able to communicate with other professionals and contribute to the overall NPI program. As this example suggests, you should not try to imitate other mental health professionals; instead you should provide educational services that are not available through any other professional group (training in social and academic skills).

If you are not working within a multidisciplinary facility, such as a hospital or residential treatment center, you will need to make referrals for services available from other agencies or persons (the question of whether these services are considered "related" under PL 94-142 is not at issue here; assume, for the present, that your employing agency or the child's parents will pay for the service). Figure 13-5 is a checklist you may find useful in deciding whether to refer the student outside

Figure 13-5.   Referral Decision-Making Checklist

		Yes	Comments

1. Does the pupil engage in any of the following in most, or all, of his ecological settings:

Language disorder (echolalia, pronomial reversal, mutism, etc.)?   _____

Self-stimulation, self-mutilation, hallucinations, catastrophic reactions?   _____

Rumination?   _____

Encopresis, enuresis, obsessive-compulsive behaviors (e.g., rituals, preoccupying thoughts)?   _____

Chronic depression?   _____

Phobias?   _____

Generalized anxiety?   _____

Suicidal behavior?   _____

Sleep disorders?   _____

Gang delinquency?   _____

Interpersonal aggression?   _____

Excessive masturbation?   _____

Sexual misconduct?   _____

Chemical intoxication?   _____

Seizures?   _____

2. Are you unable to control the consequences, or are unable to gain the cooperation of those who do control consequences affecting the pupil's target behaviors?   _____

3. Is (are) the pupil's problem behaviors not under the control of antecedent stimuli arranged by you?   _____

4. Does the pupil fail to respond (appropriately or inappropriately) to consequences administered by you?   _____

5. Are you unable to work with the parents?   _____

6. Are you unable to identify or control any of the pupil's reinforcers?   _____

7. Have you been ineffective in achieving meaningful gains with the pupil?   _____

Specify goals not met:

_____

_____

_____

_____

8. Are there other reasons why you cannot or will not work with the pupil and/or his caretakers?   _____

Note: If these problems are targeted on the student's IEP, you may be responsible as the primary treatment agent. However, you may also need to work with other agencies or professionals on these problems.

your program for help with specific problems or to a different treatment program (remember that all decisions to move a student toward a more restrictive environment, or decisions that alter a student's IEP, must follow due process). We recommend that you use Figure 13-5 in conjunction with Figures 13-1, 13-2, and 13-3 to gain a comprehensive picture of the problem, the student, and the student's ecological settings when contemplating a referral decision. The questions in Figure 13-5 are intended to be illustrative rather than exhaustive. Thus, they are only a sample of those you could ask. Those behaviors encompassed in the first question suggest a referral for related services, whereas subsequent questions imply difficulty in reaching educational objectives with the pupil.

If your decision involves making a referral, the question of to whom you refer and for what services depends on whether the student appears to need a more controlled or consistent environment, whether the parents need relief from management responsibilities, and so forth. As indicated earlier, it is wise to maintain a log of your referrals with appropriate evaluative comments. This log should be kept confidential, unless there are compelling professional reasons for making portions of it public (e.g., you are subpoenaed in litigation against a professional who has worked with some of your pupils).

Legal Constraints

CONSTRAINTS ON THE ROLE OF TEACHERS

Surely one of the most imposing threats is that of legal sanction. The long-standing common-law doctrine of in-loco parentis, giving teachers authority equivalent to that of parents, has been tested in the courts more and more often.

Increasingly, "professionals who serve children are finding themselves being sued or dismissed on such charges as malpractice, liability, and assault" (Weintraub & McCaffrey, 1976, p. 333). As a teacher, you may be liable for injury sustained by a pupil as a result of negligence on your part, or for defamatory material regarding students or fellow employees (contributory negligence must be ruled out in the case of older or more mature students). You, or your agency, may also be liable for negligence in depriving a student of appropriate treatment or due process (Weintraub & McCaffrey, 1976).

The Council for Exceptional Children (CEC) has developed a code of ethics and professional standards to guide practitioners and define their professional responsibilities (CEC Delegate Assembly, 1983). The introduction to these guidelines states that "special education professionals charge themselves with obligations to three parties: the exceptional student, the employer, and the profession" (p. 8). The CEC Code of Ethics consists of eight principles that form the basis for professional conduct.

I. Special education professionals are committed to developing the highest educational and quality of life potential of exceptional individuals.

II. Special education professionals promote and maintain a high level of competence and integrity in practicing their profession.

III. Special education professionals engage in professional activities which benefit exceptional individuals, their families, other colleagues, students, or research subjects.

IV. Special education professionals exercise objective professional judgment in the practice of their profession.

V. Special education professionals strive to advance their knowledge and skills regarding the education of exceptional individuals.

VI. Special education professionals work within the standards and policies of their profession.

VII. Special education professionals seek to uphold and improve where necessary the laws, regulations, and policies governing the delivery of special education and related services and the practice of their profession.

VIII. Special education professionals do not condone or participate in unethical or illegal acts, nor violate professional standards adopted by the Delegate Assembly of CEC (p. 8).

The professional standards derived from these principles are grouped into three categories: professionals in relation to exceptional persons and their families, professional employment, and professionals in relation to the profession and to other professionals. It is important to become familiar with these standards because they will affect your professional obligations and influence critical decisions. You may obtain a free copy of the reprint from *Exceptional Children,* Volume 50, Number 3 (November 1983) entitled "Special Education and Professional Standards" by writing Publications Sales, The Council for Exceptional Children, 1920 Association Drive, Reston, VA 22091.

As you study these standards you will see the potential for conflict with your employing agency. Thus, in following them you may be on sensitive ground. In general, teachers' rights as private citizens (freedom of speech, right to action, right to due process) have been upheld by the courts. The chief reasons for the dismissal of a teacher have included insubordination, incompetence, neglect of duty, inappropriate conduct, subversive activity, or decreased need for the person's services (Weintraub & McCaffrey, 1976). If your behavior with respect to the above principles causes your employer to level charges against you, be prepared to seek legal counsel. By the same token, you may be named in a suit brought by a child's caregivers

for failing to act in accordance with these principles. As we said, it is difficult to advocate for children while simultaneously maintaining allegiance to your employing agency.

Public Law 94-142 addresses constraints on agencies providing educational services in that it declares and protects the civil rights of the handicapped. The law guarantees handicapped persons the right to treatment, which encompasses procedural and substantive due process and equal protection, the right to equal educational opportunity, the right of access to their records, and the right to an individualized education (Turnbull, 1976). In addition, the following provisions must be guaranteed by each state in their annual program plans (Thomas, 1979):

1. Extensive child-find or child identification procedures. (The first priority is to identify children who are not receiving any type of education. The second priority is to identify those who are receiving an inadequate education).

2. A full service goal and detailed timetable designed for the education of each child.

3. A guarantee of complete due process procedures.

4. The assurance of regular parent or guardian consultation.

5. Maintenance of programs and procedures for comprehensive personnel development, including inservice training.

6. Assurance of special education being provided to all handicapped children in the least restrictive environment.

7. Assurance of nondiscriminatory testing and evaluation.

8. A guarantee of policies and procedures to protect the confidentiality of data and information.

9. Assurance of the maintenance of an individual program for all handicapped children.

10. Assurance of an effective policy guaranteeing the right of all handicapped children to a public education, at no cost to parents or guardian.

11. Assurance of a surrogate to act for any child when parents or guardians are either unknown or unavailable, or when the child is a ward of the state (p. 10).

Your state department and employing agency are accountable for the implementation of policies, procedures, and safeguards. You are accountable for providing specific educational services in accordance with these guidelines. In the event that caregivers bring suit for failure to meet these provisions, you may be named as codefendant. If your professional behavior can be construed as negligent or unethical, you may become the education agency's scapegoat; you may be sued by the caregivers and *not* supported by your agency.

CONSTRAINTS ON THE USE OF BEHAVIORAL INTERVENTIONS

Legal constraints have been specifically applied to the use of aversive procedures in educational programs. These issues were discussed at length in Chapter 4. Here, we will merely point out that although aversive procedures involve the presentation of any noxious stimulus or infringement of students' bodily or human rights, court cases have generally involved corporal punishment in the form of spankings or beatings (Wood & Lakin, 1983). The school's right to use moderate corporal punishment has been upheld and is approved by most states. However, it has not been advocated in the special education literature (Wood, 1983b), and the American Federation of Teachers, the National Education Association, the Council for Exceptional Children, and the American Psychological Association have issued statements opposing it (Wood, 1983a).

The use of seclusion time-out has also been argued in the courts, although litigation has involved mental health facilities rather than public schools (Gast & Nelson, 1977; Wood & Lakin, 1983). As indicated in Chapter 4, a growing number of states and school districts are issuing policies regulating the use of behavioral interventions, particularly those involving restrictive or intrusive procedures.

Solutions to the problems posed by legal constraints are easier to suggest than to implement. With respect to your professional conduct, we suggest that you clarify your role and specific responsibilities and stay within them. By all means try to follow the Code of Ethics and Professional Standards adopted by CEC (1983), but in so doing, make it clear that your goal is to improve pupil services, not to subvert the system or its administrators. Also carefully study PL 94-142. Several brief explanations of the law and its provisions written for laypersons (e.g., Abeson, Bolick, & Hass, 1975) are available. At some point in your training, you may be required to take a course in the legal rights and issues of the handicapped.

Guidelines for the use of aversive procedures are provided in Chapter 4, but here we emphasize that punishment is justified when the behavior it suppresses is more injurious to the individual or to others than the punishment itself and when no alternative exists (Wood, 1983b). We do *not* recommend that you use corporal punishment; it is too subjective and is likely to have a long history of misapplication with your students. Instead, we urge you to apply planned, objective, and systematic procedures such as extinction, verbal reprimands, response cost, or time-out in conjunction with positive reinforcement of incompatible behavior (see Chapter 4). If you must use a more extreme technique (overcorrection, aversive physical stimulation), we recommend consideration of Wood's (1983b) suggestions:

1. All reasonable alternatives should be considered, if not tried, first. This consideration should be documented.
2. Do not apply punishment of any type without first becoming thoroughly familiar with your state and local regulations.
3. The lines of authority for the punishment procedure should be clear.
4. Punishment should be adequately super-

vised, monitored, and externally reviewed.
5. All persons using punishment should understand its dynamics and complexities.

In addition, remember that prior parental consent to use punishment in an educational program is required by PL 94-142, and parents have the right to withdraw consent at any time (Wood, 1983b).

Stress and Burnout

The many potential hazards of special education professional practice lay the groundwork for stress and burnout. Burnout has been defined as ". . . emotional exhaustion resulting from the stress of interpersonal contact" (Maslach, 1978, p. 56). In working with persons exhibiting behavior disorders, stressful interpersonal contact is the rule. How well you are able to maintain a healthy perspective of your job and your pupils in the face of stress depends on a number of factors. Researchers are just beginning to study and delineate these variables. Furthermore, because a person's emotional reactions to job stresses are subjective and highly individualized, it is difficult to obtain reliable, objective data on the subject. However, this area has attracted a great deal of current attention.

CAUSES AND SIGNS OF STRESS

Since stress is an integral part of working with behaviorally disordered pupils, you should be aware of other variables that can be emotionally and physically draining, for these may influence your decision to accept a job, change your place of employment, or leave the field entirely. Weiskopf (1980) describes a number of environmental sources of teacher stress, including work overload from IEP development and implementation, parent conferences, meetings, excessive paperwork, and so forth;

lack of perceived success with pupils; large amounts of direct contact with clients; high student-teacher ratios, especially in mainstream classes; an open or nondirective classroom structure that places fewer restrictions on student behavior; the need to give emotional support to pupils who cannot provide any to the teacher in return; lack of administrative support; resistant parents; mislabeled and misplaced students; threats of lawsuit; and confused or ill-trained co-workers and aides. Additionally, there may be a lack of opportunity for time out on the job, and a lack of professional work relationships (Zabel & Zabel, 1980).

These are conditions that occur frequently in the work of special educators. As the discussion in this and the previous chapter suggests, such environmental problems may be particularly acute for the professional in the area of behavioral disorders. Trying to deal with the educational system; spending hours working outside the classroom; encountering recalcitrant parents, nonsupportive school administrators and staff, and negative public attitudes can leave you feeling tired and defeated. If this happens, what can you do? The first step is to recognize the symptoms of stress. Weiskopf (1980) describes a continuum of signs of potential teacher stress. Initially, you may experience a vague feeling of personal distress, followed by irritability, fatigue, boredom, mild depression, or feelings of being overworked. These initial symptoms may be so subtle that you fail to notice them. Unless conditions improve, you may later find yourself increasingly resistant to change and less flexible, and you may tend to withdraw from social contact. Others may observe that you are becoming less effective. You may adhere rigidly to routines and rely excessively on manipulative controls to defend yourself from continued emotional stress. The later stages of burnout may involve more serious symptoms such as alcohol and drug abuse, marital conflict, absenteeism, chronic depression, and even mental illness. However, Weiskopf (1980) observes that these symptoms may be related to other personal problems and that precise data on burnout are not available. Therefore, do not expect to see all of these signs or to see them appear in this particular pattern. If you find yourself extremely dissatisfied with your work, find frequent reasons to be absent, or are unable to psychologically get away from your students' problems, you should attempt to do something.

COPING WITH STRESS

Unfortunately, many of the variables that should be changed to reduce stress are controlled by your employing agency, not by you. For example, Zabel and Zabel (1980) indicate that the probability of burnout may be reduced by lowering student-teacher ratios, reducing working hours, providing opportunities for time away from the job, sharing student loads through team teaching, and training in dealing with stress. All of these tactics require organizational change, which involves policy decisions at higher administrative levels.

Evidence that organizational variables affect teacher stress was provided by Bensky et al. (1980). One hundred fourteen teachers responded to a questionnaire evaluating stress and variables related to it. Those who had a clear perception of their jobs' expectations were under less stress. Also, teachers reported less stress if they perceived their school system as clearly either in compliance or not in compliance with PL 94-142. When they saw their school system as marginally in compliance, greater stress was reported. Apparently greater role clarity existed among these teachers when their district's status regarding the law was less ambiguous.

Although you can little affect such organizational changes as compliance with PL 94-142, reducing working hours, or training in stress management, you may be able to reduce the amount of stress that you experience personally. Weiskopf (1980) gives several suggestions:

1. Know in advance what the job requires in terms of emotional demands.
2. Set realistic goals for yourself and for your students.
3. Delegate routine work, such as paperwork, to aides or volunteers.
4. Avoid becoming isolated from other staff members.
5. Break up the amount of direct contact you have with students through team teaching, the use of learning centers, and so forth.
6. Remain intellectually active off the job.
7. Get physical exercise.
8. Interject newness and variety into your day to counterbalance routine.
9. Participate in hobbies and activities not related to your job.

However, keep in mind that there is no valid evidence that these methods reduce burnout (Weiskopf, 1980). We feel that the best deterrents are adequate professional and personal support and reinforcement.

As we have tried to demonstrate throughout this text, and especially in this chapter, working with problem students, their families, and their communities is difficult. Remaining psychologically fit and professionally effective requires that you know your role and its limitations. This is not sufficient, however. To be a successful educator who works with behaviorally disordered pupils, you must also be highly skilled. We hope this text has helped you acquire the skills you need to feel, and be, effective.

Summary

The complexity and intensity of working with students exhibiting behavioral problems require high levels of dedication and expertise by professional educators. To function effectively, these persons need adequate support systems in their working and personal environments; they must also recognize and work within the limitations of their roles. Optimal programming for behaviorally disordered children and youth should address their needs, and the needs of other persons who care for and work with them, across many different ecological settings. The practice in our culture of institutionalizing human services according to specific settings and agencies, constrains those who must work within formal professional roles. This chapter has described some of these constraints and has suggested guidelines and strategies for working more effectively within them. Ultimately, the success of interventions on behalf of students with behavioral disorders will depend upon our ability to bridge professional and political boundaries in designing strategies that provide meaningful habilitative or rehabilitative experiences that ensure the skills acquired in educational settings are retained and used to facilitate lifelong patterns of success.

Discussion Questions

1. What are the constraints that affect educators working in each of the following roles: special education resource teacher, special education self-contained classroom teacher, school psychologist, school social worker?

2. As a special education teacher, how would you deal with the problem of a regular classroom teacher who uses corporal punishment with one of your students?

3. How would you respond to parents who request your help in managing their child's behavior outside of school? (The student is being seen by a psychologist in private practice.)

4. The principal of your school wants to refer one of your pupils to a residential treatment program. You disagree with this action, but the principal insists. What should you do?

5. A psychiatrist has prescribed an antipsychotic drug for a behaviorally disordered pupil in your school. You have observed that the student is lethargic, withdrawn, and experiencing trouble concentrating. The parent, however, is pleased with the child's improved behavior at home and will not

consider asking the psychiatrist to adjust the dosage. What course of action will you take?

6. You have been asked to participate in designing a study of burnout in your school district. How would you assess staff to identify signs of stress and burnout? What recommendations could you offer to reduce or prevent it?

References

Abeson, A., Bolick, N., & Hass, J. (1975). *A primer on due process: Education decisions for handicapped children.* Reston, VA: Council for Exceptional Children.

Bensky, J. M., Shaw, S. F., Gouse, A. S., Bates, H., Dixon, B., & Beane, W. E. (1980). Public Law 94-142 and stress: A problem for educators. *Exceptional Children, 47,* 24-29.

Council for Exceptional Children Delegate Assembly. (1983). Code of ethics and standards for professional practice. *Exceptional Children, 50,* 8-12.

Federal Register (1977, Tuesday, August 23). Part II, *42* (163), 42474-42518.

Frith, G. H. (1981). "Advocate" vs. "professional employee": A question of priorities for special educators. *Exceptional Children, 47,* 486-492.

Gast, D. L., & Nelson, C. M. (1977). Legal and ethical considerations for the use of timeout in special education settings. *Journal of Special Education, 11,* 457-467.

Hewett, F. M., & Taylor, F. D. (1980). *The emotionally disturbed child in the classroom: The orchestration of success* (2nd ed.). Boston: Allyn & Bacon.

Kauffman, J. M. (1985). *Characteristics of children's behavior disorders* (3rd ed.). Columbus, OH: Merrill.

Kauffman, J. M., & Lewis, C. D. (Eds.). (1974). *Teaching children with behavior disorders: Personal perspectives.* Columbus, OH: Merrill.

Maslach, C. (1978). Job burnout: How people cope. *Public Welfare, 36,* 56-58.

Rosenfield, S. J. (1980, January-February). Advocates and educators lock horns over "related services." *Amicus, 6-7,* 48.

Thomas, C. C. (1979). *PL 94-142: An instructional module for inservice training.* Frankfort, KY: Office of Education for Exceptional Children, Kentucky Department of Education.

Turnbull, H. R., III. (1976). Accountability: An overview of the impact of litigation on professionals. In F. J. Weintraub, A. Abeson, J. Ballard, & M. L. LaVor (Eds.). *Public policy and the education of exceptional children* (pp. 362-368). Reston, VA: Council for Exceptional Children.

Wahler, R. G., & Cormier, W. H. (1970). The ecological interview: A first step in outpatient behavior therapy. *Journal of Behavior Therapy and Experimental Psychiatry, 1,* 279-289.

Weintraub, F. J., & McCaffrey, M. A. (1976). Professional rights and responsibilities. In F. J. Weintraub, A. Abeson, J. Ballard, & M. L. LaVor (Eds.). *Public policy and the education of exceptional children* (pp. 333-343). Reston, VA: Council for Exceptional Children.

Weiskopf, P. E. (1980). Burnout among teachers of exceptional children. *Exceptional Children, 47,* 18-23.

Wood, F. H. (1983a). The influence of public opinion and social custom on the use of corporal punishment in the schools. In F. H. Wood & K. C. Lakin (Eds.). *Punishment and aversive stimulation in special education: Legal, theoretical, and practical issues in their use with emotionally disturbed children and youth* (pp. 29-39). Reston, VA: Council for Exceptional Children.

Wood, F. H. (1983b). Punishment and special education: Some concluding comments. In F. H. Wood & K. C. Lakin (Eds.). *Punishment and aversive stimulation in special education: Legal, theoretical, and practical issues in their use with emotionally disturbed children and youth* (pp. 119-122). Reston, VA: Council for Exceptional Children.

Wood, F. H., & Lakin, K. C. (1983). The legal status of the use of corporal punishment and other aversive procedures in the schools. In F. H. Wood & K. C. Lakin (Eds.). *Punishment and aversive stimulation in special education: Legal, theoretical, and practical issues in their use with emotionally disturbed children and youth* (pp. 3-27). Reston, VA: Council for Exceptional Children.

Zabel, R. H., & Zabel, M. K. (1980). Burnout: A critical issue for educators. *Education Unlimited, 2,* 23-25.

Glossary

activity reinforcement Providing opportunity to engage in preferred or high-probability behaviors contingent upon completion of less preferred or low-probability behaviors

addiction Compulsive use of a drug, characterized by a behavior pattern that centers on drug use, procurement, and continued use. According to this definition, evidence of physical tolerance and dependence is not necessary for establishing that a person is addicted.

admissions and release committee See *child study team*

advocacy To campaign for the services your students require

aggression A category of behavior that involves harm, injury, or damage to persons or property (e.g., kicking, pushing, throwing school books)

AIMS Assessment System Instruments used to evaluate the adequacy of students' classroom and peer social adjustments in less restrictive settings (Walker, 1986).

alcohol abuse The voluntary intake of alcohol in spite of adverse physical and social consequences

analogue measures A role-play or behavioral rehearsal in which an individual demonstrates how he or she would respond in a given social situation

anger control training An approach to help juvenile delinquents manage their aggressive behavior using modeling, role-playing, visual clues, and homework

anorexia nervosa Extreme self-starvation, despite no known physical cause of illness, brought about by an abnormal aversion to eating in which the weight of an individual (usually an adolescent girl) falls at least 25 percent below what would be normal

antecedent-behavior-consequence analysis A technique used to identify systematically functional relationships among behaviors and environmental variables

antecedent stimulus A stimulus that precedes a behavior; stimulus may or may not serve as a discriminative for a specific behavior

applied behavior analysis A systematic, performance-based, self-evaluative technology for assessing and changing behavior

assessment The process of gathering data for the purpose of making educational decisions

attempted suicide Includes some of the elements of completed suicide (i.e., having the conscious intent to die but not dying); attempters wish both to live and to die

autism (autistic) The condition characterized by extreme withdrawal and poorly developed communication/language skills

aversive procedure Any procedure involving the use of an aversive stimulus to modify behavior (e.g., lemon juice applied to a pupil's mouth following an episode of rumination)

aversive stimulus A stimulus having the effect of decreasing the rate of probability of a behavior when presented as a consequence; as such, a type of punisher; alternately, may have the effect of increasing the rate or probability of a behavior when removed as a consequence

avoidant disorder Experienced by children who go to great lengths to avoid contact with any strangers

back-up reinforcer An object or event received in exchange for a specific number of tokens, points, and so forth

413

bar graph A method of visually displaying data; may be used to show progress toward a specific goal or objective

baseline data Data points that reflect an operant level (the level of natural occurrence of the behavior before intervention) of the target behavior; serve a purpose similar to a pretest; provide a level of behavior against which the results of an intervention procedure can be compared

behavioral-ecological assessment The evaluation of observable student behaviors across the range of settings in which they occur

behavioral interview An important part of the assessment process, interviewing students, their parents, and teachers to gather information about a student's strengths and weaknesses

behaviorally disordered Behavior characteristics that (1) deviate from educators' standards of normality, and (2) impair the functioning of that student or others; manifested as environmental conflict or personal disturbances

behavioral objectives The behavior to be achieved following intervention

behavioral standard A standard for behavior based on the expectations of other persons

bulimia An eating disorder in which eating binges are accompanied by vomiting, often self-induced

burnout Emotional exhaustion (sometimes experienced by a teacher)

caffeine A stimulant drug; belongs in a chemical class named xanthines (pronounced "zanthenes") and is a methyl-xanthine compound

certification A decision to classify a pupil for special education placement

changing-criterion design A single-subject experimental design that involves successfully changing the criterion for reinforcement, systematically increasing or decreasing in a step-wise manner

chart A method of visually displaying data; displays from several to many symbols in order to represent the data

chemical abuse The self-administration of a psychoactive chemical that has not been prescribed by a physician; or the compulsive use of a chemical persisting at a high level in spite of extreme disruption of physical well-being, psychological integrity, social functioning; or a combination of these

Child Behavior Checklist A checklist developed by Echenbach and Edelbrock (1980) and used for screening children for psychiatric problems

childhood psychosis Used to denote a wide range of severe and profound disorders of children, including autism, schizophrenia, and symbiotic psychosis

child study team A group of persons designated to oversee the assessment of a handicapped student as well as the implementation and evaluation of the student's IEP

classroom adjustment code (CAC) A five-second interval recording system that measures three categories of pupil and teacher behavior; used to evaluate the adequacy of students' classroom and peer social adjustments in less restrictive settings

classroom density The crowding of a classroom that can affect aggressive behavior

clinical syndrome DSM-III classifies psychological disorders along five axes of dimensions; Axis I consists of the major pattern or symptoms or clinical syndrome that the student exhibits

clock light An environmental intervention that signals on- and off-task behavior

cocaine A narcotic with physiological effects very similar to amphetamines

cognitive behavior modification A new approach that involves teaching students cognitive strategies to help them to solve problems

collaborative approaches A multidisciplinary team approach to aid in the self-management of aggressive behavior

collaborative consultation Teacher assistance teams that promote better mobilization of the resources available in schools

collateral effect One intervention affecting several target behaviors

communicative function Maladaptive behaviors that occur because students lack more effective means of communicating their needs or obtaining reinforcement

competing explanations In single-subject design, the uncontrolled factors that influence the behavior simultaneously with the intervention

compliance training Modifying oppositional behavior and training students to respond quickly to adult directions

conditioned reinforcer A stimulus that has acquired a reinforcing function through pairing with a previously established reinforcer; including most social, activity, and generalized reinforcers (also called a secondary reinforcer)

conditions The part of an instructional objective that specifies when a terminal behavior should occur

consensual observer drift Two observers gradually changing their response definitions while recording data

consequence Any stimulus that is presented contingently following a particular response

constructs Theoretical constructions of traits or attributes

consultation Providing indirect services to pupils by helping their teachers or parents directly

contiguity The timing of reinforcement or punishment

contingency The relationship between behavior and its consequences

contingency contracting Making access to a high-probability behavior contingent on a low-probability behavior

contingent observation A form of time-out in which a child is removed from reinforcement while observing others receiving reinforcement

continuous measurement Continuous data collection for the purpose of monitoring and evaluating student progress

continuum of services A special education range with consideration given to more restrictive educational placements after interventions have been proven unsuccessful in less restrictive settings

contracting Placing contingencies for reinforcement (if-then statements) into a written document; creates a permanent product that can be referred to by both teacher and student

Council for Children with Behavioral Disorders The major professional organization for special educators serving behaviorally disordered students

criteria The part of an instructional objective that specifies the requirements for acceptable performance of the terminal behavior

criterion-based assessment (CBA) Assessment of a pupil's status with regard to specific curriculum content and objectives

criterion of functioning in the next environment Identifying the skill requirements and expectations of less restrictive environments and teaching these in order to increase students' chances of successful participation

criterion of ultimate functioning The functional skills needed by adults to participate freely in community environments

cumulative graph A graphic presentation of successive summed numbers (rate, frequency, percentage, duration) that represent behavioral occurrences

curriculum modification The modification or change of a curriculum to provide appropriate materials and instructional level

data-based decision making Using direct and frequent measures of a behavior as a basis for comparing student performance to a desired level, and making adjustments in the student's educational program based on that comparison

data decision rules Rules that suggest how to respond to patterns in student performance; developed by the teacher to facilitate the efficient and effective evaluation of instructional and behavior management programs

data level change The amount of relative change in the data within or between conditions

data stability The variability of individual data points around the trend line

data trend A pattern that tells you whether a program is working, because data paths seldom follow straight lines, nor do they increase or decrease in even increments

decertification criteria The goals and objectives for a student's special education program; when goals are met, student should be returned to regular education

dependence Compulsive drug use to ward off physical or emotional discomfort; the person depends on the drug to prevent withdrawal or abstinence-related distress; *physical and psychological dependence* are distinguished on the basis of overt and predictable withdrawal symptoms

dependency The need for maximum adult support, accompanied by minimal independent skills

dependent group contingencies The performance of certain group members determining the consequence received by the entire group

dependent group-oriented contingency A student's desired behavior earning reinforcers desired by peers; has also been observed to increase peers' positive attention to the targeted student

dependent measures A variable that is measured while another variable (the independent variable) is changed in a systematic way

dependent variable The behavior that is to be changed through intervention

depressants Depressant drugs belonging to the classes of barbiturates (phenobarbital, hexobarbital), benzodiazepine and propanediol minor tranquilizers (Librium, Valium, meprobamate), and antihistaminic sedatives (Barbiturates are commonly prescribed for sleep facilitation and for control of seizures. Benzodiazepines and propanediols are antianxiety agents. Benzodiazepines are used to control seizures and increase muscle relaxation. Antihistemines are used to control allergies and respiratory ailments.)

depression A behavioral disorder characterized by discouragement, a feeling of inadequacy, sleep loss, weight loss, loss of sexual drive, or loss of appetite

detention A behavioral correction intervention in which a student must come thirty to ninety minutes before or after school to complete assignments

developmental regression A temporary lapse in an individual's social skills

differential reinforcement Four strategies that involve reinforcement applied differentially to reduce behaviors; see *DRL, DRO, DRI,* and *DRA*

direction/adult involvement How much structure a teacher or a classroom assistant provides

direct observation Observation of a student in those settings in which the target behavior occurs

discrete learning trial A learning trial that has a discriminable beginning and end; involves the presentation of a prompt or discriminative stimulus, a pupil response, and a subsequent teacher response

discrimination Demonstration of the ability to differentiate among stimuli or environmental events

discriminative stimulus (S^D) A stimulus that is likely to occasion a particular response in that it signals the probability that reinforcement will follow certain responses made in its presence

DRA (differential reinforcement of alternate behavior) A procedure in which reinforcement is delivered to behaviors that are functionally incompatible with or simply alternatives to the target behavior

DRI (differential reinforcement of incompatible behaviors) Reinforcing a response that is topographically incompatible with a behavior targeted for reduction

DRL (differential reinforcement of low rates of behavior) A procedure in which reinforcement is delivered when the number of responses in a specified period of time is less than or equal to a prescribed limit; enables the maintenance of a behavior at a predetermined rate lower than was occurring at its baseline or naturally occurring frequency

DRO (differential reinforcement of other behaviors) A procedure in which reinforcement is delivered when the target behavior is not emitted for a specified period of time; behaviors other than the target behaviors are specifically reinforced

drug Any chemical that is consumed and is present in abnormal concentration in the body; includes substances such as insulin or other hormones found naturally within the body, which can dramatically influence emotion and behavior if their concentrations are not kept within normal limits

drug abuse The voluntary intake of a chemical in spite of adverse physical and social consequences

drug tolerance Physical adaptation to the effects of a drug so that more of the drug is necessary to produce the same effect with repeated use

DSM-III Diagnostic and Statistical Manual of Mental Disorders (3rd edition) A manual that defines and classifies mental disorders according to the American Psychiatric Association guidelines (APA, 1980)

due process Procedural safeguards established to ensure the rights of exceptional students and their parents

duration recording Recording the amount of time between the initiation of a response and its conclusion; *total duration recording* is recording cumulative time between the initiation of a response and its final conclusion (e.g., one may record cumulative time out-of-seat across several instances); *duration per occurrence* is recording each behavioral event and its duration

dysphoria Sadness, a symptom of depression

eating disorders Socially immature and inadequate behavior that involves food

echolalia The parroting repetition of words or phrases either immediately after they are heard or later; observed in psychotic, schizophrenic, or autistic children

ecological approach An approach to assessment that focuses on the student's interaction with the environment rather than on the deficits of the student

ecological ceiling Acknowledgment that it is unrealistic to expect target behaviors to increase or decrease to rates above or below those of peers in the same settings

ecological model Assumptions that behavior disorders are primarily a result of flaws in a complex social system in which various elements of the system (e.g., child, school, family, church, community) are highly interdependent, and that the most effective preventative actions and therapeutic interventions will involve changes in the entire social system

ecological setting The various subsettings in which a student's behavior occurs

edible reinforcement Providing edible items (that are reinforcing for particular students) after a state of relative deprivation for the edible item

Education of the Handicapped Act (PL 94-142) The public law that guarantees appropriate experiences for handicapped children and youth

elective mutism Refusal to talk

emphysema A disease in which the alveoli or air sacs of the lung are destroyed, thus preventing the normal exchange of oxygen and carbon dioxide; resulting in breathlessness, expansion of the rib cage, and possible heart impairment

encopresis Incontinence of feces, which may consist of passing feces into the clothing or bed at regular intervals or leaking mucus and feces into the clothing or bed almost continuously

enuresis Incontinence of urine, which may be diurnal (wetting oneself during the day) or nocturnal (bed-wetting)

environmental analysis A technique used to provide the intervention team with information on specific settings, time, and adult actions for further examination

environmentally mediated strategy Relies on changing some aspect of the environment to prevent or manage behavioral problems

equal interval graph paper A form for presenting behavioral data: vertical lines represent training sessions or calendar days, and horizontal lines may be designated to represent number, percentage, or rate (frequency); emphasizes absolute differences among data points

equal ratio graph paper A form for presenting behavioral data in terms of rate per minute or percent; semilogarithmic rather than additive, therefore changes in rate of performance that are proportionately equal are visually presented as equal.

event recording Recording a tally or frequency count of behavior as it occurs within an observation period; an observational recording procedure

expulsion A disciplinary consequence that involves exclusion from school

externalizing Acting out a behavior so that it is observable

extinction Withholding reinforcement for a previously reinforced behavior in order to reduce the occurrence of the behavior

facial screening A procedure for reducing stereotypic behaviors by covering the student's face with your hand or a cloth bib when the student engages in the target behavior

fair pair rule A way of simultaneously identifying a desired social behavior to replace the behavior to be reduced

feedback Providing the student with descriptive information regarding the student's behavior

follow-up assessment Evaluating the student's current status with regard to IEP or intervention objectives, and evaluating the effectiveness of the educational program

formative evaluation Evaluation that occurs as skills are being developed

frequency The number of times a behavior occurs during an observation period

frequency polygon A noncumulative frequency graph; may be used to report frequency, rate, or percent data

functional analysis A technique used to systematically identify functional relationships among behaviors and environmental variables

functional mediators A strategy that takes advantage of potential discriminative stimuli common to training and generalization training

functional relationship In applied behavior analysis, demonstrated when a behavior varies systematically with the application of an intervention procedure; sometimes called a cause-and-effect relationship

functional response class A class of behaviors grouped because they have the same effect on the environment (e.g., attention-seeking behaviors)

generalization Expansion of a student's capability of performance beyond those conditions set for initial acquisition; *stimulus generalization* refers to performance under conditions—that is, cues, materials, trainers, and environments—other than those present during acquisition; *maintenance generalization* refers to continued performance of learned behavior after contingencies have been withdrawn; *response generalization* refers to changes in behaviors similar to those directly treated

generalization training Successfully reintegrating your students into the mainstream of school life

good behavior game An independent, group-oriented contingency that applies consequences to a group, contingent upon each member reaching a specified level of performance

Grandma's Law See *Premack Principle*

graph A method of visually displaying data; typically uses only one or two symbols to represent data

group contingency A peer-mediated strategy in which several peers and the target student work with the teacher to modify behaviors

group goal setting An intervention that consists of two major components: first, the teacher establishes a social behavior goal for each student; and second, each student receives

feedback on his progress towards that goal during highly structured group discussions

group-oriented contingency Contingencies related to the behavior of groups of persons

hallucinogens A chemically heterogeneous group of drugs with the common property of altering sensory experiences and mood

hashish A purified resin of the marijuana plant

heroin Ciadetylmorphine; a narcotic opiate

high-probability behavior Preferred behavior

home-based contract Placing contingencies for reinforcement, in which parents have agreed to participate

IEP (individualized education program) A written educational plan developed for each student eligible for special education

ignoring The withdrawal of social attention for the length of the time-out period

independent group contingency Contingencies related to the behavior of groups with consequences for behaviors directed toward individual group members

independent variable The treatment or intervention under experimenter control that is being manipulated in order to change a behavior

inhalants and volatile solvents Chemicals that mix easily with air and can be inhaled, includes hydrocarbons (benzene, carbon tetrachloride), freons (trichlorofloromethane), keytones (acetone), esters (ethylacetate), alcohols (methyl alcohol), glycols (ethylene glycol), and gasoline; common sources of these chemicals are aerosols, fingernail polish, household cements, lacquer thinner, lighter fluid, cleaning fluid, and model cement

in-loco parentis The legal doctrine, giving teachers authority equivalent to that of parents

in-school suspension A school intervention that includes a reinforcing setting from which the student is removed, a nonreinforcing environment to which the student goes, and contingencies that govern the student's passage from one environment to the other

instructional time The amount of time that students are engaged in active learning and instruction

intellectual assessment The process of gathering data for the purpose of demonstrating that a problem is not due to cognitive impairment

intensity A measure of behavior that involves recording both its frequency and its duration

interdependent group contingency Requiring each student to reach a prescribed level of behavior before the entire group receives a consequence

intermittent schedules of reinforcement Schedules in which reinforcement follows some, but not all, correct or appropriate responses or follows when a period of appropriate behavior has elapsed; include ratio, interval, and response-duration schedules of reinforcement

interobserver agreement Comparison of observable measures to obtain reliability

interval recording An observational recording system in which an observation period is divided into a number of short intervals, and the observer counts the number of intervals during which the behavior occurs, rather than instances of the behavior

interval schedules of reinforcement A schedule for the delivery of reinforcers contingent upon the occurrence of a behavior following a specified period of time; in a *fixed interval* (FI) schedule, the interval of time is standard (e.g., FI5 indicates the delivery of reinforcement for the first occurrence of behavior following each five-minute interval of the observation period); in a *variable interval* (VI) schedule, the interval of time varies (e.g., VI5 indicates the delivery of reinforcement for the first response that occurs after intervals averaging five minutes in length)

intervention Becoming involved with the student in an official capacity in order to improve his or her performance socially, emotionally, or academically

intervention plan The components include a behavioral objective, what will be done, who will do it, how it will be done, when it will be done, when it will be reviewed, who will review it, and what will happen if the plan is ineffective or if undesired side effects occur

interviews A useful assessment tool for obtaining assessment data from both children and adults

intrusiveness The extent to which interventions impinge or encroach on students' bodies or personal rights

juvenile delinquency Pattern of behaviors that, if exhibited by an adult, would be considered criminal

latency recording Recording the amount of time between the presentation of the S^D (discriminative stimulus) and the initiation of a response

learned helplessness Acquired helplessness, ranging from anaclitic depression (infants who are suddenly bereft of their mothers) to the older child's lack of joy and interest in life

least dangerous assumption When conclusive data are not available regarding the effectiveness of an intervention, educational decisions should be based on assumptions that, if incorrect, will have the least dangerous effect on the student

least intrusive alternative See *least restrictive alternative*

least restrictive alternative Using the simplest yet most effective intervention based on available data regarding the effectiveness of a procedure

least restrictive placement The placement imposing the fewest restrictions on a student's normal academic or social functioning

levels system A method of differentiating hierarchically any aspect of an individual's performance (e.g., in a token economy or for assessment purposes); also referred to as *phase system*

limiting behaviors Behaviors that limit the student's access to public education programs

line of desired progress A line drawn on a behavior graph to depict the rate of desired pupil progress toward a terminal goal

low-probability behavior Less preferred behavior

LSD (lysergic acid diethylamide) The prototypical hallucinogen

magnitude of behavior change The quantity by which a behavior increases or decreases with respect to some prior amount of behavior

mainstreaming The integration of exceptional children and normal peers

marijuana The dried leaves and flowers of the hemp plant (genus cannabis, *cannabis sativa*)

measurement probe Measurement that provides the best data base for making intervention decisions

mediator Parent, teacher, or other person who provides direct services to a pupil or other client with the support of a consultant

medical model An assessment model used by mental health professionals; based on the identification of emotional or cognitive pathology that is presumed to underlie the student's behavior problems

mental health assessment The identification of emotional or cognitive pathology that is presumed to underlie a student's behavior problems

modeling An instructional procedure by which demonstrations of a desired behavior are presented in order to prompt an imitative response

momentary time sampling The measurement of the occurrence or nonoccurrence of a behavior immediately following a specified interval of time

monitoring teacher verbal behavior Monitoring yourself to gain control of your verbal messages

movement suppression procedure A variation of time-out from reinforcement in which the student is punished for any movement or verbalization while in a time-out area

multiple baseline design A single-subject experimental design in which a treatment is replicated across (1) two or more students, (2) two or more behaviors, or (3) two or more settings; functional relationships may be demonstrated as changes in the dependent variables occur with the systematic and sequenced introduction of the independent variable

multiple probe design A variation of the multiple baseline design in which data are collected periodically rather than continuously across settings, behaviors, or students

narcotics Practical and effective drugs for treating specific types of pain; powerful analgesics that reduce pain without seriously altering the ability of the patient to function normally in other ways

negative reinforcement Behavior that is strengthened or maintained by avoiding or terminating an aversive stimulus

nicotine A drug found in many forms of tobacco that is commercially grown; chemically classified as an alkaloid and is physically highly toxic, causing nausea, salivation, abdominal pain, vomiting, diarrhea, cold sweat, headache, dizziness, confusion, convulsions, and respiratory failure at high doses; a common active ingredient in several insecticides

noncompliance Refusal to comply with teacher's request; behavior that is not under the verbal stimulus control of an adult

norm-referenced standardized test A test that compares a student's performance to that of the students in a norm group; standard scores are identified on the basis of this group's performance

observer drift A change in the observer's response definition while observing behavior and recording data

off-task behavior When a student is not paying attention to or participating in a class activity or not working on a class assignment or project

on-task behavior When a student is working or paying attention to classroom work

operational definition Describing a behavior in terms of its observable and measurable component parts

oppositional behavior A pattern of refusal to follow directions, even when the refusal is destructive to the interests and well-being of the oppositional individual

organized games Manipulating the play of primary school children to reduce the level of aggression during recess

overanxious disorder Experienced by children who are chronically fearful or worried about future events, demands made of them, their health, or their social and academic skills

overcorrection A procedure used to reduce the occurrence of an inappropriate behavior; the student is taught the appropriate behavior in which to engage through an exaggeration of experience; in *restitutional overcorrection* students must restore or correct an environment they have disturbed to its condition before the disturbance and must then improve it beyond its original condition, thereby overcorrecting the environment; in *positive practice overcorrection* students, having engaged in an inappropriate behavior, are required to engage in exaggerated practice of appropriate behaviors

parent surrogate An adult appointed to take the role of the parent and to make decisions regarding the most appropriate educational program and placement

peer coaching A procedure involving peers and adults who provide instruction to train social isolate pupils in social skills

peer imitation training An intervention that requires an isolate child's classmate to model certain social behaviors

peer manager strategy Young socially withdrawn students being trained to play "class manager" to increase their social interactions and sociometric ratings

peer-mediated intervention An intervention that requires a member of the individual's peer group, rather than an adult, to take the primary role as the agent of behavior change

peer modeling Having the student model or imitate the behavior exhibited by peers

peer monitoring Having students issue and withdraw points from their classmates

peer reporting An intervention designed to help students improve their social interactions and reduce aggression

peer social initiation An intervention strategy to improve the social skills of withdrawn children

peer tutoring Formal instruction of one child by another

perceptual reinforcement Reinforcement by engaging in particular perceptual experiences; a key to understanding SSB is to view it as a form of perceptual reinforcement to the individual

performance deficit A skill that a student can perform but does not because of a lack of motivation

performance feedback Providing the student with descriptive information regarding role-playing activities or academic performance

performance graph A graph that plots a change on a single task or behavior

permanent product recording A measurement strategy based on permanent products (e.g., written work, numerical counts)

phase line Vertical lines drawn on a behavior graph to designate where program changes have been made

phencyclidine (PCP) Along with LSD, by far the most frequently abused hallucinogen (except for cannabis); more likely to promote aggressive behavior with concurrent increased physical vigor and lack of response to pain

phenobarbital A barbiturate sedative hypnotic; also used as antiseizure medication in children; other types of antiepileptic medication such as phenytoin (diphenylhydantoin), Cylert (pemoline) and Tegretol (carbamazepine) also have potentially negative side effects (e.g., depression, insomnia, weight loss, confusion, hallucinations)

phobias An abnormally intense dread of certain objects or specific situations that normally do not instill fear

physical aversives Substances having aversive tastes and odors, electric shock, slaps, and pinches used to reduce severe maladaptive behaviors

pica The persistent eating of nonnutritive substances

pinpointing Specifying in measurable, observable terms a behavior targeted for change

playcheck Recording which students are engaged in a particular activity at the end of specified intervals

point-by-point reliability A method used to assess the agreement between two observers when discrete units of observation are being compared

Formula: $\dfrac{\text{number of agreements}}{\text{number of agreements plus disagreements}} \times 100$

positive practice overcorrection A procedure in which the student is required to engage in a period of exaggerated alternative behaviors (e.g., exercises) after an episode of an unwanted behavior

positive reinforcement The presentation of a consequence maintaining or strengthening behavior over time

postvention Refers to a set of actions that we take to prevent contagion after a suicide and to help students and staff deal with bereavement

praise Giving positive attention or praise for appropriate behavior

predictability The amount of newness in a group experience

Premack Principle A principle stating that any high-probability activity may serve as a positive reinforcer for any low-probability activity (also called activity reinforcement and Grandma's Law)

prereferral interventions Straightforward and relatively easy program modifications that can be implemented by the regular classroom teacher

primary treatment settings Individual classrooms that afford a high degree of stimulus control over students' behavior

procedural reliability The extent to which intervention procedures are being followed

progress graph A graph that shows the time it takes a student to master a set of objectives

projective technique A psychological assessment procedure in which the client "projects" his personality through responses to ambiguous stimuli such as pictures or ink blots

prompt An added stimulus that increases the probability that the S^D (discriminative stimulus) will occasion the desired response

psychological problems Problems characterized by a sudden change in behavior or mood; a feeling of sadness, fatigue, anhedonia; a change in appetite; a change in sleep, and a feeling of worthlessness

psychopathology Mental illness; in psychiatry, the study of significant causes and development of mental illness; more generally, behavior disorder

psychosis Behavior disorder characterized by major departure from normal patterns of acting, thinking, and feeling

public posting Publicly listing the names of persons who have (or have not) engaged in a target behavior

punisher A consequent stimulus that decreases the future rate or probability of a behavior

punishment An aversive consequence following a response, or the removal of a positive consequence following a response in order to weaken behavior

rate The frequency of a behavior during a defined time period

$$\text{Formula: rate} = \frac{\text{frequency}}{\text{time}}$$

rating scale A scale using information supplied by a teacher, parent, sibling, or peer to produce a picture of a child's behavior

ratio schedules of reinforcement A schedule for the delivery of reinforcers contingent upon the number of correct responses; in a *fixed-ratio* (FR) schedule, the number of appropriate responses required for reinforcement is held constant (e.g., FR5 indicates the delivery of reinforcement following every fifth appropriate response); in a *variable-ratio* (VR) schedule, the number of appropriate reponses required for reinforcement varies (e.g., VR5 indicates that reinforcement is delivered on the average of every fifth appropriate response)

reinforcement Providing reinforcing consequences or removing or withholding aversive consequences contingent upon the occurrence of a desired pupil behavior; results in an increase or maintenance of the rate of that behavior

reinforcing event (RE) menu A pictorial or verbal list of a variety of reinforcing events

relevant behaviors A strategy that involves adding to the student's social repertoire behaviors that are likely to set up reciprocal social interactions that strengthen further social initiations on the student's part

reliability A test's consistency; types of reliability include test-retest, alternate form, split-half, and interrater

replacement behaviors Desirable skills that are strengthened as undesirable maladaptive behaviors are reduced

reprimand A verbal aversive used by adults to influence children's behavior by telling them their behavior is inappropriate

response class Behavior definitions including several related responses, as in self-injurious behavior

response cost A procedure for the reduction of inappropriate behavior through withdrawal of specific amounts of reinforcer contingent upon the behavior's occurrence

response definition The definition or description of a behavior in observable, measurable terms

response generalization Changes in untreated behaviors related to those behaviors targeted for intervention

response latency recording A measurement strategy used by starting a timer when a cue is presented and stopping a timer when the pupil complies with the request

response maintenance The continuation of durability of behavior in treatment settings after the intervention has been withdrawn

response-reinforcer procedure An intervention in which the immediate environment is manipulated so that the student, as a result of completing a task, has immediate access to a reinforcer physically imbeddded within the task

restitutional overcorrection The student must restore an environment which he or she has disturbed, to its condition before the disturbance and must then improve it beyond its original condition, thereby overcorrecting the environment

restraint devices An intervention designed to limit the harm of the stereotypic behavior, rather than preventing the self-injurious behaviors themselves

restrictiveness The extent to which an intervention inhibits a student's freedom to be treated like other students

reversal design A single-subject experimental design in which a treatment condition is removed after intervention in order to verify the existence of a functional relationship; its four phases include baseline, imposition of treatment, removal of treatment (also known as return to baseline), and reimposition of treatment; also called ABAB design

reverse tolerance Increased sensitivity to a drug; may be the result of metabolic factors that produce a buildup in the body over time with regular use

ripple/spillover effect A spreading effect; see *generalization*

ritualistic behaviors Repetitive, stereotypic acts that appear to have no function in the environment

role-playing A therapeutic procedure that helps introduce new behaviors to enhance social relationships (the adult attempts to recreate certain situations for the student in an effort to help that student practice skills that have been difficult)

rules A basic component of a school's discipline code, communicating student and teacher expectations

rumination (mercyism) Self-induced regurgitation with loss of weight or failure to thrive

SBS Checklist of Correlates of Child Handicapping Conditions A checklist by Walker and Rankin (1980) describing conditions and characteristics commonly associated with handicapping conditions

SBS Inventory of Teacher Social Behavior Standards and Expectations A rating scale by Walker and Rankin (1980) describing adaptive and maladaptive student classroom behavior

scatter plot A format that enables observers to monitor targeted behaviors across extended periods of time

schedule of reinforcement A schedule for the delivery of reinforcers for the purpose of increasing or maintaining the rate of that behavior

scheduling Posting daily activities in a clear schedule that reflects how each student should spend his time

schizophrenia A psychotic disorder characterized by distortion of thinking, abnormal perception, and bizarre behavior and emotions

school phobia Fear of going to school, usually accompanied by indications of anxiety about attendance (abdominal pain, nausea, or other physical complaints) just before leaving for school in the morning

school records Archival information helpful in assessing social skills and problem areas

school survival skills The important skills necessary to do well in school, such as classroom deportment and time management strategies

school-wide interventions Behavior management interventions that occur in the school, including rules, detention, and in-school suspension

scopolamine One of a class of drugs known as anticholinergics, because they inhibit the activity of the brain chemical acetylcholine, which is considered important for mood and sensory regulation

screening Identification of students at risk for behavioral problems

self-evaluation A student assesses his or her behavior by rating

self-injurious behaviors Behaviors that hurt the person exhibiting them; also referred to as "self-mutilating" or "self-destructive"

self-instruction A procedure through which students practice "coping statements" to themselves

self-management An intervention in which the target individual plays the primary role in changing behavior

self-mediated stimuli A strategy that involves having the student carry or deliver stimuli discriminative of appropriate responding

self-mediated strategies Strategies for behavior management in which the student controls his or her own planned intervention

self-monitoring Recording one's own behavior to increase one's academic productivity and on-task behavior

self-mutilation See *self-injurious behavior*

self-recording A procedure whereby a student records his own performance

self-regulation A range of procedures (e.g., self-monitoring, self-evaluation, and self-reinforcement) considered to be least intrusive on and least restrictive of the enhancement procedures that can be applied across a wide range of situations without interrupting ongoing activities

self-reinforcement A procedure whereby a student reinforces his own behavior

self-report A procedure whereby a student reports his own performance

self-stimulatory behavior Any repetitive, stereotypic activity that seems only to provide sensory feedback

self-verbalization A strategy used with socially immature and impulsive students to improve their academic performance by self-instruction or verbalization

sensory extinction A procedure designed to eliminate a particular sensory consequence of a given self-stimulatory behavior; based on the notion that certain individuals have a strong preference for one aspect of sensory input (e.g., tactile, proprioceptive, visual, or auditory) and engage in self-stimulatory behaviors to increase this sensory input.

sensory preferences Establishing the sensory experiences that are deemed desirable to the child

sensory reinforcement Providing the child with one or more sensory experiences that are deemed desirable to the child

separation anxiety The problem of a child who has great difficulty when separated from significant others or familiar surroundings

sequential modification Replicating the intervention procedures in other settings without systematically programming for the durability of treatment effects once intervention is withdrawn

seriously emotionally disturbed Those who exhibit one or more characteristics over a long period of time and to a marked degree which adversely affects educational performance: (1) an inability to learn that cannot be explained by intellectual, sensory, or health factors, (2) an inability to build or maintain satisfactory interpersonal relationships with peers and teachers, (3) inappropriate behavior or feelings under normal circumstances, (4) a general pervasive mood of unhappiness or depression, or (5) a tendency to develop physical symptoms or fears associated with personal or school problems

setting events Times of day or transition periods that set the occasion for certain behaviors

single-subject designs Experimental investigations in which each individual serves as his or her own control

skill deficit A target behavior that cannot be performed due to a lack of appropriate skills

social competence An ability to establish satisfactory social relationships

social interaction code (SIC) Assesses three major classes of events associated with the student's social interactions with peers

social isolation Behavior of individuals who seldom if ever interact with their peers or with adults

social learning theory Assumptions that antecedent or setting events (e.g., models, instructions), consequences (rewards and punishments), and cognitive processes (perceiving, thinking, feeling) influence behavior; includes features of behavioral model or behavior modification with additional consideration of cognitive factors

socially maladjusted Refers to students who may be considered emotionally disturbed

(delinquent behavior and predelinquent behavior are considered to be forms of social maladjustment)

social reinforcement Teacher attention (feedback, attention, and approval) to influence particular behavior positively

social skills Specific social behaviors (e.g., a greeting, a nod during a conversation, a handshake) that facilitate interpersonal interactions

social skills deficits The student's inability to perform a particular skill when a social performance deficit denotes that the individual knows how to perform the skill but does not do so

social validation Confirming that significant behavior change has occurred through the judgments of other persons concerning the importance of behavior changes

social withdrawal A cluster of behaviors that result in an individual's escaping or avoiding social contact

sociometric procedure A technique used to evaluate the social status or position of individuals in a particular social reference group

special education admissions and release committee (ARC) A team to determine whether assessment information supports the need for special education placement

static measures Assessments that provide a report of progress at discrete points in time (e.g., annual or semiannual reassessments)

stereotypic behaviors Repetitive nonfunctional movements (e.g., rocking, hand flapping) characteristic of autism and other severe handicaps

stimulants The two drugs of this category that are familiar to most people are amphetamine (speed) and cocaine; there are other drugs that fall in this category, including nicotine (cigarettes and other forms of tobacco), phenylpropanolamine, methylphenidate, pemoline, and phencyclidine (PCP)

stimulus change Altering the discriminative stimuli for a particular response

stimulus control The relationship between behavior and its antecedent in which the antecedent occasions the behavior or serves as a cue for the behavior to occur; repeated occurrences of the behavior are dependent upon its being reinforced; an antecedent that serves as an appropriate cue for occasioning a response and therefore results in reinforcement is known as a discriminative stimulus (S^D); an antecedent that does not serve as an appropriate cue for occasioning a response and therefore does not result in reinforcement is known as an S-delta (S^Δ)

stimulus fading The gradual removal of discriminative stimuli

stimulus generalization The transfer of behaviors that have been trained in one setting or in the presence of specific discriminative stimuli to new settings or the presence of stimuli for which they have not been taught

stimulus variation A procedure to increase the level of motivation and responsiveness exhibited by a student engaged in self-stimulatory behavior

stress How you feel when you cannot cope

structured learning A popular approach to teaching prosocial behaviors to aggressive students using modeling, role-playing, performance feedback and transfer of learning

structuring Clarifying the relationship between behavior and its consequences

student prompting of teacher praise Training students to modify teacher's behavior

study carrels or cubicles A study area for isolating easily distracted pupils

sufficient stimulus exemplars A strategy that involves arranging for more than one, or for a small set of, discriminative stimuli to control the target behavior

suicidal ideation Having thoughts about killing oneself

suicide When someone takes his or her life *with conscious intent*

summative evaluation Evaluation done at the end of a program

suspension A temporary exclusion from school to manage behavior

systematic desensitization A systematic procedure used to help a person relax when engaging in activities that previously were anxiety-provoking; while in a relaxed state, the individual is asked to give a list of events ranging from most comfortable to most anxiety-provoking

tactile (sensory) reinforcement The application of tactile or sensory consequences that are reinforcing primarily with severely and profoundly handicapped students

tangible reinforcement Providing nonedible items that are reinforcing for particular students

target behavior A behavior identified for change that is observable, measurable, defined so that two persons can agree as to its occurrence, and stated so that a criterion can be set for a described level of performance

task analysis The process of breaking down a complex behavior into its component parts

Teacher assistance team Staff identified with the regular education program to help with prereferral intervention

teacher expectations The rating of important adaptive behaviors and teachers' tolerance for maladaptive behaviors in terms of how they affect their willingness to work with students in their classroom

Teacher Interview for Psychiatric Symptoms (TIPS) A new instrument for identifying psychiatric problems in children (Kerr & Schaeffer, 1987)

teacher interview A method based on social criteria for identifying pupils who are not socially responsive

teacher-mediated strategy Behavior management strategies that involve a teacher's direct interaction with students

terminal behavior The desired end product or goal for change in a student's behavior

therapy A procedure for bringing about social adjustment

time delay An errorless teaching procedure in which the time interval between a task request and an instructional prompt is systematically increased until the pupil emits the correct response before the prompt is given

time management The organization of time for school tasks

time-out A procedure for the reduction of inappropriate behavior whereby the student is denied access, for a fixed period of time, to the opportunity to receive reinforcement

timer game Using a kitchen timer to shape pupil behavior and train teachers to use tokens and praise

time sampling An observational recording system in which an observation period is divided into equal intervals, and observation of the target behavior is made at the end of each interval

token economy A system of behavior modification in which tangible or token reinforcers such as points, plastic chips, metal washers, poker chips, or play money are given as rewards and later exchanged for back-up reinforcers that have value in themselves (e.g., food, trinkets, play time, books); a miniature economic system used to foster desirable behavior

topographic response class A class of behaviors that are related in terms of their form, or the movements comprising the response (e.g., handraising)

topography The physical form or description of a motor behavior

total reliability A method used to assess the agreement between the total numerical counts of behaviors or products obtained by two independent observers

$$\text{Formula: } \frac{\text{smaller frequency}}{\text{larger frequency}} \times 100$$

train-and-hope programming Assessment probes conducted in generalization settings in which generalization is not specifically programmed

transenvironmental programming A strategy consisting of four components; (1) assessing the behavioral expectations of specific generalization settings, (2) competency training in the special education environments, (3) selection and use of techniques for promoting the transfer of skills across settings, and (4) monitoring and evaluating student performance in generalization settings

transfer of training The final phases of structured learning in which overlearning is emphasized

transition plan A program designed to help students better cope with the move from one setting to another, usually including annual goals and short- and long-term plans

transition services Services and agencies designed to aid students in the move from one setting to another, including helping the individual make work and social contacts, helping him or her become established, and following up the individual in his or her progress in the new environment

transition strategies Strategies that involve transferring students and their entire repertoires of behavior to new settings

trapping effect A tactic to increase behaviors that effectively receive naturally contingent reinforcement (behaviors used to "trap" reinforcement)

trend A description of data represented on a graph (an ascending or descending trend is defined as three data points in a single direction)

trend lines Lines of progress that tell you whether a program is working, because data paths seldom follow straight lines, nor do they increase or decrease in even increments

triadic model A description of the relationship between a consultant (trainer), a mediator (direct service provider), and the target pupil

trial-by-trial recording Recording student responses to individual prompts given by the teacher over a set of discrete trials

trials to criterion recording A measurement strategy for monitoring progress through a task-analyzed sequence or for measuring skill generalization

unprompted generalization A strategy that involves monitoring in generalization settings and reinforcing spontaneous generalization

validity The degree to which a test measures what it purports to measure; types of validity include content, criterion-referenced (predictive and concurrent), and construct

variable reinforcement Observing and reinforcing students after varying time intervals, which average a designated time interval

verbal aversives A verbal reprimand used to modify behavior

vicarious reinforcement Reinforcement of another student for appropriate behavior so that observing students will imitate the desired behavior

visual analysis Evaluating the significance of behavior change through visual inspection of a behavior graph

visual screening A procedure for reducing stereotypic behaviors by covering the student's eyes with your hand when the student engages in the target behavior

volatility Drug inhalants mixing readily with air in high concentrations

Walker-Rankin Child Behavior Rating Scale A criterion-referenced scale on which the teacher in the sending setting assesses the target student's behavioral status on the items designated as critical or unacceptable (Walker, 1986)

window of variance The amount of desired stability around the trend; found by drawing parallel dotted lines representing a 15-percent range above and below the trend line

withdrawal design A single-subject experiment design that involves collecting preintervention data (A), followed by an intervention condition (B), and a withdrawal of intervention procedures (A_2)

Index